Collins
gem

WELSH
DICTIONARY

Published by Collins
An imprint of HarperCollins
 Publishers
Westerhill Road
Bishopbriggs
Glasgow G64 2QT

HarperCollins Publishers
1st Floor, Watermarque Building
Ringsend Road, Dublin 4, Ireland

Fourth Edition 2017

10 9 8 7 6 5

© HarperCollins Publishers 1992,
2006, 2009, 2017

ISBN 978-0-00-819483-3

Collins Gem® is a registered
trademark of HarperCollins
Publishers Limited

www.collinsdictionary.com

Typeset by Sharon McTeir

Printed in India by
Replika Press Pvt. Ltd.

The contents of this publication
are believed correct at the time
of printing. Nevertheless,
the Publisher can accept no
responsibility for errors or
omissions, changes in the detail
given or for any expense or loss
thereby caused.

HarperCollins does not warrant
that any website mentioned
in this title will be provided
uninterrupted, that any website
will be error-free, that defects will
be corrected, or that the website or
the server that makes it available
are free of viruses or bugs. For full
terms and conditions please refer
to the site terms provided on the
website.

A catalogue record for this book is
available from the British Library.

If you would like to comment on
any aspect of this book, please
contact us at the given address
or online.
E-mail:
dictionaries@harpercollins.co.uk
 facebook.com/collinsdictionary
 @collinsdict

Acknowledgements
We would like to thank those
authors and publishers who
kindly gave permission for
copyright material to be used in
the Collins Corpus. We would also
like to thank Times Newspapers
Ltd for providing valuable data.

CONTENTS

EDITOR/GOLYGYDD
Susie Beattie

CONTRIBUTORS/CYFRANWYR
Eurwen Booth
David Bullock
Harry Campbell
Non Jenkins
Jo Knell
Maggie Seaton

FOR THE PUBLISHER/AR RAN Y CYHOEDDWR
Gerry Breslin
Kerry Ferguson

INTRODUCTION

The first Spurrell Welsh-English dictionary appeared in 1848 published by William Spurrell (1813–89) the Carmarthen printer and publisher. One of his sons, Walter Spurrell (1858–1934), joined his father in the business and the family firm published a series of distinguished Welsh-English, English-Welsh dictionaries and influential Welsh grammars during the latter part of the nineteenth century and the first half of the last century. William Spurrell was advised by and well-acquainted with Daniel Silvan Evans (1818–1903), one of the father figures of Welsh lexicography, sometime lecturer in Welsh at St David's University College, Lampeter and the first professor of Welsh to be appointed by the University of Wales.

The Collins-Spurrell Welsh Dictionary was first published in 1960 and quickly became an essential tool of general reference for Welsh learners as well as those anxious to interpret literature. It was edited by Henry Lewis, Professor of Welsh Language and Literature at University College, Swansea, with valuable contributions from the staff of the Department of Welsh Language and Literature at St David's University College, Lampeter.

D A THORNE

NOTES ON THE PRONUNCIATION OF WELSH

VOWELS

They are sounded, long or short, as the vowels in the English words given below.

A   p**a**lm, p**a**t.
E   g**a**te (without diphthongization), g**e**t.
I   f**ee**t, f**i**t.
O   m**o**re, n**o**t.
U (1)   North Wales: like French *u* or German *ü* without rounding lips.
   (2)   South Wales: as I.
W   c**oo**l, f**u**ll.
Y (1)   In monosyllables generally, and in final syllables, as U (the 'clear' sound).
   (2)   In all but final syllables, and in **y, yr** (the), **fy** (my), **dy** (thy), **yn, yng, ym** (in), the adverbial **yn**, the preverbal and relative particle **y, yr** (**y'm, y'th** etc), **syr** (sir), **nyrs** (nurse), as English f**u**n, (the 'obscure' sound).

DIPHTHONGS

1 Falling diphthongs, in which the second
sound is consonantal: the two vowels have
the sound noted above: **ae, oe, ai, oi,** the
diphthong **ei** as English *by*, **aw, ew, iw, ow,
uw, ŵy, yw.**

2 Rising diphthongs, in which the first sound
is consonantal: **ia, ie, io, iw, iy,** ('obscure' y);
wa, we, wi, wo, wy, ('clear' y), **wy,**
('obscure' y).

CONSONANTS

Only those which differ from English need to be
noted.

CH (following C in the alphabet), as Scottish lo*ch*.
DD (following D in the alphabet), as *th* in
      English *this*, brea*the*.
F   as English *v*.
FF as English *f*.
G   always as in English *go*.
NG (following G in the alphabet), as in English
      sing.
      In some words (e.g. **dangos**), however, it is
      sounded *ng-g*, as in English lo*nger*.
      Alphabetically this follows after N.
LL produced by placing the tongue to pronounce *l*,
      then emitting breath without voice.
PH (following P in the alphabet), as English *f*.
TH always as th in English *thin*.

ACCENT

Welsh words are generally accented on the last syllable but one. There are certain exceptions:

1   The reduplicated personal pronouns **myfi, tydi, efe, efô, hyhi, nyni, chwychwi, hwynt-hwy**, accented on the final syllable.

2   Verbs in **-(h)au, -(h)oi, -eu**, accented on the final syllable.

3   A few dissyllabic words beginning **y** + consonant, accented on the final syllable.

4   Certain polysyllabic words with a diphthong resulting in contraction in the final syllable, such as **Cymraeg**.

5   Some borrowed words accented as in the language of origin, generally English.

MUTATIONS

Mutations, or letter changes, can occur at the beginning of Welsh words. Mutations are caused by the preceding word. There are three different mutations:

Llythyren wreiddiol *Original letter*	Treiglad meddal *Soft mutation*	Treiglad trwynol *Nasal mutation*	Treiglad llaes *Aspirate mutation*
	changes to:	*changes to:*	*changes to:*
p	b	mh	ph
t	d	nh	th
c	g	ngh	ch
b	f	m	
d	dd	n	
g	-	ng	
ll	l		
m	f		
rh	r		

COMMON WORDS CAUSING SOFT MUTATION – TREIGLAD MEDDAL

ei	*his*
dy	*your*
dau / dwy	*two (masculine / feminine)*
pa	*which*
neu	*or*
rhy	*too*
yn	before an adjective

Adjectives which come before the noun:	For example:
Mae'r hen **dd**yn yn byw yn y tŷ.	*The old man lives in the house.*
Dyma fy hoff **g**ân.	*This is my favourite song.*
Some prepositions:	For example:
Mae'r bws yn mynd i **G**aerdydd.	*The bus is going to Cardiff.*
Maen nhw'n chwarae dros **d**îm yr ysgol.	*They play for the school team.*

Certain words which come before a feminine noun:
y and 'r   *the*
un   *one*

Mae castell yn y **d**ref.	*There's a castle in town.*
Mae'r **dd**inas wedi gwella.	*The city has improved.*
Dim ond un **b**roblem sydd ar ôl.	*There's only one problem left.*

Any feminine noun which has an adjective immediately after it:

merch **dd**a   *a good girl*

COMMON WORDS CAUSING NASAL MUTATION – TREIGLAD TRWYNOL

fy	*my*
yn	*in*

COMMON WORDS CAUSING ASPIRATE MUTATION – TREIGLAD LLAES

a	*and*
â	*as/to/with*
chwe	*six*
ei	*her*
gyda	*with*
tri	*three*
tua	*approximately*

ABBREVIATIONS		BYRFODDAU
abbreviation	*abbr*	byrfodd
adjective	*adj*	ansoddair
anatomy	*Anat*	anatomeg
automobile	*Aut*	moduro
auxiliary verb	*aux vb*	berf atodol
British English	*BRIT*	Saesneg Prydain
collective noun	*coll n*	enw torfol
computing	*Comput*	cyfrifiadureg
conjunction	*conj*	cysylltiad
contraction	*contr*	cywasgiad
cookery	*Culin*	coginio
definite article	*def art*	bannod bendant
demonstrative	*dem*	dangosol
emphatic	*emphat*	pwyslais
exclamation	*excl*	ebychiad
formal	*form*	ffurfiol
(phrasal verb) where the particle is inseparable	*fus*	(berf ymadroddol) lle na all y rhangymeriad gael ei wahanu
imperative	*imper*	gorchmynnol
indefinite article	*indef art*	bannod amhendant
indeterminate	*indeter*	amhenderfynadwy
colloquial usage (offensive)	*inf(!)*	defnydd llafar (anweddus)

grammar, linguistics	*Ling*	gramadeg, ieithyddiaeth
masculine	*m*	gwrywaidd
mathematics	*Math*	mathemateg
medical term	*Med*	term meddygol
modal auxiliary verb	*mod aux vb*	berf atodol moddol
music	*Mus*	cerddoriaeth
noun	*n*	enw
noun dual	*nd*	enw deuol
number	*num*	rhif
old-fashioned	*old*	hen ffasiwn
derogatory, pejorative	*pej*	difrïol
plural	*pl*	lluosog
past participle	*pp*	rhangymeriad gorffennol
politics	*Pol*	gwleidyddiaeth
prefix	*pref*	rhagddodiad
preposition	*prep*	arddodiad
pronoun	*pron*	rhagenw
past tense	*pt*	amser gorffennol
relative	*rel*	perthynol
singular	*sing*	unigol
Telecommunications	*Tel*	Telathrebu
American English	*US*	Saesneg America
verb	*vb*	berf
impersonal verb	*vb imper*	berf amhersonol
intransitive verb	*vi*	berf gyflawn
transitive verb	*vt*	berf anghyflawn

WELSH–ENGLISH

a

a¹ *interrogative particle, preverbal particle, rel pron* who, that, which

a², ac *conj* and

a³ *excl* ah, oh

â¹, ag *conj* as

â², ag *prep* with

ab, ap *nm* son (*before name, in place of surname, like 'Mac'*)

abad (-au) *nm* abbot

abadaeth (-au) *nf* abbacy, abbotship

abades (-au) *nf* abbess

abatir (-oedd) *nm* abbey-land

abaty (abatai) *nm* abbey

aber (-oedd, ebyr) *nm* confluence; mouth of river, estuary; brook, stream

aberfa (-oedd) *nf* mouth of river, estuary

abergofiant *nm* forgetfulness, oblivion

aberth (-au, ebyrth) *nm* sacrifice

aberthged *nf* oblation; offering of fruits

aberthol *adj* sacrificial

aberthu *vb* to sacrifice

aberthwr (-wyr) *nm* sacrificer

aberu *vb* to flow into

abid *nmf* apparel; dress of religious order

abiéc *nmf* alphabet

abl *adj* able; well-off

abladol *adj* ablative

abledd *nm* ability; plenty

abrwysg *adj* clumsy, drunken

absen *nm* absence; slander

absennol *adj* absent

absennu *vb* to backbite, to slander

absennwr (absenwyr) *nm* backbiter

absenoldeb *nm* absence

absenoli *vb* to absent

absenoliaeth (-au) *nf* absenteeism

abwyd, abwydyn (abwydod) *nm* worm; fishing-bait

ac, a *conj* and

academaidd *adj* academic

academi (-ïau) *nm* academy

acen (-ion) *nf* accent

aceniad *nm* accentuation

acennod *nm* accent mark

acennu *vb* to accent, to stress

acenyddiaeth *nf* accentuation

acer (-i) *nf* acre

aciwbigiad (-au) *nm* acupuncture

acne *nm* acne

acrilig *adj* acrylic

act (-au) *nf* act

actio *vb* to act

actor (-ion) *nm* actor

actores (-au) *nf* actress

acw adv there, yonder
ach¹ excl ugh
ach² (**-au, -oedd**) nf degree of kinship; (pl) pedigree, ancestry
aches nm tide, flood; eloquence
achfre nmf see **achwre**
achlân adv wholly, entirely
achles (**-oedd**) nf succour, protection; manure
achlesol adj succouring
achlesu vb to succour, to cherish
achlod nm shame, disgrace
achlust nm rumour
achlysur (**-on**) nm occasion
achlysurol adj occasional
achos¹ (**-ion**) nm cause, case
achos² conj because, for
achosi vb to cause
achres (**-i, -au**) nf genealogical table
achub vb to seize, to snatch; to save, to rescue; **achub y blaen** to forestall; **achub y cyfle** to seize the opportunity
achubiaeth nf salvation
achubol adj saving
achubwr (**-wyr**), **achubydd** (**-ion**) nm saviour, rescuer
achul adj thin, emaciated
achwre, achfre nmf under-thatch, protection; covering, garment
achwyn vb to complain ▸ nm (**-ion**) complaint, plaint
achwyniad (**-au**) nm complaint, accusation
achwynwr (**-wyr**) nm complainer; complainant, plaintiff
achwynyddes (**-au**) nf complainant

achydd (**-ion**) nm genealogist
achyddiaeth nf genealogy
achyddol adj genealogical
achwyngar adj querulous
ad- prefix very; second; bad, re-
adail nf building, edifice, structure
adain, aden (**adenydd**) nf wing; fin; spoke
adamant nm adamant, diamond
adamantaidd adj adamantine
adar npl (nm **aderyn**) birds, fowls; **adar drudwy, adar yr eira** starlings; **adar y to** sparrows
adara vb to catch birds, to fowl
adardy (**-dai**) nf aviary
adareg nf ornithology
adargi (**-gwn**) nm retriever, setter, spaniel
adargraffiad (**-au**) nm reprint
adarwr (**-wyr**) nm fowler
adarwriaeth nf fowling
adarydd (**-ion**) nm ornithologist
adaryddia n birdwatching ▸ vb to go birdwatching
adaryddiaeth nf ornithology
ad-dalu vb to repay, to requite
ad-drefnu vb to rearrange
adeg (**-au**) nf time, occasion, opportunity
adeilad (**-au**) nmf building, edifice
adeiladaeth nf building; edification, construction
adeiladol adj edifying, constructive
adeiladu vb to build, to edify
adeiladwaith nm construction
adeiladwr (**-wyr**), **adeiladydd** (**-ion**) nm builder
adeiledd nm structure
adeiniog adj winged

aden (-ydd, edyn) *nf* wing; *see also* **adain**

adenedigaeth *nf* regeneration

adeni *vb* to regenerate

adennill *vb* to regain, to recover

aderyn (adar) *nm* bird

adfach (-au) *nm* barb; liver-fluke

adfail (-feilion) *nm* ruin

adfeddiannu *vb* to repossess

adfeiliad *nm* decay, ruin

adfeiliedig *adj* decayed, in ruins

adfeilio *vb* to decay, to moulder

Adfent *nm* Advent

adfer, adferu, adferyd *vb* to restore

adferf (-au) *nf* adverb

adferfol *adj* adverbial

adferiad *nm* restoration

adferol *adj* restorative; remedial

adferwr (-wyr) *nm* restorer

adflas *nm* after-taste, bad taste

adfyd *nm* adversity

adfydus *adj* adverse, miserable

adfynach *nm* renegade monk

adfyw *adj* half alive, half dead

adfywhau *vb* to revive, to reanimate

adfywiad (-au) *nm* revival

adfywio *vb* to revive, to resuscitate

adfywiol *adj* refreshing

adiad *nm* drake

adio *nm* addition ▸ *vb* to add

adiolyn (adiolion) *nm* additive

adladd, adlodd *nm* aftermath

adlais (-leisiau) *nm* echo

adlam (-au) *nm* home; rebound; **cic adlam** drop-kick

adlamu *vb* to rebound

adleisio *vb* to resound

adlewyrch, adlewyrchiad (adlewyrchiadau) *nm* reflection

adlewyrchu *vb* to reflect

adlewyrchydd (-ion) *nm* reflector

adlog (-au) *nm* compound interest

adloniadol *adj* of or for entertainment

adloniant *nm* recreation, entertainment

adlonni *vb* to entertain, to refresh

adlunio *vb* to remodel, to reconstruct

adnabod *vb* to know, to recognize

adnabyddiaeth *nf* knowledge, acquaintance

adnabyddus *adj* known, familiar; well-known

adnabyddwr *nm* knower

adnau (adneuon) *nm* deposit, pledge; **ar adnau** on deposit

adneuo *vb* to deposit

adneuol *adj* depositing

adneuwr (-wyr) *nm* depositor

adnewyddadwy *adj* renewable

adnewyddiad (-au) *nm* renewal, renovation

adnewyddu *vb* to renew, to renovate

adnewyddwr (-wyr) *nm* renewer, renovator

adnod (-au) *nf* verse

adnoddau *npl* resources

adolygiad (-au) *nm* review

adolygu *vb* to review

adolygydd (-ion) *nm* reviewer

adran (-nau) *nf* division, section, department

adref *adv* homewards, home

3

Adriatig

Adriatig nm: yr Adriatig the Adriatic (Sea)

adrodd vb to relate, to recite

adroddgan (-au) nf recitative

adroddiad (-au) nm report; recitation

adroddwr (-wyr) nm narrator, reciter

aduniad nm reunion

aduno vb to reunite

adwaith (-weithiau) nm reaction

adweithio vb to react

adweithiol adj reactionary

adweithydd (-ion) nm reactor

adwerthu vb to retail

adwr nm coward, churl

adwy (-au, -on) nf gap, breach; pass

adwyth (-au) nm evil, misfortune, illness

adwythig adj cruel; evil, baneful; sore, sick; harmful

adyn (-od) nm wretch

adysgrif (-au) nf copy, transcript

adysgrifio vb to copy, to transcribe

addas adj suitable, proper

addasiad (-au) nm adjustment, adaptation

addasrwydd nm suitableness, fitness

addasu vb to suit, to adapt, to fit

addawol adj promising

addef vb to acknowledge, to own, to admit

addefiad nm admission, confession

addewid (-ion) nf promise

addfain adj slender, shapely

addfed adj see aeddfed

addfwyn adj gentle, meek, mild

addfwynder nm gentleness, meekness

addien adj fair, beautiful

addo vb to promise

addod nm: wy addod nest-egg

addoed nm death, hurt

addoedi vb to delay, to postpone

addoediad nm prorogation

addoer adj sad, cruel; chilling

addoldy (-dai) nf place of worship

addolgar adj devout, reverent

addolgarwch nm devoutness, reverence

addoli vb to worship, to adore

addoliad nm worship

addolwr (-wyr) nm worshipper

adduned (-au) nf vow

addunedu vb to vow

addurn (-au, -iadau) nm ornament, adornment

addurnedig adj decorated

addurniad nm ornamentation

addurno vb to decorate, to adorn, to ornament

addurnol adj ornamental, decorative

addurnwr (-wyr) nm decorator

addysg nf education, instruction; addysg gorfforol PE; addysg uwch higher education

addysgiadol adj instructive, educational

addysgiaeth nf instruction, training

addysgol adj educational

addysgu vb to educate, to instruct

addysgwr (-wyr), addysgydd (-ion) nm educator, instructor, tutor

aeddfed *adj* ripe, mature
aeddfedrwydd *nm* ripeness, maturity
aeddfedu *vb* to ripen; to mature
ael (-iau) *nf* brow
aele *adj* sad, wretched
aelod (-au) *nm* member, limb; **Aelod Seneddol** Member of Parliament
aelodaeth *nf* membership
aelodi *vb* to become a member; to enrol
aelwyd (-ydd) *nf* hearth, fireside
aer¹ (-ion) *nf* heir
aer² *nm* air
aerdymheru *nm* air conditioning
aeres (-au) *nf* heiress
aerfa *nf* slaughter, battle
aerglo *nm* air-lock
aerobeg *nm* aerobics
aeron *npl* fruit, fruits, berries
aerwy (-au, -on) *nm* collar, torque; neck-chain
aes *nf* shield
aestheteg *nf* aesthetics
aesthetig *adj* aesthetic
aeth *nm* pain, grief, fear, shock
aethnen *nf* aspen, poplar
aethus *adj* poignant, grievous, severe
afal (-au) *nm* apple
afallen (-nau) *nf* apple-tree
afan *npl* (*nf-en*) raspberries
afanc (-od) *nm* beaver
afiach *adj* unwell, unhealthy, morbid
afiachus *adj* sickly; unwholesome
afiaith *nm* zest, mirth, glee
afiechyd (-on) *nm* disease, malady

afieithus *adj* mirthful, gleeful
aflafar *adj* harsh, unmelodious
aflan *adj* unclean, polluted, foul
aflawen *adj* fierce; sad, cheerless, dismal; awful
aflednais *adj* immodest, indelicate
afledneisrwydd *nm* immodesty, indelicacy
aflem *adj* obtuse
aflendid *nm* uncleanness; pollution
aflêr *adj* untidy, slovenly
aflerwch *nm* untidiness, slovenliness
afles *nm* disadvantage, hurt
aflesol *adj* disadvantageous, unprofitable
afliwiog *adj* pale, colourless
aflonydd *adj* unquiet, restless
aflonyddu *vb* to disturb, to molest
aflonyddwch *nm* disturbance, unrest
aflonyddwr (-wyr) *nm* disturber
afloyw *adj* turbid; opaque
afluniaidd *adj* mis-shapen, deformed
aflunio *vb* to disfigure, to deform
aflwydd *nm* misfortune, calamity
aflwyddiannus *adj* unsuccessful
aflwyddiant *nm* failure
aflwyddo *vb* to fail
aflywodraeth *nf* misrule, anarchy
aflywodraethus *adj* ungovernable, uncontrollable
afocado (-s) *nm* avocado
afon (-ydd) *nf* river
afonig *nf* rivulet, streamlet, brook
afradlon *adj* wasteful, prodigal
afradlonedd *nm* prodigality

afradloni

afradloni, afradu vb to waste, to lavish, to squander

afraid adj unnecessary, needless ▸ nm superfluity

afrasol adj graceless, impious

afrealaidd, afrealistig adj unrealistic

afreidiol adj needless, superfluous

afreol nf misrule, disorder

afreolaidd adj irregular; disorderly

afreoleidd-dra nm irregularity

afreolus adj unruly, disorderly

afreswm nm absurdity

afresymegol adj illogical

afresymol adj unreasonable

afresymoldeb nm unreasonableness

afrifed adj innumerable

afrllad (-au), afrlladen (-nau) nf wafer

afrosgo adj clumsy, unwieldy

afrwydd adj difficult, stiff, awkward

afrwyddineb nm difficulty

afrwyddo vb to obstruct, to hinder

afrywiog adj perverse, cross-grained, improper

afrywiogrwydd nm churlishness, roughness

afu nmf liver; **afu (g)las** gizzard

afwyn (-au) nf rein

affeithiad nm affection (in grammar)

Affganistan nf Afghanistan

afflau nm grip, hug, embrace

affliw nm shred, particle

Affrica nf Africa

Africanaidd adj African

Africanwr (-wyr) nm African

affwysol nm abysmal

ag, â conj as ▸ prep with

agen (-nau) nf cleft, chink, fissure

agendor nmf gulf, abyss

agennu vb to split, to crack

ager, agerdd nm steam, vapour

agerfad (-au) nm steamboat

agerlong (-au) nf steamship, steamer

ageru vb to steam, to evaporate

agerw adj bitter, fierce

agor, agoryd vb to open, to expand

agorawd (-au) nf overture

agored adj open; liable

agorfa (-oedd) nf opening, orifice

agoriad (-au) nm opening; key

agoriadol adj opening, inaugural

agorwr (-wyr), agorydd (-ion) nm opener; **agorwr tuniau** can-opener

agos adj near, nigh

agosaol adj approaching

agosatrwydd nm intimacy

agosáu vb to draw near, to approach

agosrwydd nm nearness, proximity

agwedd (-au) nf form; aspect; attitude

agweddi nm dowry, marriage gift

agwrdd adj strong, mighty

angall adj unwise, foolish

angau nmf death

angel (angylion, engyl) nm angel

angen (anghenion) nm need, want; **anghenion arbennig** special needs

angenrheidiol adj necessary, needful

angenrheidrwydd *nm* necessity

angerdd *nm* heat; passion; force

angerddol *adj* ardent, intense, passionate

angerddoldeb *nm* vehemence, intensity

anghaffael *nm* mishap; defect, flaw

anghallineb *nm* unwisdom, imprudence

angharedig *adj* unkind

angharedigrwydd *nm* unkindness

anghelfydd *adj* unskilful, clumsy

anghenfil (anghenfilod) *nm* monster

anghenraid (angenrheidiau) *nm* necessity

anghenus *adj* needy, necessitous, indigent

angheuol *adj* deadly, mortal, fatal

anghlod *nm* dispraise, dishonour

anghoelio *vb* to disbelieve

anghofiedig *adj* forgotten

anghofio *vb* to forget

anghofrwydd *nm* forgetfulness

anghofus *adj* forgetful, oblivious

anghred *nf* unbelief, infidelity

anghredadun (anghredinwyr) *nm* unbeliever

anghrediniaeth *nf* unbelief, infidelity

anghrediniol *adj* unbelieving

anghredu *vb* to disbelieve

anghrefyddol *adj* irreligious

anghryno *adj* incompact, prolix

anghwrtais *adj* discourteous

anghwrteisi *nm* discourtesy

anghydbwysedd *nm* imbalance

anghydfod *nm* disagreement, discord

Anghydffurfiaeth *nf* Nonconformity

Anghydffurfiwr (-wyr) *nm* Nonconformist

anghydnaws *adj* uncongenial

anghydsynio *vb* to dissent, to disagree

anghydweddol *adj* incompatible

anghyfaddas *adj* unsuitable, unfit

anghyfaddasu *vb* to disqualify

anghyfamodol *adj* uncovenanted

anghyfanhedd-dra *nm* desolation

anghyfanheddle (-aneddleoedd) *nm* desolate place

anghyfanheddol *adj* desolating; desert

anghyfannedd *adj* uninhabited, desert

anghyfansoddiadol *adj* unconstitutional

anghyfartal *adj* unequal, uneven

anghyfartaledd *nm* disparity

anghyfarwydd *adj* unfamiliar, unskilled

anghyfeillgar *adj* unfriendly

anghyfiaith *adj* foreign, alien

anghyfiawn *adj* unjust, unrighteous

anghyfiawnder *nm* injustice

anghyflawn *adj* incomplete

anghyfleus *adj* inconvenient

anghyfleustra (-terau) *nm* inconvenience

anghyflogaeth *nm* unemployment

anghyfnewidiol *adj* immutable

anghyfraith *nf* transgression, crime

anghyfranogol *adj* incommunicable

anghyfreithlon *adj* unlawful, illegal, illegitimate

anghyfrifol *adj* irresponsible

anghyffredin *adj* uncommon, rare

anghyffwrdd *adj* intangible

anghyffyrddus *adj* uncomfortable

anghymedrol *adj* immoderate

anghymen *adj* rash, coarse, untidy

anghymeradwy *adj* unacceptable

anghymeradwyo *vb* to disapprove

anghymesur *adj* inordinate

anghymharol *adj* incomparable

anghymharus *adj* ill-matched

anghymhendod *nm* foolishness, indelicacy, untidiness

anghymhwyso *vb* to unfit, to disqualify

anghymhwyster *nm* incapacity, disqualification

anghymodlon *adj* implacable

anghymwys *adj* unfit, unsuitable

anghynefin *adj* unfamiliar

anghynefindra *nm* unfamiliarity

anghynhyrchiol *adj* unproductive

anghynnes *adj* odious, loathsome

anghysbell *adj* out-of-the-way; remote

anghyson *adj* inconsistent

anghysondeb (-au), anghysonder (-au) *nm* inconsistency

anghysur (-on) *nm* discomfort

anghysuro *vb* to discomfort

anghysurus *adj* uncomfortable

anghytbwys *adj* unbalanced, lopsided

anghytgord (-iau) *nm* discord, dissension

anghytûn *adj* not agreeing, discordant

anghytundeb *nm* disagreement

anghytuno *vb* to disagree

anghywair *adj* ill-equipped; discordant ▸ *nm* disrepair

anghyweithas *adj* uncivil

anghywir *adj* incorrect, inaccurate, false

anghywirdeb (-au) *nm* inaccuracy, falseness

anghywrain *adj* unskilful; slovenly

angladd (-au) *nmf* burial, funeral

angladdol *adj* funereal

angof *nm* forgetfulness, oblivion

angor (-au, -ion) *nm* anchor

angorfa (-oedd, -feydd) *nf* anchorage

angori *vb* to anchor

angylaidd *adj* angelic

angyles (-au) *nf* female angel

ai¹ *adv* is it? what?; **ai e?** is it so?

ai² *conj* or; either; if

AID *nm* AIDS

aidd *nm* zeal, ardour, zest

Aifft *nf*: **yr Aifft** Egypt

aig¹, eigiau *nf* host, shoal

aig² *nf* sea, ocean

ail *adj* second ▸ *adv* a second time, again

ailadrodd *vb* to repeat

ailadroddiad (-au) *nm* repetition

ailarholiad (-au) *nm* resit

ailbriodi *vb* to remarry

aildrydanu *vb* to recharge

ailenedigaeth *nf* rebirth

aileni *vb* to regenerate

Ailfedyddiwr (-wyr) *nm* Anabaptist

ailgylchu *vb* to recycle ▸ *n* recycling

ailgynnig (ailgynigion) *nm* resit

ail-law *adj* second-hand

ail-lenwi *vb* to top up, to refill

ailsefyll *vb* to resit

aillt *nm* vassal, villain, slave

ais *npl (nf eisen)* laths; ribs

alaeth *nm* wailing, lamentation, grief

alaethu *vb* to lament

alaethus *adj* mournful, lamentable

alarch (-od, elyrch) *nm* swan

alaru *vb* to surfeit; to loathe

alaw (-on) *nf* lily; air, melody, tune

Alban *nf:* **yr Alban** Scotland

Albanwr (-wyr) *nm* Scot

alcali (-ïau) *nm* alkali

alcam *nm* tin

alcohol *nm* alcohol

alch (-au, eilch) *nf* grate, grill

ale (-au, -on) *nf* aisle; gangway; alley

algebra *nm* algebra

Algeraidd *adj* Algerian

Algeria *nf* Algeria

Algeriad (-iaid) *nm* Algerian

Almaen *nf:* **yr Almaen** Germany

Almaeneg *nf* German

Almaenwr (-wyr) *nm* German

almon *nm* almond

aloi (aloeon) *nm* alloy

Alpau *npl:* **yr Alpau** the Alps

Alzheimer *nm:* **clefyd Alzheimer** Alzheimer's (disease)

allan *adv* out

allanfa *nf* exit

allanol *adj* outward, external

allblyg *adj* extrovert

allbrint (-iau) *nm* printout

allforio *vb* to export

allfro *nf* foreigner; foreign land

allfudwr (-wyr) *nm* emigrant

allgarwch *nm* altruism

allgofnodi *vb* to log off, to log out

allor (-au) *nf* altar

allt (elltydd) *nf* hill; cliff; wood

alltud (-ion) *nm* alien; exile

alltudiaeth *nf* banishment, exile

alltudio *vb* to banish, to exile

allwedd (-au, -i) *nf* key, clef *(in music)*

allweddell *nf* keyboard

am¹ *prep* round, about; for; at; on ▸ *conj* for, because; so long as

am² *see* ym

amaeth *nm* husbandman; agriculture

amaethdy (-dai) *nm* farm-house

amaethu *vb* to farm, to till

amaethwr (-wyr) *nm* farmer

amaethwraig *nf* farm-wife

amaethyddiaeth *nf* agriculture

amaethyddol *adj* agricultural

amarch *nm* disrespect, dishonour

amau *vb* to doubt, to suspect ▸ *nm* (-heuon) doubt

ambell *adj* occasional; **ambell waith** sometimes

amcan (-ion) *nm* purpose, aim; guess; **ar amcan** at random, approximately, at a guess

amcangyfrif *vb* to estimate ▸ *nm* (-on) estimate

amcanu *vb* to purpose; to aim; to guess

amdo (**-oeau**) nm shroud, winding-sheet

amdoi vb to shroud, to enshroud

amdorch (**-dyrch**) nf chaplet, wreath

amddifad adj destitute, orphan

amddifadrwydd nm destitution, privation

amddifadu vb to bereave, to deprive

amddifaty (**-tai**) nm orphanage

amddifedi nm destitution, privation

amddiffyn vb to defend, to protect, to shield ► nm (**addiffynion**) defence

amddiffynfa (**-feydd**) nf fortress

amddiffyniad nm protection, defence

amddiffynnwr (**-wyr**), **amddiffynyddion** nm defender, protector

amddyfrwys adj mighty, rugged; marshy

America Ladin nf Latin America

Amerig nf: yr Amerig America

amfesur (**-au**) nm perimeter

amgáu vb to enclose, to shut in

amgen adj, adv other, else, otherwise; different; **nid amgen** that is to say, namely

amgenach adj, adv otherwise; better

amgueddfa (**-feydd**) nf museum

amgyffred vb to comprehend, to comprise ► nm (**-ion**) comprehension

amgyffrediad nm comprehension

amgylch (**-oedd**) nm circuit; environs, surroundings; **o** (**oddi**) **amgylch** round about, about

amgylchedd nm circumference; environment

amgylcheddol adj environmental; **yn amgylcheddol** environmentally; **amgylcheddol garedig** environmentally friendly

amgylchfyd nm environment

amgylchiad (**-au**) nm circumstance; occasion

amgylchiadol adj circumstantial

amgylchu vb to surround

amgylchynol adj surrounding

amgylchynu vb to surround

amharchu vb to dishonour, to disrespect

amharchus adj disrespectful, disreputable

amhariad nm impairment, damage

amharod adj unprepared, unready

amharodrwydd nm unreadiness

amharu vb to impair, to harm, to injure, to damage

amhendant adj indefinite, vague

amhenderfynol adj irresolute

amhenodol adj indefinite

amherchi vb to dishonour, to insult

amherffaith adj imperfect

amherffeithrwydd nm imperfection

amhersonol adj impersonal

amherthnasol, amherthynasol adj irrelevant

amheuaeth nf doubt, scepticism

amheugar adj suspicious; sceptical

amheuol adj doubting, doubtful

amheus *adj* doubting, doubtful, dubious

amheuthun *adj* dainty, savoury
▶ *nm* (**-ion**) dainty, delicacy, treat

amheuwr (**-wyr**) *nm* doubter, sceptic

amhlantadwy *adj* childless, barren

amhleidiol, amhleitgar *adj* impartial

amhoblog *adj* sparsely populated

amhoblogaidd *adj* unpopular

amhosibl *adj* impossible

amhriodol *adj* improper

amhrisiadwy *adj* priceless

amhrofiadol *adj* inexperienced

amhrydlon *adj* unpunctual

amhûr *adj* impure, foul

amhwrpasol *adj* irrelevant

amhwyllo *vb* to lose one's senses, to go mad

aml *adj* frequent, abundant ▶ *adv* often

amlder, amldra *nm* abundance

amldduwiad (**-iaid**) *nm* polytheist

amldduwiaeth *nf* polytheism

amleiriog *adj* wordy, verbose, prolix

amlen (**-ni**) *nf* envelope, wrapper

amlhad *nm* increasing, increase

amlhau *vb* to increase, to multiply

amlinelliad (**-au**) *nm* outline

amlinellu *vb* to outline

aml-lawr *adj* multi-storey

amlochrog *adj* many-sided

amlosgfa *nf* crematorium

amlosgi *vb* to cremate

amlwg *adj* plain, clear, manifest, evident, prominent

amlwreigiaeth *nf* polygamy

amlwreigiwr (**-wyr**) *nm* polygamist

amlygiad (**-au**) *nm* manifestation

amlygrwydd *nm* prominence, limelight

amlygu *vb* to manifest, to reveal, to evince

amnaid (**-neidiau**) *nf* beck, nod

amneidio *vb* to beckon, to nod

amnest (**-au**) *nm* amnesty

amod (**-au**) *nmf* condition

amodi *vb* to covenant, to stipulate

amodol *adj* conditional

amp (**-au**) *nm* amp

amrant (**-au, -rannau**) *nm* eyelid

amrantiad *nm* wink, twinkling, second

amrediad *nm* range

amreiniol *adj* not privileged

amrwd *adj* uncooked, raw, crude

amryddawn *adj* versatile

amryfal *adj* sundry, manifold

amryfus *adj* erroneous, inadvertent

amryfusedd (**-au**) *nm* error, oversight

amryliw *adj* variegated; multicoloured

amryw *adj* several, sundry, various

amrywiad (**-au**) *nm* variant

amrywiaeth *nm* variety, diversity

amrywio *vb* to vary, to differ

amrywiol *adj* sundry

amser (**-oedd, -au**) *nmf* time; **amser sbâr** spare time

amseriad (**-au**) *nm* timing, dating, date

amserlen (**-ni**) *nf* time-table

amserol *adj* timely; temporal

11

amseru vb to time, to date
amserydd (-ion) nm chronologist
amseryddiaeth nf chronology
amseryddol adj chronological
amwisg (-oedd) nf covering, shroud
amwisgo vb to enwrap, to shroud
amwys adj ambiguous
amwysedd nm ambiguity
amyn conj, prep unless, except, but
amynedd nm patience
amyneddgar adj patient
an- prefix un-, in-, de-, dis-
anabl adj disabled
anabledd nm disability
anad adj: **yn anad** above all, more than
anadferadwy adj irreparable
anadl (-au, -on) nfm breath
anadliad nm breath, breathing
anadlu vb to breathe
anadlydd (-ion) nm inhaler
anadnabyddus adj unknown
anaddas adj unfit, unsuitable
anaddasu vb to unfit, to disqualify
anaeddfed, anaddfed adj unripe, immature
anaeddfedrwydd nm unripeness, immaturity
anaele adj awful, direful; incurable
anaesthetig adj anaesthetic
anaf (-au) nm blemish, defect; wound
anafu vb to blemish, to maim, to hurt
anafus adj maimed, disabled
anair (-eiriau) nm ill report, slander
anallu nm inability
analluog adj unable

analluogi vb to disable
anaml adj infrequent, rare ▸ adv rarely, seldom
anamlwg adj obscure, inconspicuous
anamserol adj untimely, mistimed
anap (anhapon) nmf mischance, mishap
anarchiaeth nfm anarchy
anarchydd (-ion) nm anarchist
anarferol adj unusual, extraordinary
anarfog adj unarmed
ancr nmf anchorite, anchoress
ancwyn (-ion) nm dinner, supper; delicacy
anchwiliadwy adj unsearchable
andras nm curse; devil, deuce
andwyo vb to spoil, to ruin, to undo
andwyol adj harmful, ruinous
anedifeiriol adj impenitent
aneffeithiol adj ineffectual
aneglur adj indistinct; illegible
aneirif adj innumerable
anelu vb to bend, to aim
anenwog adj unrenowned, ignoble, mean
anerchiad (-au) nm salutation, address
anesboniadwy adj inexplicable
anesgusodol adj inexcusable
anesmwyth adj uneasy, restless
anesmwythder, anesmwythdra nm uneasiness, unrest
anesmwytho vb to be or make uneasy
anesmwythyd nm uneasiness, disquiet

anewyllysgar *adj* unwilling

anfad *adj* wicked, nefarious

anfadrwydd *nm* wickedness, villainy

anfadwaith *nm* villainy; crime

anfadwr (-wyr) *nm* villain, scoundrel

anfaddeugar *adj* unforgiving

anfaddeuol *adj* unpardonable

anfantais (-eision) *nf* disadvantage

anfanteisiol *adj* disadvantageous

anfarwol *adj* undying, immortal

anfarwoldeb *nm* immortality

anfedrus *adj* unskilful

anfedrusrwydd *nm* unskilfulness

anfeidrol *adj* infinite

anfeidroldeb *nm* infinity

anferth *adj* huge, monstrous

anferthedd *nm* hugeness, monstrosity

anfodlon *adj* unwilling

anfodloni *vb* to discontent, to dissatisfy

anfodlonrwydd *nm* discontent

anfodd *nm* unwillingness, displeasure

anfoddhaol *adj* unsatisfactory

anfoddio *vb* to displease, to disoblige

anfoddlon *see* anfodlon

anfoddog *adj* discontented, dissatisfied

anfoddogrwydd *nm* discontentment

anfoesgar *adj* unmannerly, rude

anfoesgarwch *nm* rudeness, incivility

anfoesol *adj* immoral

anfoesoldeb *nm* immorality

anfon *vb* to send, to transmit, to dispatch

anfoneb *nf* invoice

anfoneddigaidd *adj* ungentlemanly

anfonheddig *adj* ignoble, discourteous

anfoniad *nm* sending, transmission

anfri *nm* disrespect, dishonour

anfuchedddol *adj* immoral

anfuddiol *adj* unprofitable

anfwriadol *adj* unintentional

anfwyn *adj* unkind, uncivil

anfwytadwy *adj* inedible

anfynych *adj* infrequent, rare
  ▸ *adv* seldom

anffaeledig *adj* infallible

anffaeledigrwydd *nm* infallibility

anffafriol *adj* unfavourable

anffawd (-ffodion) *nf* misfortune

anffodus, anffortunus *adj* unfortunate

anffrwythlon *adj* unfruitful, barren

anffurfio *vb* to disfigure, to deform

anffurfiol *adj* informal

anffyddiaeth *nf* atheism

anffyddiwr (-wyr) *nm* infidel, atheist

anffyddlon *adj* unfaithful

anhaeddiannol *adj* unmerited, undeserved

anhaeddiant *nm* demerit, unworthiness

anhapus *adj* unhappy, unlucky

anhardd *adj* unhandsome, unseemly, ugly

13

anhawdd adj hard, difficult
anhawddgar adj unamiable, unlovely
anhawster (anawsterau) nm difficulty
anhepgor (-ion) nm essential
anhepgorol adj indispensable
anhoffter nm hatred, dislike
anhraethadwy adj unutterable
anhraethol adj unspeakable, ineffable
anhrefn nm disorder, confusion
anhrefnu vb to disorder, to disarrange
anhrefnus adj disorderly, untidy
anhreiddiol adj impervious, impenetrable
anhreuliedig adj undigested; unspent
anhrugarog adj unmerciful, merciless
anhuddo vb to cover (a fire)
anhunedd nm wakefulness, disquiet
anhwyldeb nm disorder, complaint, illness
anhwylder nm illness
anhwylus adj unwell
anhwylustod nm inconvenience
anhyblyg adj inflexible, stiff, rigid
anhydawdd adj insoluble
anhyder nm distrust, diffidence
anhyderus adj diffident
anhydrin adj unmanageable
anhydyn adj intractable, obstinate
anhyddysg adj unversed, ignorant
anhyfryd adj unpleasant
anhyfrydwch nm unpleasantness

anhygar adj unpleasant, unamiable
anhygoel adj incredible
anhygyrch adj inaccessible
anhylaw adj unhandy, unwieldy
anhynod adj indistinctive; uncertain
anhysbys adj unknown; unversed
anhywaith adj intractable, refractory
anial adj desert, wild ▸ nm wilderness
anialwch nm wilderness
anian (-au) nf nature, instinct, genius
anianawd nm temperament, disposition
anianol adj natural
anianyddol adj physical
anifail (-feiliaid) nm animal, beast
anifeilaidd adj beastly, brutish
anifeileiddio vb to animalize, to brutalize
anlwc nf bad luck, misfortune
anlwcus adj unlucky
anllad adj wanton, lascivious, lewd
anlladrwydd nm wantonness, lewdness
anllygredig adj incorrupt, incorruptible
anllygredigaeth nf incorruption
anllythrennog adj illiterate
anllywodraeth nf misrule, anarchy
annaearol adj unearthly, weird
annatodol adj indissoluble, that cannot be undone
annaturiol adj unnatural
annealladwy adj unintelligible

anneallus *adj* unintelligent
annedwydd *adj* unhappy, miserable
annedwyddwch *nm* unhappiness
annedd (anheddau) *nf* dwelling
anneddfol *adj* lawless
annefnyddiol *adj* useless; immaterial
annel (anelau) *nfm* trap; purpose, aim
annelwig *adj* shapeless, unformed; vague
anner (aneirod, -i, -au) *nf* heifer
annerbyniol *adj* unacceptable
annerch *vb* to salute, to greet, to address ▸ *nm* (**anerchion**) salutation, greeting
annewisol *adj* ineligible, undesirable, unwelcome
annhebyg *adj* unlike, dissimilar
annhebygol *adj* unlikely, improbable
annhebygolrwydd *nm* improbability
annhebygrwydd *nm* unlikeness, unlikelihood
annheg *adj* unfair
annhegwch *nm* unfairness
annheilwng *adj* unworthy
annheilyngdod *nm* unworthiness
annherfynol *adj* endless; infinitive, infinite
annhirion *adj* cruel
annhosturiol *adj* pitiless, ruthless
annhuedd *nf* disinclination
annhueddol *adj* disinclined, indisposed
anniben *adj* untidy, slovenly
annibendod *nm* untidiness

annibyniaeth *nf* independence
annibynnol *adj* independent
Annibynnwr (-wyr) *nm* Independent
annichellgar *adj* guileless, simple
annichon, annichonadwy *adj* impossible
anniddan *adj* comfortless, miserable
anniddig *adj* peevish, irritable, fretful
anniddigrwydd *nm* peevishness
anniddos *adj* leaky, comfortless
annifeiriol *adj* innumerable, countless
anniflanedig *adj* unfading, imperishable
annifyr *adj* miserable, wretched
annifyrrwch *nm* misery
anniffoddadwy *adj* unquenchable
annigonedd *nm* insufficiency
annigonol *adj* insufficient, inadequate
annigonolrwydd *nm* inadequacy
annileadwy *adj* indelible, ineffaceable
annilys *adj* unauthentic, spurious, insincere
annillyn *adj* inelegant, clumsy
annioddefol *adj* unbearable, intolerable
anniogel *adj* unsafe, insecure
anniolchgar *adj* unthankful, ungrateful
anniolchgarwch *nm* ingratitude
annirnadwy *adj* incomprehensible
annisgrifiadwy *adj* indescribable
annisgwyliadwy *adj* unexpected

15

anniwair adj unchaste, incontinent, lewd

anniwall adj insatiable

anniweirdeb nm unchastity, incontinence

anniwylliedig adj uncultured

annoeth adj unwise, imprudent

annoethineb nm unwisdom, folly

annog vb to incite, to urge; to exhort

annormal adj abnormal

annos vb to incite, to set (a dog) on

annosbarthus adj unruly, disorderly

annuw, annuwiad (annuwiaid) nm atheist

annuwiaeth nf atheism

annuwiol adj ungodly, godless

annuwioldeb nm ungodliness

annwn, annwfn nm the underworld; hell

annwyd (anwydau, -on) nm cold

annwyl adj dear, beloved

annyledus adj undue, wrongful

annymunol adj unpleasant, disagreeable

annynol adj inhuman, cruel

annysgedig adj unlearned

anobaith nm despair

anobeithio vb to despair

anobeithiol adj hopeless

anochel, anocheladwy adj unavoidable, inevitable

anodd adj hard, difficult

anoddefgar adj impatient, intolerant

anogaeth (-au) nf exhortation

anolrheinadwy adj untraceable

anolygus adj unsightly

anonest adj dishonest

anonestrwydd nm dishonesty

anorchfygol adj irresistible; unconquerable

anorecsig adj anorexic

anorfod adj insuperable; unavoidable

anorffen adj endless, unending

anorffenedig adj incomplete, unfinished

anorthrech adj invincible

anrasol adj graceless

anrhaith (-rheithiau) nf prey, spoil, booty

anrheg (-ion) nf present, gift

anrhegu vb to present, to give

anrheithio vb to prey, to spoil, to plunder

anrheithiwr (-wyr) nm spoiler, pillager

anrhydedd (-au) nm honour

anrhydeddu vb to honour

anrhydeddus adj honourable

anrhydeddwr (-wyr) nm honourer

ansad adj unsteady, unstable

ansadrwydd nm instability

ansafadwy adj unstable; fickle

ansathredig adj untrodden, unfrequented

ansawdd (-soddau) nfm quality, state

ansefydlog adj unsettled, unstable; fickle

ansefydlogi vb to unsettle

ansicr adj uncertain, doubtful

ansicrwydd nm uncertainty, doubt

ansoddair (-eiriau) nm adjective

ansoddeiriol adj adjectival

ansyber adj untidy, slovenly

Antarctig nf; yr Antarctig the Antarctic
anterliwt (-iau) nfm interlude
anterth nm meridian, zenith, prime
antur (-iau) nfm attempt, venture; adventure; enterprise; **ar antur** at random
anturiaeth (-au) nf adventure, enterprise
anturiaethus adj adventurous, enterprising
anturiaethwr (-wyr) nm adventurer
anturio vb to venture, to adventure
anturus adj adventurous
anthem (-au) nf anthem
anudon (-au) nm false oath, perjury
anudoniaeth nf perjury
anudonwr (-wyr) nm perjurer
anufudd adj disobedient
anufudd-dod nm disobedience
anufuddhau vb to disobey
anundeb nm disunion
anunion adj crooked; unjust
anuniondeb nm injustice, iniquity
anurddo vb to spoil, to mar, to disfigure
anwadal adj unstable, fickle, changeable
anwadalu vb to waver, to vacillate
anwadalwch nm fickleness
anwar adj wild, barbarous, savage
anwaraidd adj uncivilized, barbarous
anwarddyn (-wariaid) nm barbarian, savage
anwareidd-dra nm barbarity

anwastad adj uneven, unstable, fickle
anwe (-oedd) nf woof
anwedd nm vapour, steam
anweddaidd adj unseemly, indecent
anweddus adj improper, indecent
anweledig adj unseen, invisible
anwes nm indulgence; caress
anwesog adj pampered, affectionate
anwesu vb to fondle, to caress, to pamper, to indulge
anwir adj untrue, lying, false; wicked
anwiredd (-au) nm untruth; iniquity
anwireddu vb to falsify
anwireddus adj untruthful, false, lying
anwr (-wyr) nm wretch, coward
anwybod nm ignorance
anwybodaeth nf ignorance
anwybodus adj ignorant
anwybyddu vb to ignore
anwydog adj cold, chilly; having a cold
anwydwst nf influenza
anwyldeb nm belovedness, dearness
anwyliaid npl beloved ones, favourites
anwylo vb to cherish, to fondle, to caress
anwylyd (-liaid) nm beloved
anwylyn nm favourite
anwythiad nm induction
anwytho vb to induce
anwythol adj inductive

17

anymarferol adj impractical, impracticable

anymddiried vb to mistrust, to distrust

anymwybodol adj unconscious

anymwybyddiaeth nf unconsciousness

anynad adj peevish, petulant; brawling

anysgrifenedig adj unwritten

anysgrythurol adj unscriptural

anystwyth adj stiff, rigid

anystwytho vb to stiffen

anystyriaeth nf heedlessness, rashness

anystyriol adj heedless, reckless, rash

anystywallt, anystywell adj unmanageable

apelio vb to appeal

apostol (-ion) nm apostle

apostolaidd, apostolig adj apostolic

apostoliaeth nf apostleship

apwyntiad (-au) nm appointment

apwyntio vb to appoint

ar prep on, upon, over; **ar gau** closed

âr nm ploughed land, tilth; ground

Arab (-iaid) nm Arab

arab adj facetious, merry, pleasant

Arabaidd adj Arab

arabedd nm facetiousness, wit

Arabeg nf Arabic

arabus adj witty

aradr (erydr) nm plough

araf adj slow, soft, gentle, still

arafu vb to slow; to quiet; to moderate

arafwch nm slowness; moderation

arail vb to guard, to care for, to foster ▸ adj attending, careful

araith (areithiau) nf speech

arall (eraill) adj, pron another, other; else

aralleg (-au) nfm allegory

aralleiriad (-au) nm paraphrase

aralleirio vb to paraphrase

araul adj sunny, sunlit; serene

arawd nf speech, oration

arbed vb to spare, to save

arbediad (-au) nm save, salvage

arbedol adj sparing, saving

arbedwr (-wyr) nm: **arbedwr sgrin** screen saver

arbenigaeth nf expertise; specialisation

arbenigo vb to specialise

arbenigrwydd nm speciality, prominence

arbenigwr (-wyr) nm specialist

arbennig adj special

arbrawf (arbrofion) nm experiment

arbrofi vb to experiment

arbrofol adj experimental

Arctig nf: **yr Arctig** the Arctic

arch¹ (eirchion) nf request, petition; bidding

arch² (eirch) nf ark, coffin; trunk, waist

archaeoleg nf archaeology

archangel (-ylion) nm archangel

archddiacon (-iaid) nm archdeacon

archeb (-ion) nf order

archebu vb to order

archen nf shoe; clothing

archenad nm shoe; clothing

Archentaidd adj Argentinian
archesgob (-ion) nm archbishop
archesgobaeth (-au) nf archbishopric
archfarchnad (-oedd) nf supermarket
archiad nm bidding
archif (-au) nfm archive
archifdy (-dai) nm record office
archifydd (-ion) nm archivist
archoffeiriad (-iaid) nm high priest
archoll (-ion) nf wound
archolli vb to wound
archwaeth nm taste, appetite
archwaethu vb to taste, to savour
archwiliad (-au) nm audit; checkup; inspection, examination; exploration
archwilio vb to examine, to audit; to explore
archwiliwr (-wyr) nm examiner, auditor; explorer
ardal (-oedd) nf region, district
ardalydd (-ion) nm marquis
ardreth (-i) nf rent
ardrethu vb to rent
ardystiad (-au) nm pledge, attestation
ardystio vb to pledge, to attest
arddangos vb to show, to exhibit, to indicate
arddangosfa (-feydd) nf show, exhibition
arddegau npl teens
arddegol adj teenage
arddel vb to avow, to own
arddeliad nm claim, avowal; unction

ardderchog adj excellent, noble, splendid
ardderchowgrwydd nm excellency
arddodi vb to prefix; to impose
arddodiad (-iaid) nm preposition
arddu vb to plough
arddull (-iau) nf style
arddulleg nf stylistics
ardduniant nm sublimity
arddunol adj sublime
arddwr (-wyr) nm ploughman
arddwrn (-ddyrnau) nm wrist
arddywediad (-au) nm dictation
aredig vb to plough
areitheg nf rhetoric
areithio vb to speak, to make a speech
areithiwr (-wyr) nm speaker, orator
areithyddiaeth nf oratory; elocution
arel nm laurel
aren (-nau) nf kidney; (pl) reins
arestio vb to arrest
arf (-au) nmf weapon; (pl) arms; tool
arfaeth (-au) nf purpose; decree
arfaethu vb to purpose, to intend
arfbais (-beisiau) nf coat of arms
arfdy (-dai) nm armoury
arfer vb to use, to accustom ▸ nfm (-ion) use, custom, habit
arferiad nmf use, custom, habit
arferol adj usual, customary
arfod nf stroke of a weapon, fight; armour; opportunity
arfog adj armed
arfogaeth nf armour

arfogi vb to arm

arfoll (-au) nm pledge, oath

arfordir (-oedd) nm coast

arforol adj maritime

arffed (-au) nf lap

argae (-au) nm dam, embankment; enclosed place

argeisio vb to seek

argel nmf concealment, refuge ▸ adj hidden, occult

arglwydd (-i) nm lord

arglwyddaidd adj lordly

arglwyddes (-au) nf lady

arglwyddiaeth (-au) nf lordship, dominion

argoed (-ydd) nm enclosure of trees

argoel (-ion) nf sign, token, omen

argoeli vb to betoken, to portend, to augur

argoelus adj ominous

argraff (-ion,-au) nf print, impression

argraffdy (-dai) nm printer's, printing-house

argraffiad (-au) nm impression; edition

argraffu vb to print, to impress

argraffwaith nm print, typography

argraffwasg nf printing-press

argraffwr (-wyr), argraffydd (-ion) nm printer

argrwm, argrwn adj convex

argyfwng (-yngau, -yngoedd) nm crisis

argyhoeddi vb to reprove; to convince, to convict

argyhoeddiad (-au) nm conviction

argyhoeddiadol adj convincing

argymell vb to urge, to recommend

argymhelliad nm recommendation

arholi vb to examine

arholiad (-au) nm examination; arholiad mynediad entrance examination

arholwr (-wyr) nm examiner

arhosfa nf stop; arhosfa bws, arhosfa bysiau bus stop

arhosfan (-nau) nm = arhosfa

arhosiad nm staying, stay

arhosol adj abiding, permanent

arial nm vigour, mettle

arian nm silver ▸ coll n money, cash; arian breiniol currency; arian byw mercury; arian gleision silver; arian parod cash; arian pen exact money; arian treigl current money

ariandy (-dai) nm bank

ariangar adj fond of money, avaricious

ariangarwch nm love of money, avarice

ariannaid adj silver, silvern

ariannaidd adj silvery

arianneg nmf finance

Ariannin nf Argentina

ariannog adj moneyed, wealthy, rich

ariannol adj financial, monetary

ariannu vb to silver; to finance/ fund

ariannydd (arianyddion) nm banker, investor, financier

arlais (-leisiau) nf temple

arlein, ar-lein adj, adv online

arloesi vb to clear, to prepare the way, to pioneer

arloesydd (-wyr) nm pioneer

arluniaeth nf portraiture, painting

arlunio vb to draw, to paint, to portray

arlunydd (-wyr) nm artist

arlwy (-au, -on) nmf provision, feast, menu

arlwyaeth (-au) nf catering

arlwyo vb to prepare, to provide; to cook

arlywydd (-ion) nm president

arlywyddiaeth nf presidency

arlywyddol adj presidential

arlliw (-iau) nm varnish, tint, shade, trace

arlliwio vb to colour, to tint, to paint

arllwys vb to pour out, to empty

arllwysfa nf outfall, outlet, vent

armel nm second milk

armes nf prophecy; calamity

arnofio vb to float

arobryn adj worthy, prize-winning

arofun vb to intend, to purpose

arogl (-au), aroglau (-euon) nm scent, smell

arogldarth nm incense

arogldarthu vb to burn incense

arogli, arogleuo vb to scent; to smell

arogliad nm smelling, sense of smell

aroleuadau npl: **aroleuadau gwallt** highlights

aroleuydd (-ion) nm highlighter (pen)

arolwg nm survey

arolygiad (-au) nm inspection

arolygiaeth nf superintendency

arolygu vb to superintend

arolygwr (-wyr), arolygydd (-ion) nm superintendent, inspector; supervisor

aros vb to wait, to await, to stay, to stop, to tarry, to abide, to remain; **aros ar ôl** stay behind; **aros gartref** stay in

arswyd nm dread, terror, horror

arswydo vb to dread; to shudder

arswydus adj fearful, terrible, dreadful

arsylwi vb to observe

arsyllfa (-feydd) nf observatory

arsyllu vb to observe

artaith (-teithiau) nf torture, torment, pang

arteithio vb to torture, to rack

arteithiol adj racking, excruciating

artisiog (-au) nm artichoke

artistig adj artistic

arth (eirth) nfm bear

arthes (-au) nf she-bear

arthio, arthu vb to bark, to growl

aruchel adj lofty, sublime

arucheledd nm loftiness, sublimity

aruthr adj marvellous, strange

aruthredd nm amazement, horror

aruthrol adj huge, prodigious

arwahanrwydd nm uniqueness, individuality

arwain vb to conduct, to lead, to guide, to carry

arwedd (-au, -ion) nf bearing, aspect

arweddu vb to bear

arweddwr (-wyr) nm bearer

21

arweiniad *nm* guidance; introduction

arweiniol *adj* leading, introductory

arweinydd (-ion) *nm* guide, leader; conductor

arweinyddiaeth *nf* leadership

arwerthiant (-iannau) *nm* auction

arwerthu *vb* to sell by auction

arwerthwr (-wyr) *nm* auctioneer

arwisgiad *nm* investiture

arwisgo *vb* to enrobe, to array, to invest

arwr (-wyr) *nm* hero

arwraidd *adj* heroic, epic

arwres (-au) *nf* heroine

arwrgerdd (-i) *nf* epic poem

arwriaeth *nf* heroism

arwrol *adj* heroic, gallant

arwybod *nm* awareness

arwydd (-ion) *nmf* sign, signal; ensign; **arwydd ffordd** road sign

arwyddair (-eiriau) *nm* motto

arwyddbost *nm* signpost

arwyddlun (-iau) *nm* emblem, symbol

arwyddluniol *adj* emblematic, symbolic

arwyddnod (-au) *nm* mark, token

arwyddo *vb* to sign; to signify

arwyddocâd *nm* signification, significance

arwyddocaol *adj* significant

arwyddocáu *vb* to signify, to denote

arwyl (-ion) *nf* funeral, funeral rites

arwylo *vb* to mourn over the dead

arwynebedd *nm* surface, superficies

arwynebol *adj* superficial

arwyrain *nmf* praise, panegyric
▶ *vb* to rise, to extol

arwystl *nm* mortgage

arwystlo *vb* to pledge, to mortgage

arysgrif (-au), **arysgrifen (-nau)** *nf* inscription, epigraph

asb (-iaid) *nf* asp

asbri *nm* animation, vivacity, spirits

ased *nm* asset

aseiniad (-au) *nm* assignment

asen¹ (-nau) *nf* rib

asen² (-nod) *nf* she-ass

asesiad *nm*: **asesiad parhaus** continuous assessment

asesu *vb* to assess; **asesu parhaus** continuous assessment

aseth *nf* stake, spar, lath

asgell (esgyll) *nf* wing, fin; **asgell fraith** chaffinch

asgellog *adj* winged

asgellwr (-wyr) *nm* wing, outside-forward

asglod, asglodion *npl* chips

asgre *nf* bosom, heart

asgwrn (esgyrn) *nm* bone

Asia *nf* Asia

Asiad (Asiaid) *nm* Asian

asiad (-au) *nm* joint, weld

Asiaidd *adj* Asian

asiant (-au) *nm* agent

asiantaeth *nf* agency

asid *nm* acid

asidig *adj* acidic

asiedydd *nm* joiner

asio *vb* to join, to weld; to solder; to cement

astell (astyllod, estyll) *nf* plank, shelf

astroleg nf astrology
astrus adj abstruse, difficult
astud adj attentive
astudiaeth (-au) nf study;
  astudiaethau cyfrifiadurol
  computer studies
astudio vb to study
astudrwydd nm attentiveness
aswy adj left
asyn (-nod) nm he-ass
asynnaidd adj asinine
at prep to, towards; for; at; by
atafaeliad nm confiscation,
  distraint
atafaelu vb to confiscate
atal vb to stop, to hinder, to
  withhold ▸ nm (-ion) hindrance,
  impediment; atal dweud
  stammering
ataleb (-au) nf injunction
atalfa (-feydd) nf check; stoppage
ataliad (-au) nm stoppage
ataliol adj preventive
atalnod (-au) nf stop, point
atalnodi vb to point, to punctuate
atblygol adj reflexive
ateb vb to answer, to reply ▸ nm
  (-ion) answer
atebol adj answerable, responsible
ateg (-ion) nf prop, stay, support
ategiad (-au) nm affirmation
ategol adj confirming; auxiliary
ategu vb to support
atgas adj odious, hateful
atgasedd nm hatred
atgasrwydd nm odiousness,
  hatefulness
atgenhedliad nm regeneration
atgenhedlu vb to regenerate

atgno (-oeau, -oeon) nm remorse
atgof (-ion) nm remembrance,
  reminiscence
atgofio vb to recollect, to
  remember, to remind
atgofus adj reminiscent
atgoffa vb to recall, to remind
atgyfnerthion npl reinforcements
atgyfnerthu vb to reinforce
atgyfodi vb to rise, to raise again
atgyfodiad nm resurrection
atgynhyrchu vb to reproduce
atgyweiriad (-au) nm repair
atgyweirio vb to repair, to mend
atgyweiriwr (-wyr) nm repairer,
  mender
atig (-au) nmf attic
Atlantaidd adj Atlantic
Atlantig adj Atlantic
atodi vb to add, to append, to affix
atodiad (-au) nm addition,
  appendix
atodlen (-ni) nf supplement;
  schedule
atodol adj supplementary
atolwg, atolygu vb to pray, to
  beseech
atom (-au) nfm atom
atomfa (-feydd) nf nuclear power
  station
atomig adj atomic
atsain (-seiniau) nf echo
atseinio vb to resound, to echo
atwf (atyfion) nm second growth
atyniad (-au) nm attraction
atyniadol adj attractive
atynnu vb to attract
Athen nf Athens
athletau npl athletics

23

athrawes (-au) nf teacher, governess

athrawiaeth (-au) nf doctrine

athrawiaethol adj doctrinal

athrist adj very sad, pensive, sorrowful

athro (athrawon) nm teacher, master

athrod (-ion) nm slander, libel

athrodwr (-wyr) nm slanderer, libeller

athrofa (-feydd) nf college, academy, institute

athrofaol adj academic

athroniaeth nf philosophy

athronydd (-ion, -wyr) nm philosopher

athronyddol adj philosophical

athronyddu vb to philosophize

athrylith (-oedd) nf genius

athrylithgar adj of genius, talented

athrywyn nm mediation, intervention ▸ vb to mediate, to arbitrate

aur nm gold

awch nm edge; ardour, zest; relish, appetite

awchlym adj sharp, keen, acute

awchlymu vb to sharpen, to whet

awchus adj sharp, keen; eager; greedy

awdl (-au, odlau) nf ode

awdur (-on, -iaid) nm author

awdurdod (-au) nmf authority

awdurdodedig adj authorised

awdurdodi vb to authorize

awdurdodol adj authoritative

awdures (-au) nf authoress

awduriaeth nf authorship

awel (-on) nf breeze, wind

awelog adj breezy, windy

awen¹ (-au) nf muse

awen² (-au) nf rein

awenydd (-ion) nm poet

awenyddiaeth nf poetry, poesy

awenyddol adj poetical

awenyddu vb to poetize

awgrym (-au, -iadau) nm hint, suggestion

awgrymiadol adj suggestive

awgrymog adj suggestive

awgrymu vb to hint, to suggest

awr (oriau) nf hour; oriau hamdden spare time, leisure; oriau hyblyg flexitime; oriau ychwanegol overtime

Awst nm August

Awstralia nf Australia

Awstria nf Austria

awtistig adj autistic

awydd (-au) nm desire, eagerness

awyddfryd nm vehement desire, zeal

awyddu vb to desire

awyddus adj desirous, eager, zealous

awyr nf air, sky

awyrdrom (-au) nf aerodrome

awyren (-nau, -ni) nf balloon, aeroplane

awyrendy (-dai) nm hangar

awyrgylch (-au, -oedd) nmf atmosphere

awyriad nm ventilation

awyrlong (-au) nf airship

awyru vb to air, to ventilate

b

baban (-od) *adj* baby
babanaidd *adj* babyish
babandod *nm* babyhood, infancy
babi *nm* baby
bacas (bacs(i)au) *nf* footless stocking; hair on horse's fetlocks
baco *nm* tobacco
bacwn *nm* bacon
bach¹ (-au) *nm* hook; **bachau petryal** square brackets
bach² *adj* little, small
bachell (-au, -ion) *nf* nook, corner; snare
bachgen (bechgyn) *nm* boy
bachgendod *nm* boyhood
bachgennaidd *adj* boyish
bachgennyn (bechgynnos) *nm* little boy
bachigyn (bachigion) *nm* little bit, diminutive
bachog *adj* hooked
bachu *vb* to hook, to grapple
bachwr (-wyr) *nm* hooker *(in rugby)*

bad (-au) *nm* boat; **bad achub** lifeboat
badwr (-wyr) *nm* boatman
badd (-au), baddon (-au) *nm* bath
bae (-au) *nm* bay
baedd (-od) *nm* boar
baeddu *vb* to beat, to buffet; to soil
baetio *vb* to bait, to maltreat
bag (-iau) *nm* bag; **bag aer, bag awyr** airbag
bagad (-au) *nm* cluster; troop, multitude
bagl (-aul) *nf* crook; crutch; leg
baglor (-ion) *nf* bachelor
bagloriaeth *nf* bachelorship
baglu *vb* to entangle, to ensnare, to trip
bai (beiau) *nm* fault, vice; defect; blame
baich (beichiau) *nm* burden, load
bais *nm* bottom, ford; walking
bala *nm* efflux of river from lake
balch *adj* proud; glad; delighted
balchder *nm* pride
balchdra *nm* joy, gladness
balchïo *vb* to pride
baldordd *nm* babble, balderdash
baldorddi *vb* to babble
bale *nm* ballet
baled (-i) *nf* ballad
baledwr (-wyr) *nm* ballad-monger
balm *nm* balm
balmaidd *adj* balmy
balog (-au, -ion) *nf* fly, cod-piece; flap
balleg *nf* hamper, net, purse
ballegrwyd (-au) *nf* drag-net
ban (-nau) *nmf* peak; horn; corner; stanza
banadl *npl (nf* **-hadlen)** broom

banc

banc¹ (-iau) *nm* bank

banc² (bencydd) *nm* bank, mound, hill

bancaw (-iau) *nm* band, tuft

band (-iau) *nm* band; **band eang, band llydan** broadband

baner (-au, -i) *nf* banner, flag

banerog *adj* with banners, bannered

banerwr (-wyr) *nm* standard-bearer; ensign

banffagl (-au) *nf* bonfire, blaze

bangaw *adj* eloquent, melodious, skilful

Bangladesh *nf* Bangladesh

bangor (-au, bangyr) *nfm* upper row of rods in wattle fence; monastery

baniar (-ieri) *nm* shout; banner

banllawr (-lloriau) *nm* platform

banllef (-au) *nf* loud shout

bannod (banodau) *nf* article

bannog *adj* elevated, conspicuous; horned

bar (-rau) *nm* bar

bâr *nm* fury, greed

bara *nm* bread

barbaraidd *adj* barbarous

barbareidd-dra *nm* barbarity

barbareiddio *vb* to barbarize

barbariad (-iaid) *nm* barbarian

barbariaeth *nm* barbarism

barbwr (-wyr) *nm* barber

barcer (-iaid) *nm* tanner

barclod (-iau) *nm* apron

barcud (-iaid), barcutan (-od) *nm* kite

barcut *nm* kite

barcuta *vb* to hang-glide

bardd (beirdd) *nm* bard, poet

barddas *nfm* bardism

barddol *adj* bardic

barddoni *vb* to compose poetry, to poetize

barddoniaeth *nf* poetry, verse

barddonol *adj* poetic, poetical

barf (-au) *nf* beard, whiskers

barfog *adj* bearded

bargeinio, bargenna *vb* to bargain

bargen (-einion) *nf* bargain

bargod (-ion) *nm* eaves

bargyfreithiwr (-wyr) *nm* barrister

bariaeth *nmf* evil, grief, wrath; greed

baril (-au) *nf* barrel

barilaid (-eidiau) *nf* barrelful

bario *vb* to bar, to bolt

barlad *nm* drake

barlys *nm* barley

barn (-au) *nf* judgment; opinion; sentence

barnais *nf* varnish

barnedigaeth (-au) *nf* judgment

barneisio *vb* to varnish

barnol *adj* judicial, condemnatory, annoying

barnu *vb* to judge

barnwr (-wyr) *nm* judge

baromedr *nm* barometer

barrug *nm* hoar-frost

barugo *vb* to cast hoar-frost

barugog *adj* white with hoar-frost

barus *adj* voracious, greedy

barwn (-iaid) *nm* baron

barwnes (-au) *nf* baroness

barwniaeth (-au) *nf* barony

barwnig (-iaid) *nm* baronet

bas¹ *adj* shallow ▸ *npl* (**bais, beis**) shallows

bas² *adj, nm* bass

basged (-i, -au) *nf* basket

basgedaid (-eidiau) *nf* basketful

basgedwr (-wyr) *nm* basket-maker

basil *nm* basil

basn (-au, -ys) *nm* basin

bastard (-iaid) *nm* bastard

bastardiaeth *nf* bastardy

batio *vb* to bat

batri *nm* battery

bath (-au) *nm* kind, sort; stamp; coin

bathdy (-dai) *nm* mint

bathodyn (-nau) *nm* medal, badge

bathol *adj* coin, coined

bathu *vb* to coin

baw *nm* dirt, mire, dung, filth

bawaidd *adj* dirty, vile; sordid, mean

bawd (bodiau) *nf* thumb, toe

bechan *adj f* of **bychan**

bechgynnos *npl* little boys, youngsters

bedw *npl* (*nf*-**en**) birch

bedydd *nm* baptism

bedyddfa (-fâu, -feydd) *nf* baptistry

bedyddfaen (-feini) *nm* font

bedyddio *vb* to baptize

bedyddiol *adj* baptismal; baptized

Bedyddiwr (-wyr) *nm* Baptist

bedd (-au) *nm* grave, tomb, sepulchre

beddargraff (-iadau) *nm* epitaph

beddfaen (-feini) *nm* tombstone

beddgell (-oedd) *nf* vault, catacomb

beddrod (-au) *nm* tomb, sepulchre

Beibl (-au) *nm* Bible

Beiblaidd *adj* Biblical

beic (-iau) *nm* bike; **beic modur** motorbike; **beic mynydd** mountain bike

beicio *vb* to cycle

beiciwr, beicwr (-wyr) *nm* cyclist; **beiciwr modur** motorcyclist

beichio *vb* to burden; to low; to sob

beichiog *adj* pregnant

beichiogi *vb* to conceive

beichus *adj* burdensome, oppressive

beiddgar *adj* daring, audacious; outrageous

beiddgarwch *nm* daring, audacity

beiddio *vb* to dare, to presume

beili (beilïaid) *nm* bailiff

beio *vb* to blame, to censure

beirniad (-iaid) *nm* adjudicator; critic

beirniadaeth (-au) *nf* adjudication; criticism

beirniadol *adj* critical

beirniadu *vb* to adjudicate; to criticize

beisgawn (-au) *nf* stack, heap of corn sheaves

beiston *nf* sea-shore, beach; surf

beius *adj* faulty; blameworthy

bellach *adv* now, at length

bendigaid, bendigedig *adj* blessed

bendigedigrwydd *nm* blessedness

bendith (-ion) *nf* blessing, benediction

bendithio *vb* to bless

bendithiol *adj* conferring blessings

benthyca, benthycio vb to
borrow, to lend
benthyciad nm loan
benthyciwr (-wyr) nm borrower,
lender
benthyg nm loan
benyw adj female ▸ nf (**-od**)
female, woman
benywaidd adj feminine;
effeminate
benywol adj feminine, female
ber adj f of **byr**
bêr (berau, -i) nm spear; roasting-
spit
bera nfm rick; pyramid
berdys npl (nm **-yn**, nf **-en**) shrimps
berf (-au) nf verb; **berf anghyflawn**
transitive verb; **berf gyflawn**
intransitive verb
berfa (-fâu, -feydd) nf barrow
Berlin nf Berlin
berth adj beautiful, valuable
berthog adj wealthy, fair
berw nm, adj boiling, seething,
ebullition
berwedig adj boiling
berwedydd (-ion) nm boiler
berwedd-dy (-dai) nm brewery
berweddu vb to brew
berwi vb to boil, to seethe, to
effervesce
berwr coll n cress
betgwn nmf nightgown
betws nm oratory, chapel; birch
grove
betys npl beetroot
beudy (-dai) nm cow-house, byre
beunoeth, beunos adv nightly,
every night

beunydd adv daily, every day,
always
beunyddiol adj daily, quotidian
bidog (-au) nf dagger; bayonet
bing (-oedd) nm alley, bin
bil (-iau) nm bill
bilidowcar nm cormorant
bilwg (-ygau) nm billhook
bin (-iau) nm: **bin sbwriel** litter bin
biocemeg nfm biochemistry
bioleg nf biology
bir (-oedd) nm beer
bisgeden nf biscuit, cracker
biswail nm dung
blaen adj fore, foremost, first;
front ▸ nm (**-au, -ion**) point,
end, top, tip; front, van, priority,
precedence; edge
blaenasgellwr (-wyr) nm wing-
forward
blaenbrawf (-brofion) nm
foretaste
blaendal nm prepayment, deposit
blaendarddu vb to sprout
blaendir nm foreground
blaenddalen (-nau) nf title page
blaenddodi vb to prefix
blaenddodiad (-iaid) nm prefix
blaenffrwyth nm first-fruits
blaengar adj prominent,
progressive
blaengroen (-grwyn) nm foreskin
blaenllaw adj forward, prominent
blaenllym adj sharp, keen
blaenllymu adj sharpen, whet
blaenor (-iaid) nm leader; elder
blaenori vb to lead, to precede
blaenoriaeth nf preference;
precedence

blaenorol *adj* previous, antecedent

blaenu *vb* to point; to outrun; to precede

blaenwr (-wyr) *nm* leader; forward

blagur *coll n* sprouts, buds, shoots

blaguro *vb* to sprout, to bud; to flourish

blaguryn *nm* sprout, bud, shoot

blaidd (bleiddiaid, bleiddiau) *nm* wolf

blas *nm* taste, savour, relish

blasio, blasu *vb* to taste

blasus *adj* tasty, savoury, delicious

blawd (blodion, -iau) *nm* flour, meal

blêr *adj* untidy, slovenly

blerwm *nm* blabberer

blew *npl (nm* **-yn)** hairs; hair; fur

blewog *adj* hairy, shaggy

blewyn *nm* straw

bliant *nm* lawn, fine linen

blif (-iau) *nm* catapult

blingo *vb* to skin, to flay

blin *adj* tired, weary; peevish, irritable

blinder (-au) *nm* weariness; trouble

blinderog, blinderus *adj* wearisome

blinfyd *nm* tribulation

blino *vb* to tire, to weary; to trouble, to vex

blith (-ion) *nm* milk ▶ *adj* milch

blith draphlith *adv* helter-skelter

bloc (-iau) *nm*: **bloc swyddfeydd** office block

blodeugerdd (-i) *nf* anthology

blodeuglwm *nm* bunch, nosegay

blodeuo *vb* to flower, to bloom, to flourish

blodeuog *adj* flowery; flourishing

blodeuyn, blodyn (blodau) *nm* flower

blodfresychen *nf* cauliflower

blodiog *adj* floury, mealy

bloddest *nf* rejoicing, acclamation

bloedd (-iau, -iadau) *nf* shout

bloeddio, bloeddian *vb* to shout, to cry

bloeddiwr (-wyr) *nm* shouter

bloesg *adj* lisping, faltering, indistinct

bloesgi *vb* to lisp, to falter, to speak indistinctly

blog (-iau) *nm* blog

blogio *vb* to blog

blogiwr (-wyr) *nm* blogger

blwch (blychau) *nm* box; **blwch postio** mailbox

blwng *adj* angry, sullen, cheerless ▶ *nm* anger

blwydd (-au, -i) *nf, adj* year of age; year-old

blwydd-dal *nm* annuity, pension

blwyddiad (-iaid) *nm* yearling, annual

blwyddiadur (-on) *nm* yearbook, annual

blwyddyn (blynyddoedd) *nf* year; **blwyddyn bwlch** gap year

blychaid (-eidiau) *nm* boxful

blynedd *npl* years *(after numerals)*

blynyddol *adj* annual, yearly

blys *nm* craving, lust

blysig *adj* greedy, lustful

blysigrwydd *nm* greediness

blysio *vb* to crave, to lust

bocs (-ys) *nm* box

bocsach *nm* vaunt, boast, brag

29

bocsio vb to box
bocsiwr (-wyr) nm boxer
boch (-au) nf cheek
bochdew nf hamster
bochgoch adj rosy-cheeked
bod vb to be, to exist ▶ nm (-au) being, existence; **Y Bod Mawr** God
bod(olaeth) nm(f) existence
boda nmf buzzard
bodio vb to thumb, to finger
bodlon adj content, willing
bodloni vb to satisfy, to content; to be content
bodlonrwydd nm contentment
bodoli vb to exist
bodd nm pleasure, will, consent
boddfa nf flood, drenching
boddhad nm pleasure, satisfaction
boddhaol adj pleasing, satisfactory
boddhau vb to please, to satisfy
boddhaus adj pleased
boddi vb to drown; to flood
boddio vb to please, to satisfy
boddlon see bodlon
bogail (-eiliau) nmf navel; boss, hub
boglwm (boglymau), boglyn (-nau) nm boss, knob, stud, bud, bubble
bol, bola (boliau) nm belly
bolaid (-eidiau) nm bellyful
bolera vb to gorge, to guzzle; to sponge
bolerwr (-wyr) nm sponge, parasite
bolgi (-gwn) nm gourmand, glutton
bolheulo vb to bask in the sun
bolio vb to belly, to gorge

boliog adj big-bellied, corpulent
boloch nm pain, anxiety, destruction
bolrwth adj gluttonous, greedy
bolrwym adj costive, constipated
bolsothach, bolysothach nm hotchpotch; jargon
bolwst nfm gripes, colic
bollt (-au, -ydd, byllt) nf bolt
bom (-iau) nmf bomb
bomio vb to bomb
bomiwr (-wyr) nm bomber; **bomiwr hunanleiddiol** suicide bomber
bôn (bonau, bonion) nm bottom; stump; **yn y bôn** basically
boncath (-od) nm buzzard
bonclust (-iau) nm box on the ear
boncyff (-ion) nm stump, trunk, stock
bondigrybwyll adv forsooth ▶ adj hardly mentionable
bondo nm eaves
bonedd nm gentility, nobility
boneddigaidd adj noble; gentlemanly
boneddigeiddrwydd nm gentlemanliness
boneddiges (-au) nf lady
bonesig nf lady; Miss
bonet (-i) nf bonnet
bonheddig adj noble, gentle, gentlemanly
bonheddwr (-wyr) nm gentleman
bonllef (-au) nf shout
bonllwm adj bare-bottomed; bare-backed
Bonn nf Bonn
bonyn (bonion) nm stump

bord (-ydd, -au) nf table, board
bordhwylio vb to windsurf
bore (-au) nm morning ▸ adj early
boreddydd nm day-break, morning
borefwyd nm breakfast
boreol adj morning
bors nf hernia
bos nf palm of the hand, fist
Bosnia nf Bosnia
bost (-iau) nm boast, brag
bostio vb to boast, to brag
botas, en (-asau) nf boot
botwm (-ymau) nm button
botymog adj buttoned
botymu vb to button
both (-au) nf nave of wheel; boss
bowlio vb to bowl
brac adj free, frank, talkative
bracso vb to wade, to paddle
bracty (-tai) nm malt-house,
  brewery
brad (-au) nm treason; plot
bradfwriadu vb to plot, to conspire
bradlofrudd (-ion) nm assassin
bradlofruddiaeth (-au) nf
  assassination
bradlofruddio vb to assassinate
bradwr (-wyr) nm traitor
bradwriaeth (-au) nf treason,
  treachery
bradwrus adj traitorous,
  treacherous
bradychu vb to betray
braen adj rotten, corrupt
braenar (-au) nm fallow
braenaru vb to fallow, to pioneer
braenu vb to rot, to putrify
braf adj fine
brag nm malt

bragad nf army, battle; offspring
bragaldian vb to jabber, to gabble,
  to prate
bragio vb to brag, to boast
bragiwr (-wyr) nm bragger,
  boaster
bragu vb to malt, to brew
bragwair nm moorland hay, coarse
  grass
bragwr (-wyr) nm maltster, brewer
braich (breichiau) nf arm; branch,
  handle; headland
braidd adv rather, somewhat
braint (breintiau) nf privilege
braisg adj gross, thick, large;
  pregnant
braith adj f of brith
brân (brain) nf crow, rook, raven
bras (breision) adj fat; coarse; rich;
  luxuriant
brasáu vb to grow fat or gross
brasbwytho vb to baste, to tack
brasgamu vb to stride
Brasil nf Brazil
braslun (-iau) nm sketch, outline
braslun bywyd nm curriculum
  vitae
braslunio vb to sketch, to outline
brasnaddu vb to rough-hew
braster nm fat
brasterog adj fat, greasy
brat (-iau) nm rag, clout; pinafore
bratiaith nf debased language
bratiog adj ragged, tattered
brath (-au) nm stab, wound;
  sting; bite
brathog adj that bites; biting
brathu vb to stab, to wound; to
  sting; to bite

brau

brau *adj* brittle, frail, fragile; kindly; prompt

braw (-iau) *nm* terror, dread, fright

brawd¹ (brodyr) *nm* brother; friar; **brawd yng nghyfraith** brother-in-law

brawd² (brodiau) *nf* judgment

brawdgarwch *nm* brotherly love

brawdmaeth *nm* foster-brother

brawdol *adj* brotherly, fraternal

brawdoliaeth (-au) *nf* brotherhood, fraternity

brawddeg (-au) *nf* sentence

brawddegu *vb* to construct sentences

brawl *nm* boast, brag; gabble, tattle

brawychu *vb* to frighten, to terrify

brawychus *adj* frightful, terrible

brawychwr *nm* terrorist

bre (-on, -oedd) *nf* hill, highland

brebwl (-yliaid) *nm* blockhead; prattler

brêc *nm* brake

breci *nm* wort; spree

brecio *vb* to brake

brecwast (-au) *nmf* breakfast

brecwasta *vb* to breakfast

brech¹ *nf* eruption, pox; **brech yr ieir** chickenpox

brech² *adj f of* **brych**

brechdan (-au) *nf* slice of bread and butter

brechiad (-au) *nm* inoculation, vaccination

brechu *vb* to vaccinate, to inoculate

bredych (-au, -ion) *nm* betrayal; fear; rascal

bref (-iadau) *nf* lowing; bleat; bray

breferad (-au) *nm* bellowing

brefiad (-au) *nm* lowing; bleating

brefu *vb* to low; to bleat; to bray

breg *nm* guile, blemish, breach
  ▸ *adj* fragile, faulty

bregliach *vb* to jabber

bregus *adj* frail, brittle, rickety

breichled (-au) *nf* bracelet

breichrwy, breichrwyf (-au) *nmf* bracelet

breindal *nm* royalty

breinio *vb* to privilege, to enfranchise

breiniol *adj* privileged, free

breinlen (-ni) *nf* charter

breintal *nm* bonus; royalty

breintiedig *adj* patented, patent

breintio *vb* to privilege, to favour

brenhinaidd *adj* kingly, regal

brenhindod *nm* royalty

brenhindref (-i) *nf* royal city

brenhinllys (-dai) *nm* royal palace

brenhines (breninesau) *nf* queen

brenhinfainc *nf* throne

brenhiniaeth (breniniaethau) *nf* kingdom

brenhinllys *nm* basil

brenhinol *adj* royal, regal

brenin (-hinoedd) *nm* king

brest (-iau) *nf* breast, chest

bresych *npl (nf -en)* cabbages

brethyn (-nau) *nm* cloth

brethynnwr (-ynwyr) *nm* clothier; cloth-worker

breuan (-au) *nf* quern; print of butter

breuder *nm* brittleness, frailty

breuddwyd (-ion) *nmf* dream; **breuddwyd gwrach** wishful thinking

breuddwydio *vb* to dream

breuddwydiol *adj* dreaming, dreamy

breuddwydiwr (-wyr) *nm* dreamer

brëyr, brehyr (brehyrion, -iaid) *nm* nobleman, chief, baron

bri *nm* honour, renown, distinction

briallu *npl* (*nf* **briallen**) primroses

bribys *npl* fragments, scraps

bricsen *nf* brick

bricyllen *nf* apricot

brid *nm* breed

bridio *vb* to breed

brifo *vb* to hurt

brig (-au) *nm* top; (*pl*) twigs

brigâd (-au) *nf* brigade; **brigâd dân** fire-brigade

briger (-au) *nm* hair of head; top

brigo *vb* to top; to branch

brigog *adj* branching; flourishing

brigwyn *adj* white-topped, white-crested

brigyn (brigau) *nm* twig

brith (f braith) *adj* mottled, speckled

britho *vb* to mottle, to speckle; to dazzle

Brithwr (-wyr) *nm* Pict

brithyll (-od, -iaid) *nm* trout

briw *adj* broken, bruised, sore ► *nm* (**-iau**) wound, sore

briwfwyd *nm* crumbs, mince

briwgig *nm* mince

briwlaw *nm* drizzling rain

briwlio *vb* to broil

briwo *vb* to wound, to hurt

briwsion *npl* (*nm* **-yn**) crumbs, fragments

briwsioni *vb* to crumble

briwsionyn *nm* crumb

briwsyn (briwsion) *nm* crumb, morsel

bro (-ydd) *nf* land; region; vale

broch¹ *nm* badger

broch² *nm* froth, anger, tumult

brochi *vb* to chafe, to fume; to bluster

brochus *adj* fuming; blustering

brodio *vb* to embroider; to darn

brodor (-ion) *nm* native; fellow countryman

brodorol *adj* native, indigenous

broga (-od) *nm* frog

brol *nf* boast, brag

broliant *nm* blurb

brolio *vb* to boast, to brag, to vaunt

broliwr (-wyr) *nm* boaster, braggart

bron¹ (-nau, -nydd) *nf* breast; hillside

bron² *adv* almost, nearly, practically; **o'r bron** completely, in succession

bronfraith (-freithod) *nf* thrush

brongoch (-iaid) *nmf* robin redbreast

bronwen *nf* weasel

bru *nm* womb

brud (-iau) *nm* chronicle; divination

brudio *vb* to prognosticate, to divine

brudiwr (-wyr) *nm* wizard, soothsayer

brwd *adj* hot, fervent ► *nm* boil, heat

brwdfrydedd nm ardour, enthusiasm

brwdfrydig adj ardent, enthusiastic

brwmstan nm brimstone, sulphur

brwmstanaidd adj sulphury

brwnt (f**bront**) adj foul, nasty, dirty; harsh

brwyd¹ (-**au**) nm embroidering frame; skewer

brwyd² adj variegated; bloodstained; shattered

brwydo vb to embroider; to tear, to consume

brwydr (-**au**) nf battle, combat

brwydro vb to battle, to combat

brwydrwr (-**wyr**) nm fighter, combatant

brwydwaith nm embroidery

brwylio vb to broil

brwyn nm grief, sadness

brwynen (**brwyn**) nf rush

brwynog adj rushy

brwysg adj drunk; vigorous

brycan, brecan (-**au**) nfm blanket, rug

brych (f**brech**) adj mottled, brindled, freckled ▸ nm the afterbirth of a cow

brychau npl (nm -**euyn**) spots, freckles

brycheulyd adj spotted, brindled

brycheuyn nm spot

brychni nm spots, freckles

brychu vb to spot, to freckle

bryd nm mind, heart, will

brydio vb to burn, to inflame, to boil, to throb

brygawthan vb to jabber, to prate, to rant

bryn (-**iau**) nm hill

bryncyn (-**nau**) nm hillock

bryniog adj hilly

brynti, bryntni nm filthiness, filth

brys nm haste, hurry

brysio vb to hasten, to hurry

brysiog adj hurried, hasty

bryslythyr (-**au**) nm dispatch

brysneges (-**au**) nf telegram

brytheirio vb to belch; to utter oaths, threats etc

Brython (-**iaid**) nm Briton, Welshman

Brythoneg nf British language, Welsh

brythwch nm storm, tumult; groan

bryweddu vb to brew

brywes nm brewis

bual (**buail**) nm buffalo, drinking horn

buan adj fast, quick, swift, fleet; soon

buander, buandra nm swiftness, speed

buandroed adj swift-footed

buarth (-**au**) nm yard

buchdraeth (-**au**) nf biography, memoir

buchedd (-**au**) nf life, conduct

bucheddol adj right-living, virtuous

bucheddu vb to live, to flourish

buches (-**au**) nf herd of cows

buchfrechu vb to vaccinate

budr adj dirty, filthy, foul, vile

budreddi nm filthiness, filth

budro vb to dirty, to soil, to foul

budd (-ion) nm benefit, profit, gain

buddai (-eiau) nf churn

buddel (-wydd) nmf cow-house post, pillar

buddiant (-iannau) nm interest

buddio vb to profit, to avail

buddiol adj profitable, beneficial, useful

buddioldeb nm profitableness, expediency

buddran nf dividend

buddsodd (-ion), buddsoddiad (-au) nm investment

buddsoddi vb to invest

buddugol adj winning, victorious

buddugoliaeth (-au) nf victory

buddugoliaethus adj victorious, triumphant

buddugwr (-wyr) nm winner, victor

bugail (-eiliaid) nm shepherd; pastor

bugeiles (-au) nf shepherdess

bugeiliaeth (-au) nf pastorate

bugeilio, bugeilia vb to watch, to shepherd

bugeiliol adj pastoral

bugunad nm bellowing, roar

bun nf maid, maiden

burgyn (-nod, iaid) nm carcass, carrion

burman, burum nm barm, yeast

busnes (-ion) nmf business

busnesa vb to interfere, to meddle

busnesgar, busneslyd adj meddlesome

bustach (-tych) nm bullock, steer

bustachu vb to buffet about, to bungle

bustl nm gall, bile

bustlaidd adj like gall; bitter as gall

buwch (buchod) nf cow; **buwch goch gota** ladybird

bwa (bwâu) nm bow; arch

bwaog adj arched, vaulted

bwbach (-od) nm bugbear, bogey, scarecrow

bwced (-i) nmf bucket

bwci (-ïod) nm bugbear, bogey, ghost

bwcl (byclau) nm buckle

bwcled (-au) nf buckler

bwch (bychod) nm buck; **bwch dihangol** scapegoat; **bwch gafr** he-goat

Bwdhaeth nf Buddhism

Bwdhaidd adj Buddhist

bwgan (-od) nm bogey, ghost, scarecrow

bwgwl (bygylau) nm threat, menace

bwgwth see bygwth, bygythio

bwhwman vb to beat about; to vacillate

bŵl (bylau) nm globe, ball, knob

bwlch (bylchau) nm gap; pass; notch

bwled (-i) nf bullet

Bwlgaria nf Bulgaria

bwn (bynnoedd, byniaid) nm bittern

bwndel (-i) nm bundle

bwngler (-iaid) nm bungler

bwnglera vb to bungle

bwngleraidd adj bungling, clumsy

bwnglerwaith nm bungle, botch

bwnglerwch *nm* clumsiness
bwr (**byr**) *adj* fat, big, strong
bwrdais (**-deisiaid**) *nm* burgess
bwrdeistref (**-i**) *nf* borough
bwrdd (**byrddau**) *nm* table; deck; board; **bwrdd du** black-board
bwrgler *nm* burglar
bwrglera *vb* to burgle
bwrgleriaeth *nf* burglary
bwriad (**-au**) *nm* purpose, intention
bwriadol *adj* intentional
bwriadu *vb* to purpose, to intend
bwrlwm (**byrlymau**) *nm* bubble; gurgling
bwrn (**byrnau**) *nm* burden, incubus; bale
bwrw *vb* to cast; to shed; to strike; to imagine, to suppose; to spend ► *nm* cast, throw; woof
bws (**bysiau, bysys**) *nm* bus; **bws mini** minibus
bwtler (**-iaid**) *nm* butler
bwtri *nm* buttery, pantry, dairy
bwth (**bythod**) *nm* hut, booth, cot
bwthyn (**bythynnod**) *nm* cottage, cabin, hut
bwyall (**bwyeill**), **bwyell** (**bwyeill**) *nf* axe
bwyd (**-ydd**) *nm* food; **bwyd sothach** junk food; **bwyd sydyn** fast food
bwyda, bwydo *vb* to feed
bwydlen *nf* menu
bwyd-offrwm (**-ymau**) *nm* meat-offering
bwydwr (**-wyr**) *nm* feeder
bwygilydd *adv* (from one) to the other
bwylltid (**-au**) *nm* swivel

bwyllwr, bwyllwrw (**-yriau**) *nm* provisions for journey
bwysel (**-au, -i**) *nm* bushel
bwystfil (**-od**) *nm* (wild) beast
bwystfilaidd *adj* brutal
bwystfiles (**-au**) *nf* beast
bwyta *vb* to eat; to corrode
bwytadwy *adj* eatable, edible
bwytäwr (**-wyr**) *nm* eater
bwyteig *adj* greedy, voracious
bwyty (**-tai, -tyau**) *nm* restaurant
bychan (*f* **bechan**) *adj* little, small
bychander, bychandra *nm* littleness, smallness
bychanu *vb* to belittle, to minimize
bychanus *adj* derogatory
byd (**-oedd**) *nm* world; state; life
bydaf (**-au**) *nm* beehive
byd-eang *adj* worldwide
bydio *vb* to live, to fare
bydol *adj* worldly, secular
bydolddyn (**-ion**) *nm* worldling
bydolrwydd *nm* worldliness
bydwraig (**-wragedd**) *nf* midwife
bydwreigiaeth *nf* midwifery
bydysawd *nm* universe
byddag (**-au**) *nf* running knot, noose
byddar *adj* deaf ► *nm* (**-iaid, byddair**) deaf person
byddardod *nm* deafness
byddarol *adj* deafening
byddaru *vb* to deafen, to stun
byddin (**-oedd**) *nf* army, host
byddino *vb* to set army in array, to embattle
byddinog *adj* with armies

bygwth vb to threaten, to menace ▸ nm (**-ython, -ythiau**) threat, menace

bygythiad (-au) nm threat; **bygythiad bom** bomb scare

bygythio vb to threaten, to menace

bygythiol adj threatening, menacing

byl (-au) nfm edge, brim (of vessel); **hyd y fyl** to the brim

bylb (-au) nm bulb

bylchog adj gapped, gappy; notched

bylchu vb to make a gap, to breach; to notch

byngalo (-s, -au) nm bungalow

bynnag pron -ever, -soever

bynsen nf bun

byr (f **ber**) adj short, brief

byrbryd (-iau) nm luncheon, snack

byrbwyll adj impulsive, rash

byrbwylltra nm impulsiveness

byrder, byrdra nm shortness, brevity

byrdwn nm burden, refrain, chorus

byrddaid (-eidiau) nm tableful

byrddio vb to board

byrddiwr (-wyr) nm boarder

byrfodd nm abbreviation

byrfyfyr adj impromptu

byrgorn adj shorthorn

byrgyr nm burger

byrhau vb to shorten, to abridge

byrhoedlog adj short-lived

byrlymu vb to bubble, to gurgle

byrllysg (-au) nmf mace

byrnio (-u) vb to bale, to bundle

byrnwr (-wyr) nm baler

byrstio vb to burst

bys (-edd) nm finger; toe; hand of dial, latch

bysaid (-eidiau) nm pinch

byseddu vb to finger

bysled, bysledr (-au) nm finger-stall

byth adv ever, for ever ▸ nm eternity

bytheiad (-aid) nm hound

bytheirio vb to belch, to threaten

bythgofiadwy adj memorable

bythol adj everlasting, eternal, perpetual

bytholi vb to perpetuate

bytholwyrdd (-ion) adj, nm evergreen

bythynnwr (-ynwyr) nm cottager

byw vb to live ▸ adj alive, living, quick ▸ nm life

bywgraffiad (-au) nm biography

bywgraffiadol adj biographical

bywgraffiadur (-on) nm biographical dictionary

bywgraffydd (-ion) nm biographer

bywgraffyddol adj biographical

bywhau, bywiocáu vb to animate, to vivify, to quicken

bywiad nm see bywad

bywiog adj lively, animated, vivacious

bywiogi vb to enliven, to animate

bywiol adj living, animate

bywoliaeth (-oliaethau) nf living

bywyd (-au) nm life

bywydeg *nf* biology
bywydegwr (-wyr) *nm* biologist
bywydfad (-au) *nm* lifeboat
bywydol *adj* of life, vital
bywyn (-nau) *nm* pith, core

cabaets *npl* (*nf* **cabaetsen**)
cabbage
caban (-au) *nm* cabin
cabidwl *nm* consistory, chapter
cabl (-au) *nm* blasphemy, reviling
cabledd (-au) *nm* blasphemy
cableddus *adj* blasphemous
cablu *vb* to blaspheme, to revile
cablwr (-wyr), cablydd (-ion) *nm*
blasphemer
caboli *vb* to polish
cacamwci *nm* burdock
cacen (-nau, -ni) *nf* cake
cacwn *npl* (*nf* **cacynen**) wasps;
wild bees
cachfa (-feydd) *nf* excretion;
closet
cachgi (-gwn) *nm* coward; sneak
cachiad *nm* excretion; jiffy; coward
cachlyd *adj* befouled, dirty
cachu *vb* to defecate
cachwr (-wyr) *nm* coward; sneak;
one who excretes

cad (**-au, -oedd**) *nf* battle; army, host

cadach (**-au**) *nm* cloth, kerchief, clout

cadair (**-eiriau**) *nf* chair, seat; cradle; udder

cadarn (**cedyrn**) *adj* strong, mighty; firm

cadarnhad *nm* affirmation, confirmation

cadarnhaol *adj* affirmative

cadarnhau *vb* to strengthen, to confirm

cadeirfardd (**-feirdd**) *nm* chaired bard

cadeirio *vb* to chair

cadeiriog *adj* chaired

cadeiriol *adj* pertaining to a chair, cathedral

cadeirydd (**-ion**) *nm* chairman

cadernid *nm* strength; stability

cadfarch (**-feirch**) *nm* war-horse

cadfridog (**-ion**) *nm* general

cadfwyall (**-eill, -yll**) *nf* battle-axe

cadlas (**-lesydd**) *nf* close, enclosure

cadlong (**-au**) *nf* warship, battleship

cadlys (**-oedd**) *nf* camp, headquarters

cadno (**cadnoid, cadnawon**) *nm* fox

cadnöes, cadnawes (**-au**) *nf* vixen

cadoediad (**-au**) *nm* armistice, truce

cadofydd (**-ion**) *nm* tactician, strategist

cadofyddiaeth *nf* tactics, strategy

cadofyddol *adj* tactical, strategic

cadw *vb* to keep, to preserve, to save; to hold; **cadw'n heini** to keep fit

cadwedig *adj* saved

cadwedigaeth *nf* salvation

cadw-mi-gei *nm* money-box

cadwraeth *nf* keeping; observance; conservation

cadwyn (**-au, -i**) *nf* chain

cadwyno *vb* to chain

cadwynog *adj* chained, in chains

caddug *nm* darkness; mist, fog

caddugo *vb* to darken, to obscure

cae (**-au**) *nm* field; fence, hedge; brooch

caead (**-au**) *nm* cover, lid ▸ *adj* shut, closed

caeadle (**-oedd**) *nm* enclosure

caeedig *adj* closed, fenced

cael *vb* to have; to get; to find

caen (**-au**) *nf* surface; peel; coating

caenen (**-nau**) *nf* layer, film, flake

caentach (**-au**) *nf* wrangle, grumbling ▸ *vb* to wrangle, to grumble

caenu *vb* to coat, to finish

caer (**-au, ceyrydd**) *nf* wall; castle; city

Caerdydd *nf* Cardiff

Caeredin *nf* Edinburgh

caeriwrch *nm* roebuck

caerog *adj* walled, fortified; brocaded

Caersalem *nf* Jerusalem

caeth *adj* bound, captive, confined ▸ *nm* (**-ion**) bondman, slave; **caeth i gyffuriau** addicted to drugs

caethder *nm* strictness; restraint; asthma

caethfab (-**feibion**) *nm* slave
caethfasnach *nf* slave-trade
caethferch (-**ed**) *nf* slave
caethforwyn (-**forynion**) *nf* slave
caethglud *nf* captivity
caethgludiad (-**au**) *nm* captivity
caethgludo *vb* to lead captive
caethiwed *nm* slavery, bondage, captivity, detention
caethiwo *vb* to bind, to confine, to enslave
caethiwus *adj* confining; confined, tied
caethlong (-**au**) *nf* slave-ship
caethwas (-**weision**) *nm* slave
caethwasanaeth, caethwasiaeth *nm* slavery
cafell (-**au**) *nf* cell; sanctuary, oracle
cafn (-**au**) *nm* trough, gutter
cafnedd *nm* concavity
cafnio, cafnu *vb* to hollow out, to scoop, to gouge
cafod *see* **cawod**
caffael *vb* to get, to obtain
caffaeledd *nm* availability; acquisitiveness
caffaeliad (-**au**) *nm* acquisition, asset; prey, spoil
caffe (-**s**), **caffi** (-**s**) *nm* café, restaurant; **caffe rhyngrwyd** internet café, cybercafé
caffio *vb* to snatch, to grapple
cafflo *vb* to cheat; to entangle
cagl *nm* clotted dirt
caglu *vb* to befoul, to bedraggle
cangell (-**hellau**) *nf* chancel
cangelloriaeth *nf* chancellorship
cangen (-**hennau**) *nf* branch, bough

canghellor (**cangellorion**) *nm* chancellor
canghennog *adj* branching
canghennu *vb* to branch, to ramify
caib (**ceibiau**) *nf* pickaxe, mattock
cail (**ceiliau**) *nf* sheepfold, flock of sheep
caill (**ceilliau**) *nf* testicle
cain *adj* fair, fine, elegant
cainc (**cangau, ceinciau**) *nf* branch; strand; strain
cais (**ceisiadau**) *nm* application; attempt; try
cal, cala (-**iau**) *nf* penis
calan (-**nau**) *nm* first day of month; **Dydd Calan** New Year's Day
calclwlws (**calcwli**) *nm* calculus
calch *nm* lime
calchaidd *adj* calcareous
calchbibonwy *nm* stalactite
calchbost (-**byst**) *nm* stalagmite
calchen *nf* limestone; lump of lime
calchfaen (-**feini**) *nm* limestone
calcho, calchu *vb* to lime
caled *adj* hard; severe; harsh; dry
caledfwrdd *nm* hardboard
caledi *nm* hardness; hardship
caledu *vb* to harden, to dry
caledwch *nm* hardness
calen (-**nau, -ni**) *nf* whetstone; bar
calendr *nm* calendar
calennig *nmf* New Year's gift
calon (-**nau**) *nf* heart
calondid *nm* encouragement
calon-dyner *adj* tender-hearted
calon-galed *adj* hard-hearted
calon-galedwch *nm* hard-heartedness
calonnog *adj* hearty; high-spirited

calonogi vb to hearten, to encourage
calori (-ïau) nm calorie
calsiwm nm calcium
call adj wise, sensible, rational
callestr (cellystr) nf flint
callineb nm wisdom, sense
cam¹ (-au) nm step
cam² adj crooked, wry; wrong
  ▶ nm (-au) injury, wrong
cam- prefix wrong, mis-
camarfer vb to misuse, to abuse
  ▶ nmf (-ion) misuse, malpractice
camargraff nfm wrong impression
camarwain vb to mislead
camarweiniol adj misleading
Cambodia nf Cambodia
cambren (-ni) nm swingletree
camchwarae nm foul play
camdafliad (-au) nm foul throw
camdaflu vb to foul throw
camder, camdra nm crookedness
cam-drefn nf disorder
camdreuliad nm indigestion
camdreulio vb to mis-spend
cam-drin vb to ill-treat, to abuse
camdriniaeth (-au) nf ill-treatment
camdystiolaeth (-au) nf false witness
camdystiolaethu vb to bear false witness
camddeall vb to misunderstand
camddealltwriaeth nm misunderstanding
camddefnydd nm misuse
camddefnyddio vb to misuse

camedd nm bend, curvature; **camedd y droed** instep; **camedd y gar** knee-joint
cameg (-au, cemyg) nf felloe
camel (-od) nm camel
camenw (-au) nm misnomer
camenwi vb to misname
camera (camerâu) nm camera; **camera digidol** digital camera; **camera fideo** video camera
camfa (-feydd) nf stile
camfarnu vb to misjudge
camgred (-oau, -au) nf misbelief, heresy
camgredu vb to misbelieve
camgredwr (-wyr) nm heretic
camgwl nm penalty, fine; blame
camgyfrif vb to miscalculate
camgyhuddiad (-au) nm false accusation
camgyhuddo vb to accuse falsely
camgymeriad (-au) nm mistake
camgymryd vb to mistake, to err
camlas (-lesi, -lesydd) nfm canal
camliwio vb to misrepresent
camochri vb to be offside
camog (-au) nf felloe
camp (-au) nf feat, exploit; game; prize
campfa (-feydd) nf gymnasium
campus adj excellent, splendid, grand
campwaith (-weithiau) nm masterpiece, feat
campwr (-wyr) nm champion
camre nm walk, footstep(s)
camsyniad (-au) nm mistake
camsynied vb to mistake
camsyniol adj mistaken

camu¹ vb to bow, to bend, to stoop

camu² vb to step, to stride

camwedd (-au) nm iniquity, transgression

camweddu vb to transgress

camwri nm injury, wrong

camymddwyn vb to misbehave

camymddygiad (-au) nm misconduct

can adj white ► nm flour

cân (caniadau, caneuon) nf song

canabis nm cannabis

Canada nf Canada

cancr nm canker; cancer

cancro vb to canker, to corrode

candryll adj shattered, wrecked

canfasio vb to canvass

canfed adj hundredth

canfod vb to see, to perceive, to behold

canfyddadwy adj perceptible

canfyddiad nm perception

canhwyllbren (canwyllbrenni, -au) nmf candlestick

canhwyllwr (canhwyllwyr) nm chandler

caniad¹ nm singing; ringing; crowing

caniad² (-au) nf song, poem

caniadaeth nf singing, psalmody

caniatâd nm leave, permission, consent

caniataol adj permissive; granted

caniatáu vb to permit, to allow

caniedydd (-ion) nm singer; songster; song-book

canlyn vb to follow, to pursue

canlyniad (-au) nm consequence, result

canlynol adj following, consequent

canlynwr (-wyr) nm follower

canllaw (-iau) nfm hand-rail, parapet, aid

canmlwyddiant nm centenary

canmol vb to praise, to commend

canmoladwy adj praiseworthy

canmoliaeth (-au) nf praise, commendation

canmoliaethus adj eulogistic, complimentary

cannaid adj white, bright, luminous

cannu vb to whiten, to bleach

cannwr (canwyr) nm bleacher

cannwyll (canhwyllau) nf candle

canol adj, nm (-au) middle, centre, midst; **canol y ddinas** city centre

canolbarth (-au) nm middle part, midland

canolbwynt (-iau) nm centre, focus

canolbwyntio vb to centre, to concentrate

canoldir (-oedd) nm inland region

canolddydd nm mid-day, noon

canolfan (-nau) nmf centre; **canolfan chwaraeon** sports centre; **canolfan galwadau** call centre; **canolfan iechyd** health centre; **canolfan ymwelwyr** visitor centre

canoli vb to centre; to arbitrate; to centralize

canolig adj middling

canoloesol adj mediaeval

canolog adj central

canolradd (-ol) adj intermediate

canolwr (-wyr) nm mediator, referee; centre half, centre; **canolwr blaen** centre forward

canon¹ (-au) nfm canon (music)

canon² (-iaid) nm canon (priest)

canonaidd adj canonical

canoneiddio vb to canonize

canoniaeth (-au) nf canonry

canonwr (-wyr) nm canon, canonist

canradd (-au) adj, nf centigrade, percentile

canran (-nau) nm percentage

canrif (-oedd) nf century

cansen (-ni) nf cane

canser nm cancer

canslo vb to cancel

cant¹ (-au) nm circle, ring, rim; tyre

cant² (cannoedd) nm hundred

cantel (-au) nm rim, brim

cantîn (cantinoedd) nf canteen

cantor (-ion) nm singer

cantores (-au) nf songstress, singer

cantref (-i, -ydd) nm hundred

cantwr (-orion) nm singer, songster

cantwraig nf songstress, singer

canu vb to sing, to chant; to play; to crow; to ring ▶ nm, **canu gwlad** country music

canŵ (-od) nm canoe

canŵa vb to canoe, to go canoeing ▶ nm canoeing

canŵo vb to canoe

canwr (-wyr) nm singer

canwriad (-iaid) nm centurion

canwyr (-au, -ion) nm plane (in carpentry)

canys conj because, for

cap (-iau) nm cap

capan (-au) nm cap; lintel

capel (-i, -ydd, -au) nm chapel

capelwr (-wyr) nm chapel-goer

caplan (-iaid) nm chaplain

caplaniaeth (-au) nf chaplaincy

capteiniaeth nf captaincy

capten (-einiaid) nm captain

car (-ceir) nm car; **car campau** sports car; **car cefn codi** hatchback; **car llog** hire car

câr (ceraint) nm friend; relation

carafán (-nau) nf caravan

carbohydrad (-au) nm carbohydrate

carbon (-au) adj, nm carbon

carbwl adj clumsy, awkward

carco vb to take care

carcus adj solicitous, anxious, careful

carchar (-au) nm prison; restraint

carchardy (-dai) nm prison-house

carchariad nm imprisonment

carcharor (-ion) nm prisoner

carcharu vb to imprison

carden (cardiau) nf card

cardigan (-au) nf cardigan

cardod (-au) nf charity, alms, dole

cardota vb to beg

cardotyn (-wyr) nm beggar

cardydwyn, cardodwyn nm weakest of brood or litter

caredig adj kind

caredigrwydd nm kindness

caregog adj stony

caregu vb to stone; to petrify; to gather stones

carennydd nm friendship; kinship

caretsen (carets) *nf* carrot

carfaglog *adj* clumsy

carfan (-au) *nf* beam; swath; party, faction

cariad¹ (-au) *nm* love

cariad² (-au, -on) *nm* lover, sweetheart

cariadfab *nm* lover, sweetheart

cariadferch *nf* sweetheart, mistress

cariadlawn *adj* full of love, loving

cariadus *adj* loving, beloved, dear

caridým (-s) *nm* ragamuffin

cario *vb* to carry, to bear

carismatig *adj* charismatic

cariwr *nm* carrier; **y Cariwr Dŵr** Aquarius

carlam (-au) *nm* prance, gallop

carlamu *vb* to prance, to gallop

carlwm (-lymod) *nm* ermine, stoat

carn¹ (-au) *nm* hoof; hilt, haft, handle

carn² (-au), carnedd (-au) *nf* cairn

cárnifal *nm* carnival

carniforus *adj* carnivorous

carnog, carnol *adj* hoofed

carol (-au) *nmf* carol

carp (-iau) *nm* clout, rag

carped (-au, -i) *nm* carpet

carpiog *adj* ragged, tattered

carrai (careiau) *nf* lace, thong

carreg (cerrig) *nf* stone

cart (ceirt) *nmf* cart

cartaid, certaid (-eidiau) *nf* cartful

cartilag (-au) *nm* cartilage

cartref (-i, -ydd) *nm* home, abode
▸ *adj* home-made; **cartref henoed**

old people's home; **cartref symudol** mobile home

cartrefle (-oedd) *nm* abode

cartreflu *nm* militia

cartrefol *adj* homely, domestic, home; civil

cartrefu *vb* to make one's home, to settle

cartŵn (cartwnau) *nm* cartoon

cartwnydd (-ion) *nm* cartoonist

carth (-ion) *nm* tow, oakum; off-scouring

carthen (-ni, -nau) *nf* Welsh blanket, coverlet; **carthen blu** duvet

carthffos (-ydd) *nf* sewer

carthffosiaeth *nf* sewerage

carthu *vb* to cleanse, to purge, to scavenge

caru *vb* to love; to like; to court

caruaidd *adj* loving, kind

carw (ceirw) *nm* stag, deer

carwden (-ni) *nf* back-chain; tall awkward fellow

carwr (-wyr) *nm* lover, wooer

carwriaeth (-au) *nf* courtship

cas¹ *adj* hateful, odious; nasty, disagreeable ▸ *nm* hatred, aversion

cas² (caseion) *nm* hater, foe, enemy

casáu *vb* to hate, to detest, to abhor

casbeth (-au) *nm* aversion, nuisance

caseg (cesig) *nf* mare

casét (-iau) *nm* cassette

casgen (-ni, casgiau) *nf* cask

casgl *nfm* collection

casgliad (-au) nm collection; gathering

casglu vb to collect, to gather; to infer

casglwr (-wyr), **casglydd (-ion)** nm collector

casineb nm hatred

cast (-iau) nm vice, knack

castan (-au) nf chestnut

castanwydd npl (nf-en) chestnut-trees

castell (cestyll) nm castle

castellog adj castled, castellated

castellu vb to castle, to encamp

castio vb to trick, to cheat; to cast, to calculate

castiog adj full of tricks, tricky

casul (-i)au) nmf cassock

caswir nm unpalatable truth

casyn (casiau) nm case, casing

cat (-iau) nm bit, piece, fragment; pipe

catalog (-au) nm catalogue

catalogio vb to catalogue

catalydd (-ion) nm catalyst

categori (-ïau) nm category

catel coll n chattels; cattle

catgor (-(i)au) nm ember day(s)

catrawd (-rodau) nf regiment

cath (-od, -au) nf cat

cathl (-au) nf melody, hymn, lay

cathlu vb to sing, to hymn

cathod (-au) nf cathode

catholig adj catholic

Catholigiaeth nf Catholicism

catholigrwydd nm catholicity

cau[1] adj hollow, concave

cau[2] vb to shut, to close, to enclose

caul (ceulion) nm maw; rennet; curd

caw (-(i)au) nm band, swaddling-clothes

cawdel nm hotchpotch, mess

cawell (cewyll) nm hamper, basket, cradle

cawellwr (-wyr) nm basket-maker

cawg (-iau) nm basin, bowl, pitcher

cawl nm broth, soup; hotchpotch

cawn npl (nf-en) reeds

cawod (-ydd) nf shower

cawodi vb to shower

cawodog adj showery

cawr (cewri) nm giant

cawraidd adj gigantic

cawres (-au) nf giantess

caws nm cheese; curd

cawsai, cawsi nmf causeway

cawsaidd adj cheesy, caseous

cawsellt (-ydd, -i, -au) nm cheese-vat

cawsio vb to curd, to curdle

cawsiog adj curdled

CC adv BC

CD (-s, -au) nm CD

cecian vb to stammer

cecren (-nod) nf shrew, scold, cantankerous woman

cecru vb to wrangle, to bicker

cecrus adj cantankerous, quarrelsome

cecryn (-nod) nm wrangler, brawler

cedor nmf pubic hair

cedrwydd npl (nf-en) cedars

cefn (-au) nm back; support

cefndedyn nm mesentery; diaphragm; pancreas

45

cefnder (**-dyr**) *nm* first cousin

cefndir (**-oedd**) *nm* background

cefnen (**-nau**) *nf* ridge

cefnfor (**-oedd**) *nm* main sea, ocean

cefngrwm *adj* hump-backed

cefnog *adj* well-off, well-to-do

cefnogaeth *nf* encouragement, support

cefnogi *vb* to encourage, to support

cefnogol *adj* encouraging

cefnu *vb* to back, to turn the back, to forsake

cefnwlad (**-wledydd**) *nf* hinterland

cefnwr (**-wyr**) *nm* back, full-back

ceffyl (**-au**) *nm* horse

ceg (**-au**) *nf* mouth

cega *vb* to mouth, to prate

cegaid (**-eidiau**) *nf* mouthful

cegen (**-nau**) *nf* gullet, windpipe

cegid, cegiden (**cegidau**) *nf* green woodpecker, jay

cegin (**-au**) *nf* kitchen

cegrwth *adj* gaping

cegyr *npl* hemlock

cengl (**-au**) *nf* band; girth; hank

cenglu *vb* to hank; to girth; to wind

cei (**-au**) *nm* quay

ceibio *vb* to pick with pickaxe

ceidwad (**-aid**) *nm* keeper, saviour

ceidwadaeth *nf* conservatism; conservancy

ceidwadol *adj* conservative

Ceidwadwr (**-wyr**) *nm* Conservative

ceiliagwydd (**-au**) *nm* gander

ceiliog (**-od**) *nm* cock; ceiliog rhedyn grasshopper

ceinach (**-od**) *nf* hare

ceincio *vb* to branch out, to ramify

ceinciog *adj* branched, branching

ceinder *nm* elegance, beauty

ceiniog (**-au**) *nf* penny

ceiniogwerth (**-au, -i**) *nf* pennyworth

ceinion *npl* beauties, gems

ceintach *vb* to grumble, to croak

ceintachlyd *adj* querulous

ceintachwr (**-wyr**) *nm* grumbler, croaker

ceirch (*nf* **-en**) *coll n* oats

ceirios *npl* (*nf* **-en**) cherries

ceisbwll (**-byliaid**) *nm* catchpole, bailiff

ceisio *vb* to seek; to ask; to try, to attempt, to endeavour; to fetch, to get

cêl *adj* hidden, concealed ► *nm* concealment ► *npl* kale

celain (**celanedd**) *nf* dead body

celanedd *coll n* carnage, slaughter

celc *nfm* concealment; hoard

celf (**-au**) *nf* art, craft

celfi *npl* (*nm* **-cyn**) tools, gear; furniture

celfydd *adj* skilled, skilful

celfyddgar *adj* ingenious; artistic

celfyddwr (**-wyr**) *nm* artificer, artist

celfyddyd (**-au**) *nf* art, craft; skill; celfyddydau graffig graphic arts

celfyddydol *adj* relating to art/ the Arts

celu *vb* to hide, to conceal

celwrn (**-yrnau**) *nm* tub, bucket, pail

celwydd (-au) nm lie, falsehood, untruth

celwyddan nm liar

celwyddog adj lying, mendacious; false

celwyddwr (-wyr) nm liar

celyn npl (nf **-nen**) holly

cell (-oedd, -au) nf cell, chamber; **celloedd cenhedlu** germ cells; **enyniad y celloedd** cellulitis

celli (cellïau, -ïoedd) nf grove

cellog adj cellular

cellwair vb to jest, to trifle ▸ nm fun

cellweiriwr (-wyr) nm jester, trifler

cellweirus adj playful, jocular

cemeg nm chemistry

cemegol adj chemical

cemegwr (-wyr), cemegydd (-ion) nm chemist

cemegyn (cemegau) nm chemical

cen coll n skin, peel, scales, scurf, film, lichen

cenadwri nf message

cenau (cenawon) nm cub, whelp; rascal

cenedl (-hedloedd) nf nation; gender

cenedlaethol adj national

cenedlaetholdeb nm nationalism

cenedlaetholi vb to nationalize

cenedlaetholwr (-wyr) nm nationalist

cenedl-ddyn (-ion) nm gentile

cenedligrwydd nm nationality

cenfaint (-feiniau) nf herd

cenfigen (-nau) nf envy, jealousy

cenfigennu vb to envy

cenfigennus, cenfigenllyd adj envious, jealous

cenhadaeth (cenadaethau) nf mission

cenhadol adj missionary

cenhadu vb to permit; to propagate, to conduct a mission

cenhadwr (-hadon) nm missionary

cenhedlaeth (cenedlaethau) nf generation

cenhedlig adj gentile, pagan

cenhedlu vb to beget, to generate

Cenia nf Kenya

cenllif nm flood, torrent, deluge

cenllysg coll n hailstones, hail

cennad (-hadau, -hadon) nf leave; messenger

cennin npl (nf **-hinen**) leeks

cennog adj scaly, scurfy

cennu vb to scale, to scurf

centimedr (-au) nm centimetre

cêr nf gear, tools, trappings

cerameg nmf ceramics

ceramig adj ceramic

cerbyd (-au) nm chariot, coach, car

cerbydwr (-wyr) nm coachman

cerdyn (cardiau) nm card; **cerdyn adnabod** identity card; **cerdyn cof** memory card; **cerdyn crafu** scratch card; **cerdyn credyd** credit card; **cerdyn debyd** debit card; **cerdyn sweip** swipe card

cerdd (-i) nf song, poem; music, poetry

cerddbrenni npl woodwinds

cerddbresi npl brass section (orchestra)

cerdded vb to walk; to go; to travel

47

cerddediad *nm* walking, going; pace

cerddgar *adj* harmonious, musical

cerddin, cerdin *npl* (*nf* **-en**) rowan

cerddor (-ion) *nm* singer, musician

cerddorfa (-feydd) *nf* orchestra

cerddorfaol *adj* orchestral

cerddoriaeth *nf* music

cerddorol *adj* musical

cerddwr (-wyr) *nm* walker

cerfddelw (-au) *nf* graven image, statue

cerfio *vb* to carve

cerflun (-iau) *nm* statue; engraving

cerfluniaeth *nf* sculpture

cerflunydd (-lunwyr) *nm* sculptor

cerfwaith *nm* carving, sculpture

cern (-au) *nf* cheek, jaw

cernod (-iau) *nf* buffet

cernodio *vb* to buffet, to clout

Cernyw *nm* Cornwall

cerpyn (carpiau) *nm* clout, rag

cerrynt *nmf* course, road; current

cert (-i) *nf* cart

certiwr (-wyr) *nm* carter

certh *adj* right; awful

cerub, ceriwb (-iaid) *nm* cherub

cerwyn (-i) *nf* tub; vat; winepress

cerydd (-on) *nm* correction, chastisement; rebuke, reproof, censure

ceryddol *adj* chastising, chastening

ceryddu *vb* to correct, to chastise; to rebuke

ceryddwr (-wyr) *nm* chastiser; rebuker

cesail (-eiliau) *nf* arm-pit; bosom

cesair *npl, coll n* hailstones; hail

cest (-au) *nf* belly, paunch

cestog *adj* corpulent

cetyn (catiau) *nm* piece, bit; pipe

cethin *adj* dark, fierce, ugly

ceubren (-nau) *nm* hollow tree

ceubwll (-byllau) *nm* pit

ceudod *nm* cavity; abdomen; thought, heart

ceudwll *nm* cavern

ceufad *nm* canoe

ceuffordd (-ffyrdd) *nf* tunnel

ceuffos (-ydd) *nf* drain, ditch

ceugrwm *adj* concave

ceulan (-nau, -lennydd) *nf* bank, brink

ceulo *vb* to curdle, to coagulate

ceunant (-nentydd) *nm* ravine, gorge

cewyn (-nau, cawiau) *nm* napkin

ci (cŵn) *nm* dog, hound

ciaidd *adj* dog-like; brutal

cib (-au) *nm* pod, husk

cibddall *adj* purblind

cibo *vb* to frown, to scowl

cibog *adj* scowling

cibws, cibwst *nf* kibes, chilblains

cibwts (-au) *nm* kibbutz

cibyn (-nau) *nm* shell; husk; half a bushel

cic (-iau) *nfm* kick; **cic gychwyn** kick-off

cicio *vb* to kick

ciciwr (-wyr) *nm* kicker

cidwm (-ymiaid, -ymod) *nm* wolf; rascal

cieidd-dra *nm* brutality

cig (-oedd) *nm* flesh, meat

cigfran (-frain) *nf* raven

cignoeth adj touching to the quick, caustic

cigog adj fleshy

cigwain (-weiniau) nf flesh-hook

cigydd (-ion) nm butcher

cigyddiaeth nf butchery

cigysol adj carnivorous

cigysydd (-ion) nm carnivore

cil (-iau, -ion) nm back; retreat; corner

cilagor vb to open partly

cilagored adj ajar

cilbost (cilbyst) nm gate-post

cilchwyrn npl (nf-en) glands

cildrem (-iau) nf leer

cildremio vb to leer

cildroi vb to reverse

cildwrn nm tip, bribe

cildyn adj obstinate, stubborn

cildynnu vb to be obstinate

cildynnus adj obstinate, stubborn

cildynrwydd nm obstinacy

cilddant (-ddannedd) nm molar

cilfach (-au) nf nook; creek, bay

cilfilyn (-filod) nm ruminant

cilgant nm crescent

cilgnoi vb to chew the cud, to ruminate

cilgwthio vb to push, to shove, to jostle

cilgynnyrch (-gynhyrchion) nm by-product

cilio vb to retreat, to recede, to swerve

cilo nm kilo

cilocalori (-iau) nm kilocalorie

cilogram (-au) nm kilogram

cilomedr (-au) nm kilometre

cilowat nm kilowatt

cilwen (-au) nf half smile

cilwenu vb to simper, to smile, to leer

cilwg (-ygon) nm frown, scowl

cilydd (-ion) nm fellow, companion

cilyddol adj reciprocal

cimwch (-ychiaid) nm lobster

ciniawa vb to dine

cinio (ciniawau) nm dinner; **cinio gwadd** dinner party

cip (-ion) nm pluck, snatch; glimpse

cipdrem (-iau) nfm glance, glimpse

cipedrych vb to glance, to glimpse

cipio vb to snatch

cipiwr (-wyr) nm snatcher

cipolwg nmf glance, glimpse

ciprys nm scramble

cis (-iau) nmf buffet; slap, touch

cist (-iau) nf chest, coffer, box; bin

ciw (-iau) nm cue, queue

ciwb nm cube

ciwed coll n rabble, mob, crew

ciwrad (-iaid) nm curate

ciwt adj cute, clever, ingenious

claddedigaeth (-au) nmf burial

claddfa (-feydd) nf burial-ground, cemetery

claddgell nf vault

claddu vb to bury

claear adj lukewarm, tepid; mild; cool

claearineb nm lukewarmness

claearu vb to make mild or tepid; to soothe

claer adj clear, bright, shining

claerder nm clearness, brightness

claf (cleifion) adj sick, ill ► nm sick person, patient

clafdy (-dai) nm hospital, infirmary

49

clafr nm itch, mange

clafrllyd adj mangy

clafychu vb to sicken, to fall ill

clai (**cleiau**) nm clay

clais (**cleisiau**) nm stripe; bruise

clamp (**-iau**) nm mass, lump; monster

clap (**-iau**) nm lump

clapgi (**-gwn**) nm telltale

clapio vb to lump; to strike; to gossip

clapiog adj lumpy

clas nm monastic community, cloister, college

clasur (**-on**) nm classic

clasurol adj classical

clau adj quick, swift, soon; true; audible

clawdd (**cloddiau**) nm hedge; dyke, embankment

clawr (**cloriau**) nm face, surface; cover, lid; board

clebar, cleber nmf idle talk, gossip, tattle

clebran vb to chatter, to gossip, to tattle

clec (**-iau, -s**) nf click; clack; crack; gossip

cleci (**-cwn**) nf telltale

clecian vb to click; to clack; to crack, to snap

cledr (**-au**) nf pole; rail; palm (of hand)

cledren (**-nau, -ni**) nf pale, pole, rail

cleddyf, cleddau, cledd (**cleddyfau**) nm sword; brace

cleddyfwr (**-wyr**) nm swordsman

clefyd (**-au**) nm disease; fever; clefyd melys diabetes; clefyd y galon heart disease; clefyd y gwair hay fever

clegar vb to clack, to cluck, to cackle

clegyr, clegr nm rock; cairn, stony place

cleiog adj clayey

cleiriach nm decrepit one

cleisio vb to bruise

cleisiog adj bruised

clem (**-iau**) nf notion, idea; look, gaze ▸ pl grimaces

clep (**-iau**) nf clack, clap; gossip

clepgi (**-gwn**) nm babbler; telltale

clepian vb to clap; to slam; to blab

clêr[1] coll n itinerant minstrels; bards

clêr[2] npl (nf **cleren**) flies

clera vb to stroll as minstrels

clerc (**-od**) nm clerk

clercio vb to serve as clerk

cleren nf fly

clerigol adj clerical

clerigwr (**-wyr**) nm clergyman

clerwr (**-wyr**) nm itinerant minstrel

clerwriaeth nf minstrelsy

clewt (**-iau**) nm clout

clewtian vb to clout

clic (**cliciau**) nm clique

clicied (**-au**) nf clicker; trigger

cliciedu vb to latch, to fasten

clicio vb to click; clicio dwywaith double-click

clindarddach vb to crackle ▸ nm crackling

clinig (**-au**) nm clinic

clir adj clear

clirio vb to clear

clo (**cloeau, cloeon**) nm lock, conclusion

clwcian

cloben nf monster
clobyn nm monster
cloc (-iau) nm clock; **cloc larwm** alarm clock
clocian vb to cluck
clocsiau npl (nf **clocsen**) clog
cloch (clych, clychau) nf bell; **o'r/ar gloch** o'clock
clochaidd adj sonorous, noisy
clochdar vb to cluck, to cackle
clochdy (-dai) nm belfry, steeple
clochydd (-ion) nm bell-man; sexton
clod (-ydd) nmf praise, fame, renown
clodfori vb to praise, to extol
clodwiw adj commendable, praiseworthy
cloddfa (-feydd) nf quarry, mine
cloddio vb to dig, to delve; to quarry, to mine
cloddiwr (-wyr) nm digger, navvy
cloëdig adj locked, closed
cloer (-(i)au) nm locker; niche; pigeon-hole
cloff adj lame
cloffi vb to lame, to halt ▸ nm lameness
cloffni nm lameness
cloffrwym (-au) nm fetter, hobble; **cloffrwym y cythraul, cloffrwym y mwci** great bindweed
clog¹ (-au) nmf cloak
clog² (-au) nf rock, precipice
clogfaen (-feini) nm boulder
clogwyn (-i) nm cliff, crag, precipice
clogwynog adj craggy, precipitous
clogyn (-nau) nm cloak, cape

clogyrnaidd adj rough, rugged, clumsy
cloi vb to lock
clonc nf clank; gossip ▸ adj addled
clopa (-âu) nmf noddle; knob; club
cloren (-nau) nf rump, tail
clorian (-nau) nmf pair of scales
cloriannu vb to weigh, to balance
clorin nm chlorine
clorinio, clorinadu vb to chlorinate
clos¹ (-ydd) nm yard
clos² (closau) nm pair of breeches
clòs adj close
closio vb to close, to near
cludadwy adj portable
cludair (-eiriau) nf heap, load, wood-pile
cludiad nm carriage
cludiant (-nnau) nm transport, haulage
cludo vb to carry, to convey
cludwr (-wyr), cludydd (-ion) nm porter
clul (-iau) nm knell
clun (-iau) nf hip, haunch, thigh, leg; moor
cluro vb to rub, to smear
clust (-iau) nfm ear; handle
clustfeinio vb to prick up the ears; to eavesdrop
clustfys nm little finger
clustffôn (-ffonau) nm earphone
clustlws (-lysau) nm earring
clustnod (-au) nm earmark
clustog (-au) nfm cushion, pillow
clwb (clybiau) nm club
clwc adj addled
clwcian vb to cluck

51

clwm (clymau) nm knot, tie

clwpa (-od) nm knob, boss; club; dolt

clws (f clos) adj pretty, nice

clwstwr (clystyrau) nm cluster

clwt (clytiau) nm patch, clout, rag

clwyd (-au, -i, -ydd) nf hurdle; gate; roost

clwydo vb to roost

clwyf (-au) nm wound; disease

clwyfo vb to wound

clwyfus adj wounded; sore; sick

clybodeg nf acoustics

clybodig adj acoustic

clyd adj warm, sheltered, snug, cosy

clydwch, clydwr nm warmth, shelter

clyfar adj clever; pleasant, agreeable

clymblaid (-bleidiau) nf clique, cabal

clymog adj knotty, entangled

clymu vb to knot, to tie

clytio vb to patch, to piece

clytiog adj patched; ragged

clytwaith (-weithiau) nm patchwork

clyw nm sense of hearing

clywadwy adj audible

clywed vb to hear; to feel; to taste; to smell

clywedigaeth nf hearing

clywedol adj aural

clywedydd (-ion) nm hearer, auditor

clyweled adj audio-visual

clywelediad nm audition

cnaf (-on, -iaid) nm knave, rascal

cnafaidd adj knavish, rascally

cnaif (cneifion) nm shearing, fleece

cnap (-iau) nm lump, knob, boss

cnapan (-au) nm ball, bowl, kind of ball game

cnapiog adj lumpy

cnau npl (nf cneuen) nuts

cnawd nm flesh

cnawdol adj carnal, fleshly, fleshy

cneifio vb to shear, to fleece

cneifiwr (-wyr) nm shearer

cneua vb to nut

cneuen (cnau) nf nut

cnewyllyn (cnewyll) nm kernel, nucleus

cnith (-iau, -ion) nm slight touch, blow; pluck

cno nm bite, chewing, gnawing

cnoc (-iau) nmf knock

cnocio vb to knock

cnofa (-feydd) nf gnawing, pang

cnofil (-od) nm rodent

cnoi vb to gnaw, to chew, to bite; to ache

cnot (-iau) nm knot, bunch

cnu (-au), cnuf (-iau) nm fleece

cnud (-oedd) nf pack

cnùl, cnul (-iau) nm knell

cnwc nm knob

cnwd (cnydau) nm crop; covering

cnydfawr adj fruitful, productive

cnydio vb to crop, to yield increase

cnydiog adj fruitful, productive

cob (cobau) nf coat, cloak, robe

còb (-iau) nm embankment; miser; wag; cob

coban (-au) nf: coban nos nightshirt

coblyn (-nod) *nm* sprite, goblin, imp

cocos¹ *npl* cogs; **olwyn gocos** cog-wheel

cocos², cocs *npl* (*nf* **cocsen**) cockles

coch *adj*, *nm* red

coch-gam *nf* robin

cochi¹ *vb* to redden, to blush

cochi², cochder *nm* redness

cochl (-au) *nmf* mantle, cloak

cod (-au) *nf* bag, pouch

codaid (-eidiau) *nf* bagful

codi *vb* to rise, to get up; to raise, to lift; to erect

codiad (-au) *nm* rise, rising; erection

codog *adj* baggy ► *nmf* (**-ion**) rich man; miser

codwm (codymau) *nm* fall, tumble

codwr (-wyr) *nm* riser; raiser, lifter; **codwr canu** precentor

codymu *vb* to wrestle

codymwr (-wyr) *nm* wrestler

codded *nm* anger; grief

coddi *vb* to anger, to offend

coed (-ydd) *coll n* wood, timber, trees

coeden (coed) *nf* tree

coedio *vb* to timber

coediog *adj* wooded, woody

coedwig (-oedd) *nf* wood, forest

coedwigaeth *nf* forestry

coedwigo *vb* to forest

coedwigwr (-wyr) *nm* woodman, forester

coedd *adj* public

coeg *adj* empty, vain; one-eyed, blind

coegddyn (-ion) *nm* fop, coxcomb, fool

coegedd *nm* emptiness, silliness

coegen (-nod) *nf* minx, coquette

coegennaidd *adj* coquettish

coegfalch *adj* vain, foppish

coegi *vb* to jeer at, to mock

coeglyd *adj* vain, sarcastic

coegni *nm* vanity; spite; sarcasm

coegwr (-wyr) *nm* fool

coegwych *adj* gaudy, garish, tawdry

coegyn (-nod) *nm* coxcomb

coel (-ion) *nf* belief, trust, credit

coelbren (-nau, -ni) *nm* lot

coelcerth (-i) *nf* bonfire, blaze

coelgrefydd (-au) *nf* superstition

coelgrefyddol *adj* superstitious

coelio *vb* to believe, to credit, to trust

coes (-au) *nf* leg, shank ► *nfm* handle; stem, stalk

coetgae *nm* hedge; enclosure

coetmon (-myn) *nm* lumberjack

coetref *nf* woodland, homestead

coets *nm* pushchair

coeth *adj* fine, refined; elegant

coethder *nm* refinement, elegance

coethi *vb* to refine; to chastise; to babble

coethwr (-wyr) *nm* refiner

cof (-ion) *nm* memory; remembrance

cofadail (-eiladau) *nf* monument

cofbin (-nau) *nm* memory stick, pen drive

cofeb (-ion) *nf* memorandum; memorial

53

cof-gerdyn (cof-gardiau) *nm* memory card

cofgolofn (-au) *nf* monument

cofiadur (-on, -iaid) *nm* recorder

cofiadwy *adj* memorable

cofiannydd (-anyddion) *nm* biographer

cofiant (-iannau) *nm* memoir, biography

cofio *vb* to remember, to recollect

cofl (-au) *nf* embrace; bosom

coflaid (-eidiau) *nf* armful; bundle

coflech (-au) *nf* memorial tablet

cofleidio *vb* to embrace, to hug

coflyfr (-au) *nm* record, chronicle

cofnod (-ion) *nm* memorandum, minute

cofnodi *vb* to record, to register

cofrestr (-au) *nf* register, roll

cofrestrfa *nf* registry

cofrestru *vb* to register

cofrestrydd (-ion) *nm* registrar

cofrodd *nf* souvenir

cofus *adj* mindful

cofweini *vb* to prompt

cofweinydd (-ion) *nm* prompter

coffa *vb* to remember ▸ *nm* remembrance

coffâd *nm* remembrance

coffadwriaeth *nf* remembrance, memory

coffadwriaethol *adj* memorial

coffáu *vb* to remember; to remind; to commemorate

coffi *nm* coffee

coffr (-au) *nm* coffer, trunk, chest

cog¹ (-au) *nf* cuckoo

cog² (-iau) *nf* cook

coginiaeth *nf* cookery

coginio *vb* to cook

cogio *vb* to cog; to sham, to feign, to pretend

cogiwr (-wyr) *nm* pretender, swindler

cogor *vb* to chatter, to caw, to croak ▸ *nm* chattering

cogwrn (-yrnau, cegyrn) *nm* knob, cone; cock (of corn); shell

cogydd (-ion) *nm* cook

cogyddes (-au) *nf* cook

cogyddiaeth *nf* cookery

congl (-au) *nf* corner

col (-ion) *nm* awn, beard

côl *nf* bosom, embrace

coladu *vb* to collate

coledd, coleddu *vb* to cherish, to foster

coleddwr (-wyr) *nm* cherisher, fosterer, patron, supporter

coleg (-au) *nm* college; **coleg chweched dosbarth** sixth-form college; **coleg technoleg dinasol** city technology college

colegol *adj* collegiate

colegwr (-wyr) *nm* collegian

coler (-i) *nfm* collar

colfen (-nau, -ni) *nf* bough, branch; tree

colofn (-au) *nf* column, pillar

colofnydd *nm* columnist

colomen (-nod) *nf* dove, pigeon

colomendy (-dai) *nm* dove-cot

colomennaidd *adj* dove-like

coluddion *npl* (*nm* -yn) bowels

coluddyn *nm* gut

colur (-au) *nm* make-up, colour

coluro *vb* to make-up, to paint; to conceal

colwyn (-od) *nm* puppy
colyn (-nau) *nm* pivot; sting; tail
colynnog *adj* stinging; hinged
colynnu *vb* to sting
coll (-iadau) *nm* loss; failing, defect
colladwy *adj* perishable
colldddail *adj* deciduous
colled (-ion) *nfm* loss
colledig *adj* lost, damned
colledigaeth *nf* perdition
colledu *vb* to occasion loss
colledus *adj* fraught with loss
colledwr (-wyr) *nm* loser
collen (cyll) *nf* hazel
collfarn (-au) *nf* doom, condemnation
collfarnu *vb* to condemn
colli *vb* to lose; to be lost, to perish; to spill, to shed
collnod (-au) *nm* apostrophe
collwr (-wyr) *nm* loser
coma (-s) *nm* comma
côma (comâu) *nm* coma
comed (-au) *nf* comet
comedi (-ïau) *nfm* comedy
comig *adj* comic, comical ▶ *nm* comic (paper)
comin *nm* common
comisiwn (-iynau) *nm* commission
comisiynu *vb* to commission
comiwnydd (-ion) *nm* communist
comiwnyddiaeth *nf* communism
comiwnyddol *adj* communist
conach *vb* to grumble
conclaf *nm* conclave
concro *vb* to conquer
concwerwr (-wyr) *nm* conqueror
concwest (-au) *nf* conquest, victory

condemniad *nm* condemnation
condemnio *vb* to condemn
confensiwn (-iynau) *nm* convention
conffederasiwn (-asiynau) *nm* confederation
conffirmasiwn *nm* confirmation
conffirmio *vb* to confirm
conifferaidd *adj* coniferous
cono *nm* rascal; wag; old fogey
consesiwn (-iynau) *nm* concession
consol (-au) *nm* : consol gêmau games console
consuriaeth *nf* conjuring
consurio *vb* to conjure
consuriwr (-wyr) *nm* conjurer
conwydd *npl* (*nf-en*) coniferous trees
cop, copyn (-nod, -nau) *nm* spider
copa (-âu) *nf* top, crest; head
copi (-ïau) *nm* copy; copy-book
copïo *vb* to copy, to transcribe
copïwr (-wyr) *nm* copyist, transcriber
copr *nm* copper
cor (-rod) *nm* dwarf (*offensive*); spider
côr (corau) *nm* choir; stall, pew; côr-feistr choirmaster
corachaidd *adj* dwarfish, stunted
Corân *nm* Koran
corawl *adj* choral
corbwll (-byllau) *nm* whirlpool; puddle
corcyn (cyrc) *nm* cork
cord (-iau) *nm* cord; chord
cordeddu *vb* to twist, to twine
corddi *vb* to churn; to turn; to agitate

corddiad (-au) nm churning

corddwr (-wyr) nm churner

Corea nf Korea

cored (-au) nf weir, dam

coreograffiaeth nf choreography

corfan (-nau) nm metrical foot

corff (cyrff) nm body

corfflu (-oedd) nm corps

corffol adj corpulent; physical

corfflolaeth nf bodily form; stature

corfforaeth (-au) nf corporation

corffori vb to embody, to incorporate

corfforiad (-au) nm embodiment

corfforol adj bodily, corporeal, corporal

corgan (-au), **côr-gân (côr-ganau)** nf chant

corganu vb to chant

corgi (-gwn) nm cur, corgi

corgimwch (-ychiaid) nm prawn

corhwyad (-aid) nf teal; moorhen

corlan (-nau) nf fold

corlannu vb to fold

corn (cyrn) nm horn; pipe; tube; roll; corn; stethoscope; **corn gwddw(f), corn gwynt** windpipe; **corn siarad** loudspeaker

cornant (-nentydd) nm brook, rill

cornboer nm phlegm

cornchwiglen (-chwiglod) nf lapwing

cornel (-i, -au) nfm corner

cornelu vb to corner

cornicyll (-od) nm lapwing, plover, peewit

cornio vb to horn, to butt; to examine with a stethoscope

corniog adj horned

cornwyd (-ydd) nm boil, abscess, sore

coron (-au) nf crown

coroni vb to crown ▶ nm coronation

coroniad nm coronation

coronog adj crowned

corrach (corachod) nm dwarf, pygmy

corryn (corynnod) nm spider

cors (-ydd) nf bog, swamp

corsen (-nau, cyrs) nf reed; stem, stalk; cane

cortyn (-nau) nm cord, rope

corun (-au) nm crown of the head; tonsure

corwg, corwgl (-yg(l)au) nm coracle

corws nm chorus

corwynt (-oedd) nm whirlwind

cosb (-au) nf punishment, penalty; **cosb ddihenydd** capital punishment

cosbadwy adj punishable

cosbedigaeth nf punishment

cosbi vb to punish

cosbol adj punitive, penal

cosbwr (-wyr) nm punisher

cosfa (-feydd) nf itch, itching; thrashing

cosi vb to scratch, to itch ▶ nm itching

cosmetigau npl cosmetics

cosmig adj cosmic

Cosofo nf Kosovo

cost (-au) nf cost, expense

costiad (-au) nm costing

costio vb to cost

costiwm (-tiymau) nmf costume

costog (-ion) nm mastiff; cur ▸ adj surly

costowci (-cwn) nm mastiff, mongrel

costrel (-au, -i) nf bottle

costrelaid (-eidiau) nf bottleful

costrelu vb to bottle

costus adj costly, expensive

cosyn (-nau, -nod) nm a cheese

côt, cot (cotiau) nf coat

cotwm nm cotton

Coweit nf Kuwait

cownter (-au, -i) nm counter

cowntio vb to count, to account, to esteem

crac (-iau) nm crack

cracio vb to crack

craciog adj cracked

crach npl scabs ▸ adj scabby; petty

crachach npl snobs

crachboer nm phlegm

crachen nf scab

crachfardd (-feirdd) nm poetaster

crachfeddyg (-on) nm quack doctor

crachfonheddwr (-wyr) nm snob

crafangio, crafangu vb to claw, to grab

crafanc (-angau) nf claw; talon; clutch

crafellu vb to grate

crafiad (-au) nm scratch

crafog adj cutting, sarcastic

crafu vb to scrape; to scratch ▸ nm itch

crafwr (-wyr) nm scraper

craff adj close; keen; sagacious ▸ nm hold, grip

craffter nm keenness, sagacity

craffu vb to look closely, to observe intently

craffus adj keen, sagacious

cragen (cregyn) nf shell

crai adj new, fresh, raw

craidd (creiddiau) nm middle, centre

craig (creigiau) nf rock

crair (creiriau) nm relic

craith (creithiau) nf scar

cramen (-nau) nf crust, scab

cramwythen nf pancake

cranc (-od) nm crab; **y Cranc** Cancer

crand adj grand

crandrwydd nm grandeur, finery

crap (-iau) nm hold; smattering

crapio vb to grapple; to pick up

cras (creision) adj parched, dry; harsh

crasiad nm baking

craslyd adj harsh, grating

craster nm dryness; harshness

crasu vb to parch, to scorch; to bake

crau¹ (creuau) nm hole, eye, socket

crau² nmf blood, gore

crau³ (creuau) nm sty; stockade

crawcian, crawcio vb to croak, to caw

crawen (-nau) nf crust

crawn nm matter, pus

crawni vb to gather, to suppurate

crawnllyd adj purulent

cread nm creation

creadigaeth (-au) nf creation

creadigol adj creative

creadur (-iaid) nm creature; animal

creadures (-au) nf female creature

creawdwr (-wyr) nm creator

crebach adj shrunk, withered

crebachlyd adj crabbed, wrinkled

crebachu vb to shrink, to shrivel, to wrinkle, to pucker

crebwyll (-ion) nm invention, understanding, fancy

crecian vb to cluck; to crackle

crechwen nf loud laughter, guffaw

crechwenu vb to laugh loud, to guffaw

cred (-au) nf belief; trust; pledge, troth

credadun (credinwyr) nm believer

credadwy adj credible

crediniaeth nf belief

crediniol adj believing

credo (-au) nmf creed, belief

credu vb to believe

credwr (-wyr) nm believer

credyd (-on) nm credit

credydu vb to credit

cref adj f of **cryf**

crefu vb to crave, to beg, to implore

crefydd (-au) nf religion

crefydda vb to profess or practise religion

crefyddol adj religious, pious

crefyddolder nm religiousness, piety

crefyddwr (-wyr) nm religionist

crefft (-au) nf handicraft, trade; **crefftau'r cartref** DIY, do-it-yourself

crefftus adj skilled, workmanlike

crefftwaith nm craftwork

crefftwr (-wyr) nm craftsman

cregyn npl (nf **cragen**) shells

creider nm freshness

creifion npl scrapings

creigiog adj rocky

creigiwr (-wyr) nm quarryman

creigle (-oedd) nm rocky place

creinio vb to wallow, to lie or fall down; to cringe

creision npl flakes, crisps

creithio vb to scar

crempog (-au) nf pancake

crensio vb to grind (the teeth)

crepach adj numb ▸ nf numbness

crest nm crust, scurf

Creta nf Crete

creu vb to create

creulon adj cruel

creulondeb (-derau) nm cruelty

crëwr (crewyr) nm creator

crëyr (crehyrod) nm heron

cri¹ (-au) nm cry, clamour

cri² adj new, fresh, raw; unleavened

criafol, criafolen nf mountain ash

crib (-au) nfm comb, crest; ridge

cribddeilio vb to grab, to extort

cribddeiliwr (-wyr) nm extortioner; speculator

cribin (-iau) nfm rake; skinflint

cribinio vb to rake

cribo vb to comb; to card

criced nm cricket

cricedwr (-wyr) nm cricketer

cricsyn nm cricket

crimog (-au) nf shin

crimp (-(i)au) nm shin

crin adj withered, sear, dry

crino vb to wither, to dry up

crintach, crintachlyd adj niggardly, stingy

crintachrwydd nm niggardliness

crintachu vb to scrimp, to skimp, to stint

rio vb to cry, to weep

ripio vb to scratch; to climb, to creep

ris-groes nf criss-cross

risial (-au) nm, adj crystal

risialu vb to crystallise

Crist nm Christ

Cristion (-ogion), Cristnogion nm Christian

Cristionogaeth nf Christianity

Cristionogol adj Christian

Cristnogaeth nf Christianity

Cristnogol adj Christian

criw (-iau) nm crew

crïwr (-wyr) nm crier

Croatia nf Croatia

crocbont (-ydd) nf suspension bridge

crocbren (-ni) nmf gallows, gibbet

crocbris (-iau) nm exorbitant price

croch adj loud, vehement

crochan (-au) nm pot, cauldron

crochanaid (-eidiau) nm potful

crochenwaith (-weithiau) nm pottery

crochenydd (-ion) nm potter

croen (crwyn) nm skin; hide; peel, rind

croendenau adj thin-skinned

croeni, croenio vb to form skin, to skin over

croes¹ (-au) nf cross ▶ nm transept

croes² (-ion) adj cross, contrary

croesair (-eiriau) nm crossword

croesawgar adj hospitable

croesawiad nm welcome, reception

croesawu vb to welcome

croesawus adj hospitable

croesbren (-nau) nmf cross

croes-ddweud vb to contradict

croesfan (-nau) nf crossing; croesfan sebra zebra crossing

croesffordd (-ffyrdd) nf crossroads

croesgad (-au) nf crusade

croesgadwr (-wyr) nm crusader

croeshoeliad nm crucifixion

croeshoelio vb to crucify

croesholi vb to cross-examine

croesholiad (-au) nm cross-examination

croesi vb to cross

croeslinol adj diagonal

croeso nm welcome

croestorri vb to intersect

croesymgroes adj criss-cross; vice-versa

crofen (-nau, -ni) nf rind, crust

crog (-au) nf cross, rood ▶ adj hanging

crogi vb to hang, to suspend

croglath (-au) nf springe, snare, gibbet

Croglith nfm: Dydd Gwener y Groglith Good Friday

croglofft (-ydd, -au) nf garret; rood-loft

crogwr (-wyr) nm hangman

cronglwyd (-ydd) nf: tan fy nghronglwyd under my roof

crombil (-iau) nf crop; gizzard; bowels

cromen (-ni, -nau) nf dome

cromfach (-au) nf bracket, parenthesis

cromlech (-au, -i) nf cromlech

cromlin nf curve

cromosom (-au) nm chromosome

cron *adj f* of **crwn**

cronfa (-feydd) *nf* reservoir; fund; **cronfa ddata** database

cronicl (-au) *nm* chronicle

croniclo *vb* to chronicle

cronnell (cronellau) *nf* sphere, globe

cronni *vb* to collect, to hoard; to dam

cronolegol *adj* chronological

cropian *vb* to creep, to crawl, to grope

crosiet (-au, -i) *nm* crotchet

croth (-au) *nf* womb; calf (of leg)

croyw *adj* clear, plain, distinct; fresh

croywder *nm* clearness; freshness

croywi *vb* to clear; to freshen

crud (-au) *nm* cradle

crug (-iau) *nm* hillock; tumulus; heap; multitude; abscess, blister

cruglwyth (-i) *nm* heap, pile

cruglwytho *vb* to heap, to pile up; to overload

crugo *vb* to fester, to vex, to plague

crwban (-od) *nm* tortoise, turtle

crwca *adj* crooked, bowed, bent

crwm (f crom) *adj* convex, curved, bowed

crwn (f cron) *adj* round; complete

crwner (-iaid) *nm* coroner

crwsâd (-adau) *nmf* crusade

crwst (crystiau) *nm* crust

crwt (cryts) *nm* boy, lad

crwth (crythau) *nm* crowd, fiddle; purring; hump

crwybr *nm* honeycomb; mist; hoarfrost

crwydr *nm* wandering; **ar grwydr** astray

crwydro *vb* to wander, to stray, to roam

crwydrol, crwydrus *adj* wandering

crwydrwr (-wyr) *nm* rambler; wanderer, rover

crwydryn (-riaid) *nm* vagrant, tramp

crwys *nf* cross, crucifix; **dan ei grwys** laid out for burial

crybwyll *vb* to mention ▶ *nm* **(-ion)** mention

crybwylliad *nm* mention, notice

crych *adj* rippling; curly; quavering ▶ *nm* **(-au)** crease, ripple, wrinkle

crychlais (-leisiau) *nm* trill, tremolo

crychlyd *adj* wrinkled, puckered

crychnaid (-neidiau) *nf* leap, gambol

crychneidio *vb* to skip, to frisk

crychni *nm* curliness; wrinkle

crychu *vb* to wrinkle, to pucker; to ruffle, to ripple

cryd (-iau) *nm* shivering; fever; ague

crydd (-ion) *nm* cobbler, shoemaker

crydda *vb* to cobble

cryf (f cref) *adj* strong

cryfder, cryfdwr *nm* strength

cryfhaol *adj* strengthening

cryfhau *vb* to strengthen; to grow strong

cryg (f creg) *adj* hoarse

cryglyd *adj* hoarse, raucous

crygni *nm* hoarseness**

rygu vb to hoarsen

ryman (-au) nm reaping-hook, sickle

rymanwr (-wyr) nm reaper

rymu vb to bow, to bend, to stoop

ryn adj considerable, much

rŷn, cryn nm, adj shivering

rynder nm roundness

ryndod nm trembling, shivering

rynedig adj trembling, tremulous

rynfa (-feydd) nf tremble, tremor

rynhoad (-noadau) nm collection, digest

rynhoi vb to gather together, to collect

ryno adj compact; neat, tidy

rynodeb (-au) nm summary

rynodi vb to concentrate

ryno ddisg (-iau) nm CD, compact disc

rynswth nm mass, bulk, whole

rynu vb to shiver, to tremble, to quake

rynwr (-wyr) nm Quaker

rys (-au) nm shirt; **crys chwys** sweatshirt

rysbais (-beisiau) nf jacket, jerkin

rystyn (crystiau) nm crust

rythor (-ion) nm fiddler, violinist

ryw (-iau) nm creel; weir

u adj dear, fond, kind

uchio vb to scowl, to frown

uchiog adj scowling, frowning

udyll (-od) nm hawk

udyn (-nau) nm lock (of hair), tuft

udd adj hidden, concealed

uddfa (-feydd) nf hiding-place; hoard

cuddiad nm hiding

cuddiedig adj hidden, concealed

cuddio vb to hide, to conceal

cufydd (-au) nm cubit

cul (-ion) adj narrow, lean

culfor (-oedd) nm strait

culhau vb to narrow; to grow lean

culni nm narrowness

cun adj dear, beloved; lovely

cunnog (cunogau) nf pail

cur nm throb, ache, pain; care, trouble

curad (-iaid) nm curate

curadiaeth (-au) nf curacy

curfa (-feydd) nf beating, flogging

curiad (-au) nm beat, throb, pulse

curio vb to pine, to waste

curlaw nm pelting rain

curn (-au), curnen (-nau) nf mound, core, rick

curnennu vb to heap, to stack

curo vb to beat, to strike, to knock; to throb; to clap

curwr (-wyr) nm beater

curyll (-od) nm hawk

cusan (-au) nmf kiss

cusanu vb to kiss

cut (-iau) nm hovel, shed, sty

cuwch (cuchiau) nm scowl, frown

CV (-s) nm CV

cwafrio vb to quaver, to trill

cwar (-rau) nm quarry

cwarel nm windowpane

cwb (cybiau) nm kennel, coop, sty

cwbl adj, nm all, whole, total

cwblhad nm fulfilment

cwblhau vb to fulfil, to complete, to finish

cwcer (-au) nm cooker

cwcw nf cuckoo

cwcwallt (-iaid) nm cuckold

cwcwallt vb to cuckold

cwcwll (cycyllau) nm hood, cowl

cwch (cychod) nm boat; hive; **cwch gwyllt** speed boat

cwd (cydau) nm pouch, bag

cweir (-iau) nm thrashing, hiding

cweryl (-on) nm quarrel

cweryla vb to quarrel

cwerylgar adj quarrelsome

cwest (-au) nm inquest

cwestiwn (-iynau) nm question

cwestiynu vb to question

cwfaint nm convent

cwfl nm hood

cwffio vb to fight, to box

cwgn (cygnau) nm knot; knuckle; joint

cwilt (-iau) nm quilt

cwlbren (-ni) nm bludgeon

cwlff (cylffau), **cwlffyn** (cylffiau) nm chunk

cwlwm see clwm

cwlltwr (cylltyrau) nm coulter

cwm (cymau, cymoedd) nm valley

cwman nm rump; stoop; churn

cwmanu vb to stoop

cwmni (-ïau, -ïoedd) nm company

cwmnïaeth nf companionship

cwmpas (-oedd) nm round; **o gwmpas** about

cwmpasog adj round about, circuitous

cwmpasu vb to round, to wind, to surround

cwmpawd (-odau) nm compass

cwmpeini, cwmpni nm company

cwmwd (cymydau) nm commot

cwmwl (cymylau) nm cloud

cŵn see ci

cwndid (-au) nm song, carol

cwningar nf warren

cwningen (-ingod) nf rabbit

cwnsel (-au, -oedd, -i) nm council; counsel, advice, secret

cwnsela vb to counsel

cwnsler (-iaid) nm counsellor

cwnstabl (-iaid) nm constable; **cwnstabl heddlu** PC, police constable; **prif gwnstabl** chief constable

cworwm nm quorum

cwota (-âu) nm quota

cwpan (-au) nmf cup, goblet; chalice

cwpanaid (-eidiau) nm cupful

cwpl (cyplau) nm couple; tie beam

cwplâd, cwpláu see cwblhad; cwblhau

cwpled (-i, -au) nm couplet

cwplws (cyplysau) nm coupling; brace

cwpwrdd (cypyrddau) nm cupboard; **cwpwrdd ffeilio** filing cabinet

cwr (cyrrau) nm edge, border, skirt

cwrbyn nm kerb

cwrcwd nm stooping; squatting

cwrdd (cyrddau) nm meeting

cwrdd², cwrddyd vb to meet, to touch

cwrel nm coral

cwricwlwm (cwricwla) nm curriculum

cwrlid (-au) nm coverlet

cwrs (**cyrsiau**) *nm* course; fit; **prif gwrs** main course; **cwrs hyfforddiant** training course

cwrt (**cyrtiau**) *nm* court

cwrtais *adj* courteous

cwrteisi, cwrteisrwydd *nm* courtesy

cwrw (**cyrfau**) *nm* ale, beer

cwrwg, cwrwgl *see* **corwg**

cwsg *nm* sleep

cwsmer (**-iaid**) *nm* customer

cwsmeriaeth *nf* custom

cwstard (**-iau**) *nm* custard

cwstwm (**cystymau**) *nm* custom, patronage

cwt[1] (**cytiau**) *nfm* tail, skirt, queue

cwt[2] (**cytiau**) *nm* hut, sty

cwta *adj* short, curt

cwter (**-i, -ydd**) *nf* gutter, channel

cwtogi *vb* to shorten, to curtail

cwthr (**cythrau**) *nm* anus, rectum

cwthwm (**cythymau**) *nm* puff of wind, storm

cwymp (**-au**) *nm* fall, tumble

cwympo *vb* to fall; to fell

cwyn (**-ion**) *nfm* complaint, plaint

cwynfan *vb* to complain, to lament

cwynfanllyd *adj* querulous

cwynfanus *adj* plaintive, mournful

cwyno *vb* to complain, to lament

cwyr *nm* wax

cwyro *vb* to wax

cwys (**-au, -i**) *nf* furrow-slice, furrow

cybôl *nm* nonsense, rubbish

cybolfa *nf* hotchpotch, medley

cyboli *vb* to muddle; to talk nonsense; to mess, to bother

cybydd (**-ion**) *nm* miser, niggard

cybydda *vb* to stint, to hoard

cybydd-dod, cybydd-dra *nm* miserliness

cybyddlyd *adj* miserly

cycyllog *adj* hooded, cowled

cychwr (**-wyr**) *nm* boatman

cychwyn *vb* to rise, to stir, to start; to switch on

cychwynfa *nf* start, starting-point

cychwyniad (**-au**) *nm* start, beginning

cyd *adj* joint, united, common; fellow ▸ *prefix* together

cydadrodd *vb* to recite together

cydaid (**-eidiau**) *nm* bagful

cydbwysedd *nm* balance

cydbwyso *vb* to balance

cyd-destun (**-au**) *nm* context

cyd-drafodaeth *nf* negotiation

cyd-ddigwydd *vb* to coincide

cyd-ddigwyddiad *nm* coincidence

cydfod *nm* agreement, concord

cydfodolaeth *nf* coexistence

cydfyned *vb* to go with, to concur, to agree

cyd-fyw *vb* to cohabit

cydffurfio *vb* to conform

cydgordio *vb* to agree, to harmonize

cydgwmni (**-ïau**) *nm* consortium

cydiedig *adj* adjoined

cydio *vb* to join; to bite; to take hold

cydletywr (**-wyr**) *nm* roommate, flatmate, housemate

cydnabod *vb* to acknowledge ▸ *nm* acquaintance

cydnabyddiaeth *nf* acquaintance; recognition

cydnabyddus *adj* acquainted; familiar

cydnaws *adj* congenial

cydnerth *adj* well set

cydol *nmf, adj* whole

cydradd *adj* equal

cydraddoldeb *nm* equality

cyd-rhwng *prep* between

cydsyniad *nm* consent

cydsynio *vb* to consent

cydwastad *adj* level (with), even

cydweddog *adj* conjugal

cydweddu *vb* to accord, to agree

cydweithfa (-feydd) *nf* co-operative

cydweithio *vb* to cooperate

cydweithrediad *nm* co-operation

cydweithredol *adj* co-operative

cydweithredu *vb* to co-operate

cydweled *vb* to agree

cydwladol *adj* international

cyd-wladwr (-wyr) *nm* compatriot

cydwybod (-au) *nf* conscience

cydwybodol *adj* conscientious

cydwybodolrwydd *nm* conscientiousness

cydymaith (cymdeithion) *nm* companion

cydymdeimlad *nm* sympathy

cydymdeimlo *vb* to sympathize

cydymffurfiad *nm* conformity

cydymffurfio *vb* to conform

cydymgais *nm* competition, rivalry, joint effort

cydymgeisydd (-wyr) *nm* rival

cyddwysiad (-au) *nm* condensation

cyddwyso *vb* to condense

cyfadran (-nau) *nf* faculty (in college), period (in music)

cyfaddas *adj* fit, suitable, convenient

cyfaddasiad (-au) *nm* adaptation

cyfaddaster *nm* fitness, suitability

cyfaddasu *vb* to fit, to adapt

cyfaddawd (-odau) *nm* compromise

cyfaddawdu *vb* to compromise

cyfaddef *vb* to confess, to own, to admit

cyfaddefiad (-au) *nm* confession, admission

cyfaenad *nm* harmonious song
 ▸ *adj* harmonious

cyfagos *adj* near, adjacent, neighbouring

cyfaill (-eillion) *nm* friend

cyfair¹ (-eiriau) *nm* acre

cyfair², cyfer *nm* direction

cyfalaf *nm* capital

cyfalafiaeth *nf* capitalism

cyfalafol *adj* capitalistic

cyfalafwr (-wyr) *nm* capitalist

cyfamod (-au) *nm* covenant

cyfamodi *vb* to covenant

cyfamodol *adj* federal; covenanted

cyfamodwr (-wyr) *nm* covenanter

cyfamser *nm* meantime

cyfamserol *adj* timely; synchronous

cyfan *adj, nm* whole

cyfandir (-oedd) *nm* continent

cyfandirol *adj* continental

cyfanfor (-oedd) *nm* main sea, ocean

cyfanfyd *nm* whole world, universe

cyfangorff *nm* whole, bulk, mass

cyfan gwbl *adj*: **yn gyfan gwbl** altogether, completely

cyfanheddol *adj* habitable, inhabited

cyfanheddu *vb* to dwell, to inhabit

cyfannedd *adj* inhabited ▸ *nf* (**-anheddau**) inhabited place, habitation

cyfannol *adj* integrated, integral

cyfannu *vb* to make whole, to complete

cyfanrwydd *nm* wholeness, entirety

cyfansawdd *adj* composite, compound

cyfansoddi *vb* to compose, to constitute

cyfansoddiad (-au) *nm* composition; constitution

cyfansoddiadol *adj* constitutional

cyfansoddwr (-wyr) *nm* composer

cyfansoddyn (-ion) *nm* constituent, compound

cyfanswm (-symiau) *nm* total

cyfantoledd (-au) *nm* equilibrium

cyfanwaith (-weithiau) *nm* complete composition, whole

cyfanwerth *nm* wholesale

cyfarch *vb* to greet, to salute, to address

cyfarchiad (-au) *nm* greeting, salutation

cyfaredd (-ion) *nf* charm, spell

cyfareddol *adj* enchanting

cyfareddu *vb* to charm, to enchant

cyfarfod *vb* to meet ▸ *nm* (**-ydd**) meeting

cyfarfyddiad (-au) *nm* meeting

cyfarpar *nm* provision, equipment; diet; **cyfarpar rhyfel** munitions of war

cyfarparu *vb* to equip

cyfartal *adj* equal, even

cyfartaledd *nm* proportion, average

cyfartalu *vb* to proportion, to equalize

cyfarth *vb*, *nm* to bark

cyfarwydd *adj* skilled; familiar ▸ *nm* (**-iaid**) storyteller

cyfarwyddo *vb* to direct; to become familiar

cyfarwyddwr (-wyr) *nm* director

cyfarwyddyd (-iadau) *nm* direction, instruction

cyfatal *adj* unsettled, hindering

cyfateb *vb* to correspond, to agree, to tally

cyfatebiaeth (-au) *nf* correspondence, analogy

cyfatebol *adj* corresponding, proportionate

cyfathrach (-au) *nf* affinity; intercourse

cyfathrachu *vb* to have intercourse

cyfathrachwr (-wyr) *nm* kinsman

cyfathreb (-au) *nm* communication

cyfathrebu *vb* to communicate

cyfddydd *nm* day-break, dawn

cyfeb, cyfebr *adj* pregnant (*of mare, ewe*)

cyfebol *adj* in foal

cyfeddach (-au) *nf* carousal

cyfeddachwr (-wyr) *nm* carouser

cyfeiliant *nm* musical accompaniment

cyfeilio *vb* to accompany

cyfeiliorn *nm* error; wandering, lost (*person etc*); **ar gyfeiliorn** astray

cyfeiliornad (-au) *nm* error, heresy

cyfeiliorni *vb* to err, to stray

cyfeiliornus *adj* erroneous, mistaken

cyfeilydd (-ion) *nm* accompanist

cyfeillach (-au) *nf* fellowship; fellowship-meeting

cyfeillachu *vb* to associate

cyfeilles (-au) *nf* female friend

cyfeillgar *adj* friendly

cyfeillgarwch *nm* friendship

cyfeiriad (-au) *nm* direction; reference; (postal) address; **cyfeiriad ebost** email address; **cyfeiriad gwe** web address

cyfeiriannu *nm* orienteering

cyfeirio *vb* to point; to direct; to refer; to address (*letter*)

cyfeirnod (-au) *nm* mark of reference; aim; direct (*in music*)

cyfeirydd (-ion) *nm* indicator, guide

cyfenw (-au) *nm* surname; namesake

cyfenwi *vb* to surname

cyfer *nm*: **ar gyfer** opposite, for

cyferbyn *adj* opposite

cyferbyniad (-au) *nm* contrast

cyferbyniol *adj* opposing, opposite, contrasting

cyferbynnu *vb* to contrast, to compare

cyfesuryn *nm* coordinate

cyfethol *vb* to co-opt

cyfiaith *adj* of the same language

cyfiawn *adj* just, righteous

cyfiawnder (-au) *nm* justice, righteousness

cyfiawnhad *nm* justification

cyfiawnhau *vb* to justify

cyfieithiad (-au) *nm* translation, version

cyfieithu *vb* to translate, to interpret

cyfieithydd (-wyr) *nm* translator, interpreter

cyfisol *adj* of the present month, instant

cyflafan (-au) *nf* outrage; massacre

cyflafareddiad *nm* arbitration

cyflafareddu *vb* to arbitrate

cyflafareddwr (-wyr) *nm* arbitrator

cyflaith *nm* toffee

cyflasyn *nm* flavouring

cyflawn *adj* full, complete

cyflawnder *nm* fullness; abundance

cyflawni *vb* to fulfil, to perform, to commit

cyflawniad (-au) *nm* fulfilment, performance

cyfle (-oedd) *nm* place; chance; opportunity

cyfled *adj* as broad as

cyflegr (-au) *nm* gun, cannon, battery

cyflegru *vb* to bombard

cyflenwad (-au) *nm* supply

cyflenwi *vb* to supply

cyfleu *vb* to place, to set; to convey

cyfleus adj convenient

cyfleustra (-terau) nm opportunity, convenience

cyflin adj parallel

cyfliw adj of the same colour

cyflo adj in calf

cyflog (-au) nmf hire, wage, wages

cyflogaeth nf employment

cyflogedig (-ion) nm employee

cyflogi vb to hire; to engage in service

cyflogwr (-wyr) nm hirer, employer

cyflwr (-lyrau) nm condition; case

cyflwyniad nm presentation; dedication

cyflwyno vb to present; to dedicate

cyflwynydd (-ion) nm compère, presenter

cyflychwr, cyflychwyr nm evening twilight, dusk

cyflym adj quick, fast, swift

cyflymder, cyflymdra nm swiftness, speed

cyflymu vb to speed, to accelerate

cyflynu vb to stick together

cyflyru vb to condition

cyflythreniad (-au) nm alliteration

cyfnerthu vb to confirm; to aid, to help

cyfnerthydd (-ion, -wyr) nm strengthener, booster

cyfnesaf (-iaid, -eifiaid) nmf next of kin, kinsman ▸ adj next, nearest

cyfnewid vb to change, to exchange

cyfnewidfa (-oedd, -feydd) nf exchange

cyfnewidiad (-au) nm change, alteration

cyfnewidiol adj changeable

cyfnewidiwr (-wyr) nm changer, trader

cyfnither (-oedd) nf female cousin

cyfnod (-au) nm period; **cyfnod prawf** trial period

cyfnodol adj periodic(al)

cyfnodolyn (-ion) nm periodical publication

cyfnos nm evening twilight, dusk

cyfochredd nm parallelism

cyfochrog adj parallel

cyfodi vb to rise, to arise; to raise

cyfodiad nm rise, rising

cyfoed adj contemporary, of the same age ▸ nm (-ion) contemporary

cyfoes adj contemporary, up-to-date

cyfoesi vb to be contemporary

cyfoeswr (-wyr) nm contemporary

cyfoeth nm power; riches, wealth

cyfoethog adj powerful; rich, wealthy

cyfoethogi vb to make or grow rich

cyfog nm sickness

cyfogi vb to vomit

cyfor nm flood, abundance; rim, brim, edge ▸ adj entire, brim-full

cyforiog adj brim-full, overflowing

cyfosodiad nm apposition

cyfradd (-au) nf rate ▸ adj of equal rank; **cyfradd llog** rate of interest

cyfraid (-reidiau) nm necessity

cyfraith (-reithiau) nf law

cyfran (-nau) nf part, portion, share

cyfranc (-rangau) nfm meeting; combat; incident; story, tale

cyfranddaliad (-au) nm share

cyfranddaliwr (-wyr) nm shareholder

cyfraniad (-au) nm contribution

cyfrannedd nm proportion

cyfrannog adj participating, partaking

cyfrannol adj contributing

cyfrannu vb to contribute; to impart

cyfrannwr (-anwyr) nm contributor

cyfranogi vb to participate, to partake

cyfranogwr (-wyr) nm partaker

cyfredol adj current, concurrent

cyfreithio vb to go to law, to litigate

cyfreithiol adj legal

cyfreithiwr (-wyr) nm lawyer

cyfreithlon adj lawful, legitimate

cyfreithlondeb nm lawfulness

cyfreithloni vb to legalize; to justify

cyfreithus adj legitimate

cyfres (-i) nf series

cyfresol adj serial

cyfresu vb to serialise

cyfresymiad (-au) nm syllogism

cyfresymu vb to syllogise

cyfrgolli vb to lose utterly; to damn

cyfrif vb to count, to reckon; to account; to impute ▸ nm (-on) account, reckoning; **cyfrif banc** bank account

cyfrifeg nfm accountancy

cyfrifiad (-au) nm counting; census

cyfrifiadur (-on) nm computer; **cyfrifiadur personol** PC, personal computer

cyfrifiadureg nf computer science

cyfrifiaduro n computing

cyfrifiannell nf calculator

cyfrifol adj of repute; responsible

cyfrifoldeb (-au) nm responsibility

cyfrifydd (-ion) nm accountant

cyfrin adj secret, subtle

cyfrinach (-au) nf secret

cyfrinachol adj secret, private, confidential

cyfrinair (-eiriau) nm password

cyfrinfa nf lodge of friendly society or trade union

cyfrin-gyngor (-nghorau) nm privy council

cyfriniaeth nf mystery; mysticism

cyfriniol adj mysterious, mystic

cyfriniwr (-wyr) nm mystic

cyfrodedd adj twisted, twined

cyfrodeddu vb to twist, to twine

cyfrol (-au) nf volume

cyfrwng (-ryngau) nm medium, means

cyfrwy (-au) nm saddle

cyfrwyo vb to saddle

cyfrwys adj cunning

cyfrwystra nm cunning

cyfrwywr (-wyr) nm saddler

cyfryngdod nm mediation, intercession; mediatorship

cyfryngiad nm mediation; intervention

cyfryngol adj mediatorial

cyfryngu vb to mediate; to intervene

cyfryngwr (-wyr) nm mediator

cyfryngwriaeth nf mediatorship

cyfryw adj like, such

cyfuchlinedd (-au) nm contour

cyfuchliniau npl contours

cyfundeb (-au) nm union; connexion

cyfundebol adj connexional; denominational

cyfundrefn (-au) nf system

cyfundrefnol adj systematic

cyfundrefnu vb to systematize

cyfuniad (-au) nm combination

cyfuno vb to unite, to combine

cyfunol adj united

cyfunrhywiol adj homosexual

cyfuwch adj as high

cyfweld vb to interview

cyfweliad (-au) nm interview

cyfwelydd (-wyr) nm interviewer

cyfwerth adj equivalent

cyfwng (-yngau) nm space; interval

cyfwrdd vb to meet

cyfyng adj narrow, confined

cyfyngder (-au) nm trouble, distress

cyfyngdra nm narrowness; distress

cyfyngedig adj confined, restricted, limited

cyfyng-gyngor nm perplexity

cyfyngu vb to narrow, to confine, to limit

cyfyl nm neighbourhood; **ar ei gyfyl** near him

cyfyrder (-dyr) nm second cousin

cyfystlys adj side by side

cyfystyr adj synonymous

cyfystyron npl synonyms

cyff (-ion) nm stock

cyffaith (-feithiau) nm confection

cyffelyb adj like, similar

cyffelybiaeth (-au) nf likeness, similitude

cyffelybiaethol adj figurative

cyffelybrwydd nm likeness, similarity

cyffelybu vb to liken, to compare

cyffes (-ion) nf confession

cyffesgell (-oedd) nf confessional

cyffesu vb to confess

cyffeswr (-wyr), cyfesydd (-ion) nm confessor

cyffin (-iau, -ydd) nfm border, confine

cyffio vb to stiffen; to fetter, to shackle; to beat

cyffion npl stocks

cyfford (-ffyrdd) nf junction

cyffredin adj common; general

cyffredinedd nm mediocrity, banality

cyffredinol adj general, universal

cyffredinoli vb to universalize, to generalize

cyffredinolrwydd nm universality

cyffredinwch nm commonness

cyffro (-adau) nm motion, stir; excitement

cyffroi vb to move, to excite; to provoke

cyffrous adj exciting; excited

cyffur (-iau) nfm ingredient, drug

cyffuriwr (-wyr) nm apothecary, druggist

cyffwrdd vb to meet, to touch

cyffylog (-od) *nm* woodcock

cyffyrddiad (-au) *nm* touch, contact

cyffyrddus *adj* comfortable

cygnog *adj* knotted, gnarled

cyngaf, cyngaw *nm* burdock; burs

cyngan *adj* suitable, harmonious

cynganeddol *adj* in *cynghanedd*

cynganeddu *vb* to form *cynghanedd*; to harmonize

cynganeddwr (-wyr) *nm* writer of *cynghanedd*

cyngaws (cynghawsau, -ion) *nm* lawsuit, action; trial; battle

cyngerdd (-ngherddau) *nmf* concert

cynghanedd (cynganeddion) *nf* music, harmony; Welsh metrical alliteration

cynghori *vb* to counsel, to advise; to exhort

cynghorwr (-wyr) *nm* councillor; counsellor; exhorter

cynghrair (-eiriau) *nmf* alliance, league

cynghreiriad (-iaid) *nm* confederate, ally

cynghreirio *vb* to league, to confederate

cynghreiriwr (-wyr) *nm* confederate, ally

cyngor (-nghorion) *nm* counsel, advice ▸ *nm* (-nghorau) council; **Cyngor Bro** Community Council; **Cyngor Tref** Town Council; **Cyngor Sir** County Council

cyngres (-au, -i) *nf* congress

cyngresydd (-wyr) *nm* congressman

cyngwystl (-(i)on) *nmf* wager, pledge

cyhoedd *adj, nm* public

cyhoeddi *vb* to publish, to announce

cyhoeddiad (-au) *nm* publication; announcement; (preaching) engagement

cyhoeddus *adj* public

cyhoeddusrwydd *nm* publicity

cyhoeddwr (-wyr) *nm* publisher

cyhuddiad (-au) *nm* accusation, charge

cyhuddo *vb* to accuse, to charge

cyhuddwr (-wyr) *nm* accuser

cyhwfan *vb* to wave, to heave

cyhyd *adj* as long, so long

cyhydedd *nm* equator

cyhydeddol *adj* equatorial, equinoctial

cyhyr (-au) *nm* flesh, muscle

cyhyrog *adj* muscular

cylch (-au, oedd) *nm* round, circle, sphere, hoop

cylchdaith (-deithiau) *nf* circuit

cylchdro (-eon, -adau) *nm* orbit

cylchdroi *vb* to rotate, to revolve

cylched (-au) *nm* coverlet, blanket

cylchedd (-au) *nmf* compass, circle, circuit

cylchfan *nf* roundabout

cylchgrawn (-gronau) *nm* magazine

cylchlythyr (-au) *nm* circular

cylchredeg *vb* to circulate

cylchrediad *nm* circulation

cylchres (-i) *nf* round, rota

cylchwyl (-iau) *nf* anniversary, festival

cylchynol adj surrounding

cylchynu vb to surround, to encompass

cylion npl (nm **-yn**, nf **-en**) flies, gnats

cylymu vb to knot, to tie

cyll npl (nf **collen**) hazel-trees

cylla (**-on**) nm stomach

cyllell (**-yll**) nf knife

cyllid (**-au**) nm revenue, income

cyllideb (**-au**) nf budget

cyllido vb to finance

cyllidol adj financial, fiscal

cyllidwr (**-wyr**), **cyllidydd** (**-ion**) nm tax-gatherer, revenue or excise officer, financier

cymaint adj as big, as much, as many; so big etc

cymal (**-au**) nm joint; clause

cymalwst nf rheumatism

cymanfa (**-oedd**) nf assembly; festival

cymantoledd (**-au**) nm equilibrium

cymanwlad nf commonwealth

cymar (**-heiriaid**) nm fellow, partner

cymathiad nm assimilation

cymathu vb to assimilate

cymdeithas (**-au**) nf society; association; **Cymdeithas yr Iaith Gymraeg** The Welsh Language Society

cymdeithaseg nf sociology

cymdeithasegol adj sociological

cymdeithasgar adj sociable

cymdeithasol adj social

cymdeithasu vb to associate; to socialize

cymdogaeth (**-au**) nf neighbourhood

cymdogol adj neighbourly

cymedr (**-au**) nm mean (in maths), average

cymedrol adj moderate, temperate

cymedroldeb nm moderation, temperance

cymedroli vb to moderate

cymedrolwr (**-wyr**) nm moderator; moderate drinker

cymell vb to urge, to press, to persuade, to induce; to motivate
▸ nm (**cymhellion**) motivation

cymen adj wise, skilful, neat, becoming

cymer (**-au**) nm confluence

cymeradwy adj acceptable, approved, commendable

cymeradwyaeth nf approval; applause; recommendation

cymeradwyo vb to approve; to recommend

cymeradwyol adj commendatory

cymeriad (**-au**) nm character, reputation

cymesur adj proportionate, symmetrical

cymesuredd nm proportion, symmetry

cymesurol adj commensurate, proportionate

cymhareb (**cymarebau**) nf ratio

cymhariaeth (**cymariaethau**) nf comparison

cymharol adj comparative

cymharu vb to pair; to compare

cymhelliad (**-elliadau**) *nm* motive, inducement

cymhendod *nm* knowledge; proficiency; tidiness; eloquence; affection

cymhennu *vb* to put in order, to trim; to scold, to reprove

cymhercyn *adj* limping, infirm
▸ *nm* valetudinarian

cymhleth (**-au**) *adj* complex, complicated

cymhlethdod (**-au**) *nm* complexity

cymhlethu *vb* to complicate

cymhorthdal (**cymorthdaloedd**) *nm* subsidy, grant

cymhwysiad *nm* application, adjustment

cymhwyso *vb* to apply, to adjust

cymhwyster (**cymwysterau**) *nm* fitness, suitability; (*pl*) qualifications

cymod *nm* reconciliation

cymodi *vb* to reconcile; to be reconciled

cymodol *adj* reconciliatory, propitiatory

cymodwr (**-wyr**) *nm* reconciler

cymon *adj* orderly, tidy; seemly

cymorth *vb* to assist, to aid, to help
▸ *nm* assistance, aid, help

Cymraeg *nfm*, *adj* Welsh

Cymraes *nf* Welshwoman

cymrawd (**-odyr**) *nm* comrade, fellow

Cymreictod *nm* Welshness

Cymreig *adj* Welsh

Cymreiges (**-au**) *nf* Welshwoman

Cymreigio *vb* to translate into Welsh

Cymreigiwr (**-wyr**) *nm* one versed or skilled in Welsh; Welsh-speaking Welshman

Cymro (**Cymry**) *nm* Welshman

cymrodedd *nm* arbitration; compromise

cymrodeddu *vb* to compromise, to reconcile

cymrodor (**-ion**) *nm* consociate, fellow

cymrodoriaeth *nf* fellowship

Cymru *nf* Wales

cymrwd *nm* mortar, plaster

Cymry *see* Cymro

cymryd *vb* to take, to accept; cymryd ar pretend

cymudo *vb* to commute

cymun, cymundeb *nm* communion, fellowship

cymuned *nf* community; **y Gymuned Ewropeaidd** the European Community

cymunedol *adj* community

cymuno *vb* to commune

cymunwr (**-wyr**) *nm* communicant

cymwy (**-au**) *nm* affliction

cymwynas (**-au**) *nf* kindness, favour

cymwynasgar *adj* obliging, kind

cymwynasgarwch *nm* obligingness, kindness

cymwynaswr (**-wyr**) *nm* benefactor

cymwys *adj* fit, proper, suitable; exact

cymwysedig *adj* applied

cymwysiadol *adj* applicable

cymdog (**cymdogion**) (*f* **cymdoges**) *nm* neighbour

cymylog *adj* cloudy, clouded

cymylu *vb* to cloud, to dim, to obscure

cymyndod *nm* committal

cymynnu *vb* to bequeath

cymynrodd (-ion) *nf* legacy, bequest

cymynroddi *vb* to bequeath

cymynu *vb* to hew, to fell

cymynwr (-wyr) *nm* hewer, feller

cymysg *adj* mixed

cymysgedd *nmf* mixture

cymysgfa *nf* mixture, medley, hotchpotch

cymysgliw *adj* motley

cymysglyd *adj* muddled, confused

cymysgryw *adj* mongrel; heterogeneous

cymysgu *vb* to mix, to blend; to confuse

cymysgwch *nm* mixture, jumble

cymysgwr (-wyr) *nm* mixer, blender

cyn¹ *prefix* before, previous, first, former, pre-, ex-; **Cyn Crist** Before Christ, B.C.

cyn² *adv*: **cyn gynted (â phosib)** as soon (as possible) ; **cyn wynned â** as white as

cŷn (cynion) *nm* wedge, chisel

cynadledda *vb* to meet in conference

cynaeafa, cynhaeafa *vb* to dry in the sun

cynaeafu, cynhaeafu *vb* to harvest

cynaeafwr, cynhaeafwr (-wyr) *nm* harvester

cynamserol *adj* premature, untimely

cynaniad *nm* pronunciation

cynanu *vb* to pronounce

cyndad (-au) *nm* forefather, ancestor

cynderfynol *adj* semi-final

cyndyn *adj* stubborn, obstinate

cyndynnu *vb* to be obstinate

cyndynrwydd *nm* stubbornness, obstinacy

cynddaredd *nf* madness; rabies

cynddeiriog *adj* mad, rabid

cynddeiriogi *vb* to madden, to enrage

cynddeiriogrwydd *nm* rage, fury

cynddrwg *adj* as bad

cynddydd *nm* day-break, dawn

cynefin *adj* acquainted, accustomed, familiar ▸ *nm* haunt, habitat

cynefindra *nm* use, familiarity

cynefino *vb* to get used, to become accustomed

cynefinol *adj* usual, accustomed

cynfas (-au) *nfm* (bed) sheet; canvas

cynfyd *nm* primitive world, antiquity

cynffon (-nau) *nf* tail; tang

cynffonna *vb* to fawn, to toady, to cringe

cynffonnwr (-onwyr) *nm* toady, sycophant; sneak

cyn-geni *adj* antenatal

cynhadledd (cynadleddau) *nf* conference

cynhaeaf (cynaeafau) *nm* harvest

cynhaeafa *vb see* **cynaeafa**

73

cynhaeafu vb see **cynaeafu**

cynhaeafwr nm see **cynaeafwr**

cynhaliaeth nf maintenance, support

cynhaliol adj sustaining

cynhaliwr (-wyr) nm supporter, sustainer

cynhanesiol adj prehistoric

cynhebrwng (-yngau) nm funeral

cynhenid adj innate

cynhennu vb to contend, to quarrel

cynhennus adj contentious, quarrelsome

cynhennwr (-henwyr) nm wrangler

cynhesol adj agreeable, amiable

cynhesrwydd nm warmth

cynhesu vb to warm, to get warm; **cynhesu byd-eang** global warming

cynhorthwy (cynorthwyon) nm help, aid

cynhwynol adj natural, congenital, innate

cynhwysedd (cynwyseddau) nm capacity, capacitance

cynhwysfawr adj comprehensive

cynhwysiad nm contents

cynhwysydd nm container

cynhyrchiad (-au) nm production

cynhyrchiol adj productive

cynhyrchu vb to produce

cynhyrchydd (-ion, cynhyrchwyr) nm producer, generator

cynhyrfiad (cynyrfiadau) nm stirring, agitation

cynhyrfiol adj stirring, thrilling

cynhyrfu vb to stir, to agitate

cynhyrfus adj agitated; exciting

cynhyrfwr (-wyr) nm agitator, disturber

cynhysgaeth nf portion, fortune

cyni nm anguish, distress, adversity

cynifer adj, nm as many, so many

cynigiad (-au) nm proposal, motion

cynigiwr (-wyr), cynigydd (-ion) nm proposer, mover

cynildeb nm frugality, economy

cynilion npl savings

cynilo vb to save, to economise

cynio vb to chisel, to gouge

cyniwair vb to go to and fro, to frequent

cyniweirfa (-feydd) nf resort, haunt

cyniweirydd nm wayfarer

cynllun (-iau) nm pattern; plan

cynllunio vb to plan, to design

cynllunydd (-ion, -wyr) nm designer

cynllwyn vb to plot, to conspire ▸ nm (-ion) plot

cynllwynio vb to conspire, to plot

cynllwynwr (-wyr) nm conspirator

cynnal vb to hold, to uphold, to support, to sustain

cynnar adj early

cynnau vb to kindle, to light

cynneddf (cyneddfau) nf quality, faculty

cynnen (cynhennau) nf contention, strife; **asgwrn y gynnen** bone of contention

cynnes adj warm

cynnig *vb* to offer; to attempt; to propose, to move; to bid; to apply ▸ *nm* (**cynigion**) offer; attempt; motion

cynnil *adj* economical; delicate

cynnor (**cynhorau**) *nf* door-post

cynnud *nm* firewood, fuel

cynnull *vb* to collect, to gather, to assemble

cynnwrf *nm* stir, commotion, agitation

cynnwys *vb* to contain, to include, to comprise, to comprehend ▸ *nm* content(s)

cynnydd *nm* increase, growth, progress

cynnyrch (**cynhyrchion**) *nm* produce, product; (*pl*) productions

cynoesol *adj* primeval

cynorthwyo *vb* to help, to assist

cynorthwyol *adj* auxiliary; assistant

cynorthwywr (**-wyr**) *nm* helper, assistant

cynorthwyydd (**-ion**) *nm*: **cynorthwyydd dosbarth** classroom assistant

cynradd *adj* primary

cynrychioladol *adj* representative

cynrychiolaeth *nf* representation

cynrychioli *vb* to represent

cynrychiolwr (**-wyr**), **cynrychiolydd** (**-ion**) *nm* representative, delegate

cynrhon *npl* (*nm* **-yn**) maggots

cynrhoni *vb* to breed maggots

cynrhonllyd *adj* maggoty

cynt *adj* earlier, sooner, quicker ▸ *adv see* **gynt**

cyntaf *adj, adv* first

cyntedd (**-au**) *nm* court; porch, foyer

cyntefig *adj* prime, primitive

cyntun *nm* nap

cynulleidfa (**-oedd**) *nf* congregation

cynulleidfaol *adj* congregational

cynulliad (**-au**) *nm* gathering

cynuta *vb* to gather fuel

cynyddol *adj* increasing, growing

cynyddu *vb* to increase

cynysgaeddu *vb* to endow, to endue

cyplad *nm* copula

cypladu *vb* to copulate

cyplu, cyplysu *vb* to couple

cyplysnod *nm* hyphen

cyraeddadwy *adj* attainable

cyraeddiadau *npl* attainments

cyrbibion *npl* atoms, smithereens

cyrcydu *vb* to squat, to cower

cyrch (**-au**) *nm* attack

cyrchfa (**-feydd**) *nf* resort

cyrchfan *nf* destination

cyrchu *vb* to go, to resort, to repair

cyrchwr (**-wyr**) *nm* cursor

cyrens *npl* (*nf* **cyrensen**) currants

cyrhaeddgar *adj* telling, incisive

cyrhaeddiad (**cyraeddiadau**) *nm* reach, attainment

cyrliog *adj* curly

cyrraedd *vb* to reach, to attain; to arrive; to get back

cyrydiad *nm* corrosion

cyrydu *vb* to corrode

cysawd

cysawd (**-odau**) *nm* system; constellation

cysefin *adj* original, primordial

cysegr (**-au, -oedd**) *nm* sanctuary

cysegredig *adj* consecrated, sacred

cysegredigrwydd *nm* sacredness

cysegriad (**-au**) *nm* consecration

cysegr-ladrad *nm* sacrilege

cysegr-lân *adj* holy

cysegru *vb* to consecrate, to dedicate, to devote

cyseinedd *nm* alliteration

cysetlyd *adj* fastidious

cysgadrwydd *nm* sleepiness, drowsiness

cysgadur (**-iaid**) *nm* sleeper

cysglyd *adj* sleepy

cysgod (**-au, -ion**) *nm* shade, shadow; shelter; type

cysgodi *vb* to shadow, to shade; to shelter

cysgodol *adj* shady, sheltered

cysgu *vb* to sleep

cysgwr (**-wyr**) *nm* sleeper

cysidro *vb* to consider

cysodi *vb* to set type, to compose

cysodydd (**-ion,-wyr**) *nm* compositor

cyson *adj* consistent, constant

cysondeb *nm* consistency; regularity

cysoni *vb* to harmonize; to reconcile

cysonwr (**-wyr**), **cysonydd** (**-ion**) *nm* harmonist

cystadleuaeth (**-laethau**) *nf* competition

cystadleuol *adj* competitive

cystadleuwr (**-wyr**), **cystadleuydd** *nm* competitor

cystadlu *vb* to compete; to compare

cystal *adj* as good, so good ▶ *adv* as well, so well

cystrawen (**-nau**) *nf* construction, syntax

cystudd (**-iau**) *nm* affliction; illness

cystuddiedig *adj* afflicted, contrite

cystuddio *vb* to afflict, to trouble

cystuddiol *adj* afflicted

cystuddiwr (**-wyr**) *nm* oppressor

cystwyo *vb* to tell off, to chastise

cysur (**-on**) *nm* comfort, consolation

cysuro *vb* to comfort, to console

cysurus *adj* comfortable

cysurwr (**-wyr**) *nm* comforter

cyswllt (**-ylltiadau**) *nm* joint, junction

cysylltiad (**-au**) *nm* conjunction; joining, connexion; **cysylltiadau cyhoeddus** public relations

cysylltiedig *adj* connected

cysylltiol *adj* connecting; connected

cysylltnod (**-au**) *nm* ligature, hyphen

cysylltu *vb* to join, to connect

cysylltydd (**-ion**) *nm* connector, contact

cysyniad (**-au**) *nm* concept

cytbell *adj* equidistant

cytbwys *adj* of equal weight

cytbwysedd *nm* balance

cytew *nm* batter

cytgan (**-au**) *nmf* chorus

cytgord *nm* concord

cytir (-oedd) *nm* common

cytras *adj* allied, related; cognate

cytsain (-seiniaid) *nf* consonant

cytûn *adj* agreed, of one accord, unanimous

cytundeb (-au) *nm* agreement, consent

cytuno *vb* to agree, to consent

cythlwng *nm* fasting, fast, hunger

cythraul (-euliaid) *nm* devil, demon

cythreuldeb *nm* devilment

cythreulig *adj* devilish, fiendish

cythru *vb* to snatch, to rush

cythruddo *vb* to annoy, to provoke, to irritate

cythrwfl *nm* uproar, tumult

cythryblu *vb* to trouble, to agitate

cythryblus *adj* troubled, agitated

cyw (-ion) *nm* young bird, chick, chicken; baby

cywain *vb* to convey, to carry; to garner

cywair (-eiriau) *nm* order; key; tune

cywaith (-weithiau) *nm* collective work, project

cywarch *nm* hemp

cywasg, cywasgedig *adj* diminished

cywasgiad (-au) *nm* contraction, compression

cywasgu *vb* to contract, to compress

cywasgydd (-ion) *nm* compressor

cyweiriad (-au) *nm* repair

cyweiriadur (-on) *nm* modulator

cyweirio *vb* to set in order; to prepare, to dress

cyweirnod (-au) *nm* key-note

cywen (-nod) *nf* pullet, young hen

cywerth *adj* equivalent

cywilydd *nm* shame; shyness

cywilydd-dra *nm* shamefulness

cywilyddgar *adj* bashful, shy

cywilyddio *vb* to shame; to be ashamed

cywilyddus *adj* shameful, disgraceful; outrageous

cywir *adj* correct, accurate, true, faithful

cywirdeb *nm* correctness; integrity

cywiriad (-au) *nm* correction

cywiro *vb* to correct; to make good; to perform

cywirwr (-wyr) *nm* corrector

cywladu *vb* to naturalize

cywrain *adj* skilful; curious

cywreinbeth (-au, cywreinion) *nm* curiosity

cywreindeb *nm* skill, ingenuity

cywreinrwydd *nm* skill; curiosity

cywydd (-au) *nm* alliterative Welsh poem

cywyddwr (-wyr) *nm* composer of cywyddau

ch

Chechnya *nf* Chechnya
Chile *nf* Chile
China *nf* China
chwa (-on) *nf* puff, gust, breeze
chwaer (chwioydd) *nf* sister
chwaeroliaeth *nf* sisterhood
chwaeth (-au, -oedd) *nf* taste
chwaethu *vb* to taste
chwaethus *adj* tasteful; decent
chwaith *adv* nor either, neither
chwâl *adj* scattered, loose
chwalfa (-feydd) *nf* upset, rout
chwalu *vb* to scatter, to spread
chwalwr (-wyr) *nm* scatterer, demolisher
chwaneg *adj*, *nm* more
chwanegiad (-au) *nm* addition
chwanegol *adj* additional
chwanegu *vb* to add, to augment, to increase
chwannen (chwain) *nf* flea
chwannog *adj* desirous; addicted; prone

chwant (-au) *nm* desire, craving, lust
chwantu *vb* to desire, to lust
chwap *nm* sudden blow; moment ▸ *adv* instantly
chwarae, chware *vb* to play ▸ *nm* play; **chwaraeon y gaeaf** winter sports
chwaraedy (-dai) *nm* playhouse, theatre
chwaraefa (-feydd) *nf* pitch, playground
chwaraegar *adj* playful, sportive
chwaraewr (-wyr) *nm* player, actor, performer; **chwaraewr cryno-ddisgiau** CD player; **chwaraewr DVD** DVD player
chwaraeydd (-ion) *nm* actor
chwarddiad (-au) *nm* laugh
chwarel (-au, -i, -ydd) *nf* quarry
chwarelwr (-wyr) *nm* quarryman
chwareus *adj* playful
chwarren (-arennau) *nf* gland; kernel
chwart (-iau) *nm* quart
chwarter (-i, -au) *nm* quarter
chwarterol *adj* quarterly
chwarterolyn (-olion) *nm* quarterly (magazine)
chwarteru *vb* to quarter
chwe *adj* six (*before a noun*)
chweban (-nau) *nf* sestet, sextain
chwech (-au) *adj*, *nm* six
chwechawd (-au) *nm* sextet
chweched *adj* sixth; **chweched dosbarth** sixth form
chwedl (-au) *nf* story, tale
chwedleua *vb* to talk, to gossip
chwedleuwr (-wyr) *nm* story-teller
chwedloniaeth *nf* mythology

chwedlonol *adj* mythical, mythological

chwedlonydd (-wyr) *nm* mythologist

chwedyn *adv*: **na chynt na chwedyn** neither before nor after

Chwefror, Chwefrol *nm* February

chwennych, chwenychu *vb* to covet, to desire

chwenychiad (-au) *nm* desire

chweongl (-au) *nm* hexagon

chwephlyg *adj* sixfold

chwerthin *vb* to laugh ▸ *nm* laughter

chwerthiniad (-au) *nm* laugh

chwerthinllyd *adj* laughable, ridiculous

chwerthinog *adj* laughing, merry

chwerw *adj* bitter

chwerwder, chwerwdod *nm* bitterness

chwerwedd *nm* bitterness

chwerwi *vb* to grow bitter, to embitter

chwi *pron* you

chwib (-iau) *nm* whistle

chwiban *vb* to whistle ▸ *nm* whistle

chwibaniad *nm* whistling, whistle

chwibanogl (-au) *nf* whistle, flute

chwibanu *vb* to whistle

chwibon (-iaid) *nm* curlew, stork

chwifio *vb* to wave, to flourish, to brandish

chwiff (-iau) *nf* whiff, puff

chwiffiad *nm* whiff, jiffy

chwil¹ (-od) *nmf* beetle, chafer

chwil² *adj* whirling, reeling

chwilboeth *adj* scorching, piping hot

chwildroi *vb* to whirl, to spin

chwilen (chwilod) *nf* beetle

chwilenna *vb* to rummage; to pry; to pilfer

chwiler (-od) *nm* chrysalis, pupa

chwilfriw *adj* smashed to atoms

chwilfriwio *vb* to smash, to shatter

chwilfrydedd *nm* curiosity

chwilfrydig *adj* curious, inquisitive

chwilgar *adj* curious, inquisitive

chwilgarwch *nm* inquisitiveness

chwiliad (-au) *nm* search, scrutiny

chwiliadur (-on) *nm* search engine

chwilibawa, chwilibawan *vb* to - dawdle, to trifle

chwilio *vb* to search; to examine

chwiliwr (-wyr) *nm* searcher

chwil-lys *nm* inquisition

chwilmantan *vb* to pry, to rummage

chwilolau (-oleuadau) *nm* searchlight

chwilota *vb* to rummage, to pry

chwilotwr (-wyr) *nm* searcher, rummager

chwim *adj* nimble, quick, agile

chwimder, chwimdra *nm* nimbleness

chwimio *vb* to move, to stir, to accelerate

chwimwth *adj* nimble, brisk

chwinc *nm* wink

chwinciad *nm* twinkling, trice

chwiorydd *see* chwaer

chwip (-iau) *nf* whip; whipping

chwipiad (-au) *nm* whipping

chwipio *vb* to whip

chwipyn *adv* instantly

chwirligwgan *nf* whirligig

chwisgi *nm* whisky

chwisl (-au) *nm* whistle

chwistrell (-au, -i) *nf* squirt, syringe

chwistrelliad (-au) *nm* injection

chwistrellu *vb* to squirt, to syringe, to inject

chwit-chwat *adj* fickle, inconstant

chwith *adj* left; wrong; sad; strange

chwithau *pron* you (on your part), you also

chwithdod, chwithdra *nm* strangeness

chwithig *adj* strange, wrong, awkward

chwithigrwydd *nm* awkwardness

chwiw (-iau) *nf* fit, attack, malady

chwiwgar *adj* fickle

chwychwi *pron* you yourselves

chwŷd, chwydiad *nm* vomit

chwydu *vb* to vomit, to spew

chwydd, chwyddi *nm* swelling

chwyddiant (-nnau) *nm* inflation; inflammation

chwyddo *vb* to swell, to increase, to magnify

chwyddwydr (-au) *nm* microscope

chwŷl (chwylion) *nmf* turn, rotation

chwyldro (-ion) *nm* rotation; orbit

chwyldroad (-au) *nm* revolution

chwyldroadol *adj* revolutionary

chwyldroadwr (-wyr) *nm* revolutionary

chwyldroi *vb* to whirl, to revolve, to rotate

chwyldrowr *see* chwyldroadwr

chwylolwyn (-ion) *nf* flywheel

chwyn (nm chwynnyn) *coll n, npl* weeds

chwynladdwr *nm* weed-killer

chwynnu *vb* to weed

chwyrligwgan (-od) *nf* spinning top, whirligig

chwyrlïo *vb* to whirl, to spin, to speed

chwyrlwynt (-oedd) *nm* whirlwind

chwyrn *adj* rapid, swift

chwyrnellu *vb* to whirl, to whiz

chwyrnu *vb* to hum; to snore; to snarl

chwyrnwr (-wyr) *nm* snorer; snarler

chwys *nm* sweat, perspiration

chwysfa (-feydd) *nf* sweating

chwysiant *nm* exudation

chwysigen (-igod) *nf* blister, vesicle

chwyslyd *adj* sweaty

chwystyllau *npl* pores

chwysu *vb* to sweat, to perspire; to exude

chwyswr (-wyr) *nm* sweater

chwyth, chwythad *nm* breath

chwythbib (-au) *nf* blowpipe

chwythbrenni *npl* woodwinds

chwythell (-i) *nf* jet

chwythiad (-au) *nm* blow, blast

chwythu *vb* to blow, to blast; to breathe; to hiss

chwythwr (-wyr) *nm* blower

d

da adj good, well ▸ nm (**-oedd**) good; goods; stock, cattle
dacw adv there is, are; behold there
dad-, dat- prefix un-, dis-, re-, back
da-da nm sweets
dadansoddi vb to analyse
dadansoddiad (-au) nm analysis
dadansoddol adj analytic(al)
dadansoddwr (-wyr) nm analyst
dadansoddydd (-wyr) nm analyser
dadchwyddiant (-nnau) nm deflation
dad-ddyfrio vb to dehydrate
dadebriad nm resuscitation
dadebru vb to resuscitate, to revive
dadelfeniad (-au) nm decomposition
dadelfennu vb to decompose; to refine
dadeni vb to regenerate, to reanimate ▸ nm rebirth, renascence, renaissance
dadfachu vb to unhook

dadfathiad nm dissimulation
dadfeiliad nm decay
dadfeilio vb to fall to ruin, to decay
dadflino vb to rest (after exertion)
dadl (-euon) nf debate; doubt; plea
dadlaith vb to thaw; to dissolve
dadlau vb to argue, to debate; to plead
dadleniad (-au) nm disclosure, exposure
dadlennol adj revealing, disclosing, exposing
dadlennu vb to disclose, to expose
dadleoli vb to dislocate
dadleoliad (-au) nm dislocation
dadleuaeth nf polemics, controversy
dadleugar adj argumentative
dadleuol adj controversial, polemical
dadleuwr (-wyr), dadleuydd (-ion) nm debater, controversialist; advocate
dadluddedu vb to rest (after exertion)
dadlwytho vb to unload, to unburden; to download
dadlygru vb to decontaminate
dadmer vb to thaw; to dissolve
dadnitreiddiad nm denitrification
dadolwch nm propitiation ▸ vb to worship, to seek forgiveness
dadorchuddio vb to unveil, to uncover
dadreolaeth nf decontrol
dadrewlifiant nm deglaciation
dadrithiad (-au) nm disillusionment
dadrithio vb to disillusion
dadsefydlu vb to disestablish

dadwaddoli vb to disendow
dadwaddoliad nm disendowment
dadwneuthur, dad-wneud vb to undo, to unmake
dadwrdd nm noise, uproar, hubbub
dadymchwel, dadymchwelyd vb to overturn, to overthrow
daear (-oedd) nf earth, ground, soil
daeardy (-dai) nm dungeon
daeareg nf geology
daearegol adj geological
daearegwr (-wyr), **daearegydd** (-ion) nm geologist
daearen nf the earth; land, country
daearfochyn (-foch) nm badger
daeargell (-oedd) nf dungeon, vault
daeargi (-gwn) nm terrier
daeargryd (-iau) nm earth tremor
daeargryn (-fâu) nmf earthquake
daearol adj terrestrial, earthly, earthy
daearu vb to earth; to inter
daearyddiaeth nf geography
daearyddol adj geographical
daearyddwr (-wyr) nm geographer
dafad (defaid) nf sheep; wart
dafaden (-ennau) nf wart
dafn (-au) nm drop
dafnu vb to trickle
dagr (-au) nm dagger, bayonet, dirk
dagrau npl (nm **deigryn**) tears
dagreuol adj tearful, sad
dail npl (nf **dalen**, nf **deilen**) leaves
daioni nm goodness, good
daionus adj good; beneficial; beneficent

dal, dala vb to hold; to catch; to arrest; to last; **dal ati!** carry on!, don't give up!
dalen (-nau, **dail**) nf leaf
dalfa (-feydd) nf hold; arrest, custody; prison
dalgylch (-oedd) nm catchment area
daliad (-au) nm holding; tenet; spell
daliwr (-wyr) nm jig, catcher
dall (**deillion**) adj blind
dallbleidiaeth nf bigotry
dallbleidiol adj bigoted
dallbleidiwr (-wyr) nm bigot
dallineb nm blindness
dallu vb to blind; to dazzle
damcaniaeth (-au) nf theory
damcaniaethol adj theoretical
damcaniaethwr (-wyr) nm theorist
damcanu vb to theorize, to speculate
dameg (-hegion) nf parable
damhegol adj parabolic(al), allegorical
damhegwr (-wyr) nm allegorist
damnedig adj damned, damnable
damnedigaeth nf damnation, condemnation
damnio vb to damn
damniol adj damning, damnatory
damsang vb to tread, to trample
damwain (-weiniau) nf accident, chance, fate
damweinio vb to befall, to happen
damweiniol adj accidental, casual
dan see **tan**
danadl npl (nf **danhadlen**) nettles

danas *coll n* deer; **bwch danas** buck

danfon *vb* to send, to convey; to escort

dangos *vb* to show

dangoseg (-ion) *nf* index; indication

dangosol *adj* indicative, demonstrative

danheddog *adj* jagged, serrated, toothed

dannod *vb* to reproach, to upbraid, to taunt, to twit

dannoedd *nf* toothache

dansoddol *adj* abstract

dant (danneddd) *nm* tooth

danteithfwyd (-teithion) *nm* dainty

danteithiol *adj* dainty, delicious

danteithion *npl* delicacies

darbodaeth *nf* thrift

darbodus *adj* provident, thrifty

darbwyllo *vb* to persuade, to convince

darfod *vb* to finish, to end; to perish; to happen

darfodadwy *adj* transitory, perishable

darfodedig *adj* perishable, transient

darfodedigaeth *nm* consumption

darfudiad (-au) *nm* convection

darfudol *adj* convectional

darganfod *vb* to discover, to find out

darganfyddiad (-au) *nm* discovery

darganfyddwr (-wyr) *nm* discoverer

dargludedd *nm* conductivity

dargludo *vb* to conduct

dargludydd (-ion) *nm* conductor

dargyfeiredd *nm* divergence

dargyfeirio *vb* to diverge, to divert

darlith (-iau, -oedd) *nf* lecture

darlithfa (-feydd) *nf* lecture room, lecture theatre

darlithio *vb* to lecture

darlithiwr (-wyr), darlithydd (-ion) *nm* lecturer

darlun (-iau) *nm* picture

darluniad (-au) *nm* portrayal, description

darluniadol *adj* pictorial, illustrated

darluniaeth *nf* imagery

darlunio *vb* to portray, to depict, to describe

darluniol *adj* pictorial

darllediad (-au) *nm* broadcast

darlledu *vb* to broadcast

darlledwr (-wyr) *nm* broadcaster

darllen *vb* to read

darllenadwy *adj* readable, legible

darllenfa (-feydd) *nf* reading room; reading-desk; lectern

darllengar *adj* fond of reading, studious

darlleniad (-au) *nm* reading

darllenwr (-wyr), darllenydd (-ion) *nm* reader

darn (-au) *nm* piece, fragment, part

darnguddio *vb* to conceal or withhold a part

darniad (-au) *nm* fragmentation

darnio *vb* to cut up, to hack

darn-ladd *vb* to beat mercilessly

darogan *vb* to predict, to foretell, to forebode ▶ *nf* (-au) prediction, foreboding

daroganu *vb* to predict, to foretell

daroganwr (-wyr) *nm* predictor, prophet, soothsayer, forecaster

darostwng *vb* to lower; to subdue; to subject, to humiliate

darostyngiad *nm* humiliation; subjection

darpar (-ion, -iadau) *nm* preparation, provision ▸ *adj* intended, elect

darpariaeth (-au) *nf* preparation, provision

darparu *vb* to prepare, to provide

darparwr (-wyr) *nm* provider

darwden *nf* ringworm

das (-au, deisi) *nf* rick, stack

dat- *prefix see* dad-

data *nm* data

datblygiad (-au) *nm* development, evolution

datblygol *adj* nascent, developing

datblygu *vb* to develop, to evolve

datblygus *adj* developmental

datblygydd (-ion) *nm* developer

datchwyddiant *nm* deflation

datgan *vb* to declare; to recount; to render

datganiad (-au) *nm* declaration; rendering

datganoli *vb* to devolve, to decentralize ▸ *nm* devolution

datganoliad *nm* devolution

datganu *vb* to declare; to sing; to render

datgeliad (-au) *nm* detection; revelation

datgelu *vb* to detect; to reveal

datgloi *vb* to unlock

datglymu *vb* to unhitch, to undo

datgorffori *vb* to dissolve (*parliament*)

datgorfforiad *nm* dissolution

datguddiad (-au) *nm* revelation, disclosure

datguddio *vb* to reveal, to disclose

datgyffesiad *nm* recantation

datgyffesu *vb* to recant

datgymalu *vb* to dislocate, to dismember

datgysylltiad *nm* disestablishment

datgysylltu *vb* to disconnect; to disestablish

datod *vb* to undo, to untie, to dissolve

datrannu *vb* to dissect

datro *vb* to change; to undo

datrys *vb* to solve

datrysiad (-au) *nm* solution, resolution

datseinio *vb* to resound, to reverberate

datsgwar (-au) *nm* square root

datysen (datys) *nf* date

dathliad (-au) *nm* celebration

dathlu *vb* to celebrate

dau (*f* dwy) *adj, pron* two

dau-, deu- *prefix* two, bi-

dauddyblyg *adj* twofold, double

daufiniog *adj* double-edged

dauwynebog *adj* two-faced

dawn (doniau) *nmf* gift, talent

dawns (-iau) *nf* dance

dawnsio *vb* to dance

dawnsiwr (-wyr) *nm* dancer

dawnus *adj* gifted, talented

de *adj, nf* right ▸ *nm* south

De Affrica *nf* South Africa

deall vb to understand ▸ nm understanding, intellect, intelligence

dealladwy adj intelligible

deallgar adj intelligent

deallol adj intellectual

dealltwriaeth (-au) nf understanding, intelligence

deallus adj understanding, intelligent

deallusion npl intelligentsia

deallusrwydd nm intelligence

deau adj, nf right ▸ nm south

debentur (-on) nf debenture

debyd (-au) nm debit

debydu vb to debit

dec (-iau, -s) nm deck

decilitr (-au) nm decilitre

decimetr (-au) nm decimetre

decstros nm dextrose

dectant nm ten-stringed instrument, psaltery

dechrau vb to begin ▸ nm beginning

dechreuad (-au) nm beginning

dechreunos nf nightfall, dusk

dechreuol adj initial

dechreuwr (-wyr) nm beginner

dedfryd (-au) nf verdict; sentence

dedfrydu vb to sentence

dedlein (-s) nf deadline

dedwydd adj happy, blessed

dedwyddwch, dedwyddyd nm happiness, bliss

deddf (-au) nf law, statute, act

deddfeg nf jurisprudence

deddfegwr (-wyr) nm jurist

deddfol adj legal, lawful

deddfu vb to legislate, to enact

deddfwr (-wyr) nm legislator

deddfwriaeth nf legislation, legislature

deddfwriaethol adj legislative

deddlyfr (-au) nm statute book

de-ddwyrain nm southeast

defni vb to drip, to trickle

defnydd (-iau) nm material, stuff; use

defnyddio vb to use, to utilize, to employ; **defnyddio'r cwbl o, defnyddio'r cyfan o** use up

defnyddiol adj useful

defnyddioldeb nm usefulness, utility

defnyddiwr (-wyr) nm user, consumer

defnyn (-nau) nm drop

defnynnu vb to drop, to drip, to dribble, to distil

defod (-au) nf custom; rite, ceremony

defodaeth nf ritualism

defodol adj ritualistic

defosiwn (-ynau) nm devotion

defosiynol adj devotional, devout

deffro, deffroi vb to rouse; to wake

deffroad (-au) nm awakening

deg adj ten ▸ nm (-au) ten

degaidd adj denary

degawd (-au) nm decade

degiad (-au) nm decimal

degol (-ion) nm, adj decimal

degoli vb to decimalise

degoliad nm decimalisation

degolyn (degolion) nm decimal

degwm (-ymau) nm tenth, tithe

degymu vb to tithe

dehau, deheu see **deau**

deheubarth, deheudir *nm* southern region, south
deheuig *adj* dexterous, skilful
deheulaw *nf* right hand
deheuol *adj* southern
deheurwydd *nm* dexterity, skill
deheuwr (-wyr) *nm* southerner
deheuwynt *nm* south wind
dehongli *vb* to interpret
dehongliad (-au) *nm* interpretation
dehonglwr (-wyr), dehonglydd (-ion) *nm* interpreter
dehydrad (-au) *nm* dehydration
dehydru *vb* to dehydrate
deial (-au) *nm* dial
deialog (-au) *nmf* dialogue
deialu *vb* to dial
deifio *vb* to singe, to scorch; to blast; to dive
deifiol *adj* scorching, scathing
deifiwr (-wyr) *nm* diver
deigryn (dagrau) *nm* tear
deilbridd *nm* humus
deildy (-dai) *nm* bower, arbour
deilen (dail) *nf* leaf
deilgoll *adj* deciduous
deiliad (-on, deiliaid) *nm* tenant; subject
deiliant (-nnau) *nm* foliage
deilio *vb* to leaf
deiliog *adj* leafy
deillio *vb* to proceed, to emanate, to issue
deinameg *nf* dynamics
deinamig *adj* dynamic
deinamo (-s, -au) *nm* dynamo
deincod *nm* teeth on edge
deincryd *nm* chattering or gnashing of teeth

deintio *vb* to nibble
deintrod (-au) *nf* cog
deintydd (-ion) *nm* dentist
deintyddiaeth *nf* dentistry
deintyddol *adj* dental
deiseb (-au) *nf* petition
deisebu *vb* to petition
deisebwr (-wyr), deisebydd (-ion) *nm* petitioner
deisyf, deisyfu *vb* to desire, to wish; to beseech, to entreat
deisyfiad (-au) *nm* request, petition
del *adj* pretty, neat
delfryd (-au) *nm* ideal
delfrydiaeth *nf* idealism
delfrydol *adj* ideal
delfrydu *vb* to idealize
delfrydwr (-wyr) *nm* idealist
delff *nm* churl, oaf, dolt, rascal
delio *vb* to deal
delw (-au) *nf* image; form, mode, manner
delwedd (-au) *nf* image
delweddaeth *nf* imagery
delweddu *vb* to portray
delwi *vb* to pale, to be paralysed with fright
dellni *nm* blindness
dellt *npl (nf -en)* laths, lattice, splinters
democratiaeth (-au) *nf* democracy
democratig *adj* democratic
demograffeg *nf* demography
demograffig *adj* demographic
deng *adj* ten *(before certain words)*
dengar *adj* attractive
dengarwch *nm* attractiveness

deniadau *npl* attractions, allurements

deniadol *adj* attractive

denims *npl* denims

Denmarc *nf* Denmark

denu *vb* to attract, to allure, to entice

deon (-iaid) *nm* dean

deondy (-dai) *nm* deanery

deoniaeth (-au) *nf* deanery

deor *vb* to brood, to hatch, to incubate

deorfa (-fâu, -feydd) *nf* hatchery

de-orllewin *nm* southwest

deorydd (-ion) *nf* incubator

derbyn *vb* to receive; to accept; to admit

derbyniad (-au) *nm* receipt; reception

derbyniadwy *adj* admissible

derbyniol *adj* acceptable

derbyniwr (**derbynwyr**) *nm* = **derbynnydd**

derbynneb (-ynebau, -ynebion) *nf* receipt, voucher

derbynnydd (-ynddion) *nm* receiver

deri *npl* (*nf* **dâr**) oak-trees, oak

dernyn (-nau) *nm* piece, scrap

derwen (**derw, deri**) *nf* oak-tree, oak

derwydd (-on) *nm* druid

derwyddiaeth *nf* druidism

derwyddol *adj* druidic(al)

desg (-iau) *nf* desk; **desg dalu** checkout

desgant (-au) *nm* descant

desibel (-au) *nm* decibel

destlus *adj* neat

destlusrwydd *nm* neatness

detector (-au) *nm* detector

dethol *vb* to select, to pick, to choose ▸ *adj* select

detholedd *nm* selectivity

detholiad (-au, **detholion**) *nm* selection, anthology

deu- *see* **dau-**

deuawd (-au) *nfm* duet

deublyg *adj* double, twofold

deuddeg *adj*, *nm* twelve

deufin *adj* two-edged

deuffocal *adj* bifocal

deugain *adj*, *nm* forty

deugraff *nm* digraph

deunaw *adj*, *nm* eighteen

deunydd (-iau) *nm* stuff, material; **deunydd lapio** packaging

deuocsid *nm* dioxide

deuod (-au) *nm* diode, binary

deuol *adj* dual

deuoliaeth *nf* dualism, duality

deuparth *nd* two-thirds

deuris *adj* two-tier

deurudd *nd* the cheeks

deuryw *adj* bisexual

deurywiol *adj* bisexual

deusain *nd* diphthong

deutu *nd*: **o ddeutu** about

dewin (-iaid) *nm* diviner, magician, wizard

dewines (-au) *nf* witch, sorceress

dewiniaeth *nf* divination, witchcraft

dewinio *vb* to divine

dewiniol, dewinol *adj* prophetic, divinatory

dewis *vb* to choose, to select ▸ *nm* choice

dewisiad nm choice, option

dewisol adj choice, desirable; optional

dewr adj brave ▸ nm (**-ion**) brave man, hero

dewrder nm bravery, valour

di- neg prefix without, not, un-, non-, -less

diabetig adj, nm diabetic

diacon (**-iaid**) nm deacon

diacones (**-au**) nf deaconess

diaconiaeth nf diaconate

diadell (**-au, -oedd**) nf flock

diaddurn adj unadorned, plain, rude

diaelodi vb to dismember; to expel a member

diafael adj slippery, careless

diafol (**diefyl, dieifl**) nm devil

diaffram (**-au**) nm diaphragm

diagnosis nm diagnosis

diangen adj unnecessary, free from want

dianghenraid adj unnecessary, needless

di-ail adj unequalled, unrivalled

dial vb to avenge, to revenge ▸ nm vengeance, revenge

dialedd (**-au**) nm vengeance, nemesis

dialgar adj revengeful, vindictive

dialgarwch nm vindictiveness

di-alw-amdano adj redundant, uncalled for

dialwr (**-wyr**), **dialydd** (**-ion**) nm avenger

diamau adj doubtless

diamcan adj aimless, purposeless

diamedr (**-au**) nm diameter

diamedral adj diametral

diamheuol adj undoubted, indisputable

diamod adj unconditional, absolute

diamodol adj unconditional, unqualified

diamwys adj unambiguous

diamynedd adj impatient

dianc vb to escape

dianwadal adj unwavering, immutable

dianwadalwch nm immutability

diarddel vb to expel, to excommunicate

diarddeliad nm expulsion, excommunication

diarfogi vb to disarm

diarfogiad nm disarmament

diarffordd adj out of the way, inaccessible

diargyhoedd adj blameless

diarhebol adj proverbial

diaroglydd (**-ion**) nm deodorant

diarwybod adj unawares

diasbad nf cry, scream

diasbedain vb to resound, to ring

diatreg adj immediate

diau adj true, certain; doubtless

diawl (**-iaid**) nm devil

diawledig adj devilish

di-baid, dibaid adj unceasing, ceaseless

di-ball, diball adj unfailing, infallible, sure

diben (**-ion**) nm end, purpose, aim

di-ben-draw adj endless

dibeniad (**-au**) nm ending, conclusion; predicate

di-benllanw adj off-peak
dibennu vb to end, to conclude, to finish
diberfeddu vb to disembowel, to eviscerate
dibetrus adj unhesitating
dibl (-au) nm border, edge
di-blwm adj lead-free
dioblogaeth nf depopulation
diboblogi vb to depopulate
dibrin adj abundant, plentiful
dibriod adj unmarried, single
dibris adj reckless, contemptuous
dibrisio vb to depreciate, to despise
dibristod nm depreciation, contempt
dibwys adj trivial, unimportant
dibwysiant (-nnau) nm depression
dibyn (-nau) nm steep, precipice
dibynadwy adj reliable
dibynadwyedd nm reliability
dibyniad nm dependence
dibyniant nm dependence
dibynnedd nm reliability
dibynnol adj depending; subjunctive
dibynnu vb to depend, to rely
dibynnydd (dibynyddion) nm dependant
dicllon adj wrathful, angry
dicllonrwydd nm wrath, indignation
dicotomi (-iau) nm dichotomy
dicra adj squeamish, fastidious, slow
dicter nm anger, wrath, displeasure
dichell (-ion) nf wile, craft, guile
dichellgar adj wily, crafty, cunning

dichlyn vb to choose, to pick ▶ adj careful, circumspect, exact
dichon vb to be able ▶ adv perhaps, maybe
dichonol adj potential
di-dact adj tactless
didactig adj didactic
didaro adj unaffected, unconcerned, cool
di-daw adj ceaseless, clamant
diden (-nau) nf nipple, teat
diderfyn adj unlimited
didoli vb to separate, to segregate
didoliad nm separation, segregation
didolnod (-au) nm diæresis
di-dor, didor adj unbroken, uninterrupted
didoreth adj shiftless, silly, fickle
didoriad adj unbroken, untamed, rough
di-drais, didrais adj non-violent, meek
diduedd adj impartial, unbiassed
didwyll adj guileless, sincere
didwylledd nm guilelessness, sincerity
di-ddadl adj unquestionable, indisputable
diddan adj amusing, diverting, pleasant
diddanion npl pleasantries, jokes
diddanu vb to amuse, to divert; to comfort
diddanwch nm comfort, consolation
diddanwr (-wyr), diddanydd (-ion) nm comforter
diddarbod adj shiftless

di-dderbyn-wyneb adj outspoken
diddig adj contented, pleased
diddigrwydd nm contentment, placidity
diddim adj, nm void
diddordeb nm interest
diddori vb to interest
diddorol adj interesting
diddos adj watertight, sheltered; snug
diddosi vb to shelter
diddosrwydd nm shelter, safety
di-dduw, didduw adj ungodly
▶ nm atheist
di-ddweud adj taciturn, stubborn
diddwythiad nm deduction
diddwytho vb to deduce
diddyfnu vb to wean
diddymdra nm nothingness, void
diddymiad, diddymiant nm annihilation
diddymu vb to annihilate, to abolish
dieflig adj devilish, diabolical, fiendish
diegwyddor adj unprincipled
dieisiau adj unnecessary, needless
dieithr adj strange, alien, foreign
▶ nm (-iaid) stranger
dieithrio vb to estrange, to alienate
dieithrwch nm strangeness
diemwnt nm diamond
dienaid adj soulless, senseless
dienyddiad (-au) nm execution
dienyddio vb to put to death, to execute
dienyddiwr (-wyr) nm executioner
dieuog adj guiltless, innocent

difa vb to consume, to destroy, to devour
di-fai, difai adj blameless, faultless
difalch adj humble
difancoll nf total loss, perdition
difaol adj consuming, devouring
difater adj indifferent, unconcerned
difaterwch nm indifference, apathy
difeddiannu vb to dispossess, to deprive
di-feind adj heedless
difenwad (-au) nm defamation
difenwi vb to revile, to abuse, to belittle
diferlif nm stream, issue
diferol adj dripping, dropping
diferu vb to drip, to drop, to dribble, to distil
diferyn (-nau, diferion) nm drop
diferynnu vb to trickle
difesur adj huge, immeasurable, unstinted
di-feth, difeth adj infallible, certain
difetha vb to destroy, to spoil, to waste
difethwr (-wyr) nm destroyer
Difiau nm Thursday
difidend (-au) nm dividend
diflanbwynt nm vanishing point
diflanedig adj evanescent, fleeting
diflaniad nm disappearance
diflannu vb to vanish, to disappear
di-flas adj tasteless
diflas adj insipid, dull, wearisome
diflastod nm disgust

diflasu vb to disgust; to weary, to surfeit

diflin, diflino adj untiring, indefatigable

difodi vb to annihilate, to exterminate

difodiad, difodiant nm annihilation

di-foes, difoes adj rude, unmannerly

difreiniad nm disfranchisement

difreinio vb to disfranchise, to deprive

difriaeth nf abuse, calumny

difrif nm seriousness, earnestness

difrifddwys adj solemn

difrifol adj serious, earnest, solemn, grave

difrifoldeb see difrifwch

difrifoli vb to sober, to solemnize

difrifwch nm seriousness, earnestness, solemnity

difrio vb to scold, to abuse, to malign

difrod nm waste, havoc, damage

difrodi vb to waste, to spoil, to ravage

difrodol adj destructive

difrodwr (-wyr) nm spoiler, devastator

difrycheulyd adj spotless, immaculate

di-fudd, difudd adj unprofitable, useless, futile

di-fwlch, difwlch adj without a break, continuous

difwyniad (-au) nm adulteration, pollution

difwyniant nm defilement

difwyno vb to mar, to soil, to sully, to defile

difyfyr adj impromptu

difynio vb to dissect, to vivisect

difyr adj pleasant, diverting, amusing

difyrion npl diversions, amusements

difyrru vb to divert, to amuse, to beguile

difyrrus adj diverting, amusing

difyrrwch nm diversion, amusement, fun

difyrrwr (-yrwyr) nm entertainer

difyrwaith (-weithiau) nm hobby

difywyd adj inert

diffaith adj waste, desert; base, mean ► nm (-ffeithydd) wilderness, desert

diffeithdra nm dereliction

diffeithio vb to lay waste

diffeithwch (-ychau) nm desert, wilderness

diffiniad (-au) nm definition

diffinio vb to define

diffodd, diffoddi vb to put out, to quench, to extinguish; to switch off

diffoddiad nm quenching, extinction

diffoddwr (-wyr), diffoddydd (-ion) nm quencher

diffrwyth adj barren; numb, paralysed

diffrwythder, diffrwythdra nm barrenness; numbness

diffrwytho vb to make barren; to paralyse

91

diffuant adj unfeigned, sincere, genuine; **yn ddiffuant** sincerely

diffuantrwydd nm genuineness

di-ffurf adj amorphous

diffwys adj wild, waste; high, steep; huge, awful

diffyg (-ion) nm defect, want, lack; eclipse

diffygiant nm deficiency

diffygio vb to fail; to faint, to weary

diffygiol adj defective; faint, weary

diffyndoll (-au) nf tariff

diffyndollaeth nf protectionism

diffynnydd (-ynyddion) nm defendant

dig adj angry, wrathful ▸ nm anger, wrath

digalon adj disheartened, depressed, dejected, sad

digalondid nm depression, dejection

digalonni vb to dishearten, to discourage, to put off

digamsyniol adj unmistakable

digasedd nm hatred, enmity

digid (-au) nm digit

digidiad (-au) nm digitation

digidol adj digital

digio vb to anger, to offend; to take offence

di-glem adj inept

diglion see **dicllon**

digofaint nm anger, wrath, indignation

digofus adj angry, indignant

digolledu vb to indemnify, to compensate

digon nm, adj, adv enough; done (of cooking)

digonedd nm abundance, plenty

digoni vb to suffice; to satisfy; to cook

digonol adj satisfying; sufficient, adequate; satisfied

digonolrwydd nm sufficiency, abundance

digornio vb to dehorn

di-gred adj infidel

di-grefft, digrefft adj unskilled

digrif, digrifol adj mirthful, funny

digriflun (-iau) nm caricature, cartoon

digrifwas (-weision) nm clown, buffoon

digrifwch nm mirth, fun

digroeso adj inhospitable

digwydd vb to befall, to happen, to occur

digwyddiad (-au) nm happening, occurrence, event

digwyddiadol adj incidental

digyfnewid adj unchangeable

digyffelyb adj incomparable

digymysg adj unmixed

digyswllt adj incoherent

digywilydd adj impudent

digywilydd-dra nm impudence

dihafal adj unequalled, peerless

dihangfa (diangfâu) nf escape

dihangol adj escaped, safe

dihareb (diarhebion) nf proverb

dihatru vb to strip, to undress

dihefelydd adj unequalled

diheintio vb to disinfect

diheintydd (-ion) nm disinfectant, sterilizer

di-hid, di-hidio adj heedless, indifferent, reckless

ihidlo vb to drop, to distil; to shed

ihidrwydd nm indifference, recklessness

ihiryn (-hirod) nm rascal, scoundrel

ihoeni vb to languish, to pine

ihuno vb to wake, to rouse

i-hwyl adj out of sorts

ihyder adj lacking confidence

ihydradu vb to dehydrate

ihysbydd adj inexhaustible

ihysbyddu vb to empty, to exhaust

il (-iau) nm: **dil mêl** honeycomb

ilead nm abolition, deletion

ilechdid nm dialectic

iledryw adj pure, genuine

ileu vb to delete, to rub out; to blot out; to abolish

ilewyrch adj dismal; not prosperous

ilorni vb to abuse, to revile

i-lun adj slovenly

iluw see **dilyw**

ilyffethair adj unencumbered, unfettered

ilyn vb to follow, to pursue; to imitate

ilyniad nm following; imitation

ilyniant (-nnau) nm sequence, progression

ilynol adj following; consequent

ilynwr (-wyr) nm follower; imitator

ilys adj sure, certain; genuine

ilysiant (-nnau) nm validation

ilysnod (-au) nm hallmark

ilysrwydd nm genuineness

dilysu vb to certify, to warrant, to guarantee

dilyw nm flood, deluge

dillad (nm dilledyn) npl clothes, clothing; **dillad isaf** underwear

dilladu vb to clothe

dilledydd nm clothier

dilledyn nm garment

dim adj any (with negative understood); no ▸ nm anything; none, nothing

dimensiwn (-iynau) nm dimension

dimensiynol adj dimensional

di-nam, dinam adj faultless

dinas (-oedd) nf city

dinasol adj municipal

dinasyddiaeth nf citizenship

dincod see **deincod**

dinesig adj civil, civic

dinesydd (dinasyddion) nm citizen

dinistr nm destruction

dinistrio vb to destroy

dinistriol adj destroying, destructive

dinistriwr (-wyr) nm destroyer

dinistrydd (-ion) nm destroyer

diniwed adj harmless, innocent

diniweidrwydd nm innocence

di-nod, dinod adj insignificant, obscure

dinodedd nm insignificance, obscurity

dinoethi vb to bare, to denude, to expose

diod (-ydd) nf drink, beverage

diodi vb to give drink

dioddef vb to suffer, to bear; to wait ▸ nm (-iadau) suffering

dioddefaint nm suffering, passion

dioddefgar, dioddefus *adj* patient
dioddefgarwch *nm* patience
**dioddefwr (-wyr), dioddefydd
(-ion)** *nm* sufferer, patient
di-oed, dioed *adj* without delay,
immediate
diofal *adj* careless
diofalwch *nm* carelessness
diog *adj* slothful, indolent, lazy
diogel *adj* safe, secure; sure,
certain
diogelu *vb* to make safe, to secure
diogelwch *nm* safety, security
diogi *vb* to be lazy, to idle ▸ *nm*
laziness
dioglyd *adj* lazy, sluggish, indolent
diogyn *nm* lazy one, idler, sluggard
diolch *vb* to thank, to give
thanks ▸ *nm* **(-iadau)** thanks,
thanksgiving
diolchgar *adj* thankful, grateful
diolchgarwch *nm* thankfulness,
gratitude, thanksgiving
diolwg *adj* ugly
diorseddu *vb* to dethrone, to
depose
di-os *adj* without doubt
diosg *vb* to undress, to put off, to
strip, to divest
diota *vb* to tipple
diotwr (-wyr) *nm* boozer, drunkard
dioty (-tai) *nm* ale-house, public-
house
diploma (-âu) *nmf* diploma
diplomateg *nf* diplomacy
diplomydd (-ion) *nm* diplomat
diplomyddol *adj* diplomatic
dipton (-au) *nf* diphthong
dir *adj* certain, necessary

diraddiad (-au) *nm* degradation
diraddio *vb* to degrade
diraddiol *adj* degrading
di-raen *adj* shabby, dull
dirboeni *vb* to torture, to
excruciate
dirdyniad (-au) *nm* convulsion
dirdynnol *adj* excruciating
dirdynnu *vb* to rack, to torture
direidi *nm* mischievousness,
mischief
direidus *adj* mischievous
direol *adj* unruly, disorderly
direwydd *nm* defroster
direwyn *nm* antifreeze
dirfawr *adj* vast, huge, immense,
enormous
dirgel *adj* secret ▸ *nm* **(-ion)** secret
dirgelaidd *adj* mysterious
dirgeledig *adj* hidden, secret;
mystical
dirgeledigaeth (-au) *nfm* mystery
dirgelu *vb* to secrete, to conceal,
to hide
dirgelwch *nm* secrecy, mystery,
secret
dirgryniad (-au) *nm* tremor,
vibration
dirgrynol *adj* vibrating
dirgrynu *vb* to tremble, to vibrate
diriaethol *adj* concrete
dirlawn *adj* saturated
dirmyg *nm* contempt, scorn
dirmygu *vb* to despise, to scorn
dirmygus *adj* contemptuous;
contemptible
dirnad *vb* to discern, to
comprehend

dirnadaeth nf discernment, comprehension

dirnadwy adj discernible

dirprwy (-on) nm deputy; delegate

dirprwyaeth (-au) nf commission; deputation

dirprwyo vb to deputise, to delegate

dirprwyol adj vicarious

dirprwywr (-wyr) nm deputy, substitute

dirwasgiad (-au) nm depression

dirwest nm abstinence, temperance

dirwestol adj temperate

dirwestwr (-wyr) nm abstainer

dirwy (-on) nf fine

dirwyn vb to wind, to twist, to twine

dirwynwr (-wyr) nm winder

dirwyo vb to fine

di-rym adj powerless, void

dirymu vb to nullify, to annul, to cancel

diryw adj neuter

dirywiad nm degeneration, deterioration

dirywiaeth nf degeneracy

dirywiedig adj degenerate

dirywio vb to degenerate, to deteriorate

dirywiol adj decadent, retrograde

dis (-iau) nm die, dice

di-sail adj groundless, baseless

disbaddu vb to castrate, to geld, to spay

disbaddwr (-wyr) nm castrator

disberod nm: ar ddisberod wandering, astray

disbyddedig adj exhausted

disbyddu vb to empty, to exhaust

disbyddwr nm exhaust

disel nm diesel

diserch adj sullen, sulky, loveless

disg (-iau) nm disk, record; **disg caled** hard disk

disgen (disgiau) nf discus

disglair adj bright, brilliant

disgleirdeb, disgleirder nm brightness, brilliance

disgleirio vb to shine, to glitter

disgloff adj free from lameness

disgo (-au) nm disco

disgownt (-iau, -s) nm discount

disgrifiad (-au) nm description

disgrifiadol adj descriptive

disgrifio vb to describe

disgwyl vb to look, to expect, to wait

disgwylfa (-feydd) nf watch-tower

disgwylgar adj watchful, expectant

disgwyliad (-au) nm expectation

disgybl (-ion) nm disciple, pupil

disgyblaeth nf discipline

disgyblu vb to discipline

disgyblwr (-wyr) nm disciplinarian

disgyn vb to descend, to get off; to fall, to drop; to let down

disgynfa (-feydd) nf descent, declivity; landing place

disgyniad (-au) nm descent

disgynnol adj descending

disgynnydd (-ynyddion) nm descendant

disgyrchedd nm gravitation

95

disgyrchiad, disgyrchiant *nm*
gravity; **craidd disgyrchiant**
centre of gravity

disgyrchu *vb* to gravitate

di-sigl *adj* unshaken, steadfast,
firm

disiog *adj* diced

disodli *vb* to trip up, to supplant

dist (-iau) *nm* joist, beam

distadl *adj* insignificant, low, base,
mean

distadledd *nm* insignificance,
obscurity

distain (-einiaid) *nm* steward

distaw *adj* silent, quiet

distawrwydd *nm* silence, quiet

distewi *vb* to silence; to calm,
to quiet

distryw *nm* destruction

distrywgar *adj* destructive,
wasteful

distrywio *vb* to destroy

distrywiwr (-wyr) *nm* destroyer

distyll *nm* ebb; distillation

distyllio *vb* to distil

di-sut *adj* unwell; small

diswta *adj* sudden, abrupt

diswyddiad (-au) *nm* dismissal

diswyddo *vb* to dismiss from office,
to discharge

disychedu *vb* to quench thirst

di-syfl *adj* immovable,
impregnable

disyfyd *adj* sudden, instantaneous

disyml *adj* simple, artless,
ingenuous

disymud *adj* immobile

disymwth *adj* sudden,
instantaneous

disynnwyr *adj* senseless

ditectif (-s) *nm* detective

diwahân *adj* inseparable,
indiscriminate

diwair *adj* chaste; celibate

di-waith, diwaith *adj*
unemployed, idle

diwall *adj* satisfied, full, perfect

diwallu *vb* to satisfy, to supply

diwarafun *adj* unforbidden,
ungrudging

diwasgedd (-au) *nm* depression
(weather)

diwedydd (-iau) *nm* evening,
eventide

diwedd *nm* end, conclusion

diweddar *adj* late, modern

diweddaru *vb* to modernize

diweddarwch *nm* lateness

diweddeb *nf* cadence

diweddglo *nm* conclusion

diweddu *vb* to end, to finish, to
conclude

diweirdeb *nm* chastity

diweithdra *nm* unemployment

diwelfa (-feydd) *nf* watershed

diwerth *adj* worthless

diwethaf *adj* last

di-wifr *adj* wireless; **rhwydwaith
di-wifr** wireless network

diwinydd (-ion) *nm* divine,
theologian

diwinyddiaeth *nf* divinity,
theology

diwinyddol *adj* theological

diwreiddio *vb* to uproot, to
eradicate

diwrnod (-iau) *nm* day

diwrthdro *adj* inexorable

diwyd adj diligent, industrious, hard-working

diwydianfa nf industrial estate

diwydiannaeth nf industrialization, industrialism

diwydiannol adj industrial

diwydiannwr (-ianwyr) nm industrialist

diwydiant (-iannau) nm industry

diwydrwydd nm diligence, industry

diwyg nm form, dress, garb

diwygiad (-au) nm reform, reformation; revival

diwygiadol adj reformatory; revivalistic

diwygiedig adj reformed; revised

diwygio vb to amend, to reform, to revise

diwygiol adj reformatory

diwygiwr (-wyr) nm reformer; revivalist

diwylliadol adj cultural

diwylliannol adj cultural

diwylliant (-nnau) nm culture

diwylliedig adj cultured

diwyllio vb to cultivate

diymadferth adj helpless

diymadferthedd nm helplessness

diymdroi adj without delay

diymhongar adj unassuming

diymod adj steadfast, immovable

diymwad adj undeniable, indisputable

diysgog adj steadfast, firm, stable

diystyr adj contemptuous; contemptible; meaningless

diystyrllyd adj contemptuous, disdainful

diystyru vb to disregard, to despise

diystyrwch nm contempt, disdain, scorn

do adv yes (to questions in preterite tense)

doc (-iau) nm dock

docfa (-feydd) nf berth

docio vb to shorten; to dock, to berth

doctor (-iaid) nm doctor

doctora vb to doctor

dod vb to come; to become; **dod i mewn** to come in; **dod yn ôl** to come back

dodi vb to put, to place; to give; to switch on

dodrefn npl (nm -**yn**) furniture

dodrefnu vb to furnish

dodrefnwr (-wyr) nm furnisher

dodwy vb to lay eggs

doe adv yesterday

doeth (-ion) adj wise

doethineb nmf wisdom

doethinebu vb to discourse wisely, to pontificate

doethor (-iaid) nm doctor (of university)

doethur (-iaid) nm doctor (of university)

doethuriaeth (-au) nf doctorate

dof adj tame, domesticated; garden

dofednod npl fowls, poultry

dofi vb to tame, to domesticate; to assuage

dofn adj f of **dwfn**

Dofydd nm God

dogfen (-ni, -nau) nf document

dogfennaeth nf documentation

dogfennen (-ennau) *nf* documentary

dogfennol *adj* documentary

dogn (-au) *nm* share, portion; dose

dogni *vb* to ration

doili *nm* doyley

dol (-iau) *nf* doll

dôl¹ *nm* dole

dôl² (dolydd, dolau) *nf* meadow

dolbridd (-oedd) *nm* alluvium, meadow soil

doldir (-oedd) *nm* meadow-land

dolef (-au) *nf* cry

dolefain *vb* to cry out

dolefus *adj* wailing, plaintive

dolen (-nau) *nf* loop, link, ring, bow

dolennog *adj* ringed, looped; winding

dolennu *vb* to loop; to wind, to meander

doler (-i) *nf* dollar

dolffin *nm* dolphin

dolur (-iau) *nm* sore; ailment; grief

dolurio *vb* to hurt, to wound; to grieve

dolurus *adj* sore

dominyddu *vb* to dominate

donio *vb* to endow, to gift

doniol *adj* gifted; witty, humorous

donioldeb, doniolwch *nm* wit, humour

dôr (dorau) *nf* door

dos (-ys, -au) *nf* dose

dosbarth (au, -iadau) *nm* class; district

dosbarthiad *nm* distribution

dosbarthu *vb* to class, to classify; to distribute

dosbarthwr (-wyr) *nm* distributor

dosio *vb* to dose

dosran (-nau) *nf* division, section

dosrannu *vb* to separate, to analyse

dot¹ (-iau) *nmf* dot

dot² *nf* giddiness, vertigo

dotio *vb* to dote

drachefn *adv* again

dracht (-iau) *nm* draught *(of liquor)*

drachtio *vb* to drink deep

draen¹ (draeniau) *nf* drain

draen², draenen (drain) *nf* thorn

draeniad (-au) *nm* drainage

draenio *vb* to drain

draenog (-od) *nm* hedgehog

drafft (-iau) *nm* draft, draught

draffts *npl* draughts

dragio *vb* to drag, to tear, to mangle

draig (dreigiau) *nf* dragon

drain *see* **draen**

drama (dramâu) *nf* drama

dramateiddio *vb* to dramatize

dramatig *adj* dramatic

dramodiad (-au) *nm* dramatization

dramodwr (-wyr) *nm* dramatist

dramodydd *nm* playwright

drâr *nm* drawer

draw *adv* yonder, away

dreflan *vb* to dribble

dreng *adj* morose, surly, sullen, harsh

dresel (dreseli, dreselydd), dreser *nm* dresser

drewdod *nm* stink, stench

drewi *vb* to stink

drewllyd *adj* stinking

driblo *vb* to dribble

drifft (-iau) nm drift
dringad vb to climb
dringfa (-feydd) nf climb, ascent
dringo vb to climb
dringwr (-wyr) nm climber
dril (-iau) nm drill
drilio vb to drill
dripsych adj drip-dry
drôr (drors) nm drawer
dros see **tros**
drud adj dear, precious, costly; reckless
drudfawr adj costly, expensive
drudwen nf starling
drudwy nm starling
drwg adj evil, bad, naughty, wicked ▸ nm **(drygau)** evil, harm, hurt
drwgdybiaeth (-au) nf suspicion
drwgdybio vb to suspect
drwgdybus adj suspicious
drwglosgiad nm arson
drwgweithredwr (-wyr) nm evildoer
drwm (drymiau) nm drum
drws (drysau) nm door
drwy see **trwy**
drycin (-oedd) nf foul weather
drycinog adj stormy
drych (-au) nm spectacle; mirror; object, pattern
drychfeddwl (-yliau) nm idea
drychiolaeth (-au) nf apparition, phantom
drygair nm ill report; scandal
dryganadl nm halitosis
drygfyd nm adversity
drygioni nm badness, wickedness
drygionus adj bad, wicked
drygu vb to hurt, to harm, to injure

dryll (-iau) nm piece; part ▸ nmf gun, rifle
drylliad (-au) nm breaking; wreck
drylliedig adj broken, shattered
dryllio vb to break in pieces, to shatter
drylliog adj broken, contrite
drymiwr (-wyr) nm drummer
drysi npl (nf-ïen) thorns, briers
dryslwyn (-i) nm thicket
dryslyd adj perplexing; confused
drysu vb to tangle; to perplex; to be confused
dryswch nm tangle; perplexity; confusion
dryw (-od) nmf wren
DU nf UK
du adj black; (of person) Black
duc, dug (-iaid) nm duke
dugiaeth nf duchy
Dulyn nf Dublin
dull (-iau) nm form, manner, mode
dullwedd (-au) nm mannerism
duo vb to black, to blacken
dur nm steel
duw (-iau) nm god; **Duw** God
düwch nm blackness
duwdod nm godhead, divinity, deity
duwies nf goddess
duwiol (-ion) adj godly, pious
duwioldeb nm godliness, piety
duwiolfrydedd nm godliness, piety
duwiolfrydig adj god-fearing, pious
DVD (-s) n DVD
dwbio vb to daub, to plaster
dwbl adj double
dweud, dwyed see **dywedyd**

99

dwfn

dwfn (f **dofn**) adj deep, profound
dwfr, dŵr (**dyfroedd**) nm water
dwl adj dull, stupid, foolish
dwlu vb to dote
dwmbwr-dambar adv helter-skelter
dwndwr nm din, babble, hubbub
dwnsiwn (**-iynau**) nm dungeon
dŵr see **dwfr**
dwrdio vb to scold
dwrn (**dyrnau**) nm fist; knob, handle, hilt
dwsin (**-au**) nm dozen
dwst nm dust, powder
dwster (**-i**) nm duster
dwthwn nm day
dwy see **dau**
dwyfol adj divine
dwyfoldeb nm divinity, deity
dwyfoli vb to deify
dwyfron (**-nau**) nf breast, chest
dwyfronneg nf breastplate
dwyieithedd nm bilingualism
dwyieithiog nf study of bilingualism
dwyieithog adj bilingual
dwyieithrwydd nm bilingualism
dwylaw, dwylo nd, pl two hands, hands
dwyn vb to bear; to bring; to steal
dwyochredd nm bilateralism
dwyochrol adj bilateral
dwyradd adj quadratic, two-tier
dwyrain nm, adj east; **Dwyrain yr Almaen** East Germany
dwyraniad nm dichotomy
dwyrannu vb to bisect
dwyreiniol adj easterly, eastern, oriental

dwyreiniwr (**-wyr**) nm easterner
dwys adj dense, grave, deep, intense
dwysáu vb to deepen, to intensify
dwysbigo vb to prick, to sting
dwysedd (**-au**) nm density
dwyster nm gravity, solemnity
dwythell (**-au**) nf duct
dwywaith adv twice
dy pron thy, thine
dyblu vb to double; to repeat
dyblyg adj twofold, double
dyblygiad (**-au**) nm duplication, duplicate
dyblygu vb to double, to fold
dyblygydd (**-ion**) nm duplicator
dybryd adj sore, dire; flagrant
dychan (**-au**) nf lampoon, satire
dychangerdd (**-i**) nf satirical poem, satire
dychanol adj satirical
dychanu vb to lampoon, to satirize, to revile
dychanwr (**-wyr**) nm satirist
dychmygadwy adj imaginable
dychmygol adj imaginary
dychmygu vb to imagine
dychmygus adj imaginative, inventive
dychryn (**-iadau**) nm fright, terror
  ▸ vb to frighten
dychrynllyd adj frightful, terrible
dychrynu vb to frighten, to be frightened
dychweledig adj returned
dychweliad (**-au**) nm return; conversion
dychwelyd vb to return, to come back

dychymyg (dychmygion) *nm* imagination, fancy; riddle, device

dydd (-iau) *nm* day; **dyddiau cŵn** silly season; **Dydd Sant Folant** Valentine's Day

dyddfu *vb* to flag, to pine, to faint

dyddiad (-au) *nm* date

dyddiadur (-on) *nm* diary, journal

dyddiedig *adj* dated

dyddio *vb* to become day, to dawn; to date

dyddiol *adj* daily

dyddlyfr (-au) *nm* diary, journal

dyddodyn (-odion) *nm* deposit

dyfais (-feisiau) *nf* device, invention

dyfal *adj* diligent

dyfalbarhad *nm* perseverance

dyfalbarhau *vb* to persevere

dyfaliad (-au) *nm* guess, conjecture

dyfalu *vb* to guess, to conjecture

dyfalwch *nm* diligence, assiduity

dyfarniad (-au) *nm* decision, verdict

dyfarnu *vb* to adjudge; to referee

dyfarnwr (-wyr) *nm* judge, umpire, referee

dyfeisio *vb* to make up, to devise, to invent, to imagine; to guess

dyfeisiwr (-wyr) *nm* inventor

dyfnant (-nentydd) *nf* ravine

dyfnder (-au, -oedd) *nm* deep, depth

dyfnhau *vb* to deepen

dyfod *vb* to come; to become

dyfodfa *nf* access, entrance

dyfodiad¹ *nm* coming, arrival, advent

dyfodiad² (-iaid) *nm* incomer, stranger

dyfodol *adj* coming, future ▸ *nm* future

dyfradwy *adj* watered; watering

dyfredig *adj* irrigated

dyfrffos (-ydd) *nm* canal, watercourse

dyfrgi (-gwn) *nm* otter

dyfrllyd *adj* watery

dyfrwr *n* waterman, water-carrier; **y Dyfrwr** Aquarius

dyfrhad *nm* irrigation

dyfrhau, dyfrio *vb* to water

dyfyniad (-au) *nm* citation, quotation

dyfynnod (-ynodau) *nm* quotation mark

dyfynnol *adj* citatory, summoned

dyfynnu *vb* to cite, to quote; to summon

dyffryn (-noedd) *nm* valley

dyffryndir (-oedd) *nm* low country; vale

dygn *adj* hard, severe, grievous, dire

dygnu *vb* to strive, to persevere

dygnwch *nm* perseverance, assiduity

dygwyl *nm* holiday, feast day

dygymod *vb* to agree (with), to put up (with)

dyhead (-au) *nm* aspiration

dyheu *vb* to pant; to long, to yearn, to aspire

dyhiryn *see* dihiryn

dyladwy *adj* due

dylanwad (-au) *nm* influence

dylanwadol *adj* influential

dylanwadu vb to influence
dyled (-ion) nf debt, obligation
dyledog adj in debt, indebted
dyledus adj due
dyledwr (-wyr) nm debtor
dyletswydd (-au) nf duty, obligation
dylif nm flood, deluge ▸ nf warp
dylifo vb to flow, to stream, to pour
dylni nm stupidity, dullness
dyluniad (-au) nm design, drawing
dylunio vb to design
dylunydd (-ion) nm designer
dylyfu gên vb to yawn, to gape
dylluan see tylluan
dyma adv here is, here are; this is, these are
dymchweliad nm overthrow
dymchwelyd vb to overthrow, to upset, to subvert
dymuniad (-au) nm wish, desire
dymuno vb to wish, to desire
dymunol adj desirable, agreeable, pleasant
dyn (-ion) nm man, person
dyna adv there is, there are; that is, those are
dynad npl nettles
dyndod nm manhood, humanity
dyneiddiaeth nf humanism
dyneiddiol adj humanistic
dyneiddiwr (-wyr) nm humanist
dynes nf woman
dynesiad nm approach
dynesu vb to draw near, to approach
dyngar adj humane
dyngarol adj philanthropic
dyngarwch nm philanthropy

dyngarwr (-wyr) nm philanthropist
dyniawed (-iewaid) nm yearling, steer
dynladdiad nm manslaughter
dynodi vb to denote, to signify
dynodiad (-au) nm denotation
dynol adj human; man-like; manly
dynoliaeth nf humanity
dynoliaethau npl humanities
dynolryw coll n mankind
dynwared vb to imitate, to mimic
dynwarededd nm mimicry
dynwarediad (-au) nm imitation, mimicry
dynwaredol adj imitative
dynwaredwr (-wyr) nm imitator, mimic
dyraddiant nm degradation
dyraniad (-au) nm allocation
dyrchafael vb to rise, to ascend ▸ nm ascension
dyrchafedig adj exalted
dyrchafiad nm elevation, promotion
dyrchafol adj elevating
dyrchafu vb to raise, to elevate; to rise, to ascend
dyri (-iau), **dyrif (-au)** nf ballad, lyric
dyrnaid (-eidiau) nm handful
dyrnio vb to punch
dyrnod (-iau) nmf blow, stroke
dyrnu vb to thump; to thresh
dyrnwr (-wyr) nm thresher
dyrnwr medi nm combine harvester
dyrys adj tangled; difficult; perplexing

dyryslyd, dyrysu, dyryswch *see* dryslyd; drysu; dryswch
dysg *nf m* learning
dysgedig (-ion) *adj* learned
dysgeidiaeth *nf* teaching, doctrine
dysgl (-au) *nf* dish; **dysgl loeren** satellite dish
dysglaid (-eidiau) *nf* dishful, dish
dysgu *vb* to learn, to teach
dysgwr (-wyr) *nm* learner, teacher
dyslecsig *adj* dyslexic
dywalgi (-gwn) *nm* tiger
dywediad (-au) *nm* saying
dywedwst *adj* taciturn ► *nm* taciturnity
dywedyd *vb* to say, to speak, to tell
dyweddi (-ïau) *nf* betrothal; fiancé(e)
dyweddïad *nm* betrothal
dyweddïo *vb* to betroth

e

eang *adj* wide, broad, immense
eangder, eangu *see* ehangder; ehangu
eangfrydedd *nm* magnanimity
eangfrydig *adj* broad-minded, magnanimous
eb, ebe, ebr *vb* said
ebargofiant *nm* oblivion
ebill (-ion) *nm* auger, borer; peg
ebillio *vb* to bore
ebol (-ion) *nm* colt, foal
eboles (-au) *nf* foal, filly
eboni *nm* ebony
ebost (ebyst) *nm* email
ebostio *vb* to email
ebran (-nau) *nm* provender, fodder
Ebrill *nm* April
ebrwydd *adj* quick, swift, soon
ebwch (-ychau) *nm* gasp
ebychiad (-au) *nm* interjection, ejaculation
ebychnod *nm* exclamation

ebychu vb to gasp, to interject, to ejaculate

eciwmenaidd adj ecumenical

ecliptig adj, nm ecliptic

ecoleg (-au) nf ecology

ecolegol adj ecological

ecolegwr (-wyr) nm ecologist

economaidd adj economic

economeg nf economics

economegol adj economic

economegwr (-wyr) nm economist

economegydd (-ion) nm economist

economi (-ïau) nm economy

economydd nm economist

ecsbloetio vb to exploit

ecsbloetiwr (-wyr) nm exploiter

ecseis nm excise

ecseismon (-myn) nm exciseman

ecsema nm eczema

ecsentredd (-au) nm eccentricity

ecsentrig adj eccentric (in maths)

ecstasi nm ecstasy

ecstatig adj ecstatic

echblyg adj explicit, outward

echblygol adj extrovert

echdoe adv day before yesterday

echdoriad (-au) nm eruption

echdorri vb to erupt

echdynnu vb to extract

echel (-au) nf axle, axletree; axis

echelin (-au) nm axis

echnos adv night before last

echrydus adj fearful, frightful, shocking

echryslon adj dire

echwyn (-ion) nm loan

echwynna vb to borrow, to lend

echwynnwr (-wynwyr) nm lender, creditor

edau (edafedd) nf thread; (pl) yarn, wool

edefyn nm thread

edfryd vb to restore

e-diced (-i) nf e-ticket

edifar adj penitent, sorry

edifarus, edifeiriol adj repentant, penitent

edifarhau, edifaru vb to repent, to be sorry

edifeirwch nm repentance, penitence

edliw vb to upbraid, to reproach, to taunt

edmygedd nm admiration

edmygol adj admiring

edmygu vb to admire

edmygus adj impressed

edmygwr, edmygydd (edmygwyr) nm admirer

edrych vb to look, to examine; **edrych ar** to look at

edrychiad nm look

edrychwr (-wyr) nm beholder, spectator

edwi, edwino vb to fade, to wither, to decay

eddi npl thrums; fringe, nap

ef, efe pron he, him; it

efallai adv perhaps, peradventure

e-fasnach (-au) nf e-commerce

efengyl (-au) nf gospel

efengylaidd adj evangelical

efengyleiddio vb to evangelize

efengyles (-au) nf female evangelist

efengylu vb to evangelize

efengylwr, efengylydd
(efengylwyr) nm evangelist
efelychiad (-au) nm imitation
efelychiadol adj imitative
efelychu vb to imitate
efelychwr (-wyr) nm imitator
efelychydd (-ion) nm simulator
eferw adj effervescent
eferwad (-au) nm effervescence
eferwi vb to effervesce
efo prep with
efô pron he, him; it
efrau npl tares
Efrog Newydd nf New York
efrydiaeth (-au) nf study
efrydu vb to study
efrydydd (-ion, -wyr) nm student
efydd nm bronze, copper, brass
effaith (-eithiau) nf effect;
effeithiau arbennig special effects
effeithio vb to effect, to affect
effeithiol adj effectual, effective
effeithioli vb to render effectual
effeithiolrwydd nm efficacy
effeithlon adj efficient
effeithlonedd nm efficiency (of
machines etc)
effeithlonrwydd nm efficiency
effro adj awake, vigilant
eger (-au) nm bore, eagre
egin npl (nm -yn) germs, sprouts
eginhad, eginiad (-au) nm
germination, sprouting
egino vb to germinate, to shoot,
to sprout
eginol adj germinal, shooting
eginyn (egin) nm sprout
eglur adj clear, plain, evident
eglurdeb, eglurder nm clearness

eglureb (-au) nf illustration
egluro vb to make clear, to explain
eglurhad nm explanation,
demonstration
eglurhaol adj explanatory
eglwys (-i, -ydd) nf church
eglwysig adj church, ecclesiastical
eglwyswr (-wyr) nm churchman
eglwyswraig (-wragedd) nf
churchwoman
egni (-ïon) nm effort, might, energy
egnïo vb to endeavour, to make
an effort
egnïol adj energetic
egnïoli vb to energise
ego nm ego
egoistiaeth nm egoism
egosentrig adj egocentric
egöydd nm egoist
egr adj sharp; sour; severe; savage;
cheeky
egroes npl (nf-en) hips
egwan adj weak, feeble
egwyd (-ydd) nf fetlock; fetter
egwyddor (-ion, -au) nf rudiment;
principle; alphabet
egwyddorol adj high-principled
egwyl nf lull, respite; opportunity
enghraifft (-eifftiau) nf example,
instance
enghreifftiol adj exemplary,
illustrative
englyn (-ion) nm Welsh alliterative
stanza
englyna, englynu vb to compose
englynion
englynwr (-wyr) nm composer of
englynion
engyl see angel

ehangder (eangderau) nm breadth, immensity

ehangu vb to enlarge, to extend

ehedeg vb to fly; to run to seed

ehedfa (-feydd) nf flight

ehedfan vb to hover, to fly

ehediad¹ (-au) nm flight

ehediad² (-iaid) nm fowl, bird

ehedog adj flying

ehedydd (-ion) nm lark

ehofndra nm fearlessness, boldness

ei pron his, hers; its

eicon (-au) nm icon

eich pron your

Eidal nf: **yr Eidal** Italy

eidion (-nau) nm ox

eiddew nm ivy

eiddgar adj zealous, ardent

eiddgarwch nm zeal, ardour

eiddigedd nm jealousy; zeal

eiddigeddu vb to be jealous, to envy; to have zeal

eiddigeddus adj jealous, envious

eiddigus adj jealous; zealous

eiddil adj slender, feeble

eiddilwch nm slenderness, feebleness

eiddiorwg nm ivy

eiddo nm property, possessions
  ▸ pron his etc

eidduno vb to desire, to wish, to pray

Eifftaidd adj Egyptian

Eifftiwr (-wyr), **Eifftiad (-iaid)** nm Egyptian

eigion nm depth, ocean

eigioneg nf oceanography

eigionol adj pelagic

eingion (-au) nf anvil

Eingl npl Angles, Englishmen

Eingl-Gymro (-Gymry) nm Anglo-Welshman

Eingl-Sais (-Saeson) nm Anglo-Saxon

Eingl-Seisnig adj Anglo-Saxon

eil- prefix second

eilchwyl adv again

eiliad (-au) nfm second, moment

eiliadur (-on) nm alternator

eilio vb to weave, to plait; to sing; to second

eiliwr (-wyr) nm seconder

eilradd (-ol) adj secondary, inferior

eilrif (-au) nm even number

eilun (-od) nm image, idol

eilunaddolgar adj idolatrous

eilunaddoli vb to worship idols

eilunaddolwr (-wyr) nm idolator

eilwaith adv again

eilydd (-ion) nm seconder, reserve

eillio vb to shave

eilliwr (-wyr) nm shaver, barber

ein pron our

einioes nf life, lifetime

einion (-au) nf anvil

eira nm snow

eirchion see **arch**

eirias adj burning, glowing, fiery

eirin npl (nf **-en**) plums; **eirin gwlanog** peaches; **eirin duon** damsons; **eirin duon bach** sloes; **eirin Mair** gooseberries

eirinen nf plum

eiriol vb to plead, to pray, to intercede

eiriolaeth nf intercession

eiriolwr (-wyr) nm intercessor, mediator

eirlaw nm sleet

eirlin (-iau) nm snow line

eirlithrad (-au) nm avalanche

eirlys (-iau) nm snowdrop

eironi nm irony

eisen (ais) nf rib; lath

eisglwyf nm pleurisy

eisiau nm want, need, lack

eising nm icing

eisin coll n bran, husk

eisio vb to ice

eisoes adv already

eistedd vb to sit, to seat

eisteddfa (-oedd, -fâu) nf seat

eisteddfod (-au) nf session; eisteddfod

eisteddfodol adj eisteddfodic

eisteddfodwr (-wyr) nm frequenter of eisteddfodau

eisteddfota vb to frequent eisteddfodau

eisteddiad (-au) nm sitting, session

eisteddle (-oedd) nm seat, sitting, pew

eitem (-au) nf item

eithaf (-ion) adj, nm extreme; superlative ▶ adv very, quite

eithafbwynt (-iau) nm extremity; apogee

eithafiaeth nf extremism

eithafion npl extremes, extremities

eithafol adj extreme; extremist

eithafwr (-wyr) nm extremist

eithin npl (nf-en) furze, gorse

eithinog adj furzy

eithr prep except; besides ▶ conj but

eithriad (-au) nm exception

eithriadol adj exceptional

eithrio vb to except, to exclude

elastig adj, nm elastic

elastigedd nm elasticity

electromagneteg nf electromagnetism

electromedr (-au) nm electrometer

electron (-au) nm electron

electroneg nf electronics

electronig adj electronic

elegeiog adj elegiac, mournful

eleni adv this year

elfen (-nau) nf element

elfennig adj elemental

elfennol adj elementary

eli (elïoedd) nm ointment, salve

elifiant (-nnau) nm effluence

elifyn (elifion) nm effluent

eliffant (-od, -iaid) nm elephant

eliffantaidd adj elephantine

elin (-au, -oedd) nf elbow; angle, bend

elips (-au) nm ellipse

eliptig adj elliptical

elor nf bier

elusen (-nau) nf alms

elusendy (-dai) nm almshouse

elusengar adj charitable, benevolent

elusengarwch nm charity, benevolence

elusennol adj eleemosynary

elusennwr (-enwyr) nm almoner

elw nm possession, gain, profit

elwa vb to gain, to profit

elwlen (-wlod) *nf* kidney

e-lyfr *nm* e-book

ellyll (-on) *nm* fiend; goblin

ellyllaidd *adj* fiendish; elfish

ellylles (-au) *nf* fury, she-goblin

ellyn (-au, -od) *nm* razor

embryo *nm* embryo

embryoleg *nf* embryology

emosiwn (-iynau) *nm* emotion

emosiynol *adj* emotional

empeiraeth *nf* empiricism

empeiraidd *adj* empirical

empirig *adj* empirical

emrallt *nm* emerald

emyn (-au) *nm* hymn

emyn-dôn (-au) *nf* hymn-tune

emyniadur (-on) *nm* hymnal

emynwr (-wyr) *nm* hymnist

emynyddiaeth *nf* hymnody, hymnology

enaid (eneidiau) *nm* life, soul

enamel (-au) *nm* enamel

enamlio *vb* to enamel

enbyd, enbydus *adj* dangerous, perilous

enbydrwydd *nm* peril, danger, jeopardy

encil (-ion) *nm* retreat, flight

encilfa (-feydd) *nf* retreat

enciliad (-au) *nm* retreat; desertion

encilio *vb* to retreat; to desert

enciliwr (-wyr) *nm* retreater; deserter

enclitig *adj* enclitic

encôr *nm* encore

encyd *nm* space; while

enchwythu *vb* to inflate

endemig *adj* endemic

endid *nm* entity, existence

endothermig *adj* endothermic

eneidiog *adj* animate

eneidiol *adj* animate, living

eneiniad (-au) *nm* anointing, unction

eneinio *vb* to anoint

Eneiniog *nm* The Messiah, Christ

eneiniog *adj, nm* anointed

enfawr *adj* enormous, huge, immense

enfys (-au) *nf* rainbow

engiriol *adj* nefarious, cruel, terrible

engrafiad (-au) *nm* engraving

engrafu *vb* to engrave

enhuddo *see* anhuddo

enigma *nm* enigma

enigmatig *adj* enigmatic

enillfawr *adj* lucrative, remunerative

enillgar *adj* gainful; winsome

enillion *npl* profits, earnings

enillwr, enillydd (enillwyr) *nm* gainer, winner

enllib (-ion, -iau) *nm* slander, libel

enllibaidd *adj* slanderous, libellous

enllibio *vb* to slander, to libel

enllibiwr (-wyr) *nm* slanderer, libeller

enllibus *adj* slanderous, libellous

enllyn *nm* relish eaten with bread

ennaint (eneiniau) *nm* ointment

ennill *vb* to gain, to win; to earn
▸ *nm* **(enillion)** gain, profit; *(pl)* earnings; **ennill pwysau** put on weight

ennyd *nmf* while, moment

ennyn *vb* to kindle, to burn, to inflame; to excite

nsyniad (-au) nm insinuation

nsynio vb to insinuate

ntrych (-ion) nm firmament, height, zenith

nw (-au) nm name; noun; **enw bedydd** first name, Christian name

nwad (-au) nm denomination, sect

nwadaeth nf sectarianism

nwadol adj sectarian; nominative

nwadwr (-wyr) nm sectarian, sectary

nwaediad nm circumcision

nwaedu vb to circumcise

nwebai (-eion) nm nominee

nwebiad (-au) nm nomination

nwebu vb to nominate

nwedig adj: **yn enwedig** particularly, especially

nwi vb to name

nwog (-ion) adj famous, renowned, noted

nwogi vb to make famous

nwogrwydd nm fame, renown

nwol adj nominal, nominative

nwyn nm: **llaeth enwyn** buttermilk

nynfa nf inflammation; itching

nyniad (-au) nm inflammation

nynnol adj inflammatory; inflamed

ofn adj fearless, bold

og (-iaid) nm salmon

os (-au) nf nightingale

osaidd adj like a nightingale

pa (-od) nm ape, monkey

pidemig adj, nm epidemic

pig nf epic

epiglotis (-au) nm epiglottis

epigram (-au) nm epigram

epil nm offspring, brood

epilepsi nm epilepsy

epilgar adj prolific, teeming

epiliad (-au) nm reproduction

epilio vb to bring forth, to teem, to breed

epilog nm epilogue

episeicloid (-au) nm epicycloid

epistol (-au) nm epistle

eples nm leaven, ferment

eplesiad nm fermentation

eplesu vb to leaven, to ferment

er prep for, in order to; since ▸ conj though

eraill see **arall**

erbyn vb to receive, to meet ▸ prep against, by

erch adj speckled; frightful

erchi vb to ask, to pray, to command, to demand

erchwyn (-ion) nm side, bed-side

erchyll adj hideous, horrible

erchyllter (-au) nm atrocity

erchylltod, erchylltra nm hideousness, horror

eres adj wonderful, strange

erestyn nm minstrel, buffoon

erfin npl (nf -**en**) turnips

erfyn vb to beg, to pray, to implore, to expect

erfyniad (-au) nm prayer, petition

ergyd (-ion) nmf blow, stroke; shot; cast

ergydio vb to strike; to throw, to cast

ergydiwr (-wyr) nm striker

erial (-au) nm aerial

erioed adv ever
erledigaeth (-au) nf persecution
erlid vb to persecute ▸ nm **(-iau)** persecution
erlidiwr (-wyr) nm persecutor
erlyn vb to pursue, to prosecute
erlyniad nm prosecution
erlynydd (-ion) nm prosecutor
ern, ernes (-au) nf earnest, pledge, deposit
ers prep since
erthwch nm grunt, pant
erthygl (-au) nf article
erthyl (-od) nm abortion
erthylaidd adj abortive
erthyliad (-au) nm abortion, miscarriage
erthylu vb to abort, to miscarry
erw (-au) nf acre
erwain npl meadow-sweet
erwydd npl stave (in music)
erydiad (-au) nm erosion
erydol adj erosive
erydu vb to erode
erydydd (-ion) nm erosive agent
eryr (-od) nm eagle; shingles
eryraidd adj eagle-like, aquiline
esblygiad (-au) nm evolution
esblygiadaeth nf evolutionism
esblygu vb to evolve
esboniad (-au) nm explanation; commentary
esboniadaeth nf exposition, exegesis
esboniadol adj expository, explanatory
esbonio vb to explain, to expound
esboniwr (-wyr) nm expositor, commentator

esbonydd (-ion) nm exponent
esbonyddol adj exponential
escaladur (-on) nm escalator
esgair (-eiriau) nf shank, leg; ridge
esgeirlwm adj exposed, wind-swept
esgeulus adj neglectful, negligent
esgeuluso vb to neglect
esgeulustod, esgeulustra nm negligence
esgid (-iau) nf boot, shoe; **esgidiau ymarfer** trainers
esgob (-ion) nm bishop
esgobaeth (-au) nf bishopric, see, diocese
esgobyddiaeth nf episcopalianism
esgoli vb to escalate
esgor vb to bring forth, to bear
esgud adj quick, swift, active
esgus (-ion, -odion) nm excuse, pretext
esgusodi vb to excuse
esgusodol adj excusable, excused
esgymun adj execrable, excommunicate
esgymuno vb to excommunicate
esgyn vb to ascend, to rise; to take off
esgynbren (-nau) nm perch
esgynfa (-feydd) nf ascent, rise
esgynfaen nm horse-block
esgyniad nm ascension
esgynneb (esgynebau) nf climax
esgynnol adj ascending
esgyrn see **asgwrn**
esgyrnog adj bony
esiampl (-au) nf example
esmwyth adj soft, smooth; easy
esmwythâd nm ease, relief

esmwytháu *vb* to soothe, to ease
esmwythder, esmwythdra *nm* ease
esmwytho, esmwytháu *vb* to ease, to soothe, to soften
esmwythyd *nm* ease, luxury
estron¹ (-iaid) *nm* foreigner, alien
estron² *adj* foreign, strange, alien
estrones (-au) *nf* alien woman
estronol *adj* strange, foreign, alien
estrys (-od) *nfm* ostrich
estyll *npl* (*nf* **-en**) planks, boards
estyn *vb* to extend, to reach; to stretch, to prolong
estynadwy *adj* extensible
estyniad *nm* extension, prolongation
estheteg *nf* aesthetics
esthetig *adj* aesthetic
etifedd (-ion) *nm* heir, inheritor
etifeddeg *nf* heredity
etifeddes (-au) *nf* heiress
etifeddiaeth (-au) *nf* inheritance
etifeddol *adj* hereditary
etifeddu *vb* to inherit
eto *conj* yet, still ▸ *adv* again; yet, still
ether *nm* ether
ethnig *nm* ethnic
ethnoleg *nf* ethnology
ethol *vb* to elect
etholaeth (-au) *nf* constituency
etholedig (-ion) *adj* elect
etholedigaeth *nf* election (theology)
etholfraint *nf* franchise
etholiad (-au) *nm* election
etholiadol *adj* electoral, elective
etholwr (-wyr) *nm* elector, voter
ethos *nm* ethos

eu *pron* their
euog *adj* guilty
euogfarn *nf* conviction
euogfarnu *vb* to convict
euogrwydd *nm* guiltiness, guilt
euraid, euraidd *adj* golden, (of) gold
euro *vb* to apply or bestow gold; to gild
eurych (-od) *nm* goldsmith
ewig (-od) *nf* hind
ewin (-edd) *nmf* nail, talon, claw; hoof
ewino *vb* to claw
ewinog *adj* having nails or claws
ewinrhew *nf* frost-bite
ewro (-aid, -s) *nm* euro
Ewrop *nf* Europe
Ewropead (-aid) *nm* European
Ewropeaidd *adj* European
ewyllys (-iau) *nf* will
ewyllysio *vb* to will, to wish
ewyn *nm* foam, froth, surf
ewynnog *adj* foaming, foamy, frothy
ewynnu *vb* to foam, to froth
ewythr (-edd) *nm* uncle

e

111

f

fagddu *nf*: **y fagddu** gross darkness
falf (**-iau**) *nf* valve
fan (**-iau**) *nf* van
fandal (**-iaid**) *nm* vandal
fandaleiddio *vb* to vandalize
fandaliaeth *nf* vandalism
farnais (**-eisiau**) *nm* varnish
farneisio *vb* to varnish
fe *pron* he, him
feallai *adv* perhaps, peradventure
fegan (**-iaid**) *nm* vegan
feganaidd *adj* vegan
fel *adv, conj, prep* so, as, that, thus,
   like; how; **fel arall** otherwise; **fel**
   arfer, fel rheol usually
felly *adv* so, thus
festri (**-ïoedd**) *nf* vestry
fi *pron* me
ficer (**-iaid**) *nm* vicar
ficerdy (**-dai**) *nm* vicarage
fideo (**-s**) *nm* video; **gêm fideo**
   video game
figan (**-iaid**) *nm* vegan

figanaidd *adj* vegan
fila *nf* villa
finegr *nm* vinegar
fiola (**-s**) *nf* viola
firws (**-au, fira**) *nm* virus
fitamin (**-au**) *nm* vitamin
fo *pron* him
folt (**-iau**) *nf* volt
foltamedr (**-au**) *nm* voltameter
foltedd (**-au**) *nm* voltage
foltmedr (**-au**) *nm* voltmeter
fortais (**-eisiau**) *nm* vortex
fory (**yfory**) *adv* tomorrow
fry *adv* above, aloft
fwltur (**-iaid**) *nm* vulture
fy *pron* my
fyny *adv* up, upwards

ff

ffa *npl* (*nf* **ffäen,** *nf* **ffeuen**) beans;
ffa'r gors buckbeans; **ffa pob**
baked beans
ffabrigo *vb* to fabricate
ffacbys *npl* fitches, vetches
ffacbysen (**ffacbys**) *nf* chickpea
ffactor (**-au**) *nmf* factor; **fffactor**
cyffredin mwyaf highest common
factor; **fffactor cysefin** prime
factor
ffactori, -o *vb* to factorize
ffactri (**-ïoedd**) *nf* factory, mill
ffaeledig *adj* fallible, ailing
ffaeledigrwydd *nm* fallibility
ffaeledd (**-au**) *nm* failing, defect
ffaelu *vb* to fail
ffafr (**-au**) *nf* favour
ffafraeth *nf* favouritism
ffafrio *vb* to favour
ffafriol *adj* favourable
ffagl (**-au**) *nf* blaze, flame; torch
ffair (**ffeiriau**) *nf* fair, exchange;
ffair sborion jumble sale

ffaith (**ffeithiau**) *nf* fact
ffald (**-au**) *nf* fold; pound
ffals (**ffeilsion**) *adj* false, deceitful
ffalsedd *nm* falsehood, deceit
ffalster *nm* deceitfulness, cunning
ffalwm *nm* whitlow
ffan (**-nau**) *nf* fan
ffanatig *nm* fanatic
ffanatigiaeth *nf* fanaticism
ffansi *nf* fancy
ffansïo *vb* to fancy
ffansïol *adj* fanciful
ffantasi, ffantasia (**-ïau**) *nf*
fantasy
ffarm (**ffermydd**) *nf* farm
ffarmio *vb* to farm
ffarmwr (**ffermwyr**) *nm* farmer
ffarmwraig (**-wragedd**) *nf* farmer
ffârs (**-iau**) *nf* farce
ffarwél *nf* farewell
ffarwelio *vb* to bid farewell
ffas (**-ys, -au**) *nf* face, coal-face
ffasâd (**ffasadau**) *nm* facade
ffasgaeth *nf* fascism
ffasiwn (**-iynau**) *nm* fashion
ffasiynol *adj* fashionable
ffasner (**-i**) *nm* fastener
ffasnin (**-au**) *nm* fastening
ffasno *vb* to fasten
ffasnydd (**-ion**) *nm* fastener
ffatri (**-ïoedd**) *nf* factory, mill
ffatrïaeth *nf* manufacturing
ffau (**ffeuau**) *nf* den
ffawd (**ffodion**) *nf* fortune, fate
ffawdheglu *vb* to hitch-hike
ffawdheglwr (**-wyr**) *nm* hitchhiker
ffawna *nf* fauna
ffawydd *npl* (*nf* **-en**) beech trees
ffederal *adj* federal

ffederaliaeth nf federalism

ffederasiwn (-iynau) nm federation

ffedereiddio, ffedreiddio vb to federate

ffefryn (-nau) nm favourite

ffeil nf file; **ffeil sip** zip file

ffeilio vb to file

ffein, ffeind adj fine

ffeirio vb to barter, to exchange

ffeithiol adj factual

ffelt nm felt

ffelwm nm whitlow

ffemwr (ffemora) nm femur

ffendir nm fenland

ffenestr (-i) nf window; **ffenestri dwbl** double glazing

ffenigl nm fennel

ffenomen (-au) nf phenomenon

ffens (-ys) nf fence

ffensio vb to fence

ffêr (fferau) nf ankle

fferdod nm numbness

fferi (-ïau) nf ferry

fferins npl sweets

fferm (-ydd) nf farm

ffermdy (-dai) nm farm-house

ffermio vb to farm

ffermwr (-wyr) nm farmer

fferru vb to congeal, to freeze; to perish with cold

fferyllfa (-feydd) nf dispensary

fferylliaeth nf pharmacy

fferyllol adj chemical, pharmaceutical

fferyllydd (-wyr) nm chemist, pharmacist

ffesant (-s, -au) nm pheasant

ffest¹ adj fast

ffest² nf feast

ffetan (-au) nf sack, bag

ffeuen nf bean

ffi (-oedd) nf fee

ffiaidd adj loathsome, abominable

ffibr (-au) nm fibre

ffibrog, -us adj fibrous

Ffichtiad (-iaid) nm Pict

ffidil (ffidlau) nf fiddle

ffidlan vb to fiddle, to dawdle

ffidler (-iaid) nm fiddler

ffidlo vb to fiddle

ffieiddbeth (-au) nm abomination

ffieidd-dra nm abomination

ffieiddio vb to loathe, to abominate, to abhor

ffigur (-au) nf figure, type

ffigurol adj figurative

ffigys npl (nf -en) figs

ffigysbren (-nau) nm fig-tree

ffigysen nf fig

ffiled (-au, -i) nf fillet

ffilharmonig adj philharmonic

ffilm (-iau) nf film

ffilmio vb to film

ffiloreg nf rigmarole, nonsense

ffilter (-au, -i) nm filter

ffin (-iau) nf boundary, limit

Ffindir nf: **y Ffindir** Finland

ffindir (-oedd) nm borderland

ffinio vb to border (upon), to abut

ffiniol adj bordering

ffiol (-au) nf vial; cup

ffiseg nf physics

ffisegol adj physical

ffisegwr (-wyr) nm physicist

ffisig nm physic, medicine

ffisigwr (-wyr) nm physician

ffisigwriaeth nm physic, medicine

ffisioleg *nfm* physiology

ffisiotherapi *nm* physiotherapy

ffit *adj* fit ▸ *nf* (-**iau**) fit, paroxysm

ffit-ffatio *vb* to flip-flop

ffitrwydd *nm* fitness

ffiwdal *adj* feudal

ffiwg (-**iau**) *nf* fugue

ffiws (-**iau**) *nm* fuse

ffiwsio *vb* to fuse

fflach (-**iau**) *nf* flash

fflachiad (-**au**) *nm* flash

fflachio *vb* to flash

fflachiog *adj* flashing

fflag (-**iau**) *nf* flag

fflagen (-**ni**) *nf* flagon, flag-stone

fflangell (-**au**) *nf* scourge

fflangelliad (-**au**) *nm* flagellation

fflangellu *vb* to scourge, to whip, to flog

fflam (-**au**) *nf* flame

fflamadwy *adj* (in)flammable

fflamio *vb* to flame, to blaze

fflamllyd *adj* flaming, blazing

fflan (-**iau**) *nm* flan

fflap (-**iau**) *nm* flap

fflasg (-**iau**) *nf* flask, basket

fflat *adj* flat ▸ *nm* (-**iau**) flat-iron ▸ *nf* (-**au**, -**iau**) a flat

fflatio *vb* to flat, to flatten

fflatwadn *adj* flatfooted

fflaw *nm* splinter

fflecs (-**ys**) *nm* flex

fflêm, fflem *nf* phlegm

fflint *nm* flint

ffliwt (-**iau**) *nf* flute

ffloch (-**au**) *nm* floe; **ffloch iâ** ice floe

fflodiad, -iart *nf* floodgate

ffo *nm* flight

ffoadur (-**iaid**) *nm* fugitive, refugee

ffodus *adj* fortunate, lucky

ffoedigaeth *nf* flight

ffoi *vb* to flee, to run away

ffôl *adj* foolish, silly ▸ *nf* (**ffols**) fall (in a slate quarry)

ffoledd *nm* foolishness, folly, fatuity

ffolen (-**nau**) *nf* buttock

ffoli *vb* to infatuate, to dote; to fool

ffolineb *nm* foolishness, folly

ffôn (**ffonau**) *nm* phone; **ffonau clust** headphones; **ffôn camera** camera phone; **ffôn symudol** mobile phone

ffonnod (**ffonodiau**) *nf* stroke, blow, stripe

ffonodio *vb* to cudgel, to beat

fforc (**ffyrc**) *nf* (table) fork

fforch (-**au**, **ffyrch**) *nf* fork

fforchi *vb* to fork

fforchio *vb* to fork

fforchog *adj* forked, cleft, cloven

ffordd (**ffyrdd**) *nf* way, road; distance

fforddio *vb* to afford

fforddol (-**ion**) *nm* wayfarer, passer-by

fforest (-**ydd**, -**au**) *nf* forest; **fforest law** rainforest

fforffedu *vb* to forfeit

fforio *vb* to explore

ffortiwn (-**iynau**), -**un** (-**au**) *nf* fortune

fforwm (-**ymau**) *nm* forum

ffos (-**ydd**) *nf* ditch, trench

ffosffad (-**au**) *nm* phosphate

ffosil (-**au**) *nm* fossil

ff

115

ffracsiwn

ffracsiwn (-iynau) *nm* fraction

ffrae (-au) *nf* quarrel

ffraeo *vb* to quarrel

ffraeth *adj* fluent; witty, facetious

ffraetheb (-ion) *nf* joke, witticism

ffraethineb *nm* wit, facetiousness

Ffrangeg *nf* French (language)

Ffrainc *nf* France

ffrâm (fframiau) *nf* frame

fframio *vb* to frame

fframwaith *nm* framework

Ffrances (-au) *nf* Frenchwoman

Ffrancwr (-wyr, Ffrancod) *nm* Frenchman

Ffrengig *adj* French; **llygod fffrengig** rats

ffres *adj* fresh

ffresgo (-au) *nm* fresco

ffresni *nm* freshness

ffretwaith *nm* fretwork

ffreutur *nf* refectory

ffrewyll (-au) *nf* whip, scourge

ffridd (-oedd) *nf* mountain pasture

ffrimpan (-au) *nf* frying pan

ffrind (-iau) *nm* friend

ffrio *vb* to fry; to hiss

ffrîs (-iau) *nf* frieze

ffrit (-iau) *nm* frit, flop ► *adj* worthless, unsubstantial

ffrith (-oedd) *nf* mountain pasture

ffrithiant (-nnau) *nm* friction

ffroch, ffrochwyllt *adj* furious

ffroen (-au) *nf* nostril; muzzle (of gun)

ffroenell (-au) *nf* nozzle

ffroeni *vb* to snort, to snuff, to sniff

ffroenuchel *adj* haughty, disdainful

ffroes *npl* (*nf*-en) pancakes

ffrog (-iau) *nf* frock

ffrom *adj* angry, irascible, testy, touchy

ffromi *vb* to fume, to chafe, to rage

ffrostgar *adj* boastful

ffrwd (ffrydiau) *nf* stream, torrent

ffrwgwd (ffrygydau) *nm* squabble

ffrwst *nm* hurry, haste, bustle

ffrwtian *vb* to splutter

ffrwydriad (-au) *nm* explosion

ffrwydro *vb* to explode

ffrwydrol *adj* explosive

ffrwydryn (-nau, ffrwydron) *nm* mine, explosive

ffrwyn (-au) *nf* bridle

ffrwyno *vb* to bridle, to curb

ffrwyth (-au, -ydd) *nm* fruit; vigour, use

ffrwythlon *adj* fruitful, fertile

ffrwythlondeb, -der *nm* fruitfulness, fertility

ffrwythloni *vb* to become fruitful; to fertilize

ffrwytho *vb* to bear fruit

ffrydio *vb* to stream, to gush

ffrydlif *nmf* stream, flood, torrent

ffrynt *nm* front

ffuantus *adj* insincere

ffug *adj* fictitious, false, sham ► *nm* (-ion) fiction, sham

ffug-bas (-ys) *nf* dummy (pass)

ffugbasio *vb* to dummy

ffugenw (-au) *nm* pseudonym

ffugiad (-au) *nm* forgery

ffugio *vb* to feign; to forge

ffugiwr (-wyr) *nm* impostor; forger

ffuglen *nf* fiction; **ffuglen wyddonol** science fiction

ffugliw (-iau) *nm* camouflage

ffugliwio *vb* to camouflage

ffunud *nm* form, manner; **yr un ffunud â** exactly like

ffured (-au) *nf* ferret

ffureta *vb* to ferret

ffurf (-iau) *nf* form, shape

ffurfafen *nf* firmament, sky

ffurfdro (-eon) *nm* inflection

ffurfeb (-au) *nf* formula

ffurfiad (-au) *nm* formation

ffurfiant (-nnau) *nm* accidence; formation

ffurfio *vb* to form

ffurfiol *adj* formal

ffurfiolaeth *nf* formalism

ffurfioldeb *nm* formality, formalism

ffurflen (-ni) *nf* form (to fill); **ffurflen gais** application form

ffurfwasanaeth (-au) *nm* liturgy

ffurfwedd (-au) *nf* configuration

ffust (-iau) *nf* flail

ffustio, -o *vb* to beat

ffwdan *nf* fuss, bustle, flurry

ffwdanllyd *adj* fussy, bustling

ffwdanu *vb* to fuss, to bustle

ffwdanus *adj* fussy, fidgety, flurried

ffwng (ffyngoedd, ffyngau) *nm* fungus

ffwngleiddiad (-au) *nm* fungicide

ffŵl (ffyliaid) *nm* fool

ffwlbart (-iaid) *nm* polecat

ffwlbri *nm* fudge, nonsense, tomfoolery

ffwlcyn *nm* fool, nincompoop

ffwndro *vb* to founder, to become confused

ffwndrus *adj* confused, bewildered

ffwndwr *nm* confusion, hurly-burly

ffwr *nm* fur

ffwrdd *nm* way; **i ffwrdd** away

ffwrn (ffyrnau) *nf* furnace, oven

ffwrnais (-eisiau) *nf* furnace

ffwrwm (ffyrymau) *nf* form, bench

ffwythiannol *adj* functional

ffydd *nf* faith

ffyddiog *adj* strong in faith, trustful

ffyddlon *adj* faithful

ffyddlondeb *nm* faithfulness, fidelity

ffyddloniaid *npl* faithful ones

ffynhonnell (ffynonellau) *nf* fount, source

ffyniannus *adj* prosperous

ffyniant *nm* prosperity

ffynidwydd *npl* (*nf* **-en**) fir-trees, pine-trees

ffynnon (ffynhonnau) *nf* fountain, well, spring

ffynnu *vb* to prosper, to thrive

ffyrf (*f* **fferf**) *adj* thick, stout

ffyrfder *nm* thickness, stoutness

ffyrling (-au, -od) *nf* farthing

ffyrm *nf* firm

ffyrnig *adj* fierce, savage, ferocious

ffyrnigo *vb* to grow fierce; to enrage

ffyrnigrwydd *nm* fierceness, ferocity

117

g

gadael, gadu vb to leave, to forsake; to let, to allow
gaeaf (-au, -oedd) nm winter
gaeafaidd, gaeafol adj wintry
gaeafu vb to winter, to hibernate
Gaeleg nf Gaelic
gafael, gafaelyd vb to hold, to grasp ▸ nf (**gafaelion**) hold, grasp
gafaelgar adj gripping, tenacious
gafl (-au, geifl) nf fork, groin
gafr (geifr) nf goat; **yr Afr** Capricorn
gafrewig (-od) nf gazelle, antelope
gagendor see agendor
gaing (geingau) nf chisel; **gaing gau** gouge
gair (geiriau) nm word
galanas (-au) nf murder, massacre
galanastra nm slaughter; mess
galar nm mourning, grief, sorrow
galarnad (-au) nf lamentation
galarnadu vb to lament

galaru vb to mourn, to grieve, to lament
galarus adj mournful, lamentable, sad
galarwr (-wyr) nm mourner
galw vb to call ▸ nm call, demand
galwad (-au) nmf call, demand
galwedigaeth (-au) nf occupation, vocation, calling
galwedigaethol adj vocational
galwyn (-i) nm gallon
gallt (gelltydd) nf wooded slope; hill, rise
gallu vb to be able ▸ nm (**-oedd**) power, ability
galluog adj able, powerful, mighty
galluogi vb to enable, to empower
gan prep with, by; of, from
gar (-rau) nfm thigh, shank
garan (-od) nf heron, crane
Garawys nm Lent
gardas, gardys (gardysau) nfm garter
gardd (gerddi) nf garden; garth, yard
garddio vb to garden ▸ nm gardening
garddwr (-wyr) nm gardener
garddwriaeth nf horticulture
gargam adj knock-kneed
garlant (-au) nm garland
garlleg npl (nf -en) garlic
gartref adv at home
garth nm hill; enclosure
garw (geirwon) adj coarse, rough, harsh
garwedd nm roughness
garwhau vb to roughen; to ruffle
gast (geist) nf bitch (offensive)
gau adj false; hollow

gefail (-eiliau) nf smithy

gefeilldref (-i) nf twinned town

gefel (-eiliau) nf tongs, pincers

gefell (-eilliaid) n twin; **yr Efeilliaid** Gemini

gefyn (-nau) nm fetter, shackle

gefynnu vb to fetter, to shackle

geingio vb to chisel, to gouge

geilwad (-waid) nm caller

geirbrosesu n word processing

geirda nm reference

geirfa (-oedd) nf vocabulary, glossary

geiriad nm wording, phraseology

geiriadur (-on) nm dictionary, lexicon

geiriadurol adj lexicographical

geiriadurwr (-wyr) nm lexicographer

geirio vb to word, to phrase

geiriol adj verbal

geirlyfr (-au) nm word-book, dictionary

geirwir adj truthful, truth-speaking

geirwiredd nm truthfulness

gel (-iau) nmf gel; **gel cawod** shower gel

gelau, gelen (gelod) nf leech

gelyn (-ion) nm foe, enemy

gelyniaeth nf enmity, hostility

gelyniaethus adj hostile, inimical

gelynol adj hostile, adverse

gellyg npl (nf-**en**) pears

gem (-au) nf gem, jewel

gêm (gêmau, gemau) nf game; **gêm cyfrifiadur** computer game; **gêm fideo** video game

gemog adj gemmed, jewelled

gemwaith nm jewellery

gemydd (-ion) nm jeweller

gên nf jaw, chin

genau (-euau) nm mouth, orifice

genau-goeg, geneugoeg (-ion) nf lizard; newt

genedigaeth (-au) nf birth

genedigol adj native

Genefa nf Geneva

geneth (-od) nf girl

genethaidd adj girlish

genethig nf little girl, maiden

geneufor nm gulf

geni vb to be born

genni vb to be contained

genwair (-eiriau) nf fishing-rod

genweirio vb to angle, to fish

genweiriwr (-wyr) nm angler

genyn (-nau) nm gene

ger prep by, near

gêr coll n gear, tackle

gerbron prep before (place); in the presence of

gerfydd prep by

geri nm bile, gall; **geri marwol** cholera

geriach coll n gear, odds and ends

gerllaw prep near ▸ adv at hand

gerwin adj rough, severe, harsh

gerwindeb, gerwinder nm roughness, severity

gerwino vb to roughen

gewyn (-nau, gïau) nm sinew, tendon

gewynnog adj sinewy

Ghana nf Ghana

gïach (-od) nm snipe

Gibraltar n Gibraltar

gieuwst nf neuralgia

119

gig (-iau) nm gig (concert)

gildio vb to yield; to gild

gilydd nm: **ei gilydd** each other; **gyda'i gilydd** together

gimbill nf gimlet

gitarydd (-ion) nm guitarist

glafoerio vb to drivel, to slobber

glafoerion npl drivel, slobber

glaif, gleifiau nm lance, sword, glaive

glain (**gleiniau**) nm gem, jewel; bead

glan (-nau, **glennydd**) nf bank, shore

glân adj clean; holy; fair, beautiful

glanfa nf landing

glanhad nm cleansing, purification

glanhaol adj cleansing, purging

glanhau vb to cleanse, to purify

glanhäwr nm cleanser

glaniad nm landing, disembarkation

glanio vb to land, to disembark

glanwaith adj clean, tidy

glanweithdra nm cleanliness

glas (**gleision**) adj blue, green, grey, silver ▸ nm blue

glasgoch adj, nm purple

glaslanc (-iau) nm youth, stripling

glasog (-au) nf crop, gizzard

glastwr nm milk and water

glastwraidd adj watered down, feeble; muddled

glasu vb to become blue, green or grey; to turn pale

glaswellt coll n grass

glaswelltyn nm blade of grass; tigridia

glaw (-ogydd) nm rain

glawiad (-au) nm rainfall

glawio vb to rain

glawlen (-ni) nf umbrella

glawog adj rainy

gleisiad (-iaid) nm sewin

gleision npl whey

glendid nm cleanness; fairness; beauty

glesni nm blueness, verdure

glew (-ion) adj brave, daring; astute

glewdra, glewder nm courage, resource

glin (-iau) nm knee

gliniadur (-on) nm laptop, laptop computer

glo nm coal

globaleiddio nm globalization

gloddest (-au) nm carousal, revelling

gloddesta vb to carouse, to revel

gloddestwr (-wyr) nm reveller

gloes (-au, -ion) nf pang; qualm

glofa (-feydd) nf colliery

glöwr (**glowyr**) nm collier

glowty (-tai) nm cow-house, shippon

glöyn nm coal; **glöyn byw** butterfly

gloyw (-on) adj bright, clear; shiny, glossy

gloywder nm brightness, clearness

gloywi vb to brighten, to polish

glud (-ion) nm glue; bird-lime

gludio vb to glue

gludiog adj sticky

glwth[1] (**glythau**) nm couch

glwth[2] (**glython**) adj gluttonous ▸ nm glutton

glwys adj fair; holy

glyn (-noedd) nm glen, valley

glynu vb to stick, to adhere, to cleave

glythineb, glythni nm gluttony

glythinebu, glythu vb to glut

go adv rather, somewhat

goachul adj lean; puny; sickly, poorly

gobaith (-eithion) nm hope

gobeithio vb to hope

gobeithiol adj hopeful

gobeithlu (-oedd) nm Band of Hope

gobennydd (-enyddiau) nm bolster, pillow

goblygiad nm implication

goblygu vb to fold, to wrap

gochel see gochelyd

gocheladwy adj avoidable

gochelgar adj wary, cautious

gocheliad nm avoidance; **ar ei ocheliad** on his guard

gochelyd vb to avoid, to shun

godidog adj excellent, splendid

godidowgrwydd nm excellence

godineb nm adultery

godinebu vb to commit adultery

godinebus adj adulterous

godinebwr (-wyr) nm adulterer

godre (-on) nm skirt, border, edge

godriad (-au) nm milking

godro vb to milk

goddaith (-eithiau) nf fire, bonfire

goddef vb to bear, to suffer, to allow, to permit

goddefgar adj forbearing, tolerant

goddefgarwch nm forbearance, tolerance

goddefiad (-au) nm licence; toleration

goddefol adj tolerable; passive

goddiweddyd, goddiwes vb to overtake

goddrych nm subject (in grammar)

goddrychol adj subjective

gof (-aint) nm smith

gofal (-on) nm care, charge

gofalaeth nf maintenance

gofalu vb to care, to mind, to take care; **gofalu (am)** to look after

gofalus adj careful; **yn ofalus** carefully

gofalwr nm caretaker

gofaniaeth nf smith's craft

gofer (-oedd, -ydd) nm overflow of well; rill

gofid (-iau) nm grief, sorrow, trouble

gofidio vb to afflict, to grieve, to vex

gofidus adj grievous, sad

gofod nm space; **llong ofod** spaceship

gofodwr (-wyr) nm astronaut

gofyn vb to ask, to demand, to require ▸ nm (**-ion**) demand, requirement

gofyniad (-au) nm question, query

gofynnod (-ynodau) nm note of interrogation, question-mark

gofynnol adj necessary, requisite; interrogative (pronoun etc)

gogan nf defamation, satire

goganu vb to defame, to satirize, to lampoon

goganwr (-wyr) nm satirist

gogledd nm, adj north

gogledd-ddwyrain *nm* northeast

Gogledd Iwerddon *nf* Northern Ireland

gogleddol *adj* northern

gogledd-orllewin *nm* northwest

gogleddwr (-wyr) *nm* northerner; North Walian

gogleddwynt *nm* north wind

gogleisio *vb* to tickle

gogleisiol *adj* tickling, titillating, amusing

gogoneddu *vb* to glorify

gogoneddus *adj* glorious

gogoniant *nm* glory

gogor (-ion) *nf* fodder, provender

gogr (-au) *nm* sieve, riddle

gogri, gogrwn, gogryn *vb* to sift, to riddle

gogwydd *nm* slant, inclination, bent

gogwyddiad (-au) *nm* inclination

gogwyddo *vb* to incline, to slope, to lean

gogyfer *adj* opposite; for, by

gogyfuwch *adj, prep* of equal height

gogyhyd *adj* of equal length

gogymaint *adj* equal in size

gohebiaeth (-au) *nf* correspondence

gohebol *adj* corresponding

gohebu *vb* to correspond (by letter etc); to reply

gohebydd (-wyr) *nm* correspondent, reporter

gohiriad (-au) *nm* postponement

gohirio *vb* to delay, to postpone, to defer; to put off

golau *adj, nm* light ▶ *vb* to light

golau-leuad *nm* moonlight

golch (-ion) *nm* wash; coating; lye

golchdy (-dai) *nm* wash-house, laundry

golchfa *nf* wash; lathering

golchi *vb* to wash; to coat

golchiad (-au) *nm* washing; plating, coating

golchion *npl* slops; suds

golchwr (-wyr), golchydd (-ion) *nm* washer

golchwraig (-wragedd) *nf* washerwoman

golchyddes (-au) *nf* laundress

goledd, goleddf *nm* slant, slope

goleddu, goleddfu *vb* to slant, to slope

goleuad (-au) *nm* light, luminary

goleudy (-dai) *nm* lighthouse

goleuni *nm* light

goleuo *vb* to light, to enlighten, to illuminate

gôl-geidwad *nm* goalkeeper

golosg *nm* coke, charcoal

golud (-oedd) *nm* wealth, riches

goludog *adj* wealthy, rich

golwg (-ygon) *nfm* sight, look; (pl) eyes

golwr (-wyr) *nm* goalkeeper

golwyth (-ion) *nm* chop, slice, cut

golygfa (-feydd) *nf* scene, view; (pl) scenery

golygiad (-au) *nm* view

golygu *vb* to view; to mean; to edit

golygus *adj* comely, handsome

golygwedd (-au) *nf* feature, aspect

golygydd (-ion, -wyr) *nm* editor

golygyddiaeth *nf* editorship

golygyddol *adj* editorial**

gollwng vb to drop, to release, to let go; to discharge; to dismiss; to leak; to let down

gollyngdod nm release; absolution

gollyngiadau npl emissions

gomedd vb to refuse

gomeddiad nm refusal, omission

gonest, onest adj honest

gonestrwydd nm honesty

gor- prefix over-, super-

gôr nm pus

goramser nm overtime

gorau (-euon) adj best; **o'r gorau** very well

gorawen nm joy, ecstasy

gorblu npl immature feathers

gorboblogi vb to overpopulate

gorbwyso vb to outweigh, to overweigh

gorchest (-ion) nf feat, exploit

gorchestol adj excellent, masterly

gorchfygu vb to overcome, to conquer

gorchfygwr (-wyr) nm victor; conqueror

gorchmynnol adj imperative

gorchudd (-ion) nm cover, covering, veil

gorchuddio vb to cover

gorchwyl (-ion) nm task, undertaking

gorchymyn vb to command ▶ nm (**gorchmynion**) command, commandment

gor-dewdra nm obesity

gordoi vb to overspread, to cover

gordyfu vb to overgrow

gordd (gyrdd) nf sledge-hammer, mallet

gordderch (-adon) nf concubine; lover; bastard

gorddogn (-au) nm overdose

gorddrafft nm overdraft

goresgyn vb to overrun, to invade; to conquer

goresgyniad nm invasion; conquest

goresgynnydd nm invader; conqueror

goreuro vb to gild

gorfod vb to be obliged ▶ nm obligation, necessity

gorfodaeth nf obligation, compulsion

gorfodi vb to oblige, to compel

gorfodol adj obligatory, compulsory

gorfoledd nm joy, rejoicing, triumph

gorfoleddu vb to rejoice, to triumph

gorfoleddus adj jubilant, triumphant

gorffen vb to finish, to complete, to conclude

gorffeniad nm finishing, finish

Gorffennaf nm July

gorffennol adj, nm past

gorffwyll adj mad, frenzied

gorffwyllo vb to rave

gorffwyllog adj mad, insane

gorffwylltra nm madness, insanity

gorffwys, gorffwyso vb to rest, to repose ▶ nm rest, repose

gorffwysfa (-oedd) nf resting-place, rest

gorffwysfan nm lay-by

gorffwysiad (-au) nm rest, pause

123

gorffwystra *nm* rest, repose

gorhendaid *nm* great-great-grandfather

gorhennain *nf* great-great-grandmother

gori *vb* to hatch

gorifyny *nm* ascent, hill, steep climb

goris *prep* below, beneath, under

goriwaered *nm* descent, declivity

gorlawn *adj* superabundant; packed

gorlenwi *vb* to overfill

gorlifo *vb* to swamp

gorliwio *vb* to colour too highly, to exaggerate

gorllewin *nm* west; **Gorllewin yr Almaen** West Germany

gorllewinol *adj* westerly, western

gorllewinwr (-**wyr**) *nm* westerner

gormes *nm* oppression, tyranny

gormesol *adj* oppressive, tyrannical

gormesu *vb* to oppress, to tyrannize

gormeswr (-**wyr**), **gormesydd** (-**ion**) *nm* oppressor, tyrant

gormod (-**ion**) *nm* too much, excess

gormodedd *nm* excess, superfluity

gormodiaith *nf* hyperbole, exaggeration

gormodol *adj* excessive

gormwyth *nm* catarrh

gornest, ornest (-**au**) *nf* contest, match

goroesi *vb* to outlive, to survive

goroesiad (-**au**) *nm* survival

goroeswr (-**wyr**) *nm* survivor

goror (-**au**) *nm* border, coast, frontier

gorsaf (-**oedd**) *nf* station; **gorsaf dân** fire station; **gorsaf fysiau** bus station

gorsedd (-**au**), **gorseddfa** (-**oedd**), **gorseddfainc** (-**feinciau**) *nf* throne

gorseddu *vb* to throne, to enthrone, to install

gorsin, gorsing (-**au**) *nf* door-post

gorthrech *nm* oppression; coercion

gorthrechu *vb* to oppress; to coerce

gorthrwm *nm* oppression

gorthrymder *nm* oppression, tribulation

gorthrymedig *adj* oppressed

gorthrymu *vb* to oppress

gorthrymus *adj* oppressive

gorthrymwr (-**wyr**), **gorthrymydd** *nm* oppressor

goruchaf *adj* most high, supreme

goruchafiaeth *nf* supremacy; triumph

goruchel *adj* high, exalted

goruchwyliaeth (-**au**) *nf* oversight, supervision; dispensation

goruchwylio *vb* to oversee, to supervise

goruchwyliwr (-**wyr**) *nm* supervisor, steward

goruwch *prep* above, over

goruwchnaturiol *adj* supernatural

goruwchreoli *vb* to overrule

gorwedd *vb* to lie; **gorwedd i lawr** lie down

gorweddfa (-**oedd**), **gorweddfan** (-**au**) *nf* bed, couch

orweddian vb to lounge, to loll
orweiddiog adj bedridden
orwel (-ion) nm horizon
orwych adj gorgeous
orwyr (-ion) nm great-grandson
orwyres (-au) nf great-granddaughter
orymdaith (-deithiau) nf procession
orymdeithio vb to walk in procession
orynys (-oedd) nf peninsula
oryrru vb to drive too fast ▸ n speeding
osber (-au) nm vespers
osgedd (-au) nm form, figure
osgeiddig adj comely, graceful
osgordd (-ion) nf retinue, train, escort
osgorddlu (-oedd) nm bodyguard
oslef (-au) nf tone, intonation
osod vb to put, to place, to set; to let ▸ adj false, artificial
osodiad (-au) nm proposition, statement
osteg (-ion) nf silence; (pl) banns
ostegu vb to silence, to still, to quell
ostwng vb to lower, to reduce; to bow; to put down, to humble
ostyngedig adj humble
ostyngeiddrwydd nm humility
ostyngiad nm reduction; humiliation
ostyngol adj reduced
owt nm gout
radell (gredyll) nf griddle
radd (-au) nfm grade, degree, stage
raddedig adj postgraduate

graddedigion npl graduates
graddfa (-feydd) nf scale
graddiant nm gradient
graddio vb to graduate
graddol adj gradual
graddoli vb to grade, to graduate
graean coll n gravel
graeanu vb to granulate
graeanwst nf gravel (complaint)
graen nm grain, gloss, lustre
graenus adj of good grain, glossy, sleek
graff (-iau) nm graph
gramadeg (-au) nm grammar
gramadegol adj grammatical
gramadegwr (-wyr), gramadegydd nm grammarian
gran (-nau) nm cheek
gras (-au, -usau) nm grace
graslawn, graslon adj full of grace, gracious
graslonrwydd nm graciousness, grace
grasol, grasusol adj gracious
grât (gratiau) nm grate
grawn npl (nm gronyn) grain; grapes; roe
grawnfwyd (-ydd) coll n cereal
grawnffrwyth nm grapefruit
grawnwin npl grapes
Grawys nm Lent
gre (-oedd) nf stud, flock
greddf (-au) nf instinct, intuition
greddfol adj instinctive, intuitive, rooted
greddfu vb to become ingrained
grefi nm gravy
gresyn nm pity
gresyni, gresyndod nm misery, wretchedness

g

gresynu vb to commiserate, to pity
gresynus adj miserable, wretched
greyenyn nm grain, granule
gridyll (-au) nmf griddle
griddfan vb to groan, to moan
  ▶ nm (**-nau**) groan
grillian, grillio vb to squeak, to creak; to chirp; to crunch
gris (-iau) nm step, stair
grisial nm crystal
grisialaidd adj crystal, crystalline
gro coll n (nm **gröyn**) gravel, pebbles
Groeg nf Greek language; Greece
  ▶ adj Greek
Groegaidd adj Grecian, Greek
Groeges (-au) nf Greek woman
Groegwr (-wyr, -iaid) nm Greek
gronell (-au) nf roe
Grønland nf Greenland
gronyn (-nau) nm grain, particle; while
grot (-iau) nm groat, fourpence
grual nm gruel
grud nm grit
grudd (-iau) nf cheek
gruddfan see griddfan
grug nm heather
grugiar (-ieir) nf moor-hen, grouse
grugog adj heathery
grwgnach vb to grumble, to murmur
grwgnachlyd adj given to grumbling
grwgnachwr (-wyr) nm grumbler
grwn (grynnau) nm ridge (in ploughing)
grŵn, grwndi nm purr
grwnan vb to croon, to purr
grwndwal (-au) nm foundation

grydian vb to murmur; to grunt
grym (-oedd) nm force, power, might
grymial vb to mutter, to murmur, to grumble
grymus adj strong, powerful, mighty
grymuso vb to strengthen
grymuster, grymustra nm power, might
gwacáu vb to empty
gwacsaw adj trivial, frivolous
gwacsawrwydd nm levity, vanity
gwacter nm emptiness, vacuity
gwachul see goachul
gwad, gwadiad nm denial, disavowal
gwadn (-au) nm sole
gwadnu vb to sole; to foot it
gwadu vb to deny, to disown; to renounce, to forsake
gwadwr (-wyr) nm denier
gwadd¹ (-od) nf mole
gwadd² see gwahodd
gwaddod (-ion) nm sediment, lees, dregs
gwaddodi vb to deposit sediment
gwaddol (-ion, -iadau) nm endowment; dowry
gwaddoli vb to endow
gwae (-au) nmf woe
gwaed nm blood
gwaedlif, gwaedlyn nm hæmorrhage, dysentery
gwaedlyd adj bloody, sanguinary
gwaedoliaeth nf blood, consanguinity
gwaedu vb to bleed
gwaedd (-au) nf cry, shout
gwaeddi see gweiddi

gwaeg (gwaegau) nf buckle, clasp
gwael adj poor, vile; poorly, ill
gwaelder, gwaeldra nm poorness, vileness
gwaeledd nm illness
gwaelod (-ion) nm bottom; (pl) sediment
gwaelodi vb to settle, to deposit sediment
gwaelodol adj basic
gwaelu vb to sicken
gwaell (gwëyll, gweill) nf knitting-needle
gwaered nm descent; **i waered** down
gwaeth adj worse
gwaethwaeth adj worse and worse
gwaethygu vb to worsen
gwaew see gwayw
gwag (gweigion) adj empty, vacant, vain
gwagedd nm vanity
gwagelog adj wary, circumspect
gwagen (-i) nf waggon
gwagenwr (-wyr) nm waggoner
gwagfa (-feydd) nf vacuum
gwagle (-oedd) nm space, void
gwagu vb to empty
gwahadden (gwahaddod) nf mole
gwahan, gwahân nm: **ar wahân** apart, separately
gwahangleifion npl lepers
gwahanglwyf nm leprosy
gwahanglwyfus adj leprous ▸ nm leper
gwahaniaeth (-au) nm difference
gwahaniaethol adj distinguishing
gwahaniaethu vb to differ; to distinguish

gwahanol adj different
gwahanredol adj distinctive
gwahanu vb to divide, to part, to separate
gwahardd vb to forbid, to prohibit
gwaharddedig adj forbidden
gwaharddiad (-au) nm prohibition, veto
gwahodd vb to invite
gwahoddedigion npl guests
gwahoddiad (-au) nm invitation
gwahoddwr (-wyr) nm inviter, host
gwain (gweiniau) nf sheath, scabbard
gwair (gweiriau) nm hay
gwaith¹ (gweithiau) nm work
gwaith² (gweithiau) nf time, turn
gwal (-iau, gwelydd) nf wall
gwâl (gwalau) nf couch, bed; lair
gwala nf enough, plenty
gwalch (gweilch) nm hawk; rogue, rascal
gwaled (-au) nf wallet
gwalio vb to wall, to fence
gwall (-au) nm defect, want; mistake, error
gwallgof adj mad, insane
gwallgofdy (-dai) nm madhouse, lunatic asylum
gwallgofddyn (-gofiaid) nm madman
gwallgofi vb to go mad, to rave
gwallgofrwydd nm madness, insanity
gwallt (-iau) nm, coll n hair of the head
gwalltog adj hairy
gwallus adj faulty, incorrect, inaccurate

g

127

gwamal *adj* fickle, frivolous

gwamalio, gwamalu *vb* to waver; to behave frivolously

gwamalrwydd *nm* frivolity, levity

gwan (gweiniaid, gweinion) *adj* weak, feeble

gwanaf (-au) *nf* layer; row, swath

gwanc *nm* greed, voracity

gwancus *adj* greedy, voracious

gwaneg (-au, gwenyg) *nf* wave, billow

gwangalon *adj* faint-hearted

gwangalonni *vb* to lose heart

gwanhau *vb* to weaken, to enfeeble

gwanllyd, gwannaidd *adj* weakly, delicate

gwant *nm* caesura; division

gwantan *adj* unsteady, fickle; feeble, poor

gwanu *vb* to pierce, to stab

gwanwyn (-au) *nm* spring

gwanwynol *adj* vernal, spring-like

gwanychu *vb* to weaken, to enfeeble

gwar (-rau) *nfm* (nape of) neck

gwâr *adj* civilised, tame, gentle

gwaradwydd (-iadau) *nm* shame, disgrace

gwaradwyddo *vb* to shame, to disgrace

gwaradwyddus *adj* shameful, disgraceful

gwarafun *vb* to forbid, to refuse, to grudge

gwaraidd *adj* gentle, civilized

gwarant (-au) *nf* warrant

gwarantu *vb* to warrant, to guarantee

gwarchae *vb* to besiege ▶ *nm* siege

gwarcheidiol *adj* guardian, tutelary

gwarcheidwad (-waid) *nm* guardian

gwarchod *vb* to watch, to look after, to ward, to mind; **gwarchod plant** to baby-sit, to do baby-sitting

gwarchodaeth *nf* ward, custody

gwarchodfa (-feydd) *nf*: **gwarchodfa natur** nature reserve

gwarchodlu (-oedd) *nm* garrison, guards

gwarchodwr (-wyr) *nm* custodian; security guard; babysitter, childminder

gward (-iau) *nmf* ward

gwarden (-deiniaid) *nm* warden

gwared *vb* to rid; to deliver, to redeem

gwaredigaeth (-au) *nf* deliverance

gwaredigion *npl* redeemed, ransomed

gwaredu *vb* to save, to deliver, to redeem; to rid

gwaredwr (-wyr), gwaredydd (-ion) *nm* saviour

gwaredd *nm* mildness, gentleness

gwareiddiad *nm* civilization

gwareiddiedig *adj* civilized

gwareiddio *vb* to civilize

gwargaled *adj* stiff-necked, stubborn

gwargaledwch *nm* stubbornness

gwargam *adj* stooping

gwargamu *vb* to stoop

gwarged *nm* remains

gwargrwm *adj* round-shouldered

gwargrymu vb to stoop
gwariant nm expenditure
gwario vb to spend
gwarogaeth see gwrogaeth
gwarth nm shame, disgrace
gwarthaf nm top, summit; **ar warthaf** on top of, upon
gwarthafl (-au) nf stirrup
gwartheg npl cows, cattle
gwarthnod (-au) nm stigma
gwarthnodi vb to stigmatize
gwarthol (-ion) nf stirrup
gwarthrudd nm shame, disgrace
gwarthruddo vb to shame, to disgrace
gwarthus adj shameful, disgraceful, outrageous
gwas (gweision) nm lad; servant
gwasaidd adj servile, slavish
gwasanaeth (-au) nm service
gwasanaethferch (-ed) nf handmaid
gwasanaethgar adj serviceable; obliging
gwasanaethu vb to serve, to minister
gwasanaethwr (-wyr) nm manservant, servant
gwasanaethwraig (-wragedd) nf maidservant
gwasanaethydd (-ion) nm servant
gwasanaethyddes (-au) nf handmaid
gwasarn nm litter
gwaseidd-dra nm servility
gwasg (-au, -oedd, gweisg) nf press ▸ nm waist; bodice
gwasgar nm dispersion; **ar wasgar** scattered, dispersed
gwasgaredig (-ion) adj scattered

gwasgarog adj scattered; divided
gwasgaru vb to scatter, to disperse; to spread
gwasgarwr (-wyr) nm scatterer; spreader
gwasgfa (-feydd, -feuon) nf squeeze; fit
gwasgod (-au) nf waistcoat
gwasgu vb to press, to squeeze, to crush, to wring
gwasod adj in heat (of a cow)
gwastad adj level, flat; even; constant, continual
gwastadedd (-au) nm plain
gwastadol adj continual, perpetual
gwastadrwydd nm evenness
gwastatáu vb to make even, to level; to settle
gwastatir (-oedd) nm level ground, plain
gwastraff nm waste, extravagance
gwastraffu vb to waste, to squander
gwastraffus adj wasteful, extravagant
gwastrawd (-odion) nm groom, ostler
gwastrodaeth[1] nf grooming; discipline
gwastrodaeth[2], **gwastrodi** vb to discipline
gwatwar vb to mock; to mimic ▸ nm mockery
gwatwareg nf sarcasm, satire, irony
gwatwarus adj mocking, scoffing
gwatwarwr (-wyr) nm mocker, scoffer
gwau vb to knit, to weave

gwaun (**gweunydd**) *nf* moor, meadow

gwawch (**-iau**) *nf* scream, yell

gwawchio *vb* to scream, to yell

gwawd *nm* scoff, scorn, ridicule

gwawdiaeth *nf* ridicule

gwawdio *vb* to mock, to scoff, to jeer, to ridicule

gwawdiwr (**-wyr**) *nm* mocker, scoffer

gwawdlyd *adj* mocking, jeering, sneering

gwawl *nm* light

gwawn *nm* gossamer

gwawr *nf* dawn, day-break; hue, nuance

gwawrio *vb* to dawn

gwayw (**gwewyr**) *nm* pang, pain, stitch

gwaywffon (**-ffyn**) *nf* spear

gwden (**-ni, gwdyn**) *nf* withe

gwdihŵ *nm* owl

gwddf (**gyddfau**) *nm* neck, throat

gwe (**-oedd**) *nf* web; texture; **y We (Fyd-Eang)** the (World-Wide) Web

gwead *nm* weaving, knitting; texture

gwedd[1] (**-au**) *nf* aspect, form; appearance

gwedd[2] (**-oedd**) *nf* yoke; team

gweddaidd *adj* seemly, decent

gweddeidd-dra *nm* seemliness, decency

gwedder (**gweddrod**) *nm* wether; **cig gwedder** mutton

gweddgar *adj* plump, sleek

gweddi (**-ïau**) *nf* prayer

gweddigar *adj* prayerful

gweddill (**-ion**) *nm* remnant, remainder, rest; (*pl*) remains

gweddillio *vb* to leave spare, to leave a remnant

gweddïo *vb* to pray

gweddïwr (**-ïwyr**) *nm* one who prays

gweddol *adj* fair, fairly

gweddu *vb* to suit, to become, to befit

gweddus *adj* seemly, decent, proper

gweddustra *nm* decency, propriety

gweddw *adj* single; widow, widowed ▸ *nf* (**-on**) widow; **gŵr gweddw** widower

gweddwdod *nm* widowhood

gweddwi *vb* to widow

gwefan (**-nau**) *nfm* website

gwefl (**-au**) *nf* lip (*usu. of animal*)

gwefr *nmf* thrill, excitement; charge

gwefreiddio *vb* to electrify, to thrill

gwefreiddiol *adj* thrilling

gwefus (**-au**) *nf* (human) lip

gwefusol *adj* of the lip, labial

gwe-gamera (**gwe-gamerâu**) *nm* webcam

gwegi *nm* vanity, levity

gwegian *vb* to sway, to totter

gwegil *nm* back of head

gwehelyth *nmf* lineage, pedigree

gwehilion *npl* refuse, trash, riffraff

gwehydd (**-ion**) *nm* weaver

gwehyddu *vb* to weave

gwehynnu *vb* to draw, to pour, to empty

gweiddi *vb* to cry, to shout

gweilgi *nf* sea, torrent

gweili *adj* empty, idle

gweini *vb* to serve, to minister; to be in service

gweinidog (-ion) nm minister, servant

gweinidogaeth (-au) nf ministry, service

gweinidogaethol adj ministerial

gweinidogaethu vb to minister

gweinio vb to sheathe

gweinydd (-ion) nm waiter; server

gweinyddes (-au) nf attendant, nurse; waitress

gweinyddiaeth (-au) nf administration

gweinyddol adj administrative

gweinyddu vb to administer, to officiate

gweinyddwr (-wyr) nm administrator

gweirglodd (iau) nf meadow

gweitied, gweitio vb to wait

gweithdy (-dai) nm workshop

gweithfa (-oedd, -feydd) nf works

gweithfaol adj industrial

gweithgar adj hard-working, industrious

gweithgaredd (-au), **gweithgarwch** nm activity

gweithio vb to work; to ferment; to purge

gweithiol adj executive

gweithiwr (-wyr) nm workman, worker; **gweithiwr cymdeithasol** social worker

gweithle nm workspace

gweithred (-oedd) nf act, deed, work

gweithrediad (-au) nm action, operation

gweithredol adj active, actual, virtual

gweithredu vb to act, to work, to operate

gweithredwr (-wyr) nm doer

gweithredydd (-ion) nm doer, factor, agent

gweladwy adj perceptible, visible

gweled, gweld vb to see, to perceive

gwelediad nm sight, appearance

gweledig adj seen, visible

gweledigaeth (-au) nf vision

gweledol adj visual

gweledydd (-ion) nm seer

gwelw adj pale

gwelwi vb to pale

gwely (-au, gwelâu) nm bed; river basin; sea bed; stratum; flat surface; **gwely haul** sunbed

gwell adj better, superior

gwella vb to better, to mend, to improve, to recover

gwellau, gwellaif (-eifiau) nm shears

gwellen (gweill) nf knitting-needle

gwellhad nm recovery, improvement

gwellhau vb to better, to improve

gwelliant (-iannau) nm amendment, improvement

gwellt coll n grass; sward; straw

gwelltglas nm grass, greensward

gwelltog adj grassy, green

gwelltyn nm blade of grass; a straw

gwellwell adv better and better

gwen adj f of **gwyn**

gwên (gwenau) nf smile

gwenci (-iod) nf stoat, weasel

gwendid (-au) nm weakness, frailty

Gwener nf Venus; **dydd Gwener** Friday

gwenerol *adj* venereal

gwenfflam *adj* blazing, ablaze

gweniaith *nf* flattery

gwenieithio *vb* to flatter

gwenieithiwr (-wyr) *nm* flatterer

gwenieithus *adj* flattering

gwenith *npl (nf* **-en)** wheat

gwenithfaen *nm* granite

gwennol (gwenoliaid) *nf* swallow, martin; shuttle

gwenu *vb* to smile

gwenwisg (-oedd) *nf* surplice

gwenwyn *nm* poison, venom; jealousy

gwenwynig, gwenwynol *adj* poisonous, venomous

gwenwynllyd *adj* peevish; jealous

gwenwyno *vb* to poison; to fret; to be jealous

gwenyn *npl (nf* **-en)** bees

gwep *nf* visage, grimace

gwêr *nm* tallow, suet *etc*

gwêr *nm* shade

gwerchyr *nm* cover, lid, valve

gwerdd *adj f* of **gwyrdd**

gwerin *coll n* men, people; democracy; crew

gweriniaeth (-au) *nf* democracy; republic; **Gweriniaeth Tsiec** Czech Republic; **Gweriniaeth Iwerddon** Irish Republic

gwerinlywodraeth (-au) *nf* republic

gwerinol *adj* plebeian, vulgar

gwerinos *coll n* rabble, mob

gwerinwr (-wyr) *nm* democrat

gwern¹ (-i, -ydd) *nf* swamp, meadow; alder-grove

gwern² *npl (nf* **-en)** alder-trees

gwerog *adj* tallowy, suety

gwers (-i) *nf* verse; lesson; **gwers yrru** driving lesson

gwerslyfr *nm* textbook

gwersyll (-oedd) *nm* camp, encampment

gwersylla, gwersyllu *vb* to camp; to encamp

gwerth *nm* worth, value; **ar werth** for sale

gwerthfawr *adj* valuable, precious

gwerthfawredd *nm* preciousness

gwerthfawrogi *vb* to appreciate

gwerthfawrogiad *nm* appreciation

gwerthfawrogol *adj* appreciative

gwerthiant *nm* sale

gwerthu *vb* to sell

gwerthwr (-wyr) *nm* seller; **gwerthwr cyffuriau** drug dealer; **gwerthwr eiddo** estate agent

gwerthyd (-au) *nf* spindle, axle

gweryd (-au) *nm* earth, soil; sward ▶ *nf* groin

gweryriad *nm* neighing

gweryru *vb* to neigh

gwestai (-eion) *nm* guest

gwesty (-au, -tai) *nm* inn, hotel

gweu *vb* to weave, to knit

gwewyr *nm* anguish

gwg *nm* frown, scowl; disapproval

gwglo *vb* to google

gwgu *vb* to frown, to scowl, to lower

gwialen (gwiail) *nf* rod, switch

gwialennod (-enodiau) *nf* stroke, stripe

gwialenodio *vb* to beat with a rod

gwib *nf* wandering, jaunt ▶ *adj* wandering

gwibdaith (-deithiau) nf excursion

gwiber (-od) nf viper

gwibio vb to flash, to flit, to dart, to wander

gwibiog adj flitting, darting, wandering

gwiblong (-au) nf cruiser

gwich nf squeak; creak; wheeze, wheezing

gwichiad (-iaid) nm periwinkle

gwichian vb to squeak, to squeal; to creak; to wheeze

gwichlyd adj creaking; wheezy

gwiddon¹ (-od) nf witch

gwiddon² npl mites

gwif (-iau) nm lever, crowbar

gwifren nf wire

gwig (-oedd) nf wood

gwingo vb to wriggle, to fidget; to writhe; to kick, to struggle

gwin (-oedd) nm wine

gwinau adj bay, brown, auburn

gwinc (-od) nf chaffinch

gwinegr nm vinegar

gwinllan (-noedd, -nau) nf vine-yard

gwinllannwr, gwinllanydd nm vine-dresser

gwinwryf (-oedd) nm wine-press

gwinwydd npl vines

gwir adj true ► nm truth

gwireb (-au, -ion) nf truism, axiom

gwireddu vb to verify, to substantiate

gwirfodd nm goodwill; own accord

gwirfoddol adj voluntary, spontaneous

gwirfoddoli vb to volunteer

gwirfoddolwr (-wyr) nm volunteer

gwirio vb to verify

gwirion (-iaid) adj innocent; silly

gwiriondeb nm innocence; silliness

gwirionedd (-au) nm truth, verity, reality

gwirioneddol adj true, real, genuine

gwirioni vb to infatuate, to dote

gwirionyn nm simpleton

gwiriwr (-wyr) nm verifier; **gwiriwr sillafu** spellchecker

gwirod (-ydd) nm liquor, spirits

gwisg (-oedd) nf dress, garment, robe

gwisgi adj brisk, lively, nimble; ripe

gwisgo vb to dress; to wear; to put on

gwisgwr (-wyr) nm wearer

gwiw adj fit, meet; worthy

gwiwer (-od) nf squirrel

gwlad (gwledydd) nf country, land

gwladaidd adj countrified, rustic

Gwlad Belg nf Belgium

gwladfa (-oedd) nf colony, settlement

gwladgar see **gwlatgar**

gwladgarol adj patriotic

gwladgarwch nm patriotism

gwladgarwr (-wyr) nm patriot

gwladol adj of a country, civil, state

gwladoli vb to nationalize

Gwlad Thai nf Thailand

gwladweiniaeth nf statesmanship

gwladweinydd (-ion, -wyr) nm statesman

gwladwr (-wyr) nm countryman, peasant

gwladwriaeth (-au) nf state

gwladwriaethol adj state, political

gwladychfa (-oedd) nf settlement, colony

g

133

gwladychu vb to inhabit, to settle, to colonize; to rule

gwladychwr (-wyr) nm settler, colonist

Gwlad yr Iâ nf Iceland

gwlân (gwlanoedd) nm wool

gwlana vb to gather wool

gwlanen (-ni) nf flannel

gwlanog adj woolly

gwlatgar adj patriotic

gwlaw see glaw

gwledig adj countrified, country, rural

gwledd (-oedd) nf feast, banquet

gwledda vb to feast

gwleddwr (-wyr) nm feaster

gwleidydd (-ion) nm politician, statesman

gwleidyddiaeth nf politics

gwleidyddol adj political

gwleidyddol-gywir adj politically correct

gwleidyddwr (-wyr) nm politician

gwlith (-oedd) nm dew

gwlithen nf slug

gwlitho vb to dew, to bedew

gwlithog adj dewy; inspiring

gwlithyn nm dewdrop

gwlyb (-ion) adj wet, fluid, liquid ▸ nm fluid, liquid

gwlybaniaeth nm wet, moisture

gwlybwr nm wet, moisture, liquid, fluid

gwlybyrog adj wet, damp, rainy

gwlych nm wet; **rhoi yng ngwlych** steep

gwlychu vb to wet, to moisten; to get wet; to dip

gwlydd npl, coll n (nm -yn) haulm

gwn (gynnau) nm gun

gŵn (gynau) nm gown

gwndwn see gwyndwn

gwneud, gwneuthur vb to do, to make; to make up

gwneuthuriad nm make, making

gwneuthurwr (-wyr) nm maker, doer, manufacturer

gwnïad nm sewing, stitching, seam

gwniadur (-iau, on) nmf thimble

gwniadwraig nf stitcher, seamstress

gwniadyddes (-au) nf seamstress

gwnïo vb to sew, to stitch

gwnyddes (-au) nf seamstress

gwobr (-au) nm reward, prize

gwobrwy (-au, -on) nfm reward, prize

gwobrwyo vb to reward

gwobrwywr (-wyr) nm rewarder

gŵr (gwŷr) nm man; husband

gwrach (-ïod, -od) nf hag, witch; **breuddwyd gwrach** wishful thinking

gwrachïaidd adj old-womanish

gwraidd (gwreiddiau) coll n roots

gwraig (gwragedd) nf woman; wife

gwrandaw see gwrando

gwrandawiad nm listening, hearing

gwrandäwr (gwrandawyr) nm listener, hearer

gwrando vb to listen, to hearken

gwrcath (-od) nm tom-cat

gwregys (-au) nm girdle, belt, truss; zone

gwregysu vb to girdle, to gird

gwrêng (gwŷr) nm, coll n (one of the) common people

gwreichion npl (nf **-en**) sparks
gwreichioni vb to emit sparks, to sparkle
gwreiddio vb to root
gwreiddiol adj radical, rooted; original
gwreiddioldeb nm originality
gwreiddyn (**gwreiddiau**) nm root
gwres nm heat, warmth
gwresfesurydd (**-ion**) nm thermometer
gwresog adj warm, hot; fervent
gwresogi vb to warm, to heat
gwresogydd nm heater
gwrhydri nm exploit; valour
gwryd (**-oedd**), **gwryd** nm fathom
gwrhydri nm exploit; valour
gwrid nm blush, flush
gwrido vb to blush, to flush
gwridog, gwritgoch adj rosy-cheeked, ruddy
gwrogaeth nf homage
gwrogi vb to do homage
gwrol adj brave, courageous
gwroldeb nm bravery, courage
gwroli vb to hearten
gwron (**-iaid**) nm hero
gwroniaeth nf heroism
gwrtaith (**-teithiau**) nm manure, fertiliser
gwrteithiad nm cultivation, culture
gwrteithio vb to manure; to cultivate, to culture
gwrth- prefix counter-, contra-, anti-
gwrthban (**-au**) nm blanket
gwrthblaid nf (party in) opposition
gwrthbrofi vb to disprove, to refute

gwrthbwynt nm counterpoint
gwrthdaro vb to clash, to collide
gwrthdrawiad (**-au**) nm collision
gwrth-droi vb to reverse
gwrthdystiad (**-au**) nm protest
gwrthdystio vb to protest
gwrthddadl (**-euon**) nf objection
gwrthddadlau (**-au**) vb to object, to controvert
gwrth-ddweud vb to contradict
gwrthddywediad (**-au**) nm contradiction
gwrthddywedyd vb to contradict
gwrthfiotig nm antibiotic
gwrthgiliad (**-au**) nm backsliding
gwrthgilio vb to backslide, to secede
gwrthgiliwr (**-wr**) nm backslider, seceder
gwrthglawdd (**-gloddiau**) nm rampart
gwrthglocwedd adj anticlockwise
gwrthgyferbyniad (**-au**) nm contrast, antithesis
gwrthgyferbynnu vb to contrast
gwrthnaws nm antipathy ▸ adj repugnant
gwrthnysig adj obstinate, stubborn
gwrthod vb to refuse, to reject
gwrthodedig adj rejected, reprobate
gwrthodiad nm refusal, rejection
gwrthodwr (**-wyr**) nm refuser, rejecter
gwrthol nm, adv back; **ôl a gwrthol** to and fro
gwrthrych (**-au**) nm object; subject (of biography)
gwrthrychol adj objective

g

135

gwrthryfel (-oedd) nm rebellion, mutiny

gwrthryfela vb to rebel

gwrthryfelgar adj rebellious, mutinous

gwrthryfelwr (-wyr) nm rebel, mutineer

gwrthsafiad nm resistance

gwrthsefyll vb to withstand, to resist

gwrthun adj repugnant, odious, absurd

gwrthuni nm odiousness, absurdity

gwrthuno vb to mar, to deform, to disfigure

gwrthweithio vb to counteract

gwrthwenwyn nm antidote

gwrthwyneb nm opposite, contrary

gwrthwynebiad (-au) nm objection

gwrthwynebol adj opposed

gwrthwynebu vb to resist, to oppose

gwrthwynebus adj repugnant; antagonistic

gwrthwynebwr (-wyr), **gwrthwynebydd** nm opponent, adversary

gwrych¹ (-oedd) nm hedge

gwrych² npl, coll n (nm -yn) bristles

gwryd see **gwrhyd**

gwryf (-oedd) nm press

gwrym (-iau) nm seam; wale

gwrysg npl (nf -en) stalks, haulm

gwryw adj male ▸ nm (-od) male

gwrywaidd, gwrywol adj masculine

gwth nm push, thrust, shove; gust

gwthio vb to push, to thrust, to shove

gwthiwr (-wyr) nm pusher

gwyar nm gore, blood

gwybed npl (nm -yn) flies

gwybedyn nm midge

gwybod vb to know ▸ nm (-au) knowledge; **gwybodau** studies

gwybodaeth (-au) nf knowledge

gwybodeg nm epistemology

gwybodus adj knowing, well-informed

gwybyddus adj known, aware of

gwych adj fine, splendid, brilliant

gwychder nm splendour, pomp

gwŷd (gwydiau) nm vice

gwydn adj tough

gwydnwch nm toughness

gwydr (-au) nm glass

gwydraid (-eidiau) nm glassful, glass

gwydro vb to glaze; **gwydro dwbl** double glazing

gwydrwr (-wyr) nm glazier

gwydryn (gwydrau) nm drinking-glass

gwŷdd¹ (gwehyddion, gwyddion) nm loom; plough

gwŷdd² npl (nf gwydden) trees

gwŷdd³ nm presence

gŵydd² (gwyddau) nm goose

gwyddbwyll nf chess

Gwyddel (-od, Gwyddyl) nm Irishman

Gwyddeleg nf Irish language

Gwyddeles (-au) nf Irishwoman

Gwyddelig adj Irish

gwyddfa nf tumulus, grave

gwyddfid nm honeysuckle

gwyddfod nm presence

gwyddoniadur (-on) nm encyclopædia

gwyddoniaeth nf science

gwyddonol adj scientific

gwyddonydd (-wyr) nm scientist

gwyddor (-ion) nf rudiment; science; **yr wyddor** the alphabet

gwyddori vb to instruct, to ground

gwyfyn (-od) nm moth

gwŷg coll n vetch

gwygbysen (gwygbys) nf chickpea

gŵyl¹ adj bashful, modest

gŵyl² (gwyliau) nf holiday, feast, festival

gwylaidd adj bashful, modest

gwylan (-od) nf sea-gull

gwylder nm bashfulness, modesty

gwyleidd-dra nm bashfulness, modesty

gwylfa (-fâu, -feydd) nf watch; lookout

gwyliadwriaeth nfm watchfulness, caution; watch, guard

gwyliadwrus adj watchful, cautious

gwyliedydd (-ion) nm watchman, sentinel

gwylio vb to watch, to mind, to beware

gwyliwr (-wyr) nm watchman, sentinel

gwylmabsant (-au) nf wake

gwylnos (-au) nf watch-night, wake, vigil

gwyll nm darkness, gloom

gwylliad (-iaid) nm robber, bandit

gwyllt adj wild, savage, mad; rapid; **bywyd gwyllt** wildlife

gwylltineb nm wildness; rage, fury

gwylltio, gwylltu vb to frighten; to fly into a passion

gwymon (f **gwen**) nm seaweed

gwyn (f **gwen**) adj white; (of person) White; blessed

gwŷn (gwyniau) nmf ache, smart; lust

gwynder, gwyndra nm whiteness

gwyndwn nm unploughed land

gwyneb see **wyneb**

gwynegon nm rheumatism

gwynegu vb to throb, to ache

gwynfa nf paradise

gwynfyd (-au) nm blessedness, bliss; (pl) beatitudes

gwynfydedig adj blessed, happy, beatific

gwyngalch nm whitewash

gwyngalchog adj whitewashed

gwyngalchu vb to whitewash

gwyniad (-iaid) nm whiting

gwynias adj white-hot

gwyniedyn nm sewin

gwynio vb to throb, to ache

gwynnu vb to whiten, to bleach

gwynnwy nm white of egg

gwynt (-oedd) nm wind; breath; smell

gwyntell (-i) nf round basket without handle

gwyntio vb to smell

gwyntog adj windy

gwyntyll (-au) nf fan

gwyntylliad nm ventilation

gwyntyllio, gwyntyllu vb to ventilate, to winnow

gwŷr see **gŵr**

gŵyr adj crooked, oblique, sloping

gwyrdraws adj perverse

gwyrdro (-ion) nm perversion

g

gwyrdroi _vb_ to pervert, to distort
gwyrdd (-ion) _adj, nm_ green
gwyrddlas _adj_ green, verdant
gwyrddlesni _nm_ verdure
gwyrddni _nm_ greenness
gwyrgam _adj_ crooked
gwyriad _nm_ vowel mutation
gwyrni _nm_ crookedness, perverseness
gwyro _vb_ to swerve; to slope; to stoop; to tilt; to deviate
gwyrth (-iau) _nf_ miracle
gwyrthiol _adj_ miraculous
gwyry, gwyryf (gwyryfon) _nf_ virgin; y Wyryf Virgo
gwyryfdod _nm_ virginity
gwyryfol _adj_ virgin
gwŷs (gwysion) _nf_ summons
gwysio _vb_ to summon
gwystl (-on) _nm_ pledge; hostage
gwystlo _vb_ to pledge, to pawn
gwystno _vb_ to dry, to wither, to flag
gwythïen (gwythi, gwythiennau) _nf_ vein, blood vessel, artery; cwlwm gwythi cramp
gwyw _adj_ withered, faded, sere
gwywo _vb_ to wither, to fade
gyda, gydag _prep_ with
gyddfol _adj_ guttural
gyferbyn _prep_ over against, opposite
gylfin (-od) _nm_ bill, beak
gylfinir _nm_ curlew
gynfad (-au) _nm_ gunboat
gynnau _adv_ a little while ago, just now
gynt _adv_ formerly, of yore
gyr (-roedd) _nm_ drove

gyrfa (-oedd, -feydd) _nf_ race; course; career
gyrfaol _adj_ vocational
gyriant (gyriannau) _nm_ drive; gyriant disg disk drive
gyriedydd (-ion) _nm_ driver
gyrru _vb_ to drive; to send; to work, to forge; gyrru tra'n feddw drink-driving
gyrrwr (gyrwyr) _nm_ driver; sender
gyrwynt (-oedd) _nm_ hurricane, tornado

h

ha *excl* ha

hac (-iau) *nf* cut, notch, hack

hacio *vb* to hack

haciwr (-wyr) *nm* hacker

had (-au) *nm, coll n (nm* **hedyn)** seed

hadlif *nm* seminal fluid

hadog *nm* haddock

hadu *vb* to seed

hadyd *coll n* seed-corn

haearn (heyrn) *nm* iron; **haearn bwrw** cast iron; **haearn gyr** wrought iron

haearnaidd *adj* like iron

haeddiannol *adj* meritorious; merited

haeddiant (-iannau) *nm* merit, desert

haeddu *vb* to deserve, to merit

hael *adj* generous, liberal

haelfrydedd *nm* liberality

haelfrydig *adj* generous, free

haelioni *nm* generosity

haelionus *adj* generous, liberal

haen (-au) *nf* layer, stratum; seam; **haen osôn** ozone layer

haenen (-nau) *nf* layer, film

haenu *vb* to stratify

haeriad (-au) *nm* assertion

haerllug *adj* importunate; impudent

haerllugrwydd *nm* importunity; impudence

haeru *vb* to affirm, to assert

haf (-au) *nm* summer

hafaidd *adj* summer-like, summery

hafal *adj* like, equal

hafaliad *nm* equation

hafan *nf* haven

hafn (-au) *nf* hollow, gorge, ravine

hafod (-ydd) *nf* summer dwelling, upland farm

hafog *nm* havoc

hafoty (-tai) *nm* summer residence

hagr *adj* ugly

hagru *vb* to mar, to disfigure

hagrwch *nm* ugliness

haid (heidiau) *nf* swarm, drove, horde

haidd (heiddiau) *nm, coll n (nf* **heidden)** barley

haig (heigiau) *nf* shoal

haint (heintiau) *nmf* pestilence; faint

hala *vb* to send, to spend

halen *nm* salt, brine

halog, halogedig *adj* defiled, polluted

halogi *vb* to defile, to profane, to pollute

halogrwydd *nm* defilement, pollution

halogwr (-wyr) *nm* defiler, profaner

hallt *adj* salt, salty; severe
halltedd, halltrwydd *nm* saltness, saltiness
halltu *vb* to salt
halltwr (-wyr) *nm* salter
hambwrdd (-byrddau) *nm* tray
hamdden *nf* leisure, respite
hamddenol *adj* leisurely
hanerob (-au) *nf* flitch of bacon
haneru *vb* to halve
hanes (-ion) *nm* history, story, account
hanesydd (-wyr) *nm* historian
hanesyddol *adj* historical
hanesyn (-nau) *nm* anecdote
hanfod *vb* to descend from, to issue ▸ *nm* essence
hanfodion *npl* essentials
hanfodol *adj* essential
haniad *nm* derivation, descent
haniaeth *nf* abstraction
haniaethol *adj* abstract
hanner (hanerau, haneri) *nm, adj, adv* half; **hanner ffordd (i)** halfway (to); **hanner pris** half fare; **hanner tymor** half term
hanner-sgim *adj* semi-skimmed
hanu *vb* to proceed, to be derived, to be descended
hap *nf* luck
hapchwarae *nm* lottery
hapus *adj* happy
hapusrwydd *nm* happiness
hardd *adj* beautiful, handsome
harddu *vb* to beautify, to embellish, to adorn
harddwch *nm* beauty
harnais (-eisiau) *nm* harness
harneisio *vb* to harness

hatling (-au, -od) *nf* mite, half a farthing
hau *vb* to sow, to disseminate
haul (heuliau) *nm* sun
hawdd *adj* easy; **hawdd ei drin** user-friendly
hawddamor *nm, excl* good luck, welcome
hawddfyd *nm* ease, prosperity
hawddgar *adj* amiable; comely
hawddgarwch *nm* amiability
hawl (-iau) *nf* claim; right; **hawl ac ateb** question and answer
hawlfraint *nf* title; copyright
hawlio *vb* to claim, to demand
hawlydd (-ion) *nm* claimant, plaintiff
haws *adj* easier
heb *prep* without; **heb afael** hands-free
heblaw *prep* beside(s)
hebog (-au) *nm* hawk, falcon
Hebraeg *nf, adj* Hebrew *(language)*
Hebreaidd, Hebreig *adj* Hebrew, Hebraic
Hebrees (-au) *nf* Hebrew woman
Hebreigydd (-ion) *nm* Hebraist
Hebrëwr (-wyr) *nm* a Hebrew
hebrwng *vb* to accompany, to conduct, to convey, to escort
hebryngydd (-ion) *nm* conductor, guide
hedeg *vb* to fly; to run to seed
hedegog *adj* flying; high-flown
hedfa (-feydd) *nf* flight
hedfan *vb* to fly, to hover
hedydd (-ion) *nm* lark
hedyn (hadau) *nm* seed, germ
hedd *nm* peace, tranquillity

heddgeidwad (-waid) *nm* police officer

heddiw *adv* today

heddlu *nm* police force

heddwas (-weision) *nm* police officer

heddwch *nm* peace, quiet, tranquillity

heddychiaeth *nf* pacifism

heddychlon *adj* peaceful, peaceable

heddychol *adj* peaceable, pacific

heddychu *vb* to pacify, to appease

heddychwr (-wyr) *nm* pacifist, peace-maker

heddyw *see* **heddiw**

hefelydd *adj* similar

hefyd *adv* also, besides

heffer (heffrod) *nf* heifer

hegl (-au) *nf* leg, shank

heglog *adj* leggy, long-legged

heglu *vb* to foot it

heibio *adv* past

heidio *vb* to swarm, to throng, to flock

heidden *nf* grain of barley

heigio *vb* to shoal, to teem

heini *adj* active, lively, nimble, brisk

heintio *vb* to infect

heintus *adj* infectious, contagious

heislan (-od) *nf* hackle

heislanu *vb* to hackle flax

hel *vb* to gather, to collect; to drive, to chase

hela *vb* to hunt, to spend *(money, time)*; **cŵn hela** hounds

helaeth *adj* ample, abundant, extensive

helaethrwydd *nm* abundance

helaethu *vb* to enlarge, to extend, to amplify

helaethwych *adj* sumptuous

helbul (-on) *nm* trouble

helbulus *adj* troubled, troublous

helcyd *vb* to hunt ▸ *nm* worry, trouble

helfa (-fâu, -feydd) *nf* hunt, catch

helfarch (-feirch) *nm* hunter *(horse)*

helgi (-gwn) *nm* hound

heli *nm* salt water, brine

heliwr (-wyr) *nm* hunter, huntsman

helm (-au) *nf* helm, helmet, stack

help *nm* help, aid, assistance

helpio, helpu *vb* to help, to aid, to assist

helwriaeth *nf* game, hunting; chase

helyg *npl (nf-en)* willows

helynt (-ion) *nf* trouble, fuss, bother, hassle

helltni *nm* saltiness, saltness

hem¹ *nm* rivet

hem² (-iau) *nf* hem, border

hen *adj* old, aged, ancient, of old

henadur (-iaid) *nm* alderman

henaduriad (-iaid) *nm* Presbyterian, elder

henaduriaeth (-au) *nf* presbytery

henaint *nm* old age

hendaid (-deidiau) *nm* great-grandfather

hender *nm* oldness

hendref (-i, -ydd) *nf* winter dwelling, lowland farm

heneb (-ion) *nf* ancient monument

heneiddio *vb* to grow old, to age

henfam *nf* grandmother

henffasiwn *adj* old-fashioned

141

hennain (heneiniau) *nf* great-grandmother
heno *adv* tonight
henoed *coll n* elderly people
henuriad (-iaid) *nm* elder, presbyter
heol (-ydd) *nf* road
hepgor *vb* to spare, to dispense with ▸ *nm* (**-ion**) what may be dispensed with
hepian *vb* to slumber, to doze
her (-iau) *nf* challenge
herc (-iau) *nf* hop; limp
hercian *vb* to hop, to hobble, to limp
heresi (-iau) *nf* heresy
heretic (-iaid) *nm* heretic
hereticaidd *adj* heretical
herfeiddio *vb* to dare, to brave, to defy
herfeiddiol *adj* daring, defiant
hergwd *nm* push, thrust, shove
hergydio *vb* to bump
herio *vb* to challenge, to dare, to brave, to defy
heroin *nm* heroin
herw *nm* raid; outlawry
herwa *vb* to scout, to prowl, to raid
herwgipio *vb* to kidnap
herwgipiwr (-wyr) *nm* kidnapper; hijacker
herwhela *vb* to poach (game)
herwr (-wyr) *nm* scout, raider; outlaw
herwydd *see* oherwydd
hesb *adj f of* hysb
hesben (-nau) *nf* hasp
hesbin (-od) *nf* yearling ewe
hesbio *vb* to dry up
hesbwrn (-yrniaid) *nm* young ram

hesg *npl* (*nf* **-en**) sedge, rushes
het (-iau) *nf* hat
heulo *vb* to shine (as the sun); to sun
heulog *adj* sunny
heulwen *nf* sunshine
heuwr (-wyr) *nm* sower
hi *pron* she, her; it
hidio *vb* to heed
hidl¹ *adj*: **wylo yn hidl** weep abundantly
hidl² (-au) *nf* strainer, sieve
hidlen (-ni) *nf* strainer, sieve
hidlo *vb* to distil, to run; to strain, to filter
hidlydd *nm* filter
hil *nf* race, lineage, posterity
hiliaeth *nf* racism
hilio *vb* to bring forth, to teem, to breed
hiliogaeth *nf* offspring, issue, posterity
hiliol *adj* racist
hiliwr (-wyr) *nm* racist
hilydd (-ion) *nm* racist
hilyddiaeth *nf* racism
hin *nf* weather
Hindŵ (-iaid) *nm* Hindu
hinfynegydd (-ion) *nm* barometer
hiniog (-au) *nf* threshold, door-frame
hinon *nf* fair weather
hinsawdd (-soddau) *nf* climate
hinsoddol *adj* climatic
hir (hirion) *adj, prefix* long
hiraeth *nm* longing, nostalgia, grief; homesickness
hiraethu *vb* to long, to yearn, to sorrow
hiraethus *adj* longing; homesick

hirbell adj: o hirbell from afar
hirben adj long-headed, shrewd
hirymaros nm long-suffering
hirymarhous adj long-suffering
hirhoedledd nm longevity
hirhoedlog adj long-lived
hithau pron she (on her part), she also
HIV n HIV; **HIV negyddol/positif** HIV negative/positive
hobaid (-eidiau) nf peck
hobi (hobïau) nm hobby
hoced (-ion) nf deceit, fraud
hocedu vb to cheat, to deceive, to defraud
hocedwr (-wyr) nm cheat, fraud
hoci nm hockey
hocys npl mallows
hodi vb to shoot, to ear, to run to seed
hoe nf spell, rest
hoeden (-nau) nf hoyden
hoedl (-au) nf lifetime, life
hoel, hoelen (hoelion) nf nail
hoelio vb to nail
hoeliwr (-wyr) nm nailer
hoen nf joy, gladness; vigour
hoenus adj joyous, blithesome, gay
hoenusrwydd nm liveliness, sprightliness
hoenyn (-nau) nm snare
hoew see hoyw
hofran vb to hover
hofrennydd nm helicopter
hoff adj dear, fond; favourite
hoffi vb to like, to love
hoffter nm fondness; delight
hoffus adj lovable, amiable, affectionate
hogen (-nod) nf girl

hogennaidd adj girlish
hogfaen (-feini) nm whetstone, hone
hogi vb to sharpen, to whet
hogyn (hogiau) nm boy, lad
hongiad (-au) nm suspension
hongian vb to hang, to dangle
holgar adj inquisitive, curious
holi vb to ask, to question, to inquire
holiad (-au) nm interrogation, question
holiadur (-on) nm questionnaire
holwr (-wyr) nm questioner, interrogator; catechist, question-master
holwyddoreg (-au) nf catechism
holwyddori vb to catechize
holl adj all, whole
hollalluog adj almighty, omnipotent
hollalluowgrwydd nm omnipotence
hollbresennol adj omnipresent
hollbresenoldeb nm omnipresence
hollfyd nm universe
hollgyfoethog adj almighty
holliach adj whole, sound
hollol adj quite
hollt (-au) nf split, slit, cleft
hollti vb to split, to cleave, to slit
hollwybodaeth nf omniscience
hollwybodol adj omniscient
homeopatheg nf homeopathy
homili (-ïau) nf homily
hon pron f of hwn
honcian vb to waggle; to jolt; to limp
honedig adj alleged

143

honiad (**-au**) *nm* claim, assertion, allegation

honni *vb* to assert, to allege, to profess, to pretend

honno *pron f* of **hwnnw**

hopran (**-au**) *nf* mill-hopper; mouth

hosan (**-au**) *nf* stocking

hoyw *adj* alert, sprightly, lively, gay

hoywdeb, hoywder *nm* sprightliness

hoywi *vb* to brighten, to smarten

hual (**-au**) *nm* fetter, shackle

hualu *vb* to fetter, to shackle

huan *nf* the sun

huawdl *adj* eloquent

hud *nm* magic, illusion, charm, enchantment

hudlath (**-au**) *nf* magic wand

hudo *vb* to charm, to allure, to beguile

hudol *adj* enchanting ► *nm* (**-ion**) enchanter

hudoles (**-au**) *nf* enchantress, sorceress

hudoliaeth (**-au**) *nf* enchantment, allurement

hudolus *adj* enchanting, alluring

hudwr (**-wyr**) *nm* enticer, allurer

huddygl *nm* soot

hufen *nm* cream; **hufen iâ** ice cream

hufennog *adj* creamy

hugan (**-au**) *nf* cloak, covering; rug

hulio *vb* to cover, to spread

hun[1] (**-au**) *nf* sleep, slumber

hun[2] *pron* self; **ei dŷ ei hun** his own house

hunan (**-ain**) *pron* self ► *prefix* self-

hunan-dyb *nm* self-conceit

hunangar *adj* selfish

hunanhyderus *adj* self-confident

hunaniaeth *nf* identity

hunanladdiad *nm* self-murder, suicide

hunanol *adj* selfish, conceited

hunanoldeb *nm* selfishness; conceit

hunanymwadiad *nm* self-denial

hunanymwadu *vb* to deny oneself

hunanysgogol *adj* automatic

hunell (**-au**) *nf* wink (of sleep)

hunllef (**-au**) *nf* nightmare

huno *vb* to sleep

huodledd *nm* eloquence

hur (**-iau**) *nm* hire, wage

hurbwrcas *nm* hire purchase

hurio *vb* to hire

huriwr (**-wyr**) *nm* hirer; hireling

hurt *adj* stunned, stupid

hurtio *vb* to stun, to stupefy

hurtrwydd *nm* stupidity

hurtyn (**-nod**) *nm* stupid, blockhead

hwb (**hybiau**) *nm* push; effort; lift

hwde (**hwdiwch**) *vb imper* take, accept

hwdi (**-s**) *nm* hoodie

Hwngari *nf* Hungary

hwiangerdd *nf* lullaby

hwn (*f* **hon**) *adj, pron* this (one)

hwnnw (*f* **honno**) *adj, pron* that one (absent)

hwnt *adv* beyond, away, aside; **tu hwnt** beyond

hwp *nm* push

hwpio, hwpo *vb* to push

hwrdd[1] (**hyrddod**) *nm* ram; **yr Hwrdd** Aries

hwrdd² (**hyrddiau**) *nm* impulse, stroke

hwre *vb see* **hwde**

hwsmon (**-myn**) *nm* farm-bailiff

hwtio *vb* to hoot, to hiss

hwy *pron* they, them

hwyad, hwyaden (**hwyaid**) *nf* duck

hwyhau *vb* to lengthen, to elongate

hwyl! *excl* bye!

hwyl (**-iau**) *nf* sail; humour; religious fervour

hwylbren (**-nau, -ni**) *nm* mast

hwylio *vb* to sail; to prepare, to order

hwyliog *adj* fervent, eloquent

hwylus *adj* easy, convenient, comfortable

hwyluso *vb* to facilitate

hwylustod *nm* ease, facility, convenience

hwynt *pron* them, they

hwynt-hwy *pron* they, they themselves

hwyr *adj* late ▸ *nm* evening

hwyrach *adv* perhaps ▸ *adj* later

hwyrdrwm *adj* sluggish, drowsy, dull

hwyrfrydig *adj* slow, tardy, reluctant

hwyrfrydigrwydd *nm* tardiness, reluctance

hwyrol *adj* evening

hwyrhau *vb* to get late

hwythau *pron* they (on their part), they also

hy *adj* bold

hybarch *adj* venerable

hyblyg *adj* flexible, pliant, pliable

hyblygrwydd *nm* flexibility, pliancy

hybu *vb* to improve in health; to promote

hyd (**-au, -oedd**) *nm* length ▸ *prep* to, till, as far as

hydawdd *adj* soluble

hydeiml *adj* sensitive

hyder *nm* confidence, trust

hyderu *vb* to confide, to rely, to trust

hyderus *adj* confident

hydred (**-ion**) *nm* longitude

hydredol *adj* longitudinal

hydref (**-au**) *nm* autumn; **Hydref** October

hydrefol *adj* autumnal

hydrin *adj* tractable, docile

hydwyll *adj* gullible

hydwylledd *nm* gullibility

hydwyth *adj* supple, elastic

hydwythedd *nm* elasticity

hydyn *adj* tractable, docile

hydd (**-od**) *nm* stag

hyddysg *adj* well versed, learned

hyf *see* **hy**

hyfder, hyfdra *nm* boldness

hyfedr *adj* expert, skilful, clever

hyfryd *adj* pleasant, delightful, agreeable

hyfrydu *vb* to delight

hyfrydwch *nm* delight, pleasure

hyfwyn *adj* kindly, genial

hyfforddedig *adj* trainee

hyfforddi *vb* to direct, to instruct, to train

hyfforddiadol *adj* training

hyfforddiant *nm* instruction, training; **cwrs hyfforddiant** training course

hyfforddwr (-wyr) nm guide, instructor; **hyfforddwr gyrru** driving instructor

hygar adj amiable

hygarwch nm amiability

hyglod adj celebrated, renowned, famous

hyglwyf adj vulnerable

hyglyw adj audible

hygoel adj credible

hygoeledd nm credibility; credulity

hygoelus adj credulous, gullible

hygyrch adj accessible

hyhi pron she, her; herself

hylaw adj handy, convenient; dexterous

hylif (-au) nm, adj fluid, liquid

hylifydd nm liquidizer

hylithr adj slippery, fluent

hylosg adj combustible, inflammable

hylwydd adj prosperous

hyll adj ugly, hideous

hylltra nm ugliness

hyllu vb to mar, to disfigure

hyn adj, pron this; these; that

hynafgwr (-gwyr) nm old man, elder

hynafiad (-iaid) nm ancestor

hynafiaeth (-au) nf antiquity

hynafiaethol adj antiquarian

hynafiaethwr (-wyr), hynafiaethydd nm antiquary

hynafol adj ancient

hynaws adj kind, genial

hynawsedd nm kindness, geniality

hynny adj, pron that; those

hynod adj noted, notable, remarkable

hynodi vb to distinguish, to characterize

hynodion npl peculiarities

hynodrwydd nm peculiarity

hynt (-iau, -oedd) nf way, course

hyrddio, hyrddu vb to hurl, to impel

hyrddwynt (-oedd) nm hurricane

hyrwyddiad nm promotion

hyrwyddo vb to facilitate, to promote

hyrwyddwr (-wyr) nm sponsor, promoter

hysb (f hesb) adj dry, barren

hysbio vb to dry

hysbyddu vb to exhaust, to drain

hysbys adj known, evident; **dyn hysbys** wise man, sorcerer; **tra hysbys** well-known

hysbyseb (-ion) nf advertisement

hysbysebu vb to advertise

hysbysebwr (-wyr) nm advertiser

hysbysfwrdd nm noticeboard

hysbysiad (-au) nm announcement, advertisement

hysbyslen nf prospectus

hysbysrwydd nm information

hysbysu vb to inform, to announce

hysbyswr (-wyr) nm informant, informer

hysian, hysio vb to hiss; to set on, to incite

hytrach adv rather

hywaith adj industrious, dexterous

hywedd adj trained, tractable

i¹ *prep* to, into
i² *pron* I, me
iâ *nm* ice
iach *adj* healthy, well
iachâd *nm* healing
iachaol *adj* therapeutic
iacháu *vb* to heal; to save
iachawdwr (-wyr) *nm* saviour
iachawdwriaeth *nf* salvation
iachäwr (iachawyr) *nm* healer
iachus, iachol *adj* healthy,
healthful, wholesome
iachusol *adj* wholesome
iad (-au) *nf* pate, cranium
iaith (ieithoedd) *nf* language; **yr**
iaith fain English
iâr (ieir) *nf* hen
iard (ierdydd) *nf* yard
iarll (ieirll) *nm* earl
iarllaeth (-au) *nf* earldom
iarlles (-au) *nf* countess
ias (-au) *nf* shiver; thrill
iasol *adj* weird

Iau *nm* Jupiter; **dydd Iau** Thursday
iau¹ (ieuau) *nm* liver
iau² (ieuau, ieuoedd) *nf* yoke
iawn *adj* right ▸ *nm* right;
atonement ▸ *adv* very; **yn iawn**
all right
iawndal *nm* compensation
iawnder (-au) *nm* right, equity
iawnol *adj* atoning, expiatory
idealaeth *nf* idealism
ideoleg (-au) *nf* ideology
idiom (-au) *nf* idiom
Iddew (-on) *nm* Jew
Iddewes (-au) *nf* Jewish woman
Iddewiaeth *nf* Judaism
Iddewig *adj* Jewish
iddwf *nm*: **tân iddwf** erysipelas
ie *adv* yes, yea
iechyd *nm* health
iechydaeth *nf* hygiene, sanitation
iechydol *adj* hygienic, sanitary
iechydwriaeth *nf* salvation
ieitheg *nf* philology
ieithegydd (-ion, -wyr) *nm*
philologist
ieithwedd (-au, -ion) *nf* diction,
(literary) style
ieithydd (-ion) *nm* linguist
ieithyddiaeth *nf* linguistics,
philology
ieithyddol *adj* linguistic,
philological
Iesu *nm* Jesus
iet (-au, -iau) *nf* gate
ieuanc (-ainc) *adj* young
ieuenctid *nm* youth
ieuo *vb* to yoke
ifanc (-ainc) *adj* young
ifori *nm* ivory
ig (-ion) *nm* hiccup

igam-ogam *adj* zigzag

igian *vb* to hiccup

ing (-oedd) *nm* agony, anguish

ingol *adj* agonizing, agonized

ildio *vb* to give in, to give way

ill *pron* they; **ill dau** they both

impio *vb* to sprout, to shoot; to bud, to graft

impyn *nm* graft; scion

inc *nm* ink

incil (-iau) *nm* tape

incio *vb* to ink

incwm *nm* income

India *nf* India

India'r Gorllewin *npl* West Indies

Indonesia *nf* Indonesia

iod *nm* iota, jot

ioga *nmf* yoga

Iôn *nm* the Lord

Ionawr *nm* January

Iôr *nm* the Lord

Iorddonen *nf* Jordan

iorwg *nm* ivy

ir *adj* fresh, green, raw

irai *nm* ox-goad

iraid (ireidiau) *nm* grease

iraidd *adj* fresh, succulent, luxuriant

Iran *nf* Iran

Iraq *nf* Iraq

irder *nm* freshness, greenness

ireidd-dra *nm* freshness, vigour

ireiddio *vb* to freshen

iriad (-au) *nm* lubrication, greasing

iro *vb* to grease, to smear, to rub, to anoint

irwr (-wyr) *nm* greaser

is *adj* inferior, lower ▸ *prep* below, under ▸ *prefix* under-, sub-, vice-

isadran (-nau) *nf* subsection

Isalmaen *nf* Holland

is-deitl (-au) *nm* subtitle

isel *adj* low; base; humble; depressed

iselder (-au) *nm* lowness, depth; depression

iseldir (-oedd) *nm* lowland

Iseldiroedd *npl*: **yr Iseldiroedd** the Netherlands

iselfryd *adj* humble-minded

iselfrydedd *nm* humility, condescension

iselhau *vb* to lower, to abase, to degrade

isel-ysbryd *adj* despondent

isetholiad (-au) *nm* by-election

isffordd *nf* subway

is-gadeirydd *nm* vice-chairman

is-ganghellor *nm* vice-chancellor

is-gapten (-iaid, -einiaid) *nm* lieutenant

isgell *nm* broth, stock

isiarll (-ieirll) *nm* viscount

islais *nm* undertone

Islâm *nf* Islam

Islamaidd *adj* Islamic

islaw *prep* below, beneath

islawr *nm* basement

isod *adv* below, beneath

isop *nm* hyssop

isosod *vb* to sublet

isradd (-iaid) *nm* inferior, subordinate

israddol *adj* inferior

israddoldeb *nm* inferiority

Israel *nf* Israel

iswasanaethgar *adj* subservient

isymwybod *nm* subconscious

isymwybyddiaeth *nf* subconsciousness

ithfaen *nm* granite
Iwerddon *nf* Ireland
Iwerddon Rydd *nf* Eire
Iwerydd *nm*: **yr Iwerydd** the Atlantic (Ocean)
Iwganda *nf* Uganda
iwrch (iyrchod) *nm* roebuck

j

jac codi baw *nm* JCB
jac-y-do *nm* jackdaw
jam *nm* jam
Jamaica *nf* Jamaica
jamio *vb* to preserve
jar (-iau) *nf* jar, hot water bottle
jel *n* gel
jersi (-s) *nf* jersey
jest *adv* just, almost
jeti (-iau) *nm* jetty
jetlif *nm* jet stream
jet-sgi (-sgïau) *nf* jet-ski
jet-sgïo *vb* to jet-ski
ji-binc (-od) *nf* chaffinch
jîns *npl* jeans
job (-sys) *nf* job
jobyn *nm* job
jôc *nf* joke
jocan *vb* to joke
joci (-s) *nm* jockey
jwg (jygiau) *nf* jug
jyngl (-oedd) *nm* jungle

l

label (-i) *nf* label
labelu *vb* to label
labordy (-dai) *nm* laboratory
labro *vb* to labour
labrwr (-wyr) *nm* labourer
lafant *nm* lavender
lamp (-au) *nf* lamp
lamplen (-ni) *nf* lampshade
lansio *vb* to launch
lapio *vb* to lap, to wrap
larwm *nmf* alarm; **larwm lladron**
burglar alarm; **larwm mwg,
larwm fwg** smoke alarm
laser (-au, -i) *nm* laser
lawnt (-iau) *nf* lawn
lawrlwytho *vb* to download
lefain *nm* leaven
lefeinio *vb* to leaven
lefeinllyd *adj* leavened
lefel (-au) *nf* level; **Lefel A** A level
leicio *vb* to like
lein (-iau) *nf* clothes line; line-out
(rugby)

lesbiad (-iaid) *nf* lesbian
lesbiaidd *adj* lesbian
letys *npl* (*nf* **-en**) lettuce
Libanus *nf* Lebanon
libart *nm* back-yard
Libya *nf* Libya
lifrai *nmf* livery
lifft (-iau) *nm* lift
lili *nf* lily
limwsîn (-s, -au) *nm* limousine
lindys *npl* (*nm* **-yn**) caterpillars
locust (-iaid) *nm* locust
lodes *nf* girl, lass
loetran *vb* to loiter
lol *nf* nonsense
lolfa (-feydd) *nf* lounge, sitting
room; **lolfa ymadael** departure
lounge
lolian *vb* to talk nonsense
lôn (lonydd) *nf* lane
loncian *vb* to jog
lonciwr (-wyr) *nm* jogger
lori (-ïau) *nf* lorry
losin *npl* (*nf* **-en**) sweets
lot (-iau) *nf* lot
Luxembourg *nf* Luxembourg
lŵans, lwfans *nm* allowance
lwc *nf* luck
lwcus *adj* lucky
lwmp (lympiau) *nm* lump

llabed (**-au**) nf lappet, lapel, flap
llabwst (**-ystiau**) nm lubber, lout
llabyddio vb to stone
llac adj slack, loose, lax
llacio vb to slacken, to loosen, to relax
llacrwydd nm slackness, laxity
llacs nm mud, dirt
llacsog adj muddy, dirty
llach (**-iau**) nf lash, slash
llachar adj bright, brilliant, flashing
llachio vb to lash, to slash
Lladin nf Latin
lladmerydd (**-ion**) nm interpreter
lladrad (**-au**) nm theft, robbery
lladradaidd adj stealthy, furtive
lladrata vb to thieve, to steal
lladron see **lleidr**
lladrones (**-au**) nf female thief
lladronllyd adj thievish, pilfering
lladd vb to cut; to kill, to slay, to slaughter
lladd-dy (**-dai**) nm slaughter-house

lladdedig (**-ion**) adj killed, slain
lladdwr (**-wyr**) nm killer, slayer
llaes adj long, loose; **treiglad llaes** spirant mutation
llaesod, llaesodr nf litter (for animals)
llaesu vb to slacken, to loosen, to relax, to droop, to flag
llaeth nm milk
llaetha vb to yield milk
llaethdy (**-dai**) nm milk-house, dairy
llaethog adj rich in milk; milky
llafar nm utterance, speech ▸ adj vocal; loud
llafariad (**-iaid**) nf vowel
llafn (**-au**) nm blade
llafrwyn npl (nf-**en**) bulrushes
llafur (**-iau**) nm labour; corn
llafurfawr adj elaborate; laborious
llafurio vb to labour, to toil; to till
llafurlu (**-oedd**) nm manpower, labour force, workforce
llafurus adj laborious, toilsome, painstaking
llafurwr (**-wyr**) nm labourer, husbandman
llai adj smaller
llaid nm mud, mire
llain (**lleiniau**) nf patch, piece, narrow strip
llais (**lleisiau**) nm voice, vote
llaith adj damp, moist
llall (**lleill**) pron other, another
llam (**-au**) nm stride, leap, jump, bound
llamhidydd (**llamidyddion**) nm porpoise
llamsachus adj prancing, frisky
llamu vb to stride, to leap, to bound

llan (-nau) nf church; village

llanast, llanastr nm confusion, mess

llanc (-iau) nm young man, youth, lad

llances (-au, -i) nf young woman, lass

llannerch (llennyrch), llanerchau (-i, -ydd) nf spot, patch, glade

llanw nm flow (of tide) ▸ vb to flow, to fill

llaprwth nm lout

llariaidd adj mild, meek, gentle

llarieidd-dra nf meekness, gentleness

llarieiddio vb to soothe, to mollify

llarp (-iau) nf shred, clout

llarpio vb to rend, to tear, to mangle, to maul

llarpiog adj tattered, ragged

llaswyr (-au) nm psalter

llath (-au) nf yard; wand

llathen (-ni) nf yard

llathr adj bright, glossy, smooth

llathraidd adj smooth; of fine growth

llathru vb to polish

llau npl (nf lleuen) lice

llaw (dwylaw, dwylo) nf hand

llawcio vb to gulp, to gorge, to gobble

llawchwith adj left-handed

llawdde adj dexterous

llawddryll (-iau) nm pistol, revolver

llawen adj merry, joyful, glad, cheerful

llawenhau vb to rejoice, to gladden

llawenychu vb to rejoice

llawenydd nm joy, gladness, mirth

llawer (-oedd) nm, adj, adv many, much

llawes (llewys) nf sleeve

llawfaeth adj reared by hand

llawfeddyg (-on) nm surgeon

llawfeddygaeth nf surgery

llawfeddygol adj surgical

llaw-fer nf shorthand

llawfom (-iau) nf grenade

llawforwyn (-forynion) nf handmaid

llawlyfr nm manual

llawn adj full ▸ adv quite

llawnder, llawndra nm fullness, abundance

llawr (lloriau) nm floor, ground, earth

llawrydd adj freelance

llawryf (-oedd) nm laurel, bay

llawryfog, llawryfol adj laureate

llawysgrif (-au) nf manuscript

llawysgrifen nf handwriting

lle (-oedd, llefydd) nm place

lecyn (-nau) nm place, spot

llech (-au, -i) nf slab, flag, slate

llechen nf tablet

llechgi (-gwn) nm sneak

llechres (-i) nf table, catalogue, list

llechu vb to hide, to shelter; to lurk, to skulk

llechwedd (-au, -i) nf slope, hillside

llechwraidd adj stealthy, underhand, insidious

lled¹ (-au) nm breadth, width

lled² adv partly, rather

lledaenu vb to spread, to disseminate, to circulate

lleden (lledod) nf flat-fish

llediaith nf foreign accent

llednais adj modest, delicate; meek

llednant (-nentydd) nf tributary

lledneisrwydd nm modesty, delicacy

lled-orwedd vb to recline, to lounge, to loll

lledr (-au) nm leather; **lledr y gwefusau** gums

lledred (-ion) nm latitude

lledrith nm magic, illusion, phantasm

lledrithio vb to appear, to haunt

lledrithiol adj illusory, illusive

lledrwr (-wyr) nm leather-merchant

lledryw adj degenerate

lledu vb to widen, to broaden, to expand, to spread

lleddf adj slanting; flat, minor; plaintive

lleddfol adj sedative

lleddfolyn (-olion) nm sedative

lleddfu vb to flatten; to soften, to soothe, to allay

llef (-au) nf voice, cry

llefain vb to cry

llefareg nf speech training

llefaru vb to speak, to utter

llefarwr (llefarwyr), llefarydd (-ion) nm speaker

lleferydd nmf utterance, voice, speech

llefn adj of llyfn

llefrith nm sweet milk, new milk, milk

llegach adj weak, feeble, infirm, decrepit

lleng (-oedd) nf legion

lleiaf adj least, smallest

lleiafrif (-au) nm minority

lleiafswm nm minimum

lleian (-od) nf nun

lleiandy (-dai) nm nunnery, convent

lleibio vb to lap, to lick

lleidiog adj miry

lleidr (lladron) nm thief, robber

lleiddiad (-iaid) nm assassin

lleihad nm diminution, decrease

lleihau vb to lessen, to diminish, to decrease

lleill see **llall**

lleisio vb to sound, to utter, to voice

lleisiol adj vocal

lleisiwr (-wyr) nm vocalist

lleithder, lleithdra nm damp, moisture

lleithig nf couch; footstool

lleitho vb to damp, to moisten

llem adj of **llym**

llen (-ni) nf sheet; veil, curtain

llên nf literature, lore, learning

llencyn nm literary man

llencyndod nm adolescence

llengar adj literary, learned

llengig nf diaphragm, midriff; **tor llengig** rupture

llên-ladrad (-au) nm plagiarism

llenor (-ion) nm literary man

llenwi vb to fill; to fill in; to flow in

llenydda vb to practise literature

llenyddiaeth (-au) nf literature

llenyddol adj literary

lleol adj local

lleoli vb to locate; to localize

lleoliad nm location; localization

llercian vb to lurk, to loiter

lles nm benefit, profit, good, advantage; **y wladwriaeth les** the welfare state

llesâd *nm* advantage, profit, benefit

llesáu *vb* to benefit, to advantage

llesg *adj* feeble, faint; languid, sluggish

llesgâu *vb* to weaken, to languish, to faint

llesgedd *nm* weakness, languor, debility

llesmair (-meiriau) *nm* faint, swoon

llesmeirio *vb* to faint, to swoon

llesmeiriol *adj* faint

llesol *adj* advantageous, profitable, beneficial

llestair, llesteirio *vb* to hinder, to impede, to baulk

llestr (-i) *nm* vessel

llesyddiaeth *nf* utilitarianism

lletbai *adj* askew, awry; oblique

lletchwith *adj* awkward, clumsy

lletem (-au) *nf* wedge, stud, rivet

lletraws *adj* diagonal

lletwad (-au) *nf* ladle

llety (-au) *nm* lodging(s)

lletya *vb* to lodge

lletygar *adj* hospitable

lletygarwch *nm* hospitality

lletywr (-wyr) *nm* lodger; host

lletywraig (-wragedd) *nf* landlady

llethol *adj* oppressive, overpowering

llethr (-au) *nf* slope, declivity

llethrog *adj* sloping, steep, declining

llethu *vb* to overlie; to smother; to oppress, to overpower, to overwhelm

lleuad (-au) *nf* moon

lleuog *adj* lousy

llew (-od) *nm* lion; **dant y llew** dandelion; **y Llew** Leo

llewaidd *adj* lionlike, leonine

llewes (-au) *nf* lioness

llewpart (-pardiaid) *nm* leopard

llewych *nm* light, brightness

llewyg (-on) *nm* faint, swoon

llewygu *vb* to faint, to swoon

llewyrch *nm* brightness, radiance, gleam

llewyrchu *vb* to shine

llewyrchus *adj* flourishing, prosperous

lleyg (-ion) *adj* lay

lleygwr (-wyr) *nm* layman

lliain (-einiau) *nm* linen; cloth; towel

lliaws *nm* host, multitude

llibin *adj* limp, feeble; awkward, clumsy

llid *nm* wrath; irritation, inflammation

llidiart (-ardau) *nm* gate

llidio *vb* to be angry, to chafe, to inflame

llidiog *adj* angry, wrathful; inflamed

llidiowgrwydd *nm* wrath, indignation

llidus *adj* inflamed

llieiniwr (-wyr) *nm* linen-draper

llif¹ (-iau) *nf* saw

llif² (-ogydd) *nm* stream, flood, current

llifbridd *nm* alluvium

llifddor (-au) *nf* floodgate

llifddwfr (-ddyfroedd) *nm* flood, torrent

llifeiriant (-iaint) *nm* flood

llifeirio *vb* to flow, to stream

llifeiriol *adj* streaming, overflowing

llifio *vb* to saw

llifiwr (-wyr) *nm* sawyer

llifo[1] *vb* to flow, to stream

llifo[2] *vb* to grind *(tool)*

llifo[3] *vb* to dye

llifogydd *npl* flooding

llifolau (-euadau) *nm* floodlight

llifoleuo *vb* to floodlight

llifwr (-wyr) *nm* dyer

llifyn (-nau, -ion) *nm* dye

llilinio *vb* to streamline

llin *nm* flax; **had llin** linseed

llinach (-au) *nf* lineage, pedigree

llindagu *vb* to strangle, to throttle, to choke

llinell (-au) *nf* line; **llinell gais** try line; **llinell gymorth** helpline

llinelliad (-au) *nm* lineation, drawing

llinellog *adj* lined, ruled

llinellol *adj* lineal

llinellu *vb* to rule

llinglwm *nm*: **clwm llinglwm** tight knot

lliniaru *vb* to ease, to soothe, to allay

llinol *adj* linear

llinorog *adj* eruptive; purulent, suppurating

llinos (-od) *nf* linnet

llinyn (-nau) *nm* line, string, twine

llinynnu *vb* to string

llipa *adj* limp, weak

llipryn (-nod) *nm* hobbledehoy, weakling

lliprynnaidd *adj* limp, flabby

llith (-iau, -oedd) *nf* lesson, lecture; bait, mash

llithio *vb* to entice, to allure, to seduce; to feed

llithren (-nau) *nf* chute

llithriad (-au) *nm* slip, glide

llithrig *adj* slippery, glib, fluent

llithrigrwydd *nm* slipperiness, glibness

llithro *vb* to slip, to glide, to slide

lliw (-iau) *nm* colour, hue, dye

lliwgar *adj* colourful

lliwio *vb* to colour, to dye

lliwiog *adj* coloured

lliwur *nm* dye

llo (lloi) *nm* calf

lloc (-iau) *nm* fold, pen

lloches (-au) *nf* refuge, shelter, den

llochesu *vb* to harbour, to shelter

llochi *vb* to stroke, to caress, to fondle

llodig *adj* in heat *(of a sow)*

llodrau *npl* trousers, breeches

Lloegr *nf* England

lloer (-au) *nf* moon

lloeren (-ni, -nau) *nf* satellite

lloerig *adj*, *nm* lunatic

llofnod (-au), llofnodiad *nm* signature

llofnodi *vb* to sign

llofrudd (-ion) *nm* murderer; **llofrudd cyfresol** serial killer

llofruddiaeth (-au) *nf* murder

llofruddio *vb* to murder

llofruddiog *adj* guilty of murder

lloffa *vb* to glean

lloffion *npl* gleanings

llofft (-ydd) *nf* loft, bedroom, gallery

lloffwr (-wyr) *nm* gleaner

lloffyn *nm* bundle of gleanings

llog (-au) *nm* interest

llogi

llogi *vb* to hire
llogwr (-wyr) *nm* hirer
llong (-au) *nf* ship; **llong ofod** spaceship
llongddrylliad (-au) *nm* shipwreck
llongddryllio *vb* to wreck
llongwr (-wyr) *nm* sailor
llongwriaeth *nf* seamanship
llom *adj f of* **llwm**
llon *adj* glad, merry
llonaid, llond *nm* full
llonder *nm* gladness, joy
llongyfarch *vb* to congratulate
llongyfarchiad (-au, -archion) *nm* congratulation
lloniant *nm* joy, cheer
llonni *vb* to cheer, to gladden
llonydd *adj* quiet, still ▸ *nm* quiet, calm
llonyddu *vb* to quiet, to still, to calm
llonyddwch *nm* quietness, quiet
llorgynllun (-iau) *nm* ground plan
llorio *vb* to floor; to ground (rugby)
llorwedd *adj* horizontal
llosg *nm, adj* burning
llosgach *nm* incest
llosgadwy *adj* combustible
llosgfa (-fâu, -feydd) *nf* burning, inflammation
llosgfynydd (-oedd) *nm* volcano
llosgi *vb* to burn, to scorch; to smart
llosgwrn (-yrnau) *nm* tail
llosgydd (-ion) *nm* incinerator
llu (-oedd) *nm* host
lluched *npl* (*nf* **-en**) lightning
lluchfa (-feydd) *nf* snowdrift
lluchio *vb* to throw, to fling, to pelt; to throw away

lluchiwr (-wyr) *nm* thrower
lludlyd *adj* ashy
lludu, lludw *nm* ashes, ash
lludded *nm* weariness, fatigue
lluddedig *adj* wearied, tired, fatigued
lluddedu *vb* to tire, to weary
lluddias, lluddio *vb* to hinder; to forbid
lluest (-au) *nm* tent, booth
lluestfa (-feydd) *nf* encampment
lluestu *vb* to encamp
lluesty (-tai) *nm* tent, booth
llugoer *adj* lukewarm
lluman (-au) *nm* banner, standard, ensign
llumanwr (-wyr) *nm* linesman
llumon *nm* chimney stack, peak
Llun, dydd Llun *nm* Monday
llun (-iau) *nm* form, image, picture
Llundain *nf* London
llungopïo *vb* to photocopy
lluniad (-au) *nm* drawing
lluniadaeth (-au) *nf* draughtsmanship
lluniadu *vb* to draw
lluniaeth *nm* food, nourishment
lluniaethu *vb* to order, to ordain, to decree
lluniaidd *adj* shapely
lluniedydd *nm* draughtsman
llunio *vb* to form, to shape, to fashion
lluniwr (-wyr) *nm* former, maker
llun-recordydd (-ion) *nm* video-tape recorder
lluosflwydd *adj* perennial
lluosi *vb* to multiply
lluosiad *nm* multiplication

lluosill, lluosillafog *adj* polysyllabic

lluosog *adj* numerous; plural

lluosogi *vb* to multiply

lluosogiad *nm* multiplication

lluoswm *nm* product (*in maths*)

lluosydd *nm* multiplier

llurgunio *vb* to mangle, to mutilate

llurguniwr (-wyr) *nm* mangler, mutilator

llurig (-au) *nf* coat of mail, cuirass

llurigog *adj* mail-clad

llus *npl* (*nf*-**en**) bilberries, whinberries

llusern (-au) *nf* lantern, lamp

llusg (-ion) *nm* draught; drag

llusgfad (-au) *nm* tugboat

llusgo *vb* to drag; to trail; to crawl; to drawl

llusgwr (-wyr) *nm* dragger, slowcoach

llutrod *nm* mire, ashes, debris

lluwch *nm* dust; spray; snowdrift

lluwchio *vb* to drift

lluydd *nm* host, army

lluyddu *vb* to mobilise

llw (-on) *nm* oath

llwch *nm* dust, powder

llwdn (llydnod) *nm* young of animals

llwfr *adj* timid, cowardly

llwfrdra *nm* cowardice

llwfrddyn, llwfrgi *nm* coward

llwfrhau *vb* to faint

llwglyd *adj* hungry, famished

llwgr *nm* corruption ▶ *adj* corrupt

llwgrwobrwy (-on) *nm* bribe

llwgrwobrwyo *vb* to bribe

llwgu *vb* to starve, to famish

llwm (*f* **llom**) *adj* bare; destitute, poor

llwnc *nm* gulp, swallow; gullet

llwncdestun *nm* toast (*health*)

llwr, llwrw *nm* track; llwr ei ben headlong; llwr ei gefn backwards

llwy (-au) *nf* spoon, ladle

llwyaid (-eidiau) *nf* spoonful

llwybr (-au) *nm* path, track

llwybreiddio *vb* to direct, to forward

llwybro *vb* to walk

llwyd *adj* brown; grey; pale; hoary

llwydaidd *adj* greyish, palish

llwydi, llwydni *nm* greyness; mould, mildew

llwydnos *nf* dusk, twilight

llwydo *vb* to turn grey; to become mouldy

llwydrew *nm* hoar-frost

llwydrewi *vb* to cast hoar-frost

llwydd *nm* welfare

llwyddiannus *adj* successful, prosperous

llwydd, -iant *nm* success, prosperity

llwyddo *vb* to succeed, to prosper

llwyfan (-nau) *nfm* platform, stage

llwyfandir (-oedd) *nm* plateau

llwyfannu *vb* to stage

llwyfen (llwyf) *nf* elm

llwyn¹ (-i) *nm* grove; bush

llwyn² *nf* loin

llwynog (-od) *nm* fox

llwynoges (-au) *nf* vixen

llwynwst *nf* lumbago

llwyo *vb* to use a spoon; to ladle

llwyr *adj* entire, complete, total ▶ *adv* entirely, altogether ▶ *prefix* total

llwyredd nm entireness, completeness

llwyrymatal, llwyrymwrthod vb to abstain totally

llwyrymwrthodwr (-wyr) nm teetotaller

llwyth¹ (-au) nm tribe, clan

llwyth² (-i) nm load, burden

llwytho vb to load, to burden

llwythog adj laden, burdened

llychlyd adj dusty

Llychlyn nf Scandinavia

llychwino vb to spot, to tarnish, to soil, to sully

llychyn nm particle of dust, mote

llydan adj broad, wide

Llydaw nf Brittany

llydnu vb to bring forth, to foal

llyfn (f llefn) adj smooth, sleek

llyfnder, -dra nm smoothness, sleekness

llyfndew adj plump, sleek

llyfnhau vb to smooth, to level

llyfnu vb to smooth, to level; to harrow

llyfr (-au) nm book; **llyfr nodiadau** notebook

llyfrbryf (-ed) nm bookworm

llyfrfa nf (-feydd) library; book room; official publishing house of religious denomination, government etc

llyfrgell (-oedd) nf library

llyfrgellydd (-ion) nm librarian

llyfrifeg nmf book-keeping

llyfrnod (-au) nm bookmark

llyfrwerthwr (-wyr) nm bookseller

llyfrydd (-ion) nm bibliographer, transcriber of books

llyfryddiaeth nf bibliography

llyfryn (-nau) nm booklet, pamphlet

llyfu vb to lick

llyffant (-od, llyffaint) nm frog, toad

llyffethair (-eiriau) nf fetter, shackle

llyffetheirio vb to fetter, to shackle

llyg (-od) nmf shrew(-mouse)

llygad (llygaid) nm eye; **llygad y dydd** daisy

llygad-dynnu vb to bewitch

llygad-dyst nm eyewitness

llygadog adj eyed, sharp-eyed

llygadrwth adj wide-eyed, staring

llygadrythu vb to stare

llygadu vb to eye

llygatgraff adj keen-eyed, sharp-sighted

llygedyn nm ray of light

llygeidiog adj eyed

llygoden (llygod) nf mouse; **llygoden fawr, llygoden ffrengig** rat

llygota vb to catch mice

llygotwr (-wyr) (f llygotwraig) nm mouser, ratter

llygradwy adj corruptible

llygredig adj corrupt, depraved, degraded

llygredigaeth (-au) nf corruption

llygredd nm corruptness, depravity

llygriad (-au) nm corruption, adulteration

llygru vb to corrupt, to adulterate

llygrwr (-wyr) nm corrupter, adulterator

llynges (-au) nf fleet, navy

llyngeswr (-wyr) nm navy-man

llyngesydd (-ion) nm admiral

llyngyr npl (nf-**en**) (intestinal) worms

llym (f**llem**) adj sharp, keen, severe

llymaid (-eidiau) nm sip, drink

llymarch (llymeirch) nm oyster

llymder¹ nm sharpness, keenness, severity

llymder², llymdra nm bareness, poverty

llymeitian, llymeitio vb to sip, to tipple

llymeitiwr (-wyr) nm tippler, sot

llymhau¹ vb to make bare

llymhau² vb to sharpen

llymrïaid npl (nf-**ien**) sand-eels

llymru nm flummery

llymsur adj acrid

llymu vb to sharpen, to whet

llyn (-noedd) nm lake, pond, pool

llynciad (-au) nm draught, gulp

llyncu vb to swallow, to gulp, to absorb

llyncwr (-wyr) nm swallower, guzzler

llynedd nf last year

llyo vb to lick

llys (-oedd) nm court, hall, palace

llysaidd adj courtly, polite

llysblant npl step-children

llyschwaer nf step-sister

llysenw (-au) nm nickname

llysenwi vb to nickname

llysfab nm step-son

llysfam nf step-mother

llysferch nf step-daughter

llysfrawd nm step-brother

llysgenhadaeth nf embassy, legation

llysgenhadol adj ambassadorial

llysgennad (-genhadon) nm ambassador

llysiau npl (nm -**ieuyn**) herbs, vegetables

llysieueg nm botany

llysieuol adj herbal, vegetable

llysieuwr nm vegetarian

llysieuydd (-ion, llysieuwyr) nm botanist; vegetarian

llysieuyn nm plant

llysnafedd nm snivel, slime

llystad nm step-father

llystyfiant nm vegetation

llyswenwyn nm herbicide

llysysol adj herbivorous

llysywen (llysywod) nf eel

llysywenna vb to catch eels

llythrennedd nm literacy

llythrennol adj literal

llythyr (-au) nm letter, epistle

llythyrdy (-dai) nm post-office

llythyren (llythrennau) nf letter, type

llythyrwr (-wyr) nm letter-writer

llyw (-iau) nm ruler; rudder, helm

llywaeth adj hand-fed, tame, pet

llywiawdwr (-wyr) nm ruler, governor

llywio vb to rule, to govern, to direct, to steer

llywiwr (llywyr) nm steersman, helmsman

llywodraeth (-au) nf government

llywodraethol adj governing, dominant

llywodraethu vb to govern, to rule

llywodraethwr (-wyr) *nm* governor, ruler
llywydd (-ion) *nm* president
llywyddiaeth (-au) *nf* presidency
llywyddol *adj* presidential
llywyddu *vb* to preside

mab (meibion) *nm* boy, son; man, male
mabaidd *adj* filial
maban (-od) *nm* babe, baby
mabandod *nm* childhood, infancy
mabinogi *nm* tale, story
mablygad *nm* eyeball
mabmaeth (-au, -od) *nm* foster-son
maboed *nm* childhood, infancy, youth
mabolaeth *nf* sonship; boyhood, youth
mabolaidd *adj* youthful, boyish
mabolgamp (-au) *nf* game, sport, feat
mabsant *nm* patron saint
mabwysiad *nm* adoption
mabwysiadol *adj* adoptive; adopted
mabwysiadu *vb* to adopt
macrell (mecryll) *nfm* mackerel
macsu *vb* to brew

macwy (-aid) nm youth, page
machlud, machludo vb to set, to go down; **machlud haul** sunset
machludiad nm setting, going down
machnïydd nm mediator
madarch npl (nf-**en**) mushrooms
madfall (-od) nm lizard
madrondod nm giddiness, stupefaction
madroni vb to make or become giddy
madru vb to putrefy, to fester, to rot
madruddyn nm cartilage; **madruddyn y cefn** spinal cord
maddau vb to pardon, to forgive, to remit
maddeuant nm pardon, forgiveness
maddeugar adj of a forgiving disposition
maddeuol adj pardoning, forgiving
maddeuwr (-wyr) nm pardoner
mae vb tis, are; there is, there are
maeden nf slut, jade
maeddu see baeddu
maen (meini) nm stone
maenol, maenor (-au) nf manor
maentumio vb to maintain
maer (-od, meiri) nm mayor
maeres (-au) nf mayoress
maerol adj mayoral
maeryddiaeth nf mayoralty
maes (meysydd) nm field ▸ adj free-range; **i maes** out; **maes glanio** airport
maesglaf (-gleifion) nm outpatient
maeslywydd (-ion) nm field-marshal

maestir (-oedd) nm open country, plain
maestref (-i, -ydd) nf suburb
maesu vb to field
maeth nm nourishment, nutriment
maethiad nm nutrition
maethlon adj nourishing, nutritious
maethu vb to nourish, to nurture
maethydd (-ion) nm nourisher
maethyn (-nau) nm nutrient; suckling
mafon npl (nf-**en**) raspberries
magl (-au) nf snare; mesh
maglu vb to snare, to mesh, to trip
magnel (-au) nf gun, cannon
magnelaeth nf artillery
magnelwr (-wyr) nm gunner
magnesiwm nm magnesium
magnetedd nm magnetism
magneteiddio vb to magnetise
magu vb to breed, to rear, to nurse; to gain, to acquire
magwraeth nf nourishment, nurture
magwrfa nf nursery
magwyr (-ydd) nf wall
maharen (meheryn) nm ram; wether
Mai nm May
mai conj that it is
maidd nm whey
main (meinion) adj fine, slender, thin; **main y cefn** small of the back
mainc (meinciau) nf bench, form, seat
maint nm size, quantity, number
maintioli nm size, stature
Maiorca nf Majorca

maip *npl* (*nf* **meipen**) turnips
maith (**meithion**) *adj* long, tedious
mâl *adj* ground
malais *nm* malice
maldod *nm* dalliance, affection
maldodi *vb* to pet, to pamper, to indulge
Maleisia *nf* Malaysia
maleisus *adj* malicious
maleithiau *npl* chilblains
malio *vb* to care, to mind, to heed
Malta *nf* Malta
malu *vb* to grind, to mince, to chop, to smash
malurio *vb* to pound; to crumble, to moulder
malurion *npl* fragments, debris
malwen *nf* snail
malwod *npl* (*nf-***en**, *nf* **malwen**) snails
malwr (**-wyr**) *nm* grinder
mall *nf* blight; **y fall** Belial, perdition
malltod *nm* rot, blight, blast
mallu *vb* to rot, to blast
mam (**-au**) *nf* mother, mum; **mam-gu** grandmother
mamaeth (**-od**) *nf* nurse
mamal (**-iaid**) *nm* mammal
mam-gu *nf* granny
mamiaith (**-ieithoedd**) *nf* mother-tongue
mamog (**-iaid**) *nf* dam, sheep with young
mamol *adj* maternal
mamolaeth (**-au**) *nf* maternity
mamwlad (**-wledydd**) *nf* motherland
man¹ *nmf* place, spot, location
man² *nm* speck, blemish
mân *adj* small, fine, petty

mandyllog *adj* porous
maneg (**menig**) *nf* glove, gauntlet
mangre *nf* place, spot
manion *npl* scraps, trifles, minutiæ
mantais (**-eision**) *nf* advantage
manteisio *vb* to take advantage, to profit
manteisiol *adj* advantageous; profitable
mantell (**-oedd, mentyll**) *nf* mantle
mantellog *adj* mantled
mantol (**-ion**) *nf* balance; **y Fantol** Libra
mantolen (**-ni**) *nf* balance-sheet
mantoli *vb* to turn scale, to balance, to weigh
manŵaidd *adj* delicate, fine
manwerthu *vb* to retail
mân-werthu *vb* to retail
mân-werthwr *nm* retailer
manwl *adj* exact, precise, strict, particular
manwl-gywir *adj* precise
manylion *npl* particulars, details
manylrwydd *nm* exactness, precision
manylu *vb* to go into detail, to particularize
manylwch *nm* exactness, precision
map (**-iau**) *nm* map
mapio *vb* to map
mapiwr (**-wyr**) *nm* cartographer
marathon (**-au**) *nf* marathon
marblen (**marblys**) *nf* marble
marc (**-iau**) *nm* mark
marcio *vb* to mark
Marcsiaeth *nf* Marxism
march (**meirch**) *nm* horse, stallion
marchlu (**-oedd**) *nm* cavalry
marchnad (**-oedd**) *nf* market

marchnadfa (-oedd) *nf* marketplace

marchnata *vb* to market, to trade

marchnatwr (-wyr) *nm* merchant

marchnerth (-oedd) *nm* horsepower

marchocáu *vb* to ride a horse

marchog (-ion) *nm* horseman, rider; knight

marchogaeth *vb* to ride

marchogwr (-wyr) *nm* rider, horseman

marchredyn *npl* (*nf-en*) polypody fern

marchwellt *nm* tall, coarse grass

marian *nm* holm, strand, moraine

marlad *nm* drake

marmalêd (-ledau) *nm* marmalade

marmor *nm* marble

marsialydd (-ion) *nm* marshal

marsiandïaeth *nf* merchandise

marsiandïwr (-wyr) *nm* merchant

marsipan *nm* marzipan

marw¹ *vb* to die

marw² (meirw, meirwon) *nm*, *adj* dead

marwaidd *adj* lifeless, sluggish, moribund

marwdon *nf* dandruff

marweidd-dra *nm* deadness, sluggishness

marweiddio *vb* to deaden, to mortify

marwhad *nm* mortification

marwhau *vb* to deaden, to mortify

marwnad (-au) *nf* lament, elegy

marwol *adj* deadly, mortal, fatal

marwolaeth (-au) *nf* death

marwoldeb *nm* mortality

marwolion *npl* mortals

marwor *npl* (*nm-yn*) embers; charcoal

marwydos *npl* embers

masarnen (masarn) *nf* sycamore

masgl (-au) *nf* shell, pod

masglo, masglu *vb* to shell; to interlace

masnach (-au) *nf* trade, traffic, commerce; **masnach deg** fair trade

masnachol *adj* commercial, business

masnachu *vb* to do business, to trade, to traffic

masnachwr (-wyr) *nm* dealer, merchant

masw *adj* wanton

maswedd *nm* wantonness, ribaldry

masweddol *adj* wanton, ribald

maswr (-wyr) *nm* outside half

mat (-iau) *nm* mat

mater (-ion) *nm* matter

materol *adj* material; materialistic

materoliaeth *nf* materialism

matog (-au) *nf* mattock

matras (-resi) *nm* mattress

matrics (-au) *nm* matrix

matsien (matsys) *nf* match

math (-au) *nm* sort, kind

mathemateg *nm* mathematics, maths

mathru *vb* to trample, to tread

mathrwr (-wyr) *nm* trampler

mawl *nm* praise

mawn *coll n* (*nf-en*) peat

mawnog *adj* peaty ▸ *nf* peat-bog

mawr (-ion) *adj* big, great, large

mawredd *nm* greatness, grandeur, majesty

mawreddog adj grand, majestic; grandiose

mawrfrydig adj magnanimous

mawrfrydigrwydd nm magnanimity

Mawrth nm Mars; March; **dydd Mawrth** Tuesday

mawrygu vb to magnify, to extol

mawrhau vb to magnify, to enlarge

mawrhydi nm majesty

mebyd nm childhood, infancy, youth

mecaneg nf mechanics

mecanwaith (-weithiau) nm mechanism

mecanyddol adj mechanical

Mecsico nf Mexico

mechnïaeth nf surety, bail

mechnïo vb to go bail, to become surety

mechnïol adj vicarious

mechnïydd (-ion) nm surety, bail

medel (-au) nf reaping; reaping party

medelwr (-wyr) nm reaper

Medi nm September

medi vb to reap

medr nm skill, ability

medru vb to know, to be able

medrus adj clever, skilful

medrusrwydd nm cleverness, skilfulness, skill

medrydd (-ion) nm gauge

medd¹ nm mead

medd² vb says

meddal adj soft, tender

meddalhau, meddalu vb to soften

meddalwch nm softness

meddalwedd nm software

meddiannol adj possessing, possessive

meddiannu vb to possess, to occupy

meddiant (-iannau) nm possession

meddu vb to possess, to own

meddw (-on) adj drunk, intoxicated

meddwdod nm drunkenness, intoxication

meddwi vb to get drunk, to intoxicate, to inebriate

meddwl vb to think; to mean ▸ nm (**meddyliau**) thought; meaning; opinion

meddwol adj intoxicating

meddwyn (-won) nm drunkard, inebriate

meddyg (-on) nm physician, doctor; **meddyg teulu** GP, general practitioner

meddygaeth nf medicine

meddygfa (-feydd) nf surgery

meddyginiaeth (-au) nf medicine, remedy, medication

meddyginiaethol adj medicinal, remedial

meddyginiaethu vb to cure, to remedy, to heal

meddygol adj medicinal; medical

meddylfryd nm mind, affection, bent

meddylgar adj thoughtful

meddylgarwch nm thoughtfulness

meddyliol adj mental, intellectual

meddyliwr (-wyr) nm thinker

mefus npl (nf **-en**) strawberries

megin (-au) nf bellows

megino vb to work bellows, to blow

megis *conj, prep* as, so as, like a

Mehefin *nm* June

meicrobioleg *nm* microbiology

meicro-brosesydd *nm* microprocessor

meicroffon (-au) *nm* microphone

meicrosglodyn (-ion) *nm* microchip

meicrosgop (-au) *nm* microscope

meichiad (-iaid) *nm* swineherd

meichiau (-iafon) *nm* surety, bail

meidrol *adj* finite

meidroldeb *nm* finiteness

meiddio *vb* to dare, to venture

meiddion *npl* curds and whey

meiddlyd *adj* wheyey, curdled

meigryn *nm* migraine

meilart *nm* drake

meillion *npl* (*nf*-**en**) clover

meim (-iau) *nmf* mime

meimio *vb* to mime

meinder *nm* fineness, slenderness

meindio *vb* to mind, to care

meindwr *nm* spire

meinedd *nm* slender part, small

meingefn *nm* small of the back

meinhau *vb* to grow slender, to taper

meini *see* **maen**

meinllais *nm* shrill voice, treble

meintoli *vb* to quantify

meintoliad *nm* quantification

meinwe (-oedd) *nf* tissue

meipen (maip) *nf* turnip

meirch *see* **march**

meirioli *vb* to thaw

meirw *see* **marw**

meistr (-iaid, -i, -adoedd) *nm* master

meistres (-i) *nf* mistress

meistrolaeth *nf* mastery

meistrolgar *adj* masterful, masterly

meistroli *vb* to master

meitin *nm*: **ers meitin** some time since

meitr (-au) *nm* mitre

meithder *nm* length

meithrin *vb* to nurture, to rear, to foster

meithrinfa (-oedd) *nf* nursery

mêl *nm* honey

mela *vb* to gather honey

melan *nf* melancholy

melen *adj f of* **melyn**

melfaréd *nm* corduroy

melfed *nm* velvet

melin (-au) *nf* mill

melinydd (-ion) *nm* miller

melodaidd *adj* melodious

melodi *nm* melody

melyn (*f* **melen**) *adj* yellow ▶ *nm* yellow; **melyn wy** yolk of egg; **y clefyd melyn** jaundice

melynaidd *adj* yellowish, tawny

melynder, melyndra *nm* yellowness

melynddu *adj* tawny, swarthy

melyngoch *adj* yellowish red, orange

melyni *nm* yellowness; jaundice

melynu *vb* to yellow

melynwy *nm* yolk

melynwyn *adj* yellowish white, cream

melys *adj* sweet ▶ *npl* (-**ion**) sweets

melysfwyd *nm* dessert

melyster, melystra *nm* sweetness

melysu *vb* to sweeten

mellt npl (nf **-en**) lightning

melltennu vb to flash lightning

melltigaid, melltigedig adj accursed, cursed

melltith (-ion) nf curse

melltithio vb to curse

memorandwm (-anda) nm memorandum

memrwn (-rynau) nm parchment, vellum

men (-ni) nf wain, waggon, cart

mên adj mean

mendio vb to mend, to heal, to recover

menestr nm cup-bearer

menig see **maneg**

mentr nf venture, hazard

mentro vb to venture, to hazard

mentrus adj adventurous

mentrwr (-wyr) nm entrepreneur

menyw (-od) nf woman

mêr (merion) nm marrow

mercwri nm mercury

merch (-ed) nf daughter, woman

Mercher nm Mercury; **dydd Mercher** Wednesday

mercheta vb to womanise

merchetaidd adj effeminate

merch-yng-nghyfraith nf daughter-in-law

merddwr (-ddyfroedd) nm stagnant water

merf, merfaidd adj insipid, tasteless, flat

merfdra, merfeidd-dra nm insipidity

merlen nf pony

merlota vb to pony-trek

merlyn (-nod, merlod) (f **merlen**) nm pony

merllyd adj insipid

merllys nm asparagus

merthyr (-on, -i) nm martyr

merthyrdod nm martyrdom

merthyru vb to martyr

merwindod nm numbness, tingling

merwino vb to benumb, to tingle, to smart

meryw npl (nf **-en**) juniper trees

mes npl (nf **-en**) acorns

mesa vb to gather acorns

mesur¹ (-au) nm measure; metre; tune; bill

mesur², mesuro vb to measure, to mete

mesureg nf mensuration

mesuriad (-au) nm measurement

mesurwr (-wyr) nm measurer; surveyor

mesurydd (-ion) nm measurer, meter

metamorffedd nm metamorphism

metel (-oedd) nm metal; mettle

metelaidd adj metallic

metelydd (-ion) nm metallurgist

metelyddiaeth nf metallurgy

metr (-au) nm metre

metrig adj metric

metrigeiddio vb to metricate

meth (-ion) nm miss, failure

methdaliad (-au) nm bankruptcy

methdalwr (-wyr) nm bankrupt

methedig (-ion) adj decrepit, infirm, disabled

methiannus adj failing, decayed

methiant nm failure

methodoleg nf methodology

methu vb to fail, to miss

meudwy (-aid, -od) nm hermit, recluse

meudwyaidd adj hermit-like, retiring

meudwyol adj eremitic

mewian vb to mew

mewn prep in, within

mewnanadlu vb to inhale

mewnblyg adj introvert

mewnbwn nm input

mewnforio vb to import ▶ npl (-ion) imports

mewnfudwr (-wyr) nm immigrant

mewngofnodi vb to log in, to log on

mewnol adj inward, internal; subjective

mewnosod vb to insert

mewnrwyd (-i, -au) nf intranet

mewnwr (-wyr) nm scrum-half

mewnyn (mewnion) nm filling

mi pron I, me

mieri npl (nf **miaren**) brambles

mig nf: chwarae mig to play bo-peep

mign, mignen nf bog, quagmire

migwrn (-yrnau) nm knuckle; ankle

mil¹ (-od) nm animal

mil² (-oedd) nf thousand

milain adj angry, fierce, savage, cruel

mileindra nm savageness, ferocity

mileinig adj savage, ferocious, malignant

milfed adj thousandth

milfeddyg (-on) nm veterinary surgeon

milfil nf million, an indefinite number

milflwyddiant nm millennium

milgi (-gwn) nm greyhound

miliast (-ieist) nf greyhound bitch

milimedr nm millimetre

militariaeth nf militarism

militarydd nm militarist

miliwn (-iynau) nf million

milionydd (-ion) nm millionaire

milodfa (-oedd, -feydd) nf menagerie

milwr (-wyr) nm soldier

milwraidd adj soldierly

milwriad (-iaid) nm colonel

milwriaeth nf warfare

milwriaethus adj militant

milwrio vb to militate

milwrol adj military

milltir (-oedd) nf mile

min (-ion) nm edge; brink; lip

mindlws adj simpering, affected, precious

mingamu vb to grimace

minibws (-bysiau, -bysys) nm minibus

minio vb to edge, to sharpen; to make impression

miniog adj sharp, keen, cutting

minlliw (-iau) nm lipstick

minnau pron I (on my part), I also

mintai (-eioedd) nf band, troop

mintys nm mint

mirain adj fair, beautiful, comely

mireinder nm beauty, comeliness

miri nm merriment, fun, festivity

mis (-oedd) nm month

misglwyf nm period

misio vb to miss, to fail

misol (-ion) adj monthly

misolyn (-olion) nm monthly (magazine)

167

mitsio vb to mitch, to play truant

miwsig nm music

mo contr. of **dim o**; **nid oes mo'i debyg** there is none like him

moch npl (nm **-yn**) swine, pigs, hogs

mocha vb to pig, to litter

mochaidd adj swinish, hoggish

mochynnaidd adj piggish, swinish

modfedd (-i) nf inch

modiwl (-au) nm module

modrwy (-au) nf ring

modrwyo vb to ring

modrwyog adj ringed

modryb (-edd) nf aunt

modur (-on) nm motor

modurdy (-dai) nm garage

modurwr (-wyr) nm motorist

modylu vb to modulate

modylydd (-ion) nm modulator

modd (-ion, -au) nm mode, manner; means; mood

moddion npl means; medicine

moddol adj modal

moel[1] **(-ion)** adj bare, bald; hornless, polled

moel[2] **(-ydd)** nf hill

moeli vb to make or become bald; to hang (ears)

moelni nm bareness, baldness

moelyn nm bald-head

moes[1] vb imper give, bring hither

moes[2] **(-au)** nf morality; (pl) manners, morals

moeseg nf ethics

moesegol adj ethical

Moesenaidd adj Mosaic

moesgar adj mannerly, polite

moesgarwch nm politeness

moesol adj moral, ethical

moesoldeb nm morality

moesoli vb to moralize

moesolwr (-wyr) nm moralist

moeswers (-i) nf moral

moesymgrymu vb to bow

moeth (-au) nm luxury, indulgence

moethi vb to pamper, to indulge

moethlyd adj pampered, spoilt

moethus adj luxurious, pampered

moethusrwydd nm luxuriousness, luxury

molawd nm eulogy

molecwl (-cylau) nm molecule

molecwlar adj molecular

moled (-au) nf kerchief; muffler

moli, moliannu vb to praise, to laud

moliannus adj praised, praiseworthy

moliant (-iannau) nm praise

mollt (myllt) nm wether

molltgig nm mutton

moment (-au) nf moment

momentwm (momenta) nm momentum

monarchiaeth nf monarchy

monarchydd (-ion) nm monarchist

monni vb to sulk, to pout

monocsid (-au) nm monoxide

monopoli (-ïau) nm monopoly

mor adv how, so, as

môr (moroedd) nm sea, ocean; **Môr Adria** the Adriatic; **y Môr Canoldir, Môr y Canoldir** the Mediterranean; **Môr Hafren** the Bristol Channel; **Môr y Gogledd** the North Sea; **Môr Iwerddon** the Irish Sea; **y Môr Coch** the Red Sea; **y Môr Iwerydd** the Atlantic; **y Môr**

Tawel the Pacific; **y Môr Udd** the English Channel
moratoriwm (-atoria) *nm* moratorium
mordaith (-deithiau) *nf* voyage
mordeithiwr (-wyr) *nm* voyager
mordwyaeth *nf* navigation
mordwyo *vb* to go by sea, to voyage, to sail
mordwyol *adj* nautical
mordwywr (-wyr) *nm* mariner, sailor
morddwyd (-ydd) *nfm* thigh
morfa (-feydd) *nm* moor, fen, marsh
morfil (-od) *nm* whale
môr-forwyn (-forynion) *nf* mermaid
morfran (-frain) *nf* cormorant
morffoleg *nf* morphology
morffolegol *adj* morphological
morgainc (-geinciau) *nf* gulf
morgais (-geisiau) *nm* mortgage
morgeisî *nm* mortgagee
morgeisio *vb* to mortgage
môr-gerwyn *nf* whirlpool, vortex, abyss
morgi *nm* shark
morglawdd (-gloddiau) *nm* embankment, mole
morgrug *npl (nm -yn)* ants
morio *vb* to voyage, to sail
môr-ladrad (-au) *nm* piracy
môr-leidr (-ladron) *nm* pirate
morlen (-ni) *nm* chart
morlo (-loi) *nm* sea-calf, seal
morllyn (-noedd) *nmf* lagoon
Moroco *nf* Morocco
morol *adj* maritime

moron *npl (nf -en)* carrots
mortais (-eisiau) *nf* mortise
morteisio *vb* to mortise
morter (-au) *nm* mortar
morthwyl (-ion) *nm* hammer
morthwylio *vb* to hammer
morthwyliwr (-wyr) *nm* hammerer
morwr (-wyr) *nm* seaman, sailor, mariner
morwriaeth *nf* seamanship, navigation
morwydd *npl (nf -en)* mulberry-trees
morwyn (-ynion) *nf* maid, virgin; **y Forwyn** Virgo
morwyndod *nm* virginity
morwynol *adj* virgin, maiden
moryd (-iau) *nf* estuary
moryn (-nau) *nm* billow, breaker
mosaig (-au) *nm, adj* mosaic
Moscow *nf* Moscow
Moslem *nmf* Muslim
Moslemaidd *adj* Muslim
motif (-au) *nm* motive
motiff (-au) *nm* motif
MP3 *n* MP3; **peiriant MP3** MP3 player
muchudd *nm* jet
mud *adj* unable to speak; dull
mudan (-od) *nm* man who is unable to speak
mudandod *nm* speech disorder
mudanes (-au) *nf* woman who is unable to speak
mudferwi *vb* to simmer
mudiad (-au) *nm* removal; movement
mudo *vb* to move, to remove

169

mudol

mudol *adj* mobile, moving, migratory

mudwr (-wyr) *nm* remover

mul (-od) *nm* mule; donkey

mulaidd *adj* mulish, asinine

mules (-au) *nf* she-mule, she-ass

mulfran (-frain) *nf* cormorant

mun *see* bun

munud¹ (-au) *nfm* minute, moment

munud² (-iau) *nm* sign, gesture; nod

munudio *vb* to make gestures, to gesticulate

mur (-iau) *nm* wall

murddun (-od) *nm* ruin, ruins

murio *vb* to wall

murlun (-iau) *nm* mural

murmur *vb* to murmur ▸ *nm* (-on) murmur

mursen (-nod) *nf* coquette; prude

mursendod *nm* prudery, affectation

mursennaidd *adj* prudish, affected

mursennu *vb* to coquette, to mince

musgrell *adj* feeble, decrepit

musgrellni *nm* feebleness, debility

mwclis *npl* necklace

mwd *nm* mud

mwdlyd *adj* muddy

mwdwl (mydylau) *nm* cock (of hay)

mwg *nm* smoke

mwgwd (mygydau) *nm* blind mask

mwng (myngau) *nm* mane

mwngial *vb* to mumble

mwlsyn *nm* nincompoop; mule

mwlwg *nm* refuse, sweepings, chaff

mwll *adj* close, warm, sultry

mwmian *vb* to hum, to mumble

mŵn *see* mwyn

mwnci (-iod) *nm* monkey

mwnciaidd *adj* monkeyish, apish

mwnglawdd *see* mwynglawdd

mwnwgl (mynyglau) *nm* neck

mwnws *coll n* small particles, dust, debris

mwrdro *vb* to murder

mwrllwch *nm* fog, mist, vapour

mwrn *adj* sultry, close, warm

mwrndra *nm* sultriness

mwrthwl (myrthylau) *nm* hammer

mws *adj* stale, rank, stinking

mwsg *nm* musk

mwsged (-i) *nmf* musket

Mwslim = Moslem

Mwslimaidd *adj* = Moslemaidd

mwsogl, mwswgl *nm* moss

mwstard, mwstart *nm* mustard

mwstro *vb* to fidget, to hurry

mwstwr *nm* muster; bustle, commotion

mwy *adj* more, bigger ▸ *adv* more, again

mwyach *adv* any more, henceforth

mwyafrif (-au) *nm* majority

mwyalch, mwyalchen (mwyalchod) *nf* blackbird

mwyar *npl* (*nf* -en) blackberries

mwyara *vb* to gather blackberries

mwydion *npl* crumb; pith, pulp

mwydo *vb* to moisten, to soak, to steep

mwydro *vb* to moider, to bewilder

mwydyn (mwydod) *nm* worm

mwyfwy *adv* more and more

mwynglawdd (-gloddiau) *nm* mine

mwyhau *vb* to increase, to enlarge, to magnify

mwyn[1] *nm* sake

mwyn[2], **mŵn** (**-au**) *nm* ore, mineral

mwyn[3] *adj* kind, gentle, mild; dear

mwynder (**-au**) *nm* gentleness; (*pl*) delights

mwyndoddi *vb* to refine

mwyneidd-dra *nm* kindness, gentleness

mwyngloddio *vb* to mine

mwynhad *nm* enjoyment, pleasure

mwynhau *vb* to enjoy

mwyniant (**-iannau**) *nm* pleasure

mwynofydd (**-ion**) *nm* mineralogist

mwynol *adj* mineral

mwynoleg *nf* mineralogy

mwynwr (**-wyr**) *nm* miner

mwys *adj* ambiguous, equivocal

mwythau *npl* indulgence, caresses

mwytho *vb* to pet, to fondle, to pamper

mwythus *adj* pampered

myctod *nm* asphyxia

mydr (**-au**) *nm* metre, verse

mydryddiaeth *nf* versification

mydryddol *adj* metrical

mydryddu, mydru *vb* to versify

mydylu *vb* to cock

myfi *pron* I, me, myself

myfiaeth *nf* egotism

myfiol *adj* egotistic

myfyrdod (**-au**) *nm* meditation

myfyrgar *adj* studious, contemplative

myfyrgell (**-oedd**) *nf* study

myfyrio *vb* to meditate, to study

myfyriol *adj* meditative

myfyriwr (**-wyr**) *nm* student; **myfyriwr hŷn** mature student

mygedol *adj* honorary

mygfa (**-feydd**) *nf* suffocation

myglyd *adj* smoky; close; asthmatic

myglys *nm* tobacco

mygu *vb* to smoke; to suffocate, to stifle, to smother

mygydu *vb* to blindfold

mygyn *nm* a smoke

myngial *vb* to mumble, to mutter

myngog *adj* maned

myngus *adj* indistinct, mumbling

myllni *nm* sultriness

mympwy (**-on**) *nm* whim, caprice, fad

mympwyol *adj* arbitrary, capricious

mymryn (**-nau**) *nm* particle, bit, mite

myn[1] *prep* by (*in swearing*)

myn[2] (**-nod**) *nm* kid

mynach (**-od, mynaich**) *nm* monk

mynachaeth *nf* monasticism

mynachdy (**-dai**) *nm* monastery, convent

mynachlog (**-ydd**) *nf* monastery, abbey

mynawyd (**-au**) *nm* awl

mynci (**-iau**) *nm* hame(s)

myned, mynd *vb* to go, to proceed

mynedfa (**-oedd, -feydd**) *nf* entrance, passage

mynediad *nm* going; access, admission

mynegai (**-eion**) *nm* index, exponent

mynegair (**-eiriau**) *nm* concordance

mynegbost *nm* signpost
mynegfys (-edd) *nm* forefinger, index
mynegi *vb* to tell, to express, to relate, to declare
mynegiad (-au) *nm* statement, declaration
mynegiant *nm* expression
mynegol *adj* indicative
mynnu *vb* to will, to wish; to insist; to get, to obtain
mynor (-ion) *nm* marble
mynwent (-au, -ydd) *nf* churchyard, graveyard
mynwes (-au) *nf* breast, bosom
mynwesol *adj* bosom
mynwesu *vb* to cherish
mynych *adj* frequent, often
mynychder *nm* frequency
mynychiad *nm* frequenting; repetition
mynychu *vb* to frequent, to attend; to repeat
mynydd (-oedd) *nm* mountain
mynydda *n* mountaineering ▸ *vb* to go mountaineering
mynydd-dir *nm* hill-country
mynyddig *adj* mountainous, hilly
mynyddwr (-wyr) *nm* mountaineer
myrdd, myrddiwn (myrddiynau) *nm* myriad
myrndra *nm* sultriness
myrr *nm* myrrh
myrtwydd *npl* (*nf* -en) myrtles
mysg *nm* middle, midst; **ymysg** among
mysgu *vb* to loose, to undo
myswynog (-ydd) *nf* barren cow
mysyglog *adj* mossy

mytholeg *nf* mythology
mytholegol *adj* mythological

n

na *conj* nor, neither; than ▸ *adv* no, not
nac *adv* no, not ▸ *conj* nor, neither
nacâd *nm* refusal, denial
nacaol *adj* negative
nacáu *vb* to refuse, to deny
nad *adv* not
nâd (nadau) *nf* cry, howl; clamour
Nadolig *nm* Christmas
Nadoligaidd *adj* Christmassy
nadu¹ *vb* to cry (out), to howl
nadu² *vb* to stop, to hinder
nadd *adj* hewn, wrought
naddion *npl* chips; shreds; lint
naddo *adv* no (*to questions in preterite tense*)
naddu *vb* to hew, to chip, to whittle
Naf *nm* Lord
nag *conj* than
nage *adv* not so, no
nai (neiaint) *nm* nephew
naid (neidiau) *nf* jump, leap, bound
naïf *adj* naïve

naïfder *nm* naïveté
naill *dem pron* the one ▸ *conj* either
nain (neiniau) *nf* grandmother
nam (-au) *nm* mark, blemish, flaw
namyn *pron* except, but, save
nant (nentydd) *nf* brook; gorge, ravine
napcyn (-au) *nm* napkin
narcotig *nm, adj* narcotic
natur *nf* nature; temper
naturiaeth (-au) *nf* nature
naturiaethwr (-wyr) *nm* naturalist
naturiol *adj* natural
naturioldeb *nm* naturalness
naturus *adj* angry, quick-tempered
naw *adj, nm* nine
nawdd *nm* protection; patronage
nawddogaeth *nf* patronage, protection
nawfed *adj* ninth
nawn *nm* noon
naws *nf* nature, disposition; essence, tincture
nawseiddio *vb* to temper, to soften
neb *nm* any one (*with negative understood*); no one
nedd *npl* (*nf-en*) nits
neddau, neddyf (neddyfau) *nf* adze
nef (-oedd) *nf* heaven
nefi-blw *n, adj* navy blue
nefol, nefolaidd *adj* heavenly, celestial
nefoli *vb* to make or become heavenly
nefrosis *nm* neurosis
neges (-au, -euau) *nf* errand, message; **neges destun** text message; **neges lais** voicemail

negesa, negeseua vb to run errands; to trade

negeseuwr (-wyr) nm messenger

negodi vb to negotiate

negyddiaeth nf negativism

negyddol adj negative

neidio vb to leap, to jump; to throb

neidiwr (-wyr) nm leaper, jumper

neidr (nadroedd, nadredd) nf snake

neiedd nm nepotism

neillog (-ion) nm alternative

neilltu nm one side; **o'r neilltu** aside, apart

neilltuad nm separation

neilltuaeth nf separation, privacy, seclusion

neilltuedig adj separated, secluded

neilltuo vb to set apart, to separate

neilltuol adj particular, peculiar, special

neilltuolion npl peculiarities

neilltuolrwydd nm peculiarity, distinction

neis adj nice

neisied (-i) nf kerchief

neithdar nm nectar

neithior (-au) nf marriage feast

neithiwr adv last night

nemor adj few; **nid nemor** hardly any

nen (-nau, -noedd) nf ceiling; heaven; **nen tŷ** house-top

nenbren nm roof-tree

nendwr nm skyscraper

nenfwd (-fydau) nm ceiling

nenlofft nf attic

nepell adv far; **nid nepell** not far

nerf (-au) nf nerve

nerfus adj nervous

nerfwst nm neurasthenia

nerth (-oedd) nm might, power, strength

nerthol adj strong, powerful, mighty

nerthu vb to strengthen

nes¹ adj nearer; **yn nes ymlaen** further on

nes² adv till, until

nesaf adj nearest, next

nesáu vb to draw near, to approach

nesnes adv nearer and nearer

nesu vb to draw near; **nesu draw** move away

neu conj or

neuadd (-au) nf hall

newid vb to change, to alter ► nm change; **newid hinsawdd** climate change

newidiant nm variability

newidiol adj changeable, variable

newidydd (-ion) nm transformer

newidyn (-nau) nm variable

newydd adj new, novel; fresh ► nm (-ion) news

newyddbeth (-au) nm novelty

newydd-deb, newydd-der nm newness, novelty

newyddiadur (-on) nm newspaper

newyddiaduraeth nf journalism

newyddiaduriaeth nf journalism

newyddiadurwr (-wyr) nm journalist

newyddian (-od) coll n novice, neophyte

newyn nm hunger, famine

newynog adj hungry, starving

newynu vb to starve, to famish

ni¹ pron we, us

ni², nid adv not

nifer (-oedd, -i) *nmf* number
nifwl *nm* mist, fog; nebula
Nigeria *nf* Nigeria
Nihon *nf* Japan
ninnau *pron* we (on our part), we also
nionyn (nionod) *nm* onion
nis *adv* not … it; **nis cafodd** he did not find it
nitrad (-au) *nm* nitrate
nith (-oedd) *nf* niece
nithio *vb* to sift, to winnow
nithiwr (-wyr) *nm* sifter, winnower
nithlen (-ni) *nf* winnowing-sheet
niwclear *adj* nuclear
niwed (-eidiau) *nm* harm, injury
niweidio *vb* to harm, to hurt, to injure, to damage
niweidiol *adj* harmful, injurious
niwl (-oedd) *nm* mist, fog, haze
niwlen *nf* mist, fog, haze
niwliog, niwlog *adj* misty, foggy, hazy
niwmatig *adj* pneumatic
niwmonia *nm* pneumonia
niwtral *adj* neutral
niwtraleiddio *vb* to neutralise
niwtraliaeth *nf* neutrality
nobyn (nobiau) *nm* knob
nod (-au) *nmf* note; mark, token
nodachfa (-feydd) *nf* bazaar
nodedig *adj* appointed, set; remarkable
nodi *vb* to mark, to note, to appoint, to state
nodiad (-au) *nm* note
nodiadur (-on) *nm* notebook
nodiant *nm* notation
nodlyfr (-au) *nm* notebook

nodwedd (-ion) *nf* character, characteristic, feature
nodweddiadol *adj* characteristic
nodweddu *vb* to characterize
nodwydd (-au) *nf* needle
nodwyddiad *nm* acupuncture
nodyn (-nau, nodau, nodion) *nm* note
nodd (-ion) *nm* moisture; juice, sap
nodded *nm* refuge, protection
noddfa (-fâu, -feydd) *nf* refuge
noddi *vb* to protect
noddlyd *adj* juicy, sappy
noddwr (-wyr) *nm* protector; patron
noe (-au) *nf* dish; kneading-trough
noeth *adj* naked, bare, exposed, raw
noethder *nm* bareness, nakedness
noethi *vb* to bare, to denude
noethlymun *adj* nude
noethlymunwr (-wyr) *nm* streaker
noethlymunwraig *nf* stripper
noethni *nm* nakedness, nudity
noethwr (-wyr) *nm* nudist
nofel (-au) *nf* novel
nofelwr (-wyr), nofelydd *nm* novelist
nofiadwy *adj* swimmable
nofiedydd (-ion) *nm* swimmer
nofio *vb* to swim; to float
nofiwr (-wyr) *nm* swimmer
nogio *vb* to jib
noglyd *adj* jibbing
nôl *vb* to fetch, to bring
Norwy *nf* Norway
nos (-au, nosweithiau) *nf* night; **Nos Galan** New Year's Eve
nosi *vb* to become night

n

noson, noswaith (nosweithiau) *nf* night, an evening; **noson stag** stag night

noswyl (-iau) *nf* eve of festival, vigil; **Noswyl Nadolig** Christmas Eve

noswylio *vb* to cease work at eve

nudden *nf* fog, mist, haze

nwy (-on) *nm* gas; **nwy tŷ gwydr** greenhouse gas

nwyd (-au) *nm* passion; emotion

nwydwyllt *adj* passionate

nwydd (-au) *nm* substance, article; (*pl*) goods

nwyf *nm* vivacity, energy, vigour

nwyfiant *nm* vivacity, vigour

nwyfus *adj* sprightly, spirited, lively

nwyol *adj* gaseous

nychdod *nm* feebleness, infirmity

nychlyd *adj* sickly, feeble

nychu *vb* to sicken, to pine, to languish

nydd-dro (-droeau, -droeon) *nm* twist

nydd-droi *vb* to twist, to screw

nyddu *vb* to spin, to twist

nyddwr (-wyr) *nm* spinner

nyf *nm* snow

nyni *pron* we, us

nyrs (-ys) *nfm* nurse

nyrsio *adj* nurse

nytmeg *nm* nutmeg

nyth (-od) *nmf* nest

nythu *vb* to nest, to nestle

O

o¹ *prep* from; of, out of; by

o² *excl* oh!, O!

oblegid *conj, prep* because, for

obry *adv* beneath, below

obstetreg *nm* obstetrics

obstetregydd (-wyr) *nm* obstetrician

ocsid (-iau) *nm* oxide

ocsidiad *nm* oxidisation

ocsidio *vb* to oxidise

ocsidydd (-ion) *nm* oxidising agent

ocsigen *nm* oxygen

ocsiwn *nm* auction

och *excl* oh, alas, woe

ochain *vb* to moan

ochenaid (-eidiau) *nf* sigh

ocheneidio, ochneidio *vb* to sigh

ochr (-au) *nf* side

ochrgamu *vb* to sidestep

ochri *vb* to side

od *adj* odd, remarkable

ôd *nm* snow

odiaeth adj excellent, exquisite
 ▸ adv very, most, extremely
odid adv perchance, peradventure
odl (-au) nf rhyme; ode, song
odli vb to rhyme
odrif (-au) nm odd number
odrwydd nm oddity
odyn (-au) nf kiln
oddeutu prep about
oddi prep out of, from
oddieithr, oddigerth prep except,
 unless
oed (-au) nm age; time
oed-dâl (-iadau) nm
 superannuation
oedfa (-on, -feuon) nf meeting,
 service
oedi vb to delay; to postpone,
 to defer
oediad (-au) nm delay
oedolyn (-ion) nm grown-up
oedran nm age, full age
oedrannus adj aged
oedd vb was, were
oel nm oil
oen (ŵyn) nm lamb
oena vb to lamb, to yean
oenig nf ewe-lamb
oer adj cold, chill, frigid; sad
oeraidd adj cool, chilly
oerddrws (-drysau) nm wind gap
oerfel nm cold
oergell (-oedd) nf refrigerator
oeri vb to cool, to chill
oerllyd adj chilly, frigid; cool
oernad (-au) nf howl, wail,
 lamentation
oernadu vb to howl, to wail, to
 lament
oerni nm cold, coldness, chillness

oes¹ (-oedd, -au) nf age, lifetime; **yn
 oes oesoedd** for ever and ever
oes² vb there is, there are; is there?
oesoffagws nm oesophagus
oesol adj age-long, perpetual
ofer adj vain, idle; prodigal,
 dissipated; waste
ofera vb to waste, to squander,
 to idle
oferedd nm vanity, dissipation
ofergoel (-ion) nf superstition
ofergoeledd, ofergoeliaeth nm
 superstition
ofergoelus adj superstitious
oferwr (-wyr) nm idler, waster
ofn (-au) nm fear, dread
ofnadwy adj awful, terrible,
 dreadful
ofnadwyaeth nf awe, terror, dread
ofni vb to fear, to dread
ofnog adj fearful, timorous
ofnus adj timid, nervous,
 frightened
ofnusrwydd nm timidity,
 nervousness
ofwl (-au) nm ovule
ofydd (-ion) nm ovate
offeiriad (-iaid) nm priest,
 clergyman
offeiriadaeth nf priesthood
offeiriades (-au) nf priestess
offeiriadol adj priestly, sacerdotal
offeiriadu vb to officiate, to
 minister
offer npl implements, tools, gear
offeren (-nau) nf mass
offeryn (-nau, offer) nm
 instrument, tool; **offeryn cerdd**
 musical instrument
offerynnol adj instrumental

177

offerynoliaeth *nf* instrumentality

offrwm (-ymau) *nm* offering, oblation

offrymu *vb* to offer, to sacrifice

offrymwr (-wyr) *nm* offerer, sacrificer

offthalmia *nm* ophthalmia

offthalmosgop (-au) *nm* ophthalmoscope

og (-au), oged (-au, -i) *nf* harrow

ogof (-au, -fâu, -feydd) *nf* cave, cavern; den

ogylch *prep* about

ongl (-au) *nf* angle, corner

onglog *adj* angled, angular

oherwydd *conj, prep* because, for, owing to

ôl *adj* back, hind, hindmost ▸ *nm* (**olion**) mark, print, trace, track; **yn ôl** ago; according to

ôl-dâl (-oedd) *nm* back-pay

ôl-ddodiad (-iaid) *nm* suffix

ôl-ddyddio *vb* to post-date

ôl-ddyled (-ion) *nf* arrears

olew (-au) *nm* oil

olewydd *npl* (*nf* -**en**) olive-trees

olifaid *npl* olive-berries

olrhain *vb* to trace

ôl-troed (olion traed) *nm* footprint; **ôl-troed carbon** carbon footprint

olwr (-wyr) *nm* back (*in rugby*)

olwyn (-ion) *nf* wheel

olwyno *vb* to wheel, to cycle

olwynog *adj* wheeled

Olympaidd *adj* Olympic®

olyniaeth *nf* succession, sequence

olynol *adj* successive, consecutive

olynu *vb* to succeed (to)

olynwr (-wyr), olynydd (-ion) *nm* successor

ôl-ysgrif (-au) *nf* postscript

oll *adv* all, wholly; ever, at all

ombwdsman (-myn) *nm* ombudsman

omlet (-i) *nm* omelette

ond *conj* but, only ▸ *prep* except, save, but

onest *adj* honest

onestrwydd *nm* honesty

oni, onid *adv* not?, is it not? ▸ *conj* if not, unless ▸ *prep* except, save, but

onid e *adv* otherwise, else; is it not

onis *conj* if it is not; **onis caiff** if he does not get it

onnen (onn, ynn) *nf* ash

opiniwn (-ynau) *nm* opinion

opiniynllyd, opiniynus *adj* opinionated

optimistaeth *nf* optimism

optimistaidd *adj* optimistic

optimwm (-tima) *nm* optimum

oracl (-au) *nm* oracle

oraclaidd *adj* oracular

oraens *nm* orange

ordeiniad (-au) *nm* ordination, ordinance

ordeinio *vb* to ordain

ordinhad (-au) *nf* ordinance, sacrament

oren (-nau) *nfm* orange

organ (-au) *nfm* organ

organaidd *adj* organic

organeb (-au) *nf* organism

organig *adj* organic

organydd (-ion) *nm* organist

orgraff (-au) *nf* orthography

orgraffyddol *adj* orthographical

oriawr (oriorau) *nf* watch
oriel (-au) *nf* gallery
orig *nf* little while
oriog *adj* fickle, changeable, inconstant
os *conj* if
osgo *nm* slant, slope, inclination
osgoi *vb* to swerve, to avoid, to evade, to shirk
oslef *nmf* tone, voice
osôn *nmf* ozone
ow *excl* oh!, alas!

p

pa *adj* what, which
pab (-au) *nm* pope
pabell (pebyll) *nf* tent, tabernacle
pabellu *vb* to tent, to tabernacle, to encamp
pabi *nm* poppy
pabwyr[1] *npl* (*nf* **-en**, *nm* **-yn**) rushes
pabwyr[2] *nm* wick, candle-wick
pac (-iau) *nm* pack, bundle
pacio *vb* to pack
Pacistan *nf* Pakistan
padell (-au, -i, pedyll) *nf* pan, bowl
padellaid (-eidiau) *nf* panful
pader (-au) *nm* paternoster, Lord's Prayer
pae *nm* pay, wage
paediatreg *nm* paediatrics
paediatregydd *nm* paediatrician
paent *nm* paint
paentiad (-au) *nm* painting
pafiliwn *nm* pavilion
paffio *vb* to box, to fight
paffiwr (-wyr) *nm* boxer

pagan (**-iaid**) nm pagan, heathen

paganaidd adj pagan, heathen

paganiaeth nf paganism, heathenism

paham adv why, wherefore

paill nm flour; pollen

pair (**peiriau**) nm cauldron, furnace

pais (**peisiau**) nf coat, petticoat

paith (**peithiau**) nm prairie

pâl (**palau**) nf spade

paladr (**pelydr**) nm ray, beam; staff; stem

palaeolithig adj palaeolithic

palas (**-au**) nm palace

Palestina nf Palestine

palf (**-au**) nf palm, hand; paw

palfais (**-eisiau**) nf shoulder

palfalu vb to feel, to grope

palfod (**-au**) nf smack, slap, buffet

palff nm fine, well-built man

pali nm silk brocade

palis (**-au**) nm pale, partition, wainscot

palmant (**-mentydd**) nm pavement

palmantu vb to pave

palmwydd npl (nf **-en**) palm-trees

palu vb to dig, to delve

palwr (**-wyr**) nm digger

pall[1] (**-au**) nm mantle; tent

pall[2] nm fail, failing; lack; lapse

pallu vb to fail, to cease; to neglect; to refuse

pam adv why, wherefore

pamffled, pamffledyn (**pamffledi, pamffledau**) nm pamphlet

pan conj when

pannas npl (nf **panasen**) parsnips

pannwl (**panylau**) nm dimple, hollow

pant (**-iau**) nm hollow, valley

pantio vb to depress, to dent, to sink

pantiog adj hollow, sunken; dimpled

papur (**-au**) nm paper

papuro vb to paper

papurwr (**-wyr**) nm paperer, paperhanger

papuryn nm scrap of paper

pâr[1] (**parau**) nm pair; suit

pâr[2] (**peri**) nm spear, lance

para vb to last, to endure, to continue

parabl (**-au**) nm speech, discourse

parablu vb to speak

paradeim (**-au**) nm paradigm

paradwys nf paradise

parafeddyg (**-on**) nm paramedic

paragraff (**-au**) nm paragraph

paratoad (**-au**) nm preparation

paratoawl adj preparatory

paratoi vb to prepare, to get ready

parc (**-iau**) nm park, field; **parc cenedlaethol** national park

parch nm respect, reverence

parchedig (**-ion**) adj reverend; reverent

parchedigaeth nf reverence

parchu vb to respect, to revere, to reverence

parchus adj respectful; respectable

parchusrwydd nm respectability

pardwn (**-ynau**) nm pardon

pardynu vb to pardon

parddu nm fire-black, smut; soot

pardduo vb to blacken, to vilify, to defame

pared (**parwydydd**) nm partition wall, wall

paredd nm parity

arhad nm continuance, continuation

arhaol adj lasting, perpetual

arhau vb to last, to continue; to persevere

arhaus adj lasting; continual, perpetual

aris nf Paris

arlwr (-yrau) nm sitting room; parlour

arlys nm paralysis, palsy

arlysu vb to paralyse

arod adj ready, prepared; prompt

arodrwydd nm readiness, willingness

arôl (-ion) nm parole

arsel (-i, -ydd) nm parcel

arti (-ïon) nm party

artïaeth nf partisanship

artïol adj partial, biased, partisan

arth (-au) nm part, region; floor

arthed prep about, concerning

arthu vb to part, to divide

arwyden (-nau) nf wall, side; breast

as nm whooping-cough

asg nf Passover, Easter

asgedig (-ion) adj fatted, fattened, fat

asiant (-iannau) nm pageant

asio vb to pass

ast nm paste

astai (-eiod) nf pasty, pie

asturedig adj pasteurised

asturo vb to pasteurise

astwn (-ynau) nm baton, club, cudgel

astynu vb to club, to cudgel, to bludgeon

patriarch (-iaid, patrieirch) nm patriarch

patriarchaeth (-au) nf patriarchate

patriarchaidd adj patriarchal

patrwm (-ymau) nm pattern

patrymlun (-iau) nm template

pathew (-od) nm dormouse

patholeg nf pathology

patholegol adj pathological

patholegydd (-egwyr) nm pathologist

pau nf country

paun (peunod) nm peacock

pawb pron everybody, all

pawen (-nau) nf paw

pawl (polion) nm pole, stake

pe conj if

pebyll nf see **pabell**

pecyn (-nau) nm packet, package

pechadur (-iaid) nm sinner, offender

pechadures (-au) nf woman sinner

pechadurus adj sinful, wicked

pechod (-au) nm sin, offence

pechu vb to sin, to offend

ped conj if

pedair adj f of **pedwar**

pedeirongl adj foursquare

pedi vb to worry, to grieve

pedoffeil (-s), pedoffilydd (-ion) nm paedophile

pedol (-au) nf horseshoe

pedoli vb to shoe

pedrain nf haunches, crupper

pedrongl adj square ▶ nf (-au) square

pedronglog adj quadrangular

pedryfwrdd (-fyrddau) nm quarter-deck

P

pedwar (f **pedair**) adj four
pedwarawd nm quartette
pedwarcarnol (-ion) adj four-footed, quadruped
pedwaredd adj f of **pedwerydd**
pedwarplyg adj fourfold, quarto
pedwerydd (f **pedwaredd**) adj fourth
peddestr nm pedestrian
peddestrig nm walking; pedestrian
pefr adj radiant, bright, beautiful
pefrio vb to radiate, to sparkle
peg (-iau) nm peg
pegio vb to peg
pegor (-au) nm manikin; imp
pegwn (-ynau) nm pivot, pole, axis
Pegwn y Gogledd nm North Pole
pegynol adj axial, polar
peidio vb to cease, to stop, to desist
peilon (-au) nm pylon
peilot (-iaid) nm pilot
peillio vb to bolt, to sift
peint (-iau) nm pint
peintiad (-au) nm painting
peintio vb to paint
peintiwr (-wyr) nm painter
peipen (peipiau) nf pipe
peirianneg nm engineering
peiriannol adj mechanical
peiriannydd (-ianyddion) nm engineer
peiriant (-iannau) nm machine, engine; **peiriant arian** ATM, cash machine; **peiriant chwilio** search engine; **peiriant golchi** washing machine; **peiriant MP3/DVD** MP3/DVD player
peirianwaith nm mechanism
peirianyddol adj mechanical

peiswyn nm chaff
peithyn (-au) nm ridge-tile
pêl (**pelau, peli**) nf ball
pelawd (-au) nf (cricket) over
pêl-droed nf football
peldroediwr nm footballer
pelen nf pill
pel-fâs nf baseball
pêl-fasged nf basketball
pelferyn (-nau) nm ball-bearing
pêl-foli nf volleyball
pêl-rwyd nf netball
pelten (**pelts**) nf blow
pelydr (-au) nm ray, beam
pelydru vb to beam, to gleam, to radiate
pelydryn nm ray, beam
pell adj far, distant, remote, long
pellen (-nau, -ni) nf ball (of yarn)
pellennig adj far, distant, remote
pellhau vb to put or remove far away
pellter (-au, -oedd) nm distance
pen[1] (-nau) nm head; chief; end; to
pen[2] adj head, chief, supreme
penadur (-iaid) nm sovereign
penaduriaeth nf sovereignty
penagored adj open, indefinite, undecided
penarglwyddiaeth nf sovereignty
penbaladr adj general, universal
penben adv at loggerheads
penbleth nf perplexity, quandary
pen-blwydd (-i) nm birthday
penboeth adj hot-headed, fanatical
penboethni nm fanaticism
penboethyn (-boethiaid) nm fanatic

benbwl (-byliaid) *nm* blockhead;
  tadpole
bencadlys *nm* head-quarters
bencampwr (-wyr) *nm* champion
bencampwriaeth (-au) *nf*
  championship
bencerdd (-ceirddiaid) *nm* chief
  musician
benchwiban *adj* giddy, flighty
bendant *adj* positive, emphatic
bendantrwydd *nm* positiveness
bendefig (-ion) *nm* prince, peer,
  noble
bendefigaeth *nf* aristocracy,
  peerage
bendefigaidd *adj* noble,
  aristocratic
bendefiges (-au) *nf* peeress
benderfyniad (-au) *nm*
  determination, resolution
benderfynol *adj* determined,
  resolute
benderfynu *vb* to determine, to
  resolve
bendew *adj* thick-headed, stupid
bendifaddau *adj*: **yn bendifaddau**
  especially
bendil (-iau) *nm* pendulum
bendramwnwgl *adj* topsy-turvy;
  headlong
bendraphen *adj* helter-skelter,
  confused
bendro *nf* giddiness, vertigo;
  staggers
bendroni *vb* to perplex oneself, to
  worry over
bendrwm *adj* top-heavy; drowsy
bendrymu *vb* to drowse, to droop
bendwmpian *vb* to nod, to doze,
  to slumber

penddaredd *nm* giddiness
penddaru *vb* to make or become
  giddy
penddelw *nm* bust
pendduyn (-nod) *nm* botch, boil
penelin (-oedd) *nmf* elbow
penelino *vb* to elbow
penflingo *vb* to scalp
penffest (-au) *nm* headgear
penffol *adj* silly, idiotic
penffrwyn (-au) *nfm* head-stall,
  halter
pengaled *adj* headstrong ▸ *nf*
  knapweed
pengaledwch *nm* stubbornness
pengam *adj* wrong-headed,
  perverse
pen-glin (-iau) *nf* knee
penglog (-au) *nf* skull
pengryf *adj* headstrong, stubborn
pengryniad (-iaid) *nm* roundhead
peniad (-au) *nm* header
penigamp *adj* excellent, splendid
penio *vb* to head
peniog *adj* brainy
penisel *adj* downcast, crestfallen
penlinio *vb* to kneel
penllanw *nm* tide
penllwyd *adj* grey-headed
penllwydni *nm* grey hair, white
  hair
penllywydd (-ion) *nm* sovereign
penllywyddiaeth *nf* sovereignty
pennaeth (penaethiaid) *nm* chief
pennaf *adj* chief, principal
pennawd (penawdau) *nm*
  heading; headline
pennill (penillion) *nm* verse, stanza
pennod (penodau) *nf* chapter
pennoeth *adj* bare-headed

pennog (penwaig) nm herring
pennu vb to specify, to appoint, to determine
penodi vb to appoint
penodiad (-au) nm appointment
penodol adj particular, specific
penrhydd adj unbridled, loose
penrhyddid nm licence, licentiousness
penrhyn (-noedd, -nau) nm cape, foreland
pensaer (-seiri) nm architect
pensaernïaeth nf architecture
pensil (-iau) nm pencil
pensiwn (-iynau) nm pension
pensiynwr nm pensioner
pen-swyddog (-ion) nm chief officer
pensyfrdan adj stunned, dazed
pensyfrdandod nm giddiness, dizziness
pensyfrdanu vb to stun, to daze
pensyth adj perpendicular
pentan (-au) nm hob
penteulu (pennau teuluoedd) nm head of family
pentewyn (-ion) nm firebrand
pentir (-oedd) nm headland
pentis nm penthouse
pentref (-i, -ydd) nm village; homestead
pentrefan (-nau) nm hamlet
pentrefol adj village
pentrefwr (-wyr) nm villager
pentwr (-tyrrau) nm heap, pile
penty (-tai) nm cottage, shed
pentyrru vb to heap, to pile, to accumulate
penuchel adj proud, haughty
penwan adj weak-minded

penwyn adj white-headed
penwynni nm white hair, grey hair
penwythnos nm weekend
penyd (-iau) nm penance, punishment
penyd-wasanaeth nm penal servitude
penysgafn adj light-headed, giddy, dizzy
penysgafnder nm giddiness, dizziness
pêr adj sweet, delicious, luscious
peraidd adj sweet, mellow
perarogl (-au) nm perfume, fragrance
perarogli vb to perfume; to embalm
peraroglus adj fragrant, scented
percoladur (-on) nm percolator
perchen, perchennog (perchenogion) nm owner
perchenogaeth nf ownership
perchenogi vb to possess, to own
perchentywr (-wyr) nm householder
pereidd-dra nm sweetness
pereiddio vb to sweeten
pererin (-ion) nm pilgrim
pererindod (-au) nmf pilgrimage
pererinol adj pilgrim
perfedd (-ion) nm guts, bowels
perfeddwlad (-wledydd) nf interior, heartland
perffaith adj perfect
perffeithio vb to perfect
perffeithrwydd nm perfection
perffeithydd (-ion) nm perfecter
perfformiad (-au) nm performance
perfformio vb to perform
perfformiwr (-wyr) nm performer

eri vb to cause, to bid
erl (-au) nm pearl
erlewyg (-on) nm ecstasy, trance
erlysiau npl aromatic herbs; spices
erllan (-nau) nf orchard
erocsid (-au) nm peroxide
eroriaeth nf melody, music
ersawr (-au) nm fragrance; persawr eillio aftershave (lotion)
ersawrus adj aromatic
erseiniol adj melodious
ersli nm parsley
erson¹ (-au) nm person
erson² (-iaid) nm parson, clergyman
ersonadu vb to impersonate
ersonadwr (-wyr) nm impersonator
ersondy (-dai) nm parsonage
ersonol adj personal
ersonoli vb to personify
ersonoliad (-au) nm personification
ersonoliaeth (-au) nf personality
erswâd nm persuasion
erswadio vb to persuade
ert adj quaint, pretty; pert
erth (-i) nf bush, hedge
erthnasedd (-au) nm relativity, relevance
erthnasiad (-au) nm affiliation
erthnasol adj relevant
erthyn vb to belong, to pertain, to be related
erthynas (-au) nf relation; relationship
erthynol adj relative
erwyl nm purpose, effect
erygl (-on) nm danger, peril, risk

peryglu vb to endanger, to imperil
peryglus adj dangerous, perilous
pesgi vb to feed, to fatten
pesimist (-iaid) nm pessimist
pesimistaidd adj pessimistic
pesimistiaeth nf pessimism
pestl (-au) nm pestle
peswch nm cough
pesychiad (-au) nm cough
pesychu vb to cough
petris npl (nf -en) partridges
petrocemegolau (nm -yn) npl petrochemicals
petrol (-au) nm petrol
petroleg nmf petrology
petrus adj hesitating; doubtful
petruso vb to hesitate, to doubt
petruster nm hesitation, doubt
petryal nm, adj square
peth (-au) nm thing; part, some
petheuach npl odds and ends, trifles
peunes (-od) nf peahen
pianydd (-ion) nm pianist
piau vb owns, possesses
pib (-au) nf pipe, tube; diarrhœa
pibell (-au, -i) nf pipe, tube
pibgod nf bagpipe
pibgorn (-gyrn) nm recorder (music)
pibo vb to pipe; to squirt
pibonwy (nf -en) nf icicles
pibydd (-ion) nm piper
picell (-au) nf dart, javelin, spear
picellu vb to spear, to stab
picfforch (-ffyrch) nf pitchfork
picil nm pickle, trouble
picio vb to dart, to hie
piclo vb to pickle
pictiwr (-tiyrau) nm picture

p

picwns (*nf* **picwnen**) *npl* wasps
piff (**-iau**) *nm* puff, sudden blast
piffian *vb* to snigger, to giggle
pig (**-au**) *nf* point, spike; beak;
spout
pigan *vb* to drizzle
pigdwr (**-dyrau**) *nm* spire, steeple
pigiad (**-au**) *nm* prick, sting;
injection
pigion *npl* pickings, selections
pigo *vb* to pick; to peck; to prick;
to sting
pigog *adj* prickly
pigoglys *nm* spinach
pigyn *nm* thorn, prickle
pilcod *npl* (*nm* **-yn**) minnows
pilen (**-nau**) *nf* membrane, film;
cataract
piler (**-au**, **-i**) *nm* pillar
pilio *vb* to peel, to pare
pili-pala *nm* butterfly
Pilipinas *npl* the Philippines
pilsen (**pils**) *nf* pill
pilyn *nm* garment, rag, clout
pin (**-nau**) *nmf* pin ► *nm* pen; **pin
blaen ffelt** felt-tip pen
pîn *nm* pine, fir
pinacl (**-au**) *nm* pinnacle
pinaclog *adj* pinnacled
pinafal (**-au**) *nf* pineapple
pinbwyntio *vb* to pinpoint
pinc (**-od**) *nm* finch, chaffinch
pincio *vb* to pink; **parlwr pincio**
beauty parlour
pincws (**-cysau**) *nm* pincushion
pindwll (**-dyllau**) *nm* pinhole
pinsiad (**-au**) *nm* pinch
pinsio *vb* to pinch
pinwydden *nf* pine
pioden (**pïod**) *nf* magpie

piser (**-au**, **-i**) *nm* pitcher, jug, can
pistyll (**-oedd**) *nm* spout; cataract
pistyllio *vb* to spout, to gush
pisyn (**-nau**, **pisiau**) *nm* piece
piti *nm* pity
pitw *adj* petty, puny, paltry
piw (**-od**) *nm* dug, udder
Piwritan (**-iaid**) *nm* Puritan
piwritanaidd *adj* puritan,
puritanical
piwritaniaeth *nf* puritanism
pla (**plâu**) *nmf* plague; nuisance
pladur (**-iau**) *nf* scythe
pladurwr (**-wyr**) *nm* mower
plaen¹ *adj* plain, clear
plaen² (**-au**) *nm* plane
plaenio *vb* to plane
plagio *vb* to plague, to tease, to
torment
plagus *adj* annoying, troublesome
plaid (**pleidiau**) *nf* side, party; **Plaid
Cymru** the Welsh Nationalist
Party, the Party of Wales
planced (**-i**) *nf* blanket
planed (**-au**) *nf* planet
planhigfa (**-feydd**) *nf* plantation
planhigyn (**-higion**) *nm* plant;
planhigyn wy aubergine
plannu *vb* to plant; to dive
plannwr (**-wyr**) *nm* planter
plant *npl* (*nm* **plentyn**) children
planta *vb* to bear children
plantos *npl* (little) children
plas (**-au**) *nm* hall, mansion, palace
plasaidd *adj* palatial
plastr (**-au**) *nm* plaster
plastro *vb* to plaster
plastrwr (**-wyr**) *nm* plasterer
plât, plat (**-iau**) *nm* plate
platŵn (**-tynau**) *nm* platoon

platwydr nm plate-glass

ple nm plea

pledio vb to plead, to argue

pledren (-nau, -ni) nf bladder

pleidgarwch nm partisanship

pleidio vb to side with, to support

pleidiol adj favourable, partial

pleidiwr (-wyr) nm partisan, supporter

pleidlais (-leisiau) nf vote, suffrage

pleidleisio vb to vote

pleidleisiwr (-wyr) nm voter

plencyn (planciau) nm plank

plentyn (plant) nm child, infant

plentyndod nm childhood, infancy

plentyneiddiwch nm childishness

plentynnaidd adj childish, puerile

plentynrwydd nm childishness

pleser (-au) nm pleasure

pleserdaith (-deithiau) nf trip, excursion

pleserus adj pleasurable, pleasant

plesio vb to please

plet, pleten (pletiau) nf pleat

pletio vb to pleat

pletiog adj pleated

pleth (-au) nf plait

plethdorch (-au) nf wreath

plethu vb to plait, to weave, to fold

plewra (-e) nm pleura

plicio vb to pluck, to peel, to strip

plisg npl (nm -yn) shells, husks, pods

plisgo vb to shell, to husk

plisman, plismon (plismyn) nm police officer

plismones (-au) nf police officer

plith nm midst

pliwrisi nm pleurisy

plocyn (plociau) nm block

plod adj, nm plaid, tartan

ploryn (-nod) nm pimple

plorynnod npl acne

pluen (plu) nf feather; **plu eira** snow-flakes

plufyn (pluf) nm = pluen

pluo, plufio vb to pluck, to deplume; to plume

pluog adj feathered, fledged

plwc (plyciau) nm pluck; space, while

plwg (plygiau) nm plug

plwm nm lead

plws nm plus

plwtoniwm nm plutonium

plwyf (-i, -ydd) nm parish

plwyfol adj parochial

plwyfolion npl parishioners

plycio vb to pluck

plyg (-ion) nm fold, double; hollow

plygadwy adj collapsible

plygain nm cock-crow, dawn; matins

plygeiniol adj dawning; very early

plygell (-au) nf folder

plygiad (-au) nm folding, fold

plygu vb to fold; to bend, to stoop; to bow

plymio vb to plumb, to sound

plymwr (-wyr) nm plumber

po particle: **gorau po gyntaf** the sooner the better

pob adj each, every; all

pobi vb to bake; to roast; to toast

pobiad (-au) nm baking, batch

pobl (-oedd) nf people

poblog adj populous

poblogaeth (-au) nf population

poblogaidd adj popular

poblogeiddio vb to popularize

187

poblogi vb to people, to populate
poblogrwydd nm popularity
pobwr (-wyr), pobydd (-ion) nm baker
poced (-i) nf pocket
pocedu vb to pocket
pocer (-i, -au) nm poker
podlediad nm podcast
poen (-au) nmf pain, torment
poenedigaeth nf torment
poeni vb to pain, to torment; to worry, to grieve
poenus adj painful
poenwr (-wyr) nm tormentor, torturer
poenydio vb to torment, to torture; to fret, to vex
poenydiwr (-wyr) nm tormentor
poer (-ion) nm spittle, saliva
poeri vb to spit, to expectorate
poeryn nm spittle
poeth adj hot; burning; dŵr poeth heart-burn
poethder, poethni nm hotness, heat
poethdon (-nau) nf heat wave
poethi vb to heat
pôl (polau) nm poll
polaredd nm polarity
polareiddiad nm polarisation
polareiddio vb to polarise
polymorff nm polymorph
polymorffedd nm polymorphism
polyn (polion) nm pole
pomgranad (-au) nm pomegranate
pompiwn (-iynau) nm pumpkin, gourd
pompren nf plank bridge, footbridge

ponc, poncen (ponciau) nf hillock; bank
poncyn nm hillock; bank
pont (-ydd) nf bridge, arch
pontffordd (-ffyrdd) nf fly-over, viaduct
pontio vb to bridge
popeth nm everything
poplys npl (nf -en) poplar-trees
popty (-tai) nm bakehouse; oven; popty ping microwave (oven)
porc nm pork
porchell (perchyll) nm piglet
porfa (-feydd) nf pasture, grass
porfelu vb to pasture
porffor adj, nm purple
pori vb to graze, to browse; to eat
pornograffi nm pornography
pornograffiaeth nf pornography
Portiwgal nf Portugal
portread (-au) nm portrayal, pattern
portreadu vb to portray
porth[1] nm aid, help, succour
porth[2] **(pyrth)** nm gate, gateway; porch door; porth awyr airport
porthfa (-feydd) nf port, harbour; ferry
porthi vb to feed
porthiannus adj well-fed, high-spirited
porthiant nm food, sustenance, support
porthladd (-oedd) nm port, harbour, haven
porthmon (-myn) nm cattle-dealer
porthor (-ion) nm porter, door-keeper, commissionaire
pos (-au) nm riddle, conundrum, puzzle

posib, posibl *adj* possible

posibilrwydd *nm* possibility

positif *adj* positive

positifiaeth *nf* positivism

post (pyst) *nm* post; pillar; **post sothach** junk mail

poster (-i) *nm* poster

postfarc (-iau) *nm* postmark

postio *vb* to post

postman, postmon (postmyn) *nm* postman

postyn (pyst) *nm* post

pot (-iau) *nm* pot

potelaid (-eidiau) *nf* bottleful

potelu *vb* to bottle

poten (-ni) *nf* paunch; pudding

potensial (-au) *nm, adj* potential

potes *nm* pottage, broth, soup

potio *vb* to pot; to tipple

potsiar (-s) *nm* poacher

potsio *vb* to poach

pothell (-au, -i) *nf* blister

pothellu *vb* to blister

powdr (-au) *nm* powder

powl, powlen (powliau) *nf* bowl, basin

powlio *vb* to roll; to wheel; to trundle

powltis (-au) *nm* poultice

practis *nm* practice

praff *adj* thick, stout

praffter *nm* thickness, stoutness, girth

pragmatiaeth *nf* pragmatism

praidd (preiddiau) *nm* flock

pranc (-iau) *nm* frolic, prank

prancio *vb* to caper, to prance

pratio *vb* to pat, to stroke, to caress

praw, prawf (profion) *nm* test, trial, proof; **prawf gyrru** driving test

preblan *vb* to chatter, to babble

pregeth (-au) *nf* sermon, discourse

pregethu *vb* to preach

pregethwr (-wyr) *nm* preacher

pregethwrol *adj* preacher-like

pregowtha *vb* to jabber, to rant

preifat *adj* private

preifatrwydd *nm* privacy

preimin *nm* ploughing match

prelad (-iaid) *nm* prelate

preladiaeth *nf* prelacy

preliwd (-au) *nm* prelude

premiwm (-iymau) *nm* premium

pren (-nau) *nm* tree, timber; wood

prentis (-iaid) *nm* apprentice

prentisiaeth *nf* apprenticeship

prentisio *vb* to apprentice

prepian *vb* to babble, to blab

pres *nm* brass; bronze; copper; money

preseb (-au) *nm* crib, stall

presennol *adj, nm* present

presenoldeb *nm* presence; attendance

presenoli *vb* to be present (*reflexive*)

presgripsiwn (-iynau) *nm* prescription

preswyl *nm* abode, dwelling

preswylfa (preswylfeydd) *nf* abode, dwelling

preswylio *vb* to dwell, to reside, to inhabit

preswylydd (-ion, -wyr) *nm* dweller, inhabitant

pric (-iau) *nm* stick, chip

P

189

prid adj dear, costly ► nm price, value

pridwerth nm ransom

pridd nm mould, earth, soil, ground

priddell (-au, -i) nf clod

priddglai nm loam

priddio, priddo vb to earth

priddlech (-au, -i) nf tile

priddlestr (-i) nm earthenware vessel

priddlyd adj earthy

priddo vb see **priddio**

priddyn nm earth, soil, mould

prif adj prime, principal, chief; prif gwrs main course

prifardd (-feirdd) nm chief bard

prifathro (-athrawon) nm headmaster, principal

prifddinas (-oedd) nf metropolis, capital

prifiant nm growth

prifio vb to grow

priflythyren nf capital

prifodl (-au) nf chief rhyme

prifysgol (-ion) nf university

priffordd (-ffyrdd) nf highway

prin adj scarce, rare ► adv scarcely

prinder, prindra nm scarceness, scarcity

prinhau vb to make or grow scarce, to diminish

print (-iau) nm print

printiedig adj printed

printio vb to print

printiwr (-wyr) nm printer

priod adj own; proper; married ► n husband or wife, spouse

priodas (-au) nf marriage, wedding

priodasfab (-feibion) nm bridegroom

priodasferch (-ed) nf bride

priodasol adj matrimonial

priod-ddull (-iau) nm idiom

priodfab (-feibion) nm bridegroom

priodferch (-ed) nf bride

priodi vb to marry

priodol adj proper, appropriate

priodoldeb (-au) nm propriety

priodoledd (-au) nf attribute

priodoli vb to attribute

prior (-iaid) nm prior

priordy (-dai) nm priory

pris (-iau) nm price, value

prisiad, prisiant nm valuation

prisio vb to price, to value; to prize

prisiwr (-wyr) nm valuer

problem (-au) nf problem

proc (-iau) nm poke

procer (-au, -i) nm poker

procio vb to poke; to throb

procsi nm proxy

prodin (-au) nm protein

profedig adj approved, tried

profedigaeth (-au) nf trouble, tribulation

profedigaethus adj beset with trials

profi vb to prove; to taste; to try; to experience

profiad (-au) nm experience; profiad gwaith work experience

profiadol adj experienced

profiannaeth (-au) nf probation

proflen (-ni) nf proof-sheet

profocio vb to provoke, to tease

profoclyd adj provoking, provocative

profwr (-wyr) nm taster, tester

proffes (-au) nf profession

proffesiwn (-iynau) nm profession

proffesu *vb* to profess
proffid *nf* profit
proffidio *vb* to profit, to benefit
proffidiol *adj* profitable
proffwyd (-i) *nm* prophet
proffwydes (-au) *nf* prophetess
proffwydo *vb* to prophesy
proffwydol *adj* prophetic
proffwydoliaeth (-au) *nf* prophecy
project (-au) *nm* project
proses (-au) *nmf* process
prosesu *vb* to process
prosesydd *nm* processor;
  prosesydd geiriau word processor
protest (-au) *nf* protest
Protestannaidd *adj* Protestant
Protestant (-aniaid) *nm*
  Protestant
protestio *vb* to protest
protestiwr (-wyr) *nm* protestor
prudd *adj* grave, serious, sad; wise
pruddaidd *adj* sad, gloomy,
  mournful
prudd-der *nm* sadness, gloom
pruddglwyf *nm* depression,
  melancholy
pruddglwyfus *adj* depressed,
  melancholy
pruddhau *vb* to sadden, to depress
Prwsia *nf* Prussia
pryd¹ (-iau) *nm* time; season ▸ *nm*
  (-au) meal
pryd² *adv* while, when, since
pryd³ *nm* form, aspect; complexion
Prydain *nf* Britain; **Prydain Fawr**
  Great Britain
Prydeindod *nm* Britishness
Prydeinig *adj* British
Prydeiniwr (-wyr) *nm* Brit (*inf*),
  British person

pryder (-on) *nm* anxiety, solicitude
pryderu *vb* to be anxious
pryderus *adj* anxious, solicitous
prydferth *adj* beautiful, handsome
prydferthu *vb* to beautify
prydferthwch *nm* beauty
prydles (-au, -i) *nf* lease
prydlesu *vb* to lease
prydlon *adj* timely, punctual
prydlondeb *nm* punctuality
prydydd (-ion) *nm* poet
prydyddu *vb* to compose poetry,
  to poetize
pryf (-ed) *nm* insect; worm; vermin
pryfedog *adj* verminous
pryfleiddiad (-au) *nm* insecticide
pryfoclyd *adj* irritating
pryfyn *nm* worm
prŷn *adj* bought, purchased
prynedigaeth *nmf* redemption
prynhawn (-au) *nm* afternoon
prynhawnol *adj* afternoon,
  evening
pryniad *nm* purchase
pryniant *nm* purchase
prynu *vb* to buy, to purchase; to
  redeem
prynwr (-wyr) *nm* buyer; redeemer
prysg *nm* bush, wood
prysgwydd *npl* brushwood
prysur *adj* busy, hasty; diligent;
  serious
prysurdeb *nm* haste, hurry;
  busyness
prysuro *vb* to hurry, to hasten
pulpud (-au) *nm* pulpit
pum, pump *adj* five
pumawd (-au) *nm* quintet
pumed *adj* fifth
pumongl (-au) *nm* pentagon**

punt (**punnoedd, punnau**) *nf* pound (*money*)

pupur *nm* pepper

pur *adj* pure, sincere ▸ *adv* very, fairly

purdan *nm* purgatory

purdeb *nm* purity, sincerity

puredigaeth *nf* purification

puredd *nm* purity, innocence

purfa (**-feydd**) *nf* refinery

purion *adj* very well; right enough

puro *vb* to purify, to cleanse

puror *nm* harpist

purydd (**-ion**) *nm* purist

putain (**-einiaid**) *nf* prostitute

puteindra *nm* prostitution

pwdin *nm* pudding, dessert

pwdlyd *adj* sulking

pwdr *adj* rotten, corrupt, putrid

pwdu *vb* to pout, to sulk

pŵer (**-au**) *nm* power

pwerdy *nm* power station

pwerus *adj* powerful

pwff (**pyffiau**) *nm* puff, blast

pwffian *vb* to puff

pwl (**pyliau**) *nm* fit, attack, paroxysm

pŵl *adj* blunt, obtuse; dull, dim

pwll (**pyllau**) *nm* pit, pool, pond; **pwll glo** coal pit; **pwll tro** whirlpool

pwmp (**pympiau**) *nm* pump

pwn (**pynnau**) *nm* pack, burden

pwnc (**pynciau**) *nm* point, subject, question

pwniad (**-au**) *nm* nudge, dig

pwnio *vb* to nudge; to beat, to thump, to wallop

pwrcas (**-au**) *nm* purchase

pwrcasu *vb* to purchase

pwrffil *nm* train

pwrpas (**-au**) *nm* purpose

pwrpasol *adj* suitable

pwrpasu *vb* to purpose, to intend

pwrs (**pyrsau**) *nm* purse, bag; udder; scrotum

pwt[1] (**pytiau**) *nm* stump, bit

pwt[2], **pwtian** *vb* to prod, to poke

pwti *nm* putty

pwy *pron* who

Pwyl *nf* Poland

Pwylaidd *adj* Polish

Pwyleg *nf* Polish

pwyll *nm* sense, discretion

pwyllgor (**-au**) *nm* committee

pwyllgorwr (**-wyr**) *nm* committee-man

pwyllo *vb* to pause, to consider, to reflect

pwyllog *adj* discreet, prudent, deliberate

pwynt (**-iau**) *nm* point

pwyntil *nm* tab, tag; pencil

pwyntio *vb* to point; to fatten

pwyo *vb* to beat, to batter, to pound

pwys (**-au, -i**) *nm* weight, burden, pressure; pound (lb.); importance

pwysau *nm* weight

pwysedd *nm* pressure

pwysi (**-ïau**) *nm* posy

pwysig *adj* important

pwysigrwydd *nm* importance

pwyslais (**-leisiau**) *nm* emphasis

pwysleisio *vb* to emphasize, to highlight

pwyso *vb* to weigh, to press; to lean, to rest; to rely

pwyswr (**-wyr**) *nm* weigher

pwyth (**-au**) *nm* stitch

pwytho *vb* to stitch
pwythwr (-wyr) *nm* stitcher
pybyr *adj* strong, stout, staunch, valiant
pybyrwch *nm* stoutness, vigour, valour
pydew (-au) *nm* well, pit
pydredig *adj* rotten, putrid
pydredd *nm* rottenness, putridity, rot
pydru *vb* to rot, to putrefy
pyg *nm* pitch, bitumen
pygddu *adj* pitch-black
pygu *vb* to pitch
pyngad, pyngu *vb* to cluster
pylni *nm* bluntness, dullness
pylor *nm* dust, powder
pylu *vb* to blunt, to dull
pyllog *adj* full of pits
pyllu *vb* to pit
pymtheg *adj, nm* fifteen
pymthegfed *adj* fifteenth
pyncio *vb* to sing, to play, to make melody
pynio *vb* to burden, to load
pys *npl* (*nf* -**en**) peas
pysgod *npl* (*nm* **pysgodyn**) fish, fishes; **sglodion pysgod** fish fingers; **pysgod a sglodion** fish and chips; **y Pysgod** Pisces
pysgodfa (-feydd) *nf* fishery
pysgota *vb* to fish
pysgotwr (-wyr) *nm* fisherman
pystylad *vb* to stamp with the feet
pytaten (-tws) *nf* potato
pythefnos (-au) *nmf* fortnight

r

rabi (-niaid) *nm* rabbi
rabinaidd *adj* rabbinical
radio *nm* radio
radioleg *nf* radiology
radiws *nm* radius
ras (-ys) *nf* race
rasal, raser (-elydd, -erydd) *nf* razor
realaidd *adj* realistic
realistig *adj* realistic
record (-iau) *nf* record
recordiad (-au) *nm* recording
reiat *nf* row, riot
reis *nm* rice
reit *adv* right, very, quite
ridens *nf* fringe, nap
riwl *nf* ruler
robin goch *nm* robin
robin y gyrrwr *nm* gadfly
roced (-i) *nf* rocket
Romania *nf* Romania
ruban (-au) *nm* ribbon
rŵan *adv* now

rwbel *nm* rubble, rubbish
rwber *nm* rubber
rwdins *npl* (*nf* **rwden**) swedes
Rwmania *nf* Rumania
Rwsia *nf* Russia
Rwsiad (**Rwsiaid**) *nm* Russian
(citizen)
Rwsieg *nm* Russian (language)
rysáit *nf* recipe

rhaca (**-nau**) *nf* rake
rhacanu *vb* to rake
rhacs (*nm* **rhecsyn**) *npl* rags
rhad¹ *adj* free; cheap
rhad² (**-au**) *nm* grace, favour,
blessing
rhadlon *adj* gracious, kind; genial
rhadlondeb, rhadlonrwydd *nm*
graciousness, cheapness
rhadus *adj* economical
rhaeadr (**-au**) *nf* cataract, waterfall
rhaeadru *vb* to pour, to gush
rhaff (**-au**) *nf* rope, cord
rhaffo, rhaffu *vb* to rope
rhag *prep* before, against; from;
lest ▸ *prefix* pre-, fore-, ante-
rhagafon (**-ydd**) *nf* tributary
rhagair (**-au**) *nm* preface
rhagarfaethiad *nm* predestination
rhagarfaethu *vb* to predestine
rhagarweiniad *nm* introduction
rhagarweiniol *adj* introductory,
preliminary

rhagarwyddo *vb* to foretoken, to portend

rhagbaratoawl *adj* preparatory

rhagbrawf (-brofion) *nm* foretaste; preliminary test

rhagdraeth (-au) *nm* preface, introduction

rhag-dyb (-ion) *nm* presupposition

rhagdybied, rhagdybio *vb* to presuppose

rhagddodiad (-iaid) *nm* prefix

rhagddywedyd, rhag-ddweud *vb* to foretell

rhagenw (-au) *nm* pronoun

rhagenwol *adj* pronominal

rhagfarn (-au) *nf* prejudice

rhagfarnllyd *adj* prejudiced

rhagfarnu *vb* to prejudice

rhagferf (-au) *nf* adverb

rhagflaenor (-iaid) *nm* forerunner

rhagflaenu *vb* to precede, to anticipate, to forestall

rhagflaenydd (-ion, -wyr) *nm* predecessor, precursor

rhagflas *nm* foretaste

rhagfur (-iau) *nm* bulwark

rhagfyfyrio *vb* to premeditate

rhagfynegi *vb* to foretell

Rhagfyr *nm* December

rhaglaw (-iaid, -lofiaid) *nm* prefect, viceroy, governor

rhaglawiaeth *nf* prefecture, governorship

rhaglen (-ni) *nf* program(me); **rhaglen gyfrifiadur** computer program

rhaglennu *vb* to program(me)

rhaglennydd (raglenwyr) *nm* programmer

rhagluniaeth (-au) *nf* providence

rhagluniaethol *adj* providential

rhaglunio *vb* to predestine, to predestinate

rhagod *vb* to ambush, to hinder, to waylay

rhagofal *nm* precaution

rhagofnau *npl* forebodings

rhagolwg (-ygon) *nm* prospect, outlook; **rhagolygon y tywydd** weather forecast

rhagolygon *npl* forecast

rhagor (-au, -ion) *nm* difference; more

rhagorfraint (-freintiau) *nf* privilege

rhagori *vb* to exceed, to excel, to surpass

rhagoriaeth (-au) *nf* superiority; excellence

rhagorol *adj* excellent, splendid

rhagoroldeb *nm* excellence

rhagorsaf (-oedd) *nf* out-station; outpost

rhagredegydd (-ion) *nm* forerunner

rhagrith (-ion) *nm* hypocrisy

rhagrithio *vb* to practise hypocrisy

rhagrithiol *adj* hypocritical

rhagrithiwr (-wyr) *nm* hypocrite

rhagrybuddio *vb* to forewarn

rhag-weld *vb* to foresee

rhagwelediad *nm* foresight, prescience

rhagwybod *vb* to foreknow

rhagwybodaeth *nf* foreknowledge

rhagymadrodd (-ion) *nm* introduction

rhai *pron* ones ▸ *adj* some

rhaib *nm* rapacity, greed; spell

rhaid (rheidiau) *nm* need, necessity

rh

rhaidd (**rheiddiau**) *nf* antler

rhain *pron* these

rhamant (**-au**) *nf* romance

rhamantu *vb* to romance

rhamantus *adj* romantic

rhan (**-nau**) *nf* part, portion; fate

rhanbarth (**-au**) *nm* division, district

rhanbarthol *adj* regional

rhandir (**-oedd**) *nfm* division, district

rhangymeriad (**-iaid**) *nm* participle

rhaniad (**-au**) *nm* division

rhannu *vb* to divide, to share, to distribute

rhannwr (**rhanwyr**) *nm* divider, sharer

rhanrif *nm* fraction

rhathell (**-au**) *nf* rasp

rhathiad *nm* friction, chafing

rhathu *vb* to rub, to rasp, to file

rhaw (**-iau, rhofiau**) *nf* spade, shovel

rhawd *nf* course, career

rhawg *adv* for a long time (to come)

rhawio, rhofio *vb* to shovel

rhawn *coll n* coarse long hair, horse-hair

rhech *nf* fart

rhechain *vb* to fart

rhedeg *vb* to run; to flow; **rhedeg allan (o)** run out (of); **rhedeg i ffwrdd, rhedeg ymaeth** run away

rhedegfa (**-feydd**) *nf* racecourse, race

rhedegog *adj* running, flowing

rhedegydd (**-ion, -wyr**) *nm* runner

rhedfa *nf* running, course, race

rhediad *nm* running, trend; slope

rhedweli (**-ïau**) *nf* artery

rhedyn *npl* (**nf -en**) fern

rheffyn (**-nau**) *nm* cord; string; rigmarole

rheg (**-au, -feydd**) *nf* curse; swearword

rhegen yr ŷd, rhegen ryg *nf* corncrake

rhegi *vb* to curse

rheglyd *adj* given to cursing, profane

rheng (**-au, -oedd**) *nf* row, rank

rheibio *vb* to raven, to ravage, to ravish

rheibus *adj* rapacious, of prey

rheidiol *adj* necessary, needful

rheidrwydd *nm* necessity, need

rheidus *adj* necessitous, needy

rheiddiadur *nm* radiator

rheilen *nf* rail

rheilffordd (**-ffyrdd**) *nf* railway

rheini *pron* those

rheitheg *nf* rhetoric

rheithfarn (**-au**) *nf* verdict

rheithgor (**-au**) *nm* jury

rheithiwr (**-wyr**) *nm* juryman, juror

rheithor (**-ion, -iad**) *nm* rector

rhelyw *nm* residue, rest, remainder

rhemp *nf* excess; defect

rhent (**-i**) *nm* rent

rhentu *vb* to rent

rheol (**-au**) *nf* rule, regulation

rheolaeth *nf* rule, management, control; **rheolaeth bell** remote control

rheolaidd *adj* regular; **yn rheolaidd** regularly

rheoleiddio *vb* to regulate; to regularize

rheoli vb to rule, to govern, to control

rheoliadur (-on) nm: rheoliadur calon, rheoliadur y galon pacemaker

rheolwr (-wyr) nm ruler, controller

rhes (-i) nf line, stripe; row, rank

rhesen (rhesi) nf line, parting, streak, stripe

rhesin (-au, -ingau) nm raisin

rhesog adj striped; ribbed

rhestl (-au) nf rack

rhestr (-au, -i) nf list; row

rhestru vb to list

rheswm (-ymau) nm reason

rhesymeg nf logic

rhesymegol adj logical

rhesymol adj reasonable, rational

rhesymoldeb nm reasonableness

rhesymolwr (-wyr) nm rationalist

rhesymu vb to reason

rhetoreg, rhethreg nf rhetoric

rhew (-oedd, -ogydd) nm frost, ice

rhewfryn (-iau) nm iceberg

rhewgell (-oedd) nf freezer

rhewgist nf freezer

rhewi vb to freeze

rhewlif nm glacier

rhewllyd adj icy, frosty, frigid

rhewyn (-au) nm ditch, stream

rhewynt (-oedd) nm freezing wind

rhi nm king, lord

rhiain (rhianedd) nf maiden

rhialtwch nm pomp; festivity; jollity

rhiant (rhieni) nm parent; **rhiant sengl** single parent

rhibidirês nf rigmarole

rhibin nm streak

rhic (-iau) nm notch, nick; groove

rhicio vb to score

rhiciog adj notched; grooved; ribbed

rhidyll (-iau) nm riddle, sieve

rhidyllio, rhidyllu vb to riddle, to sift

rhieingerdd (-i) nf love-poem

rhieni npl parents

rhif (-au) nm number

rhifo vb to number, to count, to reckon

rhifol (-ion) nm numeral

rhifyddeg, rhifyddiaeth nf arithmetic

rhifyddwr (-wyr) nm arithmetician

rhifyn (-nau) nm number

rhigol (-au, -ydd) nf rut, groove

rhigwm (-ymau) nm rigmarole; rhyme

rhigymu vb to rhyme, to versify

rhigymwr (-wyr) nm rhymester

rhingyll (-iaid) nm sergeant, bailiff

rhimyn (-nau) nm strip, string

rhin (-iau) nf virtue, essence

rhincian vb to creak; to gnash

rhiniog (-au) nm threshold

rhinwedd (-au) nfm virtue

rhinweddol adj virtuous

rhip nm strickle

rhisgl nm bark

rhith (-iau) nm form, guise, appearance, image; foetus

rhithio vb to appear

rhithyn nm atom, particle, scintilla

rhiw (-iau) nf hill, acclivity

rhoch nf grunt, groan; death rattle

rhochain, rhochian vb to grunt

rhod (-au) nf wheel, orb; ecliptic

rhodfa (-feydd) nf walk, promenade, avenue

rh

197

rhodiad *nm* walk

rhodianna *vb* to stroll

rhodio *vb* to walk, to stroll

rhodres *nm* ostentation, affectation

rhodresa *vb* to behave ostentatiously

rhodresgar *adj* ostentatious, affected

rhodreswr (-wyr) *nm* swaggerer

rhodd (-ion) *nf* gift, present

rhoddi *vb* to give, to bestow, to yield; to put

rhoddwr (-wyr) *nm* giver, donor

rhoi *vb* to give, to bestow, to yield; to put; **rhoi yn ôl, rhoi nôl** put back

rhol, rhôl (-iau) *nf* roll

rholbren (-ni) *nm* rolling-pin

rholen (rholiau) *nf* roll; roller

rholio *vb* to roll

rholyn (rholion) *nm* roll; roller; **rholyn bara, rholyn o fara** bread roll; **rholyn tŷ bach, rholyn toiled** toilet roll

rhombws (rhombi) *nm* rhombus

rhonc *adj* rank, stark, out-and-out

rhos¹ (-ydd) *nf* moor, heath; plain

rhos² *npl* (*nm* **-yn**) roses

rhost *adj* roast, roasted

rhostio *vb* to roast

rhosyn (-nau) *nm* rose

rhu *nm* roar

rhuad (-au) *nm* roaring, roar

rhuadwy *adj* roaring

rhuchen (rhuchion) *nf* husk; film, pellicle

rhudd *adj* red, crimson

rhuddell *nf* rubric

rhuddem (-au) *nf* ruby

rhuddin *nm* heart of timber

rhuddion *npl* bran

rhuddygl *nm* radish

Rhufain *nf* Rome

Rhufeinaidd *adj* Roman

Rhufeiniad (-iaid), Rhufeiniwr (-wyr) *nm* Roman

Rhufeinig *adj* Roman

rhugl *adj* free, fluent, glib

rhuglen (-ni) *nf* rattle

rhuglo *vb* to rattle

rhuo *vb* to roar, to bellow, to bluster

rhusio *vb* to start, to scare, to take fright

rhuthr (-au) *nm* rush; attack; sally

rhuthro *vb* to rush; to attack, to assault

rhwbio *vb* to rub, to chafe; **rhwbio allan** rub out

rhwd *nm* rust

rhwng *prep* between, among

rhwnc *nm* snort, snore; death-rattle

rhwth *adj* gaping, distended

rhwyd (-au, -i) *nf* net, snare

rhwydo *vb* to net, to ensnare

rhwydog *adj* reticulated, netted

rhwydwaith (-weithiau) *nm* network

rhwydweithio *vb* to network ▸ *nm* networking; **rhwydweithio cymdeithasol** social networking

rhwydd *adj* easy, expeditious, prosperous

rhwyddhau *vb* to facilitate

rhwyddineb *nm* ease, facility

rhwyf (-au) *nf* oar

rhwyflong (-au) *nf* galley

rhwyfo *vb* to row; to sway; to toss about

rhwyfus adj restless
rhwyfwr (-wyr) nm rower, oarsman
rhwyg (-iadau) nf rent, rupture; schism
rhwygo vb to rend, to tear
rhwyllwaith nm fretwork, lattice-work
rhwym adj bound ▸ nm (-au) bond, tie; obligation
rhwymedig adj bound, obliged
rhwymedigaeth (-au) nf bond, obligation
rhwymedd nm constipation
rhwymiad (-au) nm binding
rhwymo vb to bind, to tie; to constipate
rhwymwr (-wyr) nm binder
rhwymyn (-nau) nm band, bond, bandage
rhwysg (-au) nm sway; pomp
rhwysgfawr adj pompous, ostentatious
rhwystr (-au) nm hindrance, obstacle
rhwystro vb to hinder, to prevent, to obstruct
rhwystrus adj embarrassed, confused
rhy adv too
rhybedio vb to rivet
rhybudd (-ion) nm notice, warning
rhybuddio vb to warn, to admonish, to caution
rhybuddiwr (-wyr) nm warner
rhych (-au) nmf furrow, rut, groove
rhychog adj furrowed, seamed
rhychwant (-au) nm span
rhychwantu vb to span
rhyd (-au, -iau) nf ford

rhydio vb to ford
rhydlyd adj rusty
rhydu vb to rust
rhydwytho vb to reduce
rhydd adj free; loose; liberal
rhyddfraint nf freedom
Rhyddfrydiaeth nf Liberalism
rhyddfrydig adj liberal, generous
Rhyddfrydol adj Liberal (in politics)
Rhyddfrydwr (-wyr) nm Liberal, Radical
rhyddhad nm liberation, emancipation
rhyddhau vb to free, to release, to liberate
rhyddhäwr (rhyddhawyr) nm liberator
rhyddiaith nf prose
rhyddid nm freedom, liberty
rhyddieithol adj prose, prosaic
rhyddni nm looseness, diarrhoea
rhyfedd adj strange, queer, wonderful
rhyfeddnod (-au) nm note of exclamation
rhyfeddod (-au) nmf wonder, marvel
rhyfeddol adj wonderful, marvellous
rhyfeddu vb to wonder, to marvel
rhyfel (-oedd) nmf war, warfare
rhyfela vb to wage war, to war
rhyfelgar adj warlike, bellicose
rhyfelgri nm war-cry, battle-cry
rhyfelgyrch (-oedd) nm campaign
rhyfelwr (-wyr) nm warrior
rhyferthwy nm torrent, inundation
rhyfon npl currants

rh

199

rhyfyg *nm* presumption, foolhardiness

rhyfygu *vb* to presume, to dare

rhyfygus *adj* presumptuous; foolhardy

rhyg *nm* rye

rhyglyddu *vb* to deserve, to merit

rhygnu *vb* to rub, to grate, to jar; to harp

rhygyngu *vb* to amble; to caper, to mince

rhyngrwyd *nf* internet

rhyngu *vb*: rhyngu bodd to please

rhyngweithiol *adj* interactive

rhyngwladol *adj* international

rhyndod *nm* shivering, chill

rhynion *npl* grits, groats

rhynllyd *adj* shivering, chilly

rhysedd *nm* abundance, excess

rhython *npl* cockles

rhythu *vb* to gape; to stare

rhyw *adj* some, certain ▸ *nmf* (-iau) sort; sex

rhywbeth *nm* something

rhywfaint *nm* some amount

rhywfodd, rhywsut *adv* somehow

rhywiaeth *nf* sexism

rhywiaethol *adj* sexist

rhywiog *adj* kindly, genial; fine; tender

rhywiol *adj* sexual

rhywioldeb *nm* sexuality

rhywle *adv* somewhere, anywhere

rhywogaeth (-au) *nf* species, sort, kind

rhywun (rhywrai) *nm* someone, anyone

S

Sabath, Saboth (-au) *nm* Sabbath

Sabothol *adj* Sabbath, sabbatic(al)

sacrament (-au) *nmf* sacrament

sacramentaidd *adj* sacramental

sach (-au) *nfm* sack

sachaid (-eidiau) *nf* sackful

sachu *vb* to sack, to bag

sad *adj* firm, steady, solid; sober

sadio *vb* to firm, to steady

sadistiaeth *nf* sadism

sadrwydd *nm* firmness, steadiness

Sadwrn (-yrnau) *nm* Saturn; dydd Sadwrn Saturday

saer (seiri) *nm* wright, mason, carpenter

saerniaeth *nf* workmanship, construction

saernïo *vb* to fashion, to construct

Saesneg *nf, adj* English

Saesnes (-au) *nf* Englishwoman

saets *nm* sage

saeth (-au) *nf* arrow, dart

saethiad (-au) *nm* shooting

saethu *vb* to shoot, to dart; to blast

saethwr (-wyr) *nm* shooter, shot

saethydd (-ion) *nm* shooter, archer; **y Saethydd** Sagittarius

saethyddiaeth *nf* archery

saethyn (-nau) *nm* projectile

safadwy *adj* stable

safanna *nm* savannah

safbwynt (-iau) *nm* standpoint

safiad *nm* standing; stature; stand

safio *vb* to save

safle (-oedd) *nm* position, station, situation; **safle gwe** website

safn (-au) *nf* mouth, jaws

safnrhwth *adj* open-mouthed, gaping

safnrhythu *vb* to gape, to stare

safon (-au) *nf* standard, criterion; **safon byw** standard of living

safoni *vb* to standardise

safonol *adj* standard

saff *adj* safe

saffir *nm* sapphire

saffrwm, saffron *nm* crocus

sagrafen (-nau) *nf* sacrament

sang (-au) *nf* pressure, tread

sangu, sengi *vb* to tread, to trample

saib (seibiau) *nm* leisure; pause, rest

saig (seigiau) *nf* meal, dish

sail (seiliau) *nf* base, foundation

saim (seimiau) *nm* grease

sain (seiniau) *nf* sound, tone

Sais (Saeson) *nm* Saxon, Englishman

saith *adj, nm* seven

sâl *adj* poor; poorly; ill; **sâl môr** seasick

salad (-au) *nm* salad

saldra *nm* poorness; illness

salm (-au) *nf* psalm

salmydd (-ion) *nm* psalmist

salw *adj* poor, mean, vile; ugly

salwch *nm* illness

Sallwyr *nm* Psalter

sampl (-au) *nf* sample

samplu *vb* to sample

Sanct *nm* the Holy One

sanctaidd *adj* holy

sancteiddio *vb* to sanctify, to hallow

sancteiddrwydd *nm* holiness, sanctity

sandal (-au) *nm* sandal

sant (saint, seintiau) *nm* saint

santes (-au) *nf* female saint

sarff (seirff) *nf* serpent

sarhad (-au) *nm* insult, disgrace, injury

sarhau *vb* to insult, to affront, to injure

sarhaus *adj* insulting, offensive, insolent

sarn (-au) *nf* causeway ▶ *nm* litter, ruin, destruction

sarnu *vb* to trample; to litter; to spoil, to ruin

sarrug *adj* gruff, surly, morose

sarugrwydd *nm* gruffness, surliness

sasiwn (-iynau) *nm* C.M. Association

satan (-iaid) *nm* satan

sathredig *adj* common, vulgar

sathru *vb* to tread, to trample

Saudi Arabia, Sawdi Arabia *nf* Saudi Arabia

sawdl (sodlau) *nmf* heel

sawl *pron* whoso, he that; **pa sawl** how many

sawr, sawyr *nm* savour

sawrio, sawru *vb* to savour

sawrus *adj* savoury

saws *nm* sauce

sba (-on) *nm* spa

Sbaen *nf* Spain

sbageti *nm* spaghetti

sbam *nm* spam

sbamio *vb* to spam

sbamiwr (-wyr) *nm* spammer

sbaner (-i) *nf* spanner

sbâr (sbarion) *nm* spare; (pl) leavings

sbario *vb* to spare, to save

sbectol *nf* spectacle(s)

sbeit *nf* spite

sbeitio *vb* to spite

sbeitlyd *adj* spiteful

sbel (-iau) *nf* spell

sbon *adv*: **newydd sbon** brand-new

sbonc (-iau) *nm* leap, jerk

sboncen *nf* squash

sbort *nf* sport, fun, game

sbri *nm* spree, fun

sbring *nm* spring

sbwylio *vb* to spoil

sebon (-au) *nm* soap

seboni *vb* to soap, to lather; to soft-soap, to flatter

sebonwr (-wyr) *nm* flatterer

secsist *adj* sexist

sect (-au) *nf* sect

sectyddiaeth *nf* sectarianism

sectyddol *adj* sectarian

sech *adj* f of **sych**

sedd (-au) *nf* seat, pew

sef *conj* that is to say, namely, to wit

sefnig *nm* pharynx

sefydledig *adj* established

sefydliad (-au) *nm* establishment, institution

sefydlog *adj* fixed, settled, stationary, stable

sefydlogrwydd, sefydlowgrwydd *nm* stability

sefydlu *vb* to establish, to found, to settle

sefyll *vb* to stand; to stop; to stay

sefyllfa (-oedd) *nf* situation, position

sefyllian *vb* to stand about, to loiter

sefyllwyr *npl* bystanders

segur *adj* idle

segura *vb* to idle

segurdod *nm* idleness

segurwr (-wyr) *nm* idler

seguryd *nm* idleness

seguryn, segurwr (-wyr) *nm* idler

sengi *vb* to tread, to trample

sengl *adj* single

seiat (-adau) *nf* fellowship meeting, 'society'

seiber-fwlio *vb* to cyberbully

seibiant *nm* leisure, respite; **seibiant salwch** sick leave

seibio *vb* to pause

seiciatreg *nf* psychiatry

seiciatrydd *nm* psychiatrist

seicoleg *nf* psychology

seicolegydd (-wyr) *nm* psychologist

seidin *nm* sidings

seilio *vb* to ground, to found

seilwaith *nm* infrastructure

seimio *vb* to grease

seimllyd *adj* greasy

seinber *adj* melodious, euphonious

seindorf (-dyrf) nf band
seineg nf phonetics
seinfawr adj loud
seinfforch (-ffyrch) nf tuning-fork
seinio vb to sound, to resound; to pronounce
seintio vb to saint, to canonize
seintwar nf sanctuary
seinyddol adj phonetic
Seisnig adj English
Seisnigaidd adj English, Anglicized
Seisnigeiddio, Seisnigo vb to Anglicize
seithblyg adj sevenfold
seithfed adj seventh
seithongl (-au) nf heptagon
seithug adj futile, fruitless, bootless
sêl¹ nf zeal
sêl² (seliau) nf seal
sêl³ (-s) nf sale; **sêl cist car** car boot sale
Seland Newydd nf New Zealand
seld (-au) nf dresser, sideboard, bookcase
seler (-au, -i, -ydd) nf cellar
selio vb to seal
selni nm illness
selog adj zealous, ardent
selsig (-od) nf black-pudding, sausage
semanteg nf semantics
seminar (-au) nf seminar
seml adj f of **syml**
sen (-nau) nf reproof, rebuke, censure, snub
senedd (-au) nf senate; parliament
seneddol adj senatorial, parliamentary
seneddwr (-wyr) nm senator

sennu vb to rebuke, to censure
sentimentaleiddiwch nm sentimentality
sêr see **seren**
seraff (-iaid) nm seraph
Serbia nf Serbia
serch¹ conj, prep although, notwithstanding
serch² (-iadau) nm affection, love
serchog adj affectionate, loving
serchowgrwydd nm affection, love
serchu vb to love
serchus adj loving, affectionate, pleasant
sêr-ddewin (-iaid) nm astrologer
sêr-ddewiniaeth nf astrology
seremoni (-ïau) nf ceremony
seremonïol adj ceremonial
seren (sêr) nf star; asterisk; **seren ffilmiau** film star
serennog adj starry
serennu vb to sparkle, to scintillate
serfyll adj unsteady
seri nm causeway, pavement
serio vb to sear
sero (-au) nm zero
serth adj steep, precipitous; obscene
serthedd nm ribaldry, obscenity
serwm nm serum
seryddiaeth nf astronomy
seryddol adj astronomical
seryddwr (-wyr) nm astronomer
sesbin nm shoehorn
sesiwn (sesiynau) nm session; **sesiwn ymarfer** workout
set (-iau) nf set
sêt (seti) nf seat, pew; **sêt fawr** deacons' pew

S

203

setl (-au) nf settle

setlo vb to settle

sethrydd (-ion) nm treader, trampler

sew (-ion) nm juice; pottage; delicacy

sffêr nf sphere

sg- see also **ysg-**

sgaldan(u) vb to scald

sgâm (sgamiau) nf scheme, dodge, scam

sgamio vb to scheme, to dodge

sgamiwr (-wyr) nm scammer

sganiwr (-wyr) nm scanner; **sganiwr feirws** virus scanner

sgaprwth adj uncouth, rough

sgarff (-iau) nf scarf

sgêri adj scary

sgil nm pillion; **sgil effaith** side effect

sgil-effaith nf side effect

sgïo vb to ski

sgipio vb to skip

sgiw nf settle; **ar y sgiw** askew

sglefren nf slide

sglefrio vb to skate, to slide

sglefrolio vb to roller-skate

sgolor (-ion) nm scholar

sgon nf scone

sgôr nfm score

sgori(o) vb to score

sgorpion (-au) nm scorpion y **Sgorpion** Scorpio

sgrafell (-i) nf scraper

sgrechian nf to shriek

sgrech y coed nf jay

sgrin nf screen

sgriw (-iau) nf screw

sgwâr (-iau) nm square

sgwd (sgydiau) nf cataract, waterfall

sgwrs (sgyrsiau) nf talk, chat, conversation

sgwrsio vb to talk, to chat

sgwter (-i) nm scooter

si nm whiz, buzz; rumour, murmur

siaced (-i) nf jacket, coat

siâd (siadau) nf pate

sialc nm chalk

sialens nf challenge

sialensio vb to challenge

siambr nf chamber

sianel (-i, -ydd) nf channel

siant (-au) nf chant

siâp nm shape

siapio vb to shape

siâr nf share

siarad vb to talk, to speak ▸ nm talk

siaradus adj talkative, garrulous

siaradwr (-wyr) nm talker, speaker

siario vb to share

siars nf charge, command

siarsio vb to charge, to enjoin, to warn

siart (-iau) nm chart

siartr (-au) nf charter

siasbi nm shoehorn

siawns nf chance

siawnsio vb to chance

sibrwd vb to whisper, to murmur ▸ nm **(-ydion)** whisper, murmur

sicr adj sure, certain; secure

sicrwydd nm certainty, assurance

sicrhau vb to assure, to affirm, to confirm; to secure

sidan (-au) nm silk

sidanaidd adj silky

sidanbryf (-ed) nm silkworm

sidydd nm zodiac

sied (-au) nf shed

siêd nm escheat, forfeit

siew nf show

siffrwd vb to rustle, to shuffle

sigâr nf cigar

sigarét (sigaretau) nf cigarette

sigledig adj shaky, rickety, unstable

siglen (-nydd) nf swing; bog, swamp

siglo vb to shake, to quake, to rock, to swing, to wag

sil (-od) nm spawn, fry

silff (-oedd) nf shelf

silwair nm silage

sill (-iau), sillaf (-au) nf syllable

sillafiad nm spelling

sillafiaeth nf spelling

sillafu vb to spell

sillgoll (-au) nf apostrophe

simnai (-neiau) nf chimney

simsan adj unsteady, tottering, rickety

simsanu vb to totter

sinach (-od) nf balk, waste ground; skinflint

sinc nm zinc

sinema (sinemâu) nf cinema

sinig nm cynic

sinigaidd adj cynical

sinsir nm ginger

sïo vb to hiss, to whiz; to murmur, to purl

sioe (-au) nf show; **sioe gêm, sioe gêmau** game show; **sioe sgwrsio** chat show

siofinydd nm chauvinist

siol (-au) nf skull, pate

siôl (siolau) nf shawl

siom (-au) nm disappointment

siomedig adj disappointed, disappointing

siomedigaeth (-au) nf disappointment

siomi vb to disappoint, to let down; to balk, to thwart; to deceive

siomiant nm disappointment

sionc adj brisk, nimble, agile, active

sioncio vb to brisk

Siôn Corn nm Father Christmas

sioncrwydd nm briskness, agility

sioncyn y gwair nm grasshopper

siop (-au) nf shop; **dyn siop** shop assistant; **merch siop** shop assistant

siopa vb to shop

siopladrad (-au) nm shoplifting

siopwr (-wyr) nm shopkeeper

sipian vb to sip, to sup, to suck

sipio vb to zip

siprys nm mixed corn (oats and barley)

sipsiwn npl gypsies

sir (-oedd) nf shire, county

siriol adj cheerful, bright, pleasant

sirioldeb nm cheerfulness

sirioli vb to cheer, to brighten

sirydd (-ion), siryf (-ion) nm sheriff

siryddiaeth nf shrievalty

sisial vb to whisper

siswrn (-yrnau) nm scissors

siwgr nm sugar

siwgro vb to sugar

siwmper (-i) nf jumper

siwr, siŵr adj sure, certain

siwrnai (-eiau) nf journey ▸ adv once

siwt (-iau) nf suit

siwtio vb to suit

slaf (slafiaid) nm slave, drudge
slei adj sly
sleifio vb to slink
sleisen nf slice
slic adj slick
Slofacia nf Slovakia
Slofenia nf Slovenia
slotian vb to paddle, to dabble; to tipple
slumyn see **ystlum**
slwt nf slut (offensive)
smala adj droll
smalio vb to joke
sment nm cement
smocio vb to smoke (tobacco)
smociwr (-wyr) nm smoker
smotiog adj spotty
smotyn (smotiau) nm spot
smwddio vb to iron
smwt adj snub
smyglo vb to smuggle
smygu see **smocio**
snisin nm snuff
snwffian vb to snuff, to sniff; to snuffle; to whimper
sobr adj sober, serious
sobreiddio, sobri vb to sober
sobrwydd nm sobriety, soberness
socas (-au) nf gaiter, legging
sodli vb to heel
sodomiaeth nf sodomy
sodr nm solder
soddi vb to submerge
soeg nm brewers' grains, draff
sofl npl stubble
sofliar (-ieir) nf quail
sofraniaeth nf sovereignty
sofren (sofrod) nf sovereign (coin)
solas nm solace, joy
sol-ffa nm sol-fa

solffaeo vb to sol-fa
sôn vb to talk, to mention ▸ nm report, mention, word
soned (-au) nf sonnet
sonedwr (-wyr) nm composer of sonnets
soniarus adj melodious, tuneful; loud
soriant nm indignation, displeasure
sorod npl dross, dregs, refuse
sorri vb to chafe, to sulk, to be displeased
sosban (-nau, -benni) nf saucepan
sosej (-ys) nf sausage
soser (-i) nf saucer; **soser lloeren** satellite dish
sosialaeth nf socialism
sosialydd nm socialist
sothach nfm refuse, rubbish, trash
sownd adj fast
st- see also **yst-**
stac (-iau) nf stack
stad (-au) nf estate; state; **stad ddiwydiannol** industrial estate
staen (-au) nm stain
staenio vb to stain
staer nm stair
stafell (-oedd) nf room; **stafell sgwrsio** chat room
stâl (-au) nf stall
stamp (-iau) nmf stamp
stampio vb to stamp
starts nm starch
steil (-iau) nf style; surname; **steil gwallt** hairdo
stên (stenau) nf pitcher
stesion (-au) nf station
sticil, sticill nf stile
stilio vb to question

stiward (-iaid) nm steward

stiwdio nf studio

stoc (-au) nf stock

stomp nf bungle, mess, muddle

stompio vb to beat, to pound; to bungle, to mess

stompiwr (-wyr) nm bungler

stôr nf storage

stori (-ïau, -iâu, straeon) nf story, tale

storm, storom (stormydd) nf storm

stormus adj stormy

storom nf see **storm**

straegar adj gossiping, gossipy

strancio vb to play tricks

strategaeth nf strategy

strategol adj strategic

strategydd (-ion) nm strategist

streic (-iau) nf strike

stremp nf streak

striplun nm strip

strwythur nm structure

stryd (-oedd) nf street; **stryd fawr** high street

stumog nf stomach

stwc (stycau) nm pail, bucket

stwff (styffiau) nm stuff

stwffio vb to stuff, to thrust

stwffwl (styffylau) nm post; staple

stŵr nm stir

styffylwr nm stapler

styffylydd (-ion) nm stapler

styntiwr nm stuntman

su nm buzz, murmur, hum

suad nm buzzing, lulling; hum

sucan nm gruel

sudd (-ion) nm juice, sap

suddgloch (-glychau) nf diving-bell

suddlong (-au) nf submarine

suddo vb to sink, to dive; to invest (money)

sug (-ion) nm juice, sap

sugn nm suck; suction; sap

sugno vb to suck, to imbibe, to absorb

Sul (-iau) nm: **dydd Sul** Sunday

Sulgwyn nm Whitsunday

suo vb to buzz, to hum; to lull, to hush

sur adj sour, acid

surbwch nm spoilsport

surdoes nm leaven

surni nm sourness, staleness, tartness

suro vb to sour

suryn nm acid

sut nm manner; plight; **(pa) sut?** how? what sort of?

sw nf zoo

swalpio vb to flounder, to jump, to bounce

swci adj tame, pet

swcro vb to succour

swcwr nm succour

swch (sychau) nf ploughshare; tip; lips

Sweden nf Sweden

swil adj shy, bashful

swilder nm shyness, bashfulness

Swistir nf: **y Swistir** Switzerland

switsfwrdd (switsfyrddau) nm switchboard

swllt (sylltau) nm shilling

swm (symiau) nm sum, bulk

swmbwl (symbylau) nm goad

swmer (-au) nm beam; pack

swmp nm bulk

swmpus adj bulky

207

swn nm noise, sound

swnian vb to murmur, to grumble, to nag

swnio vb to sound, to pronounce

swnllyd adj peevish, querulous

swnt nm sound, strait

swoleg nf zoology

swp (sypiau) nm mass, heap; cluster

swper (-au) nmf supper

swrn (syrnau) nf fetlock, ankle
  ▸ **nm** good number

swrth adj heavy, sluggish; sullen

sws (-ys) nf kiss

swta adj abrupt, curt

swydd (-au, -i) nf office; county

swyddfa (-feydd) nf office

swyddog (-ion) nm officer, official

swyddogaeth nf office, function

swyddogol adj official

swyngyfaredd (-ion) nf sorcery, witchcraft

swyngyfareddwr (-wyr) nm sorcerer

swyn (-ion) nm charm, fascination, spell, magic

swyno vb to charm, to enchant, to bewitch

swynol adj charming, fascinating

swynwr (-wyr) nm magician, wizard

swynwraig (-wragedd) nf sorceress

sy see **sydd**

syber adj sober, decent; clean, tidy

sych (f sech) adj dry

sychder nm dryness, drought

sychdir (-oedd) nm dry land

sychdwr nm drought

syched nm thirst

sychedig adj thirsty, parched, dry

sychedu vb to thirst

sychin nf drought

sychlyd adj dry

sychu vb to dry, to dry up; to wipe dry, to wipe

sychwr nm dryer

sychydd nm dryer

sydyn adj sudden, abrupt

sydynrwydd nm suddenness

sydd vb is, are

syfi npl (nf syfien) strawberries

syflyd vb to stir, to move, to budge

syfrdan adj giddy, dazed, stunned

syfrdandod nm giddiness, stupor

syfrdanol adj stunning

syfrdanu vb to daze, to bewilder, to stupefy, to stun

sylfaen (-feini) nf foundation

sylfaenol adj basic

sylfaenu vb to found

sylfaenwr (-wyr), sylfaenydd (-ion) nm founder

sylw (-adau) nm notice, attention, remark

sylwadaeth nf observation

sylwebaeth nf commentary

sylwebydd nm commentator

sylwedydd (-ion) nm observer

sylwedd (-au) nm substance, reality

sylweddol adj substantial, real

sylweddoli vb to realize

sylweddoliad nm realization

sylwi vb to observe, to regard, to notice

syllu vb to gaze

symbal (-au) nm cymbal

symbol nm symbol

symboliaeth nf symbolism

ymbyliad *nm* stimulus, encouragement

ymbylu *vb* to goad, to spur, to stimulate

ymbylydd (-ion) *nm* stimulant

ymio *vb* to sum

yml (*f* **seml**) *adj* simple

ymledd *nm* simplicity

ymleiddiad *nm* simplification

ymleiddio *vb* to simplify

ymlrwydd *nm* simplicity

ymol *adj* middling, fair

ymud *vb* to move, to remove

ymudiad (-au) *nm* movement, removal

ymudol *adj* moving, movable, mobile

yn *adj* amazed; astonishing, surprising

ynagog (-au) *nm* synagogue

ynamon *nm* cinnamon

yndod *nm* marvel, amazement, surprise

yndrom (-au) *nm* syndrome

syndrom Down Down's syndrome

ynfyfyrdod *nm* reverie

ynfyfyrio *vb* to muse

ynfyfyriol *adj* vacant

ynhwyro *vb* to sense

ynhwyrol *adj* sensible

ynhwyrus *adj* sensuous

yniad (-au) *nm* notion, idea, view

yniadaeth *nf* conception

ynied, synio *vb* to think, to believe, to feel

synnu *vb* to marvel, to be amazed, to surprise, to be surprised

ynnwyr (synhwyrau) *nm* sense; **synnwyr digrifwch** sense of humour

synwyroldeb *nm* sensibleness

synwyrusrwydd *nm* sensuousness

sypio *vb* to pack, to heap, to bundle

sypyn (-nau) *nm* package, packet

syr *nm* sir

syrcas *nf* circus

syrffed *nm* surfeit

syrffedu *vb* to surfeit

syrffio *vb* to surf

Syria *nf* Syria

syrthiedig *adj* fallen

syrthio *vb* to fall, to tumble

syrthni *nm* listlessness, sloth; inertia

system *nmf* system

systematig *adj* systematic

syth *adj* stiff; straight

sythu *vb* to stiffen, to straighten

sythwelediad *nm* intuition

s

t

tabernacl (-au) nm tabernacle
tabl (-au) nm table
tablen nf ale, beer
tabŵ nm taboo
tabwrdd (-yrddau) nm drum
tabyrddu vb to drum, to thrum
taclau npl (nm **teclyn**) tackle, gear
taclo vb to tackle
taclu vb to put in order, to trim
taclus adj neat, trim, tidy
tacluso vb to trim, to tidy
taclusrwydd nm tidiness
tacsi (-s) nm taxi; **gyrrwr tacsi** taxi driver
tacteg (-au) nf tactic
Tachwedd nm November
tad (-au) nm father
tad-cu nm grandpa, grandfather
tadmaeth (-au, -od) nm foster father
tadogaeth nf paternity; derivation
tadogi vb to father
tadol adj fatherly, paternal

tad-yng-nghyfraith nm father-in-law
taenelliad nm sprinkling, affusion
taenellu vb to sprinkle
taenellwr (-wyr) nm sprinkler
taenlen (-ni) nf spreadsheet
taenu vb to spread, to expand, to stretch
taenwr (-wyr) nm spreader, disseminator
taeog adj churlish, blunt ▸ nm (-au, -ion) churl
taeogaidd adj churlish, rude
taer adj earnest, importunate, urgent
taerineb, taerni nm earnestness, importunity
taeru vb to insist, to maintain; to contend, to wrangle
tafarn (-au) nfm tavern, inn, public-house
tafarndy (-dai) nm public-house
tafarnwr (-wyr) nm inn-keeper, publican
tafell (-au, -i, tefyll) nf slice
tafellu vb to slice
tafl (-au) nf cast; scale; **ffon dafl** sling
tafladwy adj disposable
tafledigion npl projectiles
taflegryn (taflegrau) nm missile
tafleisiaeth nf ventriloquism
tafleisydd (-ion, -wyr) nm ventriloquist
taflen (-nau, -ni) nf table, list, leaflet; **taflen waith** worksheet
taflennu vb to tabulate
tafliad (-au) nm throw; set-back
taflod (-ydd) nf loft; **taflod y genau** palate

taflodol *adj* palatal
taflu *vb* to throw, to fling, to cast, to hurl; to throw away
tafluniad *nm* projection
taflunio *vb* to project
taflunydd *nm* projector
tafod (-au) *nm* tongue
tafodi *vb* to berate, to scold
tafodiaith (-ieithoedd) *nf* speech, language, dialect
tafod-leferydd *nm* speech, utterance; **ar dafod-leferydd** by rote
tafol¹ *nf* scales, balance
tafol² *npl* dock
tafoli *vb* to weigh up, to assess
tafotrwg *adj* foul-mouthed, abusive
tafotrydd *adj* garrulous, flippant
Tafwys *nf* Thames
taffi *nm* toffee
tagell (-au, tegyll) *nf* gill; wattle; dewlap; double chin
tagellog *adj* wattled; double-chinned
tagfa (-feydd) *nf* choking, strangling
tagu *vb* to choke, to stifle; to strangle
tangnefedd *nmf* peace
tangnefeddu *vb* to make peace; to appease
tangnefeddus *adj* peaceable, peaceful
tangnefeddwr (-wyr) *nm* peacemaker
tai *see* **tŷ**
taid (teidiau) *nm* grandfather
tail *nm* dung, manure
tair *adj f of* **tri**

taith (teithiau) *nf* journey, voyage, progress
tal *adj* tall, high, lofty
tâl¹ (talau, taloedd) *nm* end, forehead
tâl² (taliadau) *nm* pay, payment; **taloedd** rates
talaith (-eithiau) *nf* diadem; province, state
talar (-au) *nf* headland in field
talcen (-nau, -ni) *nm* forehead; gable
taldra *nm* tallness, loftiness, stature
taleb (-au, -ion) *nf* receipt, voucher
taledigaeth *nf* payment, recompense
taleithiol *adj* provincial
talent (-au) *nf* talent
talentog *adj* talented
talfyriad (-au) *nm* abbreviation, abridgement
talfyrru *vb* to abbreviate, to abridge
talgryf *adj* sturdy, robust; impudent
taliad (-au) *nm* payment
talm *nm* space, while; quantity, number; **er ys talm** long ago
talog *adj* jaunty
talp (-au, -iau) *nm* mass, lump
talpiog *adj* lumpy
talu *vb* to pay, to render; to answer, to suit; to be worth
talu-wrth-ddefnyddio *adj* pay-as-you-go
talwr (-wyr) *nm* payer
talwrn *nm* threshing floor; poetic contest

211

tamaid (**-eidiau**) *nm* morsel, bit, bite

tan *prep* to, till, until, as far; under

tân (**tanau**) *nm* fire

tanbaid *adj* fiery, hot, fervent; brilliant

tanbeidrwydd *nm* fierce heat, ardour

tanchwa (**-oedd**) *nf* fire-damp; explosion

tanddaearol *adj* underground, subterranean

tanddwr *adj* underwater

tanforol *adj* submarine

tanffordd *nf* underpass

taniad *nm* ignition, firing

tanio *vb* to fire, to stoke

taniwr (**-wyr**) *nm* firer, firefighter, stoker

tanlinellu *vb* to underline

tanlwybr *nm* subway

tanlli *adj*: **newydd sbon danlli** brand new

tanllwyth (**-i**) *nm* blazing fire

tanllyd *adj* fiery

tannu *vb* to adjust, to spread, to make (bed)

tanodd *adv* below, beneath

tanosodiad (**-au**) *nm* understatement

Tansanïa *nf* Tanzania

tant (**tannau**) *nm* chord, string

tanwent *nm* fuel

tanwydd *coll n* firewood, fuel

tanysgrifiad (**-au**) *nm* subscription

tanysgrifio *vb* to subscribe

tanysgrifiwr (**-wyr**) *nm* subscriber

taradr (**terydr**) *nm* auger; **taradr y coed** woodpecker

taran (**-au**) *nf* (peal of) thunder

taranfollt (**-au**) *nf* thunderbolt

taranu *vb* to thunder

tarddell *nf* source, spring

tarddiad (**-au**) *nm* source, derivation

tarddle (**-oedd**) *nm* source

tarddu *vb* to sprout, to spring; to derive, to be derived

tarfu *vb* to scare, to scatter

targed (**-au**) *nm* target

tarian (**-au**) *nf* shield

tario *vb* to tarry

taro *vb* to strike, to smite, to hit, to knock; to tap; to stick; to hot; to suit

tarren (**tarenni, -ydd**) *nf* knoll, rock

tarth (**-oedd**) *nm* mist, vapour

tarw (**teirw**) *nm* bull; **y Tarw** Taurus

tarwden *nf* ringworm

tas (**teisi**) *nf* rick, stack

tasel *nm* tassel

tasg (**-au**) *nf* task

tasgu *vb* to task; to start, to jump; to splash, to spirt

tato, tatws *npl* (*nf* **taten,** *nf* **tatysen**) potatoes

taw[1] *nm* silence; **rhoi taw ar** silence

taw[2] *conj* that

tawch *nm* vapour, haze, mist, fog

tawdd *adj* melted, molten, dissolved

tawedog *adj* silent, taciturn

tawedogrwydd *nm* taciturnity

tawel *adj* calm, quiet, still, tranquil

tawelu *vb* to calm; to grow calm

tawelwch *nm* calm, quiet, tranquillity

tawelydd *nm* silencer

tawelyn *nm* tranquillizer

tawlbwrdd nm draughtboard, backgammon

tawtologiaeth nf tautology

te nm tea; **te llysieuol** herbal tea

tebot (-au) nm teapot

tebyg adj similar, like, likely

tebygol adj likely, probable

tebygolrwydd nm likelihood, probability

tebygrwydd nm likeness, resemblance

tebygu vb to liken, to resemble; to suppose

tecáu vb to beautify, to adorn, to embellish

teclyn (taclau) nm tool, instrument; **teclyn heb afael** hands-free kit

tecstio vb to text

techneg nf technique

technegol adj technical

technegydd nm technician

technoleg (-au) nf technology; **technoleg gwybodaeth** information technology, IT

technolegol adj technological

teg adj fair, beautiful, fine

tegan (-au) nm plaything, toy, bauble

tegell (-au, -i) nm kettle, teakettle

tegwch nm fairness, beauty

tei nmf tie

teiar nm tyre

teigr (-od) nm tiger

teilchion npl fragments, atoms, shivers

teiliwr (-eilwriaid) nm tailor

teilo vb to dung, to manure

teilsen nf tile

teilwng adj worthy; deserved

teilwra vb to tailor

teilwres (-au) nf tailoress

teilwriaeth nf tailoring

teilyngdod nm worthiness, merit

teilyngu vb to deserve, to merit; to deign

teim nm thyme

teimlad (-au) nm feel, feeling, sensation, emotion

teimladol adj emotional

teimladrwydd nm feelingness, sensibility

teimladwy adj feeling; sensitive

teimlo vb to feel, to touch, to handle, to manipulate

teimlydd (-ion) nm feeler, antenna, tentacle

teios npl cottages

teip (-iau) nm type

teipiadur (-ion) nm typewriter

teipio vb to type

teipydd (-ion) nm typist

teisen (-nau) nf cake

teitl (-au) nm title

teithi npl traits, characteristics, qualities

teithio vb to travel, to journey

teithiol adj travelling, itinerant

teithiwr (-wyr) nm traveller, passenger

telathrebiaeth nf telecommunication

teledu nm television ▸ vb to televise; **teledu cylch cyfyng** CCTV

teleffon (-au) nm telephone

teler (-au) nm term, condition

teligraff nm telegraph

telm (-au) nf snare

telori vb to warble; to quaver

telyn (-au) nf harp

213

telyneg (-ion) *nf* lyric
telynegol *adj* lyrical
telynegwr *nm* lyric poet
telynor (-ion) *nm* harpist
telynores *nf* female harpist
teml (-au) *nf* temple
tempro *vb* to temper
temtasiwn (-iynau) *nfm* temptation
temtio *vb* to tempt
temtiwr (-wyr) *nm* tempter
tenant (-iaid) *nm* tenant
tenantiaeth *nf* tenancy
tenau *adj* thin, lean; slender; rarified; sensitive
tendio *vb* to tend, to mind
teneuad *nm* dilution
teneuo *vb* to thin, to become thin, to dilute
teneuwch *nm* thinness, leanness; tenuity
tenewyn (-nau) *nm* flank
tenlli, tenllif *nm* lining
tennis *nm* tennis
tennyn (tenynnau) *nm* cord, rope, halter
têr *adj* clear, refined, pure, fine
teras (-au) *nf* terrace
terfyn (-au) *nm* end, extremity, bound
terfyniad (-au) *nm* ending, termination
terfynol *adj* final; conclusive
terfynu *vb* to end, to terminate, to determine
terfysg (-oedd) *nm* tumult, riot
terfysgaeth *nf* terrorism
terfysgaidd, terfysglyd *adj* riotous, turbulent

terfysgu *vb* to riot, to rage, to surge
terfysgwr (-wyr) *nm* rioter, insurgent
term (-au) *nm* term
terminoleg *nf* terminology
tes *nm* sunshine, warmth, heat; haze
tesog *adj* sunny, hot, close, sultry
testament (-au) *nm* testament
testamentwr (-wyr) *nm* testator
testun (-au) *nm* text, theme, subject
testunio *vb* to taunt, to deride
tetanws *nm* tetanus
teth (-au) *nf* teat
teulu (-oedd) *nm* family; **teulu-yng nghyfraith** in-laws
teuluaidd *adj* family, domestic
tew *adj* thick, fat, plump
tewdra, tewdwr *nm* thickness, fatness
tewhau *vb* to thicken, to fatten
tewi *vb* to keep silence, to be silent
tewychu *vb* to thicken, to fatten; to condense
tewychydd *nm* condenser
tewyn (-ion) *nm* ember, brand
teyrn (-edd, -oedd) *nm* monarch, sovereign
teyrnas (-oedd) *nf* kingdom, realm; **y Deyrnas Gyfunol, y Deyrnas Unedig** the United Kingdom
teyrnasiad (-au) *nm* reign
teyrnasu *vb* to reign
teyrnfradwr (-wyr) *nm* traitor
teyrnfradwriaeth *nf* (high) treason
teyrngar *adj* loyal
teyrngarwch *nm* loyalty

teyrnged (-au) nf tribute
teyrnwialen (-wiail) nf sceptre
TG n IT
ti pron you
ticed (-i) nmf ticket
tician vb to tick
tid (-au) nf chain
tila adj feeble, puny, insignificant
tim (timau) nm team
tin (-au) nf bottom; rump; tail
tinc (-iadau) nm clang, tinkle
tincian vb to tinkle, to chink, to
  click, to clank
tip (-iadau) nm tick (of clock)
tipian vb to tick
tipyn (-nau, tipiau) nm bit
tir (-oedd) nm land, ground,
  territory
tirio vb to land, to ground
tiriog adj landed
tiriogaeth (-au) nf territory
tiriogaethol adj territorial
tirion adj kind, tender, gentle,
  gracious
tiriondeb nm kindness, tenderness
tirlun (-iau) nm landscape
tirol adj relating to land
tirwedd nf relief (geographic)
tisian vb to sneeze
tithau pron thou (on thy part),
  thou also
tiwmor nm tumour
tiwn (-iau) nf tune
tiwnio vb to tune
tlawd (tlodion) adj poor
tlodaidd adj poorish, mean, dowdy
tlodi vb to impoverish ▸ nm
  poverty
tlos adj f of tlws

tloty (-ai) nm poorhouse,
  workhouse
tlotyn (tlodion) nm pauper
tlws¹ (ftlos) adj pretty
tlws² (tlysau) nm jewel, gem;
  medal
tlysni nm prettiness
to (toeau) nm roof; generation
toc adv shortly, presently, soon
tocio vb to clip, to dock, to prune
tocyn¹ (tociau) nm pack, heap,
  hillock; slice of bread
tocyn² (-nau) nm ticket
tocynnwr (-ynwyr) nm bus
  conductor
toddadwy adj soluble
toddedig adj molten; melting
toddi vb to melt, to dissolve, to
  thaw
toddiant (-nnau) nm solution
toddion npl dripping
toddwr (-wyr), toddydd (-ion)
  nm melter
toes nm dough
toesen nf doughnut
toi vb to cover; to roof; to thatch
toili nm spectral funeral
tolach vb to fondle
tolc (-iau) nm dent, dinge
tolcio vb to dent, to dinge
tolciog adj dented, dinged
tolchen (-au) nf clot
tolchennu vb to clot
toll (-au) nf toll, custom
tolli vb to take toll
tom nf dirt, mire, dung
tomen (-nydd) nf heap; dunghill
tomlyd adj dirty, miry
ton¹ (-nau) nf wave, billow, breaker
ton² (-nau) nm lay-land

215

tôn

tôn (**tonau**) *nf* tone; tune; **tôn ffôn** ring tone

tonc (**-iau**) *nf* tinkle, ring, clash

toncio, -ian *vb* to tinkle, to ring

tonfedd (**-i**) *nf* wavelength

tonig (**-iau**) *adj* tonic

tonnen (**tonennydd, -au**) *nf* skin; sward; bog

tonni *vb* to wave, to undulate

tonnog *adj* wavy, billowy

tonyddiaeth *nf* tone, intonation

topio *vb* to plug, to stop up

topyn *nm* plug, stopper

tor¹ (**-ion**) *nm* break, interruption

tor² (**-rau**) *nf* belly; palm (of hand)

torcalonnus *adj* heartbreaking

torch (**-au**) *nf* wreath; coil

torchi *vb* to wreathe; to coil; to roll, to tuck

torchog *adj* wreathed; coiled

tordyn *adj* tight-bellied; hectoring

toredig *adj* broken

toreithiog *adj* abundant, teeming

toreth *nf* abundance

torf (**-eydd**) *nf* crowd, multitude

torfynyglu *vb* to break neck of; to behead

torgoch (**-ion**) *nm* roach

torgwmwl *nm* cloudburst

torheulo *vb* to bask, to sunbathe

Tori (**-ïaid**) *nm* Tory

toriad (**-au**) *nm* cut, break; fraction

Torïaeth *nf* Toryism

Torïaidd *adj* Tory, Conservative

torlan (**-nau, -lennydd**) *nf* river bank

torllengig *nm* rupture

torllwyth (**-i**), **torraid** *nf* litter

torogen (**-ogod**) *nf* tick (in cattle)

torri *vb* to break, to cut; to dig; to write, to trace; **torri i lawr** break down

torrwr (**torwyr**) *nm* breaker, cutter

tors *nmf* torch

torsyth *adj* swaggering

torsythu *vb* to strut, to swagger

torth (**-au**) *nf* loaf

tost¹ *adj* severe, sharp, sore; ill

tost² *nm* toast

tosturi (**-aethau**) *nm* compassion, pity

tosturio *vb* to be compassionate, to pity

tosturiol *adj* compassionate

tosyn (**tosau**) *nm* pimple

tôwr (**towyr**) *nm* roofer, tiler

tra *adv* over; very ▸ *conj* while, whilst

tra-arglwyddiaeth (**-au**) *nf* tyranny

tra-arglwyddiaethu *vb* to tyrannize

tra-awdurdodi *vb* to lord it over, to domineer

trabludd *nm* trouble, tumult, turmoil

trac (**-iau**) *nm* track

tractor (**-s, -au**) *nm* tractor

tracwisg *nf* tracksuit

trachefn *adv* again

trachwant (**-au**) *nm* lust, covetousness

trachwanta, trachwantu *vb* to lust, to covet

trachwantus *adj* covetous

tradwy *adv* three days hence

traddodi *vb* to deliver; to commit

traddodiad (**-au**) *nm* tradition; delivery

traddodiadol adj traditional

traddodwr (-wyr) nm deliverer

traean nm one third, the third part

traed see **troed**

traeth (-au) nm strand, shore, beach

traethawd (-odau) nm treatise, essay; tract

traethell (-au) nf strand, sandbank

traethiad (-au) nm predicate

traethodydd (-ion) nm essayist

traethu vb to utter, to declare; to treat

trafael (-ion) nf travail, trouble

trafaelio vb to travel

trafaeliwr (-wyr) nm traveller

trafaelu vb to travel; to travail

traflyncu vb to guzzle, to gulp, to devour

trafnidiaeth nf traffic

trafod vb to handle; to discuss; to transact

trafodaeth (-au) nf discussion, transaction

trafodion npl transactions

trafferth (-ion) nmf trouble

trafferthu vb to trouble

trafferthus adj troublesome; troubled

traffordd nf motorway

tragwyddol adj everlasting, eternal

tragwyddoldeb nm eternity

tragywydd adj everlasting, eternal

traha nm arrogance, presumption

trahaus adj arrogant, haughty

trahauster nm arrogance, presumption

trai nm ebb

trais nm oppression, force, violence

trallod (-ion, -au) nm trouble, tribulation

tralloddi vb to afflict, to vex, to trouble

trallodus adj troubled; troublous

trallodwr (-wyr) nm troubler

tramgwydd (-iadau) nm stumbling; offence

tramgwyddo vb to stumble; to offend; to take offence

tramgwyddus adj scandalous; offensive

tramor adj foreign

tramorwr (-wyr) nm foreigner

trampolîn (trampolinau) nm trampoline

tramwy, tramwyo vb to pass, to traverse

tramwyfa (-feydd) nf passage, thoroughfare

tranc nm end, dissolution, death

trancedig adj deceased

trancedigaeth nf death, decease

trannoeth adv next day ► nm the morrow

trapio vb to trap

traphlith adv: **blith draphlith** higgledy-piggledy

tras nf kindred, affinity

traserch nm great love, infatuation

trasiedi (trasiedïau) nf tragedy

traul (treuliau) nf wear; cost, expense; digestion

traw nm pitch

trawiad (-au) nm stroke, beat, flash

trawiadol adj striking, spectacular

traws adj cross; froward, perverse

trawsblannu vb to transplant

trawsenwad nm metonymy

trawsfeddiannu vb to usurp

217

t

trawsfudo vb to transmigrate
trawsffurfio vb to transform
trawsgludo vb to transport, to conduct
trawsgyweiriad nm transposition, modulation
trawsgyweirio vb to transpose, to change key
trawslif (-**iau**) nm cross-saw
trawslythrennu vb to transliterate
traws-sylweddiad nm transubstantiation
trawst (-**iau**) nm beam
trawstoriad nm cross-section
trebl nm, adj treble
treblu vb to treble
trech adj superior, stronger, mightier
trechu vb to overpower, to overcome, to conquer
tref (-**i, -ydd**) nf home; town
trefedigaeth (-**au**) nf settlement, colony
trefgordd (-**au**) nf township
treflan (-**nau**) nf small town, townlet
trefn (-**au**) nf order, method, system
trefniad (-**au**) nm arrangement, ordering
trefniadaeth nf organization
trefniant nm arrangement, organization
trefnlen (-**ni**) nf schedule
trefnu vb to order, to arrange, to dispose
trefnus adj orderly, methodical
trefnusrwydd nm orderliness
trefnydd (-**ion**) nm arranger; Methodist

trefol adj town, urban
treftadaeth nf patrimony, inheritance
trengi vb to die, to perish, to expire
treial (-**on**) nm trial
treiddgar adj penetrating, keen
treiddgarwch nm penetration, acumen
treiddio vb to pass, to penetrate
treiddiol adj penetrating
treigl (-**au**) nm turn, revolution, course
treiglad, treigliad (-**au**) nm mutation; inflection
treiglo vb to roll; to mutate; to inflect; to decline
treio[1] vb to ebb
treio[2] vb to try
treisiad (-**iedi**) nf heifer
treisio vb to force, to ravish, to violate, to oppress, to rape
treisiwr (-**wyr**) nm violator, oppressor; rapist
trem (-**iau**) nf sight, look, aspect
tremio vb to look, to gaze
trên (**trenau**) nm train
trenars, treners npl trainers
trennydd adv day after tomorrow
tres (-**i**) nf trace, chain; tress
tresbasu, tresmasu vb to trespass
tresglen nf thrush
treth (-**i**) nf rate; tax; **treth ffordd** road tax; **treth y pen** poll tax
trethadwy adj rateable, taxable
trethdalwr (-**wyr**) nm ratepayer
trethu vb to tax, to rate, to assess
trethwr (-**wyr**) nm taxer
treuliad nm digestion
treulio vb to wear, to consume; to spend; to digest

tri (f **tair**) adj, nm three

triagl nm treacle, balsam, balm

triawd (-**au**) nm trio

triban (-**nau**) nm triplet (metre)

tribiwnlys (-**oedd**) nm tribunal

tric (-**iau**) nm trick

tridiau npl three days

trigain adj, nm sixty

trigfa (**trigfeydd**), **trigfan** (-**au**) nf dwelling-place, abode

trigiannol adj residentiary

trigiannu vb to reside, to dwell

trigiannydd (-**ianwyr**) nm resident

trigo vb to stay, to abide; to dwell; to die (animals)

trigolion npl inhabitants, dwellers

trimio vb to trim

trin[1] (-**oedd**) nf battle

trin[2] vb to handle; to treat; to dress; to till; to transact

trindod (-**au**) nf trinity

tringar adj skilful, tender

triniaeth (-**au**) nf treatment

trioedd npl triads

triongl (-**au**) nm triangle

trionglog adj triangular

triphlyg adj triple

trist adj sad, sorrowful

tristáu vb to sadden, to grieve

tristwch nm sadness, sorrow

triw adj loyal, faithful

tro (**troeau**, **troeon**) nm turn, twist; conversion

troad (-**au**) nm bend, turning; figure of speech

trobwll (-**byllau**) nm whirlpool

trobwynt (-**iau**) nm turning-point

trochfa (-**feydd**) nf plunge, immersion

trochi vb to dip, to plunge, to immerse; to soil

trochion npl lather, suds, foam

trochioni vb to lather, to foam

trochwr (-**wyr**) nm immerser, immersionist

troed (**traed**) nmf foot, base; leg; handle

troedfainc (-**feinciau**) nf footstool

troedfedd (-**i**) nf foot (=12 inches)

troedfeddyg nm chiropodist

troëdig adj turned, converted, perverse

troëdigaeth (-**au**) nf turning, conversion

troedio vb to foot, to tread, to trudge

troednodyn nm footnote

troednoeth adj barefoot, barefooted

troedwisg nf footwear

troedwst nf gout

troell (-**au**) nf wheel, spinning-wheel

troelli vb to spin; to twist, to wind

troellog adj winding, tortuous

troellwr (-**wyr**) nm disc-jockey

troetffordd (-**ffyrdd**) nf footway, footpath

troeth nm urine

trofa (-**feydd**) nf turn; bend; turning

trofan (-**nau**) nf tropic

trofannol adj tropical

trofaus adj perverse

trofwrdd (-**fyrddau**) nm turntable

trogen see **torogen**

trogylch (-**au**) nm orbit

troi

troi vb to turn, to revolve; to convert; to plough; **troi ymlaen** switch on

trol (-iau) nf cart

trolian, trolio vb to roll

troliwr (-wyr) nm carter

trom adj f of **trwm**

trôns nm underpants; trunks; **trôns bocsiwr** boxer shorts

tros prep over, for, instead of, on behalf of

trosadwy adj convertible

trosedd (-au) nm transgression, offence, crime

troseddol adj criminal

troseddu vb to transgress, to trespass, to offend

troseddwr (-wyr) nm transgressor, trespasser, offender; criminal

trosgais (**trosgeisiau**) nm converted try (in rugby)

trosglwyddiad nm transference, transfer

trosglwyddo vb to hand over, to transfer

trosgynnol adj transcendental

trosi vb to turn; to translate; to convert (a try)

trosiad (-au) nm translation; metaphor; conversion (in rugby)

trosodd adv over, beyond

trosol (-ion) nm lever, crow-bar, bar; staff

trostan (-au) nf pole

trotian vb to trot

trothwy (-au) nm threshold

trowr (-wyr) nm ploughman

trowsus (-au) nm trousers; **trowsus nofio** swimming trunks

trowynt (-oedd) nm whirlwind, tornado

truan (**truain**) (f **truanes**) adj poor, wretched, miserable ► nm (**trueiniaid**) wretch

trueni nm wretchedness; misery; pity

truenus adj wretched, miserable

trugaredd (-au) nmf mercy, compassion

trugarhau vb to have mercy, to take pity

trugarog adj merciful, compassionate

trugarowgrwydd nm mercifulness

trulliad (-iaid) nm butler, cupbearer

trum (-au, -iau) nm ridge

truth nm flattery; rigmarole

trwbl nm trouble

trwblo vb to trouble

trwch[1] nm thickness; **trwch y blewyn** hair's breadth

trwch[2] adj broken; unfortunate; wicked

trwchus adj thick

trwm (**trymion**) (f **trom**) adj heavy

trwnc (**trynciau**) nm trunk

trwodd adv through

trwsgl adj awkward, clumsy, bungling

trwsiad nm dress, attire

trwsiadus adj well-dressed, smart

trwsio vb to dress, to trim; to mend, to repair

trwsiwr (-wyr) nm mender, repairer

trwst nm noise, din, tumult

trwstan adj awkward, clumsy, untoward

trwstaneiddiwch *nm* awkwardness

trwy *prep* through, by, by means of

trwyadl *adj* thorough

trwydded (-au) *nf* leave, licence

trwyddedig *adj* licensed

trwyddedu *vb* to license

trwyn (-au) *nm* nose, snout; point, cape

trwyno *vb* to nose, to nuzzle, to sniff

trwynol *adj* nasal

trwynsur *adj* sour, morose

trwyth (-i) *nm* decoction, infusion, urine

trwytho *vb* to steep, to saturate, to imbue

trybedd, trybed *nf* tripod, trivet

trybelid *adj* bright, brilliant

trybestod *nm* commotion, bustle, fuss

trybini *nm* trouble, misfortune, misery

tryblith *nm* muddle, chaos

trychfil (-od) *nm* insect, animalcule

trychiad (-au) *nm* cutting, fracture, section

trychineb (-au) *nmf* disaster, calamity

trychinebus *adj* disastrous, calamitous

trychu *vb* to cut, to hew, to pierce, to lop

trydan *nm* electric fluid, electricity

trydaneg *nmf* electrical engineering

trydaniaeth *nf* electricity; thrill

trydanol *adj* electric, electrical

trydanu *vb* to electrify

trydar *vb* to chirp, to chatter ▸ *nm* chirping, twittering

trydydd (f trydedd) *adj* third

tryfer (-i) *nf* harpoon, trident

tryferu *vb* to spear, to harpoon

tryfesur *nm* diameter

tryfrith *adj* speckled; swarming, teeming

trylediad (-au) *nm* diffusion

tryledu *vb* to diffuse

tryloyw *adj* pellucid, transparent

tryloywder *nm* transparency

trylwyr *adj* thorough

trylwyredd *nm* thoroughness

trymaidd *adj* heavy, close, oppressive

trymder *nm* heaviness, drowsiness

trymfryd *nm* sadness, sorrow

trymhau *vb* to make or grow heavy

trymllyd *adj* heavy, close, oppressive

tryryw *adj* thoroughbred

trysor (-au) *nm* treasure

trysordy (-dai) *nm* treasure house

trysorfa (-feydd) *nf* treasury, fund

trysori *vb* to treasure

trysorlys *nm* treasury, exchequer

trysorydd (-ion) *nm* treasurer

trystio *vb* to make a noise; to trust

trystiog *adj* noisy, rowdy

trythyll *adj* wanton, lascivious

trythyllwch *nm* lasciviousness

trywanu *vb* to transfix, to stab, to pierce

trywel *nm* trowel

trywydd *nm* scent, trail

Tsiecaidd *adj* Czech

Tsieceg *nf* Czech

Tsieciad *nm* Czech

Tsiecoslofacia *nf* Czechoslovakia

221

Tsieina

Tsieina *nf* China

Tsieinead (-eaid) *nmf* Chinese person

Tsieineaidd *adj* Chinese

tsili *nm* chilli

tu *nm* side, part, direction

tua, tuag *prep* towards; about

tuchan *vb* to grumble, to groan, to murmur

tudalen (-nau) *nmf* page; **tudalen cartref, tudalen gartref, tudalen hafan** home page; **tudalen we** web page

tudded (-i) *nf* covering; pillowcase

tuedd¹ (-iadau) *nf* tendency, inclination

tuedd² (-au) *nm* district, region

tueddfryd *nm* inclination, bent

tueddol *adj* inclined, apt

tueddu *vb* to incline, to tend, to trend

tufewnol *adj* inward, internal

tulath (-au) *nf* beam, rafter

tun *nm* tinned

Tunisia *nf* Tunisia

tunnell (tunelli) *nf* ton; tun

turio *vb* to root up, to burrow, to delve

turn *nm* lathe

turniwr (-wyr) *nm* turner

turtur (-od) *nf* turtle-dove

tusw (-au) *nm* wisp, bunch

tuth (-iau) *nm* trot

tuthio *vb* to trot

twb (tybiau) *nm* tub

twca *nm* tuck-knife

twf *nm* growth

twffyn (twffiau) *nm* tuft

twlc (tylciau) *nm* sty

twlcio *vb* to horn, to butt, to gore

twlciog *adj* given to horning

twll (tyllau) *nm* hole

twmpath (-au) *nm* tump, hillock; bush; folk-dance

twndis (-au) *nm* funnel

twndra (-âu) *nm* tundra

twnffed (-i) *nm* funnel

twnnel (twnelau, twneli) *nm* tunnel; **Twnnel y Sianel** the Channel Tunnel

twp *adj* stupid, dull, obtuse

twpdra *nm* stupidity

twpsyn *nm* stupid person

twr (tyrrau) *nm* heap; group, crowd

tŵr (tyrau) *nm* tower

Twrc (Tyrciaid) *nm* Turk

Twrci *nf* Turkey

twrci (-od) *nm* turkey

twrch (tyrchod) *nm* hog; **twrch daear** mole

twrf (tyrfau) *nm* noise; *(pl)* thunder

twrist *nm* tourist

twrnai (-eiod) *nm* attorney, lawyer

twrw *nm* noise

twt¹ *excl* tut!

twt² *adj* tidy, neat, smart

twtio *vb* to tidy

twyll *nm* deceit, deception, fraud

twyllo *vb* to deceive, to cheat, to swindle

twyllodrus *adj* deceitful, false

twyllresymeg *nf* sophism

twyllresymiad (-au) *nm* sophistry

twyllwr (-wyr) *nm* deceiver

twym *adj* warm, hot, sultry

twymder, twymdra *nm* warmness, warmth

twymgalon *adj* warm-hearted

twymo, twymno vb to warm, to heat

twymyn (-au) nf fever; **y dwymyn goch** scarlet fever; **y dwymyn doben** mumps

twyn (-i) nm hill, hillock, knoll; bush

twysged nf lot, quantity

tŷ (tai, teiau) nm house; **tŷ pâr** semidetached (house)

tyaid (-eidiau) nm houseful

tyb (-iau) nmf opinion, notion, surmise

tybaco nm tobacco

tybed adv I wonder; is that so?

tybiaeth (-au) nf supposition

tybied, tybio vb to suppose, to think, to imagine

tybiedig adj supposed, putative

tycio vb to prosper, to succeed, to avail

tydi pron thou, thyself

tyddyn (-nod) nm (small) farm, holding

tyddynnwr (-ynwyr) nm smallholder

tyfadwy adj growing

tyfiant nm growth

tyfu vb to grow; **tyfu i fyny, tyfu lan** grow up

tyfwr (-wyr) nm grower

tynged nf destiny, fate

tyngedfennol adj fateful, fatal

tynghedu vb to destine, to fate; to adjure

tyngu vb to swear, to vow

tyngwr (-wyr) nm swearer

tylath see **tulath**

tyle nm slope, hill

tylino vb to knead; **tylino y corff** massage

tylinwr (-wyr) nm kneader, masseur

tylwyth (-au) nm household, family; **tylwyth teg** fairies

tyllog adj holey

tyllu vb to hole, to bore, to perforate, to pierce

tylluan (-od) nf owl

tyllwr (-wyr) nm borer

tymer (-herau) nf temper

tymestl (-hestloedd) nf tempest, storm

tymheredd nm temperature

tymherus adj temperate

tymhestlog adj tempestuous, stormy

tymhoraidd adj seasonable

tymhorol adj temporal

tymor (-horau) nm season; **tymor y gaeaf** wintertime

tymp nm (appointed) time, season

tympan (-au) nf drum; timbrel

tyn adj tight

tynder, tyndra nm tightness, tension

tyndro (tyndroeon) nm wrench

tyner adj tender, gentle

tyneru vb to make tender, to soften

tynerwch nm tenderness, gentleness

tynfa (-feydd) nf draw, attraction

tynfaen (-feini) nm loadstone, magnet

tynhau vb to tighten, to strain

tynnu vb to draw, to pull; to take off, to remove

tyno nm hollow; tenon

tyrchu vb to root up, to burrow

tyrchwr (-wyr) nm mole-catcher

t

tyrfa (-oedd) *nf* multitude, host, crowd

tyrfau *npl* thunder

tyrfedd (-au) *nm* turbulence, thunder

tyrfo, tyrfu *vb* to make a noise or commotion

tyrpant *nm* turpentine

tyrpeg *nm* turnpike

tyrru *vb* to heap, to amass; to crowd together

tyst (-ion) *nm* witness

tysteb (-au) *nf* testimonial

tystio *vb* to testify, to witness

tystiolaeth (-au) *nf* testimony, evidence

tystiolaethu *vb* to bear witness, to testify

tystlythyr (-au) *nm* testimonial

tystysgrif (-au) *nf* certificate

tywallt *vb* to pour, to shed, to spill

tywalltiad (-au) *nm* outpouring

tywarchen (tywyrch) *nf* sod, turf

tywel (-ion) *nm* towel

tywod *nm* sand

tywodfaen *nm* sandstone

tywodlyd, tywodog *adj* sandy

tywodyn *nm* grain of sand

tywydd *nm* weather

tywyll *adj* dark, obscure; blind

tywyllu *vb* to darken, to obscure

tywyllwch *nm* darkness

tywyn (-au) *nm* sea-shore, strand

tywynnu *vb* to shine

tywys *vb* to lead, to guide

tywysen (-nau, tywys) *nf* ear of corn

tywysog (-ion) *nm* prince

tywysogaeth (-au) *nf* principality

tywysogaidd *adj* princely

tywysoges (-au) *nf* princess

tywysydd (-ion) *nm* leader, guide

th u

theatr (**-au**) *nf* theatre
thema (**themâu**) *nf* theme
theorem (**-au**) *nf* theorem
theori (**-ïau**) *nf* theory
thermomedr *nm* thermometer
thesis (**-au**) *nm* thesis
thus *nm* frankincense

ubain *vb* to howl, to wail, to moan; to sob
uchaf *adj* uppermost, highest
uchafbwynt (**-iau**) *nm* climax; zenith
uchafiaeth *nf* supremacy; ascendancy
uchafion *npl* heights
uchafrif (**-au**) *nm* maximum
uchafswm *nm* maximum
uchder *nm* height; top
uchdwr *nm* storey
uchel *adj* high, lofty; uppish; loud
uchelbwynt (**-iau**) *nm* highlight
uchelder (**-au**) *nm* highness, height
ucheldir (**-oedd**) *nm* highland
uchelfryd *adj* high-minded
uchelgais *nf* ambition
uchelgeisiol *adj* ambitious
uchelion *npl* heights
uchelradd *adj* of high degree, superior

uchelseinydd (-ion) nm loudspeaker

uchelwr (-wyr) nm gentleman, nobleman

uchelwydd nm mistletoe

uchgapten (-teiniaid) nm major

uchod adv above

UDA n US, USA

udo vb to howl

udd nm lord

UE nf EU, European Union

ufudd adj obedient, humble

ufudd-dod nm obedience, humility

ufuddhau vb to obey

uffern nf hell

uffernol adj infernal, hellish

ugain (ugeiniau) adj, nm twenty, score

Uganda nf Uganda

Ulster nf Ulster

ulw coll n ashes, powder ▸ adv utterly

un adj one, only; same ▸ coll n (-au) one, unit

unawd (-au) nm solo

unawdydd (-wyr) nm soloist

unben (-iaid, unbyn) nm sovereign lord, despot

unbenaethol adj despotic

unbennaeth nf sovereignty, despotism

undeb (-au) nm unity; union; **yr Undeb Ewropeaidd** the European Union; **yr Undeb Sofietaidd** the Soviet Union

undebaeth nf unionism

undebol adj united, union

undebwr (-wyr) nm unionist

undod (-au) nm unity; unit

Undodaidd adj Unitarian

Undodiaeth nf Unitarianism

Undodwr (-wyr, -iaid) nm Unitarian

undonedd nm monotony

undonog adj monotonous

uned (-au) nf unit

unedig adj united

unfan nm same place

unfarn adj unanimous

unfryd, unfrydol adj unanimous

unfrydedd nm unanimity

unffurf adj uniform

unffurfiaeth nf uniformity

uniad nm union

uniaethu vb to identify

uniaith adj monoglot

uniawn adj straight; right, upright; just

unig adj sole, only; alone, lonely

unigedd nm loneliness, solitude

unigol adj singular; individual ▸ nm (-ion) individual

unigoliaeth nf individuality

unigolrwydd nm individuality

unigolyn nm individual

unigrwydd nm loneliness, solitude

union adj straight, direct; just, exact

uniondeb nm straightness; rectitude

uniongred adj orthodox

uniongrededd nm orthodoxy

uniongyrch, uniongyrchol adj immediate, direct

unioni vb to straighten; to rectify; to make for

unionsgwar adj perpendicular

unionsyth adj straight; direct; erect

unllygeidiog adj one-eyed

unman *adv* anywhere
unnos *adj* of one night
uno *vb* to join, to unit, to amalgamate
unochrog *adj* unilateral, biased
unodl *adj* of the same rhyme
unol *adj* united; **yr Unol Daleithiau** the United States
unoli *vb* to unify
unoliaeth *nf* unity, oneness, identity
unplyg *adj* of one fold; folio; simple, ingenuous
unplygrwydd *nm* sincerity
unrhyw *adj* same; any
unrhywiol *adj* unisexual
unsain *adj* unison; **yn unsain** in unison
unsill *adj* monosyllabic
unswydd *adj* of one purpose
unwaith *adv* once
unwedd *adj* like ► *adv* likewise
urdd (-au) *nf* order; rank
urddas (-au) *nm* dignity, honour
urddasol *adj* dignified, noble
urddo *vb* to ordain, to confer degree or rank
us *nm* chaff
ust *excl, nm* hush
ustus (-iaid) *nm* justice, magistrate
usuriaeth *nf* usury
utganu *vb* to sound a trumpet
utganwr (-wyr) *nm* trumpeter
utgorn (-gyrn) *nm* trumpet
uwch *adj* higher ► *prep* above, over
uwchbridd (-oedd) *nm* topsoil
uwchgapten (-iaid) *nm* major
uwchradd *nm, adj* superior

uwchsonig *adj* ultrasonic, supersonic
uwd *nm* porridge

u

W

wadi (-iau) *nm* wadi
wado *vb* to beat, to thrash
wagen (-ni) *nf* truck, waggon
waldio *vb* to wallop, to beat
warws (**warysau**) *nm* warehouse
wats (-iau) *nm* watch
wedi *prep* after ► *adv* afterwards
wedyn *adv* afterwards, then
weiren *nf* wire
weirio, weiro *vb* to wire
weithian, weithion *adv* now, now at length
weithiau *adv* sometimes
wel *excl* well
wele *excl* behold, lo
wermod *nf* wormwood
wfft *excl* fie, for shame
wfftio *vb* to cry fie, to flout, to scout
wiced (-i) *nf* wicket
wicedwr (-wyr) *nm* wicket-keeper
widw *nf* widow
wlser (-au) *nm* ulcer
wmbredd *nm* abundance

wraniwm *nm* uranium
wrth *prep* by; with; to; because, since
wy (-au) *nm* egg
wybr (-au), **wybren** (-nau, -nydd) *nf* sky; cloud
wybrol *adj* ethereal
wyf *vb* I am
wygell (-oedd) *nf* ovary
wylo *vb* to weep, to cry
wylofain *vb* to wail, to weep ► *nm* wailing
wylofus *adj* wailing, doleful, tearful
ŵyn *see* oen
wyna *vb* to lamb
wyneb (-au) *nm* face, surface; front
wyneb-ddalen *nf* title-page
wynebgaled *adj* barefaced, impudent
wyneblun (-iau) *nm* frontispiece
wynebu *vb* to face, to front
wynepryd *nm* countenance
wynwyn *npl* onions
ŵyr (**wyrion**) *nm* grandchild, grandson
wyres *nf* granddaughter
wysg *nm* track; **yn wysg ei gefn** backwards
wystrys *npl* oysters
wyth (-au) *adj, nm* eight
wythawd (-au, -odau) *nf* octave
wythblyg *adj* octavo
wythfed *adj* eighth
wythnos (-au) *nf* week
wythnosol (-ion) *adj* weekly
wythnosolyn (-olion) *nm* weekly paper
wythongl (-au) *nf* octagon
wythwr (-wyr) *nm* number eight (in rugby)

y

y¹, yr, 'r *adj* the

y², yr *conj* that

ych (-en) *nm* ox

ychwaith *adv* (nor) either, neither

ychwaneg *nm* more

ychwanegiad (-au) *nm* addition

ychwanegol *adj* additional

ychwanegu *vb* to add, to augment, to increase

ychydig *adj, adv* little, few

ŷd (ydau) *nm* corn

ydfran *nf* rook

ydwyf *vb* I am

ydys *vb*: **yr ydys yn disgwyl** it is expected

ydyw *vb* is, are

yfed *vb* to drink; to absorb

yfory *adv* tomorrow

yfwr (-wyr) *nm* drinker

yfflon *npl* (*nm* **yfflyn**) shivers, pieces, bits ▸ *adj* highly annoyed

yng *prep* in **yn**

yngan, ynganu *vb* to utter, to speak

ynghyd *adv* together

ynghylch *prep* about, concerning

ynglŷn â *prep* in connection with

ym *prep* in **yn**

ym- *prefix* usu. reflexive or reciprocal

yma *adv* here, in this place; this

ymadael, ymadaw *vb* to depart

ymadawedig *adj* departed, deceased

ymadawiad *nm* departure; decease

ymadawol *adj* farewell, valedictory

ymado *vb* to depart

ymadrodd (-ion) *nm* speech, saying, expression

ymadroddus *adj* eloquent

ymaddasu *vb* to adjust, to adapt

ymaelodi *vb* to become a member, to join

ymaelyd, ymafael, ymaflyd *vb* to take hold

ymageru *vb* to evaporate

ymagor *vb* to open, to unfold, to expand

ymagweddiad (-au) *nm* demeanour, attitude

ymaith *adv* away, hence

ymarfer *vb* to practise, to exercise ▸ *nf* (**-ion**) practice, exercise

ymarferiad (-au) *nm* exercise

ymarhous *adj* dilatory; long-suffering, patient

ymaros *vb* to bear with, to endure ▸ *nm* long-suffering, patience

ymarweddiad *nm* conduct, behaviour

ymatal

ymatal vb to forbear, to refrain, to abstain

ymateb vb to answer, to respond, to correspond

ymbalfalu vb to grope

ymbaratoi vb to get oneself ready

ymbarél nm umbrella

ymbelydredd nm radiation

ymbelydrol adj radioactive

ymbellhau vb to go further away

ymbil¹ (-iau) nm supplication, entreaty

ymbil², ymbilio vb to implore, to beseech, to entreat

ymboeni vb to take pains

ymborth nm food, sustenance

ymbortheg nf dietetics

ymborthi vb to feed

ymbriodi vb to marry; to intermarry

ymbwyllo vb to pause, to reflect

ymchwelyd vb to turn, to return; to overturn

ymchwil nf search, research, quest

ymchwiliad (-au) nm investigation

ymchwilio vb to research

ymchwydd (-iadau) nm swelling, surge

ymchwyddo vb to swell; to surge

ymdaith vb to journey, to march ▸ nf (-deithiau) journey, march

ymdebygu vb to grow like; to resemble

ymdeimlad nm feeling, sense

ymdeimlo vb to feel; to be conscious of

ymdeithio vb to travel, to journey; to sojourn

ymdoddi vb to melt, to become dissolved

ymdopi vb to manage

ymdrech (-ion) nfm effort, endeavour, struggle

ymdrechgar adj striving, energetic

ymdrechu vb to wrestle; to strive, to endeavour

ymdrin vb to treat, to deal with

ymdriniaeth nf treatment; discussion

ymdrochi vb to bathe

ymdrochwr (-wyr) nm bather

ymdroi vb to linger, to loiter, to dawdle

ymdrybaeddu vb to wallow

ymdynghedu vb to vow

ymddangos vb to appear, to seem

ymddangosiad (-au) nm appearance

ymddangosiadol adj seeming, apparent

ymddarostwng vb to submit

ymddarostyngiad nm humiliation, submission

ymddatod vb to dissolve

ymddeol vb to resign, to retire

ymddeoliad (-au) nm retirement; **ymddeoliad cynnar** early retirement

ymddiddan vb to talk, to converse ▸ nm (-ion) talk, conversation

ymddihatru vb to divest, to undress

ymddiheuriad (-au) nm apology

ymddiheuro vb to apologize

ymddisgo vb to strip, to undress

ymddiried vb to trust ▸ nm trust, confidence

ymddiriedaeth nf trust, confidence

ymddiriedolwr (-wyr) nm trustee

ymddiswyddo vb to resign

ymddwyn vb to behave, to act

ymddygiad (-au) nm behaviour, conduct; (pl) actions

ymddyrchafu vb to exalt oneself; to rise, to ascend

ymegnïo vb to exert oneself

ymehangu vb to become enlarged, to expand

ymennydd (ymenyddiau) nm brain

ymenyn nm butter

ymerawdwr (-wyr) nm emperor

ymerodraeth (-au) nf empire

ymerodres (-au) nf empress

ymerodrol adj imperial

ymesgusodi vb to excuse oneself, to apologize

ymestyn vb to stretch, to extend, to reach

ymestyniad (-au) nm extension

ymestynnol adj extensive

ymfalchïo vb to pride oneself

ymfodloni vb to acquiesce

ymfudo vb to emigrate

ymfudwr (-wyr) nm emigrant

ymffrost nm boast

ymffrostio vb to boast, to vaunt

ymffrostiwr (-wyr) nm boaster

ymgadw vb to keep oneself (from), to forbear

ymgais nmf effort, attempt

ymgasglu vb to gather together

ymgecru vb to quarrel, to wrangle

ymgeisio vb to try, to apply; to aim at

ymgeisydd (-wyr) nm applicant, candidate

ymgeledd nm succour, care

ymgeleddu vb to cherish, to succour

ymgeleddwr (-wyr) nm succourer; tutor, guardian

ymgilio vb to retreat, to recede

ymgiprys vb, nm to scramble

ymglymu vb to involve, to bind together

ymglywed vb to feel (oneself), to be inclined

ymgnawdoliad nm incarnation

ymgodymu vb to wrestle, to fight

ymgofleidio vb to mutually embrace

ymgom (-ion) nf chat, conversation

ymgomio vb to chat, to converse

ymgorffori vb to incorporate

ymgorfforiad nm embodiment

ymgreinio vb to prostrate oneself; to grovel

ymgroesi vb to cross oneself; to beware

ymgryfhau vb to strengthen oneself, to be strong

ymgrymu vb to bow down, to stoop

ymguddfa nf shelter, hiding-place

ymguddio vb to hide (oneself)

ymgydio vb to copulate

ymgydnabod vb to acquaint oneself

ymgyfathrachu vb to have dealings with

ymgyfeillachu vb to associate

ymgyfoethogi vb to get rich

ymgynghori vb to consult, to confer

ymgynghoriad nm consultation

ymgymeriad (-au) *nm* undertaking

ymgymryd *vb* to undertake

ymgynefino *vb* to become familiar, to get used to

ymgynnal *vb* to bear up; to support oneself; to control oneself

ymgynnull *vb* to assemble, to congregate

ymgyrch (-oedd) *nmf* campaign, expedition

ymgyrraedd *vb* to stretch, to strive after

ymgysegriad *nm* devotion, consecration

ymgysegru *vb* to devote oneself

ymhél *vb* to meddle

ymhelaethu *vb* to abound; to enlarge

ymhell *adv* far, afar

ymhellach *adv* further, furthermore

ymherodr *see* ymerawdwr

ymhlith *prep* among

ymhlyg *adj* implicit

ymhoelyd *vb* to overturn, to topple

ymhoffi *vb* to take delight; to boast

ymholi *vb* to inquire

ymholiad (-au) *nm* inquiry

ymhonni *vb* to lay claim to, to pretend

ymhonnwr (-honwyr) *nm* pretender

ymhwedd *vb* to beseech; to implore, to crave

ymhyfrydu *vb* to delight (oneself)

ymiacháu *vb* to become healed, to get well

ymlacio *vb* to relax

ymladd *vb* to fight ▸ *nm* **(-au)** fighting

ymlâdd *vb* to kill oneself (with exertion), to tire oneself out; **wedi ymlâdd** dead beat

ymladdfa (-feydd) *nf* fight

ymladdgar *adj* pugnacious, warlike

ymladdwr (-wyr) *nm* fighter, combatant

ymlaen *adv* on, onward

ymlafnio *vb* to toil, to strive, to struggle

ymlawenhau *vb* to rejoice

ymledu *vb* to spread, to expand

ymlenwi *vb* to fill oneself

ymlid *vb* to pursue, to chase

ymlidiwr (-wyr) *nm* pursuer

ymlonyddu *vb* to grow calm or still

ymlosgiad *nm* combustion

ymlusgiad (-iaid) *nm* reptile

ymlusgo *vb* to creep, to crawl

ymlwybro *vb* to make one's way

ymlyniad *nm* attachment

ymlynu *vb* to attach, to adhere, to cleave (to)

ymlynwr (-wyr) *nm* adherent

Ymneilltuaeth *nf* Nonconformity

ymneilltuo *vb* to retire

Ymneilltuol *adj* Nonconformist

Ymneilltuwr (-wyr) *nm* Nonconformist

ymnesáu *vb* to approach, to draw near

ymochel, ymochelyd *vb* to shelter; to beware

ymod, ymodi *vb* to move, to stir

ymofyn *vb* to ask, to inquire, to seek ▸ *nm* **(-ion)** inquiry

ymofynnydd (-ofynwyr) *nm* inquirer

ymolchfa (-feydd) *nf* wash; lavatory

ymolchi *vb* to wash oneself, to bathe

ymollwng *vb* to sink, to drop, to give way, to collapse

ymorchestu *vb* to strive, to labour

ymorffwys *vb* to rest, to repose

ymorol *vb* to seek; to take care, to attend to, to see to it

ymosod *vb* to attack, to assail, to assault

ymosodiad (-au) *nm* attack, assault

ymosodol *adj* aggressive, offensive, forward

ymosodwr (-wyr) *nm* attacker, assailant

ymostwng *vb* to stoop; to humble oneself; to submit

ymostyngar *adj* submissive

ymostyngiad *nm* submission

ympryd (-ion) *nm* fast

ymprydio *vb* to fast

ymprydiwr (-wyr) *nm* faster

ymrafael (-ion) *nm* quarrel, contention

ymrafaelgar *adj* quarrelsome, contentious

ymraniad (-au) *nm* division, schism

ymrannu *vb* to part, to divide, to separate

ymrannwr (-ranwyr) *nm* separatist

ymreolaeth *nf* self-government, Home Rule

ymrestru *vb* to enlist

ymresymiad (-au) *nm* reasoning, argument

ymresymu *vb* to reason, to argue

ymresymwr (-wyr) *nm* reasoner

ymrithio *vb* to appear

ymroad *nm* application, devotion

ymroddedig *adj* devoted

ymroddgar *adj* of great application

ymroddi, ymroi *vb* to apply or devote oneself; to yield or resign oneself, to surrender, to do one's best

ymroddiad *nm* application, devotion

ymron *adv* nearly, almost

ymrous *adj* assiduous

ymrwyfo *vb* to struggle, to toss about

ymrwygo *vb* to tear, to burst

ymrwymiad (-au) *nm* engagement

ymrwymo *vb* to commit or bind oneself

ymrysongar *adj* contentious

ymryson *vb* to contend, to strive ► *nm* (**-au**) contention, strife, rivalry

ymsefydlu *vb* to establish oneself, to settle

ymsefydlwr (-wyr) *nm* settler

ymserchu *vb* to cherish, to dote

ymson *vb* to soliloquize ► *nm* (**-au**) soliloquy

ymsuddiant *nm* subsidence

ymswyno *vb* to cross oneself; to beware

ymsymud *vb* to move

ymuno *vb* to join, to unite

ymwacâd *nm* kenosis

ymwacáu *vb* to empty oneself

ymwadiad *nm* denial, abnegation

233

ymwadu *vb* to deny (oneself); to renounce

ymwahanu *vb* to part, to divide, to separate

ymwahanwr (-wyr) *nm* separatist

ymwared *nm* deliverance

ymwasgu *vb* to embrace, to hug

ymweithydd (-ion) *nm* reactor

ymweld (-au) *vb* to visit

ymweliad (-au) *nm* visit, visitation

ymwelwr, ymwelydd (ymwelwyr) *nm* visitor, visitant; **canolfan ymwelwyr** visitor centre

ymwneud *vb* to involve

ymwrando *vb* to hearken

ymwroli *vb* to take heart, to be of good courage

ymwrthod *vb* to abstain; to renounce

ymwrthodiad *nm* abstinence

ymwthgar *adj* pushing, obtrusive

ymwthio *vb* to push oneself, to obtrude

ymwthiol *adj* obtrusive, intrusive

ymwybodol *adj* conscious

ymwybyddiaeth *nf* consciousness

ymwylltio *vb* to fly into a passion

ymyl (-au, -on) *nmf* edge, border, margin

ymylu *vb* to border

ymylwe *nf* selvedge

ymyrgar *adj* meddlesome, officious

ymyrraeth¹, ymyrru, ymyrryd *vb* to meddle, to interfere

ymyrraeth² *nf* interference

ymyrrwr (-yrwyr) *nm* meddler

ymyrryd *vb* to meddle

ymysg *prep* among, amid

ymysgaroedd *npl* bowels

ymysgwyd *vb* to bestir oneself

yn¹ *prep* in, at, into; for *(also introduces verb-nouns)*

yn² *particle*

yna *adv* there; then; thereupon; that

ynad (-on) *nm* judge, justice, magistrate

yn awr *adv* now, at present

yndeintiad (-au) *nm* indentation

ynfyd (-ion) *adj* foolish, rash

ynfydrwydd *nm* foolishness, folly

ynfydu *vb* to rave, to be mad

ynfytyn (-fydion) *nm* fool, madman

ynni *nm* energy, vigour; **ynni haul, ynni'r haul** solar power

yno *adv* there

yntau *pron* he (on his part), he also

ynteu, ynte *conj* or, or else, otherwise; then

Ynyd *nm* Shrovetide

ynys (-oedd) *nf* island, river meadow; **Ynys Cyprus** Cyprus; **yr Ynysoedd Dedwydd** the Canary Islands

ynysfor (-oedd) *nm* archipelago

ynysol *adj* island, insular

ynysu *vb* to insulate

ynyswr (-wyr) *nm* islander

ynysydd (-ion) *nm* insulator

yr *see* **y**

yrŵan *adv* now

yrhawg *adv* for a long time (to come)

ys *vb* it is ▸ *conj* as

ysbaddu *vb* to castrate

ysbaid (-beidiau) *nfm* space (of time)

ysbail (-beiliau) *nf* spoil, plunder

ysbardun nmf spur

ysbarduno vb to spur

ysbeidiol adj occasional, intermittent

ysbeilio vb to spoil, to plunder

ysbeiliwr (-wyr) nm spoiler, robber

ysbienddrych (-au) nm spying-glass

ysbïo vb to spy, to look

ysbïwr (ysbiwyr) nm spy

ysblander nm splendour

ysblennydd adj splendid

ysbonc (-iau) nf jump, bound; spurt

ysboncio vb to jump, to bounce; to spurt, to splash

ysborion npl cast-offs

ysbrigyn nm sprig, twig

ysbryd (-ion, -oedd) nm spirit, ghost

ysbrydegaeth nf spiritualism

ysbrydegol adj spiritualistic

ysbrydegydd (-ion) nm spiritualist

ysbrydiaeth nf encouragement, inspiration

ysbrydol adj spiritual; high-spirited

ysbrydoli vb to spiritualize; to inspire; to inspirit

ysbrydoliaeth nf inspiration

ysbwng nm sponge

ysbwrial, ysbwriel nm rubbish, refuse

ysbwylio vb to spoil

ysbyty (-tai) nm hospital; hospice; **ysbyty'r meddwl** psychiatric hospital

ysfa (-feydd) nf itching; hankering

ysg- see sg-

ysgadan npl (nm -enyn) herrings

ysgafala adj secure, careless, free

ysgafn adj light ▸ nm stack

ysgafnder nm lightness, levity

ysgafnhau, ysgafnu vb to lighten

ysgafnu vb to heap, to pile

ysgall npl (nf -en) thistles

ysgar(u) vb to divorce

ysgariad nm separation, divorce

ysgariadaeth nf separation, divorce

ysgarlad nm scarlet

ysgarmes (-oedd, -au) nf skirmish; punch-up

ysgaru vb to part, to separate, to divorce

ysgatfydd adv perhaps, peradventure

ysgathru vb to spread, to scatter

ysgaw npl (nf -en) elder (tree)

ysgeintio vb to sprinkle

ysgeler adj wicked, villainous, infamous

ysgerbwd (-bydau) nm skeleton, carcase

ysgithr (-edd) nm tusk, fang

ysgithrog adj fanged, tusked; craggy, rugged

ysgiw (-ion) nf settle

ysglefrio vb to slide (on ice); to skate

ysglyfaeth (-au) nf prey, spoil; carrion, filth

ysglyfaethus adj of prey; rapacious

ysgogi vb to move, to stir; to motivate

ysgogiad (-au) nm movement, motion

ysgogol adj motive

ysgogul nm motive

ysgol¹ (-ion) nf school; schooling; **ysgol breswyl** boarding school;

235

ysgol fach infant school; **ysgol feithrin** nursery school; **ysgol fonedd** public school; **ysgol ganolraddol** middle school

ysgol² (**-ion**) nf ladder

ysgoldy (**-dai**) nm schoolhouse, schoolroom

ysgolfeistr (**-i, -iaid**) nm schoolmaster

ysgolfeistres (**-i**) nf schoolmistress

ysgolhaig (**-heigion**) nm scholar

ysgolheictod nm scholarship

ysgolheigaidd adj scholarly

ysgolor (**-ion**) nm scholar

ysgoloriaeth (**-au**) nf scholarship

ysgorpion (**-au**) nm scorpion

Ysgotyn (**-gotiaid**) nm Scot, Scotsman

ysgrafell (**-od, -i**) nf scraper; curry-comb

ysgrafellu vb to scrape, to curry

ysgraff (**-au**) nf boat, barge, ferry-boat

ysgraffinio vb to scarify, to graze, to abrade

ysgrech (**-feydd**) nf scream, shriek

ysgrechian, ysgrechin vb to scream, to shriek

ysgrepan (**-au**) nf wallet, scrip

ysgrif (**-au**) nf writing, article, essay

ysgrifbin (**-nau**) nm pen

ysgrifell (**au**) nf pen

ysgrifen, ysgrifeniad (**ysgrifeniadau**) nf writing

ysgrifennu vb to write

ysgrifennwyr (**-enwyr**) nm writer

ysgrifennydd (**-enyddion**) nm scribe, secretary

ysgrifenyddiaeth nf secretaryship

ysgriw (**-iau**) nf screw

ysgriwio vb to screw

ysgrwbio vb to scrub

ysgryd nm shiver

ysgrythur (**-au**) nf scripture

ysgrythurol adj scriptural

ysgrythurwr (**-wyr**) nm scripturist

ysgub (**-au**) nf sheaf; broom

ysgubo vb to sweep

ysgubol adj sweeping

ysgubor (**-iau**) nf barn, granary

ysgubwr (**-wyr**) nm sweeper, sweep

ysgutor (**-ion**) nm executor

ysguthan (**-od**) nf wood-pigeon; jade

ysgwâr adj, nf square

ysgwario vb to square

ysgŵd nm jerk, toss, fling, shove

ysgwïer (**ysgwieriaid**) nm squire

ysgwrfa nf scouring, lathering

ysgwrio vb to scour, to scrub; to lather

ysgwyd vb to shake; to flutter; to wag

ysgwydd (**-au**) nf shoulder

ysgwyddo vb to shoulder, to jostle

ysgydwad nm shaking, shake

ysgyfaint npl lungs, lights

ysgyfarnog (**-od**) nf hare

ysgymun adj excommunicate, accursed

ysgymundod nm excommunication, ban

ysgymuno vb to excommunicate

ysgyrion npl staves, splinters, shivers

ysgyrnygu vb to grind the teeth, to snarl

ysgytiad (**-au**) nm shock

ysgytio *vb* to shake violently, to shock

ysgytiol *adj* shocking

ysgythru *vb* to cut, to carve; to prune

ysictod *nm* contusion; sprain

ysig *adj* bruised, sore, sprained

ysigo *vb* to bruise, to crush; to sprain

yslotian *vb* to dabble, to tipple

ysmala *adj* droll, funny, amusing

ysmaldod *nm* fun, drollery

ysmalio *vb* to joke, to jest

ysmaliwr (-wyr) *nm* joker, wit

ysmotyn (ysmotiau) *nm* spot

ysmwddio *vb* to iron

ysmygu *vb* to smoke (tobacco)

ysmygwr (-wyr) *nm* smoker

ysol *adj* consuming, devouring; corrosive

yst- *see also* **st-**

ystabl (-au) *nf* stable

ystad (-au) *nf* state; estate; furlong

ystadegau *npl* statistics

ystadegol *adj* statistical

ystadegydd (-ion) *nm* statistician

ystafell (-oedd) *nf* chamber, room; **ystafell fyw** living room; **ystafell molchi** bathroom

ystalwyn (-i) *nm* stallion

ystanc (-iau) *nm* stake, bracket

ystarn (-au) *nf* stern

ystelcian *vb* to skulk, to loaf, to loiter

ystelciwr (-wyr) *nm* loafer, loiterer

ystên (-enau) *nf* pitcher, ewer, milk-can

ystinos *nm* asbestos

ystiwart (-wardiaid) *nm* steward

ystlum (-od) *nm* bat

ystlys (-au) *nf* side, flank

ystlyswr (-wyr) *nm* linesman

ystod (-ion) *nf* course; swath; **yn ystod** during

ystof *nmf* warp

ystofi *vb* to warp; to weave, to plan

ystôl (-olion) *nf* stool, chair

ystôr (-orau) *nm* store, abundance

ystordy (-dai) *nm* storehouse, warehouse

ystorfa (-feydd) *nf* store, storehouse

ystorio *vb* to store

ystoriwr (-iwyr) *nm* storyteller

ystorm (-ydd) *nf* storm

ystormus *adj* stormy

ystrad (-au) *nfm* vale, flat

ystranc (-iau) *nf* trick

ystrancio *vb* to play tricks; to jib

ystrodur (-iau) *nf* cart-saddle

ystryd (ystrydoedd) *nf* street

ystrydebol *adj* stereotyped

ystryw (-iau) *nf* wile, craft, ruse

ystrywgar *adj* wily, crafty

ystum (-iau) *nmf* bend; form; posture; *(pl)* grimaces

ystumio *vb* to bend, to distort; to pose

ystumog (-au) *nf* stomach

ystŵr *nm* stir, noise, bustle, fuss

Ystwyll *nm* Epiphany

ystwyrian *vb* to stretch and yawn, to stir

ystwyth *adj* flexible, pliant, supple

ystwythder *nm* flexibility, pliancy

ystwytho *vb* to make flexible; to bend, to soften

ystyfnig *adj* obstinate, stubborn

ystyfnigo *vb* to behave obstinately

ystyfnigrwydd *nm* obstinacy

ystyr (-on) *nmf* sense, meaning
ystyrgar *adj* thoughtful, meditative
ystyriaeth (-au) *nf* consideration, heed
ystyried *vb* to consider, to regard, to heed
ystyriol *adj* mindful, heedful
ysu *vb* to eat, to consume; to hanker; to itch
yswain (-weiniaid) *nm* esquire
yswil *adj* shy, bashful, timid
yswildod *nm* shyness, bashfulness
yswiriant *nm* insurance
yswirio *vb* to insure
ysywaeth *adv* more's the pity
yw¹ *vb* is, are
yw² *npl* (*nf* **-en**) yew

CYFATHREBU YN GYMRAEG

COMMUNICATING IN WELSH

Contents

Cynnwys

NUMBERS/RHIFAU

0	dim	20	dau ddeg
1	un	21	dau ddeg un
2	dau	22	dau ddeg dau
3	tri	23	dau ddeg tri
4	pedwar	24	dau ddeg pedwar
5	pump	25	dau ddeg pump
6	chwech	26	dau ddeg chwech
7	saith	27	dau ddeg saith
8	wyth	28	dau ddeg wyth
9	naw	29	dau ddeg naw
10	deg	30	tri deg
11	un deg un	40	pedwar deg
12	un deg dau	50	pum deg
13	un deg tri	60	chwe deg
14	un deg pedwar	70	saith deg
15	un deg pump	80	wyth deg
16	un deg chwech	90	naw deg
17	un deg saith	100	cant
18	un deg wyth	1 000	mil
19	un deg naw	1 000 000	miliwn

DATES/DYDDIADAU

t	1af	y cyntaf
d	2il	yr ail
d	3ydd	y trydydd
h	4ydd	y pedwerydd
h	5ed	y pumed
h	6ed	y chweched
h	7fed	y seithfed
h	8fed	yr wythfed
h	9fed	y nawfed
th	10fed	y degfed
th	11eg	yr unfed ar ddeg
th	12fed	y deuddegfed
th	13eg	y trydydd ar ddeg
th	14eg	y pedwerydd ar ddeg
th	15fed	y pymthegfed
th	16eg	yr unfed ar bymtheg
th	17eg	yr ail ar bymtheg
th	18fed	y deunawfed
th	19eg	y pedwerydd ar bymtheg
th	20fed	yr ugeinfed
st	21ain	yr unfed ar hugain
nd	22ain	yr ail ar hugain
rd	23ain	y trydydd ar hugain
th	24ain	y pedwerydd ar hugain
th	25ain	y pumed ar hugain
th	26ain	y chweched ar hugain
th	27ain	y seithfed ar hugain
th	28ain	yr wythfed ar hugain
th	29ain	y nawfed ar hugain
th	30ain	y degfed ar hugain
st	31ain	yr unfed ar ddeg ar hugain

DAYS OF THE WEEK

Monday
Tuesday
Wednesday
Thursday
Friday
Saturday
Sunday

DYDDIAU'R WYTHNOS

Dydd Llun
Dydd Mawrth
Dydd Mercher
Dydd Iau
Dydd Gwener
Dydd Sadwrn
Dydd Sul

MONTHS OF THE YEAR

January
February
March
April
May
June
July
August
September
October
November
December

MISOEDD Y FLWYDDYN

Ionawr
Chwefror
Mawrth
Ebrill
Mai
Mehefin
Gorffennaf
Awst
Medi
Hydref
Tachwedd
Rhagfyr

ME	AMSER
...hat time is it?	Faint o'r gloch ydy hi?
...s ...	Mae hi'n ...
...e o'clock	un o'r gloch
...o o'clock	ddau o'r gloch
...ree o'clock	dri o'r gloch
...ur o'clock	bedwar o'r gloch
...e o'clock	bump o'r gloch
...o'clock	chwech o'r gloch
...ven o'clock	saith o'r gloch
...ht o'clock	wyth o'r gloch
...e o'clock	naw o'r gloch
...o'clock	ddeg o'r gloch
...ven o'clock	un ar ddeg o'r gloch
...elve o'clock	ddeuddeg o'r gloch
...arter past one (1:15)	chwarter wedi un
...lf past one (1:30)	hanner awr wedi un
...arter to two (1:45)	chwarter i ddau
...e past one (1:05)	bum munud wedi un
...n past one (1:10)	ddeg munud wedi un
...enty past one (1:20)	ugain munud wedi un
...enty-five past one (1:25)	bum munud ar hugain wedi un
...enty-five to two (1:35)	bum munud ar hugain i ddau
...enty to two (1:40)	ugain munud i ddau
...n to two (1:50)	ddeg munud i ddau
...ve to two (1:55)	bum munud i ddau
...idday (12:00)	ganol dydd
...idnight (0:00)	ganol nos

7

TIME VOCABULARY	GEIRFA AMSER
day	diwrnod / dydd
week	wythnos
fortnight	pythefnos
month	mis
year	blwyddyn
today	heddiw
tonight	heno
this morning	y bore 'ma
this afternoon	y prynhawn 'ma
yesterday	ddoe
last night	neithiwr
the day before yesterday	echdoe
the night before last	echnos
tomorrow	yfory
tomorrow afternoon	prynhawn yfory
tomorrow night	nos yfory
the day after tomorrow	trennydd
every day	pob dydd
last Tuesday	dydd Mawrth diwethaf
a week on Saturday	wythnos i ddydd Sadwrn
a fortnight tomorrow	pythefnos i yfory
a month on Thursday	mis i ddydd Iau
in September	ym mis Medi

EVERYDAY GREETINGS	CYFARCHION POB DYDD
Hello!	Helo!
Hiya!	Shwmae!
Good morning.	Bore da.
Good afternoon.	Prynhawn da.
Good evening.	Noswaith dda.
This is Tom.	Dyma Tom.
This is my friend Sali.	Dyma fy ffrind Sali.
Nice to meet you. *(informal)*	Braf cwrdd â ti
Nice to meet you. *(formal)*	Braf cwrdd â chi
How are you? *(informal)*	Sut wyt ti?
How are you? *(formal)*	Sut dych chi?
Very well thanks.	Da iawn diolch
On top of the world!	Ar ben y byd!
OK.	Iawn.
Tired.	Wedi blino.
Not very well.	Ddim yn dda iawn.
What about you? *(informal)*	Beth amdanat ti?
What about you? *(formal)*	Beth amdanoch chi?
How is John?	Sut mae John?
He is very well.	Mae e'n dda iawn.
How is Siân?	Sut mae Siân?
She's fine too.	Mae hi'n dda hefyd.
What's wrong?	Beth sy'n bod?
I'm sorry.	Mae'n ddrwg 'da fi.
I'm sorry to hear that.	Mae'n ddrwg 'da fi glywed hynny

9

Do you speak Welsh? (*informal*)	Wyt ti'n siarad Cymraeg?
Do you speak Welsh? (*formal*)	Dych chi'n siarad Cymraeg?
I'm learning Welsh.	Dw i'n dysgu Cymraeg.
Good bye.	Hwyl fawr.
Good night.	Nos da.
See you.	Wela i di.
See you again.	Wela i di eto.

QUESTION WORDS	GEIRIAU CWESTIWN
Who? Who is the best player?	Pwy? **Pwy** ydy'r chwaraewr gorau?
How? How do you know James?	Sut? **Sut** rwyt ti'n nabod James?
Where? Where is Haverfordwest?	Ble? **Ble** mae Hwlffordd?
What? What do you want to do tomorrow?	Beth? **Beth** rwyt ti eisiau gwneud yfory?
Why? Why do you like vegetarian food?	Pam? **Pam** rwyt ti'n hoffi bwyd llysieuol?
Which? Which boy plays ice hockey?	Pa? **Pa** fachgen sy'n chwarae hoci iâ?
What kind of ...? What kind of music do you like?	Pa fath o ...? **Pa fath** o gerddoriaeth rwyt ti'n hoffi?
When? When is half term?	Pryd? **Pryd** mae hanner tymor?
How much? / How many? How much do the tickets cost?	Faint? **Faint** mae'r tocynnau yn costio?
What time? What time do you go to bed?	Faint o'r gloch? **Faint o'r gloch** rwyt ti'n mynd i'r gwely?

How many ...?

In Welsh there are two ways to ask 'How many ...?'
Both forms translate in the same way in English.

(i) **Sawl** ...? (+ singular noun)

How many cats?	**Sawl** <u>cath</u>?
How many children are in the class?	**Sawl** <u>plentyn</u> sydd yn y dosbarth?

(ii) **Faint o** ...? (+ plural noun)

How many cats?	**Faint o** <u>gathod</u>?
How many children are in the class?	**Faint o** <u>blant</u> sydd yn y dosbarth?

THE PRESENT TENSE	YR AMSER PRESENNOL
To be:	**Bod:**
Positive	**Cadarnhaol**
I / I am	Dw i
You / You are	Rwyt ti *(singular informal)*
He / He is It / It is	Mae e
She / She is It / It is	Mae hi
John / John is	Mae John
We / We are	Rydyn ni
You / You are	Rydych chi *(plural, or singular formal)*
They / They are	Maen nhw
Negative	**Negyddol**
I do not / I am not	Dw i ddim
You do not / You are not	Dwyt ti ddim *(singular informal)*
He/It does not / He/It is not	Dydy e ddim
She/It does not / She/It is not	Dydy hi ddim
John does not / John is not	Dydy John ddim
We do not / We are not	Dydyn ni ddim
You do not / You are not	Dydych chi ddim *(plural, or singular formal)*
They do not / They are not	Dydyn nhw ddim

Examples of sentences	Enghreifftiau o frawddegau
I like playing rugby.	Dw i'n hoffi chwarae rygbi.
You are tall.	Rwyt ti'n dal.
He lives in Swansea.	Mae e'n byw yn Abertawe.
She is very funny.	Mae hi'n ddoniol iawn.
John is driving to the party.	Mae John yn gyrru i'r parti.
We are winning the game.	Rydyn ni'n ennill y gêm.
You are polite.	Rydych chi'n gwrtais.
They work hard.	Maen nhw'n gweithio'n galed.

CONVERSATIONAL VOCABULARY

GEIRFA SGWRS

Hello, how are you? Very well thanks. And you?	Helo, sut wyt ti? Da iawn diolch. A ti?
What is your name? I'm Ffion.	Beth ydy dy enw di? Ffion ydw i.
Do you speak Welsh? A little, I'm learning	Wyt ti'n siarad Cymraeg? Tipyn bach, dw i'n dysgu.
Speak slowly please!	Siaradwch yn araf os gwelwch yn dda!
I understand. I don't understand.	Dw i'n deall. Dw i ddim yn deall.
Where do you live? I live in Aberystwyth.	Ble rwyt ti'n byw? Dw i'n byw yn Aberystwyth.
Do you like Aberystwyth? Yes I do. No I don't.	Wyt ti'n hoffi Aberystwyth? Ydw. Nac ydw.
How old are you? I'm fourteen.	Faint ydy dy oed di? Dw i'n un deg pedwar oed.
When is your birthday? My birthday is August 15.	Pryd mae dy ben-blwydd di? Mae fy mhen-blwydd i ar Awst 15.
Have you got any brothers or sisters? Yes, I've got two brothers. No, I'm an only child.	Oes brawd neu chwaer gyda ti? Oes, mae dau frawd gyda fi. Nac oes, unig blentyn ydw i.
What do you like doing? I like shopping.	Beth rwyt ti'n hoffi gwneud? Dw i'n hoffi siopa.

15

| What is your favourite subject? | Beth ydy dy hoff bwnc? |
| My favourite subject is geography. | Fy hoff bwnc ydy daearyddiaeth. |

| Can you play the guitar? | Wyt ti'n gallu chwarae'r gitâr? |
| Yes, quite well. | Ydw, yn eitha da. |

| What did you do last night? | Beth wnest ti neithiwr? |
| I listened to music. | Gwrandawais i ar gerddoriaeth. |

| What did you do on Saturday? | Beth wnest ti ddydd Sadwrn? |
| I went to Wrexham. | Es i i Wrecsam. |

Did you see Sara?	Welaist ti Sara?
Yes, she was there.	Do, roedd hi yno.
No, she wasn't there.	Naddo, doedd hi ddim yno.

| What was the weather like? | Sut roedd y tywydd? |
| It was fine. | Roedd hi'n braf. |

Was it sunny?	Oedd hi'n heulog?
Yes, it was sunny all day.	Oedd, roedd hi'n heulog trwy'r dydd.
No, it was raining.	Nac oedd, roedd hi'n bwrw glaw.

Were you ok in the car?	Oeddet ti'n iawn yn y car?
Yes, I was fine.	Oeddwn, roeddwn i'n iawn.
No, I was ill.	Nac oeddwn, roeddwn i'n sâl.

What would you like to do tomorrow?	Beth hoffet ti wneud yfory?
I'd like to go out.	Hoffwn i fynd allan.
Would you like to go to town?	Hoffet ti fynd i'r dre?
Yes, I would, thank you.	Hoffwn, diolch yn fawr.
Would you like to go and see the match?	Hoffet ti fynd i weld y gêm?
No, I wouldn't, I don't like football.	Na hoffwn, dw i ddim yn hoffi pêl-droed.
What will the weather be like tomorrow?	Sut bydd y tywydd fory?
It will be cold.	Bydd hi'n oer.
Will it be busy?	Fydd hi'n brysur?
Yes, it will.	Bydd.
No, it won't.	Na fydd.

CONNECTIVES/CYSYLLTEIRIAU

and	a / ac	**a** is used before a consonant
		ac is used before a vowel

- afal **a** banana — apple and banana
- afal **ac** oren — apple and orange

with	gyda
without	heb

- Dw i'n gwisgo'r trowsus **gyda** gwregys. — I wear the trousers with a belt.
- Dw i'n gwisgo'r sgert **heb** wregys. — I wear the skirt without a belt.

in	yn
in a	mewn

- Dw i'n byw **yn** Abertawe. — I live in Swansea.
- Dw i'n byw **mewn** fflat. — I live in a flat.

here	yma
there	yna

- Mae e'n byw **yma** gyda fi. — He lives here with me.
- Mae hi'n byw **yna** gyda Ben. — She lives there with Ben.

| at/about | am |
| approximately | tua |

- Dw i'n darllen llyfr **am** bysgota.

  I'm reading a book about fishing.

- Dw i'n dal trên mewn **tua** deg munud.

  I'm catching a train in about ten minutes.

| such as/like | fel |
| unlike | yn wahanol i |

- **Fel** Sara dw i'n siarad Sbaeneg.

  Like Sara I speak Spanish.

- **Yn wahanol i** Sara dw i ddim yn siarad Ffrangeg.

  Unlike Sara I don't speak French.

DYWEDIADAU	IDIOMATIC EXPRESSIONS
a dweud y gwir	to be honest
am byth	forever
ar fy mhen fy hun	on my own
ar hyn o bryd	at the moment
ar y cyfan	on the whole
ar y llaw arall	on the other hand
beth bynnag	whatever
byth eto	never again
cadw sŵn	make a noise
cyn bo hir	before long
chwarae teg	fair play
dal ati	keep at it
dim ond	only
diolch byth	thank goodness
does dim ots	it doesn't matter
dros ben	extremely
dros ben llestri	over the top
erbyn hyn	by now
fel arfer	usually
gorau glas	very best
gwaetha'r modd	worse luck
gwell hwyr na hwyrach	better late than never
gwneud hwyl ar ben	to make fun of
gyda llaw	by the way
heb os nac onibai	without a doubt
hen bryd	high time

...ond bol	a bellyful
...nynd o ddrwg i waeth	to go from bad to worse
...ewydd sbon	brand new
...hag ofn	in case
...hoi'r gorau i	to give up
...arad trwy ei het	to talk nonsense
...rwy'r amser	all the time
...u chwith	inside out
...nwaith ac am byth	once and for all
...wedi blino'n lân	exhausted
...wrth gwrs	of course
...wyneb i waered	upside down
...n awr ac yn y man	now and again

EXPRESSING OPINIONS	MYNEGI BARN
I like ...	Dw i'n hoffi ...
I enjoy ...	Dw i'n mwynhau ...
I'm mad about ...	Dw i'n dwlu ar ...
I love ...	Dw i wrth fy modd yn ...
I don't enjoy.	Dw i ddim yn mwynhau.
I prefer ...	Mae'n well gyda fi ...
I hate.	Mae'n gas gyda fi.
I hate.	Dw i'n casáu.
In my opinion ...	Yn fy marn i mae ...
I think that ...	Dw i'n meddwl bod ...
I believe that ...	Dw i'n credu bod ...
I feel that ...	Dw i'n teimlo bod ...
I'm sure that ...	Dw i'n sicr bod ...
I agree with ...	Dw i'n cytuno gyda ...
I disagree with ...	Dw i'n anghytuno gyda ...
Like Gareth I think that ...	Fel Gareth dw i'n meddwl bod ..
Unlike Gareth I think that ...	Yn wahanol i Gareth dw i'n meddwl bod ...
I'm in favour.	Dw i o blaid.
I'm against.	Dw i yn erbyn.
On the other hand ...	Ar y llaw arall ...
I would like to.	Hoffwn i.
My favourite ...	Fy hoff ...
What do you think of/about ...?	Beth rwyt ti'n feddwl am ...?
I think that ...	Dw i'n meddwl bod ...
What about you?	Beth amdanat ti?
Me too.	Fi hefyd.

ASKING FOR AND EXPRESSING OPINIONS

GOFYN A MYNEGI BARN

What do you think of Michael?
I think that he is lovely.

Beth rwyt ti'n feddwl am Michael?
Dw i'n meddwl ei fod e'n hyfryd.

What do you think of Alice?
I think that she is funny.

Beth rwyt ti'n feddwl am Alice?
Dw i'n meddwl ei bod hi'n ddoniol.

What do you think of the Wales team?
I think that they are great.

Beth rwyt ti'n feddwl am dîm Cymru?
Dw i'n meddwl eu bod nhw'n wych.

What is your favourite sport?
My favourite sport is basketball.

Beth ydy dy hoff chwaraeon?
Fy hoff chwaraeon ydy pêl-fasged.

Why?
Because I think that it is exciting!

Pam?
Achos dw i'n meddwl ei fod e'n gyffrous!

What is your opinion of Welsh TV programmes?
In my opinion they are quite interesting.

Beth ydy dy farn di am raglenni teledu Cymraeg?
Yn fy marn i maen nhw'n eitha diddorol.

Do you agree?
Yes, I agree, I think that Welsh programmes are a big help to people learning Welsh.

Wyt ti'n cytuno?
Ydw, dw i'n cytuno, dw i'n meddwl bod rhaglenni Cymraeg yn help mawr i bobl sy'n dysgu Cymraeg.

ENGLISH–WELSH

a

(KEYWORD)

a (before vowel and silent h **an**) indef art **1** (no equivalent word in Welsh): a book llyfr; an apple afal; she's a doctor meddyg yw hi

2 (in expressing ratios, prices etc): three a day/week tri y diwrnod/yr wythnos; **10 km an hour** 10 km yr awr; **£5 a person** £5 yr un/£5 y pen; 30p a kilo 30c y cilo

aback adv yn ôl; **taken aback** wedi synnu

abandon vt rhoi'r gorau i, gadael

abandoned adj wedi ei adael

abate vb gostwng, lleihau; gostegu

abattoir n lladd-dy

abbey n abaty, mynachlog

abbreviate vt byrhau, talfyrru

abbreviation n byrfodd

abdomen n bol

abdominal adj perthynol i'r bol

abduct vt dwyn ymaith drwy drais, cipio

abhor vt ffieiddio, casáu

abide vb aros, trigo; goddef

ability n gallu, medr

able adj abl, galluog

abnormal adj anghyffredin, annormal

aboard adv ar fwrdd (llong)

abolish vt diddymu, dileu

abominable adj ffiaidd

abomination n ffieidd-dra

abort vb erthylu, atal

abortion n erthyliad

(KEYWORD)

about adv **1** (approximately) tua, oddeutu, o gwmpas, rhyw; **about a hundred/thousand** tua chant/ mil; it takes about 10 hours mae'n cymryd tua/oddeutu/o gwmpas/ rhyw 10 awr; **at about 2 o'clock** tua 2 o'r gloch; I've just about finished rwyf bron â gorffen

2 (referring to place) o gwmpas/ yma ac acw; **to run about** rhedeg o gwmpas/rhedeg yma ac acw; **to walk about** cerdded o gwmpas; they left all their things lying about gadawsant eu pethau ar hyd y lle

3: to be about to do sth bod ar wneud rhth/bod ar fin gwneud rhth

▶ prep **1** (relating to) am, ynghylch, ynglŷn â; **a book about Cardiff** llyfr am Gaerdydd/llyfr ynghylch Caerdydd/llyfr ynglŷn â Chaerdydd; **what is it about?** beth sydd dan sylw?; **we talked about**

it buom yn siarad am y peth; **what**
or how about doing this? beth
amdani?
2 (referring to place) o amgylch/o
gwmpas; **to walk about the town**
cerdded o amgylch y dref/cerdded
o gwmpas y dref

above prep uwch, uchlaw ▸ adv
fry
abroad adv allan, ar led, dros y dŵr
abrupt adj disymwth; serth
abscess n cornwyd, crynhofa
absence n absenoldeb
absent adj absennol ▸ vt absenoli
absenteeism n absenoliaeth
absent-minded adj anghofus
absolute adj cwbl, hollol; diamodol
▸ n diamod, absolwt
absolutely adv yn hollol
absorb vt yfed, llyncu, sugno, sychu
absorbent adj amsugnol ▸ n
amsugnydd
abstain vb ymatal, ymgadw
abstract adj haniaethol ▸ n
crynodeb
absurd adj gwrthun, afresymol
abundance n digonedd,
helaethrwydd
abundant adj aml, helaeth, digonol
abuse¹ vt camddefnyddio, cam-
drin; difrïo
abuse² n camddefnydd,
camdriniaeth; difriaeth
abusive adj sarhaus, gwatwarus
abysmal adj diwaelod, dwys; enbyd
academic adj athrofaol, academig
academy n ysgol, athrofa, academi
accelerate vt cyflymu, chwimio

accelerator n ysbardun,
chwimiadur
accent n acen; llediaith ▸ vt
acennu
accept vt derbyn (yn gymeradwy)
acceptable adj derbyniol,
cymeradwy
acceptance n derbyniad
access n mynedfa, mynediad
accessary n cynorthwywr,
cefnogydd
accessible adj hygyrch; hawdd
dod ato
accessory adj cynorthwyol,
cyfranogol; atodol
accident n damwain, anap
accidental adj damweiniol
accidentally adv yn ddamweiniol
acclaim vt datgan cymeradwyaeth
accommodate vt cymhwyso;
lletya
accommodating adj cyfaddasol
accommodation n lle, llety
accompaniment n cyfeiliant
accompany vb hebrwng; cyfeilio
accomplice n cynorthwywr mewn
trosedd
accomplish vt cyflawni, cwblhau
accomplishment n medr, dawn,
camp
accord vb cytuno; cyflwyno ▸ n
cydfod
accordance n: **in accordance with**
yn unol â
according adv: **according to** yn ôl
accordingly adv felly, gan hynny
according to prep yn ôl
account vb cyfrif ▸ n cyfrif; hanes
accountable adj cyfrifol, atebol
accountant n cyfrifydd

account number n rhif cyfrif
accumulate vb casglu, pentyrru, cronni
accuracy n cywirdeb
accurate adj cywir
accurately adv yn gywir
accusation n cyhuddiad
accuse vt cyhuddo
accustomed adj cyfarwydd, cyffredin
ace n as; mymryn
ache vi poeni, gwynio ▸ n poen, cur
achieve vt cyflawni, gorffen, cwblhau
achievement n cyflawniad, camp
acid adj siarp, sur ▸ n suryn, asid
acid rain n glaw asid
acknowledge vt cydnabod, cyfaddef
acknowledgment n cydnabyddiaeth
acne n acne, plorynnod
acorn n mesen
acoustic adj clybodig
acquaintance n cydnabod
acquire vt cael, ennill
acquisition n caffaeliad
acquit vt rhyddhau
acre n erw, cyfair, acer
across adv, prep yn groes, ar draws; trosodd
acrylic adj acrylig
act vb gweithredu; actio ▸ n act, gweithred; deddf
action n gweithred, gweithrediad
activate vb gweithredoli
active adj bywiog; gweithredol
activity n gweithgarwch, gweithgaredd

actor n actor, actiwr
actress n actores
actual adj gwir, gwirioneddol
actually adv mewn gwirionedd
acupuncture n nodwyddiad, aciwbigiad
acute adj llym, tost; craff
ad n hysbys
A.D. abbr (= Anno Domini) O.C., A.D.
adamant adj pendant, sicr
adapt vt cyfaddasu
adapter n adaptydd
add vb chwanegu, atodi; adio; **add up** vt adio; **to add up to** gwneud
addict vt ymroddi, gorddibynnu
addicted adj: **addicted (to sth)** caeth (i rywbeth), dibynnol (ar rywbeth)
addiction n ymroddiad, gorddibyniaeth, tueddiad
addition n ychwanegiad
additional adj ychwanegol
additive n adiolyn
address vb annerch; cyfeirio ▸ n anerchiad; cyfeiriad
adequate adj digonol
adhere vi ymlynu, glynu wrth
adhesive adj glynol, ymlynol ▸ n adlyn, glud
adjacent adj cyfagos, gerllaw
adjective n ansoddair
adjourn vt gohirio, oedi
adjust vt cymhwyso, addasu
administer vt gweinyddu
administration n gweinyddiaeth
administrative adj gweinyddol
administrator n gweinyddwr
admirable adj rhagorol, campus
admiral n llyngesydd
admiration n edmygedd

admire vt edmygu
admission n derbyniad; addefiad
admit vt derbyn; addef, cyfaddef
admittance n derbyniad; trwydded
adolescence n llencyndod, adolesens
adolescent n adolesent, llencyn, llances
adopt vb mabwysiadu
adopted adj mabwysiedig; **he's adopted** mae e wedi'i fabwysiadu
adoption n mabwysiad
adore vt addoli
adorn vt addurno
Adriatic n: **the Adriatic (Sea)** Môr Adria, yr Adriatig
adrift adv yn rhydd, diangor
adult n (un) mewn oed, oedolyn
adultery n godineb
advance vb symud ymlaen; rhoi benthyg ▸ n benthyg, echwyn
advanced adj ar y blaen
advantage n mantais
advantageous adj manteisiol
advent n dyfodiad; yr Adfent
adventure n antur, anturiaeth
adverb n adferf
adversary n gwrthwynebydd
adverse adj adfydus, gwrthwynebus, croes
advert n hysbyseb
advertise vt hysbysu, hysbysebu
advertisement n hysbysiad, hysbyseb
advertiser n hysbysydd
advertising adj hysbysebol
advice n cyngor, cyfarwyddyd
advisable adj doeth, buddiol
advise vt cynghori; hysbysu

advisory adj ymgynghorol
advocate n eiriolwr, bargyfreithiwr ▸ vt eiriol, cefnogi, pleidio
aerial adj awyrol, wybrol
aerobics n aerobeg
aeroplane n awyren
aerosol n erosol
affair n achos, mater; helynt
affect vt effeithio; cymryd arno, ffugio
affection n serch, cariad; clefyd
affectionate adj serchog, caruaidd
afflict vt cystuddio
affluence n cyfoeth, digonedd
affluent adj goludog, cyfoethog, cefnog
afford vt rhoddi; fforddio
Afghanistan n Affganistan, Afghanistan
afraid adj ag ofn arno, ofnus
Africa n Affrica
African adj Affricanaidd ▸ n Affricanwr
after prep, conj wedi, ar ôl, yn ôl ▸ adv wedyn
aftercare n gofal wedyn, ôl-ofal
after-effects n ôl-effeithiau
aftermath n adladd, adlodd
afternoon n prynhawn
afters n (Brit, inf: dessert) y cwrs terfynol
aftershave, aftershave lotion n persawr eillio
aftersun, aftersun cream, aftersun lotion n hufen i drin llosg haul, hylif ar ôl haul
afterthought n syniad diweddar
afterwards adv wedi hynny, wedyn
again adv eilwaith, drachefn, eto
against prep erbyn, yn erbyn

a

age *n* oed, oedran; oes; henaint
▸ *vb* heneiddio

aged *adj* hen, oedrannus

agency *n* cyfrwng, asiantaeth

agenda *n* agenda

agent *n* asiant, gwithredydd,
cynrychiolydd

aggravate *vt* gwneuthur yn waeth

aggression *n* ymosodiad, gormes

aggressive *adj* ymosodol

agile *adj* heini, sionc, gwisgi

ago *adv* yn ôl; **long ago** ers talm

agony *n* ing, poen

agree *vi* cytuno; dygymod; cyfateb

agreeable *adj* clên, dymunol

agreement *n* cytundeb

agricultural *adj* amaethyddol

agriculture *n* amaethyddiaeth

ahead *adv* ymlaen, o flaen

aid *vt* cynorthwyo, helpu ▸ *n*
cymorth, cynhorthwy

AIDS *n abbr* AID, afiechyd
imiwnedd diffygiol

ailment *n* dolur, afiechyd,
anhwyldeb

aim *vb* anelu, amcanu ▸ *n* amcan,
nod

air *n* awyr; osgo; cainc, alaw ▸ *vt*
awyru

airbag *n* bag awyr, bag aer

air-conditioned *n* gyda system
dymheru

air conditioning *n* aerdymheru

aircraft *n* awyren

airforce *n* llu awyr

airline *n* cwmni hedfan

air mail *n* post awyr

airport *n* maes glanio

airtight *adj* aerglos, aerdyn

aisle *n* ystlys eglwys; llwybr; eil

ajar *adv* cilagored

à la carte *adv* à la carte

alarm *vt* dychrynu ▸ *n* braw,
dychryn; rhybudd; larwm

alarm clock *n* cloc larwm

albeit *conj* er, er hynny, eto

album *n* albwm

alcohol *n* alcohol

alcoholic *adj*, *n* alcoholig

alcove *n* cilfach, alcof

ale *n* cwrw

alert *adj* effro, gwyliadwrus

A level *n* Lefel A

algebra *n* algebra

Algeria *n* Algeria

Algerian *adj* Algeraidd ▸ *n*
Algeriad

alias *adv* mewn modd, dan enw
arall

alibi *n* alibi

alien *adj* estronol ▸ *n* estron

alight *vi* disgyn

align *vb* cyfunioni

alike *adj* yr un fath ▸ *adv* yn
gyffelyb

alive *adj*, *adj* yn fyw, byw

alkali *n* alcali

(KEYWORD)

all *adj* (*the whole of*) cyfan, oll, i gyd;
all Wales Cymru gyfan; **all day**
trwy gydol y dydd; **all night** trwy
gydol y nos; **all men** y dynion i gyd;
all five pob un o'r pump; **all the
books** pob un o'r llyfrau; **all his life**
trwy gydol ei oes
▸ *pron* **1** (*everyone*) pawb/pob un
2 (*everything*) y cyfan/y cwbl/pob
dim/popeth; **I ate it all**, **I ate all of
it** bwyteais y cyfan; **all of us went**

243

aethom bawb; **all of the boys
went** aeth pob un o'r bechgyn; **is
that all?** ai dyna'r cyfan?
3 (in phrases): **above all** uwchlaw
pob dim/yn anad dim/yn bennaf
oll; **after all** wedi'r cyfan; **at all,
not at all** (in answer to question) dim o
gwbl (in answer to thanks) croeso!
I'm not at all tired nid wyf wedi
blino o gwbl **anything at all will
do** bydd unrhyw beth o gwbl yn
gwneud y tro; **all in all** ar ei gilydd,
rhwng popeth
▸ adv: **all alone** ar eich pen eich
hun bach; **it's not as hard as all
that** nid yw mor anodd â hynny i
gyd; **all the better** gorau oll, gorau
i gyd; **all but** popeth ond; **the score
is 2 all** 2 yr un yw'r sgôr

allegedly adv yn honedig
allegiance n teyrngarwch,
gwrogaeth
allergic adj alergig
allergy n alergedd
alleviate vt ysgafnhau, esmwytho
alley n llwybr, ale
alliance n cyfathrach, cynghrair
allied adj cynghreiriol
all-night adv drwy'r nos
allocate vt rhannu, dosbarthu
allot vb gosod, penodi
all-out adv yn llwyr, a'i holl egni
allow vt caniatáu, goddef
allowance n dogn; lwfans
all right adv yn iawn
ally vt cynghreirio ▸ n cynghreiriad
almighty adj hollalluog,
hollgyfoethog
almond n almon

almost adv bron
alone adv, adj unig, ar ei ben ei hun
along adv ymlaen; ar hyd; **all along**
o'r cychwyn
aloof adv, adj yn cadw draw; pell
aloud adv uchel, yn groch
alphabet n egwyddor, abiéc
alphabetical adj yn nhrefn yr
wyddor
Alps npl: **the Alps** yr Alpau
already adv eisoes, yn barod
also adv hefyd
altar n allor
alter vb newid, altro
alteration n newid, cyfnewidiad
alternate adj bob yn ail ▸ vb
digwydd bob yn ail
alternative n dewis arall
alternatively adv o ddewis arall
although conj er
altitude n uchder
altogether adv oll, i gyd, yn gyfan
gwbl
aluminium n alwminiwm
always adv yn wastad(ol), bob
amser
Alzheimer's, Alzheimer's disease
n clefyd Alzheimer
a.m. abbr (= anti meridiem) a.m.
amalgamate vb cymysgu, cyfuno,
uno
amass vt casglu, cronni, pentyrru
amateur n amatur
amaze vt synnu, rhyfeddu
amazement n syndod
amazing adj rhyfeddol
ambassador n llysgennad
amber n ambr
ambiguous adj amwys
ambition n uchelgais

ambitious adj uchelgeisiol

ambulance n ambiwlans

ambush n, vb cynllwyn, rhagod

amend vb gwella, diwygio

amendment n gwelliant

amenities n mwynderau

America n yr Amerig

American adj Americanaidd ▸ n Americanwr

amiable adj hawddgar, serchus

amicable adj cyfeillgar

amid, amidst prep ynghanol, ymhlith, ymysg

ammunition n pylor

amnesty n maddeuant

amok adv yn wyllt, yn ddilywodraeth

among, amongst prep ymhlith; among you/them yn eich/eu plith

amount vi cyrraedd; codi ▸ n swm

amp n amp

ample adj helaeth, eang, digon

amputate vt torri aelod, trychu

amuse vt difyrru, diddanu

amusement n difyrrwch, digrifwch

amusement arcade n arcêd difyrion

an see a

anaemia n diffyg gwaed

anaemic adj di-waed, diwryg

anaesthetic adj, n anesthetig

analogy n cyfatebiaeth, cydweddiad

analyse vt dadansoddi, dadelfennu

analysis n dadansoddiad

analyst n dadansoddwr

analytical adj dadansoddol

anarchic, anarchical adj anarchol

anarchy n anhrefn, anarchaeth

anatomy n anatomeg

ancestor n cyndad, hynafiad

anchor n angor ▸ vb angori

ancient adj hen, hynafol; oesol

and conj a, ac

angel n angel

anger n dicter, llid ▸ vt digio, llidio

angle n ongl ▸ vi genweirio, pysgota

Anglican adj perthynol i Eglwys Loegr, Anglicanaidd

angling n pysgota

angry adj dig, llidiog

anguish n ing

animal n anifail, mil ▸ adj anifeilaidd

animation n (of person) bywiogrwydd; (Cinema) animeiddiad

ankle n migwrn, ffêr

annex vt cysylltu, cydio; meddiannu

annihilate vt diddymu, difodi

annihilation n diddymiant, difodiant

anniversary n pen blwydd

annotate vb gwneud nodiadau

announce vt datgan, cyhoeddi

announcement n cyhoeddiad, hysbysiad

announcer n cyhoeddwr

annoy vt poeni, blino, cythruddo

annoying adj trafferthus, blinderus

annual adj blynyddol

anonymous adj dienw, anhysbys

anorak n anorac

anorexic adj anorecsig

another pron, n arall

answer vb ateb ▸ n ateb, atebiad

answerable adj atebol, cyfrifol

answering machine n peiriant ateb

ant n morgrugyn

Antarctic n: the Antarctic yr Antarctig

antarctic adj o gylch y pegwn deheuol

antelope n gafrewig, antelop

antenatal adj cyn-geni

anthem n anthem

anthology n blodeugerdd

anthropology n anthropoleg

anti- prefix gwrth-, yn erbyn

antibiotic n, adj gwrthfiotig

anticipate vt achub y blaen, disgwyl

anticlimax n disgynneb

anticlockwise adj o chwith, gwrthglocwedd ▸ adv yn wrthglocwedd

antics npl ystumiau, stranciau

antidote n gwrthwenwyn

antifreeze n, adj gwrthrew, direwyn

antique¹ adj hen, hynafol

antique² n hen beth

antique shop n siop hen bethau

anti-Semitism n gwrth-Iddewiaeth

antiseptic adj, n antiseptig

antisocial adj gwrthgymdeithasol

anxiety n pryder

anxious adj pryderus, awyddus

any adj 1 (in questions etc; often no equivalent word in Welsh): **do you have any butter/children/ink?** a oes gennych fenyn/blant/inc? 2 (with negative): **I don't have any**

money/books nid oes gennyf arian/lyfrau 3 (no matter which) unrhyw; **choose any book you like** dewiswch unrhyw lyfr a ddymunwch; **any teacher you ask will tell you** bydd unrhyw athro a holwch yn dweud wrthych 4 (in phrases): **in any case** beth bynnag; **any day now** unrhyw ddiwrnod nawr; **at any moment** unrhyw eiliad; **at any rate** beth bynnag; **any time** unrhyw bryd; **he might come (at) any time** gallai ddod unrhyw bryd; **come (at) any time** dewch unrhyw bryd ▸ pron 1 (in questions etc; often no equivalent word in Welsh): **have you got any milk?** a oes gennych laeth?; **can any of you sing?** a all unrhyw rai ohonoch ganu? 2 (with negative) ddim; **they aren't any better** nid ydynt ddim gwell 3 (no matter which) unrhyw; **take any of those books (you like)** cymerwch unrhyw rai o'r llyfrau hynny (a ddymunwch) ▸ adv 1 (in questions etc): **do you want any more soup/sandwiches?** gymerwch chi ragor o gawl/frechdanau?; **are you feeling any better?** a ydych yn teimlo rywfaint yn well? 2 (with negative): **I can't hear him any more** ni allaf ei glywed bellach, ni allaf ei glywed mwyach; **don't wait any longer** peidiwch ag aros bellach

anybody pron unrhyw un, rhywun

anyhow *adv* (*anyway*) beth bynnag; (*haphazardly*) unrhyw sut

anyone *pron* rhywun

anything *pron* dim, rhywbeth, rhywfaint

anyway *adv* beth bynnag

anywhere *adv* rhywle

apart *adv* o'r neilltu, ar wahân

apartment *n* rhandy, llety

apathetic *adj* difater, didaro

apathy *n* difrawder, difaterwch

ape *n* epa ▸ *vt* dynwared

aperture *n* bwlch, twll, agorfa

apex *n* blaen, brig

apocalypse *n* datguddiad

apologize *vi* ymddiheuro, ymesgusodi

apology *n* ymddiheuriad, esgusawd

apostrophe *n* sillgoll, collnod (')

app *n* (*inf, Comput*) (*application*) ap

appal *vt* brawychu, digalonni

appalling *adj* arswydus, gwarthus

apparatus *n* offer, aparatws

apparent *adj* amlwg, eglur

apparently *adv* mae'n debyg

appeal *vi* apelio, erfyn ▸ *n* apêl

appear *vi* ymddangos, ymrithio

appearance *n* ymddangosiad

appease *vt* llonyddu, tawelu, dofi

appendicitis *n* enyniad y coluddyn crog, apendiseitis

appendix *n* atodiad, ychwanegiad

appetite *n* archwaeth, chwant, awydd

appetizer *n* lluniaeth i greu blas, blasyn

applaud *vt* cymeradwyo, curo dwylo

applause *n* cymeradwyaeth

apple *n* afal; **apple of the eye** cannwyll llygad

appliance *n* offeryn, dyfais

applicant *n* ymgeisydd

application *n* cymhwysiad; cais; ymroddiad

application form *n* ffurflen gais

apply *vb* cymhwyso; ymroi; ymgeisio

appoint *vb* gosod, penodi, pennu

appointment *n* cyhoeddiad; penodiad

appreciate *vt* prisio, gwerthfawrogi

appreciation *n* gwerthfawrogiad

appreciative *adj* gwerthfawrogol

apprehend *vt* ymaflyd mewn; dirnad; ofni

apprehension *n* dirnadaeth; ofn

apprehensive *adj* ofnus, pryderus

apprentice *n* prentis, dysgwr ▸ *vt* prentisio

approach *vb* nesáu, dynesu ▸ *n* dyfodfa

approachable *adj* hawdd mynd ato

appropriate *vt* meddiannu ▸ *adj* priodol, addas

approval *n* cymeradwyaeth

approve *vt* cymeradwyo; profi

approximate *vi* agosáu ▸ *adj* agos

approximately *adv* oddeutu, tua, yn agos i

apricot *n* bricyllen

April *n* Ebrill

apron *n* (ar)ffedog, barclod

apt *adj* tueddol; cymwys

aquarium *n* pysgodlyn, pysgoty

Aquarius *n* y Cariwr Dŵr

Arab *n* Arab ▸ *adj* Arabaidd

Arabic

Arabic n Arabeg
arbitrary adj gormesol, mympwyol
arc n bwa, arc
arcade n arcêd
arch n bwa, pont ▸ vt pontio
archaeologist n archaeolegwr
archaeology n archaeoleg
archbishop n archesgob
architect n pensaer
architecture n pensaerniaeth
archive n archif
Arctic n: the Arctic yr Arctig
arctic adj gogleddol
area n arwynebedd; wyneb
Argentina n Ariannin
Argentinian adj Archentaidd;
  o'r Ariannin ▸ n Archentwr
  (Archentwraig)
argue vb dadlau, ymresymu
argument n dadl, ymresymiad
Aries n yr Hwrdd
arise (pt **arose**, pp **arisen**) vi
  cyfodi, codi
aristocracy n pendefigaeth
aristocratic adj pendefigaidd,
  bonheddig
arithmetic n rhifyddeg
arm¹ n braich; cainc
arm² n (weapon) arf ▸ vb arfogi
armchair n cadair freichiau
armed adj arfog
armour n arfogaeth, arfwisg
armpit n cesail
armrest n man i orffwys braich
army n byddin
aroma n peraroglau(au)
around adv, prep am, o amgylch
arouse vt deffro(i), dihuno; cyffroi
arrange vb trefnu

arrangement n trefn, trefniad,
  trefniant
array vt trefnu; gwisgo ▸ n trefn;
  gwisg
arrears npl ôl-ddyled
arrest vt atal; dal, restio
arrival n dyfodiad, cyrhaeddiad
arrive vi cyrraedd, dyfod
arrogance n balchder, traha
arrogant adj balch, trahaus
arrow n saeth
arson n llosgiad, llosg
art n celfyddyd; ystryw
artery n rhedweli
art gallery n oriel gelf
arthritis n gwynegon,
  crydcymalau
artichoke n artisiog
article n erthygl; nwydd; bannod
articulate vb cymalu; cynanu
  ▸ adj â meddwl clir, trefnus
artificial adj gosod, ffug
artillery n offer rhyfel, magnelau
artist n celfyddydwr, arlunydd,
  artist
artistic adj celfydd, celfyddgar,
  artistig

(KEYWORD)

as conj 1 (time, moment) fel y, pan,
wrth, tra; **he came in as I was
leaving** daeth i mewn wrth imi
ymadael; **as the years went by**
wrth i'r blynyddoedd fynd heibio;
as from tomorrow o fory ymlaen
2 (because) gan; **he left early as he
had to be home by 10** ymadawodd
yn gynnar gan fod rhaid iddo fod
gartref erbyn 10
3 (referring to manner, way) fel; **do as

you wish gwnewch fel y mynnoch;
as she said fel y dywedodd
▶ adv 1 (in comparisons): as big
as cymaint â, mor fawr â; twice
as big as dwywaith mor fawr â;
as much as cymaint â; as many
as cynifer â; as much money as
cymaint o arian â; as many books
as cynifer o lyfrau â; as soon as cyn
gynted â
2 (concerning): as for or to that o
ran hynny, gyda golwg ar hynny
3: as if or though fel pe; he looked
as if he was ill edrychai fel petai'n
sâl see also long, such, well
▶ prep (in the capacity of) fel; he
works as a driver mae'n gweithio
fel gyrrwr; as chairman of the
company, he ... yn rhinwedd ei
swydd fel cadeirydd y cwmni,
...; he gave me it as a present fe'i
rhoddodd imi yn anrheg

a.s.a.p. abbr (= as soon as possible)
cyn gynted, cyn gynted â phosib
asbestos n ystinos, asbestos
ascent n esgynfa, rhiw, gorifyny
ash[1] n onnen, onn
ash[2] n (powder) lludw, ulw
ashamed adj ag arno gywilydd
ashore adv i'r lan, ar y lan
ashtray n plat lludw
Asia n Asia
Asian n Asiad ▶ adj Asiaidd
aside adv o'r neilltu
ask vb gofyn, holi; ceisio
asleep adv yng nghwsg, yn cysgu
asparagus n merllys, asbaragws
aspect n golwg, wyneb, agwedd
aspire vi dyheu

aspirin n asbrin
ass n asyn
assailant n ymosodwr
assassin n bradlofrudd, llofrudd
assassinate vt bradlofruddio
assault n ymosodiad ▶ vt ymosod
assemble vb cynnull, ymgynnull
assembly n cynulliad, cymanfa
assert vt haeru, honni, mynnu
assess vt asesu
assessment n asesiad
asset n ased
assets npl eiddo, meddiannau
assign vt gosod, penodi;
trosglwyddo
assignment n aseiniad
assimilate vb cymathu; tebygu
assist vb cynorthwyo, helpu
assistance n cymorth
assistant n cynorthwyydd
associate vb cymdeithasu,
cyfeillachu, cysylltu ▶ n
cydymaith
association n cymdeithas,
cymdeithasfa
assorted adj amrywiaeth
assortment n dosbarthiad, pigion
assume vt cymryd ar; tybied;
honni
assumption n tyb (iaeth), honiad;
dyrchafiad (Mair i'r nefoedd)
assurance n sicrwydd; hyder
assure vt sicrhau; yswirio
asterisk n serennig
asthma n y fogfa
asthmatic adj asthmatig
astonish vt synnu
astonished adj syn
astonishing adj syfrdanol
astound vt synnu, syfrdanu

249

astray adv ar gyfeiliorn, ar grwydr
astrologer n sêr-ddewin
astrology n sêr-ddewiniaeth
astronaut n gofodwr
astronomer n serydd, seryddwr
astronomy n seryddiaeth
astute adj craff, cyfrwys, call
asylum n noddfa; **lunatic asylum** gwallgofdy

(KEYWORD)

at prep **1** (referring to position, direction) ar, yn; **at the top** ar y brig; **at home** gartref; **at school** yn yr ysgol; **at the baker's** yn siop y pobydd; **to look at sth** edrych ar rth
2 (referring to time): **at 4 o'clock** am 4 o'r gloch; **at Christmas** adeg y Nadolig; **at night** gyda'r nos, yn ystod y nos; **at times** ar adegau
3 (referring to rates, speed etc): **at £1 a kilo** am £1 y cilo; **two at a time** dau ar y tro; **at 50 km/h** am 50km/a
4 (referring to manner): **at a stroke** ar amrantiad; **at peace** mewn heddwch
5 (referring to activity): **to be at work** (in the office etc) bod yn y gwaith (working) gweithio; **to play at cowboys** chwarae cowbois; **to be good at sth** bod yn dda am wneud rhth
6 (referring to cause): **shocked/surprised at sth** synnu/rhyfeddu at rhth; **I went at his suggestion** euthum ar ei awgrym ef

atheist n anffyddiwr
Athens n Athen

athlete n mabolgampwr
athletic adj athletaidd
athletics npl mabolgampau
Atlantic adj Atlantaidd, Atlantig
  ▸ n: **the Atlantic (Ocean)** yr Iwerydd, Môr Iwerydd
atlas n llyfr mapiau, atlas
ATM n abbr peiriant arian
atmosphere n awyrgylch
atom n atom
atomic adj atomig
atrocious adj erchyll, anfad, ysgeler
attach vb gosod, glynu; atafaelu
attached adj: **attached to** (fond of) hoff iawn o
attachment n ymlyniad, serch
attack vt ymosod ar ▸ n ymosodiad
attain vt ennill; cyrraedd; cael gafael
attempt vt ceisio, cynnig ▸ n cynnig, ymgais
attend vb gweini; ystyried; dilyn, mynychu
attendance n gwasanaeth; presenoldeb
attendant n gweinydd ▸ adj yn dilyn, ynghlwm wrth
attention n sylw, ystyriaeth
attic n nenlofft, nenlawr
attitude n ystum, agwedd, osgo
attorney n twrnai
attract vt tynnu, denu, hudo
attraction n atyniad
attractive adj atyniadol
attribute¹ n priodoledd
attribute² vt priodoli, cyfrif i
aubergine n planhigyn wy
auburn adj gwinau, browngoch

auction n arwerthiant, ocsiwn
audible adj hyglyw, clywadwy
audience n gwrandawyr, cynulleidfa
audit vt archwilio cyfrifon ▸ n archwiliad
audition n clywelediad
auditor n archwilydd
August n Awst
august adj urddasol, mawreddog
aunt n modryb
au pair n au pair
aura n naws, awyrgylch
austerity n gerwindeb, llymder
Australia n Awstralia
Australian n Awstraliad ▸ adj Awstralaidd
Austria n Awstria
Austrian n Awstriad ▸ adj Awstraidd
authentic adj dilys, gwir
author n awdur, awdwr
authority n awdurdod
authorize vt awdurdodi
autobiography n hunangofiant
autograph n llofnod
automatic adj hunanysgogol, awtomatig
automatically adv yn awtomatig
automobile n cerbyd, modur
autonomy n ymreolaeth
autumn n hydref
auxiliary adj cynorthwyol, ategol ▸ n cynorthwywr
avail vb llesáu, tycio ▸ n lles, budd
available adj ar gael
avalanche n syrthfa, cwymp (eira etc)
avenge vt dial cam
avenue n mynedfa, rhodfa

average n canolbris; cyfartaledd; cyffredin
aversion n gwrthwynebiad; casbeth
avert vt troi heibio, gochel, osgoi
avocado n afocado
avoid vt osgoi
await vt disgwyl, aros
awake (pt **awoke**, pp **awoken**) vb deffro, dihuno ▸ adj effro
award vt dyfarnu ▸ n dyfarniad
aware adj hysbys, ymwybodol
awareness n arwybod, ymwybyddiaeth
away adv ymaith, i ffwrdd
awe n (parchedig) ofn ▸ vt rhoi arswyd
awful adj ofnadwy, arswydus
awkward adj trwsgl, lletchwith, anghyfleus
axe n bwyall, bwyell
axle n echel
ay adv ie
aye adv yn wastad(ol), byth

b

baby n baban, babi
babysit vi gwarchod plant ▸ vt gwarchod
babysitter n gwarchodwr plant
babysitting n gwarchod plant
bachelor n dyn dibriod, hen lanc; baglor
back n cefn ▸ vb cefnogi; bacio ▸ adv yn ôl; **back out** vi bacio allan; **back up** vt cefnogi
backache n poen cefn
backbone n asgwrn cefn
backfire vi bacffeirio
background n cefndir
backing n (support) cefnogaeth
backpack n cefnbwn
backpacker n bacpacwr
backside n (inf) pen-ôl
backup n (support) cefnogaeth
backward adv yn ôl, ar ôl
bacon n cig moch, bacwn
bad adj drwg, drygionus; gwael, sâl
badge n bathodyn

badger n mochyn daear, broch ▸ vt profocio, poeni
badly adv (poorly) yn wael; (seriously) yn ddifrifol
badminton n badminton
bad-tempered adj â thymer ddrwg
bag n cwd, cod, bag
baggage n celfi, pac
bagpipe n pibgod
bail n meichiau, gwystl ▸ vt mechnïo
bait vt abwydo ▸ n abwyd
bake vb pobi, crasu
baked adj pob; wedi'i bobi; **baked beans** ffa pob
baked potato n taten bob
baker n pobydd
bakery n popty
balance n clorian, mantol; gweddill ▸ vt mantoli; cydbwyso
balanced adj cytbwys, cymesur
balcony n oriel, balcon
bald adj moel, penfoel
baleful adj alaethus
ball¹ n pêl, pellen
ball² n (dance) dawns, dawnsfa
ballerina n balerina
ballet n bale
ballet dancer n dawnsiwr bale
ballet shoes n esgidiau bale
balloon n balŵn
ballot n balot, tugel
ballpoint pen n beiro
ban vt gwahardd, ysgymuno
banana n banana
band n band, rhwymyn; mintai; seindorf
bandage n rhwymyn ▸ vb rhwymo, rhwymynnu
Band-Aid n plastr glynu

bandit n herwr, ysbeiliwr

bang vb (inf) curo ▸ n ergyd, twrf

Bangladesh n Bangladesh

bangle n breichled

banish vt alltudio, deol

bank¹ n (shore) glan, torlan; traethell

bank² n (building) banc ▸ vb bancio

bank account n cyfrif banc

banker n bancwr

bank holiday n gŵyl banc

banknote n papur banc

bankrupt n methdalwr

bankruptcy n methdaliad

bank statement n datganiad banc, adroddiad banc

banner n baner, lluman

banquet n gwledd ▸ vb gwledda

banter n ysmaldod, cellwair ▸ vb cellwair, profocio

baptism n bedydd

baptize vt bedyddio

bar n bar, bollt; rhwystr; traethell ▸ vt bario; eithrio

barbaric adj barbaraidd

barbecue n rhostfa

barbed wire n weiar bigog

barber n barbwr

bare adj noeth, llwm, moel, prin ▸ vt dinoethi

barefoot adj troednoeth

barefooted adj troednoeth

barely adv prin, o'r braidd

bargain n bargen ▸ vb bargeinio

barge n bad mawr

bark¹ vi cyfarth, coethi ▸ n cyfarthiad

bark² n rhisgl ▸ vt dirisglo, digroeni

barley n haidd, barlys

barmaid n barferch

barman n barmon

barn n ysgubor

barometer n hinfynegydd, baromedr

baron n barwn, arglwydd

barrage n argae, clawdd

barrel n baril, casgen

barren adj diffrwyth

barricade n atalglawdd ▸ vt cau

barrier n atalfa, rhwystr

barrister n bargyfreithiwr

barrow n berfa, whilber; crug

base¹ adj isel, gwael

base² n sylfaen, sail; bôn ▸ vt sylfaenu, seilio

baseball n pel-fâs

based adj (based on) wedi'i seilio ar

basement n islawr

bash (inf) n: to have a bash (at sth) rhoi cynnig (ar rth) ▸ vt pwnio

basic adj gwaelodol, sylfaenol

basically adv yn y bôn

basics npl: the basics yr hanfodion

basil n brenhinllys, basil

basin n basn, cawg, dysgl

basis n sail, sylfaen

basket n basged, cawell

basketball n pêl-fasged

bass n bas; bàs, draenogiad y môr

bass drum n drwm bas

bastard n (inf) bastard, plentyn gordderch

bat¹ n (mammal) ystlum

bat² n bat ▸ vi batio

batch n pobiad, ffyrnaid; swp, sypyn

bath n baddon; bàth

bathe vb ymdrochi, ymolchi, golchi

bathroom n ystafell ymolchi

bath towel n tywel bàth

baton n baton

batter vt curo, pwyo ▸ n defnydd crempog, cytew

battery n magnefa; batri

battle n brwydr, cad ▸ vi brwydro

battlefield n maes y gad

bay[1] n bae

bay[2] vb, n cyfarth; **to hold at bay** rhoi cyfarth

bay[3] (tree) llawryf

bay[4] adj gwinau, gwineugoch

bazaar n basâr

B.C. abbr (= before Christ) CC, Cyn Crist

(KEYWORD)

be (pt **was, were**, pp **been**) aux vb
1 (with present participle; forming continuous tenses): **what are you doing?** beth rydych yn ei wneud?; **they're coming tomorrow** maent yn dod yfory; **I've been waiting for you for 2 hours** rwyf yn aros amdanoch ers 2 awr
2 (with pp; forming passives): **to be killed** cael eich lladd; **the box had been opened** roedd y blwch wedi [cael] ei agor; **he was nowhere to be seen** nid oedd i'w weld yn unman
3 (in tag questions): **it was fun, wasn't it?** roedd yn hwyl onid oedd?; **he's good-looking, isn't he?** mae'n olygus, on'd yw e?; **she's back, is she?** mae yn ôl, ydy hi?
4 (+to +infinitive): **the house is to be sold** (necessity) rhaid i'r tŷ gael ei werthu (future) mae'r tŷ i'w werthu; **he's not to open it** rhaid

iddo beidio â'i agor
▸ vb + complement 1 (gen) bod; **I'm Welsh** Cymro/Cymraes ydw i; **I'm tired** rwyf wedi blino; **I'm hot/cold** rwy'n boeth/oer; **he's a doctor** meddyg yw e; **be careful/good/quiet!** byddwch yn ofalus/yn dda/yn dawel!; **2 and 2 are 4** 2 a 2 yw 4
2 (of health) bod; **how are you?** sut rydych chi?; **I'm better now** rwy'n well bellach; **he's very ill** mae'n sâl iawn
▸ vi 1 (exist, occur etc) bod, bodoli; **the prettiest girl that ever was** y ferch bertaf a fu erioed; **is there a God?** a oes yna Dduw?; **be that as it may** bid a fo am hynny; **so be it** boed/bydded felly, felly y bo
2 (referring to place) bod; **I won't be here tomorrow** ni fyddaf yma yfory
▸ vb imper 1 (referring to time) bod; **it's 5 o'clock** mae'n 5 o'r gloch; **it's the 28th of April** yr 28ain o Ebrill yw hi
2 (referring to distance): **it's 10 km to the village** mae'n 10 km i'r pentref
3 (referring to the weather): **it's too hot/cold** mae'n rhy boeth/oer; **it's windy today** mae'n wyntog heddiw
4 (emphatic: to emphasize a word or words they are placed first in Welsh): **it's me/the postman** fi sydd yma/y postmon sydd yna; **it was Maria who paid the bill** Maria a dalodd y bil

beach n traeth, traethell ▸ vt gyrru ar y traeth

beacon n coelcerth

bead n glain; **beads** npl paderau

beak n pig, gylfin

beam n trawst; pelydryn ▶ vi pelydru

bean n ffäen, ffeuen

bear¹ n arth; arthes

bear² (pt **bore**, pp **borne**) vt dwyn, cludo; geni; goddef
▶ **bear up** vi: **bear up!** daliwch ati!

beard n barf; col ŷd

bearded adj barfog; â barf

bearing n ymddygiad; traul

beast n bwystfil, anifail

beat (pt **beat**, pp **beaten**) vt curo
▶ n cur, curiad

beautiful adj prydferth, hardd, teg

beautifully adv yn hardd

beauty n prydferthwch, harddwch, tegwch

beaver n afanc, llostlydan

because adv, conj oherwydd, oblegid, o achos, gan, am

beckon vb amneidio

become vb dyfod; gweddu

bed n gwely; cefn, pâm

bed and breakfast n gwely a brecwast

bedclothes n dillad gwely

bedding n dillad gwely

bedraggled adj wedi caglo; aflêr

bedroom n ystafell wely, llofft

bedsit n fflat un ystafell

bedspread n cwrlid

bedtime n amser gwely

bee n gwenynen

beech n ffawydden

beef n eidion; cig eidion

beer n cwrw

beet n betys

beetle n chwilen

beetroot n betys

before prep o flaen, gerbron, cyn
▶ adv o'r blaen

beforehand adv ymlaen llaw

befriend vt ymgeleddu, bod yn gefn

beg vb erfyn, deisyf, ymbil; cardota

beggar n cardotyn ▶ vt tlodi, llymhau

begin (pt **began**, pp **begun**) vb dechrau

beginner n dechreuwr

beginning n dechreuad

behalf n plaid, rhan, achos, tu

behave vb ymddwyn

behaviour n ymddygiad

behind adv, prep ar ôl, yn ôl, tu ôl, tu cefn

beige adj beis

being n bod

belated adj diweddar, hwyr

belch vb bytheirio

Belgian adj Belgaidd; o Wlad Belg
▶ n Belgiad

Belgium n Gwlad Belg

belief n cred, crediniaeth, coel

believe vb credu, coelio

believer n credwr, credadun

belittle vt bychanu

bell n cloch

belligerent adj rhyfelog ▶ n rhyfelblaid

bellow vb rhuo, bugunad

belly n bol, cest, tor ▶ vb bolio

belong vi perthyn

belongings n meddiannau, eiddo

beloved adj annwyl, cu ▶ n anwylyd

below adv, prep is, islaw, isod

belt

belt *n* gwregys
bemused *adj* syfrdan
bench *n* mainc
bend (*pt, pp* bent) *vb* plygu, camu
  ▸ *n* tro, camedd; **bend down** *vi*
  plygu drosodd; **bend over** *vi*
  plygu drosodd
beneath *adv, prep* is, tan, oddi
  tanodd
beneficial *adj* buddiol, llesol
benefit *n* budd, lles, elw ▸ *vb*
  llesáu, elwa
benign *adj* tirion, mwyn
bent *n* tuedd, gogwydd
beret *n* bere
Berlin *n* Berlin
berry *n* aeronen, mwyaren
berth *n* lle llong; gwely llongwr;
  swydd
beside *prep* gerllaw, wrth, yn ymyl;
  to be beside oneself o'i bwyll
besides *adv, prep* heblaw, gyda
best *adj, adv* gorau
best man *n* gwas priodas
bet (*pt, pp* bet, betted) *vb* betio,
  dal am ▸ *n* bet, cyngwystl
betray *vt* bradychu
betrayal *n* brad
better *adj* gwell, rhagorach ▸ *adv*
  yn well ▸ *vt* gwella
between *prep* rhwng, cydrhwng
beverage *n* diod
beware *vi* gochel, ymogelyd
beyond *adv, prep* tu hwnt
bias *n* tuedd, gogwydd, rhagfarn
  ▸ *vt* tueddu
Bible *n* Beibl
bicker *vi* ffraeo, ymgecru
bicycle *n* beic

bid *vt* (*pt* bade, *pp* bidden) erchi
  ▸ *vi* (*pt, pp* bid) gwahodd; cynnig
big *adj* mawr
bigheaded *adj* bras, mawreddog
bike *n* beic
bikini *n* bicini
bilingual *adj* dwyieithog
bilingualism *n* dwyieithedd,
  dwyieithrwydd; dwyieitheg
bill¹ *n* bil; mesur; rhaglen
bill² *n* (beak) pig, gylfin
billiards *n* biliards
billion *n* biliwn
bin *n* cist
bind (*pt, pp* bound) *vt* rhwymo,
  caethiwo
binge *n* (*inf*) gloddest, sbri
bingo *n* bingo
binoculars *n* deulygadur
biochemistry *n* biocemeg
biography *n* bywgraffiad, cofiant
biological *adj* biolegol
biology *n* bywydeg, bioleg
birch *n* bedwen; gwialen fedw
bird *n* aderyn
birdwatching *n* adarydda, gwylio
  adar
Biro® *n* Biro
birth *n* genedigaeth
birth certificate *n* tystysgrif geni
birth control *n* atal cenhedlu
birthday *n* pen-blwydd
birthday card *n* carden pen-
  blwydd
birthmark *n* man geni
bisexual *adj* deurywiol
bishop *n* esgob
bit *n* tamaid; tipyn; genfa
bitch *n* (dog) gast

bite (*pt* **bit**, *pp* **bitten**) *vb* cnoi, brathu ▸ *n* cnoad, brath; tamaid
bitter *adj* chwerw, bustlaidd, tost
bitterness *n* chwerwedd, chwerwder
bizarre *adj* rhyfedd, od, chwithig
black *adj* du; (*ethnicity*): **Black person** person du
blackberry *n* mwyaren, mwyaren ddu
blackbird *n* aderyn du, mwyalchen
blackboard *n* bwrdd du
blackcurrant *n* cyrensen ddu ▸ *adj* cwrens du
black ice *n* iâ du
blackmail *n* arian bygwth, blacmel
black pudding *n* pwdin gwaed
bladder *n* pledren, chwysigen
blade *n* llafn; eginyn, blewyn
blame *vt* beio ▸ *n* bai
bland *adj* mwyn, tyner, tirion
blank *adj* gwag, syn; **blank verse** mesur di-odl
blank cheque *n* siec wag
blanket *n* blanced, gwrthban
blast *n* chwa, chwythiad, deifiad ▸ *vt* deifio; saethu
blatant *adj* digywilydd, haerllug
blaze *n* fflam, ffagl ▸ *vi* fflamio, ffaglu
blazer *n* blaser
bleach *vb* cannu, gwynnu
bleak *adj* oer, digysgod, noeth, noethlwm
bleed (*pt*, *pp* **bled**) *vb* gwaedu
blemish *vt* anafu, anurddo ▸ *n* anaf, bai, mefl
blend *vb* cymysgu ▸ *n* cymysgedd
blender *n* hylifydd

bless (*pt*, *pp* **blessed**, **blest**) *vt* bendithio
blessing *n* bendith
blight *n* malltod ▸ *vt* mallu, deifio
blind *adj* dall, tywyll ▸ *vt* dallu ▸ *n* llen, bleind
blindness *n* dallineb
blink *vb* cau'r llygaid, ysmicio, amrantu
bliss *n* gwynfyd, dedwyddyd
blister *n* chwysigen, pothell ▸ *vb* pothellu
blizzard *n* storm erwin o wynt ac eira
blob *n* ysmotyn, bwrlwm
block *n* plocyn, cyff ▸ *vt* cau, rhwystro
blockade *n* gwarchae ▸ *vb* gwarchae ar
blog *n* blog
blogger *n* blogiwr
blonde *adj* o bryd golau
blood *n* gwaed; gwaedoliaeth
blood pressure *n* pwysedd gwaed
blood test *n* prawf gwaed
bloody *adj* gwaedlyd
bloom *n* blodeuyn; gwawr, gwrid ▸ *vi* blodeuo
blossom *n* blodeuyn ▸ *vi* blodeuo
blot *n* ysmotyn du, blot, mefl ▸ *vb* blotio
blouse *n* blows
blow¹ *n* dyrnod, ergyd
blow² (*pt* **blew**, *pp* **blown**) *vb* chwythu
▸ **blow up** *vi* (*explode*) ffrwydro
▸ *vt* (*inflate*) llenwi
blow-dry *vb* chwythu'n sych
blue *adj*, *n* glas ▸ *vt* glasu
bluff *adj* garw, brochus

257

blunder n amryfusedd ▸ vb amryfuso

blunt adj pŵl, di-fin; plaen ▸ vt pylu

blur n ysmotyn, ystaen

blush vi cochi, gwrido ▸ n gwrid

board n bwrdd, bord; ymborth ▸ vb byrddio

board game n gêm fwrdd

boarding card n cerdyn byrddio

boarding school n ysgol breswyl

boast n ymffrost ▸ vt ymffrostio

boat n bad, cwch

body n corff

bog n cors, mignen

bogus adj ffug, gau, ffuantus

boil¹ n cornwyd, casgliad

boil² vb berwi
  ▸ **boil over** vi berwi drosodd

boiled adj berw; wedi'i ferwi

boiler n pair, crochan

boiling n berwedig

bold adj hy, eofn; eglur

bollard n bolard

bolt n bollt ▸ vb bolltio; dianc; trafluncu

bomb n bom

bomber n (person) bomiwr bomwraig); (plane) bomiwr

bombing n bomio

bomb scare n bygythiad bom

bond n rhwymyn; ysgrifrwym ▸ adj caeth

bone n asgwrn

bonfire n coelcerth, banffagl

bonnet n bonet

bonus n bonws, ychwanegiad

book n llyfr

bookcase n cwpwrdd llyfrau

book cover n clawr llyfr

booklet n llyfryn

bookshelf n silff lyfrau

bookshop n siop lyfrau

boom¹ n (on boat) bŵm

boom² vb trystio, utganu ▸ n trwst, swae

boost vb gwthio, hybu

boot n botasen, esgid

booth n bwth, lluest

booze (inf) vi diota, meddwi ▸ n diod feddwol

border n ffin, goror, ymyl ▸ vb ymylu

bore¹ vb (drill) tyllu, ebillio

bore² n rhywun diflas ▸ vt blino, diflasu

bored adj wedi syrffedu ar beth, wedi alaru

boring adj diflas, annifyr

born adj wedi ei eni

borough n bwrdeistref

borrow vt benthyca

bosom n mynwes, côl

boss n meistr

bossy adj tra-awdurdodus

both adj, pron, adv y ddau, ill dau

bother vb blino, trafferthu ▸ n helynt, trafferth

bottle n potel, costrel ▸ vt potelu, costrelu

bottle bank n banc poteli

bottle opener n agorwr poteli

bottom n gwaelod, godre; pen ôl, tin

boulder n carreg fawr, clogfaen

bounce vb neidio, adlamu

bouncer n (inf) bownsyr

bound¹ vt ffinio

bound² vi llamu, neidio

boundary n ffin, terfyn

b

bouquet n blodeuglwm, pwysi

bout n sbel; ornest, ffrwgwd

bow¹ n bwa; dolen

bow² vb plygu, crymu, ymgrymu ▸ n moesymgrymiad

bow³ n (of ship) pen blaen llong, bow

bowels npl ymysgaroedd, perfedd

bowl n cawg, basn

bowler n het galed; bowliwr

bowling n bowlio

box¹ n bocs, pren bocs

box² n bocs, blwch; sedd, côr

box³ vb taro bonclust; paffio

boxer n paffiwr, bocsiwr

boxer shorts npl trôns bocsiwr

boxing n (Boxing) paffio, bocsio

Boxing Day n Gŵyl San Steffan

box office n swyddfa docynnau

boy n bachgen, hogyn

boycott n boicot ▸ vb boicotio

boyfriend n cariadfab, anwylyd

bra n bra

brace n rhwymyn; pâr ▸ vt tynhau, cryfhau

bracelet n breichled

bracket n braced, cromfach

brag n brol, ymffrost, bocsach ▸ vb brolio, ymffrostio

braid n pleth, brwyd ▸ vt plethu, brwydo

brain n ymennydd

brainy adj peniog

brake n brêc ▸ vt brecio

bran n eisin, bran

branch n cangen, cainc ▸ vi canghennu

brand n pentewyn; nod ▸ vt gwarthnodi

brand-new adj newydd sbon

brandy n brandi

brash adj byrbwyll, ehud

brass n pres, efydd

brat n (infl) cnaf bach, cenau bach

brave adj dewr, gwrol, glew ▸ vt herio

brawl vi ffraeo, terfysgu ▸ n ffrae, ffrwgwd

bray vi brefu (megis asyn), nadu

Brazil n Brasil

breach n adwy, rhwyg, tor; trosedd

bread n bara

breadth n lled

break (pt **broke**, pp **broken**) vb torri ▸ n toriad, tor; **break down** vi (car) torri i lawr; **break in** vi torri i mewn; **break off** vt torri; **break open** vt: **to break sth open** torri rhywbeth i'w agor; **break out** vi torri allan; **break up** vb chwalu

breakfast n brecwast ▸ vb brecwasta

break-in n lladrad

breast n bron, dwyfron, mynwes ▸ vt wynebu, ymladd â

breath n anadl, gwynt

Breathalyser® n Breathalyser

breathe vb anadlu, chwythu; **breathe in** vi mewnanadlu; **breathe out** vi allanadlu

breathing n anadliad

breed (pt, pp **bred**) vb magu; epilio; bridio ▸ n brid

breeze n awel, awelan, chwa

brew vt darllaw, bragu

brewery n bragdy

bribe n llwgrwobrwy ▸ vt llwgrwobrwyo

brick n bricsen, priddfaen ▸ vt bricio

bride n priodferch, priodasferch
bridegroom n priodfab
bridesmaid n morwyn briodas
bridge n pont ▸ vt pontio
bridle n ffrwyn ▸ vt ffrwyno
brief adj byr
briefcase n briffces
briefly adv am ychydig; (in a few words) mewn ychydig eiriau
briefs n briffs
bright adj disglair, claer, gloyw
brilliant adj disglair, llachar ▸ n gem
brim n ymyl, min; cantel
brine n heli
bring (pt, pp **brought**) vt dwyn, dod â; **bring back** vt: to bring sth back dod â rhywbeth yn ôl; **bring forward** vt: to bring sth forward dod â rhywbeth ymlaen; **bring up** vt (child) magu
brink n min, ymyl, glan
brisk adj bywiog, heini, sionc
bristle n gwrychyn, gwrych ▸ vi codi gwrychyn
Britain n Prydain
British adj Prydeinig, Brytanaidd
Briton n Brython, Prydeiniwr
Brittany n Llydaw
brittle adj brau, bregus
broad adj llydan, eang, bras
broadband n band llydan, band eang
broadcast (pt, pp **broadcast**) n darllediad ▸ vb darlledu
broaden vb lledu, ehangu
broccoli n brocoli, math o fresych
brochure n llyfryn
broke adj (inf) heb arian
broken adj toredig, briw, drylliedig

broker n brocer, dyn canol
bronchitis n bronceitis
bronze n pres, efydd
brooch n tlws
brood n nythaid; hil, epil ▸ vi deor; synfyfyrio
broom n banadl; ysgub
broth n potes, cawl
brothel n puteindy
brother n brawd
brother-in-law n brawd yng nghyfraith
brow n talcen; crib
brown adj brown, llwyd, gwinau
brown paper n papur llwyd
brown sugar n siwgr coch
browse vi pori
bruise vb cleisio, ysigo ▸ n clais
brunette n gwineuferch
brush n brws ▸ vt brwsio, ysgubo
Brussels n Brwsel
Brussels sprouts npl ysgewyll Brwsel
brutal adj creulon, bwystfilaidd
bubble n bwrlwm ▸ vb byrlymu
bubble gum n gwm chwythu
buck n bwch; coegyn ▸ vb llamsachu
bucket n bwced, ystwc
buckle n bwcl, gwäeg ▸ vb byclu, gwaegu
bud n blaguryn, eginyn ▸ vb blaguro, egino
Buddhism n Bwdhaeth
Buddhist n Bwdhaidd
budge vb syflyd, chwimio
budget n cyllideb
buff adj llwydfelyn
buffalo n bual

b

buffet n cernod ► vt cernodio, baeddu
buffet car n cerbyd bwffe
bug n drewbryf, bwg
build (pt, pp **built**) vt adeiladu ► n corffolaeth; **build up** vt cynyddu
builder n adeiladwr
building n adeilad
bulb n bwlb
Bulgaria n Bwlgaria
bulge n chwydd ► vt chwyddo
bulk n swm, crynswth
bull n tarw
bulldozer n peiriant clirio ffordd, tarw dur
bullet n bwled, bwleden
bulletin n bwletin
bullfight n ymladdfa deirw
bully n gormeswr, bwli ► vt gormesu, erlid
bum n (inf) tin
bumble-bee n cacynen
bump vb bwmpio, hergydio ► n bwmp, hergwd; **bump into** vt taro ar
bumper adj llawn, helaeth
bumpy adj anwadal, garw
bun n bynsen
bunch n swp; pwysi ► vb sypio
bundle n bwndel, coflaid ► vt bwndelu
bungalow n tŷ unllawr, byngalo
bunion n corn ar fys troed
bunk n bync
bunker n bwncer
buoy n bwi ► vt cynnal, cadw rhag suddo
buoyant adj hynawf; calonnog

burden n baich ► vt beichio, llwytho
bureau n ysgrifgist; swyddfa
bureaucracy n biwrocratiaeth
burger n byrgyr
burglar n bwrgler, lleidr
burglar alarm n larwm lladron
burglary n bwrgleriaeth
burgle vt bwrglera
burial n claddedigaeth
burn (pt, pp **burned**, **burnt**) vb llosgi, ysu ► n llosg, llosgiad; **burn down** vt llosgi i lawr
burrow n twll cwningen ► vb tyllu, tyrchu
burst (pt, pp **burst**) vb byrstio, torri ► n rhwyg
bury vt claddu
bus n bws
bush n perth, llwyn, prysgwydd, drysi
business n busnes
businessman n gŵr busnes
business trip n taith fusnes
businesswoman n gwraig fusnes
bus station n gorsaf fysiau, gorsaf bws
bus stop n arhosfan bysiau, arhosfan bws
bust n penddelw; mynwes
busy adj prysur

(KEYWORD)

but conj ond; I'd love to come, but I'm busy fe hoffwn ddod, ond rwy'n brysur; he's not Welsh but English nid Cymro mohono ond Sais; but that's far too expensive! ond mae hynny'n llawer rhy ddrud!

butcher

▶ prep (apart from, except) ond, ac eithrio, heblaw; **nothing but** dim [byd] ond; **we've had nothing but trouble** dim ond trafferth a gawsom; **no-one but him can do it** dim ond ef a all ei wneud; **who but a lunatic would do such a thing?** pwy ond y gwallgofddyn a wnâi sut beth?; **but for you/your help** heblaw amdant ti/heblaw am dy gymorth di; **anything but that** unrhyw beth ond hynny, unrhyw beth heblaw hynny

▶ adv (just, only) dim ond; **she's but a child** dim ond plentyn yw hi; **had I but known** petawn i ond yn gwybod; **I can but try** ni allaf ond rhoi cynnig arni; **all but finished** bron iawn â gorffen

butcher n cigydd ▶ vt cigyddio, lladd

butcher's (shop) n siop gig

butler n trulliad, bwtler

butt vt cornio, hyrddu, twlcio

butter n ymenyn ▶ vt rhoi ymenyn ar

buttercup n blodyn yr ymenyn

butterfly n glöyn byw, iâr fach yr haf, pili-pala

button n botwm ▶ vt botymu

buy (pt, pp **bought**) vt prynu

buzz vb suo, sisial, mwmian ▶ n su, sŵn gwenyn

by prep **1** (referring to cause, agent) gan; **killed by lightning** wedi'i ladd gan fellt; **surrounded by a fence** wedi'i amgylchynu gan ffens; **a painting by Picasso** darlun gan Picasso

2 (referring to method; manner; means): **by bus/car** mewn bws/car; **by train** mewn trên; **to pay by cheque** talu â siec; **by moonlight/candlelight** yng ngolau'r lleuad/gannwyll; **by saving hard** drwy gynilo'n ddiwyd

3 (via, through) trwy; **we came by Holyhead** daethom trwy Gaergybi

4 (close to, past) yn ymyl, ger, heibio; **the house by the school** y tŷ yn ymyl yr ysgol; **a holiday by the sea** gwyliau ger y môr; **she went by me** aeth heibio yn fy ymyl; **I go by the post office every day** rwy'n mynd heibio swyddfa'r post bob dydd

5 (with time, not later than) erbyn; (during) yn ystod golau dydd **by night** yn ystod y nos, liw nos; **by 4 o'clock** erbyn 4 o'r gloch; **by this time tomorrow** erbyn yr amser hwn yfory; **by the time I got here it was too late** erbyn imi gyrraedd roedd yn rhy hwyr

6 (amount) fesul; **by the kilo/metre** fesul kilo/metr; **paid by the hour** talu fesul awr

7 (Math): (measure): **to divide/multiply by 3** rhannu/lluosi â 3; **a room 3 metres by 4** ystafell 3 metr wrth 4; **it's broader by a metre** mae fetr yn lletach

8 (according to) yn ôl, gan; **it's 3 o'clock by my watch** mae'n 3 o'r gloch yn ôl fy oriawr i; **it's all right by me** mae'n iawn gennyf i

9: **(all) by oneself** ar fy mhen fy hun
▶ *adv* **1** *see* **go, pass**
2: **by and by** maes o law, ymhen amser; **by and large** ar y cyfan, at ei gilydd

bye *excl* hwyl!
by-election *n* isetholiad
bypass *n* ffordd osgoi
bystander *n* un yn sefyll gerllaw

cab *n* cab
cabaret *n* cabare
cabbage *n* bresychen
cabin *n* caban ▶ *vt* cabanu, caethiwo
cabinet *n* cabinet
cable *n* cebl
cable car *n* car codi
cable television *n* teledu cebl
cactus *n* cactws
café *n* tŷ bwyta, caffe
cage *n* cawell, caets ▶ *vt* cau, carcharu
cake *n* teisen, cacen ▶ *vb* torthi; caglu
calculate *vb* cyfrif, bwrw cyfrif
calculation *n* cyfrif
calculator *n* cyfrifiannell
calendar *n* calendr, almanac
calf[1] *n* llo
calf[2] *n* (of the leg) croth (coes)
calibre *n* calibr
call *vb* galw ▶ *n* galwad; ymweliad; **call back** *vb* (telephone)

galw yn ôl; **call for** vt galw am;
call off vt canslo
call box n blwch ffôn
call centre n canolfan galwadau
callous adj croendew, dideimlad,
caled
calm adj tawel ► vb tawelwch ► vb
tawelu; **calm down** vb tawelu
calorie n calori, uned gwres
Cambodia n Cambodia
Cambrian adj Cymreig
camel n camel
camera n ystafell; camera
camera phone n ffôn camera
camouflage n camliw, dull o
ddieithrio ► vb dieithrio, cuddio
camp n gwersyll ► vi gwersyllu
campaign n ymgyrch, rhyfelgyrch
camp bed n gwely plyg
camper n (person) gwersyllwr
gwersyllwraig); (van) cerbyd
gwersylla
camping n gwersylla; **to go
camping** gwersyllu
campsite n maes gwersylla
campus n campws
can[1] n tyn, piser, stên

(KEYWORD)

can[2] (negative **cannot, can't,**
conditional, pt **could**) aux vb **1** (be
able to) gallu, medru; **you can
do it if you try** gallwch ei wneud
os rhowch gynnig arno; **I can't
hear you** ni allaf eich clywed,
rwy'n methu'ch clywed; **can you
speak Welsh?** allwch chi siarad
Cymraeg?, ydych chi'n medru
Cymraeg?
2 (may) cael; **can I use your phone?**

a ga i ddefnyddio'ch ffôn?
3 (expressing disbelief, puzzlement
etc): **it can't be true!** does bosibl!;
what can he want? beth all fod
arno ei eisiau?
4 (expressing possibility, suggestion
etc): **he could be in the library** fe
allai fod yn y llyfrgell; **she could
have been delayed** fe allai fod
wedi'i dal yn ôl

Canada n Canada
Canadian adj Canadaidd ► n
Canadiad
canal n camlas; pibell
Canaries n: **the Canaries** yr
Ynysoedd Dedwydd
canary n caneri
cancel vt dileu, dirymu, diddymu
cancer n cancr; **Cancer** y Cranc
candidate n ymgeisydd
candle n cannwyll
candlestick n canhwyllbren
candy n candi
cane n corsen, cansen ► vt curo
â chansen
canister n tun cadw te, bocs (te)
cannabis n canabis
canned adj ar gadw mewn can, tun
cannon n magnel
canoe n ceufad, canŵ
canoeing n canŵa
canon n canon, rheol
can-opener n agorwr tuniau
canteen n cantîn
canter vi rhygyngu ► n rhygyng
canvas n cynfas, lliain bras
canvass vb trafod; canfasio
canyon n ceunant, canion
cap n cap, capan ► vt capio

capable *adj* galluog, cymwys

capacity *n* gallu, cymhwyster; cynnwys

cape¹ *n (headland)* penrhyn, pentir, trwyn

cape² *n (cloak)* mantell, cêp

caper *n* pranc ▸ *vi* prancio

capital *adj* prif, pen ▸ *n* priflythyren; prifddinas; cyfalaf

capitalism *n* cyfalafiaeth

capital punishment *n* y gosb eithaf

Capricorn *n* yr Afr

capsize *vb* dymchwelyd, troi

capsule *n* capswl

captain *n* capten

caption *n* pennawd, teitl

captivity *n* caethiwed

capture *n* daliad ▸ *vt* dal

car *n* car, cerbyd; **car wash** golchfa geir

caramel *n* caramel

caravan *n* carafán

caravan site *n* maes carafannau

carbohydrate *n* carbohydrad

carbohydrates *npl* carbohydradau

carbon *n* carbon

carbon footprint *n* ôl troed carbon

car boot sale *n* sêl cist car

carburettor *n* carburadur

carcass *n* celain, ysgerbwd

card¹ *n* cerdyn, carden

card² *vt* cribo gwlân

cardboard *n* cardbord

Cardiff *n* Caerdydd

cardigan *n* cardigan

cardinal *adj* prif, arbennig ▸ *n* cardinal

care *n* gofal, pryder ▸ *vi* gofalu, malio

career *n* gyrfa, hynt ▸ *vi* carlamu

careful *adj* gofalus, gwyliadwrus

carefully *adv* yn ofalus

careless *adj* diofal, esgeulus

caretaker *n* gofalwr

car-ferry *n* fferi geir

cargo *n* llwyth (llong), cargo

car hire (company) *n* cwmni llogi ceir

Caribbean *adj*: **the Caribbean (Sea)** y Caribî

caring *adj* gofalus

carnation *n* blodyn cigliw

carnival *n* carnifal

carol *n* carol ▸ *vi* caroli, canu

car park *n* maes parcio

carpenter *n* saer coed

carpentry *n* saerniaeth

carpet *n* carped ▸ *vt* carpedu

carriage *n* cerbyd; cludiad

carrier *n* cariwr, cludydd

carrier bag *n* cludfag

carrot *n* moronen

carry *vb* cario, cludo; **carry on** *vi* mynd ymlaen, dal ati; **carry out** *vt* gweithredu

carrycot *n* cot cario

cart *n* trol, cert, cart

carton *n* carton

cartoon *n* digriflun, cartŵn

cartridge *n* cetrisen

carve *vt* cerfio, naddu; torri cig

case¹ *n* achos; cyflwr; dadl

case² *n (holder)* cas, gwain

cash *n* arian parod

cash desk *n* safle talu

cashier *n* ariannwr, trysorydd

cashmere *n* cashmir

cash point *n* peiriant arian

casino *n* casino

casket

casket *n* cistan, blwch
casserole *n* llestr coginio a dal bwyd
cassette *n* casét
cast *vb* bwrw, taflu ▸ *n* tafliad; **cast iron** haearn bwrw
castle *n* castell ▸ *vi* castellu
casual *adj* damweiniol, achlysurol
casualty *n* un wedi ei anafu
cat *n* cath
catalogue *n* catalog
cataract *n* rhaeadr; pilen
catarrh *n* llif annwyd, gormwyth
catastrophe *n* trychineb
catch (*pt, pp* **caught**) *vt* dal ▸ *n* bach, cliced; dalfa; **catch up** *vi*: **to catch up with sb** dal rhywun
catching *adj* heintus
category *n* trefn, dosbarth
cater *vi* arlwyo, darparu
caterpillar *n* lindysyn
cathedral *n* eglwys gadeiriol
catholic *adj* catholig ▸ *n* catholigydd
cattle *npl* gwartheg, da
cauliflower *n* blodfresychen
cause *n* achos ▸ *vt* achosi, peri
caution *n* pwyll; rhybudd ▸ *vt* rhybuddio
cautious *adj* gwyliadwrus
cave *n* ogof
caviar, caviare *n* grawn pysgod, cafiâr
cavity *n* ceudod, gwagle
CCTV *n abbr* teledu cylch cyfyng
CD *n abbr* CD, crynoddisg
CD player *n* chwaraewr cryno-ddisgiau
CD-ROM *n* CD-ROM
cease *vb* peidio, darfod

cedar *n* cedrwydden
ceiling *n* nen, nenfwd
celebrate *vt* dathlu; gweinyddu
celebrity *n* bri, enwogrwydd; person o fri
celery *n* seleri
cell *n* cell
cellar *n* seler
cello *n* sielo
cement *n* sment ▸ *vt* smentio; cadarnhau
cemetery *n* mynwent, claddfa
censor *n* sensor
census *n* cyfrifiad
cent *n* sent
centenary *n* canmlwyddiant
centigrade *adj* canradd, sentigred
centimetre *n* sentimedr
central *adj* canol, canolog
central heating *n* gwres canolog
centre *n* canol, canolfan ▸ *vb* canolbwyntio
centre forward *n* canolwr blaen
century *n* canrif
ceramic *adj* perthynol i grefft y crochenydd, ceramig
cereal *n* grawn, ŷd
ceremony *n* seremoni, defod
certain *adj* sicr; neilltuol; rhyw, rhai
certainly *adv* yn sicr, yn siwr
certainty *n* sicrwydd
certificate *n* tystysgrif
certify *vt* hysbysu, tystio
chain *n* cadwyn ▸ *vt* cadwyno
chair *n* cadair ▸ *vt* cadeirio
chairlift *n* cadair godi
chairman *n* cadeirydd
chalet *n* bwthyn (haf)
chalk *n* sialc ▸ *vt* sialcio

challenge n her, sialens ▸ vt herio, sialensio

chamber n ystafell, siambr

champagne n gwin Champagne

champion n pencampwr; pleidiwr ▸ vt cymryd plaid

championship n pencampwriaeth

chance n damwain, siawns ▸ vt digwydd

chancellor n canghellor

chandelier n canhwyllyr

change vb newid, cyfnewid ▸ n newid

changing-room n ystafell newid

channel n sianel, gwely; rhigol

Channel Tunnel n: the Channel Tunnel Twnel y Sianel

chant vt corganu ▸ n corgan, salmdon

chaos n tryblith, anhrefn

chap vt agennu, torri (am ddwylo)

chapel n capel

chapter n pennod; cabidwl

character n cymeriad; nod, arwydd

characteristic adj nodweddiadol ▸ n nodwedd

charcoal n marwor, golosg, sercol

charge vb cyhuddo; rhuthro; codi; llwytho ▸ n cyhuddiad; rhuthr; pris; ergyd

charger n (old) march rhyfel, cadfarch

charity n cariad; elusen

charity shop n siop elusennol

charm n swyn, cyfaredd ▸ vt swyno

charming adj cyfareddol, swynol, cwrtais

chart n siart

charter n siarter, breinlen ▸ vt breinio; llogi

charter flight n hediad siartr

chase vt ymlid, erlid, hel ▸ n helwriaeth

chat vi sgwrsio, ymgomio ▸ n sgwrs, ymgom

chat room n (Internet) stafell sgwrsio

chat show n sioe sgwrsio

chatter vi trydar; clebran; rhincian

chauffeur n gyrrwr

chauvinist n siofinydd

cheap adj rhad, isel

cheat n twyll; twyllwr ▸ vt twyllo

Chechnya n Chechnya

check n rhwystr, atalfa ▸ vt atal, ffrwyno; **check in** vi cofrestru

checkout n (in supermarket) desg dalu

checkup n (Med) archwiliad

cheek n grudd, boch; digywilydd-dra

cheeky adj digywilydd, haerllug, eg(e)r

cheer n calondid; arlwy ▸ vb llonni, sirioli

cheerful adj llon, siriol

cheese n caws

chef n prif gogydd

chemical adj cemegol ▸ n cyffur

chemist n fferyllydd; cemegydd

chemistry n cemeg

cheque n archeb (ar fanc), siec

cheque book n llyfr siec

cheque card n carden siec

cherry n ceiriosen

chess n gwyddbwyll

chessboard n bwrdd gwyddbwyll

chest n cist, coffr; brest

chestnut

chestnut n castan
chew vb cnoi; to chew the cud cnoi cil
chewing gum n gwm cnoi
chick n cyw
chicken n cyw iâr
chickenpox n brech yr ieir
chickpea n gwygbysen, ffacbysen
chickpeas n gwygbys
chief adj pen, pennaf, prif ▸ n pennaeth
child n plentyn
childhood n plentyndod, mebyd
childish n plentynnaidd
child minder n gwarchodwr
Chile n Chile
chill n oerni; annwyd ▸ adj oer; anwydog ▸ vb oeri, fferru, rhynnu
chilli n tsili
chilly adj (weather) oer; (manner) oeraidd
chimney n corn mwg, simnai
chin n gên
China n China, Tseina
china n llestri te (tsieni)
Chinese adj Tsieineaidd ▸ n Tsieinead
chip vb hacio, naddu ▸ n asglodyn, pric
chips npl sglodion
chiropodist n troedfeddyg
chisel n cŷn, gaing
chives n cennin sifi
chocolate n siocled
choice n dewis, dewisiad ▸ adj dewisol, dethol
choir n côr
choke vb tagu; mygu; cau
choose (pt chose, pp chosen) vb dewis, dethol, ethol

chop vt torri ▸ n golwyth
chopsticks n gweill bwyta
chord n tant; cord
chore n y dwt
chorus n côr, cytgan, corws
Christ n Crist
christen vt bedyddio, enwi
christening n bedydd
Christian adj Cristnogol ▸ n Cristion
Christianity n Cristnogaeth
Christian name n enw bedydd
Christmas n Nadolig
Christmas Eve n Noswyl Nadolig
chrome n crôm
chronic adj parhaol (am anhwyldeb)
chrysanthemum n ffarwel haf
chubby adj wynepgrwn, tew
chuck vt (inf) taflu, lluchio
chuckle vi chwerthin yn nwrn dyn
chum n cyfaill mebyd ▸ vi cyfrinachu
chunk n tafell dew, toc
church n eglwys, llan ▸ vt eglwysa
churchyard n mynwent
churn n buddai ▸ vb corddi
chutney n picl cymysg
cider n seidr
cigar n sigâr
cigarette n sigarét
cigarette lighter n taniwr sigaréts
cinema n sinema
cinnamon n sinamon
circle n cylch ▸ vb cylchu
circuit n cylch; cylchdaith
circular adj crwn ▸ n cylchlythyr
circulate vb cylchredeg, lledaenu
circumstances npl amgylchiadau
circus n syrcas

cite vt gwysio; dyfynnu

citizen n dinesydd

citizenship n dinasyddiaeth

city n dinas

city centre n canol y ddinas

city technology college n coleg technoleg dinasol

civic adj dinesig

civil adj dinesig, gwladol; moesgar

civilian n dinesydd (anfilwrol)

civilization n gwareiddiad

civil servant n gwas sifil

civil service n gwasanaeth sifil, gwasanaeth gwladol

civil war n rhyfel cartref

claim vt hawlio ▸ n hawl

clamp n ystyffwl, craff

clan n tylwyth, llwyth

clap n twrf, trwst ▸ vb curo; taro

claret n claret

clarify vt gloywi, puro; egluro

clarinet n clarinet

clash vb taro, gwrthdaro ▸ n gwrthdrawiad

clasp n bach, clesbyn ▸ vt cofleidio

class n dosbarth ▸ vt dosbarthu

classic n clasur, campwaith ▸ adj clasurol

classical adj clasurol

classify vb dosbarthu

classmate n cyd-ddisgybl

classroom n ystafell ddosbarth

classroom assistant n cynorthwyydd dosbarth

clatter vb clewtian, clepian, trystio ▸ n trwst

clause n adran, cymal

claw n crafanc, ewin ▸ vt crafangu, cripio

clay n clai

clean adj glân, glanwaith ▸ vt glanhau

cleaner n glanhâwr, glanhëydd

cleaner's n siop glanhau dillad

cleaning n glanhad, glanheuad

cleanser n glanhawr

cleansing lotion n hufen glanhau

clear adj clir, eglur, gloyw; croyw ▸ vt clirio; **clear off** vi (inf) **clear off!** hel dy bac!; **clear up** vi (weather) codi'n braf

clearly adv yn glir

clench vt cau yn dynn, clensio

clergy n offeiriaid

clerk n clerc

clever adj medrus, clyfar

cleverness n medr, clyfrwch

click n clician, clepian ▸ n clic

client n cyflogydd cyfreithiwr, cwsmer

cliff n clogwyn, allt

climate n hinsawdd

climate change n newid hinsawdd

climax n uchafbwynt

climb vb dringo

climber n dringwr

climbing adj dringol

clinch vt clensio; cau, cloi

cling (pt, pp **clung**) vi glynu, cydio

clingfilm n clingffilm

clinic n meddygfa, clinig

clip vt tocio, clipio

cloak n mantell, clogyn ▸ vt cuddio, celu

cloakroom n ystafell ddillad

clock n cloc

clog n closen ▸ vt llesteirio; tagu; clocsio

close¹ vb cau; terfynu ▸ n diwedd, diweddglo

close

close² *adj* agos, clòs; tyn
close³ *n (courtyard)* clas, clos, buarth
closed *adj* ar gau
closely *adv* yn agos
closet *n* cell, ystafell; geudy
close-up *n* llun agos
closure *n* cau, gorffen, darfod
clot *n* tolchen ▸ *vb* tolchi, ceulo
cloth *n* brethyn, lliain
clothes *npl* dillad, gwisgoedd
clothes peg *n* bachyn dillad
clothing *n* dillad
cloud *n* cwmwl ▸ *vt* cymylu
cloudy *adj* cymylog
clown *n* lleban; clown
club *n* pastwn; clwb ▸ *vb* pastynu; clybio; **club together** *vi* casglu arian
clubbing *n* clybio
clue *n* pen llinyn, arwydd
clump *n* clwmp, clamp, cyff
clumsy *adj* trwsgl, lletchwith
cluster *n* clwstwr, swp ▸ *vb* casglu, tyrru
clutch *n* crafanc; gafael; hafflau ▸ *vb* crafangu
coach *n* coets, bws; hyfforddwr ▸ *vb* hyfforddi
coal *n* glöyn, glo
coalition *n* cyfuniad; cynghrair, clymblaid
coarse *adj* garw, bras; aflednais
coast *n* arfordir, glan ▸ *vi* hwylio gyda'r lan
coastal *adj* arfordirol
coastguard *n* gwyliwr y glannau
coastline *n* morlin
coat *n* cot
coat hanger *n* cambren (dillad)

coating *n* caen, golchiad
coax *vb* hudo, denu, perswadio
cobweb *n* gwe pryf cop, gwe'r cor
cock *n* ceiliog; mwdwl; cliced (dryll) ▸ *vb* mydylu; codi cliced
cockerel *n* cyw ceiliog, ceiliogyn
cockpit *n* sedd peilot; ymladdfan ceiliogod
cockroach *n* chwilen ddu
cocktail *n* coctêl
cocoa *n* coco
coconut *n* cneuen goco, coconyt
cod *n* penfras; còd
code *n* cod
coffee *n* coffi
coffee table *n* bwrdd coffi
coffin *n* arch, ysgrîn
cog *n* dant olwyn, còg
coil *vb* torchi ▸ *n* torch
coin *n* arian bath ▸ *vb* bathu
coincide *vi* cyd-ddigwydd, cyd-daro
coincidence *n* cyd-ddigwyddiad
coke *n* golosg
colander *n* hidl
cold *adj* oer ▸ *n* oerfel, oerni; annwyd; **to catch a cold** dal annwyd
coleslaw *n* colsio
colic *n* bolwst, colig
collapse *vb* disgyn, cwympo ▸ *n* cwymp, methiant
collar *n* coler ▸ *vb* coleru
collarbone *n* pont yr ysgwydd
colleague *n* cydweithiwr
collect *n* colect ▸ *vb* crynhoi, hel, casglu; ymgynnull
collection *n* casgliad
collector *n* casglwr
college *n* coleg

:ollide vb gwrthdaro

:ollision n gwrthdrawiad

:olon n colon (:); coluddyn mawr

:olonel n cyrnol

:olonial adj trefedigaethol

:olony n trefedigaeth, gwladfa

:olour n lliw, baner ▸ vb lliwio; cochi; **colour blind** lliwddall

:olourful adj lliwgar

:olouring n lliwiad

:olumn n colofn

:oma n hunglwyf, côma

:omb n crib ▸ vb cribo

:ombat n brwydr, gornest ▸ vb brwydro

:ombination n cyfuniad

:ombine vb cyfuno; **combine harvester** cynaeafydd, combein

KEYWORD

come (pt **came**, pp **come**) vi **1** (movement towards) dod; **to come running** dod dan redeg; **he's come here to work** mae wedi dod yma i weithio; **come with me** dewch gyda mi

2 (arrive) cyrraedd; **to come home** dod adref; **we've just come from Cardiff** rydym newydd gyrraedd o Gaerdydd

3 (reach): **to come to** (decision etc) dod i; **the bill came to £40** £40 oedd y bil

4 (occur): **an idea came to me** daeth syniad imi, cododd syniad yn fy mhen

5 (be, become): **to come loose/ undone** dod yn rhydd, mynd yn rhydd; **I've come to like him** rwyf

wedi dod i'w hoffi

▸ **come across** vt fus dod ar draws

▸ **come along** vi (pupil, work) dod ymlaen

▸ **come back** vi dod yn ôl, dychwelyd

▸ **come down** vi dod i lawr; (prices) disgyn, syrthio; (buildings) disgyn, syrthio; (be demolished) cael ei ddymchwel

▸ **come from** vt fus (source) dod o, tarddu o; (place) dod o, hanu o

▸ **come in** vi dod i mewn; (fashion) dod i mewn i ffasiwn; (on deal etc) ymuno â, cymryd rhan mewn

▸ **come off** vi (button) dod yn rhydd, datod; (attempt) llwyddo

▸ **come on** vi (lights, electricity) dod ymlaen; (pupil, work, project) dod ymlaen, gwneud cynnydd; **come on!** (singular) dere!, tyrd! (plural) dewch!

▸ **come out** vi dod allan

▸ **come round** vi (after faint, operation) dod at ei hun, dadebru

▸ **come to** vi dadebru

▸ **come up** vi codi; (sun) codi; (problem) codi; (event) codi; (in conversation) codi

▸ **come up with** vt fus (money) darparu; **he came up with an idea** cafodd syniad, cynigiodd syniad

comedian n comedïwr

comedy n comedi

comfort n cysur, diddanwch ▸ vt cysuro, diddanu

comfortable *adj* cysurus, cyffyrddus

comic *adj* comic, digrif, ysmala

comma *n* atalnod, coma

command *vb* gorchymyn ► *n* gorchymyn, awdurdod

commander *n* cadlywydd, comander

commemorate *vt* coffáu, dathlu

commence *vb* dechrau

commend *vt* cymeradwyo, canmol

comment *vi* sylwi, esbonio ► *n* sylw

commentary *n* sylwebaeth

commentator *n* esboniwr, sylwebydd

commerce *n* masnach

commercial *adj* masnachol

commission *n* comisiwn, dirprwyaeth ► *vb* comisiynu

commissioner *n* comisiynydd

commit *vt* cyflawni; traddodi; cyflwyno

commitment *n* ymrwymiad; traddodiad

committee *n* pwyllgor

commodity *n* nwydd (masnachol)

common *adj* cyffredin ► *n* tir cyffredin, comin

commonplace *adj* dibwys, cyffredin

commons *npl* y cyffredin; **House of Commons** Tŷ'r Cyffredin

common sense *n* synnwyr cyffredin

commonwealth *n* cymanwlad

communal *adj* cymunol, cymunedol

commune *vi* ymddiddan; cymuno ► *n* cymundod

communicate *vb* cyfathrebu; cymuno

communication *n* cyfathrebiad, cysylltiad, neges

communion *n* cymun, cymundeb

communism *n* comiwnyddiaeth

communist *n* comiwnydd

community *n* cymdeithas, cymuned; **community centre** canolfan gymuned

commute *vb* cymudo, pendilio

commuter *n* cymudwr, pendiliwr

compact *n* cytundeb, cyfamod; compact ► *adj* cryno ► *vt* crynhoi

compact disc *n* cryno-ddisg, CD

companion *n* cydymaith

company *n* cymdeithas, cwmni; **to keep company with** cadw cwmni â

comparative *adj* cymharol

comparatively *adv* yn gymharol

compare *vt* cymharu, cyffelybu

comparison *n* cymhariaeth

compartment *n* adran, cerbydran

compass *n* cwmpawd; cwmpas ► *vt* amgylchu

compassion *n* tosturi

compatible *adj* cydweddol, cyson

compel *vt* cymell, gorfodi

compensate *vt* talu iawn, digolledu

compensation *n* iawndal

compete *vi* cystadlu

competent *adj* cymwys, digonol

competition *n* cystadleuaeth

competitive *adj* cystadleuol

competitor *n* cystadleuydd

complacent *adj* hunan-foddhaus, digonol

complain vi cwyno, achwyn, grwgnach

complaint n cwyn, achwyniad; anhwyldeb

complement n cyflawnder, cyflenwad

complementary adj cyflenwol

complete adj cyflawn ▸ vt cyflawni

completely adv yn llwyr

completion n cwblhad

complex adj cymhleth, dyrys

complexion n gwedd, pryd, gwawr

compliance n cydsyniad

complicate vt cymhlethu; drysu

complicated adj cymhleth, dyrys

complication n cymhlethdod

compliment n cyfarchiad; canmoliaeth

comply vi cydsynio, ufuddhau

component n cydran, cyfansoddyn

compose vt cyfansoddi; cysodi; tawelu

composer n cyfansoddwr

composition n cyfansoddiad, traethawd

composure n tawelwch, hunanfeddiant

compound adj cyfansawdd ▸ n cymysg ▸ vb cymysgu

comprehension n amgyffred, dirnadaeth

comprehensive adj cynhwysfawr

comprehensive school n ysgol gyfun

compress vt gwasgu, crynhoi ▸ n plastr

comprise vt amgyffred, cynnwys

compromise n cymrodedd, cyfaddawd ▸ vb cymrodeddu, cyfaddawdu

compulsive adj trwy orfod, o anfodd

compulsory adj gorfodol

computer n cyfrifiadur

computer game n gêm gyfrifiadur

computer programmer n rhaglennydd cyfrifiaduron

computer science n cyfrifiadureg

computer studies npl astudiaethau cyfrifiadurol

computing n cyfrifiaduro

conceal vb cuddio, celu, dirgelu

concede vt caniatáu, addef

conceited adj hunandybus, hunanol, balch

conceive vb dirnad; tybied; beichiogi

concentrate vt crynodi, canolbwyntio

concentration n crynodiad, ymroddiad

concept n cysyniad

concern vt ymwneud (â), pryderu, bod a wnelo â ▸ n busnes, diddordeb; gofal, pryder

concerned adj pryderus, gofalus

concerning prep ynglŷn â, ynghylch

concert n cyngerdd ▸ vt cyd-drefnu

conclude vb diweddu; casglu, barnu

conclusion n diwedd; casgliad

concrete adj diriaethol ▸ n concrit

concussion n cyd-drawiad, ysgytiad

condemn vb condemnio, collfarnu

273

condensation

condensation n cywasgiad, cyddwysedd

condense vb cywasgu, cyddwyso, cwtogi

condition n cyflwr, ansawdd; amod ▸ vb cyflyru; amodi

conditional adj amodol

conditioner n cyflyrydd

condom n condom

condominium n cydlywodraeth, condominiwm

condone vt maddau, esgusodi

conduct¹ n ymddygiad, ymarweddiad

conduct² vt arwain

conductor n arweinydd; tocynnwr

cone n pigwrn, côn

confer vb ymgynghori, cyflwyno

conference n cynhadledd

confess vb cyffesu, cyfaddef

confession n cyffesiad, cyffes

confide vb ymddiried

confidence n ymddiried, hyder; self-confidence hunanhyder

confident adj hyderus

confidential adj cyfrinachol

confine vt cyfyngu, carcharu, caethiwo

confined adj caeth, cyfyng

confirm vt cadarnhau; cyffrmio

confirmation n cadarnhad; bedydd esgob, conffirmasiwn

confiscate vt atafaelu

conflict¹ n gwrthdrawiad, ymryson

conflict² vi anghytuno, gwrthdaro

conform vb cydymffurfio

confront vt wynebu

confrontation n gwrthdaro

confuse vt cymysgu, drysu

confused adj cymysg; didrefn; dyrys

confusing adj dryslyd

confusion n anhrefn

congestion n gorlenwad, tagfa, crynhoad

congratulate vt llongyfarch

congratulations n llongyfarchiadau

congregation n cynulleidfa

congress n cyngres, cymanfa

conjunction n cysylltiad

conjure vb consurio

connect vb cysylltu, cydio

connection n cysylltiad, perthynas; **in connection with** ynglŷn â

conquer vt gorchfygu, trechu

conquest n buddugoliaeth, concwest

conscience n cydwybod

conscientious adj cydwybodol

conscious adj ymwybodol

consciousness n ymwybyddiaeth

consecutive adj olynol

consent vi cydsynio ▸ n cydsyniad, caniatâd

consequence n canlyniad

consequently adv o ganlyniad

conservation n cadwraeth, gwarchodaeth

conservative adj ceidwadol ▸ n ceidwadwr

conservatory n tŷ gwydr

consider vb ystyried

considerable adj cryn

considerate adj ystyriol, tosturiol

consideration n ystyriaeth

considering prep ac ystyried

consist vt cynnwys

consistency n cysondeb
consistent n cyson
consolation n cysur, diddanwch
console vt cysuro, diddanu
consonant adj cysain; cyson ▸ n cytsain
conspicuous adj amlwg
conspiracy n cynllwyn
constable n cwnstabl, heddgeidwad
constant adj cyson
constantly adv yn gyson
constipated adj rhwym
constipation n rhwymedd
constituency n etholaeth
constitution n cyfansoddiad
constraint n cyfyngydd, cyfyngiad
construct vt llunio, adeiladu, saernio
construction n adeiladwaith, lluniad; cystrawen
constructive adj ymarferol, adeiladol
consul n ynad, conswl
consulate n consuliaeth
consult vb ymgynghori
consultant n ymgynghorwr
consume vb treulio, difa, ysu; nychu
consumer n prynwr, treuliwr, defnyddiwr
consumption n traul; darfodedigaeth
contact n cyffyrddiad, cyswllt
contact lenses npl lensys cyffwrdd
contagious adj heintus
contain vt cynnwys, dal
container n cynhwysydd
contaminate vt halogi, llygru

contemplate vb ystyried, myfyrio; bwriadu
contemporary adj cyfoes(ol) ▸ n cyfoeswr
contempt n dirmyg, diystyrwch; contempt of court dirmyg llys
contend vb ymryson, cystadlu
content¹ adj bodlon ▸ vt bodloni
content² n cynnwys
contented adj bodlon
contest¹ n cystadleuaeth, ymryson
contest² vb amau, ymryson, ymladd
contestant n cystadleuydd
context n cyd-destun
continent n cyfandir
continental adj cyfandirol
continental breakfast n brecwast cyfandirol
continual adj parhaus, gwastadol
continue vb parhau, para, dal (i)
continuous adj parhaol, di-fwlch, di-dor
continuous assessment n asesiad parhaus, asesu parhaus
contour n amlinell, cyfuchlinedd
contraceptive n cyfarpar gwrth-genhedlu
contract¹ n cytundeb, cyfamod, contract
contract² vb byrhau; cytuno, cyfamodi
contractor n contractwr, adeiladydd
contradict vt gwrth-ddweud
contrary adj gwrthwyneb, croes; on the contrary i'r gwrthwyneb
contrast n gwrthgyferbyniad ▸ vb gwrthgyferbynnu
contribute vb cyfrannu

contribution

contribution n cyfraniad
contributor n cyfrannwr
control vt llywodraethu, rheoli ▸ n rheolaeth, awdurdod; **self control** hunanreolaeth
controversial adj dadleuol
controversy n dadl
convenience n cyfleustra, hwylustod
convenient adj cyfleus, hwylus
convent n cwfaint, lleiandy
convention n confensiwn, cynhadledd
conventional adj confensiynol
conversation n ymddiddan, sgwrs
conversion n tröedigaeth, tro
convert vt troi, newid, trosi; **converted try** trosgais
convertible adj trosadwy
convey vt cludo; trosglwyddo; cyfleu
conveyor belt n cludfelt
convict[1] vt barnu'n euog, euogfarnu; argyhoeddi
convict[2] n troseddwr
conviction n euogfarn; argyhoeddiad
convince vt argyhoeddi
convincing adj argyhoeddiadol
cook n cogydd, cogyddes ▸ vb coginio, gwneud bwyd
cooker n cwcer; **pressure cooker** gwascogydd, sosban wyllt
cookery n coginiaeth
cookie n (biscuit) bisgeden; (Comput) cwci
cooking n coginiaeth

cool adj oer, oeraidd; hunanfeddiannol ▸ vb oeri, claearu
cooperate vi cydweithio, cydweithredu
cooperation n cydweithrediad
cop (inf) n plismon ▸ vt dal
cope vi ymdaro â, ymdopi â
copper n copr, copor
copy n copi ▸ vt copïo
copyright n hawlfraint
coral n cwrel
cord n cortyn, rheffyn ▸ vt rheffynnu
corduroy n melfaréd, rib
core n calon, perfedd, craidd
cork n corc, corcyn ▸ vt corcio
corkscrew n corcsgriw
corn[1] n ŷd, llafur
corn[2] n (on foot) corn (ar droed)
corned beef n corn-biff
corner n congl, cornel, cil ▸ vt cornelu; **corner kick** cic gornel
cornflakes npl creision ŷd
cornflour n blawd corn
Cornwall n Cernyw
coronation n coroniad
coroner n crwner
corporal adj corfforol
corporate adj yn un corff, corfforedig
corporation n corfforaeth
corps n corfflu
corpse n corff (marw), celain
correct adj cywir ▸ vt cywiro; ceryddu
correction n cywiriad; cerydd
correctly adv yn gywir
correspond vi cyfateb; gohebu

correspondence n cyfatebiaeth; gohebiaeth
correspondent n gohebydd
corridor n coridor
corrode vb cyrydu, ysu, rhydu, treulio
corrupt adj llygredig, pwdr ▸ vb llygru
corruption n llygredigaeth
cosmetic n cosmetig
cosmetics npl cosmetigau
cosmetic surgery n llawfeddygaeth gosmetig
cost (pt, pp **cost**) vi costio ▸ n cost, traul
costly adj drudfawr, drud
costume n gwisg, costiwm
cosy adj cysurus, clyd
cot n gwely bychan, cot
cottage n bwthyn
cotton n cotwm; edau; **cotton wool** gwlân cotwm
couch n glwth, soffa ▸ vb gorwedd
cough n peswch ▸ vb pesychu
council n cyngor; **council house** tŷ cyngor
councillor n cynghorwr
counsel n cyngor ▸ vt cynghori
counsellor n cynghorwr, cyfarwyddwr
count¹ n cyfrif ▸ vb rhifo, cyfrif; **count the cost** bwrw'r draul ▸ **count on** vt dibynnu ar
count² n (title) iarll
counter n cownter
counter- adj croes ▸ adv yn erbyn, yn groes
counterfeit n ffug, twyll ▸ adj gau, ffug ▸ vt ffugio

counterpart n rhan gyfatebol, cymar
countess n iarlles
countless adj aneirif, di-rif
country n gwlad, bro ▸ adj gwladaidd, gwledig; **country music** canu gwlad
countryside n cefn gwlad
county n sir, swydd
coup n ergyd, trawiad; llwyddiant
couple n cwpl ▸ vt cyplu, cyplysu
coupon n cwpon
courage n gwroldeb, dewrder
courgette n corbwmpen
courier n cennad; tywyswr
course n cwrs, hynt ▸ vt hela, ymlid; **of course** wrth gwrs; **in the course of** yn ystod; **in due course** yn ei bryd; **crash course** cwrs carlam
court n llys; cwrt; cyntedd ▸ vt caru
courtesy n cwrteisrwydd, cwrteisi
courtyard n cwrt, clos, iard
cousin n cefnder; cyfnither
cover vt gorchuddio, toi; amddiffyn ▸ n gorchudd, clawr; **to take cover** cuddio, cysgodi
cover charge n tâl am wasanaeth
covert adj cêl, cudd, dirgel
cow n buwch; **barren cow** myswynog; **milking cow** buwch odro; **cow in calf** buwch gyflo
coward n llwfrgi
cowardly adj llwfr
cowboy n cowboi
crab n cranc

crack

crack *vb* cracio, hollti ▸ *n* crac; **crack down on** *vi* syrthio'n drwm ar

cracked *adj* wedi cracio

cracker *n* cracer; bisgeden

crackle *vi* clindarddach

cradle *n* crud, cawell; cadair fagu

craft *n* crefft; cyfrwystra, dichell; llong, bad

craftsman *n* crefftwr

craftsmanship *n* crefftwriaeth

cram *vb* gorlenwi, stwffio, saco

cramp *n* cwlwm gwythi, cramp ▸ *vt* caethiwo, gwasgu

cramped *adj* clòs

crane *n* garan, crëyr, crychydd; craen ▸ *vt* estyn (gwddf)

crash *vb* gwrthdaro, cwympo ▸ *n* gwrthdrawiad, cwymp

crash helmet *n* helmed ddiogelwch

crate *n* cawell

crave *vb* deisyf, dyheu

crawl *vi* ymlusgo, cropian; crafu

crayon *n* creon

craze *n* ysfa

crazy *adj* penwan, gorffwyll, o'i gof

creak *vi* gwichian

cream *n* hufen

creamy *adj* hufennog

crease *n* ôl plygiad, plyg ▸ *vt* crychu

creased *adj* crychlyd

create *vt* creu

creation *n* cread, creadigaeth

creative *adj* creadigol

creator *n* crëwr, creawdwr

creature *n* creadur

credentials *npl* credlythyrau

credible *adj* credadwy

credit *n* coel, cred; clod, credyd ▸ *vt* coelio

credit card *n* cerdyn credyd

creek *n* cilfach

creep (*pt, pp* **crept**) *vi* ymlusgo, cropian; **creep** *vi* ymlusgo, cropian

cremate *vt* amlosgi

crematorium *n* amlosgfa

crescent *n* hanner lleuad; cilgant ▸ *adj* cynyddol

cress *n* berwr

crest *n* crib; arwydd ar arfbais

crew *n* criw; haid

crib *n* preseb; gwely plentyn ▸ *vt* (*inf*) copïo

cricket *n* criced; cricsyn

crime *n* trosedd

criminal *adj* troseddol ▸ *n* troseddwr

crimson *adj, n* rhuddgoch

cringe *vi* cynffonna, ymgreinio

cripple *n* (*offensive*) cloff, efrydd ▸ *vt* cloffi, efryddu

crisis *n* argyfwng

crisp *adj* cras, crych

crisps *npl* creision tatws

criterion *n* maen prawf, safon

critic *n* beirniad

critical *adj* beirniadol; pryderus; peryglus

criticism *n* beirniadaeth

criticize *vt* beirniadu

Croatia *n* Croatia

crockery *n* llestri

crocodile *n* crocodil

crocus *n* saffrwn, crocus

crook n crwca, ffon fugail; *(inf)* troseddwr

crooked adj crwca, cam

crop n cnwd, cynnyrch; crombil ▸ vt tocio, torri

cross n, adj croes ▸ vb croesi; **cross out** vt croesi allan; **cross over** vi croesi

cross-country n, adj traws gwlad

crossing n croesfan

crossroads n croesffordd

crossword n croesair

crouch vi cyrcydu ▸ n cwrcwd; **crouch down** vi cyrcydu

crow¹ n brân

crow² vi canu fel ceiliog; ymffrostio

crowd n torf, tyrfa ▸ vb tyrru, heidio

crowded adj llawn o bobl

crown n coron; corun ▸ vt coroni

crucial adj hanfodol, terfynol

crucifix n croeslun

crude adj cri, crai; llymrig, amrwd

cruel adj creulon

cruelty n creulondeb

cruise vi morio ▸ n mordaith

crumb n briwsionyn

crumble vb briwsioni, malurio ▸ n briwsiongrwst

crumpet n crymped

crumple vb crychu, gwasgu

crunch vb creinsio

crush vb gwasgu, llethu ▸ n gwasgiad, torf

crust n crawen, crofen, crystyn

crutch n bagl, ffon fagl

cry vb llefain, wylo, crio ▸ n llef, sgrech, cri

crystal n grisial ▸ adj grisialaidd

cub n cenau

cube n ciwb ▸ vb ciwbio

cubicle n cuddygl

cuckoo n cog, cwcw; gwirionyn

cucumber n cucumer

cuddle vb anwylo, anwesu

cue n awgrym; ciw

cuff n torch llawes

cul-de-sac n pen ffordd, heol hosan

cull vt dewis, pigo

culminate vi cyrraedd ei anterth, diweddu

culprit n troseddwr, drwgweithredwr

cult n addoliad, cwlt

cultivate vt diwyllio, trin, meithrin

cultural adj diwylliannol

culture n diwylliant; gwrtaith

cunning adj dichellgar, cyfrwys ▸ n cyfrwystra

cup n cwpan

cupboard n cwpwrdd

curator n curadur

curb n atalfa; cwrbyn ▸ vt ffrwyno

curdle vb ceulo, cawsio

cure n iachâd, gwellhad; meddyginiaeth ▸ vb iacháu, gwella; hallti

curfew n hwyrgloch

curiosity n cywreinrwydd, chwilfrydedd

curious adj cywrain; chwilfrydig; hynod

curl n cwrl, cudyn ▸ vb cyrlio

curly adj cyrliog, crych

currency n arian breiniol

current adj cyfredol, cyfoes ▸ n ffrwd, llif; **current account** cyfrif

279

cyfredol; **current affairs** materion cyfoes
currently adv ar hyn o bryd
curriculum n cwricwlwm; **National Curriculum** Cwricwlwm Cenedlaethol
curriculum vitae n braslun bywyd, manylion personol
curry vt trin lledr ▸ n cyrri; **to curry favour** cynffonna, ceisio ffafr
curse n melltith, rheg ▸ vb melltithio, rhegi
cursor n (Comput) cyrchwr
curt adj cwta, byr
curtain n llen
curve vb camu, gwyro, troi ▸ n tro; cromlin
cushion n clustog
custard n cwstard
custody n dalfa, cadwraeth
custom n defod; cwsmeriaeth; toll
customer n cwsmer
customs npl y tollau
customs officer n swyddog tollau
cut (pt, pp cut) vb torri ▸ n toriad, archoll, briw; **cut back** torri yn ôl; **cut in** torri ar draws; **cut out** torri allan; **cut through** torri trwodd; **cut down** vt (tree) torri; **cut off** vt torri; **cut up** vt torri
cute adj ciwt, cyfrwys
cutlery n cwtleri
cutlet n golwyth, cydled
CV n abbr (= curriculum vitae) CV, braslun bywyd
cyberbullying n seiber-fwlio
cybercafé n caffi rhyngrwyd, caffe rhyngrwyd

cycle n cylch; cyfres; beic ▸ vb beicio, seiclo
cycling n beicio, seiclo
cyclist n beiciwr
cyclone n trowynt
cylinder n rhol; silindr
cynical adj gwawdlyd, dirmygus
Cyprus n Ynys Cyprus
cyst n coden
cystitis n llid y bledren
Czech n (person) Tsieciad; (language) Tsieceg ▸ adj Tsieciaidd; (in language) Tsieceg
Czech Republic n: the Czech Republic y Weriniaeth Tsiec

d

dab vt dabio ► n dab
dad, daddy n tad, tada, dada
daffodil n cenhinen Bedr
daft adj (inf) hurt, gwirion
dagger n dagr, bidog
daily adj dyddiol, beunyddiol ► adv beunydd, bob dydd
dairy n llaethdy; **dairy products** cynhyrchion llaeth
daisy n llygad y dydd
dam n argae, cronfa ► vt argáu, cronni
damage n niwed, difrod ► vt niweidio, difrodi; **damages** npl iawn
damn vb damnio
damp adj llaith ► n lleither ► vb lleithio
dance vb dawnsio ► n dawns; **folk dance** dawns werin; **public folk dance** twmpath dawns
dancer n dawnsiwr

dandelion n dant y llew
dandruff n marwdon, cen
Dane n brodor o Ddenmarc, Daniad
danger n perygl, enbydrwydd
dangerous adj peryglus, enbyd
dangle vb hongian; siglo
Danish n (language) Daneg ► adj Danaidd; (in language) Daneg
dare vb beiddio, mentro
daring adj beiddgar, mentrus ► n beiddgarwch
dark adj tywyll ► n tywyllwch, nos
darken vb tywyllu
darkness n tywyllwch
darling n anwylyd, cariad ► adj annwyl
dart n dart ► vb dartio, rhuthro
dash vb rhuthro; chwalu, chwilfriwio ► n rhuthr; llinell (-)
dashboard n dashfwrdd
data npl data
database n cronfa ddata
date n dyddiad, amseriad; datysen ► vb dyddio; **out of date** henffasiwn, wedi dyddio; **up to date** hyd yn hyn, cyfoes
dated adj dyddiedig
daughter n merch; **daughter-in-law** merch yng nghyfraith
dawn vi gwawrio, dyddio ► n gwawr
day n diwrnod, dydd; **by day** liw dydd; **today** heddiw; **next day** trannoeth; **the day before yesterday** echdoe
day-dream vb pensynnu, synfyfyrio
daylight n golau dydd
day-time n y dydd
dazzle vb disgleirio; dallu

dazzling *adj* disglair, llachar
dead *adj* marw ▸ *adv* hollol; **the dead** y meirw; **dead centre** yn ei ganol; **dead tired** wedi blino'n lân; **dead heat** cwbl gyfartal
deadline *n* dedlein
deadly *adj* marwol, angheuol
Dead Sea *n*: **the Dead Sea** y Môr Marw
deaf *adj* byddar
deafen *vb* byddaru
deafening *adj* byddarol
deal (*pt, pp* **dealt**) *vb* delio; trin ▸ *n* trafodaeth, dêl; **a great deal** llawer iawn; **to deal with** ymwneud â
dealer *n* masnachwr
dean *n* deon
dear *adj* annwyl, hoff; drud ▸ *n* anwylyd, cariad; **dear me** o'r annwyl!
death *n* angau, marwolaeth, tranc; **Black Death** y Pla Du
debate *vb* dadlau, ymryson ▸ *n* dadl
debit *n* debyd
debit card *n* cerdyn debyd
debt *n* dyled
decade *n* degawd
decaffeinated *adj* digaffein
decay *vi* dadfeilio, pydru ▸ *n* dadfeiliad
deceased *n* ymadawedig, trancedig
deceit *n* twyll, dichell, hoced
deceive *vt* twyllo, hocedu, siomi
December *n* Rhagfyr
decent *adj* gweddus, gweddaidd
deception *n* twyll, ffug, dichell

deceptive *adj* twyllodrus, dichellgar
decide *vb* penderfynu
decimal *adj* degol ▸ *n* degolyn; **decimal system** system ddegol; **decimal point** pwynt degol; **recurring decimal** degolyn cylchol
decision *n* penderfyniad
decisive *adj* penderfynol, pendant
deck *n* bwrdd llong, dec
deck chair *n* cadair haul
declaration *n* datganiad; cau batiad
declare *vb* mynegi, datgan, cyhoeddi
decline *vb* dadfeilio, dirywio; gwrthod ▸ *n* dadfeiliad; darfodedigaeth
decorate *vt* addurno, arwisgo
decoration *n* addurn, tlws
decorator *n* addurnwr, peintiwr tai
decrease *vb* lleihau, gostwng ▸ *n* lleihad
decree *n* gorchymyn, dyfarniad ▸ *vb* gorchymyn, dyfarnu
dedicate *vt* cysegru, cyflwyno
dedication *n* cysegriad, cyflwyniad
deduce *vt* tynnu, casglu
deduct *vt* tynnu ymaith, didynnu
deduction *n* diddwythiad, didyniad
deed *n* gweithred
deem *vt* (*form*) ystyried, barnu
deep *adj* dwfn; dwys ▸ *n* dwfn, dyfnder
deep freeze *n* rhewgell
deeply *adv* yn ddwys
deer *n* carw, hydd
default *n* diffyg ▸ *vb* methu, torri

d

defeat vt gorchfygu, trechu ▸ n gorchfygiad

defect n diffyg, nam

defective adj diffygiol

defence n amddiffyn, amddiffyniad

defend vt amddiffyn

defendant n diffynnydd

defender n amddiffynnwr

defer vb oedi, gohirio

defiance n her, herfeiddiad

defiant adj herfeiddiol

deficient adj diffygiol, prin, yn eisiau

deficit n diffyg

defile vt halogi, difwyno

define vt diffinio

definite adj penodol, pendant

definitely adv yn bendant, heb os

definition n diffiniad

deflate vb dadchwythu

deflect vb gwyro, osgoi

defraud vt twyllo, hocedu

defrost vt (fridge) dadrewi

defy vt beiddio, herfeiddio, herio

degree n gradd

delay vb oedi, gohirio ▸ n oediad

delegate vt dirprwyo ▸ n dirprwy, cynrychiolydd

delete vt dileu

deliberate vb ystyried yn bwyllog ▸ adj pwyllog, bwriadol

deliberately adv yn fwriadol

delicacy n amheuthun, danteithfwyd; **delicacies** danteithion

delicate adj tyner; cain; gwanllyd

delicatessen n delicatesen

delicious adj danteithiol, blasus

delight vb difyrru; ymhyfrydu ▸ n hyfrydwch

delighted adj balch; **I'd be delighted to ...** Mi fyddai'n bleser gen i ...

delightful adj hyfryd, braf

delinquent n troseddwr, tramgwyddwr ▸ adj troseddol, tramgwyddus

deliver vt traddodi; gwaredu; danfon; cludo

delivery n traddodiad; danfoniad

delusion n twyll, cyfeiliornad; lledrith

delve vb cloddio, palu, ymchwilio

demand vt gofyn, hawlio, mynnu ▸ n gofyn, hawl

demise n marwolaeth

democracy n democratiaeth

democrat n gwerinydd, gweriniaethwr

democratic adj gwerinol, democratig

demolish vt dymchwelyd, distrywio

demonstrate vb arddangos, profi; gwrthdystio

demonstration n arddangosiad; gwrthdystiad

demonstrator n arddangoswr; gwrthdystiwr

demote vb darostwng

den n ffau, gwâl, lloches

denial n gwadiad; nacâd, gwrthodiad; **self-denial** hunanymwadiad

denim n denim

Denmark n Denmarc

denomination n enw, enwad

denounce vt lladd ar, cyhuddo, condemnio

dense adj tew, dwys; (inf) pendew, hurt

density n dwysedd, trwch

dent n tolc ▸ vt tolcio

dental adj deintiol

dentist n deintydd

dentures npl dannedd gosod

deny vt gwadu

deodorant n diaroglydd

depart vi ymadael; cychwyn

department n adran, dosbarth

department store n siop adrannol

departure n ymadawiad; cychwyniad

departure lounge n lolfa ymadael

depend vi dibynnu

dependant n dibynnydd

dependent adj dibynnol

depict vt darlunio

deport vt alltudio

deposit vt dodi i lawr; adneuo; gwaddodi ▸ n adnau, blaendal; gwaddod; **deposit account** cyfrif cadw

depot n storfa; gorsaf

depreciate vb dibrisio

depress vt gostwng, iselu; digalonni

depressed adj digalon, iselfryd

depressing adj trist

depression n iselder (ysbryd); dibwysiant (tywydd); pant; dirwasgiad (diwydiant)

deprive vt amddifadu

deprived adj amddifadus

depth n dyfnder

deputy n dirprwy

deputy head n dirprwy brifathro

derail vb taflu oddi ar gledrau

derelict adj wedi ei adael, diberchen, diffaith

derive vb derbyn, cael; tarddu, deillio

descend vi disgyn

descent n disgyniad, disgynfa; hil, ach

describe vt disgrifio, darlunio

description n disgrifiad, darluniad

desert[1] n diffaith, anial ▸ n diffeithwch

desert[2] vb gadael, cefnu ar; encilio

deserve vb haeddu, teilyngu

design n arfaeth; cynllun ▸ vb arfaethu; cynllunio

designer n cynllunydd, dylunydd

desirable adj dymunol, dewisol

desire vb dymuno ▸ n dymuniad, chwant

desk n desg

desktop n (Comput) cyfrifiadur desg

despair n anobaith ▸ vi anobeithio

desperate adj diobaith, anobeithiol

desperately adv (try, fight) yn enbyd; (ill, worried, poor) ofnadwy

desperation n anobaith

despise vt dirmygu, diystyru

despite prep er, er gwaethaf

dessert n pwdin, melysfwyd

destination n cyrchfan, pen y daith

destiny n tynged, tynghedfen

destroy vt distrywio, dinistrio

destruction n distryw, dinistr

detach vt datod, gwahanu, datgysylltu

detached adj ar wahân

detached house n tŷ ar wahân

detail n manylyn ▸ vb manylu, neilltuo; **details** npl manylion; **in detail** yn fanwl

detailed adj manwl

detain vt cadw, caethiwo

detect vt canfod, darganfod

detection n darganfyddiad, datgeliad

detective n cuddswyddog, ditectif; **detective story** stori dditectif

detention n carchariad, ataliad

deter vt cadw rhag, atal, rhwystro

detergent n golchydd

deteriorate vb dirywio, gwaethygu

determination n penderfyniad

determine vb penderfynu, pennu

determined adj penderfynol

deterrent n atalrym, ataliad

detest vt ffieiddio, casáu

detour n cylch

detract vt tynnu oddi wrth, bychanu

detrimental adj niweidiol

devastated adj difrodedig

devastating adj difrodus

develop vb datblygu

development n datblygiad

device n dyfais

devil n diafol, diawl, cythraul

devious adj diarffordd, troellog; cyfeiliornus

devise vt dyfeisio

devolution n datganoli

devote vt cysegru, cyflwyno, ymroddi

devoted adj ffyddlon, ymroddgar

devotion n defosiwn, ymroddiad

devour vt ysu, difa, traflyncu

devout adj duwiol, crefyddol, defosiynol

dew n gwlith ▸ vb gwlitho

diabetes n clefyd melys

diabetic adj, n diabetig

diagnosis n diagnosis

diagonal n croeslin ▸ adj croeslinol

diagram n darlun eglurhaol, diagram

dial n deial ▸ vb deialu

dialect n tafodiaith

dialling tone n tôn deialu

dialogue n ymddiddan, deialog

diameter n tryfesur, diamedr

diamond n diemwnt

diarrhoea n rhyddni, dolur rhydd

diary n dyddiadur, dyddlyfr

dice n dîs

dictate vb arddywedyd; gorchymyn

dictation n arddywediad

dictionary n geiriadur

die vi marw, trengi, trigo, darfod

diesel n disel

diet n deiet

differ vi gwahaniaethu

difference n gwahaniaeth

different adj gwahanol

differentiate vb gwahaniaethu

difficult adj anodd, caled

difficulty n anhawster

dig (pt, pp **dug**) vb palu, cloddio, ceibio

digest vb treulio, toddi; cymathu

digestion n treuliad, traul

digit n digid, bys

digital adj digidol

digital camera n camera digidol

digital radio n radio digidol

digital television *n* teledu digidol
digital watch *n* oriawr ddigidol
dignified *adj* urddasol
dignity *n* urddas, teilyngdod
dilemma *n* dilema
dilute *vt* cymysgu â dwfr, gwanhau
dim *adj* pŵl, aneglur ▸ *vb* tywyllu, cymylu
dimension *n* dimensiwn
diminish *vb* lleihau, prinhau
din *n* twrf, dadwrdd, mwstwr
dine *vi* ciniawa
diner *n* ciniawr
dinghy *n* dingi
dingy *adj* tywyll, dilewyrch; tlodaidd
dining room *n* ystafell fwyta
dinner *n* cinio
dinner jacket *n* cot ginio, cot giniawa
dinner party *n* cinio gwadd
dinner time *n* amser cinio
dinosaur *n* deinosor
dip *vb* trochi, gwlychu; gostwng ▸ *n* trochfa
diploma *n* tystysgrif, diploma
diplomacy *n* diplomyddiaeth
diplomat *n* diplomydd
diplomatic *adj* diplomyddol
dire *adj* dygn, arswydus, echryslon
direct *adj* union, uniongyrchol ▸ *vt* cyfarwyddo, cyfeirio
direction *n* cyfarwyddyd; cyfeiriad
directly *adv* yn union, yn ddi-oed
director *n* cyfarwyddwr
directory *n* cyfarwyddiadur
dirt *n* baw, llaid, llaca
dirty *adj* budr, brwnt ▸ *vt* budro, difwyno, maeddu
disability *n* anabledd

disabled *adj* anabl
disadvantage *n* anfantais
disagree *vi* anghytuno
disagreeable *adj* annymunol, cas
disagreement *n* anghytundeb
disappear *vi* diflannu
disappearance *n* diflaniad
disappoint *vt* siomi
disappointed *adj* siomedig
disappointing *adj* siomedig
disappointment *n* siomedigaeth
disapprove *vb* anghymeradwyo
disarm *vb* diarfogi
disarmament *n* diarfogiad
disaster *n* trychineb, aflwydd
disastrous *adj* trychinebus
disbelief *n* anghrediniaeth, angoel
disc *n* disg(en)
discard *vt* rhoi heibio, gwrthod
discharge *vb* dadlwytho, rhyddhau ▸ *n* gollyngdod, rhyddhad
discipline *n* disgyblaeth ▸ *vt* disgyblu
disc jockey *n* troellwr disgiau
disclose *vt* dadlennu, datguddio
disco *n* disgo
discomfort *vt* anghysuro ▸ *n* anghysur
disconnect *vb* datgysylltu
discontent *n* anfodlonrwydd
discontinue *vb* torri, atal
discount *n* disgownt
discourage *vt* digalonni
discover *vt* darganfod, canfod
discovery *n* darganfyddiad
discredit *n* anfri, anghlod, amarch ▸ *vt* anghoelio; amau, difrio
discreet *adj* call, pwyllog
discrepancy *n* anghysondeb
discretion *n* barn, pwyll

discriminate vb gwahaniaethu
discrimination n gwahaniaethu, anffafriaeth
discuss vt trin, trafod
discussion n trafodaeth, sgwrs
disease n afiechyd, clefyd, clwyf
disembark vb glanio
disgrace vt gwaradwyddo ► n gwaradwydd, gwarth
disgraceful adj gwaradwyddus, gwarthus
disguise vt dieithrio, ffugio, lledrithio ► n rhith, dieithrwch
disgust n diflastod, ffieidd-dod ► vt diflasu, ffieiddio
disgusted adj wedi ffieiddio
disgusting adj ffiaidd, gwrthun
dish n dysgl; dysglaid
dishcloth n cadach llestri
dishonest adj anonest
dishwasher n peiriant golchi llestri
disillusion vb dadrithio
disinfectant n diheintydd
disintegrate vb datod, chwalu
disk n disg(en)
disk drive n gyriant disg
dislike vt casáu ► n casineb
dislocate vt rhoi o'i le, datgymalu
dismal adj tywyll, dilewyrch, digalon
dismay vt siomi, digalonni ► n siom, chwithdod
dismiss vt gollwng; diswyddo
disobedient adj anufudd
disobey vb anufuddhau
disorder n anhrefn; anhwyldeb ► vt anhrefnu
disown vt gwadu, diarddel
dispatch vb anfon; diweddu ► n neges

dispel vt chwalu, gwasgaru
dispense vb rhannu; gweinyddu; hepgor
disperse vb gwasgaru, chwalu, taenu
display vt arddangos ► n arddangosiad
displease vt anfodloni, digio
disposable adj tafladwy
dispose vt hepgor, gwaredu
disposition n anianawd
dispute vb dadlau, ymryson ► n dadl
disqualify vb difreinio, atal
disregard vt diystyru, esgeuluso ► n diystyrwch, esgeulustra
disrupt vb rhwygo, amharu ar
dissatisfaction n anfodlonrwydd
dissect vb difynio, trychu; dadansoddi
dissent vi anghytuno ► n anghytundeb; ymneilltuaeth
dissertation n traethawd
dissolve vb toddi; datod, diddymu
distance n pellter
distant adj pell, pellennig; oeraidd
distil vb distyllu, dihidlo
distillery n distyllty
distinct adj gwahanol; eglur
distinction n rhagoriaeth, gwahaniaeth
distinctive adj gwahanrédol, arbennig
distinguish vb gwahaniaethu; hynodi
distinguished adj enwog, amlwg
distort vt ystumio, anffurfio, gwyrdroi
distract vb tynnu ymaith, drysu, mwydro

distraction n dryswch, diffyg sylw

distress n ing, trallod

distressing adj trallodus, blin, poenus

distribute vt rhannu, dosbarthu

distribution n dosbarthiad, rhaniad

distributor n dosbarthydd, dosbarthwr

district n dosbarth, ardal; **district council** cyngor dosbarth

distrust n drwgdybiaeth ▸ vb drwgdybio

disturb vt aflonyddu, cyffroi

disturbance n aflonyddwch, cyffro

disturbed adj blinderus, cynhyrfus

ditch n ffos

ditto adv eto, yr un, yr un peth

dive vi ymsuddo, deifio

diver n deifiwr

diverse adj gwahanol; annhebyg

diversion n difyrrwch, adloniant; dargyfeiriad, gwyriad

divert vt dargyfeirio, difyrru

divide vb rhannu, gwahanu ▸ n gwahanfa

divine adj dwyfol ▸ n diwinydd ▸ vb dewinio, dyfalu

diving n deifio

division n rhan, rhaniad, adran; cyfraniaeth; **long division** rhannu hir

divorce vt ysgar(u) ▸ n ysgariad

divorced adj wedi ysgaru

DIY n abbr (= do-it-yourself) crefftau'r cartref, DIY

dizzy adj penysgafn, pensyfrdan

DJ n troellwr

KEYWORD

do (pt **did**, pp **done**) n (inf) (party etc) achlysur m, parti m
▸ aux vb **1** (in negative constructions) no equivalent; **I don't understand** nid wyf yn deall
2 (to form questions) no equivalent; **didn't you know?** oni wyddech?, wyddech chi ddim?; **what do you think?** beth yw'ch barn chi?
3 (for emphasis; in polite expressions): **people do make mistakes sometimes** fe fydd pobl yn cymryd cam gwag weithiau, fe fydd pobl yn gwneud camgymeriad weithiau; **she does seem rather late** mae hi'n braidd yn hwyr yn fy marn i; **do sit down/help yourself** eisteddwch/helpwch eich hunain da chi; **do take care!** cymerwch ofal da chi!
4 (used to avoid repeating vb): **she swims better than I do** mae'n nofio'n well na mi; **do you agree? — yes, I do/no I don't** a ydych yn cytuno? ydw/nac ydw; **she lives in Swansea — so do I** mae'n byw yn Abertawe — a minnau hefyd; **he didn't like it and neither did we** nid oedd yn hoffi'r peth, na ninnau ychwaith; **who broke it? — I did** pwy a'i torrodd? — minnau; **he asked me to help him and I did** gofynnodd imi ei helpu, ac fe wnes
5 (in question tags): **you like him, don't you?** rydych yn ei hoffi, on'd ydych?; **I don't know him, do I?** dwy ddim yn ei adnabod, ydw i?
▸ vt **1** (gen, carry out, perform etc) gwneud; **what are you doing**

tonight? beth wnewch chi heno?, beth fyddwch chi'n ei wneud heno; **what do you do?** *(job)* beth yw'ch gwaith chi?; **what can I do for you?** a gaf i'ch helpu?; **to do the cooking** gwneud y [gwaith] coginio; **to do one's teeth/hair/ nails** brwsio'ch dannedd/gwneud eich gwallt/gwneud eich ewinedd

2 *(Aut, etc, distance):* gwneud, teithio; *(speed)* gwneud, mynd; **we've done 200 km already** rydym wedi teithio 200 km yn barod; **the car was doing 100** roedd y car yn mynd 100 (milltir yr awr); **he can do 100 in that car** mae'n gallu gwneud 100 (milltir yr awr) yn y car yna

▸ vi **1** *(act, behave)* gwneud; **do as I do** gwnewch yr un fath â minnau **2** *(get on, fare)* dod ymlaen; **the firm is doing well** mae'r ffyrm yn gwneud yn dda; **he's doing well/ badly at school** mae'n gwneud yn dda/wael yn yr ysgol; **how do you do?** sut [r]wyt ti?, sut [r]ydych chi? *(in reply)* iawn diolch

3 *(suit)* gwneud; **will it do?** a wnaiff y tro?

4 *(be sufficient)* bod yn ddigon; **will £10 do?** a fydd £10 yn ddigon?; **that'll do** bydd hynny'n ddigon, bydd hynny'n gwneud y tro; **that'll do!** *(in annoyance)* dyna ddigon!; **to make do (with)** bodloni (ar)

▸ **do up** vt *(laces, dress)* cau, clymu; *(buttons)* botymu, cau; *(zip)* cau; *(renovate: room)* ail-wneud, atgyweirio, cyweirio

▸ **do with** vt fus *(need)* I could do

with a drink/some help mae arnaf angen diod/cymorth; **it could do with a wash** byddai golchi'r peth yn gwneud lles; *(be connected with)* that has nothing to do with you does a wneloch chi ddim â'r peth; **I won't have anything to do with it** rwy'n gwrthod ymwneud â'r peth

▸ **do without** vi gwneud y tro heb; **if you're late for tea then you'll do without** os byddwch yn hwyr i de yna rhaid ichi wneud y tro hebddo

▸ vt fus ymdopi; **I can do without a car** gallaf ymdopi heb gar

dock[1] n *(dail)* tafol

dock[2] vt tocio, cwtogi

dock[3] n doc ▸ vt docio; cwtogi

doctor n doctor, meddyg; doethur

document n dogfen

documentary adj dogfennol

dodge vb osgoi, twyllo ▸ n cast, ystryw

dog n ci ▸ vb dal i ddilyn

do-it-yourself n crefftau'r cartref, DIY

dole n dôl, dogn ▸ vt dogni, rhannu; **on the dole** yn ddi-waith, ar y clwt

doll n dol, doli

dollar n doler

dolphin n dolffin

dome n cromen, crynddo

domestic adj teuluaidd, cartrefol; gwâr, dof

dominant adj trech

dominate vb dominyddu

dominoes npl dominos

donate vb rhoddi

289

donation n rhodd
donkey n asyn, mul
donor n rhoddwr
doodle vb dwdlan
doom n dedfryd, tynged ▸ vt dedfrydu, tynghedu
door n drws, dôr, porth
doorbell n cloch drws
door-step n rhiniog, trothwy
doorway n porth, drws
dope (inf) n cyffur ▸ vb rhoi cyffur
dormitory n ystafell gysgu, hundy
dose n dogn ▸ vt dogni
dot n dot ▸ vb dotio
double adj, n dwbl ▸ vb dyblu, plygu; **double flat** meddalnod dwbl
double-bass n bas dwbl
double-click vi clicio dwywaith
double glazing n gwydro dwbl, ffenestri dwbl
doubles n parau
doubt vb amau, petruso ▸ n amheuaeth
doubtful adj amheus, petrus
doubtless adv yn ddiamau, diau
dough n toes
doughnut n toesen
dove n colomen
down¹ n manblu
down² adv i lawr, i waered; **down and out** digalon, truenus
downcast adj digalon, prudd
downfall n cwymp, codwm
download vt lawrlwytho, dadlwytho
downright adj diamheuol
Down's syndrome n syndrom Down

downstairs n y llawr ▸ adv ar y llawr
downwards adv i lawr, i waered
doze vi hepian ▸ n cyntun; **doze off** vi pendwmpian
dozen n deuddeg, dwsin
drab adj llwydaidd, salw
draft n drafft, braslun ▸ vb drafftio, braslunio
drag vb llusgo ▸ n car llusg
dragon n draig
dragon-fly n gwas y neidr
drain¹ n draen
drain² vb draenio, diferu, yfed; **draining board** bwrdd diferu
drainage n draeniad; **drainage basin** dalgylch afon
drama n drama
dramatic adj dramatig
drape vt gwisgo, gorchuddio
drastic adj cryf, llym
draught n dracht, llymaid; drafft(en); tynfa (llong)
draughts npl drafftiau
draw n atyniad, tynfa ▸ vb tynnu; lluniadu, darlunio; **draw to scale** graddluniadu; **drawn game** gêm gyfartal
drawback n anfantais
drawer n drâr, drôr
drawing n lluniad, llun
drawing pin n pin bawd
drawing room n ystafell groeso
dread vb ofni, arswydo ▸ n ofn, arswyd
dreadful adj ofnadwy
dream (pt, pp **dreamed, dreamt**) vb breuddwydio ▸ n breuddwyd
dreary adj llwm, diflas
drench vt gwlychu; drensio

dress vb gwisgo, dilladu ▸ n gwisg; **dress up** vi gwisgo'n ffansi

dresser n dreser, gwisgwr

dressing n dresin; **salad dressing** dresin salad; **dressing gown** gŵn gwisgo

dressing table n bwrdd gwisgo

dressmaker n gwniadwraig

dribble n dribl(ad), drefl ▸ vb driblo, dreflu, glafoerio

drier n peiriant sychu

drift n drifft, lluwch; tuedd ▸ vb drifftio, lluwchio

drill vb drilio ▸ n dril

drink (pt **drank**, pp **drunk**) vb yfed ▸ n diod, llymaid

drink-driving n gyrru tra'n feddw

drinker n yfwr, diotwr

drinking water n dŵr yfed

drip vb diferu, defnynnu ▸ n diferiad

drive (pt **drove**, pp **driven**) n dreif, gyriant, cymhelliad ▸ vb dreifio, gyrru

driver n gyrrwr

driving adj grymus ▸ n gyrru

driving instructor n hyfforddwr gyrru

driving lesson n gwers gyrru

driving licence n trwydded gyrru

driving test n prawf gyrru

drizzle vb briwlan ▸ n glaw mân

droop vi laesu, ymollwng; nychu

drop n diferyn, dafn; cwympiad ▸ vb diferu, cwympo, gollwng; **drop goal** gôl adlam

drought n sychder, sychdwr

drown vb boddi

drowsy adj cysglyd

drug n cyffur

drug addict n caeth i gyffuriau

drug dealer n gwerthwr cyffuriau

drum n tabwrdd, drwm ▸ vb tabyrddu

drummer n drymiwr

drunk adj meddw, brwysg

dry adj sych, cras ▸ vb sychu

dry cleaner's n sychlanhawyr

dryer n sychwr

dual adj deuol; **dual carriageway** ffordd ddeuol

dubious adj amheus, petrus

duck¹ n hwyaden

duck² vb trochi; gostwng pen

due adj dyledus, dyladwy ▸ n dyled, haeddiant

duel n gornest

duet n deuawd

duke n dug

dull adj hurt; marwaidd; diflas; cymylog; pŵl ▸ vb pylu, lleddfu

dumb adj (infl) mud

dummy n dymi; delw; ffug-bas (rygbi) ▸ vb ffug-basio

dump n dymp, storfa ▸ vb dympio

dumpling n tymplen, poten

dune n twyn

dungarees npl dyngarîs

dungeon n dwnsiwn

duplex adj dwplecs

duplicate adj dyblyg ▸ n copi ▸ vt dyblygu

durable adj parhaol, parhaus, cryf

duration n parhad

during prep yn ystod

dusk n cyfnos, gwyll

dust n llwch ▸ vt taenu neu sychu llwch, dwstio

dustbin n bin sbwriel

duster n cadach, dwster

dustman *n* dyn lludw
dusty *adj* llychlyd
Dutch *n (language)* Iseldireg
Dutchman *n* Iseldirwr
Dutchwoman *n* Iseldirwraig
duty *n* dyletswydd; toll; **customs duty** tolldal; **import duty** toll fewnforio; **export duty** toll allforio
duty-free *adj* di-doll
duvet *n* carthen blu
DVD *n abbr* DVD
DVD player *n* chwaraewr DVD
dwarf *n (infl)* cor, corrach ► *adj* corachaidd
dwell *(pt, pp* **dwelt***) vi* trigo, preswylio
dwindle *vi* darfod, lleihau, dirywio
dye *vb* lliwio, llifo ► *n* lliw, lliwur
dynamic *adj* dynamig
dyslexia *n* dyslecsia
dyslexic *adj* dyslecsig

e

each *adj, pron* pob, pob un; **each other** ei gilydd
eager *adj* awyddus, awchus
eagle *n* eryr
ear *n* clust, dolen; tywysen
earache *n* pigyn clust, clust dost
earl *n* iarll
earlier *adv* gynt
early *adj* cynnar, bore ► *adv* yn fore
early retirement *n* ymddeoliad cynnar
earmark *n* clustnod, nod clust ► *vb* clustnodi, neilltuo
earn *vt* ennill, elwa
earnest *adj* difrif, difrifol, taer
earnings *npl* enillion
earphone *n* ffôn clust
earring *n* clustdlws
earth *n* daear, pridd ► *vt* priddo
earthquake *n* daeargryn
ease *n* esmwythdra; rhwyddineb ► *vb* esmwytho
easily *adv* yn hawdd

east n dwyrain ▸ adj dwyreiniol
Easter n y Pasg
Easter egg n wy Pasg
eastern adj dwyreiniol
easy adj hawdd, rhwydd
easy-going adj didaro, di-hid
eat (pt **ate**, pp **eaten**) vt bwyta, ysu
eavesdrop vb clustfeinio
e-book n e-lyfr
eccentric adj od, hynod; echreiddig
echo n atsain, carreg ateb ▸ vb atseinio
eclipse n eclips, diffyg, clip ▸ vb tywyllu
eco-friendly adj amgylcheddol-gyfeillgar
ecological adj ecolegol
ecology n ecoleg
e-commerce n e-fasnach
economic adj economaidd
economical adj cynnil, darbodus
economics n economeg
economist n economegydd
economize vb cynilo
economy n darbodaeth, economi
ecstasy n gorfoledd, gorawen
eczema n ecsema
edge n min, ymyl ▸ vb minio, hogi;
  to be on edge bod ar bigau'r drain
edible adj bwytadwy
Edinburgh n Caeredin
edit vt golygu, paratoi i'r wasg
edition n argraffiad
editor n golygydd
editorial adj golygyddol
educate vt addysgu
education n addysg
educational adj addysgol
eel n llysywen
eerie adj iasol, annaearol

effect n effaith ▸ vb peri; after-effects sgil-effeithiau
effective adj effeithiol
effectively adv (in an effective way) yn effeithiol; (in effect) mewn gwirionedd
efficiency n effeithlonrwydd
efficient adj effeithiol, cymwys
effort n ymdrech, ymgais
e.g. abbr (= exempli gratia) er enghraifft, e.e.
egg n wy; scrambled egg cymysgwy
egg cup n cwpan wy
egg shell n masgl/plisgyn wy
ego n ego, yr hunan
Egypt n yr Aifft
eight adj, n wyth
eighteen adj, n deunaw, un deg wyth
eighteenth adj deunawfed
eighth adj wythfed
eighty adj, n pedwar ugain, wyth deg
Eire n Iwerddon Rydd, Gweriniaeth Iwerddon
either adj un o'r ddau ▸ conj naill ai ▸ adv, conj na, nac, ychwaith
eject vt bwrw allan; diarddel
elaborate[1] adj llafurfawr, manwl
elaborate[2] vb manylu
elastic adj hydwyth, ystwyth
elastic band n cylch lastig
elbow n elin, penelin
elder n henuriad, hynafgwr ▸ adj hŷn
elderly adj oedrannus
eldest adj hynaf
elect vt ethol, dewis ▸ adj etholedig

e

election n etholiad
electorate n etholaeth
electric adj trydanol, electrig
electrical adj trydanol
electric blanket n blanced drydan
electric fire n tân trydan
electrician n trydanwr
electricity n trydan
electrify vt gwefreiddio, trydanu
electronic adj electronig
electronics n electroneg
elegant adj cain, lluniaidd
element n elfen
elementary adj elfennol
elephant n cawrfil, eliffant
elevate vt dyrchafu, codi
eleven adj, n un ar ddeg
eleventh adj unfed ar ddeg
eligible adj cymwys
eliminate vt dileu, deol
elm n llwyf, llwyfen
eloquent adj huawdl
else adv arall, amgen
elsewhere adv mewn lle arall
elusive adj di-ddal, gwibiog
email n ebost ▸ vt ebostio
email address n cyfeiriad ebost
embankment n clawdd, cob
embargo n gwaharddiad
embark vb mynd/gosod ar long;
hwylio; **to embark on** ymgymryd
â, dechrau
embarrass vt rhwystro, drysu
embarrassed adj mewn penbleth,
trafferthus
embarrassing adj dyrys, anffodus
embarrassment n chwithedd,
embaras
embassy n llysgenhadaeth

embrace vt cofleidio; cynnwys ▸ n
cofleidiad
embroider vt brodio
embroidery n brodwaith
embryo n cynelwad, embryo
emerald n emrallt
emerge vi dyfod allan, dyfod i'r
golwg
emergency n argyfwng
emigrate vi allfudo, ymfudo
eminent adj enwog, amlwg, o fri
emissions npl gollyngiadau
emit vt rhoddi neu fwrw allan
emotion n emosiwn
emotional adj emosiynol
emperor n ymerawdwr, ymherodr
emphasis n pwys, pwyslais
emphasize vt pwysleisio
empire n ymerodraeth
employ vt cyflogi; arfer, defnyddio
▸ n gwasanaeth
employee n gŵr cyflog
employer n cyflogwr
employment n cyflogaeth, gwaith
empower vt awdurdodi, galluogi
empress n ymerodres
empty adj gwag ▸ vb gwacáu
empty-handed adj gwaglaw
emulsion n emwlsiwn
enable vt galluogi
enclose vt amgáu
enclosure n lle caeëdig, lloc
encore n encôr ▸ adv eto
encounter vt cyfarfod, taro ar ▸ n
ymgyfarfod, brwydr
encourage vt calonogi, annog
encyclopaedia n gwyddoniadur
encyclopedia n gwyddoniadur

end n diwedd ▸ vb diweddu,
terfynu; **end point** pwynt terfyn;
from end to end o ben bwy gilydd
endanger vt peryglu
endeavour vi ymdrechu ▸ n
ymdrech
ending n diwedd; terfyniad
endless adj diddiwedd
endorse vt cefnogi, arnodi
endorsement n arnodiad,
ardystiad
endurance n dycnwch
endure vb parhau; dioddef, goddef
enemy n gelyn
energetic adj grymus, egniol
energy n ynni, egni
enforce vt gorfodi
engaged adj wedi dyweddio;
prysur
engagement n dyweddïad; brwydr
engaging adj deniadol
engine n peiriant, injan
engineer n peiriannydd
engineering n peirianneg
England n Lloegr
English adj Saesneg, Seisnig ▸ n
(language) Saesneg; **English
Channel** Môr Udd
Englishman n Sais
Englishwoman n Saesnes
engrave vt ysgythru
engraving n ysgythrad
enhance vb mwyhau, chwyddo,
gwella
enjoy vt mwynhau; meddu
enjoyable adj pleserus
enjoyment n mwynhad
enlarge vt ehangu, helaethu
enlist vb ymrestru, listio
enormous adj anferth, enfawr

enough adj, n, adv digon
enquire vb ymholi, gofyn, holi
enquiry n ymholiad
enrage vt ffyrnigo, cynddeiriogi
enrich vt cyfoethogi
enrol vt cofrestru
enrolment n cofrestrad
ensure vt diogelu, sicrhau
entail vt gorfodi, gofyn
enter vb mynd i mewn, treiddio;
cofnodi
enterprise n anturiaeth, menter
enterprising adj anturiaethus,
mentrus
entertain vt difyrru; croesawu
entertainer n difyrrwr, diddanwr
entertaining adj difyrrus, diddan
entertainment n difyrrwch,
adloniant
enthusiasm n brwdfrydedd
enthusiast n: **she's a real
enthusiast** mae hi'n frwdfrydig
iawn
enthusiastic adj brwdfrydig,
eiddgar
entire adj cyfan, hollol, llwyr
entirely adv yn gyfan gwbl, yn llwyr
entrance¹ n mynediad, mynedfa;
entrance examination arholiad
mynediad; **entrance fee** tâl
mynediad
entrance² vt swyno
entrust vt ymddiried
entry n mynediad, mynedfa;
cofnodiad
entry phone n intercom
envelope n amlen
envious adj cenfigennus
environment n amgylchedd,
amgylchfyd

environmental adj amgylcheddol
environmentally adv yn amgylcheddol; **environmentally friendly** yn amgylcheddol garedig
environment-friendly adj amgylcheddol-gyfeillgar
envisage vb rhagweld
envoy n cennad, negesydd
envy n cenfigen, eiddigedd ▸ vt cenfigennu, eiddigeddu
epic adj arwrol, arwraidd ▸ n arwrgerdd, epig
epidemic adj heintus ▸ n haint
epilepsy n epilepsi
epileptic adj epileptig
episode n digwyddiad, episôd
equal adj cyfartal ▸ n cydradd ▸ vt bod yn gyfartal; **without equal** heb ei ail
equality n cydraddoldeb, cyfartaledd
equalize vb cydraddoli, cyfartalu
equally adv yn ogystal â, yn llawn, yn gyfartal
equate vt cyfartalu, cymharu
equation n hafaliad; **simple equation** hafaliad syml; **quadratic equation** hafaliad dwyradd; **simultaneous equation** hafaliad cydamserol
equator n y cyhydedd
equip vt taclu, paratoi, cymhwyso, cyfarparu
equipment n cyfarpar, offer
equivalent adj cyfwerth, cyfartal
era n cyfnod
erase vt dileu, rhwbio allan
eraser n dilëydd, rwber
erect adj syth, unionsyth ▸ vt codi, adeiladu

erode vb ysu, treulio, erydu
erosion n erydiad
errand n neges, cenadwri
erratic adj ansefydlog, crwydraidd
error n cyfeiliornad, camgymeriad; gwall; **in error** ar gam
erupt vb echdorri, torri allan
eruption n echdoriad, tarddiad
escalator n escaladur
escape vb dianc, osgoi ▸ n dihangfa
escort vt hebrwng ▸ n gosgordd
especially adv yn arbennig, yn enwedig
espionage n ysbïaeth
essay n ymgais; traethawd, ysgrif
essence n hanfod; rhinflas
essential adj hanfodol, anhepgor ▸ n hanfod, anghenraid
essentially adv yn hanfodol
essentials npl hanfodion, anhepgorion
establish vt sefydlu
establishment n sefydliad
estate n stad, ystad, eiddo; **industrial estate** stad ddiwydiannol
estate agent n gwerthwr eiddo
estate car n car ystad
estimate vt, n amcangyfrif
etc abbr (= et cetera) ayyb
eternal adj tragwyddol, bythol
eternity n tragwyddoldeb
ethical adj moesegol
ethics npl moeseg
Ethiopia n Ethiopia
ethnic adj ethnig, cenhedlig
e-ticket n e-docyn, e-diced
etiquette n moesau, arfer
EU n abbr (= European Union) UE

euro n ewro
Europe n Ewrob, Ewrop
European adj Ewropeaidd ▸ n Ewropead
European Union n Undeb Ewropeaidd
evacuate vt ymgilio, ymadael (â)
evade vt gochelyd, osgoi
evaporate vb ymageru, anweddu
eve n min nos, noswyl
even adj gwastad, llyfn; cyfartal ▸ adv hyd yn oed; **even number** eilrif
evening n noswaith, yr hwyr, min nos
evening class n dosbarth nos
event n digwyddiad; **in the event of** os bydd
eventful adj llawn digwyddiadau
eventually adv o'r diwedd
ever adv bob amser, erioed, byth; **ever and anon** byth a hefyd
evergreen n, adj bythwyrdd, anwyw

(KEYWORD)

every adj 1 (each) pob; **every one of them** pob un ohonynt; **every shop in town was closed** roedd pob siop yn y dref ynghau
2 (all possible) pob, yr holl; **I gave you every assistance** rhoddais bob cymorth ichi; **I have every confidence in him** mae gennyf bob ffydd ynddo; **we wish you every success** dymunwn bob llwyddiant ichi
3 (showing recurrence) pob; **every day** bob dydd/diwrnod; **every other car** bob yn ail gar; **every**

other/third day bob yn dridiau; **every now and then** bob hyn a hyn

everybody pron pawb, pob un
everyday adj bob dydd, beunyddiol
everyone pron pawb, pob un
everything pron popeth
everywhere adv ym mhobman
evict vt troi allan, dadfeddiannu
evidence n tystiolaeth, prawf
evident adj amlwg, eglur
evil adj drwg, drygionus ▸ n drwg, drygioni
evoke vt galw allan, tynnu allan; gwysio
evolution n esblygiad
evolve vb datblygu; esblygu
ewe n dafad, mamog
ex n (inf) ex; **my ex** fy ex
ex- prefix allan o; cyn-
exact¹ adj manwl, cywir, union
exact² vt hawlio, mynnu
exactly adv yn union, i'r dim
exaggerate vt chwyddo, gorliwio
exaggeration n gormodiaith, gorliwiad
exam n arholiad
examination n arholiad, archwiliad
examine vt arholi, archwilio
examiner n arholwr, archwiliwr
example n esiampl, enghraifft
excavate vt cloddio
exceed vt rhagori ar, bod yn fwy na
exceedingly adv tros ben, tra
excel vb rhagori
excellent adj rhagorol, ardderchog, godidog, campus
except prep ac eithrio, eithr, namyn, heblaw

exception n eithriad
exceptional adj eithriadol
excerpt n dyfyniad, detholiad
excess n gormod, gormodedd
excessive adj gormodol, eithafol
exchange vt cyfnewid, ffeirio ▸ n cyfnewid, cyfnewidfa; **exchange rate** cyfradd cyfnewid
excite vt cynhyrfu, cyffroi
excited adj cynhyrfus
excitement n cynnwrf
exciting adj cyffrous
exclaim vt ebychu
exclamation n ebychiad; **exclamation mark** ebychnod
exclude vt cau allan, bwrw allan
exclusion n gwaharddiad, gwrthodiad
exclusive adj cyfyngedig
excruciating adj dirdynnol
excursion n gwibdaith, pleserdaith
excuse vt esgusodi ▸ n esgus
execute vt cyflawni, gweithredu; dienyddio
execution n cyflawniad; dienyddiad
executive n gweithiol, gweithredol ▸ n gweithredwr; **executive committee** pwyllgor gwaith
exempt adj rhydd, esgusodol ▸ vt rhyddhau, esgusodi
exercise n ymarfer, ymarferiad ▸ vb ymarfer; **exercise book** llyfr ysgrifennu, ymarfer
exert vt ymegnio, ymdrechu
exertion n ymdrech, ymroddiad
exhale vb anadlu allan
exhaust vt disbyddu, diffygio, gwacáu ▸ n disbyddwr, gwacäwr

exhausted adj lluddedig, wedi ymlâdd
exhaust fumes n nwy gwacáu
exhaustion n gorludded
exhibit vt dangos, arddangos
exhibition n arddangosfa
exile n alltud; alltudiaeth ▸ vt alltudio
exist vi bod, bodoli
existence n bod(olaeth), hanfod; **in existence** mewn bod, ar glawr
exit n allanfa ▸ vb mynd allan, ymadael
exotic adj estron, egsotig
expand vb lledu, ehangu
expansion n ehangiad, ymlediad
expect vb disgwyl
expectation n disgwyliad
expedition n ymgyrch, alldaith
expel vt bwrw allan, diarddel
expenditure n gwariant
expense n traul, cost
expenses npl treuliau
expensive adj drud, costus
experience n profiad ▸ vt profi
experienced adj profiadol
experiment n arbrawf ▸ vi arbrofi
expert n arbenigwr ▸ adj medrus, deheuig
expertise n arbenigaeth
expire vb anadlu allan; darfod, marw
expiry n diwedd, terfyn
explain vt egluro, esbonio
explanation n eglurhad, esboniad
explicit adj eglur, manwl, echblyg
explode vb ffrwydro, chwalu
exploit n camp, gorchest ▸ vt gweithio, gwneud elw o, ymelwa ar

exploitation n ymelwad

explore vt fforio, chwilio

explorer n fforiwr

explosion n ffrwydriad; tanchwa

explosive n ffrwydrydd, ffrwydryn ► adj ffrwydrol

export vt allforio ► n allforyn

exporter n allforiwr

expose vt amlygu, dinoethi

express vt mynegi, datgan ► adj cyflym, clir ► n trên cyflym

expression n mynegiant

expressway n traffordd

exquisite adj odiaeth, rhagorol, coeth

extend vb estyn, ymestyn; ehangu

extension n helaethiad, ehangiad, (ym)estyniad

extensive adj ymestynnol, helaeth

extent n ehangder, maint, hyd, mesur; **to some extent** i raddau

exterior adj allanol ► n tu allan

external adj allanol

extinct adj wedi darfod, diflanedig

extinguish vt diffodd; diddymu, dileu

extra adj ychwanegol ► adv tu hwnt, dros ben ► n peth dros ben, ychwanegiad

extract vt echdynnu, tynnu; dyfynnu, rhinio ► n echdyniad; dyfyniad; rhin, darn

extraordinary adj hynod, anghyffredin

extravagant adj gwastraffus, afradlon

extreme adj i'r eithaf, eithafol ► n eithaf

extremely adv dros ben, gor-

extremist adj eithafol ► n eithafwr

extrovert adj allblyg, alltro ► n alltröedydd, person allblyg

eye n llygad; crau; dolen ► vt llygadu

eyeball n cannwyll y llygad

eyebrow n ael

eyelid n amrant

eyeliner n pensel llinellu

eye shadow n colur llygaid

eyesight n golwg

eyewitness n llygad-dyst

e

299

f

fabric n ffabrig, defnydd

fabulous adj chwedlonol, diarhebol

face n wyneb, wynepryd ▸ vb wynebu

Facebook® vt: I'll Facebook her Mi wna i gysylltu â hi ar Facebook ▸ n Facebook

face cloth n clwtyn ymolchi

face value n arwynebwerth

facilitate vt hwyluso, hyrwyddo

facilities npl cyfleusterau

fact n ffaith, gwirionedd; **as a matter of fact** mewn gwirionedd

factor n ffactor; **prime factor** ffactor cysefin

factory n ffatri

factual adj ffeithiol

faculty n cynneddf; cyfadran

fad n mympwy, chwilen

fade vb diflannu, gwywo; colli ei liw

fag n caledwaith, lludded; gwas bach

fail vi ffaelu, methu, pallu, diffygio; **without fail** yn ddi-ffael

failure n methiant

faint adj llesmeiriol, gwan, llesg ▸ vi llewygu ▸ n llesmair, llewyg

fair¹ n ffair

fair² adj teg, glân; gweddol; golau

fairground n cae ffair

fairly adv yn deg/lân, yn weddol

fair trade n masnach deg

fairy n un o'r tylwyth teg

fairy-tale n stori hud, chwedl werin

faith n ffydd

faithful adj ffyddlon, cywir

faithfully adv yn ffyddlon, yn gywir; **yours faithfully** yr eiddoch yn gywir

fake n ffug ▸ vb ffugio

falcon n hebog, cudyll

fall (pt fell, pp fallen) vi cwympo, syrthio ▸ n cwymp; **fall out** cweryla; **fall through** methu; **fall down** vi syrthio i lawr; **fall for** vt (person) syrthio mewn cariad â; (trick) llyncu; **fall out** vi (quarrel) anghytuno

false adj gau, ffug, ffals, twyllodrus; **false teeth** danedd gosod/dodi

fame n enwogrwydd, clod, bri

familiar adj cynefin, cyfarwydd

family n teulu, tylwyth

famine n newyn

famous adj enwog

fan n gwyntyll; ffan ▸ vt gwyntyllio, chwythu

fanatic n penboethyn, ffanatig

fancy n dychymyg, ffansi, serch
▶ vt dychmygu, ffansïo, serchu;
fancy dress gwisg ffansi
fantastic adj ffantastig, rhyfeddol
fantasy n ffantasi
far adj pell(ennig) ▶ adv ymhell; **as far as** hyd at
farce n ffars
fare n cost, pris; ymborth ▶ vi bod, dod ymlaen, byw
Far East n: **the Far East** y Dwyrain Pell
farewell excl yn iach, ffarwel ▶ n ffarwel; **to bid farewell** canu'n iach
farm n fferm ▶ vt amaethu, ffarmio
farmer n ffarmwr, ffermwr, amaethwr; **Young Farmers' Club** Clwb y Ffermwyr Ifainc
farmhouse n ffermdy
farming n ffermio; **intensive farming** ffermio dwys
farmyard n buarth, clos
fascinate vt hudo, swyno
fascinating adj hudol, swynol
fashion n ffasiwn, arfer, dull ▶ vt llunio, gwneud
fashionable adj ffasiynol
fast¹ vi ymprydio ▶ n ympryd
fast² adj tyn, sownd; buan, cyflym, clau
fasten vb sicrhau, cau, clymu
fast food n bwyd sydyn
fat adj tew, bras ▶ n braster, bloneg
fatal adj angheuol, marwol
fatality n trychineb, marwolaeth
fate n tynged, ffawd ▶ vt tynghedu
father n tad ▶ vt tadogi

Father Christmas n Siôn Corn
father-in-law n tad-yng-nghyfraith
fatigue n lludded, blinder ▶ vt lluddedu, blino
fatty adj seimlyd, brasterog
fault n bai, diffyg, nam; **at fault** ar fai
faulty adj gwallus, diffygiol
favour n ffafr, cymwynas ▶ vt ffafrio; **in favour of** o blaid
favourable adj ffafriol
favourite adj, n ffefryn ▶ adj hoff
fawn¹ n elain ▶ adj llwyd
fawn² vi cynffonna, gwenieithio
fax n ffacs ▶ vt ffacsio
fear n ofn, braw, arswyd ▶ vb ofni, arswydo
fearful adj ofnus, brawychus, arswydus
feasible adj dichonadwy
feast n gwledd, gŵyl ▶ vb gwledda
feat n camp, gorchest
feather n pluen, plufyn ▶ vt pluo, plufio
feature n arwedd, nodwedd
February n Chwefror, Mis Bach
federal adj cynghreiriol, ffederal
fed up adj wedi cael llond bol
fee n ffi
feeble adj gwan, eiddil
feed (pt, pp **fed**) vb porthi, ymborthi, bwydo ▶ n porthiant, ffîd, ymborth; gwledd
feedback n adborth, ymateb ▶ vb adborthi
feel (pt, pp **felt**) vb teimlo
feeling n teimlad, synhwyriad
fell vb cwympo, cymynu ▶ n ffridd, rhos

fellow n cymar; cymrawd ▸ *prefix* cyd-

fellowship n cymdeithas, cyfeillach; cymrodoriaeth

felt n ffelt ▸ vb ffeltio

female adj, n benyw

feminine adj benywaidd, benywol

feminist n ffeminist

fence n clawdd, ffens ▸ vb cau, amgáu

fencing n ffensio, cleddyfaeth

fend vb cadw draw; ymdopi

ferment n eples, cynnwrf ▸ vb eplesu, cynhyrfu

fern n rhedynen, rhedyn

ferocious adj ffyrnig, milain

ferret n ffured ▸ vt ffuredu, chwilota

ferry n fferi ▸ vb cludo dros

fertile adj ffrwythlon, toreithiog

fertilize vb ffrwythloni; gwrteithio

fertilizer n gwrtaith

festival n gŵyl, dydd gŵyl; **singing festival** cymanfa ganu

festive adj llawen, llon

fetch vt cyrchu, hôl, ymofyn, nôl

fête n gŵyl, miri ▸ vi gwledda

feud n cynnen, ffiwd

fever n twymyn

feverish adj â thwymyn

few adj ychydig, prin, anaml

fiancé n darpar-ŵr

fiancée n darpar-wraig

fib n anwiredd, celwydd

fibre n edefyn, ffibr

fibreglass n ffibr gwydrog

fickle adj anwadal, oriog, gwamal

fiction n ffuglen

fiddle n ffidil ▸ vi canu'r ffidl; ffidlan

fidelity n ffyddlondeb, cywirdeb

fidget vt ffwdanu, aflonyddu ▸ n un ffwdanus, un aflonydd

field n cae, maes ▸ vb maesu

field marshal n maeslywydd

fierce adj ffyrnig, milain; tanbaid

fifteen adj, n pymtheg

fifteenth adj pymthegfed

fifth adj, n pumed

fifty adj, n hanner cant, deg a deugain

fig n ffigysen

fight (pt, pp **fought**) vb ymladd, cwffio, brwydro, rhyfela ▸ n ymladdfa, brwydr

fighting n ymladd

figure n ffigur; llun, ffurf ▸ vb cyfrif; llunio; ymddangos; **figure of speech** troad ymadrodd; **figure out** vt deall

file n ffeil, rhathell; rhes ▸ vb ffeilio, rhathu

filing cabinet n cwpwrdd ffeilio

fill vb llenwi ▸ n llenwad, llonaid, gwala; **fill in** vt (hole) llenwi

fillet n llain, ffiled

fillet steak n stêc ffiled

filling n llenwad, mewnyn

film n pilen, caenen; ffilm ▸ vb ffilmio

film star n seren ffilmiau

filter n hidl, hidlydd ▸ vb hidlo, ffiltro

filter tip n hidl difaco

filth n brynti, budreddi, baw

filthy adj brwnt, budr, aflan

fin n adain, asgell, ffin

final adj terfynol, olaf; **semi-final** cynderfynol

finale n ffinale, diweddglo

finally adv o'r diwedd, yn olaf

finance n cyllid ▸ vb cyllido, codi arian

financial adj cyllidol, ariannol

find (pt, pp **found**) vt darganfod ▸ n darganfyddiad; **find out** vb darganfod

fine¹ adj main; mân; gwych; braf

fine² n dirwy ▸ vt dirwyo

finger n bys ▸ vt bysio, bodio; **little finger** bys bach; **third finger** bys y fodrwy; **middle finger** y bys canol

fingernail n ewin

fingerprint n bysbrint, ôl bys

finish vb diweddu, gorffen, cwblhau ▸ n diwedd; gorffeniad

finished adj gorffenedig

Finland n y Ffindir

Finn n Ffiniad

Finnish n (language) Ffinneg ▸ adj Ffinnaidd; (in language) Ffinneg

fir n ffynidwydden

fire n tân ▸ vb tanio, ennyn; **wild fire** tân gwyllt; **fire precautions** rhagofalon tân

firearm n arf-tân

fire brigade n brigâd dân

fire engine n peiriant tân

fire escape n grisiau tân

fire-extinguisher n diffoddydd tân

firefighter n diffoddwr tân

fireman n taniwr, diffoddwr tân

fireplace n lle tân

fire station n gorsaf dân

firewood n coed tân, cynnud

fireworks npl tân gwyllt

firm n cwmni, ffyrm ▸ adj cadarn, diysgog

firmly adv yn gadarn, yn ddiysgog

first adj cyntaf, blaenaf, prif ▸ adv yn gyntaf

first aid n cymorth cyntaf

first class adj dosbarth cyntaf

first floor n llawr cyntaf

first-hand adj o lygad y ffynnon

firstly adv yn gyntaf

first-rate adj campus, ardderchog, rhagorol

fish n pysgodyn, pysgod ▸ vb pysgota; **fish and chips** pysgodyn a sglodion

fisherman n pysgotwr

fish fingers npl sglodion pysgod

fishing n pysgota

fishing boat n cwch pysgota

fishing tackle n offer pysgota

fishmonger n gwerthwr pysgod

fishy adj (inf) amheus; pysgodol

fist n dwrn

fit¹ n llewyg, ffit; mesur

fit² adj addas, cymwys, gweddus; heini ▸ vb ffitio ▸ **fit in** vi (person) ffitio i mewn

fitness n ffitiad ▸ vb ffitio ▸ adj

fitting n ffitiad ▸ vb ffitio ▸ adj priodol, gweddus, addas; **fittings** npl mân daclau, ffitiadau

five adj pum ▸ n pump

fix vb sicrhau, sefydlu, gosod ▸ n cyfyngder, cyfyng-gyngor

fixed n sefydlog

fixture n gosodyn, peniant (byd chwarae)

fizzy adj byrlymog

flag n baner, lluman; fflagen ▸ vb llumanu; llaesu

flake n fflaw, caenen; (snow) pluen (eira)

flamboyant

flamboyant *adj* coegwych
flame *n* fflam ▸ *vi* fflamio, ffaglu
flan *n* fflan
flank *n* ystlys, ochr ▸ *vb* ymylu, ystlysu
flannel *n* gwlanen
flap *n* llabed, fflap ▸ *vb* fflapio
flare *vb* fflêr, fflach; fflerio, fflachio
flash *vb* fflachio ▸ *n* fflach
flashback *n* ôl-fflach
flashlight *n* fflachlamp
flask *n* costrel, fflasg
flat *n* fflat, gwastad; meddalnod ▸ *adj* fflat, gwastad, lleddf ▸ *vb* fflatio
flatten *vb* gwastatáu
flatter *vt* gwenieithio
flaunt *vb* fflawntio, rhodresa
flavour *n* blas, cyflas ▸ *vt* blasu, cyflasu
flavouring *n* cyflasyn
flaw *n* bai, diffyg, nam
flea *n* chwannen
flee (*pt*, *pp* **fled**) *vb* ffoi, cilio
fleece *n* cnu ▸ *vt* cneifio; (*inf*) ysbeilio
fleet *n* llynges, fflyd ▸ *adj* cyflym, buan
fleeting *adj* diflanedig
flesh *n* cig, cnawd; **flesh and blood** cig a gwaed; **flesh and bones** cnawd ac esgyrn
flex *n* fflecs
flexible *adj* hyblyg, ystwyth
flexitime *n* oriau hyblyg
flick *vt* cyffwrdd â blaen chwip, cnithio
flight *n* hediad, ffo; rhes
flight attendant *n* gweinydd awyren

flimsy *adj* tenau, simsan, bregus
flinch *vi* cilio yn ôl, gwingo, llwfrhau
fling (*pt*, *pp* **flung**) *vt* taflu, bwrw, lluchio ▸ *n* tafliad
flint *n* callestr, carreg dân, fflint
flip *vb* cnithio ▸ *n* cnith
flipper *n* asgell
flirt *vb* cellwair caru, fflyrtan ▸ *n* fflyrten, fflyrtyn
float *n* arnofyn, fflôt ▸ *vb* arnofio
flock *n* diadell, praidd ▸ *vi* heidio
flood *n* llif, dilyw, cenllif ▸ *vt* llifo, gorlifo
flooding *n* llifogydd
floodlight *n* llifolau ▸ *vb* llifoleuo
floor *n* llawr ▸ *vt* llorio; **ground floor** daearlawr; **first floor** llawr cyntaf
flop *n* methiant ▸ *vb* ymollwng
flora *n* fflora, planhigion
floral *adj* fflurol
florist *n* tyfwr neu werthwr blodau
flour *n* blawd, can
flourish *vb* blodeuo; ffynnu; ysgwyd ▸ *n* rhwysg; cân cyrn
flow *n* llifo, lliferio ▸ *n* llif, llanw
flower *n* blodeuyn, blodyn ▸ *vi* blodeuo; **flowerpot** pot blodau
flu *n* ffliw, anwydwst
fluctuate *vi* amrywio, anwadalu
fluency *n* huodledd, llithrigrwydd
fluent *adj* llithrig, rhugl
fluff *n* fflwcs, fflwff ▸ *vb* bwnglera, methu
fluid *adj* hylif, llifol ▸ *n* hylif, llifydd
fluke *n* pry'r afu; ffliwc, lwc
fluoride *n* fflworid
flurry *n* cyffro, ffwdan

flush n gwrid; rhuthr dŵr ▸ adj cyfwyneb, gorlawn ▸ vb gwrido, cochi; gorlifo

flute n ffliwt

flutter vb dychlamu, siffrwd ▸ n dychlamiad, siffrwd

fly¹ n gwybedyn, cleren, pryf

fly² (pt **flew**, pp **flown**) vb eheday, ehedfan
▸ **fly away** vi hedfan i ffwrdd

flying adj hedegog, cyflym

flyover n pontffordd, trosffordd

foal n ebol, eboles ▸ vb bwrw ebol; **in foal** cyfebol

foam n ewyn ▸ vi ewynnu, glafoerio

focus n canolbwynt, ffocws ▸ vb canolbwyntio

fog n niwl

foggy adj niwlog

foil vt rhwystro, trechu ▸ n ffoil, ffwyl, dalen

fold n plyg; corlan ▸ vb plygu; corlannu

folder n plygell

folding n plygiant

foliage n dail, deiliant

folk npl pobl, gwerin

folklore n llên gwerin

folk song n cân werin

follow vb canlyn, dilyn

follower n dilynwr, canlynwr

following adj dilynol, canlynol ▸ n dilyniad, canlynwyr

fond adj hoff, annwyl

food n bwyd, ymborth; **tinned food** bwyd tun

food poisoning n gwenwyn bwyd

fool n ffŵl, ynfytyn ▸ vb ynfydu, twyllo

foolish adj ffôl, ynfyd

foot n troed; troedfedd ▸ vb troedio

foot and mouth disease n clwyf y traed a'r genau

football n pêl-droed

footballer n peldroediwr

footbridge n pont gerddded, pompren

foothold n gafael troed, troedle

footie n ffwtbol

footing n sylfaen, safle

footnote n troednodiad

footpath n llwybr troed

footprint n ôl troed

footstep n cam, ôl troed

footwear n troedwisg

(KEYWORD)

for prep **1** (indicating destination, intention, purpose) i; **the train for London** y trên i Lundain; **he left for Rome** ymadawodd i fynd i Rufain; **he went for the paper** aeth i gasglu'r papur; **is this for me?** i mi y mae hwn?; **it's time for lunch** mae'n amser cinio; **what's it for?** i beth y mae'n dda?; **what for?** (why?) pam? (to what end?) i ba ddiben?; **for sale** ar werth; **to pray for peace** gweddïo dros heddwch **2** (on behalf of, representing) dros, ar ran; **the MP for Anglesey** yr Aelod dros Fôn; **to work for sb/sth** gweithio dros rhn/rhth; **I'll ask him for you** gofynnaf iddo ar eich rhan; **A for Apple** A am Afal **3** (because of) o achos, oherwydd, oblegid; **for this reason** am y rheswm hwn; **for fear of being**

forbid

criticized rhag ofn ichi gael eich beirniadu

4 (with regard to) o, o ran; **he is big for his age** mae'n fawr o'i oed; **a gift for languages** dawn o ran ieithoedd

5 (in exchange for): **I sold it for £5** fe'i gwerthais am £5; **to pay 50 pence for a ticket** talu 50 ceiniog am docyn

6 (in favour of) dros, o blaid; **are you for or against us?** a ydych o'n plaid ynteu yn ein herbyn?; **I'm all for it** rwy'n gadarn o blaid y peth; **vote for X** pleidleisiwch dros X

7 (referring to distance) am; **there are roadworks for 5 km** mae yna waith ar y ffordd am 5 km; **we walked for miles** cerddasom filltiroedd

8 (referring to time) am; ers; erbyn; **he was away for 2 years** bu i ffwrdd am 2 flynedd; **she will be away for a month** bydd i ffwrdd am fis; **it hasn't rained for 3 weeks** mae hi heb fwrw glaw ers 3 wythnos; **I have known her for years** rwy'n ei hadnabod ers blynyddoedd; **can you do it for tomorrow?** alli di ei wneud erbyn yfory?

9 (with infinitive clauses): **it would be best for you to leave** byddai'n well ichi ymadael; **there is still time for you to do it** mae amser ar gael o hyd ichi wneud y peth; **for this to be possible ...** er mwyn i hyn fod yn bosibl ...

10 (in spite of): **for all that** er gwaethaf hynny, serch hynny; **for all his work/efforts** er gwaethaf/serch ei holl waith/ymdrechion; **for all his complaints, he's very fond of her** er/serch ei gwynion, mae'n hoff iawn ohoni

▶ conj (since, as) (form) achos, canys, oblegid, oherwydd

forbid (pt **forbad, forbade**, pp **forbidden**) vt gwahardd, gwarafun, gomedd

forbidden adj gwaharddedig

force n grym; trais ▶ vt gorfodi; **centrifugal force** grym allgyrchol; **centripetal force** grym mewngyrchol; **the forces** y lluoedd arfog

forceful adj grymus, egniol

ford n rhyd ▶ vt rhydio

fore adj blaen, blaenaf ▶ adv ymlaen ▶ prefix cyn-, rhag-, blaen-; **to the fore** amlwg, blaenllaw

forearm n elin ▶ vb rhagarfogi

forecast n rhagolygon, rhagolwg ▶ vb rhagddewud, darogan

forefinger n mynegfys

forefront n lle blaen ▶ adj blaen

foreground n blaendir

forehead n talcen

foreign adj estron, tramor; **foreign affairs** materion tramor

foreigner n estron, tramorwr

foreman n fforman

foremost adj blaenaf ▶ adv ym mlaenaf

forensic adj fforensig

forerunner n rhagredegydd

foresee vt rhagweld, rhagwybod

foreseeable adj rhagweladwy

forest n coedwig, fforest ▸ vt coedwigo, fforestu

forestry n coedwigaeth; **forestry commission** Comisiwn Coedwigaeth

forever adv am byth

foreword n rhagair, rhagymadrodd

forfeit n fforffed ▸ vt fforffedu, colli

forge n gefail ▸ vb gofannu; ffugio

forget (pt **forgot**, pp **forgotten**) vt anghofio

forgetful adj anghofus

forgive vt maddau

fork n fforch, fforc ▸ vb fforchio

forlorn adj amddifad, truan, anobeithiol

form n ffurf; mainc; fflurflen ▸ vb ffurfio; **application form** ffurflen gais

formal adj ffurfiol, defodol

former adj blaenaf, blaenorol

formerly adv gynt, yn flaenorol

formidable adj arswydus, ofnadwy, grymus

formula n rheol, fformwla

fort n caer

forthcoming adj ar ddod, gerllaw

fortify vt cadarnhau, cryfhau

fortnight n pythefnos

fortnightly adj, adv bob pythefnos

fortress n amddiffynfa, caer

fortunate adj ffodus, ffortunus

fortunately adv yn ffodus, yn lwcus

fortune n ffawd; ffortun

fortune teller n un sy'n dweud ffortun

forty adj, n deugain

forum n fforwm

forward n blaenwr ▸ adj eofn, hy; blaen ▸ adv ymlaen ▸ vb anfon ymlaen; hwyluso, hyrwyddo; **inside forward** mewnwr; **wing forward** blaenasgellwr

forward slash n blaenslaes

fossil n ffosil ▸ adj ffosilaidd

foster vt magu, meithrin, coleddu

foster-child n plentyn maeth

foul adj aflan; annheg; afiach ▸ n ffowl(en) ▸ vb ffowlio, llychwino; **foul play** anfadwaith

found vt dechrau, sylfaenu, sefydlu

foundation n sail, sylfaen

founder vb ymddryllio, suddo ▸ n sylfaenydd

fountain n ffynnon, ffynhonnell

fountain pen n pin llenwi

four adj, n pedwar; pedair

fourteen adj, n pedwar (pedair) ar ddeg

fourteenth adj pedwerydd (pedwaredd) ar ddeg

fourth adj pedwerydd; pedwaredd

four-wheel drive n (car) gyriant pedair-olwyn

fowl n dofedn, ffowlyn, ffowl

fox n cadno, llwynog

foyer n cyntedd

fraction n ffracsiwn; **improper fraction** ffracsiwn pendrwm; **vulgar fraction** ffracsiwn cyffredin; **proper fraction** ffracsiwn bondrwm

fracture n toriad, drylliad ▸ vt torri, dryllio

fragile adj brau, bregus

fragment n dryll, darn

fragrance n perarogl, persawr

frail adj brau, bregus, gwan, eiddil

307

frame

frame n ffrâm; agwedd ▸ vt fframio, llunio; **frame of mind** agwedd meddwl
framework n fframwaith
France n Ffrainc
franchise n etholfraint ▸ vb etholfreinio
frank adj didwyll, agored
frantic adj cyffrous, gwallgof
fraud n twyll, hoced
fraught adj llwythog, llawn
fray n ymryson, ymgiprys, ffrae ▸ vb treulio
freak n mympwy, peth od
freckle n brych, brychni
free adj rhydd; hael; di-dâl, rhad ▸ vb rhyddhau
freedom n rhyddid, rhyddfraint
free kick n cic rydd
freelance adj llawrydd ▸ adv n llawrydd; **a freelance translator** cyfieithydd llawrydd
freely adv yn rhydd, yn hael
free-range adj maes
free trade n masnach rydd
freeway n trafforrdd
free will n ewyllys rydd, o'i fodd
freeze (pt **froze**, pp **frozen**) vb rhewi, fferru
freezer n rhewgist, rhewgell
freezing adj rhewllyd
freezing point n rhewbwynt
freight n llwyth llong ▸ vt llwytho llong
French n (language) Ffrangeg ▸ adj Ffrengig; (in language) Ffrangeg
French beans npl ffa Ffrengig
Frenchman n Ffrancwr
Frenchwoman n Ffrances
frenzy n gorffwylltra, cynddaredd

frequency n amlder, mynychder
frequent adj mynych, aml ▸ vt mynychu
frequently adv yn fynych, yn aml
fresh adj ffres, crai, cri, croyw, newydd
freshen vb ffresáu, ireiddio
fret vb sorri, poeni ▸ n soriant, trallod; ffret
friction n ffrithiant, ymrafael
Friday n dydd Gwener
fridge n oergell, rhewadur
fried adj ffriedig
friend n cyfaill, ffrind
friendly adj cyfeillgar
friendship n cyfeillgarwch
fright n dychryn, ofn, braw
frighten vb dychrynu, brawychu, codi ofn ar
frightened adj ofnus
frightening adj dychrynllyd
frightful adj dychrynllyd, brawychus
frill n ffril
fringe n ymyl, rhidens ▸ vb ymylu; **fringe benefits** cilfanteision
fritter vt afradu, ofera, gwastraffu
frivolous adj gwamal; disylwedd
fro adv: **to and fro** yn ôl ac ymlaen
frock n ffrog
frog n llyffant (melyn), broga

┌─────────────┐
│ **KEYWORD** │
└─────────────┘

from prep 1 (indicating starting place, origin etc) o; **where do you come from? where are you from?** un o ble ydych chi?, o ble rydych chi'n dod?; **where has he come from?** o ble y daeth ef?; **from London to Cardiff** o Lundain i Gaerdydd; **to**

escape from sb/sth dianc rhag
rhn/rhth; **a letter/telephone call
from my sister** llythyr/galwad ffôn
gan fy chwaer; **to drink from the
bottle** yfed o'r botel; **tell him from
me that ...** dywed wrtho fy mod
i'n dweud ...

2 (indicating time) o; **from one
o'clock to** or **until two** o un
o'r gloch tan ddau o'r gloch; **from
January (on)** o fis Ionawr (ymlaen)

3 (indicating distance) o; **the hotel
is one kilometre from the beach**
mae'r gwesty un cilometr o'r
traeth

4 (indicating price, number etc) o;
prices range from £10 to £50 mae'r
prisiau'n amrywio o £10 i £50; **the
interest rate was increased from
9% to 10%** codwyd y gyfradd log
o 9% i 10%

5 (indicating difference): **he can't tell
red from green** ni all wahaniaethu
rhwng coch a gwyrdd; **to be
different from sb/sth** bod yn
wahanol i rn/rhth

6 (because of, on the basis of): **from
what he says** o'r hyn y mae'n ei
ddweud, ar sail yr hyn y mae'n ei
ddweud; **weak from hunger** gwan
oherwydd eisiau bwyd

front n wyneb, blaen, ffrynt, talcen
▶ vb wynebu ▶ adj blaen; **front
door** drws ffrynt; **front page**
tudalen flaen
frontier n ffin, terfyn, goror
frost n rhew
frostbite n ewinrhew
frosty adj rhewllyd

froth n ewyn ▶ vi ewynnu
frown vi cuchio, gwgu ▶ n cuwch,
gwg
frozen adj wedi rhewi
fruit n ffrwyth, ffrwythau; **fruit
juice** sudd ffrwyth; **fruit salad**
salad ffrwythau
fruit machine n peiriant ffrwythau
frustrate vt rhwystro, llesteirio
frustrated adj rhwystredig
fry (pt, pp **fried**) vb ffrio ▶ n sil,
silod; **small fry** (inf) pobl ddibwys
frying-pan n ffrimpan, padell ffrio
fudge n cyffug
fuel n tanwydd; cynnud; **fuel cell**
cynudydd
fulfil vt cyflawni
full adj llawn, cyflawn ▶ n llonaid
full stop n atalnod llawn
full-time adj amser llawn
fully adv yn gyfan gwbl, yn gyflawn,
yn hollol
fumble vb palfalu, bwnglera
fume n tarth, mwg; llid ▶ vb mygu;
llidio, sorri
fumes n mwg
fun n difyrrwch, digrifwch, hwyl
function n swydd, swyddogaeth;
(mathematics) ffwythiant
fund n cronfa, trysorfa
fundamental adj sylfaenol
funds npl arian
funeral n angladd, cynhebrwng,
claddedigaeth
funfair n ffair bleser
fungus n ffwng
funnel n twmffat, twndis
funny adj digrif, ysmala; rhyfedd,
hynod
fur n blew, ffwr

fur coat n cot ffwr
furious adj cynddeiriog, ffyrnig
furnish vt dodrefnu, rhoddi
furnishings npl dodrefn
furniture n dodrefn, celfi
furry adj blewog
further adj pellach ▸ adv
  ymhellach ▸ vt hyrwyddo;
  further education addysg bellach
fury n cynddaredd, ffyrnigrwydd
fuse n ffiws ▸ vb ffiwsio
fuss n ffwdan, helynt, stŵr ▸ vb
  ffwdanu
fussy adj ffwdanus
future adj, n dyfodol
fuzzy adj blewog, aneglur

g

gadget n dyfais
Gaelic n (language) Gaeleg ▸ adj
  Gaelaidd
gag n smaldod; safnglo ▸ vb
  smalio; safngloi, cau ceg
gain vb ennill, elwa ▸ n ennill,
  elw, budd
gale n gwynt cryf; tymestl
gallery n oriel, llofft
gallon n galwyn
gallop n carlam ▸ vb carlamu
gamble vb hapchwarae, gamblo
  ▸ n gambl
gambling n gamblo
game n gêm, chwarae, camp;
  helwriaeth ▸ adj dewr, glew
gamer n person sy'n chwarae
  gêmau cyfrifiadurol
games console n consol gêmau
game show n sioe gêm, sioe
  gêmau
gammon n gamwn
gang n mintai, haid, gang

gangster n troseddwr

gap n bwlch, adwy

gape vi rhythu, syllu ▸ n rhythiad

gap year n blwyddyn bwlch

garage n modurdy, garej

garbage n ysbwriel, sothach

garden n gardd ▸ vi garddio

gardener n garddwr

gardening n garddwriaeth

garlic n garlleg

garment n dilledyn, gwisg

garnish vt addurno, harddu

gas n nwy ▸ vb gwenwyno â nwy; **gas cooker** ffwrn nwy; **gas fire** tân nwy; **gas ring** cylch nwy

gasket n gasged

gasp vb ebychu, anadlu'n drwm

gate n porth, llidiart, clwyd, gât, iet

gateway n mynedfa

gather vb casglu, cynnull, crynhoi, hel

gathering n casgliad, cynulliad

gauge n mesur; lled ▸ vt mesur

gay adj hoyw

gaze vi syllu, tremio ▸ n golwg, trem

GCSE n abbr TGAU = Tystysgrif Gyffredinol Addysg Uwchradd

gear n gêr, offer, taclau ▸ vb taclu, harneisio

gearbox n gerbocs

gear lever n lifer gêr

gel n gel

gem n glain, gem, tlws

Gemini n yr Efeilliaid

gender n cenedl

gene n genyn

general adj cyffredin, cyffredinol ▸ n cadfridog

general election n etholiad cyffredinol

generalize vb cyffredinoli

general knowledge n gwybodaeth gyffredinol

generally adv yn gyffredinol

general practitioner n meddyg teulu

generate vt cenhedlu, cynhyrchu, generadu

generation n cenhedliad; cenhedlaeth, to

generator n cynhyrchydd; generadur

generosity n haelioni

generous adj hael, haelionus, haelfrydig

genetic adj genetig

genetically modified adj: **genetically modified food** bwyd a addaswyd yn enynnol

genetics n geneteg

Geneva n Genefa

genitals npl organau cenhedlu

genius n athrylith

gentle adj bonheddig; mwyn, tyner

gentleman n gŵr bonheddig

gently adv yn dyner, addfwyn; gan bwyll

gents npl toiledau dynion

genuine adj dilys, diffuant

geography n daearyddiaeth

geology n daeareg

geometry n geometreg

gerbil n gerbil

germ n hedyn, eginyn, germ

German adj Almaenaidd ▸ n Almaenwr; (language) Almaeneg; **German measles** y frech Almeinig

Germany

Germany n yr Almaen

gesture n ystum, arwydd, mosiwn

(KEYWORD)

get (pt, pp **got**, (US) pp **gotten**) vi
1 (become, be) dod, mynd; **to get
old/tired** mynd yn hen/flinedig,
heneiddio/blino; **to get drunk**
meddwi; **to get dirty** mynd yn
frwnt, baeddu; **to get married**
priodi; **when do I get paid?** pa bryd
y caf fy nhalu?; **it's getting late**
mae'n mynd yn hwyr
2 (go): **to get to/from** mynd i/o; **to
get home** cyrraedd adref/mynd
adref; **how did you get here?** sut
cyrhaeddest ti yma?, sut dest
ti yma?
3 (begin) dechrau; **to get to know
sb** dod i adnabod rhn; **I'm getting
to like him** rwy'n dechrau dod i'w
hoffi; **let's get going** or **started**
gadewch inni ddechrau
4 (modal aux vb): **you've got to do it**
rhaid ichi ei wneud; **I've got to tell
the police** rhaid imi ddweud wrth
yr heddlu
▸ vt **1**: **to get sth done** (do) cyflawni
rhth, gwneud rhth; **to get sth/
sb ready** paratoi rhth/rhn; **to get
one's hair cut** cael torri'ch gwallt;
to get the car going or **to go**
cychwyn y car; **to get sb to do sth**
gofyn i rn wneud rhth, cael gan rn
wneud rhth
2 (obtain: money, permission, results)
cael, sicrhau; (buy) prynu; (find:
job, flat) dod o hyd i; (fetch: person,
doctor, object) nôl; **to get sth**

for sb cael rhth i rn; **get me Mr
Jones, please** (on phone) rhowch
fi drwodd i Mr Jones, os gwelwch
yn dda; **can I get you a drink?** ga i
gynnig diod ichi?
3 (receive: present, letter) cael,
derbyn; **what did you get for your
birthday?** beth gest ti ar dy ben-
blwydd?; **how much did you get
for the painting?** faint gawsoch
chi am y darlun?
4 (catch) dal; (hit: target etc) taro;
to get sb by the arm/throat dal
rhn gerfydd y fraich/y gwddf; **get
him!** daliwch ef!; **the bullet got
him in the leg** trawodd y bwled ef
yn y goes
5 (take, move): **to get sth to sb**
cael rhth i rn, mynd â rhth i rn; **do
you think we'll get it through the
door?** ydych chi'n credu y cawn ni
ef trwy'r drws?
6 (catch, take: plane, bus etc) dal;
**where do I get the train for
Birmingham?** ble mae dyn yn dal y
trên i Birmingham?
7 (understand) deall; (hear) clywed;
I've got it! rwy'n deall!, mi wn i!; **I
don't get your meaning** dwy ddim
yn eich deall; **I didn't get your
name** chlywes i mo'ch enw
8 (have, possess): **to have got** bod
gennych rth; **how many have you
got?** faint sydd gennych?
9 (illness) bod arnoch rth; **I've got
a cold** mae arnaf i annwyd; **she
got pneumonia and died** cafodd
niwmonia a bu farw
▸ **get away** vi mynd i ffwrdd;
(escape) dianc

▶ **get away with** vt fus (crime etc) cael maddau rhth

▶ **get back** vi (return) dychwelyd; vt adennill, adfer; **when do we get back?** pryd byddwn yn cyrraedd yn ôl?

▶ **get in** vi dod i mewn, mynd i mewn; (arrive home) cyrraedd adref; (train) cyrraedd

▶ **get into** vt fus mynd i mewn i; (car, train etc) mynd i mewn i; (clothes) gwisgo, gwisgo amdanoch; **to get into bed** mynd i'r gwely; **to get into a rage** cynddeiriogi, gwylltio

▶ **get off** vi (from train etc) disgyn; (depart: person, car) ymadael

▶ vt (remove: clothes, stain) tynnu, codi

▶ vt fus (train, bus) disgyn, dod i lawr [oddi ar rth]; **where do I get off?** ble dylwn i ddisgyn?

▶ **get on** vi (at exam etc) mynd ati; (agree) **to get on (with)** dod ymlaen (gyda); **how are you getting on?** sut mae'n mynd?

▶ vt fus dringo, esgyn; (horse) mynd ar gefn

▶ **get out** vi ymadael; (of vehicle) dod allan

▶ vt tynnu

▶ **get out of** vt fus dod allan [o rth], dianc; (duty etc) osgoi

▶ **get over** vt fus (illness) gwella [ar ôl rhth]

▶ **get through** vi (Tel) mynd trwodd; **to get through to sb** egluro/esbonio rhth i rn

▶ **get together** vi: **you must get together** (meet) rhaid ichi ddod at eich gilydd

▶ **get up** vi (rise) codi

▶ vt fus codi

Ghana n Ghana

ghastly adj erchyll, gwelw

ghost n ysbryd, drychiolaeth, bwgan

giant n cawr ▶ adj cawraidd

gift n rhodd, dawn, anrheg, gwobr

gifted adj dawnus, talentog

gig n (inf, concert) gig

gigantic adj cawraidd, dirfawr, anferth

giggle vb lledchwerthin, giglan

gimmick n gimig

gin n jin; hoenyn

ginger n sinsir

gipsy n sipsi

giraffe n siráff

girl n merch, geneth, hogen

girlfriend n cariadferch, anwylyd

gist n ergyd, sylwedd

give (pt gave, pp given) vb rhoddi, rhoi; **give back** vt rhoi nôl; **give in** vi ildio; **give out** vt dosbarthu; **give up** vb rhoi'r gorau i

glacier n rhewlif, glasier

glad adj llawen, llon, balch

gladly adv yn llawen, â phleser

glamorous adj swynol, cyfareddol, hudol

glamour n swyn, cyfaredd, hud

glance vb ciledrych, tremio ▶ n cipolwg, trem, cip

gland n chwarren, gland

glare vb disgleirio; rhythu ▶ n disgleirdeb, tanbeidrwydd

glass n gwydr; gwydraid

▶ **glasses** npl gwydrau, sbectol

glaze

glaze *vt* gwydro; sgleinio ▸ *n* sglein, gwydredd

gleam *n* pelydryn, llewyrch ▸ *vi* pelydru, llewyrchu

glen *n* glyn, cwm, dyffryn

glide *vi* llithro, llifo ▸ *n* llithr, llithrad

glimmer *vi* llewyrchu'n wan ▸ *n* llewyrchyn, llygedyn

glimpse *n* trem, cipolwg

glint *vb* fflachio ▸ *n* fflach, llewyrch

glisten *vi* disgleirio

glitter *vi* tywynnu, pelydru ▸ *n* pelydriad

gloat *vb* llawenhau

global *adj* hollfydol, cyffredinol

globalization *n* globaleiddio

global warming *n* cynhesu byd-eang

globe *n* pêl, pelen

gloom *n* caddug, prudd-der, tywyllwch

gloomy *adj* prudd, digalon, tywyll

glorious *adj* gogoneddus

glory *n* gogoniant ▸ *vi* ymffrostio, gorfoleddu

gloss *n* sglein; glòs

glossary *n* geirfa

glossy *adj* llathraidd

glove *n* maneg

glow *vi* twymo, gwrido ▸ *n* gwres, gwrid

glue *n* glud ▸ *vt* gludio, asio

GM *abbr*: **GM food** bwyd a addaswyd yn enynnol

gnaw *vb* cnoi, cnewian

go (*pt* **went**, *pp* **gone**) *vi* mynd ▸ *n* tro; **go after** *vt* dilyn; **go ahead** *vi* mynd ymlaen; **go away** *vi*

mynd i ffwrdd; **go back** *vi* mynd yn ôl; **go by** *vi* mynd heibio; **go down** *vi* mynd i lawr; *(decrease)* disgyn; **go for** *vt* mynd am; **go in** *vi* mynd i mewn; **go off** *vi* *(depart)* mynd i ffwrdd; **go on** *vi* *(happen)* digwydd; **to go on doing sth** dal i wneud rhth; **go out** *vi* mynd allan; **go past** *vi* mynd heibio ▸ *vt* mynd heibio i; **go round** *vi* mynd o gwmpas; **go through** *vi* mynd trwodd ▸ *vt* mynd trwy; **go up** *vi* *(ascend)* mynd i fyny; *(increase)* codi; **go with** *vt* *(match)* cyd-fynd â

goal *n* gôl, nod

goalkeeper *n* gôl-geidwad, golwr

goat *n* gafr

god *n* duw; **God** Duw

godchild *n* mab bedydd, merch fedydd

goddaughter *n* merch fedydd

goddess *n* duwies

godfather *n* tad bedydd

godmother *adj* mam fedydd

godson *n* mab bedydd

goggles *npl* gwydrau

gold *n* aur ▸ *adj* aur, euraid

golden *adj* euraid

goldfish *npl* eurbysg, pysgod aur

golf *n* golff; **golf links** maes golff

golf course *n* maes golffio

golfer *n* golffwr

gong *n* gong, cloch fwyd

good *adj* da, daionus; cryn ▸ *n* da, daioni, lles; **good morning** bore da; **good afternoon** prynhawn da; **good evening** noswaith dda; **good night** nos da; **good enough** digon da; **no good** dim gwerth, da i

ddim; **Good Friday** Dydd Gwener y
Groglith; **good humour** natur dda
good-bye *excl*, n da boch chi, yn
iach!, ffarwel
Good Friday n Dydd Gwener y
Groglith
good-looking *adj* golygus
good-natured *adj* hynaws,
rhadlon
goodness n daioni
goods *npl* nwyddau, eiddo
goodwill n ewyllys da; braint
(masnachol)
google *vb* gwglo
goose n gŵydd
gooseberry n eirinen Fair,
gwsbersen
gorge n hafn, ceunant ▶ *vb* safnio,
traflyncu
gorgeous *adj* ysblennydd, gwych
gorilla n gorila
gospel n efengyl
gossip n clec, clonc, clebryn,
clebran ▶ *vb* clebran, clecian, hel
straeon
govern *vb* llywodraethu
government n llywodraeth
governor n llywodraethwr
gown n gŵn
GP n abbr meddyg teulu
grab *vb* crafangu, cipio ▶ n gwanc,
crap
grace n gras, rhad; gosgeiddrwydd
▶ *vt* harddu, prydferthu
graceful *adj* graslon, rhadlon;
gosgeiddig, lluniaidd
gracious *adj* graslon, grasol,
rhadlon, hynaws
grade n gradd, safon ▶ *vb* graddio
gradient n graddiant

gradual *adj* graddol
gradually *adv* yn raddol
graduate *vb* graddio, graddoli ▶ n
gŵr gradd, graddedig
graduation n graddedigaeth,
graddnod
graffiti n graffiti
graft n impyn, hunan-les ▶ *vt*
impio, grafftio
grain n grawn, gronyn; mymryn;
graen
gram n gram
grammar n gramadeg
grammar school n ysgol ramadeg
grammatical *adj* gramadegol
gramme n gram
grand *adj* mawreddog, crand;
prif, uchel
grandchild n ŵyr, wyres
granddad (*inf*) n taid, tad-cu
granddaughter n wyres
grandfather n taid, tad-cu
grandma (*inf*) n nain, mam-gu
grandmother n nain, mam-gu
grandpa (*inf*) n taid, tad-cu
grandparents n taid a nain, tad-cu
a mam-gu
grandson n ŵyr
granite n gwenithfaen, ithfaen
granny (*inf*) n nain, mam-gu
grant *vt* rhoddi, caniatáu ▶ n
rhodd, grant; **to take for granted**
cymryd yn ganiataol
grapefruit n grawnffrwyth
graph n graff
graphic *adj* graffig; byw
graphics *npl* graffigwaith, graffeg
grasp *vb* gafael; amgyffred ▶ n
gafael; amgyffrediad
grass n glaswellt, porfa

315

g

grasshopper n ceiliog y rhedyn, sioncyn y gwair

grate n grat ▸ vb rhygnu, crafellu; merwino

grateful adj diolchgar; dymunol

grater n grater, crafellydd

gratitude n diolchgarwch

grave[1] adj dirifol, dwys

grave[2] n bedd, beddrod

gravel n graean, gro, grafel

gravestone n beddfaen, carreg fedd

graveyard n mynwent

gravity n disgyrchiant; pwysigrwydd; **centre of gravity** craidd disgyrchiant

gravy n grefi

graze vb pori, crafu, rhwbio

grease n saim, iraid ▸ vt iro, seimio

greasy adj seimllyd, ireidlyd

great adj mawr; **a great many** llawer iawn

Great Britain n Prydain Fawr

great grandfather n hen daid, hen-dad-cu

greatly adv yn fawr

Greece n Groeg

greed n trachwant, gwanc

greedy adj barus, trachwantus, gwancus

Greek n (language) Groeg; Groegwr ▸ adj Groegaidd

green adj gwyrdd, glas, ir ▸ vb glasu

greengrocer n grîngroser, gwerthwr llysiau

greengrocer's n siop ffrwythau a llysiau

greenhouse n tŷ gwydr

greenhouse gas n nwy tŷ gwydr

Greenland n Yr Ynys Las

greet vt annerch, cyfarch

greeting n cyfarchiad

greetings card n cerdyn cyfarch

grey adj llwyd

greyhound n milgi

grid n grid, alch; **grid reference** cyfeirnod grid

grief n galar

grievance n cwyn

grieve vb galaru

grill n gril, gridyll ▸ vb grilio, gridyllu; **mixed grill** gril cymysg

grille n gril, dellt

grim adj sarrug, milain, difrifol

grin vb lledwenu ▸ n gwên

grind (pt, pp **ground**) vb (corn etc) malu

grip vb gafael, gwasgu ▸ n gafael, crap

grit n grit; pybyrwch

groan vi, n griddfan

grocer n groser

groceries npl nwyddau

grocer's n siop groser

groin n cesail morddwyd, gwerddyr

groom n priodfab; gwastrawd ▸ vb trwsio

groove n rhigol, rhych ▸ vt rhigoli, rhychu

grope vi ymbalfalu

gross n gros; crynswth ▸ adj bras, aflednais; **gross profit** elw gros

ground n llawr, daear, tir; sail; gwaelod ▸ vt daearu, llorio

ground floor n daearlawr

groundwork n sylfaen, sail

group n grŵp ▸ vt grwpio; **discussion group** cylch trafod

grouse n grugiar ▸ vb grwgnach

grovel vi ymgreinio

grow (pt **grew**, pp **grown**) vb tyfu, prifio, cynyddu, codi; **grow up** vi tyfu i fyny, tyfu lan

growl vi chwyrnu

grown-up n rhywun mewn oed, oedolyn

growth n twf, tyfiant, cynnydd

grub n pryf, cynrhonyn; (inf) bwyd

grubby adj budr, brwnt

grudge vt gwarafun, grwgnach ▸ n dig

gruesome adj erchyll, ffiaidd

grumble vi grwgnach, tuchan

grumpy adj sarrug, diserch

grunt vi rhochian ▸ n rhoch

guarantee n gwarant, ernes ▸ vt gwarantu, mechnïo

guard n gard, gwarchodydd; sgrin ▸ vb gwarchod

guardian n gwarcheidwad

guess vb dyfalu, dyfeisio ▸ n amcan

guest n gwestai, gŵr/gwraig (g)wadd

guesthouse n gwesty

guidance n cyfarwyddyd

guide n arweinydd ▸ vt arwain, cyfarwyddo

guide book n teithlyfr

guide-dog n arweingi

guide-lines npl canllawiau

guild n urdd

guilt n euogrwydd, bai

guilty adj euog

guinea pig n mochyn cwta

guitar n gitâr

guitarist n gitarydd

gulf n gwlff, geneufor; gagendor

gull n gwylan

gulp vt llwncian, traflyncu ▸ n llawc, traflwnc

gum n gwm, glud ▸ vt gymio, gludio

gun n gwn, dryll

gunpoint n: **at gunpoint** o flaen gwn

gunpowder n powdr gwn

gunshot n ergyd gwn

gush vb ffrydio, llifeirio ▸ n ffrwd, hyrddwynt

gust n chwythwm

gut n perfeddyn, coluddyn ▸ vt diberfeddu; difrodi, ysbeilio

gutter n ffos, cwter, cafn

guy n (inf, man) boi

gym n campfa

gymnasium n gymnasiwm, campfa

gymnast n mabolgampwr

gymnastics n gymnasteg

gynaecologist n gynaecolegydd

gypsy n sipsi

g

h

haberdashery *n* dilladach, siop ddillad
habit *n* arferiad; anian; gwisg ▸ *vt* gwisgo, dilladu
habitat *n* cartref, cynefin
habitual *adj* arferol, cyson
hack *vb* hacio, torri ▸ *n* hac
hacker *n* (*Comput*) haciwr
haddock *n* corbenfras, hadog
haemorrhage *n* gwaedlif
haemorrhoids *npl* clwyf y marchogion
haggle *vi* bargeinio'n daer
hail¹ *n* cenllysg, cesair ▸ *vb* bwrw cesair
hail² *vb* cyfarch, galw
hair *n* gwallt, blew, rhawn; **hair's breadth** trwch y blewyn; **hair splitting** hollti blew
hairbrush *n* brws gwallt
haircut *n* triniaeth gwallt, toriad, crop
hairdo *n* steil gwallt

hairdresser *n* triniwr gwallt
hairdresser's *n* siop trin gwallt
hair dryer *n* sychwr gwallt
hair gel *n* jel gwallt
hair spray *n* chwistrelliad gwallt
hairstyle *n* steil gwallt
hairy *adj* blewog
hake *n* cegddu
half *n* hanner
half-brother *n* hanner brawd
half fare *n* hanner pris
half-hearted *adj* diawydd, llugoer
half-hour *n* hanner awr
half-price *adj* hanner pris
half-sister *n* hanner chwaer
half term *n* (*school*) hanner tymor
half-time *n* hanner amser
halfway *adv*: **halfway (to)** hanner ffordd (i)
hall *n* llys, neuadd, plas; cyntedd
hallmark *n* dilysnod
hallo *excl* helô
Halloween *n* nos Galangaeaf
Hallowe'en *n* Calan Gaeaf
hallucination *n* geuddrych, rhithwelediad
halo *n* corongylch, halo, lleugylch
halt *vb* sefyll ▸ *n* safiad; gorsaf, arosfa
halve *vt* haneru
ham *n* morddwyd, ham
hamburger *n* hambyrgyr
hamlet *n* pentref
hammer *n* morthwyl ▸ *vb* morthwylio
hammock *n* hamog, gwely crog
hamper *vt* rhwystro, llesteirio
hamster *n* bochdew
hamstring *n* llinyn y gar

hand n llaw; (of clock) bys ▸ vt estyn, trosglwyddo; **to be on hand** bod with law

handbag n bag llaw

handbook n llawlyfr

handbrake n brec llaw

handcuffs n gefynnau

handful n dyrnaid, llond llaw

handicap n rhwystr, llestair, anfantais

handkerchief n cadach poced, hances, macyn, neisied

handle n carn, coes, troed, dolen, clust, dwrn ▸ vt trin, trafod; **to fly off the handle** colli tymer

handlebars npl cyrn

handmade adj wedi ei wneud â llaw

hands-free adj heb afael; **hands-free kit** teclyn heb afael

handsome adj golygus, hardd

handwriting n llawysgrifen

handy adj hylaw, deheuig, cyfleus

hang (pt, pp **hung**) vb crogi, hongian; **hang around** vi loetran; **hang on** vi dal; **hang up** vt rhoi ar y hoel

hanger n cambren

hang-gliding vb barcuta

hangover n blinder ddoe, pen mawr

happen vi digwydd

happily adv yn hapus

happiness n dedwyddwch, hapusrwydd

happy adj dedwydd, hapus

harass vt poeni, blino

harassment n poen, blinder

harbour n porthladd, harbwr ▸ vb llochesu

hard adj caled, anodd; **hard of hearing** trwm ei glyw; **to be hard done by** cael cam; **hard headed** hirben

hardboard n caledfwrdd

hard disk n (Comput) disgen galed, disg caled

harden vb caledu

hardly adv: **she hardly speaks English** prin ei bod hi'n siarad Saesneg; **hardly anyone came** ni ddaeth braidd neb

hardship n caledi

hard shoulder n llain galed

hard-up adj (inf) prin o arian

hardware n nwyddau metel

hard-working adj gweithgar, diwyd

hardy adj caled, gwydn

hare n ysgyfarnog, ceinach

harm n niwed, drwg ▸ vt niweidio

harmful adj niweidiol

harmless adj diniwed, diddrwg

harmony n harmoni, cynghanedd

harness n harnais, gêr ▸ vt harneisio

harp n telyn ▸ vi canu'r delyn

harsh adj garw, gerwin, aflafar

harvest n cynhaeaf ▸ vt cynaeafu

hassle n (inf) helynt, trafferth

haste n brys, hast ▸ vi brysio, prysuro

hasten vb brysio, prysuro, hastu

hastily adv yn frysiog

hasty adj brysiog, byrbwyll

hat n het

hatch¹ vb deor, gori ▸ n deoriad

hatch² n gorddrws, rhagddor, dôr

hatchback

hatchback n car cefn codi
hate vt casáu ▸ n cas, casineb
hatred n cas, casineb
haul vb tynnu, llusgo ▸ n dalfa
haunt vt mynychu; trwblu,
  aflonyddu ▸ n cynefin, cyrchfa
haunted adj: **a haunted house**
  tŷ â bwgan

(KEYWORD)

have (pt, pp **had**) aux vb 1 bod wedi
  gwneud rhth; **to have eaten/slept**
  bod wedi bwyta/cysgu; **to have
  arrived/gone** bod wedi cyrraedd/
  mynd; **having finished** or **when
  he had finished, he left** ar ôl iddo
  orffen, ymadawodd; **we'd already
  eaten** roedden ni wedi bwyta
  eisoes
  2 (in tag questions): **you've done
  it, haven't you?** rydych chi wedi'i
  wneud, on'd ydych?
  ▸ modal aux vb (be obliged): **to have
  (got) to do sth** gorfod gwneud
  rhth; **she has (got) to do it** rhaid
  iddi ei wneud; **you haven't to
  tell her** rhaid ichi beidio â dweud
  wrthi; **do you have to book?** oes
  rhaid archebu lle?
  ▸ vt 1 (possess) bod gennych rth; **he
  has (got) blue eyes/dark hair** mae
  ganddo lygaid glas/wallt brown
  2 (referring to meals etc): **to have
  breakfast** bwyta brecwast;
  to have dinner/lunch bwyta
  cinio, ciniawa; **to have a drink**
  cymryd diod, yfed diod; **to have a
  cigarette** cymryd sigarét, ysmygu
  sigarét
  3 (receive): cael, derbyn; (obtain)

sicrhau; **may I have your address?**
  a ga i ch cyfeiriad?; **you can have
  it for £5** fe'i cewch am £5; **I must
  have it for tomorrow** rhaid imi
  ei gael at yfory; **to have a baby**
  esgor ar blentyn, cael plentyn,
  geni plentyn
  4 (maintain, allow) **I won't have it!**
  wnaiff hyn mo'r tro!; **we can't have
  that** allwn ni ddim caniatáu hyn
  5 (by sb else): **to have sth done** cael
  gwneud rhth; **to have one's hair
  cut** cael torri'ch gwallt; **to have sb
  do sth** cael gan rn wneud rhth
  6 (experience, suffer) bod â rhth
  arnoch; **to have a cold/flu** bod
  ag annwyd/ffliw arnoch; **to have
  an operation** cael llawdriniaeth;
  she had her bag stolen cafodd
  ddwyn ei bag
  7 (+noun): **to have a swim/walk**
  nofio/mynd am dro; **to have a
  bath/shower** cael bath/cawod;
  let's have a look gadewch inni
  weld; **to have a meeting** cyfarfod,
  cynnal cyfarfod; **to have a party**
  cynnal parti; **let me have a try**
  gadewch i mi roi cynnig arni

haven n hafan, porthladd
havoc n hafog, difrod
hawk n hebog, cudyll, curyll ▸ vb
  heboca
hawthorn n draenen wen
hay n gwair
hay fever n y dwymyn wair, clefyd
  y gwair
hazard n perygl ▸ vt peryglu
hazardous adj peryglus, enbydus
haze n niwl, tarth, tawch

hazel *n* collen ► *adj* gwinau golau
hazelnut *n* cneuen gyll
hazy *adj* aneglur, niwlog
he *pron* ef, efe; efo, fo, o
head *n* pen ► *vb* blaenori, penio
headache *n* dolur (cur) yn y pen, pen tost
heading *n* pennawd
headlamp *n* lamp fawr
headlight *n* prif olau
headline *n* pennawd
headmaster *n* prifathro
headmistress *n* prifathrawes
headphones *npl* ffonau clust
headquarters *npl* pencadlys
headteacher *n* (man) prifathro; (woman) prifathrawes
heal *vb* iacháu, meddyginiaethu
health *n* iechyd
health centre *n* canolfan iechyd
health food shop *n* siop bwyd iach
Health Service *n* y Gwasanaeth Iechyd
healthy *adj* iach, iachus
heap *n* crug, pentwr ► *vt* crugio, pentyrru
hear (*pt, pp* **heard**) *vb* clywed
hearing *n* clyw
hearing aid *n* cymorth clywed
hearse *n* hers
heart *n* calon
heart attack *n* trawiad y galon
heartbroken *adj* calonddrylliog
heartburn *n* dŵr poeth
heart disease *n* clefyd y galon
hearth *n* aelwyd
hearty *adj* calonnog, cynnes
heat *n* gwres, poethder ► *vb* twymo, poethi; **heat up** *vb* twymo

heater *n* gwresogydd
heather *n* grug
heating *n* gwres
heaven *n* nef, nefoedd
heavenly *adj* nefol, nefolaidd
heavily *adv* yn drwm, yn drymaidd
heavy *adj* trwm, trymaidd, trymllyd
Hebrew *n* Hebrëwr; (language) Hebraeg ► *adj* Hebraeg; Hebreig
hectare *n* hectar
hectic *adj* prysur
hedge *n* clawdd, gwrych, perth
hedgehog *n* draenog
heed *vt* ystyried, talu sylw ► *n* ystyriaeth
heel *n* sawdl ► *vb* sodli
height *n* uchder, taldra
heir *n* etifedd, aer
heiress *n* etifeddes, aeres
helicopter *n* hofrennydd
hell *n* uffern
hello *excl* helô!, hylô!
helmet *n* helm
help *vt* helpu, cynorthwyo ► *n* help, cymorth, cynorthwy
helper *n* cynorthwywr, helpwr
helpful *adj* defnyddiol, cymwynasgar, buddiol
helping *n* dogn, cyfran (o fwyd)
helpless *adj* diymadferth
helpline *n* llinell gymorth
hem *n* hem, ymyl ► *vt* hemio
hemisphere *n* hemisffer
hen *n* iâr
hence *adv* oddi yma ► *excl* ymaith!
henceforth *adv* rhag llaw, mwyach, o hyn ymlaen
hen night, hen party *n* noson merched (cyn priodas)

321

hepatitis n hepatitis
her pron ei, hi, hithau
herb n llysieuyn, sawr-lysieuyn
herbal adj llysieuol
herbal tea n te llysieuol
herd n gyr, cenfaint, gre ▸ vb heidio
here adv yma
hereditary adj etifeddol
heritage n etifeddiaeth, treftadaeth
hernia n hernia, torllengig
hero n arwr, gwron
heroic adj arwrol
heroin n heroin
heroine n arwres
heron n crëyr, crychydd
herring n pennog, ysgadenyn
hers pron (her one) un hi; **the house is hers** hi sy biau'r tŷ
herself pron ei hun
hesitant adj petrusgar
hesitate vi petruso
hesitation n petruster
heterosexual n heterorywiol
heyday n anterth
hi excl heia
hibernate vi gaeafu
hiccup n yr ig ▸ vi igian
hiccups n: **I've got hiccups** mae'r ig arnaf i
hide¹ (pt **hid**, pp **hidden**) vb cuddio, celu, ymguddio
hide² n croen
hideous adj hyll, erchyll
hi-fi n hei-ffei
high adj uchel; mawr; cryf; llawn
high chair n cadair ar gyfer plentyn
higher education n addysg uwch
high jump n naid uchel

highlight vt pwysleisio ▸ n uchelbwynt; **highlights** npl (hair) aroleuadau
highlighter n (pen) aroleuydd
highly adv yn fawr, yn uchel
highness n uchelder
high-rise n: **high-rise flats** twˆr fflatiau
high street n stryd fawr
highway n priffordd, ffordd fawr
hijack vb cipio
hijacker n herwgipiwr
hike vb crwydro ▸ n taith gerdded
hiking n heicio
hilarious adj llawen, llon, siriol, hoenus
hill n bryn, allt
hill-walking n dringo bryniau
hilly adj bryniog, mynyddig
him pron ef, efe; efo, fo; yntau
himself pron ei hun
hind¹ adj ôl
hind² n ewig
hinder vt rhwystro, atal, llesteirio
Hindu n Hindw ▸ adj Hindwaidd
hinge n colyn drws ▸ vb troi, dibynnu
hint n awgrym ▸ vt awgrymu
hip n clun, pen uchaf y glun
hippie n hipi
hippo n hipo
hire vt cyflogi, hurio, llogi ▸ n cyflog, hur
hire car n car llog
hire purchase n hurbwrcas
his adj ei ▸ pron (his one) un fe; **the car is his** fe sy biau'r car; **his car** ei gar e
hiss vb hisian
historian n hanesydd

historic adj hanesyddol

historical adj hanesyddol

history n hanes

hit (pt, pp **hit**) vb taro ▸ n ergyd, trawiad

hitch vb bachu ▸ n cwlwm; atalfa, rhwystr

hitchhike vb bodio

hitchhiker n bodiwr

hitchhiking vb bodio

HIV n abbr HIV; **HIV-negative/positive** HIV negyddol/positif

hive n cwch gwenyn; **hive off** vb (inf) rhannu, trosglwyddo, newid

HIV-negative adj HIV-negyddol

HIV-positive adj HIV-positif

hoard n cronfa, cuddfa ▸ vt cronni

hoarse adj cryg, cryglyd

hoax vt twyllo ▸ n cast, tric, twyll

hob n pentan

hobble vb hercian

hobby n difyrwaith, hobi

hockey n hoci

hog n mochyn

hoist vt codi, dyrchafu

hold¹ (pt, pp **held**) vb dal, credu; atal; cadw ▸ n gafael, dalfa ▸ **hold on** vt (grip) gafael; (wait) aros; **to hold onto sth** gafael yn rhth

hold² n ceudod llong, howld

holdall n celsach

hole n twll, ffau

holiday n gŵyl, dygwyl

Holland npl Yr Iseldiroedd

hollow adj cau, gwag ▸ n ceudod, pant ▸ vt tyllu, cafnio

holly n celyn, celynnen

holocaust n lladdfa

holy adj sanctaidd, glân

home n, adj cartref ▸ adv adref; **at home** gartref

homeland n mamwlad

homeless adj digartref

homely adj cartrefol

home-made adj cartref

homeopathy n homeopatheg

home page n (Internet) tudalen gartref, tudalen hafan

homesick adj hiraethus

homework n gwaith cartref

homicide n dynleiddiad, llofruddiaeth

homosexual n rhn cyfunrhywiol

homosexuality n cyfunrhywioldeb

honest adj (g)onest, didwyll

honestly adv yn onest

honesty n (g)onestrwydd

honey n mêl

honeymoon n mis mêl

honeysuckle n gwyddfid

honorary adj mygedol

honour n anrhydedd ▸ vt anrhydeddu

honourable adj anrhydeddus

hood n cwfl, cwcwll

hoodie n (hooded top) hwdi

hoof n carn

hook n bach ▸ vb bachu

hooligan n adyn, dihiryn

hoop n cylch, cant ▸ vt cylchu, cantio

hooray excl hwrê

hoot vb hwtian, hwtio ▸ n hŵt

Hoover® n hwfer

hoover vt hwfro

hop vb hercian ▸ n llam, herc

hope n gobaith ▸ vb gobeithio

hopefully adv (let's hope) gobeithio

hopeless adj anobeithiol; diobaith

horizon n gorwel
horizontal adj llorwedd
hormone n hormon
horn n corn ▸ vt cornio, twlcio
horoscope n horosgôp
horrible adj erchyll, ofnadwy
horrid adj erchyll, echrydus
horrifying adj brawychus
horror n arswyd, erchylltod
horse n march, ceffyl
horse-racing n rasio ceffylau
hose n pibell ddŵr
hospital n ysbyty
hospitality n lletygarwch, croeso
host n lletywr, gwesteiwr
hostage n gwystl
hostel n llety efrydwyr, neuadd breswyl
hostess n croesawferch
hostile adj gelyniaethus
hot adj poeth, twm
hot dog n ci poeth
hotel n gwesty
hot-water bottle n potel dŵr twym
hound n bytheiad, helgi ▸ vt hela, erlid
hour n awr
hourly adj, adv bob awr
house n tŷ, annedd ▸ vb lletya
household n teulu, tylwyth
householder n deiliad tŷ
housekeeper n gofalyddes
housewife n gwraig tŷ
housework n gwaith tŷ
housing n tai
hover vi hofran
hovercraft n hofrenfad
how adv pa mor, pa fodd, pa sut, sut

however adv pa fodd bynnag, sut bynnag
howl vi udo, oernadu ▸ n udiad, oernad
huddle vb tyrru, gwthio
huff vb sorri, tramgwyddo ▸ n soriant
hug vt cofleidio, gwasgu
huge adj anferth, enfawr, dirfawr
hull n corff llong; cibyn, plisgyn
hum vb mwmian ▸ n si, sibrwd
human adj dynol
human being n bod dynol
humane adj tirion, tosturiol, trugarog
humanist n dyneiddiwr
humanitarian n dyngarwr
humanity n dynoliaeth, dynolryw
humble adj gostyngedig, ufudd ▸ vt darostwng
humid adj llaith
humiliate vt bychanu, gwaradwyddo, darostwng
humiliation n darostyngiad
humour n hwyl, donioldeb ▸ vt boddio
hump n crwmach, crwmp, crwb
hunch n syniad, tybiaeth
hundred adj cant, can ▸ n cant; cantref
Hungarian n (person) Hwngariad; (language) Hwngareg ▸ adj Hwngaraidd; (in language) Hwngareg
Hungary n Hwngari
hunger n newyn, chwant bwyd ▸ vi newynu
hungry adj newynog
hunt vb hela, erlid ▸ n helwriaeth, hela

hunter n heliwr; ceffyl hela
hunting n hela
hurdle n clwyd
hurl vt hyrddio
hurricane n corwynt
hurry vb brysio ► n brys
hurt (pt, pp **hurt**) vb niweidio,
    dolurio, brifo ► n niwed, dolur
husband n gŵr, priod ► vt cynilo
hush excl ust ► vb distewi ► n
    distawrwydd
husky adj sych, cryglyd
hut n caban, cwt
hyacinth n croeso haf
hygiene n iechydaeth, hylendid
hymn n emyn ► vb emynu
hypermarket n archfarchnad
hyphen n cyplysnod, cysylltnod
hypnotize vt swyno, rheibio
hypocrite n rhagrithiwr
hypothesis n damcaniaeth
hysterical adj hysterig

I pron mi, myfi; fi, i; minnau,
    innau
ice n iâ, rhew ► vt taenu (megis)
    â rhew
iceberg n mynydd rhew
ice cream n hufen iâ
ice cube n ciwb iâ
ice hockey n hoci iâ
Iceland n Gwlad yr Iâ
ice lolly n loli iâ
ice rink n llain iâ
ice-skating n sglefrio iâ
icing n eising
icon n eicon
ICT n TGCh
icy adj rhewllyd
ID card n cerdyn adnabod
idea n drychfeddwl, syniad
ideal adj delfrydol, ideal ► n
    delfryd
identical adj yr un (yn union)
identification n (recognition)
    adnabyddiaeth

identify vt adnabod; uniaethu;
  identify with uniaethu â
identity n unfathiant, hunaniaeth
identity card n cerdyn adnabod
idiom n priod-ddull, idiom
idiot n gwirionyn, hurtyn
idiotic adj gwirion
idle adj segur, ofer ▸ vb segura,
  ofera
idol n eilun
i.e. abbr (= id est) h.y.
if conj os, pe
ignite vb ennyn, tanio, cynnau
ignition n taniad
ignorance n anwybodaeth
ignorant adj anwybodus
ignore vt anwybyddu, diystyru
ill adj drwg; gwael, claf ▸ adv yn
  ddrwg ▸ n drwg, niwed
illegal adj anghyfreithlon
illegible adj annarllenadwy,
  aneglur
illegitimate adj anghyfreithlon
illiterate adj anllythrennog
illness n afiechyd, salwch
illuminate vt goleuo, addurno
illusion n rhith, lledrith
illustrate vt darlunio
illustration n darlun
image n delw, llun, delwedd
imaginary adj dychmygol
imagination n dychymyg,
  darfelydd
imaginative adj dychmygus
imagine vt dychmygu, tybio
imbalance n anghydbwysedd
imitate vt dynwared, efelychu
imitation n dynwarediad ▸ adj
  ffug
immaculate adj difrycheulyd, pur

immature adj anaeddfed
immediate adj agos, presennol
immediately adv ar unwaith
immense adj anferth, eang
immerse vt trochi, suddo
immigrant n mewnfudwr
immigration n mewnfudiad
imminent adj gerllaw, agos
immoral adj anfoesol
immortal adj anfarwol
immune adj rhydd rhag
immunize vb gwrtheintio
impact n ardrawiad,
  gwrthdrawiad
impair vt amharu
impartial adj diduedd, amhleidiol
impatience n diffyg amynedd
impatient adj diamynedd
impatiently adv yn ddiamynedd
impeccable adj di-fai
impending adj agos, gerllaw
imperative n gorchymyn ▸ adj
  gorchmynnol, gorfodol
imperfect adj amherffaith
imperial adj ymerodrol
impersonal adj amhersonol
impersonate vt personoli
impetus n cymhelliad, symbyliad
implant vt plannu, gwreiddio
implement n offeryn, arf ▸ vb
  gweithredu
implication n ymhlygiad,
  goblygiad
implicit adj dealledig, ymhlyg,
  goblygedig
imply vt arwyddo, awgrymu
impolite adj anfoesgar
import vt mewnforio ▸ n
  mewnforyn; arwyddocâd, pwys
importance n pwys, pwysigrwydd

important adj pwysig

importer n mewnforiwr

impose vb gosod

imposing adj llethol, mawreddog

impossible adj amhosibl

impotent adj di-rym, analluog

impress vt argraffu, pwyso, dylanwadu ▶ n argraffiad

impressed adj edmygus

impression n argraff

impressive adj trawiadol

imprison vt carcharu

improbable adj annhebygol

improper adj anweddus

improve vb gwella, diwygio

improvement n gwelliant

improvise vb addasu ar y pryd

impulse n cymhelliad, ysgogiad

impulsive adj byrbwyll

(KEYWORD)

in prep **1** (followed by a definite object or a proper noun) yn; **in the house/ the fridge** yn y tŷ/yn oergell; **in the garden** yn yr ardd; **in town** yn y dref; **in the country** yn y wlad; **in school** yn yr ysgol; **in here/there** yma/acw

2 (followed by an indefinite object) mewn; **in a house** mewn tŷ; **in a garden** mewn gardd; **in a town** mewn tref; **in a school** mewn ysgol

3 (with place names: of town, region, country) in **Cardiff** yng Nghaerdydd; **in Wales** yng Nghymru; **in Japan** yn Japan; **in the United States** yn yr Unol Daleithiau

4 (indicating time: during): **in spring** yn y gwanwyn; **in summer** yn yr haf; **in May/2017** ym mis Mai/yn 2017; **in the afternoon** yn y prynhawn; **at 4 o'clock in the afternoon** am 4 o'r gloch y prynhawn

5 (indicating time: in the space of) mewn; (: future) ymhen; **I did it in 3 hours/days** fe'i gwnes mewn 3 awr/diwrnod; **I'll see you in 2 weeks** or **in 2 weeks' time** fe wela i ti ymhen pythefnos

6 (indicating manner etc) mewn/ yn; **in a loud/soft voice** mewn llais cryf/tawel; **in pencil** mewn pensel; **in writing** mewn ysgrifen; **in Welsh** yn Gymraeg; **the boy in the blue shirt** y bachgen yn y crys glas

7 (indicating circumstances): **in the sun** yn yr haul; **in the shade** yn y cysgod; **in the rain** yn y glaw; **a change in policy** newid polisi

8 (indicating mood, state): **in tears** mewn dagrau; **in his/her anger** yn ei ddagrau; **in anger** mewn dicter; **in despair** mewn anobaith; **in good condition** mewn cyflwr da; **to live in luxury** byw yn fras

9 (with ratios, numbers): **1 in 10 households, 1 household in 10** 1 aelwyd mewn 10; **20 pence in the pound** 20 ceiniog yn y bunt; **they lined up in twos** safasant mewn rhes fesul dau/mewn deuoedd; **in hundreds** fesul cant; **10** (referring to people, works) mewn, ymysg; **the disease is common in children** mae'r clefyd yn gyffredin ymysg plant; **in (the works of) Owen** yng

inability

ngwaith Owen; **11** (*with present participle*): **in saying this** wedi dweud hynny
► *adv*: **to be in** (*person: at home, work*) bod yno (*train, ship, plane*) bod wedi cyraedd (*in fashion*) bod mewn ffasiwn; **to ask sb in** gwahodd rhywun [i ddod] i mewn; **to run/limp in** dod i mewn gan redeg/hercian
► *n*: **the ins and outs (of)** (*of proposal, situation etc*) manylion

inability *n* anallu
inaccurate *adj* anghywir, anfanwl
inadequate *adj* annigonol
inadvertent *adj* anfwriadol, amryfus
inappropriate *adj* amhriodol
inaugurate *vt* urddo, agor, dechrau
inbox *n* blwch derbyn
incapable *adj* analluog
incense[1] *n* arogldarth
incense[2] *vt* llidio, cythruddo
incentive *adj* cymelliadol ► *n* cymelliad
inch *n* modfedd
incident *n* digwyddiad
incidentally *adv* gyda llaw
inclination *n* tuedd, gogwydd
incline *vb* tueddu, gogwyddo ► *n* llethr
include *vt* cynnwys
including *prep* gan gynnwys
inclusive *adj* cynwysedig, gan gynnwys
income *n* incwm; **income tax** treth incwm
income tax *n* treth incwm

incompatible *adj* anghytûn
incompetent *n* anghymwys
incomplete *adj* anghyflawn
inconsistent *adj* anghyson
inconspicuous *adj* anamlwg
inconvenience *n* anghyfleustra
inconvenient *adj* anghyfleus
incorporate *vb* corffori, ymgorffori
incorporated *adj* corfforedig
incorrect *adj* anghywir
increase *vb* cynyddu ► *n* cynnydd
incredible *adj* anhygoel, anghredadwy
incur *vt* ysgwyddo; achosi
indecent *adj* anweddus
indeed *adv* yn wir; iawn; dros ben
independence *n* annibyniaeth
independent *adj* annibynnol ► *n* annibynnwr
index *n* mynegai; **index finger** mynegfys
India *n* India
Indian *adj* Indiaidd ► *n* Indiad
indicate *vt* dangos, arwyddo
indicative *adj* arwyddol, mynegol
indicator *n* dangosydd
indict *vt* cyhuddo
indifference *n* difaterwch, difrawder
indifferent *adj* difater; dibwys
indigenous *adj* cynhenid
indigestion *n* diffyg traul, camdreuliad
indignant *adj* dig, dicllon
indirect *adj* anuniongyrchol
indispensable *adj* anhepgorol
individual *adj* unigol ► *n* un, unigolyn
Indonesia *n* Indonesia
indoor *adj, adv* dan do

doors adv dan do
duce vt denu, cymell
dulge vb boddio; maldodi
dulgence n ymfoddhad; maldod
dulgent adj ffafriol, maldodus
dustrial adj diwydiannol, gweithfaol
dustrial estate n stad ddiwydiannol
dustry n diwydrwydd; diwydiant
efficient adj aneffeithlon
equality n anghysondeb
evitable adj anochel, anesgorol
expensive adj rhad
experienced adj amhrofiadol, dibrofiad
famous adj gwaradwyddus, gwarthus
fant n baban; un dan oed
fantry n gwŷr traed, milwyr traed
fant school n ysgol fach
fect vt heintio, llygru
fection n haint
fectious adj heintus
fer vt casglu
ferior adj is, israddol ▸ n isradd
fertile adj anffrwythlon
fertility n anffrwythlondeb
finite adj anfeidrol
firmary n ysbyty, clafdy
flamed adj llidus
flammation n enyniad, llid
flatable adj y gellir ei chwyddo neu ei chwythu
flate vt chwyddo
flation n chwyddiant
flexible adj anhyblyg
flict vt peri, gweinyddu (cosb, poen etc)

influence n dylanwad ▸ vt dylanwadu
influenza n ffliw
influx n dylifiad
inform vb hysbysu
informal adj anffurfiol
information n gwybodaeth, hysbysrwydd
information technology n technoleg gwybodaeth
infra-red adj is-goch
infrastructure n seilwaith
infrequent adj anaml
infuriate vt ffyrnigo, cynddeiriogi
infuriating adj: he's infuriating mae o'n ddigon i'ch gwylltio
ingenious adj medrus, celfydd
ingredients npl cynhwysion
inhabit vt cyfaneddu, preswylio
inhabitable adj cyfannedd, trigadwy
inhabitant n preswyliwr
inhale vt anadlu
inhaler n anadlydd
inherent adj cynhenid, greddfol
inherit vt etifeddu
inheritance n etifeddiaeth
inhibit vt gwahardd, atal
inhibition n ataliad, atalnwyd
initial adj dechreuol ▸ n llythyren gyntaf
initiate vt derbyn; dechrau
initiative n cynhoredd, menter
inject vt chwistrellu
injection n chwistrelliad, pigiad
injure vt niweidio, anafu
injury n niwed, cam, anaf
injustice n anghyfiawnder, cam
ink n inc ▸ vt incio
inland adj canoldirol ▸ n canoldir

329

Inland Revenue n Cyllid y Wlad
in-laws npl teulu-yng-nghyfraith
inmate n trigiannydd, preswylydd
inn n tafarn, tafarndy
inner adj mewnol
innocence n diniweidrwydd
innocent adj diniwed, gwirion, dieuog
innovation n newyddbeth
input n mewnbwn, cyfraniad
inquest n cwest; trengholiad
inquire vb ymofyn, ymholi, gofyn
inquiry n ymholiad
insane adj gwallgof, gorffwyll, ynfyd
insect n pryf, trychfil
insect repellent n eli ymlid pryfed
insert vb mewnosod
inside n tu mewn ▸ adj mewnol
▸ prep y tu mewn i ▸ adv i mewn, o fewn
inside-out adv o chwith
insight n mewnwelediad
insignificant adj di-nod, distadl, dibwys
insincere adj annidwyll, ffuantus
insist vi mynnu
insomnia n anhunedd
inspect vt arolygu, archwilio
inspection n archwiliad, arolygiad
inspector n arolygwr
inspiration n ysbrydoliaeth
inspire vb ysbrydoli
instability n ansadrwydd
install vt sefydlu, gorseddu
instalment n cyfran, rhandal
instance n enghraifft ▸ vt enwi, nodi
instant adj taer, ebrwydd ▸ n eiliad, moment

instant coffee n coffi powdr
instantly adv ar drawiad
instead adv yn lle
instinct n greddf
institute n athrofa
institution n sefydliad
instruct vt hyfforddi
instruction n hyfforddiant
instructor n hyfforddwr
instrument n offeryn
insufficient adj annigonol
insulate vt ynysu, inswleiddio
insulin n inswlin
insult vt sarhau ▸ n sarhad
insurance n yswiriant
insurance policy n polisi yswiriant
insure vb yswirio
intact adj cyfan, dianaf
integral adj cyfan, cyflawn
integrate vb cyfannu
integrity n cywirdeb, gonestrwydd
intellect n deall
intellectual n deallusyn ▸ adj deallus, deallgar
intelligence n deallusrwydd; hysbysrwydd
intelligent adj deallus
intend vt bwriadu
intense adj angerddol, dwys
intensive adj dwys
intensive care unit n uned gofal arbennig
intent n bwriad, amcan; ystyr; diben
intention n bwriad
intentional adj bwriadol
interaction n rhyngweithiad
interactive adj rhyngweithiol
intercept vt rhyng-gipio

nterchange vt cyfnewid, ymgyfnewid

ntercourse n cyfathrach

nterest n budd, buddiant; diddordeb; llog ▸ vt diddori

nterested adj â chanddo ddidordeb

nteresting adj diddorol

nterest rate n cyfradd llog

nterface n cydwyneb

nterfere vt ymyrryd, ymhél

nterference n ymyrraeth

nterim adj dros dro ▸ n cyfamser

nterior adj mewnol ▸ n tu mewn, canol, perfeddwlad

nterior designer n cynllunydd tai

ntermediate adj canol, canolradd

ntern vt carcharu

nternal adj mewnol

nternational adj cydwladol, rhyngwladol

nternet n rhyngrwyd; internet café caffi rhyngrwyd, caffe rhyngrwyd

nternet café n caffi/caffe rhyngrwyd

nternet user n defnyddiwr rhyngrwyd

nterpret vt dehongli; cyfieithu

nterpretation n dehongliad; cyfieithiad

nterpreter n lladmerydd, cyfieithydd

nterrogate vt holi

nterrogative adj gofynnol

nterrupt vt torri ar, torri ar draws, ymyrryd

nterruption n toriad

ntersection n croesdoriad

nterval n egwyl, saib

intervene vi ymyrryd

interview n cyfweliad ▸ vb cyfweld

interviewer n cyfwelydd

intimate¹ adj cyfarwydd, agos ▸ n cydnabod

intimate² vt arwyddo, hysbysu

intimidate vt dychrynu, brawychu

into prep i, i mewn i

intranet n intranet, mewnrwyd

intransitive adj (grammar) cyflawn

intricate adj dyrys, cymhleth, astrus

intrigue vi, n cynllwyn

introduce vt cyflwyno

introduction n cyflwyniad, rhagarweiniad

introductory adj dechreuol, agoriadol, rhagarweiniol

introvert adj mewnblyg

intrude vb ymyrryd

intruder n ymyrrwr, ymwthiwr

intuition n sythwelediad

inundate vt gorlifo, boddi

invade vt goresgyn

invalid¹ adj di-rym, annilys

invalid² n un afiach, un methedig

invaluable adj amhrisiadwy

invariably adv yn ddieithriad

invasion n goresgyniad

invent vt dyfeisio, dychmygu

invention n dyfais

inventory n rhestr, stocrestr

inverted commas npl dyfynodau

invest vt buddsoddi; arwisgo

investigate vt chwilio, archwilio, ymchwilio

investigation n ymchwiliad

investigator n ymchwiliwr

investment n buddsoddiad

331

investor n buddsoddwr
invisible adj anweledig, anweladwy
invitation n gwahoddiad
invite vt gwahodd
invoice n anfoneb
involve vt drysu; cynnwys, ymwneud
involvement n ymwneud, ymglymiad
inward adj mewnol
iPad® n iPad®
iPhone® n iPhone®
iPod® n iPod®
IQ n abbr IQ, CD, cyneirydd deallusrwydd
Iran n Iran
Iraq n Irac
Iraqi n Iraciad ▸ adj Iracaidd
Ireland n Iwerddon
iris n iris; gellesgen
Irish adj Gwyddelig ▸ n (language) Gwyddeleg
Irishman n Gwyddel
Irishwoman n Gwyddeles
iron n, adj haearn ▸ vt smwddio
ironic adj eironig
ironing n smwddio
ironing board n bwrdd smwddio
irony n eironi
irrational adj direswm, afresymol
irregular adj afreolaidd
irrelevant adj amherthnasol
irresistible adj anorchfygol
irresponsible adj anghyfrifol
irritable n croendenau, anniddig, llidiog
irritate vt blino, poeni, cythruddo
irritating adj pryfoclyd
is vi mae, sydd, yw, ydy(w), oes

Islam n Islam
Islamic adj Islamaidd
island, isle n ynys
isolated adj wedi ei neilltuo, wedi ei wahanu
isolation n neilltuaeth, arwahanrwydd
ISP n abbr (= Internet Service Provider) ISP, Darparydd Gwasanaeth Rhyngrwyd
Israel n Israel
Israeli n Israeliad ▸ adj Israelaidd
issue n llif; agorfa, arllwysfa; hiliogaeth, plant; canlyniad, pwnc ▸ vb tarddu, deillio; cyhoeddi
IT n abbr (= information technology) TG, technoleg gwybodaeth

(KEYWORD)

it pron 1 (in a single word answer to a question, it is conveyed by the 3rd sing. ending of the appropriate verb): **it is** ydyw; **it may** caiff; **it can** gall; **it did** gwnaeth
2 (after prep): **about/from/of it** y peth; **I spoke to him about it** siaradais ag ef am y peth; **what did you learn from it?** beth ddysgest ti o'r peth?; **I'm proud of it** rwy'n falch o'r peth
3 (impersonal, usually) hi; **it's Friday tomorrow** dydd Gwener yw hi yfory; **it's 6 o'clock** mae hi'n 6 o'r gloch; **how far is it?** — **it's 10 miles** pa mor bell yw hi? — mae'n 10 milltir; **who is it?** — **it's me** pwy sy yna? — fi sy yma; **it's raining** mae hi'n bwrw [glaw]
4: **it was a book he lost** llyfr a

gollodd ef; **it was Wales who won the match** Cymru a enillodd y gêm

Italian *adj* Eidalaidd ▸ *n* Eidalwr; *(language)* Eidaleg
italics *npl* llythrennau italaidd
Italy *n* Yr Eidal
itch *vi* ysu, cosi ▸ *n* y crafu, ysfa
itchy *adj* coslyd
item *n* eitem
itinerary *n* taith, teithlyfr
its *adj* ei
itself *pron* ei hun, ei hunan
ivory *n* ifori
ivy *n* eiddew, iorwg

jab *n (inf)* jab, pigiad ▸ *vb* procio, gwanu
jack *n* jac
jacket *n* siaced
jagged *adj* danheddog, ysgithrog
jail *n* carchar
jam¹ *n* jam; tagfa
jam² *vt* jamio, tagu
Jamaica *n* Jamaica
janitor *n* porthor
January *n* Ionawr
Japan *n* Japan, Siapan
Japanese *adj* Japaneaidd, Siapaneaidd ▸ *n* Japanead, Siapanead; *(language)* Japaneg, Siapaneg
jar *n* jar
jargon *n* jargon
javelin *n* picell, gwaywffon
jaw *n* gên, cern; **jaws** safn
jazz *n* jas
jealous *adj* eiddigus, cenfigennus
jealousy *n* cenfigen, eiddigedd

jeans n jîns

jelly n jeli

jellyfish n slefren fôr

jerk n plwc, ysgytiad ▸ vb plycio, ysgytio

jersey n siersi

Jesus n Iesu

jet n ffrwd, jet; muchudd

jetlag n jetludded

jet-ski n jet-sgi ▸ vi jet-sgio

jetty n jeti, glanfa

Jew n Iddew

jewel n gem, tlws

jeweller n gemydd

jeweller's shop n siop gemydd

jewellery n gemwaith, gemau

Jewish adj Iddewig

jib n hwyl flaen llong, jib

jig-saw n jig-so

job n gorchwyl, gwaith

Job Centre n Canolfan Gwaith

jobless adj diwaith

jockey n joci

jog vb loncian

jogging n loncian

join vb cydio, cysylltu, uno

joiner n asiedydd, saer coed

joint n cyswllt, cymal ▸ adj cyd; **joint of meat** darn o gig

joke n cellwair, maldod ▸ vb cellwair, ysmalio

jolly adj braf, difyr, llawen

jolt n ysgytiad ▸ vb ysgytio

Jordan n Iorddonen

jotter n nodlyfr

journal n newyddiadur

journalism n newyddiaduraeth

journalist n newyddiadurwr

journey n taith, siwrnai ▸ vt teithio

joy n llawenydd, gorfoledd

judge n barnwr, beirniad ▸ vb barnu, beirniadu

judo n jwdo

jug n jwg

juggle vb siwglo

juggler n siwglwr

juice n sudd

juicy adj llawn sudd

July n Gorffennaf

jumble vb cymysgu, cyboli ▸ n cymysgfa, cybolfa

jumble sale n ffair sborion

jump vb neidio, llamu ▸ n naid, llam

jumper n neidiwr; siwmper

junction n cydiad; uniad; cyffordd

June n Mehefin

jungle n jyngl, coedwig; drysi

junior adj iau, ieuengach; ieuaf

junior school n ysgol iau

junk n sothach

junk food n bwyd sothach

junk mail n post sothach

jurisdiction n awdurdod

juror n rheithiwr

jury n rheithgor

just adj cyfiawn, uniawn, teg ▸ adv yn union; prin, braidd; newydd; **just now** gynnau (fach)

justice n cyfiawnder; ynad, ustus

justice of the peace n ynad heddwch

justify vt cyfiawnhau

jut vi taflu allan, ymwthio

juvenile adj ieuanc

k

kangaroo *n* cangarŵ
karaoke *n* karaoke
karate *n* karate
kebab *n* cebab
keel *n* cêl, trumbren, cilbren
keen *adj* craff, llym, awchus
keep (*pt, pp* **kept**) *vb* cadw, cynnal
  ▶ *n* cadw; amddiffynfa; **keep**
  on *vi*: to keep on doing sth dal
  i wneud rhywbeth; **keep up** *vi*
  dal i fyny
keeper *n* ceidwad
keep-fit *n* cadw'n heini
kennel *n* cenel, cwb ci
Kenya *n* Cenia
kerb *n* cwrbyn
kettle *n* tegell
key *n* agoriad, allwedd; cywair
keyboard *n* allweddell
keyhole *n* twll clo
key ring *n* cylch allweddi
khaki *adj, n* caci
kick *vb* cicio, gwingo ▶ *n* cic

kick-off *n* cic gychwyn
kid *n* myn; (*inf*) plentyn
kidnap *vt* herwgipio
kidney *n* aren
kidney beans *npl* ffa dringo,
  cidnebêns
kill *vt* lladd
killer *n* lladdwr
killing *n* lladd
kiln *n* odyn
kilo *n* cilo
kilogram *n* cilogram
kilometre *n* cilomedr
kilowatt *n* cilowat
kilt *n* cilt
kin *n* perthynas, tras, carennydd
kind¹ *n* rhyw, rhywogaeth, math
kind² *adj* caredig
kindergarten *n* ysgol feithrin
kindle *vb* ennyn, cynnau
kindly *adj* caredig, hynaws
kindness *n* caredigrwydd
king *n* brenin
kingdom *n* teyrnas
kingfisher *n* glas y dorlan
kiosk *n* ciosg, bwth
kipper *n* ciper, ysgadenyn hallt
  (neu sych)
kiss *vt* cusanu ▶ *n* cusan
kit *n* cit, pac
kitchen *n* cegin
kite *n* barcut
kitten *n* cath fach ▶ *vb* bwrw
  cathod
knack *n* cnac, medr
knee *n* pen-lin, pen-glin
kneel (*pt, pp* **knelt**) *vi* penlinio;
  kneel down *vi* penlinio
knickers *npl* nicers
knife *n* cyllell

knight *n* marchog ▸ *vt* urddo yn farchog

knit *vb* gwau; clymu

knitting *n* gwaith gwau; **I like knitting** Dw i'n hoffi gwau

knitting needle *n* gwaell

knob *n* cnap, cnwc; dwrn

knock *vb* cnocio, taro, curo ▸ *n* cnoc, ergyd; **knock down** *vt* taro i lawr; **knock out** *vt* llorio

knot *n* cwlwm ▸ *vt* clymu

know (*pt* **knew**, *pp* **known**) *vb* gwybod, adnabod

knowing *adj* gwybodus

knowingly *adv* yn fwriadol

knowledge *n* gwybodaeth

knowledgeable *adj* gwybodus

knuckle *n* cymal, migwrn, cwgn

Koran *n* Coran

Korea *n* Corea

kosher *adj* kosher

Kosovo *n* Cosofo

Kuwait *n* Kuwait, Coweit

label *n* llabed, label ▸ *vt* llabedu, enwi

laboratory *n* labordy

labour *n* llafur; gwewyr esgor ▸ *vb* llafurio; **the Labour Party** y Blaid Lafur

labourer *n* gweithiwr, labrwr

lace *n* las, les; carrai ▸ *vb* cau (esgidiau)

lack *n* eisiau, diffyg ▸ *vb* bod mewn eisiau

lacquer *n* lacer ▸ *vb* lacro

lad *n* bachgen, hogyn, llanc

ladder *n* ysgol; rhwyg (mewn hosan)

ladies *npl* toiledau merched

ladle *n* lletwad, llwy

lady *n* arglwyddes; boneddiges, bonesig

ladybird *n* buwch goch gota

lag *vi* llusgo ar ôl, ymdroi, llercian

lagoon *n* morlyn, lagŵn

laid-back *adj* didaro

lake n llyn
lamb n oen ▸ vb bwrw ŵyn, wyna
lame n cloff ▸ vt cloffi
lament vb galaru, cwynfan
lamp n lamp, llusern
lamppost n polyn lamp
lampshade n lamplen
land n tir, gwlad ▸ vb tirio, glanio
landing n glaniad, glanio; glanfa; pen y grisiau
landlady n perchennog llety, gwraig llety
landlord n meistr tir; lletywr, tafarnwr
landscape n tirlun
lane n lôn
language n iaith
language laboratory n labordy iaith
lantern n llusern
lap¹ n (knee) arffed, glin
lap² vb llepian, lleibio
lapel n llabed
lapse n methiant, gwall ▸ vi llithro, methu
laptop, laptop computer n gliniadur
lard n bloneg ▸ vt blonegu
larder n bwtri, pantri
large adj mawr, helaeth, eang
largely adv gan mwyaf
lark¹ n (bird) ehedydd
lark² n sbort, miri ▸ vi cellwair, prancio
laryngitis n gwddf tost, laringitis
lasagne n lasagne
laser n laser
lash n llach, fflangell ▸ vb llachio, fflangellu; rhwymo
lass n llances

last¹ adj olaf, diwethaf ▸ adv yn olaf, yn ddiwethaf; **at last** o'r diwedd; **last night** neithiwr; **last week** yr wythnos ddiwethaf
last² vi parhau, para
lastly adv yn olaf
latch n cliced ▸ vt clicedu
late adj hwyr, diweddar; **late developers** plant hwyrgynnydd
lately adv yn ddiweddar
later adv wedyn, eto, yn ddiweddarach
latest adj diweddaraf
lather n trochion ▸ vb seboni, trochioni; golchi
Latin adj, n Lladin
Latin America n America Ladin
Latin American adj Lladin-Americanaidd
latitude n lledred; penrhyddid
latter adj diwethaf
laugh vb chwerthin ▸ n chwerthiniad; **laugh at** vt (joke, situation) chwerthin am; (person) chwerthin am ben
laughter n chwerthin
launch vb lansio
laundry n golchdy; dillad golch
lavatory n tŷ bach
lavender n lafant
lavish adj hael, afradlon, gwastraffus ▸ vb afradu, gwastraffu
law n cyfraith, deddf; **law and order** cyfraith a threfn; **law of the land** cyfraith gwlad
lawful adj cyfreithlon
lawless adj digyfraith
lawn n lawnt, llannerch
lawnmower n peiriant torri porfa

337

lawsuit n cyngaws, cyfraith
lawyer n cyfreithiwr, twrnai
lax adj llac, esgeulus
laxative n carthlyn
lay¹ (pt, pp **laid**) vt gosod, dodi; dodwy
  ▸ **lay off** vt (dismiss) danfon adref
lay² adj lleyg
lay-by n gorffwysfan
layer n haen
layout n cynllun
lazy adj diog, dioglyd
lead¹ n plwm
lead² (pt, pp **led**) vb arwain, tywys
  ▸ n blaenoriaeth
leader n arweinydd; erthygl flaen
leadership n arweinyddiaeth
lead-free adj di-blwm
lead singer n prif ganwr
leaf n deilen, dalen
leaflet n taflen
league n cynghrair ▸ vi cynghreirio
leak n agen, coll ▸ vi gollwng, diferu, colli
lean¹ adj main, tenau, cul
lean² (pt, pp **leaned**, **leant**) vb pwyso, gogwyddo
  ▸ **lean forward** vi pwyso ymlaen
  ▸ **lean on** vi pwyso ar
  ▸ **lean over** vi pwyso
leap (pt, pp **leaped**, **leapt**) vb neidio, llamu ▸ n naid, llam
leap year n blwyddyn naid
learn (pt, pp **learned**, **learnt**) vb dysgu
learner n dysgwr
learner driver n dysgwr gyrru
learning n dysg, dysgeidiaeth
lease n prydles ▸ vt prydlesu

leash n cynllyfan, tennyn ▸ vt cynllyfanu
least adj lleiaf; **at least** o leiaf
leather n lledr
leave¹ n cennad, caniatâd
leave² (pt, pp **left**) vb gadael, ymadael
  ▸ **leave out** vi gadael allan
Lebanon n Libanus
lecture n darlith ▸ vb darlithio
lecturer n darlithydd
lecture theatre n darlithfa
ledge n silff, ysgafell; crib
leek n cenhinen
left adj aswy, chwith
left-hand adj chwith
left-handed adj llawchwith
left luggage n lle cadw bagiau
left-luggage office n storfa baciau
leg n coes
legacy n etifeddiaeth, cymynrodd
legal adj cyfreithiol, cyfreithlon
legalize vb cyfreithloni
legend n chwedl
leggings n legins
legible adj darllenadwy, eglur
legislation n deddfwriaeth
legislative adj deddfwriaethol
legitimate adj cyfreithlon
leisure n hamdden
leisure centre n canolfan hamdden
leisurely adj hamddenol
lemon n lemwn
lemonade n diod lemwn, lemonêd
lend (pt, pp **lent**) vt benthyca, rhoi benthyg
length n hyd, meithder
lengthen vb estyn, hwyhau
lengthy adj hir, maith

lens *n* lens; **concave lens** lens ceugrwm; **convex lens** lens amgrwm

Lent *n* y Grawys

lentil *n* corbysen, lentil

Leo *n* y Llew

leopard *n* llewpart

leprosy *n* gwahanglwyf

lesbian *n* lesbiad ▸ *adj* lesbiaidd

less *adj, adv* llai

lessen *vb* lleihau

lesson *n* gwers; llith

let (*pt, pp* **let**) *vt* gadael, goddef; gollwng; gosod, rhentu; **let down** *vt* gollwng; siomi; **let in** *vt*: **to let sb in** gadael rhywun i mewn

lethal *adj* marwol, angheuol

letter *n* llythyren; llythyr

letterbox *n* bocs llythyrau

lettuce *n* letysen

level *n, adj* lefel, gwastad ▸ *vt* lefelu, gwastatáu; **spirit level** lefelydd

level crossing *n* croesfan

lever *n* trosol

levy *vt* codi, trethu ▸ *n* treth

liability *n* cyfrifoldeb, rhwymedigaeth

liable *adj* atebol

liar *n* gŵr celwyddog, celwyddgi

libel *n* athrod, enllib ▸ *vt* athrodi, enllibio

liberal *adj* hael, rhyddfrydig, rhyddfrydol ▸ *n* rhyddfrydwr

liberate *vt* rhyddhau

liberation *n* rhyddhad

liberty *n* rhyddid

Libra *n* y Fantol

librarian *n* llyfrgellydd

library *n* llyfrgell

Libya *n* Libya

licence *n* trwydded; penrhyddid; **driving licence** trwydded yrru

license *vt* trwyddedu

licensed *adj* trwyddedig

lick *vt* llyfu, llyo; (*inf*) curo

lid *n* caead, clawr

lie¹ (*pt, pp* **lied**) *vi* (*tell lies*) dweud celwydd ▸ *n* celwydd, anwiredd

lie² (*pt* **lay**, *pp* **lain**) *vi* gorwedd ▸ **lie down** *vi* gorwedd i lawr

lie-in *n*: **to have a lie-in** cysgu'n hwyr

lieutenant *n* is-gapten; rhaglaw

life *n* bywyd, einioes, oes

lifeboat *n* bad achub

lifeguard *n* achubwr

life insurance *n* yswiriant bywyd

life jacket *n* siaced achub

lifestyle *n* ffordd o fyw

lifetime *n* oes, einioes, hoedl

lift *vt* codi, dyrchafu ▸ *n* lifft

light¹ (*pt, pp* **lighted**, **lit**) *n* golau, goleuni ▸ *adj* golau ▸ *vb* goleuo, cynnau

light² *adj* ysgafn

light bulb *n* bwlb golau

lighter *n* goleuydd, taniwr

light-hearted *adj* ysgafnfryd

lighthouse *n* goleudy

lightning *n* mellt, lluched

like¹ *adj* tebyg, cyffelyb

like² *vb* caru, hoffi

likeable *adj* hoffus; dymunol

likelihood *n* tebygolrwydd

likely *adj, adv* tebygol, tebyg

likewise *adv* yn gyffelyb, yn yr un modd

lilac *n* lelog

lily *n* lili, alaw

limb n aelod, cainc
lime n calch
limelight n amlygrwydd
limestone n carreg galch
limit n terfyn, ffin ▸ vt cyfyngu
limited adj cyfyngedig
limousine n limwsîn
limp¹ adj llipa
limp² vi hercian, cloffi
line n llinell, lein, rhes; llinach ▸ vt llinellu, rhesu
linear adj llinellog, llinellaidd, llinol
linen n lliain
liner n leiner
linger vb ymdroi, aros
lingo (inf) n iaith ddieithr, cleber
linguist n ieithydd
lining n leinin
link n dolen, cyswllt ▸ vb cydio, cysylltu
lion n llew
lip n gwefus, min, gwefl
lip-read vi darllen gwefusau
lipstick n minlliw
liquid n hylif ▸ adj gwlyb, hylif
liquidizer n hylifydd
liquor n diod, gwirod
lisp n bloesgni ▸ vb siarad yn floesg
list¹ n rhestr ▸ vt rhestru
list² n (incline) gogwydd, goledd ▸ vi pwyso, gwyro, gogwyddo
listen vi gwrando
listener n gwrandawr
literacy n llythrennedd
literal adj llythrennol
literary adj llenyddol
literature n llenyddiaeth
lithe adj ystwyth, hyblyg
litre n litr

litter n elorwely; ysbwriel, gwasarn; torllwyth, tor
litter bin n bin sbwriel
little adj bach, bychan; mân, ychydig ▸ n ychydig, tipyn
live¹ adj byw, bywiol, bywiog
live² vi byw
  ▸ **live on** vt byw ar
  ▸ **live together** vi cyd-fyw
livelihood n bywoliaeth
lively adj bywiog, heini, sionc
liver n iau, afu
living n bywoliaeth
living room n ystafell fyw
lizard n madfall, modrchwilen
load n llwyth ▸ vb llwytho
loaf n torth
loan n benthyg, benthyciad
loathe vt ffieiddio, casáu
lobby n cyntedd, lobi
lobster n cimwch
local adj lleol
local government n llywodraeth leol
locate vt lleoli, sefydlu, gosod
location n lleoliad
loch n llyn
lock n clo; llifddor ▸ vb cloi, cau;
  lock out vt: **to lock sb out** cloi rhn allan
locker n cwpwrdd clo
locomotive adj ymsymudol ▸ n peiriant rheilffordd
lodge n lluest, llety; cyfrinfa ▸ vb lletya
lodger n lletywr
lodging n, **lodgings** npl llety
loft n taflod, llofft
log n cyff, boncyff, pren; **log in, log on** vi (Comput) mewngofnodi,

logio i mewn; **log off, log out** vi (Comput) allgofnodi, logio allan

logic n rhesymeg

logical adj rhesymegol

lollipop n lolipop

London n Llundain

Londoner n Llundeiniwr

loneliness n unigrwydd

lonely adj unig

long[1] adj, adv hir, maith, llaes

long[2] vi hiraethu, dyheu

longing n hiraeth, dyhead

longitude n hydred

long jump n naid hir

long-term adj yn y tymor hir

loo n (inf) tŷ bach

look vb edrych, syllu ▸ n edrychiad, golwg; **look after** vt gwarchod, gofalu (am); **look at** vt edrych ar; **look for** vt chwilio am; **look round** vi (turn head) edrych yn ôl; **look up** vi edrych i fyny ▸ vt (in dictionary etc) edrych; **things are looking up** mae pethau'n gwella

lookout n gwyliwr

loom[1] n gwŷdd

loom[2] vi ymrithio, ymddangos

loop n dolen ▸ vb dolennu

loophole n dihangdwll

loose adj rhydd, llac ▸ vt gollwng

loosen vb rhyddhau, llacio

loot n anrhaith, ysbail ▸ vb ysbeilio, anrheithio

lopsided adj unochrog, anghymesur, anghyfartal

lord n arglwydd ▸ vb arglwyddiaethu

lorry n lori

lorry driver n gyrrwr lori

lose (pt, pp **lost**) vb colli

loser n: **we are the losers** ni sy'n colli

loss n colled

lost adj ar goll

lost-and-found n swyddfa eiddo colledig

lot n coelbren; rhan, tynged; **a lot** llawer

lotion n golchdrwyth, eli

lottery n hapchwarae, raffl

loud adj uchel, croch

loudly adv yn uchel

loud speaker n corn siarad

lounge n lolfa ▸ vi segura, gorweddian

louse n lleuen

lousy adj (inf) lleuog, brwnt

love n cariad, serch ▸ vt caru

lovely adj hawddgar, teg, hyfryd

loving adj cariadus, serchog

low[1] adj isel

low[2] vi brefu ▸ n bref (buwch)

lower vb gostwng, darostwng, iselu

loyal adj teyrngar

loyalty n teyrngarwch, ffyddlondeb

loyalty card n cerdyn teyrngarwch

luck n lwc

luckily adv yn ffodus

lucky adj ffodus, lwcus

ludicrous adj chwerthinllyd, gwrthun

luggage n bagiau

luggage rack n silff eiddo

lukewarm adj claear, llugoer

lull vt suo, gostegu ▸ n gosteg

lullaby n hwiangerdd

lumber *vb* pentyrru; llusgo
luminous *adj* golau, disglair, llachar
lump *n* lwmp, clamp, clap, talp; **lump sum** cyfandaliad
lunatic *n (offensive)* lloerigyn, gwallgofddyn
lunch *n* byrbryd, cinio canol dydd ▶ *vi* ciniawa (ganol dydd)
lung *n* ysgyfaint
lure *n* hud ▶ *vt* hudo, denu
lurk *vi* llercian, llechu
lush *adj* toreithiog, ffrwythlon
lust *n* chwant, trachwant ▶ *vi* trachwantu
Luxembourg *n* Lwcsembwrg
luxurious *adj* moethus
luxury *n* moeth, moethusrwydd
lying *adj* celwyddog
lyrics *n* geiriau

macaroni *n* macaroni
machine *n* peiriant
machine gun *n* gwn peiriant
machinery *n* peiriannau
mackerel *n* macrell
mackintosh *n* cot law
mad *adj* cynddeiriog, gwallgof, ynfyd
madam *n* madam
made-to-measure *adj* wedi ei dorri gan deiliwr
madman *n* ynfytyn, gwallgofddyn
madness *n* ynfydrwydd, gwallgofrwydd
magazine *n* ystorfa, arfdy; cylchgrawn
maggot *n* cynrhonyn
magic *adj* cyfareddol ▶ *n* hud, swyngyfaredd
magician *n* swynwr, dewin
magistrate *n* ynad
magnet *n* magned
magnetic *n* magnetig

magnificent adj gwych, ysblennydd

magnify vt mawrhau, mwyhau, chwyddo

magnifying-glass n chwyddwydr

magpie n pioden

maid n merch, morwyn

maiden name n enw morwynol

mail n y post

mailbox n blwch postio

main[1] n prif bibell; prif gebl; cefnfor; **in the main** yn bennaf, gan mwyaf

main[2] adj pennaf, prif, mwyaf

main course n prif gwrs

mainland n y tir mawr

mainly adv yn bennaf

main road n priffordd, ffordd fawr

maintain vt dal, cynnal, maentumio

maintenance n cynhaliaeth, gofalaeth

maize n indrawn, india corn

majesty n mawrhydi, mawredd

major adj mwy, mwyaf, pennaf ▸ n uwchgapten

Majorca n Maiorca, Mallorca

majority n mwyafrif; oedran llawn

make (pt, pp **made**) vt gwneud, gwneuthur, peri ▸ n gwneuthuriad; **make out** vt (understand, decipher) deall; **make up** vt (invent) dyfeisio; (constitute) gwneud; **to be made up of** cynnwys

maker n gwneuthurwr, creawdwr

make-up n colur

making n gwneuthuriad, ffurfiad

Malaysia n Maleisia

male n, adj gwryw

malicious adj maleisus

malignant adj malaen; maleisus

mall n canolfan siopa

mallet n gordd

malnutrition n gwallfaethiad, camluniaeth

malt n brag ▸ vb bragu

Malta n Malta

mammal n mamal

mammoth n mamoth ▸ adj anferth

man n dyn, gŵr

manage vb rheoli; ymdopi, llwyddo

manageable adj hydrin

management n rheolaeth, goruchwyliaeth

manager n goruchwyliwr, rheolwr

manageress n rheolwraig

mandarin n (fruit) mandarin; (language) Mandarin

mandate n gorchymyn, arch

mane n mwng

mango n mango

manhood n dyndod

mania n gwallgofrwydd, gorawydd

maniac n gwallgofddyn

manifest adj amlwg ▸ vt amlygu, dangos

manifesto n datganiad, maniffesto

manipulate vt trin, trafod

mankind n dynolryw

manly adj dynol, gwrol

manner n modd; moes

mansion n plas

manslaughter n dynladdiad

mantelpiece n silff ben tân

manual adj perthynol i'r llaw ▸ n llawlyfr

manufacture n gwaith, nwydd ▸ vt gwneuthur, gwneud

manufacturer n cynhyrchwr
manure n tail, gwrtaith
manuscript n llawysgrif
many adj aml, sawl, llawer; **as many** cymaint, cynifer; **how many** sawl
map n map
maple n masarnen
mar vt difetha, andwyo, hagru
marathon n marathon
marble n marmor; marblen
March n (mis) Mawrth
march¹ vb ymdeithio ▸ n ymdaith
march² n mers, goror
mare n caseg
margarine n margarîn
margin n ymyl, cwr, goror
marigold n gold Mair
marijuana n mariwana
marine adj morol ▸ n môr-filwr; llynges
marital n priodasol
maritime adj morol, arforol
mark n nod, marc ▸ vt nodi, marcio, sylwi
market n marchnad ▸ vb marchnata
marketing n marchnata
marmalade n marmalêd
maroon vb rhoi a gadael ar ynys anial ▸ adj coch tywyll
marriage n priodas
married adj priod
marrow n mêr; (vegetable) pwmpen
marry vb priodi
Mars n Mawrth
marsh n morfa, cors, mignen
marshal n cadlywydd, marsialydd ▸ vt byddino, trefnu
martyr n merthyr ▸ vt merthyru

marvel n rhyfeddod ▸ vi rhyfeddu, synnu
marvellous adj rhyfeddol, gwych
Marxism n marcsiaeth
Marxist adj marcsaidd
mascara n masgara, colur llygaid
masculine adj gwryw, gwrywaidd
mash n cymysg, stwnsh ▸ vt stwnsio
mashed potatoes n tatws stwnsh
mask n mwgwd ▸ vt mygydu, cuddio
mason n saer maen
mass¹ n pentwr, talp, crynswth, màs; **the masses** y werin
mass² n offeren
massacre n cyflafan ▸ vt cyflafanu
massage n, vb tylino
massive adj anferth
mast n hwylbren
master n meistr, athro, capten (llong) ▸ vt meistroli
masterpiece n campwaith, gorchest
mat n mat ▸ vt matio, plethu
match¹ n (for fire) matsien
match² n cymar; priodas; ymrysonfa, gêm ▸ vb cystadlu; cyfateb
mate n cymar, cydymaith; (inf) mêt ▸ vt cymharu
material adj materol; perthnasol, o bwys ▸ n defnydd
maternal adj mamol; o du'r fam
maternity n mamolaeth
mathematics npl mathemateg
maths n mathemateg
matron n metron
matter n mater; crawn ▸ vi bod o bwys

mattress n matras
mature adj aeddfed; mewn oed
▸ vb aeddfedu
mature student n myfyriwr hŷn
maturity n aeddfedrwydd
maul vt baeddu, pwyo ▸ n sgarmes
mauve n lliw porffor, piws
maximum n uchafswm
May n Mai
may n blodau drain gwynion
maybe adv efallai, hwyrach, dichon
May Day n Calan Mai
mayonnaise n mayonnaise
mayor n maer
mayoress n maeres
me pron myfi, mi, fi, i; minnau
meadow n dôl, gwaun, gweirglodd
meagre adj prin, tlodaidd, llwm
meal¹ n (flour) blawd
meal² n pryd o fwyd
mean¹ n cyfrwng, modd; cymedr
mean² (pt, pp **meant**) vt meddwl, golygu, bwriadu
mean³ adj gwael, isel, crintach
meaning n ystyr, meddwl
meantime, meanwhile adv yn y cyfamser
measles npl y frech goch
measure vt, n mesur
meat n cig
Mecca n Mecca
mechanic n peiriannydd
mechanical adj mecanyddol
mechanism n peirianwaith
medal n bathodyn, medal
meddle vi ymyrryd, busnesa, ymhél
media npl cyfryngau
mediaeval adj canoloesol

mediate vi canoli, cyfryngu
medical adj meddygol
medication n meddyginiaeth
medicine n meddyginiaeth; ffisig, moddion
mediocre adj canolig, cyffredin
meditate vb myfyrio
meditation n myfyrdod
Mediterranean n: the Mediterranean Môr y Canoldir
medium n canol; cyfrwng ▸ adj canol, canolig
medium-sized adj o faint canolig
meek adj llariaidd, addfwyn
meet (pt, pp **met**) vb cyfarfod, cwrdd ▸ adj addas; **meet up** vb cwrdd
meeting n cyfarfod, cyfarfyddiad
mega adv (inf) **mega rich** cyfoethog dros ben
melancholy adj prudd, pruddglwyfus ▸ n pruddglwyf, y felan
melody n peroriaeth, melodi
melon n melon
melt vb toddi, ymdoddi
member n aelod
Member of Parliament n Aelod Seneddol
membership n aelodaeth
memento n cofarwydd
memorable adj cofiadwy, bythgofiadwy
memorandum n cofnod, cofnodiad
memorial adj coffadwriaethol ▸ n coffadwriaeth; cofeb
memory n cof; coffadwriaeth
memory card n cerdyn cof, cof-gerdyn

m

memory stick *n* cof bach

menace *n* bygythiad ▸ *vt* bygwth

mend *vb* gwella, cyweirio, trwsio

meningitis *n* llid yr ymennydd

menstruation *n* y misglwyf

mental *adj* meddyliol

mental hospital *n* (*old, pej*) ysbyty'r meddwl

mention *vt* crybwyll, sôn ▸ *n* crybwylliad

menu *n* bwydlen, arlwy

mercenary *adj* ariangar, chwannog i elw ▸ *n* huriwr, milwr cyflog

merchandise *n* marsiandïaeth

merchant *n* masnachwr, marsiandwr

merciless *adj* didrugaredd

mercury *n* arian byw, mercwri

mercy *n* trugaredd

mere *adj* unig, pur, hollol

merge *vb* soddi, colli, ymgolli

merger *n* ymsoddiad, cyfuniad, ymdoddiad

merit *n* haeddiant, teilyngdod ▸ *vt* haeddu, teilyngu

mermaid *n* môr-forwyn

merry *adj* llawen, llon

merry-go-round *n* ceffylau bach

mesh *n* masgl, magl, rhwydwaith

mess *n* llanastr, annibendod ▸ *vb* ymhél; maeddu; **mess about** *vb* (*inf*) stwna; **mess up** *vt* (*inf*) gwneud cawl o

message *n* cenadwri, neges

messenger *n* cennad, negesydd

messy *adj* (*dirty*) brwnt; (*untidy*) anniben

metabolism *n* metaboleg, metabolaeth

metal *n* metel ▸ *adj* metelaidd

metaphor *n* trosiad

meteor *n* seren wib

meter *n* mesurydd; metr

method *n* trefn, method, dull

Methodist *n* Methodist ▸ *adj* Methodistaidd

meticulous *adj* gorfanwl

metre *n* mesur, mydr

metric *adj* metrig

Mexico *n* Mecsico

micro-chip *n* meicro-sglodyn

microphone *n* meicroffon, meic

microscope *n* chwyddwydr, meicrosgop

microwave *n* meicrodon; **microwave oven** ffwrn meicrodon, popty ping

mid *adj* canol

midday *n* canol dydd, hanner dydd

middle *n, adj* canol

middle-aged *adj* canol oed

middle-class *adj* dosbarth canol

Middle East *n* Dwyrain Canol

middle name *n* enw canol

middle school *n* ysgol ganolraddol

midge *n* gwybedyn

midget *n* (*inf!*) corrach

midnight *n* canol nos, hanner nos

midst *n* canol, plith

midsummer *n* canol haf

Midsummer Day *n* gŵyl Ifan

midwife (*pl* **midwives**) *n* bydwraig

might *n* nerth, cadernid, gallu

mighty *adj* cadarn, galluog, nerthol

migraine *n* meigryn

migrant *n* mudwr, ymfudwr, crwydrwr ▸ *adj* mudol, crwydrol

migrate *vi* symud, mudo

migration n mudiad, ymfudiad
mike n meic
mild adj tyner, tirion, mwyn; gwan, ysgafn
mile n milltir
mileage n milltiredd
milestone n carreg filltir
military adj milwrol
milk n llaeth, llefrith ▸ vt godro
milk chocolate n siocled llaeth
milkman n dyn llaeth
mill n melin ▸ vt melino, malu
millennium n mil blynyddoedd
millimetre n milimedr
million n miliwn
millionaire n miliynydd
mime n meim
mimic n dynwared, gwatwar
mince vt malu ▸ n briwgig, briwfwyd
mind n meddwl, bryd, cof ▸ vb gofalu, cofio
mine n mwynglawdd, pwll
miner n mwynwr, glöwr
mineral adj mwynol ▸ n mwyn
mineral water n dŵr pistyll
mingle vb cymysgu, britho
miniature n mân ddarlun ▸ adj bychan
minibus n bws mini, minibws
minimize vt lleihau, bychanu
minimum n lleiafswm, isafrif
mining n mwyngloddiaeth;
  opencast mining mwyngloddio brig
miniskirt n scyrt fini
minister n gweinidog ▸ vb gwasanaethu, gweinidogaethu
ministry n gweinidogaeth; gweinyddiaeth

minor adj llai, lleiaf; lleddf ▸ n un dan oed
minority n minoriaeth; lleiafrif
mint[1] n bathdy ▸ vt bathu
mint[2] n (plant) mintys
minus adj, pron llai, heb ▸ n minws
minute[1] adj bach, bychan, mân; manwl
minute[2] n munud; cofnod
miracle n gwyrth
miraculous adj gwyrthiol
mirage n rhithlun, lleurith
mirror n drych ▸ vt adlewyrchu
misbehave vi camymddwyn
miscarriage n erthyliad
miscarriage of justice n aflwyddo cyfiawnder
miscellaneous adj amrywiol
mischief n drwg, drygioni, direidi
mischievous adj drygionus, direidus
misconception n camsyniad, cam-dyb
misconduct n camymddygiad ▸ vb camymddwyn
miser n cybydd
miserable adj truenus, gresynus, anhapus
misery n trueni, gresyni, adfyd
misfortune n anffawd, aflwydd
mishap n anap, anffawd, aflwydd
misinterpret vb camddehongli
misjudge vb camfarnu, camddeall
mislead vb camarwain, twyllo
misprint n cambrint ▸ vb camargraffu
misrepresent vt camddarlunio, camliwio
miss vt methu, ffaelu, colli ▸ n meth

347

missile n saethyn, taflegryn

missing adj yn eisiau, yngholl, ar goll

mission n cenhadaeth

missionary n cenhadwr ▸ adj cenhadol

misspell vb camsillafu

mist n niwl, nudden, tarth, caddug

mistake vt camgymryd, methu ▸ n camgymeriad, gwall

mistletoe n uchelwydd

mistress n meistres; athrawes; Mrs

mistrust vt drwgdybio, amau

misty adj niwlog

misunderstand vt camddeall

misunderstanding n camddealltwriaeth

mix vb cymysgu; **mix up** vt cymysgu

mixed adj cymysg

mixer n: **he's a good mixer** mae e'n gymdeithaswr da

mixture n cymysgedd, cymysgfa

mix-up n dryswch

moan n, vb ochain, griddfan, udo

moat n ffos (castell)

mob n torf, tyrfa, haid ▸ vt ymosod ar

mobile adj symudol, symudadwy; mudol (cemeg)

mobile home n cartref symudol

mobile phone n ffôn symudol

mobilize vt dygyfor, byddino

mock vb gwatwar ▸ adj gau, ffug

mockery n gwatwar

mode n modd, dull

model n cynllun, patrwm ▸ vt llunio

modem n modem

moderate adj cymedrol ▸ vt cymedroli

moderation n cymedroldeb

modern adj modern, diweddar

modernize vb moderneiddio

modest adj gwylaidd, diymhongar

modesty n gwylder, gwyleidd-dra

modify vt newid, lleddfu

module n modiwl

moist adj llaith, gwlyb

moisture n lleithder, gwlybaniaeth

moisturizer n lleithydd

mole¹ n (birthmark) man geni

mole² n (mammal) gwadd, twrch daear

molecule n molecwl ▸ adj molecylig

molest vt molestu, aflonyddu

molten adj tawdd

moment n moment; pwys, pwysigrwydd

momentum n momentwm

monarch n brenin, brenhines, teyrn

monarchy n brenhiniaeth

monastery n mynachlog, mynachdy

Monday n dydd Llun

monetary adj ariannol

money n arian, pres

mongrel adj cymysgryw ▸ n mwngrel

monitor n monitor

monk n mynach

monkey n mwnci

monologue n ymson

monopoly n monopoli

monotonous adj undonog

monsoon n monsŵn

monster n anghenfil; clamp ▸ adj anferth

month n mis

monthly adj misol ▸ n misolyn

monument n cofadail, cofgolofn

mood n hwyl, tymer; modd

moody adj oriog, cyfnewidiol

moon n lleuad, lloer; **harvest moon** lleuad fedi

moonlight n golau leuad

moor¹ n morfa, rhos

moor² vt angori, bachu, sicrhau

mop n mop ▸ vt mopio, sychu

mope vi pendrymu, delwi

moped n moped

moral adj moesol ▸ n moeswers, addysg

morality n moesoldeb

morbid adj afiach

(KEYWORD)

more adj 1 (greater in number etc) mwy (na), rhagor (na); **more people/work (than)** mwy o bobl/ waith (na)

2 (additional) rhagor, ychwaneg (o); **do you want (some) more tea?** gymerwch chi ychwaneg o de?; **is there any more wine?** a oes rhagor o win?; **I have no** or **I don't have any more money** nid oes gennyf ragor o arian; **it'll take a few more weeks** bydd yn cymryd ychydig wythnosau'n rhagor

▸ pron rhagor, ychwaneg, mwy; **more than 10** mwy na 10; **it cost more than we expected** costiodd fwy na'r disgwyl; **I want more** mae arnaf eisiau ychwaneg; **is there any more?** a oes ychwaneg?;

there's no more nid oes ychwaneg; **a little more** ychydig yn rhagor; **many/much more** llawer mwy

▸ adv 1 for most adjectives of one or two syllables in Welsh the comparative degree is formed by the ending -ach; **more ready (than)** parotach (na)

2 (for most adjectives of more than two syllables the comparative is formed by using the word mwy): **more pleasant (than)** mwy dymunol (na); **more and more expensive** mwy a mwy drud; **more or less** mwy neu lai; **more than ever** mwy nag erioed; **once more** unwaith eto, unwaith yn rhagor

moreover adv heblaw hynny, hefyd

morning n bore ▸ adj bore, boreol

Morocco n Moroco

mortal adj marwol, angheuol ▸ n dyn marwol

mortar n morter

mortgage n morgais, arwystl ▸ vt morgeisio, arwystlo

mortuary n marwdy

mosaic adj brith, amryliw ▸ n brithwaith, mosaig

Moscow n Moscow

Moslem n, adj = Muslim

mosque n mosg

mosquito n mosgito

moss n mwswgl, mwsogl

most adj mwyaf, amlaf

mostly adv gan mwyaf, fynychaf

moth n gwyfyn

mother n mam

mother-in-law n mam yng nghyfraith, chwegr
Mother's Day n dydd Sul y Mamau
motion n symudiad; cynigiad
motivate vt ysgogi, cymell
motivated adj brwdfrydig
motivation n ysgogiad
motive adj symudol, ysgogol ▸ n cymhelliad, motif
motor n modur
motorbike n beic modur
motorboat n cwch modur
motor cycle n beic modur
motorcyclist n beicwr (modur)
motorist n modurwr
motor racing n rasio modur
motorway n traffordd
motto n arwyddair
mould¹ n mold; delw ▸ vt moldio, llunio, delweddu
mould² n (mildew) llwydni, llwydi
mouldy adj wedi llwydo
mound n twmpath, crug
mount¹ n mynydd, bryn
mount² vb esgyn, mynd ar gefn; gosod
mountain n mynydd
mountain bike n beic mynydd
mountaineer n mynyddwr
mountaineering n mynydda
mountainous adj mynyddig
mourn vb galaru
mourning n galar; galarwisg
mouse (pl **mice**) n llygoden ▸ vb llygota
mouse mat n mat llygoden
mousse n mousse
moustache n trawswch, mwstas
mouth n ceg ▸ vb cegu, safnu
mouthful n cegaid

move vb symud; cymell; cynnig; cyffroi; **move forward** vb symud ymlaen; **move in** vi symud i mewn; **move over** vb symud
movement n symudiad; mudiad
movie n ffilm
moving adj (in motion) yn symud
mow (pt **mowed**, pp **mowed**, **mown**) vt lladd (gwair) ▸ n mwdwl, medel
MP n abbr AS (aelod seneddol)
MP3 n MP3
MP3 player n peiriant MP3
mph abbr (= miles per hour) mya
Mr n Mr
Mrs n Mrs
MS n (= multiple sclerosis) sglerosis ymledol
Ms n Ms
much adj llawer ▸ adv yn fawr
muck n tail, tom, baw ▸ vt tomi, baeddu
mucus n llys, llysnafedd
mud n mwd, llaid
muddle vi drysu ▸ n dryswch; **muddle up** vt drysu
muddy adj mwdlyd
muesli n mwsli
mug n cwpan, godart ▸ vt mygio
mugging n ysbeiliad
mule n mul, bastard mul
multiple adj amryfal ▸ n cynhwysrif, lluosrif
multiple choice n amlddewis, dewis lluosog
multiplication n amlhad, lluosogiad
multiply vb amlhau, lluosogi, lluosi
multi-storey adj aml-lawr
mum n mam

mumble *vb* grymial, myngial
mummy *n* mwmi
mumps *n* clwy'r pennau, y dwymyn doben
munch *vt* cnoi
municipal *adj* dinesig, bwrdeisiol
mural *adj* murol ▸ *n* murlun
murder *vt* llofruddio ▸ *n* llofruddiaeth
murderer *n* llofrudd
murky *adj* tywyll, cymylog, dudew
murmur *vb, n* murmur, grwgnach
muscle *n* cyhyr, cyhyryn
muscular *adj* cyhyrog
muse *vi* myfyrio, synfyfyrio
museum *n* amgueddfa
mushroom *n* madarch
music *n* miwsig, cerdd, cerddoriaeth
musical *adj* cerddorol
musical instrument *n* offeryn cerdd
musician *n* cerddor
Muslim *adj* Moslemaidd, Mwslimaidd ▸ *n* Moslem, Mwslim
mussel *n* misglen; **mussels** *npl* cregyn gleision
must *vb def* rhaid
mustard *n* mwstart
mute *adj* mud
mutilate *vt* anafu, hagru, llurgunio
mutiny *n* terfysg, gwrthryfel
mutter *vb* mwmian
mutton *n* cig dafad, cig mollt
mutual *adj* cyd, o boptu, y naill a'r llall
muzzle *n* genau, ffroen ▸ *vt* cau safn, rhoi taw ar
my *pron* fy

myself *pron* myfi fy hun
mysterious *adj* dirgel, rhyfedd, dirgelaidd
mystery *n* dirgelwch
mystify *vt* synnu, syfrdanu
myth *n* chwedl, myth
mythology *n* chwedloniaeth

m

n

nag vb cadw sŵn ▸ n ceffyl
nail n hoel, hoelen; ewin ▸ vt hoelio
nailbrush n brws ewinedd
nail file n ffeil/rhathell ewinedd
nail scissors n siswrn ewinedd
nail varnish n farnis ewinedd
naïve adj diniwed
naked adj noeth
name n enw ▸ vt enwi, galw
namely adv sef, nid amgen
nanny n nani
nap vi cysgu, pendwmpian ▸ n cyntun
napkin n napcyn, cewyn
nappy n cewyn, clwt
narrative n naratif
narrow adj cul, cyfyng ▸ vb culhau, cyfyngu
nasal adj trwynol
nasty adj cas
nation n cenedl
national adj cenedlaethol

national anthem n anthem genedlaethol
nationalism n cenedlaetholdeb
nationalist n cenedlaetholwr
nationality n cenedl, cenedligrwydd
nationalize vb gwladoli, cenedlaetholi
National Lottery n Loteri Genedlaethol
national park n parc cenedlaethol
native n brodor ▸ adj brodorol; cynhenid
natural adj anianol, naturiol
naturally adv yn naturiol
nature n anian, natur
nature reserve n gwarchodfa natur
naughty adj drwg, drygionus
nausea n cyfog
naval adj llyngesol, morol
nave n corff eglwys
navel n bogail
navigate vt mordwyo, llywio
navy n llynges
navy blue n, adj nefi-blw
near adj, adv, prep agos, ger, gerllaw ▸ vb agosáu, nesu
nearby adv gerllaw, yn ymyl
nearly adv bron
neat adj destlus, twt; pur
neatly adv yn daclus
necessarily adv o angenrheidrwydd
necessary adj angenrheidiol
necessity n anghenraid
neck n gwddf
necklace n mwclis
need n, vb (bod mewn) angen, eisiau

needle n nodwydd; gwaell

needless adj afreidiol, dianghenraid

needlework n gwniadwaith

negative adj nacaol, negyddol

neglect vt esgeuluso ▸ n esgeulustra

neglected adj esgeulusedig

negotiate vb negodi

negotiation n trafodaeth, cyd-drafodaeth

neighbour n cymydog

neighbourhood n cymdogaeth

neither conj na, nac, ychwaith ▸ adj, pron na'r naill na'r llall, nid yr un o'r ddau

nephew n nai

nerve n nerf

nervous adj nerfus

nest n nyth ▸ vb nythu

Net n: the Net (Internet) y Rhyngrwyd

net¹ n rhwyd, rhwyden

net² adj union, net ▸ vt rhwydo

netball n pêl rwyd

Netherlands npl: the Netherlands yr Iseldiroedd

nettle n danadl

network n rhwydwaith

networking n rhwydweithio; social networking rhwydweithio cymdeithasol

neuter adj diryw

neutral adj amhleidiol ▸ n amhleidydd

never adv ni ... erioed, ni ... byth

nevertheless adv, conj eto, er hynny

new adj newydd

newcomer n newydd-ddyfodiad

news n newydd, newyddion

newsagent n gwerthwr papurau newyddion

newspaper n papur newydd, newyddiadur

newsreader n darllenydd newyddion

newt n madfall

New Year n Y Calan, Y Flwyddyn Newydd

New Year's Eve n Nos Galan

New York n Efrog Newydd

New Zealand n Seland Newydd

New Zealander n Selandwr Newydd

next adj nesaf ▸ adv yn nesaf

NHS n GIG

nibble vb deintio, cnoi

nice adj neis, hardd; cynnil

niche n cloer, cilfach

nickname n llysenw ▸ vt llysenwi

niece n nith

Nigeria n Nigeria

night n nos; noson, noswaith; by night liw nos

night club n clwb nos

nightdress n gŵn nos, coban

nightie n coban

nightmare n hunllef

nil n dim

nine adj, n naw

nineteen adj, n pedwar (pedair) ar bymtheg, un deg naw

nineteenth adj pedwerydd (pedwaredd) ar bymtheg

ninety adj, n deg a phedwar ugain, naw deg

ninth adj nawfed

nip vb brathu, cnoi; deifio

nipple n teth

nitrogen n nitrogen

no

no adv (answer to unemphatic question: na/nac + verb) **are you coming? — no (I'm not)** a ydych yn dod? — nac ydw; **would you like some more? — no thank you** a hoffech gael rhagor? — na hoffwn; (question in past tense): **did you see the programme? — no (I did not)** a welsoch y rhaglen? — naddo; (emphatic question: na, nage): **are you the owner of this dog? — no** ai chi yw perchennog y ci hwn? — nage
▸ adj (not any) dim, yr un, unrhyw; **I have no money/books** nid oes gennyf unrhyw arian/nid oes gennyf yr un llyfr; **no student would have done it** ni fyddai'r un myfyriwr wedi gwneud y peth; **"no smoking" "dim ysmygu"; "no dogs" "dim cŵn"**
▸ n y na m

nobility n bonedd
noble adj pendefigaidd ▸ n pendefig
nobody n neb
nod vb amneidio; pendrymu ▸ n amnaid
noise n sŵn
noisy adj swnllyd
nominal adj enwol, mewn enw
nominate vt enwi, enwebu
nomination n enwebiad
none pron neb, dim, dim un
nonsense n lol
non-smoking adj dim ysmygu
non-stop adv yn ddi-baid ▸ adj di-baid

noodles n nwdls
noon n hanner dydd, canol dydd
no-one pron neb
nor conj na, nac
normal adj cyffredin, safonol
normally adv fel arfer
Normandy n Normandi
north n gogledd ▸ adj gogleddol
North America n Gogledd America
northeast n gogledd-ddwyrain ▸ adj gogledd-ddwyreiniol
northern adj gogleddol
Northern Ireland n Gogledd Iwerddon
North Pole n Pegwn y Gogledd
North Sea n Môr y Gogledd
northwest n gogledd-orllewin
Norway n Norwy
Norwegian n (person) Norwyad; (language) Norwyeg ▸ adj Norwyaidd
nose n trwyn ▸ vb trwyno
nosebleed n gwaedlif o'r trwyn
nostalgia n hiraeth
nostril n ffroen
nosy adj (inf) busneslyd
not adv na, nac, nad, ni, nid
notable adj nodedig, enwog
notch n rhic
note n nod, nodyn ▸ vt nodi, sylwi; **note down** vt nodi
notebook n llyfr nodiadau, nodlyfr
noted adj nodedig
note pad n pad ysgrifennu
notepaper n papur ysgrifennu
nothing n dim; **nothing at all** dim byd, dim byd o gwbl
notice n sylw, rhybudd ▸ vt sylwi

noticeboard *n* hysbysfwrdd
notify *vt* hysbysu, rhoi rhybudd
notion *n* amcan, syniad
notorious *adj* hynod, rhemp
notwithstanding *conj* er ▸ *prep* er,
er gwaethaf
nought *n* dim; gwagnod (o)
noun *n* enw
nourish *vt* maethu, meithrin
nourishment *n* maeth
novel *adj* newydd ▸ *n* nofel
novelist *n* nofelydd
November *n* Tachwedd
novice *n* newyddian, nofis
now *adv, conj, n* yn awr, rŵan,
bellach; **just now** gynnau; **now
and then** yn awr ac yn y man
nowadays *adv* yn y dyddiau hyn
nowhere *adv* dim yn unlle
nozzle *n* ffroenell
nuclear *adj* niwclear
nucleus *n* cnewyllyn, bywyn
nude *adj* noeth, noethlymun
nudge *vt* pwnio, penelino
nuisance *n* pla, poendod
numb *adj* diffrwyth, cwsg ▸ *vt*
fferru, merwino
number *n* nifer, rhif; rhifyn ▸ *vt*
rhifo, cyfrif
number plate *n* plât rhif
numerical *adj* rhifiadol
numerous *adj* niferus
nun *n* lleian, mynaches
nurse *n* gweinyddes, nyrs ▸ *vt*
magu, meithrin, nyrsio
nursery *n* magwrfa, meithrinfa
nursery school *n* ysgol feithrin
nurture *n* maeth, magwraeth ▸ *vt*
maethu, meithrin

nut *n* cneuen
nutrition *n* maeth, maethiad
nutritious *adj* maethlon
nuts *adj* (inf, mad) gwirion
nylon *n* neilon

n

355

O

oak n derwen; derw
oar n rhwyf
oatcake n bara ceirch, teisen geirch
oath n llw
oatmeal n blawd ceirch
oats npl ceirchen, ceirch
obedience n ufudd-dod
obedient adj ufudd
obese adj tew, corffol
obesity n gor-dewdra
obey vb ufuddhau
obituary n marwgoffa
object n gwrthrych; amcan ▸ vb gwrthwynebu
objection n gwrthwynebiad
objective adj gwrthrychol ▸ n amcan, nod
obligation n dyled, rhwymau
oblige vt rhwymo; boddio; gorfodi
oblique adj lleddf, ar osgo
obliterate vt dileu
oblong adj hirgul ▸ n oblong

obnoxious adj atgas, ffiaidd
oboe n obo
obscene adj anllad, anniwair
obscure adj tywyll; anhysbys ▸ vt tywyllu
observation n sylw; sylwadaeth
observatory n arsyllfa
observe vb sylwi, arsyllu; cadw
observer n sylwedydd, arsyllwr
obsessed adj obsesedig
obsession n obsesiwn
obsolete adj anarferedig, ansathredig
obstacle n rhwystr, atalfa
obstinate adj cyndyn, ystyfnig
obstruct vt cau, tagu; rhwystro, lluddio
obtain vt cael, ennill
obvious adj eglur, amlwg
obviously adv yn amlwg; (of course) wrth gwrs; **he's obviously happy** mae'n amlwg ei fod yn hapus
occasion n achlysur ▸ vt achlysuro
occasional adj achlysurol, anaml
occasionally adv ambell waith
occult adj cudd, dirgel
occupation n galwedigaeth; meddiant
occupy vt meddu, meddiannu; llenwi; dal
occur vi digwydd; taro i'r meddwl
occurrence n digwyddiad
ocean n cefnfor, eigion
o'clock adv o'r gloch
October n Hydref
octopus n octopws
odd adj od, hynod; **odd number** odrif
odds npl ots, gwahaniaeth
odour n aroglau

KEYWORD

of prep 1 (gen): **a friend of ours** ffrind i ni; **a boy of 10** bachgen 10 oed; **that was kind of you** buoch yn garedig iawn
2 (expressing quantity, amount, dates etc) o; **a kilo of flour** cilogram o flawd; **how much of this do you need?** faint ohono y mae arnoch ei angen?; **there were three of them** roedd 3 ohonynt; **three of us went** aeth 3 ohonom; **the 5th of July** y 5ed o Orffennaf
3 (from, out of) o; **a statue of marble** cerflun o farmor; **made of wood** (wedi'i wneud) o goed

off adv ymaith, i ffwrdd ▸ prep oddi, oddi wrth, oddi ar; **off and on** yn awr ac yn y man

offence n tramgwydd, trosedd

offend vb tramgwyddo, troseddu; digio

offender n troseddwr

offensive adj atgas, ffiaidd; ymosodol

offer vb cynnig, cyflwyno; offrymu ▸ n cynnig

office n swydd; swyddfa

office block n bloc swyddfeydd

officer n swyddog, swyddwr

official adj swyddogol ▸ n swyddog

off-licence n siop diodydd

offside n camochr, camsefyll ▸ vb camochri, camsefyll

offspring n epil

often adv yn amlwg

oh excl O!

oil n olew, oel ▸ vt iro, oelio

oil rig n llwyfan olew

ointment n ennaint, eli

okay excl popeth yn iawn

old adj hen, oedrannus; **of old** gynt; **old age** henaint, henoed; **old and infirm** hen a methedig

old-fashioned adj henffasiwn, od

old people's home n cartref henoed

old stager n hen law

olive n olewydden

olive oil n olew olewydd

Olympic® adj Olympaidd; **the Olympic Games**®, **the Olympics**® y Chwaraeon Olympaidd

omelette n crempog wyau

omen n argoel, arwydd

ominous adj argoelus, bygythiol

omit vt gadael allan, esgeuluso

KEYWORD

on prep 1 (indicating position) ar; **on the table** ar y bwrdd; **on the wall** ar y wal; **on the left** ar y chwith
2 (indicating means, method, condition etc): **on foot** ar ddeudroed; **on the train/plane** (be) ar y trên/awyren; **on the telephone/radio/television** ar y ffôn/radio/teledu; **to be on drugs** bod ar gyffuriau; **on holiday** ar eich gwyliau
3 (referring to time): **on Friday** ddydd Gwener; **on Fridays** ar ddydd Gwener; **on June 20th** ar yr 20fed o Fehefin; **a week on Friday** wythnos i ddydd Gwener; **on arrival** ar ôl cyrraedd; **on seeing this** o weld hyn
4 (about, concerning): **a book on**

once

Dylan Thomas/physics llyfr am
Dylan Thomas/ffiseg
▸ *adv* **1** (*referring to dress*): **to
have one's coat on** bod â'ch cot
amdanoch; **to put one's coat on**
gwisgo'ch cot; **what's she got on?**
beth mae'n ei wisgo?
2 (*further*): (*continuously*): **to walk
on** cerdded ymlaen; **from that day
on** o'r diwrnod hwnnw ymlaen
▸ *adj* **1** (*in operation*): (*machine*)
ymlaen; (*radio, TV, light*) ymlaen;
(*tap*) yn agored; (*brakes*) wedi'u
cau [yn dynn]; **is the meeting still
on?** (*not cancelled*) a yw'r cyfarfod
yn dal ymlaen?; **when is this film
on?** pryd mae'r ffilm hon ymlaen?
2 (*inf*): **that's not on!** (*not
acceptable*) wnaiff hyn mo'r tro!
(*not possible*) amhosibl!

once *adv* unwaith; gynt
one *num* un; **one hundred and fifty**
cant a hanner; **one by one** fesul
un, o un i un, bob yn un; **one day**
un diwrnod ▸ *adj* (*sole*) unig; **the
one book which** yr unig lyfr a; **the
one man who** yr unig ddyn a;
(*same*) yr un; **they came in the one
car** daethant yn yr un car ▸ *pron*:
this one hwn (hon); **that one**
hwnnw (honno); **I've already got
one/a red one** mae un/un coch
gennyf eisoes; **which one do you
want?** pa un a hoffech ei gael?; **one
another** y naill a'r llall; **to look at
one another** edrych ar eich gilydd;
(*impersonal*) rhywun, chi, dyn; **one
never knows** wyddoch chi byth,

ŵyr neb byth, does wybod; **to cut
one's finger** torri'ch bys; **one needs
to eat** rhaid i ddyn fwyta
oneself *pron* ei hun
onion *n* wynwynyn, nionyn
online *adj adv* ar-lein
only *adj* unig ▸ *adv* yn unig; ond
onset *n* ymosodiad, cyrch;
cychwyn
onward, onwards *adj, adv* ymlaen
onwards *adv* ymlaen
ooze *n* llaid, llysnafedd ▸ *vi*
chwyzu
opaque *adj* afloyw, tywyll
open *adj* agored ▸ *vb* agor, ymagor
open-air *n, adj* awyr agored
opening *n* agoriad, agorfa
opening hours *n* oriau agor
opera *n* opera
operate *vb* gweithredu, gweithio
operation *n* gweithrediad;
gweithred, triniaeth lawfeddygol
operator *n* gweithredydd,
trafodwr
opinion *n* barn, opiniwn
opinion poll *n* arolwg barn
opponent *n* gwrthwynebydd
opportunity *n* cyfle, egwyl
oppose *vt* gwrthwynebu,
cyferbynnu
opposed *n*: **to be opposed to sth**
gwrthwynebu rhywbeth; **as
opposed to** yn hytrach na
opposite *adj, adv, prep*
gwrthwyneb, cyferbyn
opposition *n* gwrthwynebiad,
gwrthblaid
oppress *vt* gorthrymu, llethu
optician *n* optegydd

optimism n optimistiaeth
optimist n optimist
optimistic adj optimistaidd
option n dewisiad, dewis
optional adj dewisol
or conj neu, ai, ynteu, naill ai
oral adj geneuol; llafar
orange n oren, oraens ▸ adj melyngoch
orbit n rhod, tro, cylchdro
orchard n perllan
orchestra n cerddorfa
ordeal n prawf llym
order n trefn; gorchymyn, archeb; urdd ▸ vb trefnu, gorchymyn; archebu; urddo; **in order to** er mwyn
orderly adj trefnus ▸ n gwas milwr
ordinary adj cyffredin, arferol
ore n mwyn
organ n organ, offeryn
organic adj organaidd
organization n trefn, cyfundrefn, trefniadaeth; sefydliad
organize vb trefnu
organized adj trefnus
organizer n trefnydd
orgy n gloddest, cyfeddach
oriental adj dwyreiniol
orientate vb cyfeirio
origin n dechreuad, tarddiad
original adj, n gwreiddiol
originally adv yn wreiddiol
originate vb dechrau, tarddu
ornament n addurn ▸ vt addurno
ornate adj addurnedig, mawrwych
orphan adj, n amddifad
orthodox adj uniongred

osteopath n osteopath
ostrich n estrys
other adj, pron arall, llall
otherwise adv amgen, fel arall
otter n dyfrgi, dwrgi
ought vb: **I ought to do it** dylwn i ei wneud; **she ought to win** dylai hi ennill
ounce n owns
our pron ein, ein ... ni
ours pron un ni; **the garden is ours** ni sy biau'r ardd
ourselves pron ein hun
oust vt disodli
out adv allan, i maes; **out of date** (passport; ticket) â'r dyddiad wedi mynd heibio
outcast n alltud, gwrthodedig
outcome n canlyniad, ffrwyth
outcry n gwaedd; dadwrdd
outdoor adj yn yr awyr agored
outdoors adv yn yr awyr agored
outer adj allanol
outfit n dillad
outing n pleserdaith, gwibdaith
outlaw n herwr
outlay n traul, cost
outlet n allfa
outline n amlinelliad, amlinell ▸ vb amlinellu
outlook n rhagolwg, argoel; golygfa
outrageous adj gwarthus; beiddgar, cywilyddus
outset n dechrau, dechreuad
outside n tu allan, tu faes ▸ adj, adv allan(ol), oddi allan ▸ prep tu allan i, tu faes i
outskirts npl cyrrau, maestrefi

outstanding *adj* amlwg; dyledus
outward *adj* allanol
outwards *adv* tuag allan
outweigh *vt* gorbwyso
oval *adj* hirgrwn
ovary *n* ofari
oven *n* ffwrn, popty
over *prep* uwch, tros ► *adv* gor, rhy, tra
overall *adj* o ben i ben ► *n* troswisg
overcast *adj* cymylog
overcharge *vt* gorbrisio, codi gormod
overcoat *n* cot fawr/uchaf
overcome *vt* gorchfygu, trechu
overdo *vb* gorwneud
overdose *n* gor-ddogn
overdraft *n* gorddrafft
overflow *n* gorlif(iad) ► *vb* gorlifo
overhead *adj, adv* uwchben
overheat *vi* gorboethi
overload *vb* gorlwytho
overlook *vb* edrych dros; esgeuluso
overnight *adv* dros nos
overpower *vb* trechu
overrun *vb* goresgyn
overseas *adv* tramor, dros y môr
overtake *vt* goddiweddyd
overthrow *n* dymchweliad ► *vt* dymchwelyd
overtime *n* goramser, oriau ychwanegol
overturn *vt* troi, dymchwelyd
overweight *adj* dros bwysau
overwhelm *vt* llethu, gorlethu
owe *vb* bod mewn dyled
owing to *prep* oherwydd
owl *n* tylluan, gwdihŵ

own *adj* eiddo dyn ei hun, priod ► *vt* meddu; arddel; **own up** *vi* cyfaddef
owner *n* perchen, perchennog
ox *n* ych, eidion
oxygen *n* ocsigen
oyster *n* llymarch, wystrysen
ozone layer *n* haen osôn

p

pace n cam; cyflymdra ▸ vb camu, cerdded
pacemaker n (device) rheoliadur y galon, rheoliadur calon
Pacific n: **the Pacific (Ocean)** Môr Tawel
pack n pac, swp ▸ vb pacio
package n pecyn
packaging n deunydd lapio
packed adj (crowded) gorlawn
packed lunch n tocyn, pryd wedi ei bacio
packet n sypyn, paced
pact n cyfamod, cynghrair
pad n pad ▸ vt padio
paddle n padl ▸ vb padlo
paddling pool n pwll padlo
paddock n marchgae, cae bach
padlock n clo clap
paedophile n pedoffeil, pedoffilydd
page n tudalen
pain n poen, dolur ▸ vt poeni
painful adj poenus

painkiller n lladdwr poen
painstaking adj gofalus, trylwyr
paint n paent, lliw ▸ vt peintio, lliwio
paintbrush n brwsh paent
painter n peintiwr; arlunydd
painting n llun, darlun
pair n pâr, dau, cwpl ▸ vb paru
Pakistan n Pacistan
Pakistani adj Pacistanaidd ▸ n Pacistaniad
palace n palas
pale adj gwelw ▸ vb gwelwi
Palestine n Palestina
Palestinian adj Palestiniaid ▸ n Palestiniad
palm[1] n (of hand) palf, cledr llaw
palm[2] n (tree) palmwydden; **Palm Sunday** Sul y Blodau
pamper vt mwytho, maldodi
pamphlet n pamffled, llyfryn
pan n padell
pancake n crempog, cramwythen, ffroisen
pane n cwarel, paen
panel n panel
panic n dychryn, panig
pansy n triliw, llysiau'r Drindod
pant vi dyheu
panther n panther
panties npl pantos
pantomime n pantomeim
pants npl pants
paper n papur ▸ vb papuro; **blotting paper** papur sugno; **brown paper** papur llwyd; **tissue paper** papur sidan
paperback n llyfr clawr meddal
paperclip n clip papur
paper round n rownd bapurau

par *n* cyfartaledd, llawn werth
parachute *n* parasiwt
parade *n* rhodfa; rhodres, rhwysg
paradise *n* paradwys, gwynfyd
paradox *n* gwrthddywediad, paradocs
paraffin *n* paraffin
paragraph *n* paragraff
parallel *adj* cyfochrog, paralel
paralysed *adj* parlysedig
paralysis *n* parlys
paramedic *n* parafeddyg
parasite *n* un yn byw ar gefn un arall, cynffonnwr
parcel *n* parsel
pardon *n* maddeuant, pardwn ▸ *vt* maddau, pardynu
parent *n* rhiant; **parents** *npl* rhieni
Paris *n* Paris
parish *n* plwyf ▸ *adj* plwyf, plwyfol
park *n* parc ▸ *vb* parcio
parking *n*: **no parking** dim parcio
parking meter *n* amserydd parcio, rheolydd parcio
parking ticket *n* tocyn parcio
parliament *n* senedd
parliamentary *adj* seneddol
parole *n* gair, addewid, parôl
parrot *n* parot, perot
parsley *n* persli
parsnip *n* panasen
parson *n* person, offeiriad
part *n* rhan; parth ▸ *vb* rhannu, parthu; gwahanu; ymadael
partial *adj* rhannol; tueddol
participate *vb* cyfranogi
particle *n* mymryn, gronyn; geiryn
particular *adj* neilltuol, penodol ▸ *n* pwnc; **particulars** *npl* manylion

particularly *adv* yn arbennig
parting *n* ymadael
partition *n* gwahanfur, palis
partly *adv* mewn rhan, yn rhannol
partner *n* partner; cymar
partridge *n* petrisen
part-time *adj* rhan amser
party *n* plaid; parti, mintai
pass *vb* mynd heibio, llwyddo, pasio; treulio ▸ *n* bwlch; trwydded; pas; **pass away** *vi* marw; **pass out** *vi* llewygu
passable *adj* y gellir mynd heibio iddo; purion
passage *n* tramwyfa; mordaith; cyfran
passenger *n* teithiwr
passion *n* dioddefaint; gwŷn, nwyd
passionate *adj* angerddol, nwydwyllt
passive *adj* goddefol
passport *n* trwydded deithio, pasbort
password *n* cyfrinair
past *adj, n* gorffennol ▸ *prep* wedi ▸ *adv* heibio
pasta *n* pasta
paste *n* past ▸ *vt* pastio, gludio
pasteurized *adj* wedi ei basteureiddio
pastime *n* difyrrwch, adloniant
pastor *n* bugail (eglwys), gweinidog
pastry *n* crwst
pasture *n* porfa
pasty *n* pastai
pat *vt* patio
patch *n* clwt, darn ▸ *vt* clytio
patent *n* agored, amlwg; breintiedig ▸ *n* breintlythyr

paternal adj tadol
path n llwybr
pathetic adj gresynus, pathetig
patience n amynedd
patient adj amyneddgar, dioddefus
▸ n dioddefydd, claf
patio n patio
patriotic adj gwladgarol
patrol n patrôl
patrol car n car patrôl
patron n noddwr
patronizing adj nawddogol
patter vb curo (fel glaw ar ffenestr)
pattern n patrwm, cynllun
pause n saib, seibiant ▸ vi aros
pave vt palmantu
pavement n palmant, pafin
pavilion n pabell, pafiliwn
paw n palf, pawen ▸ vb palfu,
pawennu
pawn n gwystl; (chess) gwerinwr
▸ vt gwystlo
pay (pt, pp **paid**) vb talu ▸ n tâl,
pae; **back pay** ôl-dâl
pay-as-you-go adj talu-wrth-
ddefnyddio
payment n taliad, tâl
payphone n ffôn talu
PC n abbr (= personal computer) PC,
cyfrifiadur personol; (= police
constable) cwnstabl (heddlu)
▸ adj abbr (= politically correct) PC,
gwleidyddol-gywir
PE n abbr (= physical education) AG,
addysg gorfforol
pea n pysen
peace n heddwch, tangnefedd
▸ excl gosteg!, ust!
peaceful adj heddychol,
tangnefeddus, llonydd

peach n eirinen wlanog
peacock n paun
peak n pig; copa; uchafbwynt
peanut n cneuen ddaear
peanut butter n menyn pysgnau
pear n gellygen
pearl n perl
peasant n gwladwr, gwerinwr
peat n mawn
pebble n carreg lefn, cerrigyn
peck vb pigo, cnocellu ▸ n cnoc,
pigiad
peculiar adj priod, priodol; hynod
pedal n pedal ▸ vb pedalu
pedestal n troed, gwaelod
pedestrian adj ar draed, pedestrig
▸ n gŵr traed, cerddwr
pedestrian crossing n croesfan
cerddwyr
pedigree n achau, bonedd
pee (inf) n pisiad ▸ vb pisio
peel n pil, croen, rhisgl ▸ vb pilio,
plicio, crafu
peep vi cipedrych, sbïo ▸ n
cipolwg, cip
peer[1] vi ciledrych, syllu
peer[2] n cydradd; pendefig
peg n hoel bren, peg ▸ vt pegio
pelt vt lluchio, taflu, peledu
pelvis n pelfis
pen[1] n pin, ysgrifbin
pen[2] n (enclosure) lloc, ffald ▸ vt
ffaldio, llocio
penalty n cosb, cosbedigaeth
penalty (kick) n cic gosb
pence npl ceiniogau, pres
pencil n pensel, pensil
pencil case n cas pensiliau
pencil sharpener n naddwr
pensiliau

pendant

pendant n tlws
pending prep hyd, nes, yn ystod
penetrate vb treiddio; dirnad
penfriend n cyfaill llythyru
penguin n pengwin
penicillin n penisilin
peninsula n gorynys
penis n cala, pidyn
penitentiary n carchar
penknife n cyllell boced
penniless adj heb geiniog
penny (pennies) n ceiniog
pension n blwydd-dal, pensiwn
pensioner n pensiynwr
people npl pobl, gwerin
pepper n pupur
peppermill n melin bupur
peppermint n mintys poethion
per prep trwy, wrth, yn ôl
perceive vt canfod, dirnad, deall
per cent adv y cant
percentage n canran
perception n canfyddiad, canfod
perch n perc; clwyd ▶ vb clwydo
percussion n trawiad,
  gwrthdrawiad; **percussion band**
  seindorf daro
perennial adj bythol, lluosflwyddol
perfect adj perffaith ▶ vt
  perffeithio
perfection n perffeithrwydd
perfectly adv yn berffaith
perform vb cyflawni; perfformio
performance n perfformiad
performer n perfformiwr
perfume n perarogl, persawr ▶ vt
  perarogli
perhaps adv efallai, hwyrach
perimeter n amfesur, perimedr

period n cyfnod; cyfadran
  (miwsig); diweddnod; misglwyf
periodical n cyfnodolyn
perish vi trengi, marw, darfod;
  llygru
perjury n anudon, anudoniaeth
perk (inf) n mantais; **perk up** vb
  bywhau, adfywio
permanent adj parhaol
permission n caniatâd, cennad
permit vb caniatáu ▶ n trwydded
perplex vt drysu
persecute vt erlid
persevere vi dyfalbarhau
persist vi dal ati; mynnu, taeru
persistent adj dyfal, taer, cyndyn,
  parhaus
person n person
personal adj personol
personal assistant n
  cynorthwyydd personol
personality n personoliaeth
personally adv yn bersonol
perspective n persbectif, safbwynt
perspiration n chwys
persuade vt darbwyllo, perswadio
perverse adj gwrthnysig
pervert vt gwyrdroi, llygru ▶ n
  cyfeiliornwr
pessimism n pesimistiaeth
pessimist n pesimist
pessimistic adj pesimistaidd
pest n pla, poendod
pester vt blino, aflonyddu, poeni
pet n anwylyn, ffafryn ▶ adj
  llywaeth, swci ▶ vt anwesu,
  canmol
petal n petal
petite adj bychan
petition n deisyfiad; deiseb

petrified *adj* stond
petrol *n* petrol
petroleum *n* petroliwm
petrol pump *n* pwmp petrol
petrol station *n* gorsaf betrol
petticoat *n* pais
petty *adj* bach, bychan, mân
pew *n* eisteddle, côr, sedd
pewter *n* piwter
phantom *n* rhith, drychiolaeth
pharmacy *n* fferylliaeth; fferyllfa
phase *n* gwedd; tro
pheasant *n* ffesant
phenomenon *n* ffenomen
Philippines *n* Pilipinas
philosopher *n* athronydd
philosophical *adj* athronyddol
philosophy *n* athroniaeth
phlegm *n* llysnafedd, fflem
phobia *n* ffobia
phone *n* ffôn, teleffon ▸ *vb* ffonio
phone bill *n* bil ffôn
phone book *n* cyfeiriadur ffôn
phone box *n* caban ffôn
phone call *n* galwad ffôn
phone number *n* rhif ffôn
phonetics *n* seineg
phoney *adj* ffug
photo *n* ffoto
photocopier *n* llungopïydd
photocopy *n* llungopi ▸ *vb*
  llungopio
photograph *n* llun, ffotograff
photographer *n* ffotograffydd
photography *n* ffotograffiaeth
phrase *n* ymadrodd; cymal ▸ *vt*
  geirio
phrase book *n* llyfr ymadroddion
physical *adj* corfforol; ffisegol

physical education *n* addysg
  gorfforol
physician *n* meddyg, ffisigwr
physicist *n* ffisegydd
physics *n* ffiseg
physiotherapist *n* ffisiotherapydd
physiotherapy *n* ffisiotherapi
physique *n* corffolaeth,
  cyfansoddiad
pianist *n* pianydd
piano *n* piano
pick[1] *n* (*tool*) caib
pick[2] *vb* dewis, dethol ▸ *n* dewis
  ▸ **pick on** *vt* pigo ar
  ▸ **pick out** *vt* (*choose*) dewis
  ▸ **pick up** *vt* (*person, object*) codi;
  (*information, language*) dysgu
pickle *n* picl, heli ▸ *vt* piclo, halltu
pickpocket *n* pigwr pocedi,
  codleidr
picnic *n* picnic
picture *n* llun, darlun; **picture book**
  llyfr lluniau
picture messaging *n* negeseuon
  llun
picturesque *adj* darluniaidd,
  gwych
pie *n* pastai
piece *n* darn, dryll
pie chart *n* siart olwyn
pier *n* pier
pierce *vb* brathu, gwanu
pig *n* mochyn
pigeon *n* colomen
piggy bank *n* cadw-mi-gei, blwch
  cynilo
pigsty *n* twlc mochyn
pigtail *n* pleth
pike *n* gwaywffon; penhwyad

365

pile

pile¹ n (heap) crug, pentwr ▸ vt pentyrru

pile² n (of carpet) blew, ceden

piles npl clwyf y marchogion

pilgrim n pererin

pilgrimage n pererindod

pill n pelen, pilsen

pillar n colofn, piler

pillar box n bocs postio

pillow n gobennydd, clustog

pillow case n cas gobennydd

pilot¹ n cyfarwyddwr llongau, peilot

pimple n ploryn, tosyn

PIN n abbr (= personal identification number) PIN, Rhif Adnabod Personol

pin n pin ▸ vt pinio, hoelio

pinafore n brat, piner

pinch vb pinsio, gwasgu ▸ n pins, pinsiad; cyfyngder

pine¹ n pinwydden

pine² vi dihoeni, nychu

pineapple n afal pîn

pink adj, n pinc

pinpoint vb pinbwyntio

pint n peint

pioneer n arloeswr, arloesydd

pious adj duwiol, duwiolfrydig

pip n hedyn afal etc

pipe n pib, pibell ▸ vb canu pibell

pirate n môr-leidr

Pisces n y Pysgod

piss vi (pej) pisio

pissed adj (pej) meddw

pistol n llawddryll, pistol

pit n pwll, pydew ▸ vt pyllu; **coal pit** pwll glo

pitch¹ n (tar) pyg ▸ vt pygu

pitch² vb bwrw; gosod; taro (tôn) ▸ n gradd, mesur, traw

pitfall n magl, perygl

pith n bywyn; mwydion; mêr; grym

pitiful adj truenus, tosturiol

pity n tosturi, trueni, gresyn ▸ vt tosturio, pitio

pizza n pitsa

placard n murlen, hysbyslen

place n lle, man ▸ vt gosod; **to take place** digwydd; **in the first place** yn y lle cyntaf

placement n (during studies) lleoliad

placid adj tawel, llonydd

plague n pla, haint ▸ vt poeni, blino

plaice n lleden

plain adj plaen, eglur ▸ n gwastadedd

plain chocolate n siocled tywyll

plaintiff n achwynwr, hawlydd

plait n pleth ▸ vt plethu

plan n cynllun, plan ▸ vt cynllunio, planio

plane¹ adj, n (even) gwastad, lefel

plane² n plaen; awyren ▸ vt plaenio

planet n planed

plank n astell, planc

planning n cynllunio; **planning permission** caniatâd cynllunio

plant n planhigyn; offer; ffatri ▸ vt plannu

plaster n plaster ▸ vt plastro

plastic n, adj plastig; **plastic bag** cwdyn plastig

plate n plât; llestri aur etc ▸ vt platio

plateau n gwastatir uchel

platform n llwyfan, esgynlawr

platoon n platŵn

platter n plât

plausible adj teg neu resymol yr olwg, ffals

play vb chwarae; canu (offeryn) ▶ n chwarae; **play down** vt bychanu

player n chwaraewr

playful adj chwareus

playground n chwaraele

playgroup n grŵp chwarae

playing card n cerdyn chwarae

playing field n maes chwarae

playtime n amser chwarae

playwright n dramodydd

plea n ple; esgus

plead vb pledio, ymbil

pleasant adj hyfryd, pleserus

please vb boddhau, boddio; **if you please** os gwelwch yn dda

pleased adj boddhaus, bodlon; **pleased to meet you** mae'n dda gen i gwrdd â chi

pleasure n pleser, hyfrydwch

pleat n plet, pleten ▶ vt pletio

pledge n gwystl, ernes ▶ vt gwystlo

plenty n digon, helaethrwydd

pliers npl gefel fechan

plight n cyflwr

plod vb troedio, ymlafnio

plot n darn o dir; cynllwyn; cynllun, plot ▶ vb cynllwynio; cynllunio

plough n aradr, gwŷdd ▶ vb aredig, troi

ploy n cynllun, strategaeth

pluck vt tynnu; pluo ▶ n glewder

plug n topyn, plwg ▶ vt topio, plygio; **plug in** vt plygio i mewn

plum n eirinen

plumber n plymwr

plumbing n gwaith plymwr

plump adj tew ▶ vb pleidleisio i un (yn unig)

plunge n plymiad ▶ vb plymio, trochi

pluperfect adj gorberffaith

plural adj lluosog

plus n plws, ychwaneg ▶ prep, adj ychwanegol

ply vb arfer, defnyddio

plywood n pren haenog (tair-haen, pum-haen)

p.m. abbr (= post meridiem) y.h.

pneumonia n llid yr ysgyfaint, niwmonia

poach[1] vb herwhela, potsio

poach[2] vt (egg) berwi (wy) heb ei blisg

poached adj: **poached egg** wŷ wedi ei botsio

pocket n poced, llogell ▶ vt pocedu; **pocket knife** cyllell boced; **pocket money** arian poced

pod n coden, cibyn

podcast n podlediad

poem n cerdd, cân

poet n bardd, prydydd

poetry n barddoniaeth, prydyddiaeth

poignant adj ingol, aethus

point n pwynt; man; blaen ▶ vb pwyntio; dangos; **to be on the point of doing sth** bod ar fin gwneud rhywbeth; **to get the point** deall; **there's no point (in doing)** does dim diben (gwneud); **point out** vt nodi

pointer n cyfeirydd; mynegfys

pointless

pointless *adj* dibwynt, diystyr
point of view *n* safbwynt
poison *n* gwenwyn ▸ *vt* gwenwyno
poisonous *adj* gwenwynig
poke *vb* pwnio, procio
poker *n* pocer
Poland *n* Gwlad Pwyl
polar *adj* pegynol
polar bear *n* arth wen
pole *n* pawl, polyn; pegwn
police *n* heddlu
police car *n* car heddlu
policeman *n* heddwas, plismon
police officer *n* swyddog heddlu
police station *n* gorsaf heddlu
policewoman *n* heddferch, plismones
policy *n* polisi
Polish *adj* Pwylaidd; *(in language)* Pwyleg ▸ *n (language)* Pwyleg
polish *vb* cwyro, caboli, gloywi, llathru ▸ *n* cwyr
polite *adj* moesgar, boneddigaidd
politely *adv* yn gwrtais
political *adj* gwleidyddol
politician *n* gwleidydd, gwleidyddwr
politics *n* gwleidyddiaeth
poll *n* pen, copa; pôl ▸ *vb* cneifio; pleidleisio, polio
pollen *n* paill
polling station *n* gorsaf bleidleisio
pollute *vt* difwyno, llygru
polluted *adj* llygredig
pollution *n* llygredd
polo neck *n* jersi polo
polythene bag *n* bag polythen
pomegranate *n* pomgranad
pompous *adj* rhwysgfawr, balch

pond *n* llyn, pwll
ponder *vb* ystyried, myfyrio
pony *n* merlyn, poni, merlen; **pony trekking** merlota
ponytail *n* cynffon merlen
poodle *n* pwdl
pool¹ *n* pwll, llyn
pool² *n (fund)* cronfa; pwll ▸ *vt* cydgyfrannu
poor *adj* tlawd, truan, gwael, sâl
poorly *adj* sâl, gwael
pop *vb* ffrwydro; picio; **pop in** *vi* picio i mewn; **pop out** *vi* picio allan; **pop round** *vi* picio heibio
popcorn *n* popgorn
pope *n* pab
poplar *n* poplysen
poppy *n* pabi (coch), llygad y bwgan
popular *adj* poblogaidd
population *n* poblogaeth
porcelain *n* porslen
porch *n* porth, cyntedd
pore¹ *n* mandwll
pore² *vi* myfyrio
pork *n* cig moch, porc
pornography *n* pornograffi
porridge *n* uwd
port¹ *n* porth, porthladd
port² *n (on ship)* ochr chwith llong
port³ *n (drink)* port
portable *adj* cludadwy
porter *n* porthor
portfolio *n* cas papurau, portffolio
portion *n* rhan, cyfran
portrait *n* llun, darlun
portray *vt* portreadu, darlunio
Portugal *n* Portiwgal

Portuguese adj Portiwgalaidd; (in language) Portiwgaleg ▸ n (language) Portiwgaleg
pose vb sefyll, cymryd ar ▸ n ystum, rhodres
posh adj (inf) hardd, coeth
position n safle, sefyllfa; swydd
positive adj cadarnhaol, pendant
possess vt meddu, meddiannu
possession n meddiant
possibility n posibilrwydd
possible adj posibl, dichonadwy
possibly adv dichon, efallai
post¹ n (stake) post, cledr ▸ vt gosod, cyhoeddi
post² n post, llythyrfa; safle, swydd ▸ vb postio
postage n cludiad (llythyr, etc.)
postal adj post
postal order n archeb bost
postbox n bocs postio
postcard n cerdyn post
postcode n cod post
poster n hysbyslen, poster
postgraduate adj graddedig
postman n postmon
postmark n postfarc
post office n llythyrdy, swyddfa'r post
postpone vt gohirio, oedi
posture n ystum, osgo
postwoman n merch post
pot n pot, potyn; crochan ▸ vb potio
potato n taten, pytaten
potent adj grymus, nerthol
potential adj dichonadwy, dichonol ▸ n potensial
pothole n ceubwll
potter vb diogi, swmera

pottery n llestri pridd; crochendy
potty n pot
pouch n cod
poultry n dofednod, ffowls
pounce vb disgyn ar, dod ar warthaf
pound¹ n pwys; punt
pound² vb pwnio
pour vb tywallt, arllwys
pout vi pwdu, sorri
poverty n tlodi
powder n powdr ▸ vt powdro
powdered milk n llaeth powdr
power n grym; pŵer
power cut n toriad yn y cyflenwad
power failure n pall ar y cyflenwad
powerful adj nerthol, grymus
powerless adj dirym
power station n pwerdy
PR n abbr (= public relations) PR, cysylltiadau cyhoeddus
practical adj ymarferol
practically adv (almost) bron; **practically certain** bron yn sicr
practice n arfer, arferiad
practise vb arfer, ymarfer
practising adj ymarferol; yn dilyn ei swydd
practitioner n meddyg; cyfreithiwr
prairie n paith
praise vt canmol, moli ▸ n canmoliaeth, mawl
pram n coets, pram
prank n cast, pranc
prawn n corgimwch
pray vb gweddïo
prayer n gweddi
preach vb pregethu
preacher n pregethwr
precarious adj ansicr, peryglus

precaution *n* rhagofal, gofal
precede *vb* blaenori, rhagflaenu
precedent *n* cynsail
precinct *n* cyffin, rhodfa
precious *adj* gwerthfawr
precise *adj* penodol, manwl
precisely *adv* yn union
predecessor *n* rhagflaenydd
predicament *n* helynt
predict *vt* rhagfynegi
preface *n* rhagymadrodd, rhaglith
prefect *n* rhaglaw; swyddog
prefer *vt* dewis yn hytrach, bod yn well gan
preferable *adj* gwell
preference *n* dewis, hoffter
prefix *n* rhagddodiad
pregnancy *n* beichiogrwydd
pregnant *adj* beichiog, llawn
prehistoric *adj* cynhanesol
prejudice *n* rhagfarn; niwed ▸ *vt* rhagfarnu, niweidio
prejudiced *adj* rhagfarnllyd
preliminary *adj* arweiniol, rhagarweiniol
prelude *n* rhagarweiniad; preliwd
premature *adj* anaeddfed, cynamserol
premier *adj* blaenaf, pennaf, prif ▸ *n* prif weinidog
premises *npl (building)* adeilad; *(site)* safle
premium *n* premiwm
preoccupied *adj* wedi ymgolli
prep *n* gwaith paratoi
prepaid *adj* wedi ei dalu ymlaen llaw, rhagdalwyd
preparation *n* paratoad, darpariaeth
prepare *vb* paratoi

prepared *adj* parod; effro
preposition *n* arddodiad
prep school *n* ysgol baratoi
prerequisite *n* rhaganghenraid
prescribe *vb* gorchymyn, cyfarwyddo
prescription *n* presgripsiwn
presence *n* gŵydd, presenoldeb
present[1] *adj*, *n* presennol
present[2] *n (gift)* anrheg ▸ *vt* anrhegu; cyflwyno; dangos
presentation *n* cyflwyniad
presenter *n* cyflwynydd
presently *adv* yn fuan
preserve *vt* cadw, diogelu ▸ *n* jam
preside *vi* llywyddu
president *n* llywydd, arlywydd
press *vb* gwasgu ▸ *n* gwasg; cwpwrdd
pressing *adj* taer, dwys
press-up *n* ymwythiad
pressure *n* pwysau; gwasgedd, pwysedd
prestige *n* bri, braint
presumably *adv* yn ôl pob tebyg, gellid tybio
presume *vb* tybio; beiddio, rhyfygu
pretence *n* rhith, esgus
pretend *vb* ffugio, cymryd ar, cogio; honni hawl
pretext *n* esgus, cochl
pretty *adj* pert ▸ *adv* cryn, go
prevail *vi* tycio, ffynnu; gorfod, trechu
prevalent *adj* cyffredin; nerthol
prevent *vt* atal, rhwystro
preview *n* rhagolwg
previous *adj* blaenorol, cynt
previously *adv* gynt

prey n ysglyfaeth, aberth ▸ vi ysglyfaethu

price n pris ▸ vt prisio

price list n rhestr prisiau

prick n pigyn, swmbwl ▸ vb pigo; picio, codi

pride n balchder ▸ vt balchio, ymfalchïo

priest n offeiriad

primarily adv yn bennaf

primary adj prif, cyntaf, cysefin; cynradd

primary school n ysgol gynradd

prime[1] adj prif, cyntaf; gorau ▸ n anterth

prime[2] vt llwytho, llenwi

prime minister n prif weinidog

primitive adj cyntefig; garw, amrwd

primrose n briallen

prince n tywysog

princess n tywysoges; **Princess Charlotte** y Dywysoges Charlotte

principal adj prif ▸ n pen; prifathro; corff

principle n egwyddor, elfen

print n argraff, print, ôl ▸ vb argraffu, printio

printer n argraffydd

printout n allbrint

prior adj cynt, blaenorol ▸ n prior, priol

priority n blaenoriaeth

prison n carchar, carchardy

prisoner n carcharor

pristine adj cyntefig, cysefin

private adj preifat

private enterprise n menter breifat

privilege n braint, rhagorfraint

prize n (reward) gwobr ▸ vt prisio, gwerthfawrogi

prize-giving n cyfarfod gwobrwyo

prizewinner n enillydd gwobr

probability n tebygolrwydd

probable adj tebygol, tebyg

probably adv mae'n debyg, yn ôl pob tebyg; **it will probably be all right** bydd hi'n iawn, mae'n debyg or yn ôl pob tebyg

probation n prawf

probe n profiedydd ▸ vt profi, chwilio

problem n problem

procedure n trefn, gweithdrefn

proceed vi myned, deillio; erlyn

proceeds npl enillion, elw

process n proses

procession n gorymdaith

proclaim vt cyhoeddi, datgan

prod vt procio

produce vt cynhyrchu, epilio; dwyn ▸ n cynnyrch, ffrwyth

producer n cynhyrchydd

product n cynnyrch, ffrwyth

production n cynhyrchiad

profession n proffes, galwedigaeth

professional adj proffesiynol

professor n proffeswr; athro

profile n ystlyslun, cernlun

profit n elw, proffid ▸ vb llesáu, proffidio

profitable adj (financially) proffidiol, yn dwyn elw; (advantageous) proffidiol, manteisiol

profound adj dwfn, dwys

program n rhaglen ▸ vb rhaglennu

programme n rhaglen

programmer n rhaglennydd

progress n cynnydd; taith ▸ vi cynyddu

progressive adj cynyddgar, blaengar

prohibit vt gwahardd

project¹ n project

project² vb bwrw; bwriadu; ymestyn; taflunio

projector n taflunydd

prolific adj ffrwythlon, toreithiog

prolong vt hwyhau, estyn

promenade n rhodfa ▸ vb rhodianna

prominent adj yn sefyll allan, amlwg

promise n addewid ▸ vb addo, argoeli

promote vt hyrwyddo, dyrchafu

promotion n (at work) dyrchafiad; (of event) hyrwyddiad

prompt adj parod, buan ▸ vt cofweini; cymell

prone adj â'i wyneb i waered; tueddol

prong n fforch, pig fforch

pronoun n rhagenw

pronounce vb cynanu, yngan; cyhoeddi, datgan

pronunciation n cynaniad

proof n prawf; proflen

prop n ateg, prop ▸ vt ategu

propaganda n propaganda

proper adj priod, priodol

properly adv yn iawn

property n priodoledd; eiddo; priodwedd (cemeg)

prophecy n proffwydoliaeth

prophet n proffwyd

proportion n cyfartaledd, cyfrannedd

proportional adj cyfrannol

proportionate adj cymesur

proposal n cynnig

propose vb cynnig, bwriadu

proposition n cynigiad; gosodiad

proprietor n perchen, perchennog

prose n rhyddiaith

prosecute vt erlyn

prosecutor n erlynydd

prospect n rhagolwg

prospectus n prosbectws

prosper vb llwyddo, ffynnu

prosperity n llwyddiant, ffyniant

prostitute n putain

protect vt amddiffyn, noddi

protection n amddiffyn, diogelwch

protective adj amddiffynnol

protein n protein

protest vb gwrthdystio ▸ n gwrthdystiad

Protestant n Protestant ▸ adj Protestannaidd

protester n protestiwr

proud adj balch

prove vb profi

proverb n dihareb

provide vt darparu; **provide for** vt darparu ar gyfer

province n talaith; cylch, maes

provision n darpariaeth; **provisions** npl darbodion; ymborth

provoke vt cythruddo, profocio

prowl vi ysglyfaetha, prowlan

proximity n agosrwydd

proxy n dirprwy

prudent adj pwyllog, doeth

prune n eirinen sych

pry vi chwilota, chwilenna

pseudonym n ffugenw

psychiatrist *n* seiciatrydd
psychological *adj* seicolegol, meddyliol
psychologist *n* seicolegydd
psychology *n* seicoleg
PTO *abbr* (= *please turn over*) trosodd
pub *n* tafarn
puberty *n* blaenaeddfedrwydd
public *adj* cyhoeddus ▶ *n* y cyhoedd
public house *n* tŷ tafarn
publicity *n* cyhoeddusrwydd
public relations *npl* cysylltiadau cyhoeddus
public school *n* ysgol fonedd
public transport *n* cludiant cyhoeddus
publish *vt* cyhoeddi
publisher *n* cyhoeddwr
pudding *n* pwdin
puddle *n* pwll, pwllyn
puff *n* pwff, chwa, chwyth ▶ *vb* pwffio, chwythu
puff pastry *n* crwst pwff
pull *vt* tynnu ▶ *n* tynfa, tyniad; **pull down** *vt* tynnu i lawr; **pull out** *vb* tynnu allan; **pull through** *vi* dod trwyddi; **pull up** *vi* (*stop*) stopio
pulley *n* troell, pwli
pullover *n* gwasgod wlân
pulp *n* bywyn, mwydion
pulpit *n* pulpud
pulse¹ *n* (*of heart*) curiad y galon, curiad y gwaed
pulse² *n* (*vegetables*) pys, ffa *etc*
pump *n* sugnedydd, pwmp ▶ *vb* pwmpio; **pump up** *vt* pwmpio gwynt i
pumpkin *n* pwmpen

pun *n* gair mwys, mwysair
punch *n* pwns; dyrnod ▶ *vt* pwnsio, dyrnodio
punch-up *n* (*inf*) ysgarmes
punctual *adj* prydlon
punctuation *n* atalnodiad
puncture *n* twll ▶ *vt* tyllu
punish *vt* cosbi; poeni
punishment *n* cosb, cosbedigaeth
pupil *n* disgybl; cannwyll llygad
puppet *n* pyped; gwas
puppy *n* ci bach
purchase *vt* prynu, pwrcasu ▶ *n* pryniant, pwrcas
pure *adj* pur, noeth
purify *vt* puro
purity *n* purdeb
purple *adj, n* porffor
purpose *n* pwrpas, bwriad, arfaeth
purr *vb* canu crwth, grwnan
purse *n* pwrs, cod ▶ *vt* crychu
pursue *vb* dilyn, erlyn, erlid, ymlid
pursuit *n* ymlidiad; ymchwil, gorchwyl
pus *n* crawn, gôr
push *vb* gwthio ▶ *n* gwth, ysgŵd; ymdrech; **push around** *vt* gwthio o gwmpas; **push through** *vt* gwthio trwodd
pushchair *n* coets
push-up *n* ymwythiad
put (*pt, pp* **put**) *vb* gosod, dodi, rhoddi, rhoi; **put aside** *vt* rhoi o'r neilltu; **put away** *vt* rhoi i gadw; **put back** *vt* (*replace*) rhoi yn ôl; (*postpone*) gohirio; **put down** *vt* (*object*) gosod; (*animal*) difa; **put in** *vt* (*install*) gosod; **put off** *vt* (*postpone*) gohirio; (*discourage*)

digalonni; *(switch off)* diffodd; **put on** *vt* gwisgo; troi ymlaen; **to put on weight** ennill pwysau; **put out** *vt (fire; light)* diffodd; **put through** *vt (on phone)* rhoi drwodd; **put up** *vt (tent)* gosod; *(price)* codi

puzzle *n* pos ▸ *vb* drysu, pyslo
puzzled *adj* dryslyd
pyjamas *npl* pyjamas, gwisg nos
pyramid *n* pyramid, bera
Pyrenees *pl*: **the Pyrenees** y Pyreneau

q

quack¹ *n* crachfeddyg, cwac
quack² *vi* cwacian
quadruple *adj* pedwarplyg
quail *n* sofliar
quaint *adj* od, henffasiwn
quake *vi* crynu
qualification *n* cymhwyster; cymhwysiad
qualified *adj* cymwys
qualify *vt* cymhwyso, cyfaddasu
quality *n* ansawdd, rhinwedd
qualm *n* petruster, amheuaeth
quantity *n* swm, maint, mesur
quarantine *n* cwarant, neilltuaeth
quarrel *n* ymrafael, ffrae, cweryl ▸ *vi* ffraeo
quarry *n* chwarel, cwar
quart *n* chwart, cwart
quarter *n* chwarter; man; trugaredd; **quarters** *npl* lletty; **a quarter of an hour** chwarter awr; **quarter final** rownd gogynderfynol

quarter final n: the quarter-finals y rownd gogynderfynol
quartet, quartette n pedwarawd
quartz n creigrisial, cwarts
quay n cei
queen n brenhines
queer adj od, hynod
quench vt diffodd, dofi, torri
query n holiad, gofyniad ▸ vb holi, amau
quest n ymchwiliad, cwest
question n gofyniad, cwestiwn ▸ vt holi, amau
questionable adj amheus
question mark n gofynnod
questionnaire n holiadur
queue n ciw
quick adj byw; buan, cyflym; **to the quick** i'r byw
quickly adv (rapidly) yn gyflym; (promptly) yn ddi-oed
quid n (inf) punt
quiet adj llonydd, tawel, distaw ▸ n llonyddwch, tawelwch ▸ vt llonyddu, tawelu
quietly adv yn dawel
quilt n cwilt, cwrlid ▸ vt cwiltio
quirky adj od, hynod
quit (pt, pp **quit**, **quitted**) vt gadael, symud ▸ adj rhydd
quite adv eithaf; cwbl, llwyr, hollol
quits adj yn gyfartal
quiver¹ n cawell saethau
quiver² vi crynu, dirgrynu
quiz vt holi
quota n cwota
quotation n dyfyniad; prisiant
quote vt dyfynnu; nodi (prisiau)

r

rabbi n rabi
rabbit n cwningen
rabies n y gynddaredd
race¹ n ras ▸ vi rasio
race² n (ancestry) hil
racecourse n cae rasys
racetrack n trac rasio
racial adj hiliol
racing car n car rasio
racing driver n gyrrwr rasio
racism n hiliaeth
racist adj hiliol ▸ n hilydd, hiliwr
rack n rac; arteithglwyd ▸ vt arteithio, dirdynnu
racket n twrf, mwstwr; (for tennis etc) raced
racquet n raced
radar n radar
radiation n ymbelydredd
radiator n rheiddiadur
radical adj gwreiddiol, cynhenid; trylwyr ▸ n radical
radio n radio

radioactive

radioactive *adj* ymbelydrol
radio station *n* gorsaf radio
radish *n* rhuddygl, radis
RAF *n* RAF
raffle *n* raffl
raft *n* rafft
rag *n* carp, clwt
rage *n* cynddaredd ▸ *vi* terfysgu, cynddeiriogi
ragged *adj* carpiog, bratiog
raid *n* rhuthr, cyrch ▸ *vb* anrheithio, ysbeilio
rail *n* canllaw, cledren, rheilen
railcard *n* cerdyn rheilffordd
railway *n* rheilffordd
railway station *n* gorsaf reilffordd
rain *n* glaw ▸ *vb* glawio, bwrw glaw
rainbow *n* enfys
raincoat *n* cot law
rainforest *n* fforest law
rainy *adj* glawog
raise *vt* codi, dyrchafu
raisin *n* rhesinen
rake *n* cribin, rhaca ▸ *vb* cribinio, rhacanu
rally *vb* atgynnull; adgyfnerthu, gwella ▸ *n* cynulliad
ram *n* hwrdd, maharen ▸ *vt* hyrddio, pwnio
ramble *vi* gwibio, crwydro ▸ *n* gwib
rambler *n* crwydrwr
ramp *n* ramp
random *n* siawns, damwain ▸ *adj* damweiniol
range *n* amrediad; ystod; lle tân â ffwrn ▸ *vb* rhestru, cyfleu; crwydro
ranger *n* coedwigwr, ceidwad parc

rank¹ *n* rheng, gradd ▸ *vb* rhestru; **the rank and file** y bobl gyffredin
rank² *adj* mws; gwyllt; rhonc
ransom *n* pridwerth ▸ *vt* prynu, gwaredu
rant *vi* bragaldian, brygawthan
rap *n* cnoc ▸ *vt* cnocio, curo
rape *vt* treisio ▸ *n* trais
rapid *adj* cyflym, buan
rapids *n* dyfroedd gwyllt
rapist *n* treisiwr
rare *adj* prin; godidog; tenau
rash¹ *adj* byrbwyll
rash² *n* brech, tarddiant
rasher *n* tafell
raspberry *n* afanen, mafonen
rat *n* llygoden fawr, llygoden ffrengig ▸ *vi* llygota
rate¹ *vt* dwrdio, dweud y drefn
rate² *n* cyflymder; treth; *(of interest)* cyfradd
rather *adv* braidd, hytrach, go, lled
ratio *n* cymhareb
ration *n* dogn, saig ▸ *vt* dogni
rational *adj* rhesymol
rattle *vb* rhuglo, trystio ▸ *n* rhugl, rhwnc
rave *vi* gwallgofi, ynfydu
raven *n* cigfran
ravine *n* hafn, ceunant
raw *adj* amrwd; crai, cri; noeth, dolurus, garw; dibrofiad ▸ *n* cig noeth, dolur
ray¹ *n* paladr, pelydryn
ray² *n (fish)* cath fôr
razor *n* ellyn, rasal ▸ *vt* eillio
razor blade *n* llafn ellyn
re *prep* ym mater, mewn perthynas â

reach *vb* cyrraedd, estyn ▸ *n* cyrraedd

react *vi* adweithio

reaction *n* adwaith

reactor *n* adweithydd

read (*pt, pp* **read**) *vb* darllen; **read out** *vt* darllen yn uchel

reader *n* darllenydd

readily *adv* yn barod, yn ddiffwdan

reading *n* darllen

ready *adj* parod, rhwydd

real *adj* gwir, real, go-iawn

realistic *adj* realistig, realaidd

reality *n* gwirionedd, sylwedd; dirwedd, realiti

realize *vt* sylweddoli; gwireddu

really *adv* gwir, hollol, mewn difrif

realm *n* teyrnas, gwlad

reappear *vb* ailymddangos

rear¹ *n* cefn, pen ôl

rear² *vb* codi, magu; codi ar ei draed ôl

reason *n* rheswm ▸ *vb* rhesymu

reasonable *adj* rhesymol

reasonably *adv*: **reasonably good/ quick** eitha da/cyflym

reassurance *n* calondid

reassure *vt* calonogi, cysuro

reassuring *adj*: **to be reassuring** twaleu'r meddwl

rebate *n* ad-daliad

rebel *vi* gwrthryfela ▸ *n* gwrthryfelwr

rebellion *n* gwrthryfel

rebellious *adj* gwrthryfelgar

recall *vt* galw yn ôl; galw i gof, cofio

receipt *n* derbyniad; derbynneb

receive *vt* derbyn

receiver *n* derbynnydd

recent *adj* diweddar

recently *adv* yn ddiweddar

reception *n* derbyniad, croeso

reception desk *n* man croeso, man derbyn

receptionist *n* croesawferch, croesawydd

recharge *vt* aildrydanu

recipe *n* rysáit

recipient *n* derbyniwr, derbynnydd

recital *n* adroddiad, datganiad

recite *vb* adrodd

reckless *adj* anystyriol, rhyfygus, dibris

reckon *vb* cyfrif, barnu, bwrw

reclaim *vt* adennill, diwygio

recline *vb* lledorwedd, gorwedd, gorffwys

recognition *n* adnabyddiaeth, cydnabyddiaeth

recognize *vt* adnabod, cydnabod

recommend *vt* cymeradwyo, argymell

recommendation *n* cymeradwyaeth

reconcile *vt* cymodi, cysoni

reconsider *vb* ailfeddwl

record *vt* cofnodi, recordio ▸ *n* cofnod, record

recorded delivery *n* dosbarthiad cofnodedig

recorder *n* (*musical instrument*) recordydd

recording *n* recordiad

record player *n* chwaraewr recordiau

recount *vt* adrodd

re-count *vb* ailgyfrif

recover *vb* adennill; ymadfer; adferiad

recovery *n* gwellhad

r

377

recreation n difyrrwch, adloniant

recruit n recriwt; newyddian ▸ vt recriwtio

rectangle n petryal

rectangular adj petryalog

rectify vt unioni, cywiro; puro, coethi

rector n rheithor

recur vi ailddigwydd, dychwelyd

recurring adj cylchol

recycle vb ailgylchu

recycling n ailgylchu

red adj, n coch, rhudd

Red Cross n: **the Red Cross** y Groes Goch

redcurrants npl cyrans coch

redecorate vb ailaddurno

redeem vt prynu (yn ôl), gwaredu

reduce vt lleihau, gostwng; rhydwytho

reduced adj gostyngol

reduction n lleihad, gostyngiad

redundancy n anghyflogaeth

redundant adj gormodol; anghyflog, digyflog

reed n cawnen, corsen

reef n creigle (yn y môr), creigfa, rîff

reel¹ n ril ▸ vb dirwyn

reel² vi troi, chwyldroi ▸ n (dance) dawns

refectory n ffreutur

refer vb cyfeirio, cyfarwyddo

referee n dyfarnwr; canolwr ▸ vt dyfarnu

reference n cyfeiriad; geirda

refill n adlenwad ▸ vt adlenwi

refine vb puro, coethi

reflect vb adlewyrchu; myfyrio

reflection n adlewyrchiad, myfyrdod

reflex n adweithred, atgyrch

reform vb diwygio, gwella ▸ n diwygiad

refrain¹ vb ymatal

refrain² n byrdwn

refresh vt adfywio

refreshing adj adfywiol

refreshments npl ymborth, lluniaeth

refrigerator n rhewgell, oergell

refuge n noddfa, lloches

refugee n ffoadur

refund n ad-daliad ▸ vb ad-dalu

refurbish vb adnewyddu

refusal n gwrthodiad, nacâd

refuse¹ vb gwrthod

refuse² n ysbwriel

regain vt adennill

regard vt edrych ar, ystyried ▸ n sylw, parch, hoffter

regarding prep ynglŷn â, ynghylch

regardless adj heb ofal, diofal

regenerate vt aileni

regiment n catrawd

region n ardal, bro, rhanbarth

regional adj rhanbarthol

register n cofrestr ▸ vt cofrestru

registered adj cofrestredig

registrar n cofrestrydd

registration n cofrestriad

registration number n rhif cofrestru, rhif trethiant

regret vt gofidio, edifaru ▸ n gofid

regular adj rheolaidd, cyson

regularly adv yn rheolaidd

regulate vt rheoleiddio

regulation n rheol, trefniant

rehabilitation n adferiad

rehearsal n rihyrsal, practis

rehearse *vt* adrodd; ymarfer ymlaen llaw

reign *vi* teyrnasu ▸ *n* teyrnasiad

reimburse *vt* talu yn ôl, ad-dalu

rein *n* afwyn, awen ▸ *vt* ffrwyno

reindeer *n* carw

reinforce *vt* atgyfnerthu

reinstate *vt* adfer i safle/braint

reject *vt* gwrthod, bwrw ymaith

rejection *n* gwrthodiad

rejoice *vb* llawenhau, gorfoleddu

relate *vb* adrodd, mynegi; perthyn

related *adj* yn perthyn; wedi ei ddweud

relating to *prep* yn ymwneud â

relation *n* adroddiad; perthynas

relationship *n* perthynas

relative *adj* perthnasol ▸ *n* perthynas; **relative pronoun** rhagenw perthynol

relatively *adv* yn gymharol

relax *vb* llacio, llaesu, ymlacio

relaxation *n* ymlacio

relaxed *adj* ymlaciedig

relaxing *adj* ymlaciol

relay *n* cyfnewidian newydd, cyfnewid; darlledu ▸ *vb* ailosod

relay race *n* ras gyfnewid

release *vt* rhyddhau, gollwng ▸ *n* rhyddhad

relegate *vt* darostwng

relent *vi* tyneru, tirioni

relevant *adj* perthnasol

reliable *adj* y gellir dibynnu arno, dibynadwy

relic *n* crair; gweddillion

relief *n* cynhorthwy; gollyngdod, ymwared; tirwedd

relieve *vt* cynorthwyo; esmwytho, ysgafnhau; rhyddhau, gollwng

relieved *adj*: **to feel relieved** teimlo rhyddhad

religion *n* crefydd

religious *adj* crefyddol

relish *n* blas; enllyn, mwyniant ▸ *vb* blasio, hoffi

reluctance *n* amharodrwydd, anfodlonrwydd

reluctant *adj* anfodlon, anewyllysgar

reluctantly *adv* yn amharod

rely *vi* hyderu, ymddiried, dibynnu; **rely on** *vt* dibynnu ar

remain *vi* aros, parhau

remainder *n* gweddill, rhelyw

remaining *adj* ar ôl

remains *npl* olion, gweddillion

remand *vt* aildraddodi

remand home *n* cartref i droseddwyr ifanc

remark *vb* sylwi ▸ *n* sylw

remarkable *adj* nodedig, hynod

remarkably *adv*: **remarkably good** hynod o dda

remarry *vi* ailbriodi

remedy *n* meddyginiaeth ▸ *vt* meddyginiaethu, gwella

remember *vt* cofio

remind *vt* atgoffa

remnant *n* gweddill, gwarged

remorse *n* edifeirwch

remote *adj* pell, pellennig, anghysbell

remote control *n* rheolaeth bell

remotely *adv* o bell

removal *n* symudiad, diswyddiad

remove *vb* symud, dileu; mudo

renaissance *n* dadeni

render *vb* talu; datgan; gwneud; troi, cyfieithu

rendezvous

rendezvous *n* cyrchfa, man cyfarfod

renew *vt* adnewyddu

renewable *adj* adnewyddadwy

renovate *vt* adnewyddu

rent *n* rhent ▸ *vt* rhentu

rental *n* rent

reorganize *vt* ad-drefnu

rep *n* cynrychiolydd; **sales rep** gwerthwr/gwerthwraig

repair *vi* atgyweirio, trwsio ▸ *n* cywair

repay *vt* ad-dalu

repeat *vb* ailadrodd, ailgyflawni

repeatedly *adv* dro ar ôl tro

repetition *n* ailadroddiad

repetitive *adj* ailadroddus

replace *vb* ailosod, dodi'n ôl; cymryd lle (arall)

replacement *n* un sy'n cymryd lle arall

replay *vb* ailchwarae

replica *n* copi cywir, cyflun

reply *vi* ateb ▸ *n* ateb, atebiad

report *vt* adrodd, hysbysu ▸ *n* adroddiad; sŵn ergyd

reporter *n* gohebydd

represent *vt* portreadu; cynrychioli

representative *adj yn* cynrychioli ▸ *n* cynrychiolydd

repress *vt* atal, gostegu, llethu

repression *n* ataliad, darostyngiad

reprimand *n* cerydd ▸ *vt* ceryddu

reproduce *vt* atgynhyrchu, epilio

reproduction *n* atgynhyrchiad, copi; epiliad

reptile *n* ymlusgiad

republic *n* gweriniaeth, gwerinlywodraeth

repulsive *adj* atgas, ffiaidd

reputable *adj* parchus, cyfrifol

reputation *n* gair, cymeriad, enw da

request *n* cais ▸ *vt* ceisio, gofyn

require *vt* gofyn, mynnu

rescue *vt* achub ▸ *n* achubiad

research *n* ymchwil, ymchwiliad ▸ *vb* ymchwilio

resemblance *n* tebygrwydd

resemble *vt* tebygu i

resent *vt* tramgwyddo, digio

resentful *adj* digofus, llidiog

resentment *n* dig, dicter

reservation *n* cadw, cadfa

reserve *vt* cadw yn ôl, cadw wrth gefn ▸ *n yr* hyn a gedwir, cronfa; swildod

reserved *adj* swil; wedi ei gadw; **reserved seat** sedd gadw

reservoir *n* cronfa, llyn

reshuffle *vb* aildrefnu

resident *adj* preswylydd

residential *adj* preswyl

residue *n* gweddill

resign *vb* ymddiswyddo

resignation *n* ymddiswyddiad

resilient *adj* hydwyth, ystwyth

resin *n* ystor, rhwsin

resist *vb* gwrthsefyll, gwrthwynebu

resistance *n* gwrthwynebiad, gwrthsafiad

resit *vt (exam)* ailsefyll ▸ *n* ailarholiad, ailgynnig

resolution *n* penderfyniad

resolve *vb* penderfynu ▸ *n* penderfyniad

resort *vi* cyrchu ▸ *n* cyrchfa; ymwared

resource n sgil, dyfais; **resources** npl adnoddau

respect vt parch ▸ n golwg; parch

respectable adj parchus

respectful adj boneddigaidd, yn dangos parch

respective adj priodol, ar wahân

respite n saib, seibiant

respond vi ateb, ymateb; porthi

response n ateb, atebiad

responsibility n cyfrifoldeb

responsible adj atebol, cyfrifol

responsive adj ymatebol

rest¹ n, vb gorffwys ▸ n (in music) tawnod

rest² n (remainder) gweddill

restaurant n tŷ bwyta, bwyty

restless adj aflonydd, rhwyfus

restore vt adfer; atgyweirio

restrain vt atal, ffrwyno

restraint n atalfa, ffrwyn

restrict vt cyfyngu, caethiwo

restriction n cyfyngiad

result vi deillio, canlyn ▸ n canlyniad

resume vt ailddechrau

résumé n crynodeb

resuscitate vb adfywhau, dadebru

retail vt manwerthu, adwerthu ▸ n adwerth

retailer n manwerthwr

retain vb cadw, dal; llogi

retaliation n dial

retire vi ymneilltuo, encilio, cilio, ymddeol

retired adj wedi ymddeol

retirement n ymddeoliad

retort vb gwrthateb ▸ n ateb parod; ritort (cemeg)

retreat vi cilio, encilio, ffoi ▸ n encil, ffo

retrieve vt olrhain; adennill, adfer

retrospect n ad-drem, adolwg

return vb dychwelyd ▸ n dychweliad; enillion

return (ticket) n tocyn dwyffordd

reunion n aduniad

reveal vt datguddio

revel vi gloddesta; ymhyfrydu ▸ n gloddest

revenge vb, n dial

revenue n refeniw

reverend adj parchedig

reversal n dymchweliad, cwymp

reverse adj gwrthwyneb, chwith ▸ vb troi, gwrthdroi ▸ n gwrthdro, aflwydd

reverse (gear) n gêr ôl

reverse charge call n galwad y telir amdani'r pen arall

revert vb troi yn ôl, dychwelyd

review vt adolygu ▸ n adolygiad

revise vt cywiro, diwygio

revision n cywiriad; adolygiad

revival n adfywiad, diwygiad

revive vb adfywio, adnewyddu

revolt vb gwrthryfela ▸ n gwrthryfel

revolting adj atgas, ffiaidd

revolution n chwyldro, chwyldroad

revolutionary adj chwildroadol ▸ n chwildrowr

revolve vb troi, cylchdroi

revolver n llawddryll

reward n gwobr ▸ vt gwobrwyo

rewarding adj buddiol

rewind vt ailweindio

r

rheumatism n cryd cymalau, gwynegon

Rhine n Rhein

rhinoceros n rhinoseros

Rhone n Rhôn

rhubarb n rhiwbob

rhyme n odl, rhigwm ▸ vb odli, rhigymu

rhythm n rhythm, rhediad

rib n asen, eisen

ribbon n rhuban, ysnoden

rice n reis

rich adj cyfoethog, goludog, bras

rid (pt, pp **rid**) vt gwared

riddle n dychymyg, pos

ride (pt **rode**, pp **ridden**) vb marchogaeth, marchocáu

rider n marchogwr; atodiad

ridge n trum, cefn, crib

ridicule n gwawd ▸ vt gwawdio, chwerthin am ben

ridiculous adj chwerthinllyd

riding n marchogaeth

riding school n ysgol farchogaeth

rife adj cyffredin, rhemp

rifle n dryll, reiffl

rift n agen, hollt

rig vb rigio, taclu ▸ n rig

right adj iawn, uniawn; deau ▸ adv yn iawn ▸ vt unioni, cywiro ▸ n iawnder, hawl; **right wing** (politics) asgell dde

right angle n ongl sgwâr

rightful adj cyfreithlon, iawn

right-hand adj llaw dde

right-handed adj llawdde

rightly adv yn gywir

rigid adj anhyblyg

rim n ymyl, cylch, cant

rind n croen, crawen, rhisgl

ring¹ n (jewellery) modrwy; (circle) cylch ▸ vb modrwyo

ring² (pt **rang**, pp **rung**) vb (sound) canu cloch, atseinio; (person; by phone) ffonio ▸ n swn cloch, tinc ▸ **ring back** vt, vi ffonio'n ôl ▸ **ring up** vt, vi ffonio

ring binder n ffeil fodrwy

ring road n cylchffordd

ring tone n tôn ffôn

rinse vt golchi, trochi

riot n terfysg, gloddest ▸ vi terfysgu

rip vb rhwygo ▸ n rhwyg; **rip up** vt rhwygo

ripe adj aeddfed

rip-off n (inf) lladrad amlwg

ripple n crych ▸ vb crychu

rise (pt **rose**, pp **risen**) vi codi, cyfodi ▸ n codiad

risk n perygl, risg ▸ vt peryglu, mentro

rite n defod

ritual adj defodol ▸ n defod

rival n cydymgeisydd ▸ vb cystadlu

river n afon

rivet n rhybed, rifet ▸ vb rhybedu, rifetio

road n ffordd, heol; angorfa

road map n map ffyrdd, map moduro

road rage n cythraul gyrru

road sign n arwydd ffordd

road tax n treth ffordd

road works npl gwaith cynnal y ffordd

roam vi crwydro, gwibio

roar vi rhuo ▸ n rhu, rhuad

roast vb rhostio

rob *vt* lladrata, ysbeilio
robber *n* lleidr, ysbeiliwr
robbery *n* lladrad
robe *n* gwisg, gŵn
robin *n* brongoch
robot *n* robot
robust *adj* cadarn, cryf
rock¹ *vb* siglo
rock² *n* craig
rocket *n* roced
rocky *adj* creigiog; sigledig
rod *n* gwialen, llath
rodent *n* cnofil
roe¹ *n* (*deer*) iyrches, ewig
roe² *n* (*of fish*) grawn pysgod, gronell
rogue *n* gwalch, cnaf
role *n* rhan, rôl
roll *vb* rholio, treiglo ▸ *n* rhôl
roll call *n* galw enwau (ar restr)
Rollerblading *n* llafnrolio
roller skates *npl* esgidiau sglefrolio
roller-skating *n* sglefrolio
rolling pin *n* rholbren
Roman *n* Rhufeiniwr ▸ *adj* Rhufeinaidd, Rhufeinig
Roman Catholic *n* Pabydd
romance *n* rhamant ▸ *vi* rhamantu
Romania *n* Rwmania
Romanian *n* (*person*) Rwmaniad; (*language*) Rwmaneg ▸ *adj* Rwmanaidd; (*in language*) Rwmaneg
romantic *adj* rhamantus
Rome *n* Rhufain
roof *n* to, nen ▸ *vt* toi
rook *n* ydfran, brân
room *n* lle; ystafell
roommate *n* cydletywr

room service *n* gwasanaeth ystafell
roomy *adj* helaeth, eang
rooster *n* ceiliog
root *n* gwraidd, gwreiddyn ▸ *vb* gwreiddio; diwreiddio; **root around** *vi* chwilota; **root out** *vt* gwaredu
rope *n* rhaff ▸ *vt* rhaffu, rhwymo; **rope in** *vt* rhwydo
rose *n* rhosyn
rose hips *npl* egroes
rosy *adj* rhosynnaidd, gwritgoch
rot *vb* pydru, braenu ▸ *n* pydredd; (*inf*) lol
rota *n* rhod, trefn
rotate *vi* troi, cylchdroi
rotten *adj* pwdr, pydredig
rough *adj* garw, gerwin, bras
roughly *adv* (*not gently*) yn arw; (*approximately*) yn fras
round *adj* crwn ▸ *n* crwn, tro, rownd ▸ *adv, prep* o glych, o amgylch ▸ *vb* crynio, rowndio; **round off** *vt* terfynu; **round up** *vt* talgrynnu
roundabout *n* cylchfan; ceffylau bach ▸ *adj* cwmpasog
rounders *n* rownders
round trip *n* taith mynd a dod
rouse *vb* dihuno, deffroi
route *n* llwybr, hynt
routine *n* defod, arfer
row¹ *n* rhes, rhestr
row² *vb* rhwyfo
row³ *n* cythrwfl, ffrae
rowing *n* rhwyfo
rowing boat *n* cwch rhwyfo
royal *adj* brenhinol
royalty *n* brenhiniaeth; breindal

r

rub

rub vb rhwbio; **rub out** vt rhwbio
allan, dileu
rubber n rwber
rubbish n ysbwriel, sothach; lol
rubbish bin n bin ysbwriel
  ► **rubbish dump** n tomen
  ysbwriel
rubbish dump n tomen ysbwriel
rubble n rhwbel
ruby n rhuddem ► adj coch, rhudd
rucksack n rhycsach
rudder n llyw
rude adj anfoesgar; anghelfydd,
garw
ruffle vb crychu, cyffroi, aflonyddu
rug n ryg
rugby n rygbi
rugged adj garw, gerwin,
clogyrnog
ruin n distryw, dinistr; adfail ► vb
difetha, andwyo
rule n rheol ► vb rheoli; llinellu;
rule out vt diystyru
ruler n llywodraethwr; pren mesur,
rhiwl
ruling n dyfarniad, barn ► adj
llywodraethol, mewn grym
rum n rym ► adj od, rhyfedd
Rumania n Rwmania
rumble vi trystio, tyrfu
rumour n si, sôn
run (pt **ran**, pp **run**) vb rhedeg, llifo
  ► n rhediad, rhedfa; **in the long
  run** yn y pen draw; **run away** vi
  ffoi, rhedeg i ffwrdd; **run out** vi
  dod i ben; **run out of** vt rhedeg
  allan o; **run over** vt: **she was run
  over by a car** cafodd ei tharo i lawr
  gan gar
rung n ffon ysgol

runner n rhedwr
runner-up n: **the runner-up** yr ail
running n rhedeg
runway n rhedfa
rupture n rhwyg; torllengig ► vb
rhwygo
rural adj gwledig, gwladaidd
rush¹ n brwynen, pabwyryn
rush² vb rhuthro ► n rhuthr
rush hour n awr brysur
Russia n Rwsia
Russian n (person) Rwsiad;
(language) Rwseg ► adj Rwsiaidd;
(in language) Rwseg
rust n rhwd ► vb rhydu
rusty adj rhydlyd
ruthless adj didostur, diarbed,
creulon
rye n rhyg

S

Sabbath n Sabath, Saboth
sabotage n difrod bwriadol ▸ vb difrodi
sack n sach, ffetan ▸ vt sachu; difrodi; diswyddo
sacred adj cysegredig, glân, sanctaidd
sacrifice n aberth, offrwm ▸ vb aberthu
sad adj trist
saddle n cyfrwy ▸ vt cyfrwyo; beichio
sadness n tristwch, prudd-der
safe adj diogel, saff ▸ n sêff
safety n diogelwch; **safety belt** gwregys diogelwch; **safety pin** pin cau
saffron n saffrwm ▸ adj melyn
sag vb sagio, ymollwng
sage n saets
Sagittarius n y Saethydd
Sahara n Sahara
sail n hwyl ▸ vb hwylio

sailing n hwylio
sailing boat n llong hwylio
sailor n morwr, llongwr
saint n sant
sake n mwyn; **for the sake of** er mwyn
salad n salad
salami n salami
salary n cyflog
sale n gwerth, gwerthiant
sales assistant n (man) dyn siop; (woman) merch siop
salesman n gwerthwr
saleswoman n gwerthwraig
saline adj heliaidd, hallt ▸ n heli
saliva n poer
salmon n eog, samwn
saloon n neuadd, salŵn
salt n halen; (Chem) halwyn ▸ adj hallt ▸ vt halltu
salt cellar n llestr halen
salt water n dŵr hallt, dŵr y môr
salty adj hallt
salute vt cyfarch; saliwtio ▸ n cyfarchiad; saliwt
Salvation Army n: **the Salvation Army** Byddin yr Iachawdwriaeth
same adj yr un, yr un fath
sample n sampl, enghraifft ▸ vt samplu, samplo
sanction n caniatâd; cosb; sancsiwn (moeseg) ▸ vt caniatáu; cosbi
sanctuary n cysegr; noddfa, nawdd
sand n tywod ▸ vt tywodi
sandal n sandal
sand castle n castell tywod
sandpaper n papur gwydrog
sandpit n pwll tywod

sandwich n brechdan
sandy adj tywodlyd; melyngoch
sane adj iach, call
sanity n iechyd meddwl, iawn bwyll
Santa Claus n Siôn Corn
sap¹ n nodd, sugn
sap² vb tangloddio, diseilio
sapphire n saffir ▸ adj glas
sarcasm n gwawdiaith, coegni
sarcastic adj gwawdlyd, coeglyd
sardine n sardîn
satchel n sachell, cod lyfrau
satellite n canlynwr, cynffonnwr; lleuad; lloeren
satellite dish n dysgl loeren, soser lloeren
satin n satin, pali
satire n dychan, gogan
satisfaction n bodlonrwydd; iawn
satisfactory adj boddhaol; iawnol
satisfied adj bodlon
satisfy vt bodloni, diwallu, digoni
sat nav n offer llywio lloeren
Saturday n dydd Sadwrn
sauce n saws; haerllugrwydd
saucepan n sosban
saucer n soser
Saudi Arabia n Saudi Arabia, Sawdi Arabia
sausage n selsig, selsigen
savage adj milain, anwar ▸ n anwariad
save vb achub, arbed, gwaredu; cynilo ▸ prep ond; **save up** vi cynilo
saving adj achubol, darbodus
savoury n blasusfwyd ▸ adj sawrus

saw (pt **sawed**, pp **sawed**, **sawn**) n llif ▸ vb llifio
sawdust n blawd llif
saxophone n sacsoffon
say (pt, pp **said**) vb dweud
saying n dywediad, ymadrodd, gair
scab n crachen, cramen; clafr
scald vt ysgaldio, sgaldan(u)
scale¹ n (balance) clorian, tafol, mantol
scale² n graddfa ▸ vb dringo
scales npl clorian
scallop n gylfragen; gwlf ▸ vt gylfu, minfylchu
scalp n copa, croen y pen ▸ vt penflingo
scam n (inf) sgam
scampi n sgampi
scan vb corfannu; sganio
scandal n tramgwydd, gwarth
Scandinavia n Llychlyn
Scandinavian n Sgandinafiad ▸ adj Sgandinafaidd
scanner n sganydd; sganiwr; **virus scanner** sganiwr feirws
scapegoat n bwch dihangol
scar n craith ▸ vt creithio
scarce adj, adv prin
scarcely adv prin, braidd
scare vt brawychu, tarfu ▸ n dychryn
scarecrow n bwgan brain
scared adj wedi cael ofn, wedi brawychu
scarf n crafat, sgarff
scarlet adj ysgarlad
scary adj (inf) sgêri
scatter vb gwasgaru, chwalu, taenu
scene n lle; golwg, golygfa

scenery n golygfa
scenic adj hardd, golygfaol
scent n aroglau, perarogl; trywydd ▸ vt arogli
sceptical adj amheugar
schedule n atodlen, cofrestr
scheduled flight n ehediad rhestredig
scheme n cynllun ▸ vb cynllunio
scholar n ysgolhaig, ysgolor
scholarship n ysgolheictod; ysgoloriaeth
school n ysgol, ysgoldy ▸ vt addysgu
schoolbag n bag ysgol
schoolbook n llyfr ysgol
schoolboy n bachgen ysgol
schoolchildren npl plant ysgol
schoolgirl n merch ysgol
school uniform n gwisg ysgol
science n gwyddor, gwyddoniaeth
science fiction n ffuglen wyddonol
scientific adj gwyddonol
scientist n gwyddonydd
scissors npl siswrn
scold vb dwrdio, tafodi, ceryddu, cymhennu ▸ n cecren
scone n sgon
scoop n lletwad ▸ vt cafnu, cafnio
scooter n sgwter
scope n ergyd, bwriad; cwmpas
score¹ n rhic; cyfrif; sgôr; ugain
score² vb rhicio, cyfrif, sgori(o)
scorn n dirmyg ▸ vb dirmygu, gwatwar
Scorpio n y Sgorpion
scorpion n ysgorpion
Scot n Ysgotyn, Albanwr
Scotch adj Ysgotaidd, Albanaidd
scotch vt hacio, darnio, trychu

Scotland n Yr Alban
Scots adj Albanaidd; *(in language)* Scoteg
Scotsman n Albanwr
Scotswoman n Albanes
Scottish adj Albanaidd
scour¹ vt *(scrub)* carthu, ysgwrio
scour² vb rhedeg; chwilio
scout n sgowt, ysbïwr ▸ vt sgowta, ysbïo
scowl vb cuchio, gwgu ▸ n cilwg, gwg
scramble vi, n ciprys, ymgiprys
scrambled egg n cymysgwy
scrap n tamaid, dernyn
scrapbook n llyfr lloffion
scrape vb crafu ▸ n helynt, helbul, crafiad
scratch vb crafu, cripio
scratch card n cerdyn crafu
scream vi ysgrechian ▸ n ysgrech, gwawch
screen n llen, cysgod; sgrin ▸ vt cysgodi
screen saver n arbedwr sgrin
screw n sgriw, hoel dro ▸ vb ysgriwio
screwdriver n tyrnsgriw
scribble n ysgribl ▸ vb ysgriblo, ysgriblan
script n sgript
scroll n rhôl, plyg llyfr
scrub n prysgwydd; ysgwrfa ▸ vt ysgwrio
scrum, scrummage n sgrym, ysgarmes
scrutiny n archwiliad
sculptor n cerflunydd
sculpture n cerfluniaeth; cerflun ▸ vb cerflunio, torri

scum n sgum; (inf) gwehilion, sorod

scurry vi ffrystio ▸ n ffrwst, ffwdan

scuttle vi heglu ffoi, dianc

sea n môr

seafood n bwyd môr

seagull n gwylan

seal¹ n (animal) morlo

seal² n sêl, insel ▸ vt selio

sea level n lefel y môr

seam n gwniad, gwrym; haen, gwythïen; craith

search vb chwilio, profi ▸ n ymchwil

search engine n peiriant chwilio, chwiliadur

search party n criw chwilio

seashore n glan y môr

seasick adj sâl môr; **to be seasick** dioddef o salwch môr

seaside n glan y môr

season n tymor ▸ vb tymheru; halltu; **high/low season** tymor prysur/llac

seasonal adj tymhorol

season ticket n tocyn tymor

seat n sedd, sêt ▸ vi eistedd

seat belt n gwregys diogelwch

sea water n dŵr y môr

seaweed n gwymon, gwmon

second adj ail ▸ n ail; eiliad ▸ vt eilio

secondary adj eilradd, uwchradd

secondary school n ysgol uwchradd

second class adj ail ddosbarth; isradd

second-hand adj ail-law

secondly adv yn ail

secret adj dirgel, cyfrinachol ▸ n cyfrinach

secretary n ysgrifennydd

Secretary of State n Ysgrifennydd Gwladol

secretive adj yn celu, tawedog

secretly adv yn gyfrinachol

sect n sect, enwad

section n toriad, trychiad; rhan, adran

sector n sector

secular adj seciwlar

secure adj sicr, diogel ▸ vt sicrhau, diogelu

security n diogelwch, sicrwydd, gwystl

security guard n gwarchodwr

sedate adj tawel, digyffro ▸ vb rhoi i gysgu, tawelu

sedative n lleddfol, lliniarol

seduce vt llithio, hudo, twyllo

seductive adj llithiol, deniadol

see (pt saw, pp seen) vb gweld, canfod

seed n had, hedyn ▸ vb hadu, hedeg

seek (pt, pp sought) vb ceisio, ymofyn, chwilio

seem vi ymddangos

seesaw n siglenydd

segment n segment

segregate vt didoli, neilltuo, gwahanu

seize vb gafael mewn, atafaelu

seizure n daliad; ymosodiad, strôc

seldom adv anfynych, anaml

select vt dewis, dethol

selection n detholiad

self n hun, hunan

self- prefix hunan-, ym-

self-catering *adj* hunan arlwy
self-confidence *n* hunanhyder
self-confident *adj* hunanhyderus
self-conscious *adj*
hunanymwybodol, swil
self-contained *adj* annibynnol,
ar wahân
self-control *n* hunanlywodraeth
self-defence *n* hunanamddiffyniad
self-employed *adj*
hunangyflogedig
self-interest *n* hunan-les
selfish *adj* hunanol
self-respect *n* hunan-barch
self-service *n* hunanwasanaeth
sell (*pt, pp* **sold**) *vb* gwerthu; siomi
▸ *n* siom; **sell off** *vt* gwerthu; **sell
out** *vi*: they've sold out maen
nhw wedi gwerthu'r cwbl
sell-by date *n* dyddiad olaf
gwerthu
seller *n* gwerthwr
semicircle *n* hanner cylch
semidetached (house) *n* tŷ pâr
semi-final *n*: the semi-finals y
rownd cynderfynol
seminar *n* seminar
semi-skimmed *adj* hanner-sgim
semi-skimmed milk *n* llaeth
hanner sgim
senate *n* senedd
send (*pt, pp* **sent**) *vt* anfon, danfon,
gyrru; **send back** *vt* anfon yn
ôl; **send off** *vt*: he was sent off
cafodd ei anfon o'r cae; **send out**
vt anfon allan
senile *adj* hen a methedig,
heneiddiol
senior *adj* hŷn ▸ *n* hynaf
senior citizen *n* henwr

sensation *n* ymdeimlad, teimlad;
cyffro, ias, syndod
sensational *adj* iasol, cyffrous
sense *n* synnwyr, pwyll, ystyr;
sense of humour synnwyr
digrifwch
senseless *adj* dienaid, disynnwyr,
hurt
sensible *adj* synhwyrol; teimladwy
sensitive *adj* teimladwy; hydeiml
sensual *adj* cnawdol; trythyll,
chwantus
sensuous *adj* teimladol,
synhwyrus
sentence *n* brawddeg; dedfryd
▸ *vt* dedfrydu
sentiment *n* syniad, teimlad
sentimental *adj* sentimental
separate *adj* ar wahân ▸ *vb*
gwahanu, neilltuo, ysgar;
ymwahanu
separately *adv* ar wahân
separation *n* gwahaniad
September *n* Medi
septic *adj* braenol, pydrol,
madreddol
sequel *n* canlyniad
sequence *n* trefn, dilyniad
Serbia *n* Serbia
sergeant *n* rhingyll, sarsiant
serial *adj* cyfresol, bob yn rhifyn
▸ *n* stori gyfres
serial killer *n* llofrudd cyfresol
series *n* rhes, cyfres
serious *adj* difrifol
seriously *adv* yn ddifrifol
sermon *n* pregeth
servant *n* gwas; morwyn
serve *vb* gwasanaethu, gweini
server *n* gweinydd

service n gwasanaeth, oedfa; llestri
service charge n tâl am wasanaeth
service station n gorsaf gwasanaethau
serviette n napcyn
session n eisteddiad; sesiwn; tymor
set (pt, pp **set**) vb gosod, dodi; plannu; sadio; sefydlu; machlud ▸ n set; impyn, planhigyn; **set off** vi cychwyn; **set out** vi cychwyn
settee n sgiw, setl
setting n lleoliad, safle; machludiad
settle vb sefydlu; penderfynu; cytuno, setlo; plwyfo; talu; **settle down** vi (calm down) tawelu; **settle down!** byddwch yn llonydd!; **settle in** vi setlo
settlement n cytundeb; gwladfa, anheddiad
seven adj, n saith
seventeen adj, n dau (dwy) ar bymtheg, un deg saith
seventeenth adj ail ar bymtheg
seventh adj seithfed
seventy adj, n deg a thrigain, saith deg
sever vb gwahanu, datod, torri
several adj amryw; gwahanol
severe adj caled, tost, llym, gerwin
sew (pt **sewed**, pp **sewn**) vb gwnïo, pwytho; **sew up** vt gwnïo
sewage n carthffosiaeth, carthion
sewer n ceuffos, carthffos
sewing n gwnïo
sewing machine n peiriant gwnïo
sex n rhyw

sex education n addysg ryw
sexism n rhywiaeth
sexist adj rhywiaethol, secsist
sexual adj rhywiol
sexuality n rhywioldeb
sexy adj rhywiol
shabby adj carpiog, gwael, aflêr
shack n caban
shade n cysgod; ysbryd ▸ vt cysgodi
shadow n cysgod ▸ vt cysgodi
shady adj cysgodol; amheus
shaft n paladr; braich; siafft; gwerthyd
shake (pt **shook**, pp **shaken**) vb ysgwyd, siglo, crynu
shaky adj ansad, crynedig
shallow adj bas ▸ n basle, beisle
sham vb ffugio ▸ adj ffug, gau, coeg ▸ n ffug, ffugbeth
shambles npl galanastra
shame n cywilydd, gwaradwydd, gwarth ▸ vb cywilyddio, gwaradwyddo
shameful adj cywilyddus, gwarthus
shampoo vt golchi pen ▸ n siampŵ
shandy n siandi
shape n siâp, llun ▸ vt siapio, llunio
share n rhan, cyfran ▸ vb rhannu; cyfranogi; **share out** vt rhannu
shareholder n cyfranddaliwr
shark n siarc, morgi; twyllwr
sharp adj siarp, llym, miniog ▸ n llonnod (cerdd)
sharpen vb hogi, minio
sharpener n naddwr
sharply adv yn sydyn

shatter vb dryllio, chwilfriwio; ysigo

shattered adj drylliedig; (inf) wedi blino'n lân

shave vb eillio; rhasglio

shaver n: (**electric**) **shaver** eilliwr (trydan)

shaving cream n sebon eillio

shaving foam n ewyn eillio

shavings npl naddion

shawl n siôl

she pron hi ▸ adj prefix benyw

sheath n gwain; (contraceptive) maneg atal cenhedlu

shed¹ n penty, sied

shed² (pt, pp **shed**) vt tywallt; gollwng; colli; dihidlo, bwrw

sheep n dafad

sheepdog n ci defaid

sheer¹ vi gwyro o'r ffordd, cilio

sheer² adj pur, glân, noeth, syth, serth

sheet n llen; cynfas; hwylraff; dalen

shelf n silff, astell

shell n cragen; plisgyn, masgl; tân-belen

shellfish npl cregynbysg

shelter n cysgod, lloches ▸ vb cysgodi, llochesu; ymochel; llechu

shelve vi llechweddu, llethru

shepherd n bugail ▸ vt bugeilio

sheriff n sirydd, siryf

sherry n sieri

Shetland n Shetland

shield n tarian ▸ vt cysgodi, amddiffyn

shift vb newid, symud; ymdaro ▸ n newid; tro, stem, shifft

shin n crimog, crimp coes

shine (pt, pp **shone**) vb disgleirio, llewyrchu, tywynnu ▸ n disgleirdeb, sglein, llewyrch

shingle n graean, gro

shingles npl yr eryr, yr eryrod

shiny adj gloyw, disglair

ship n llong ▸ vt trosglwyddo

shipping n llongau (gwlad)

shipwreck n llongddrylliad

shirt n crys

shiver vi crynu

shoal n haig ▸ vi heigio

shock n sioc, ergyd, ysgytiad ▸ vt ysgytio

shocking adj arswydus, ysgytiol

shoe (pt, pp **shod**) n esgid; pedol ▸ vt pedoli

shoelace n carrai/lasen esgid

shoe polish n cwyr esgidiau

shoe shop n siop esgidiau

shoot (pt, pp **shot**) vb tarddu, blaguro; saethu ▸ n ysbrigyn, blaguryn

shooting n saethu

shop n siop ▸ vb siopa

shop assistant n (man) dyn siop; (woman) merch siop

shopkeeper n siopwr

shoplifting n siopladrad

shopping n siopa

shop window n ffenestr siop

shore n glan, traeth

short adj byr, cwta, prin

shortage n prinder, diffyg

shortcoming n diffyg, bai

short cut n llwybr tarw, llwybr llygad, ffordd fer

shorthand n llaw-fer

shortly adv ymhen ychydig

shorts npl trowsus cwta

S

short-sighted adj (person) â golwg byr; (action, attitude) byrweledol

shot n ergyd; saethwr

shotgun n gwn haels

shoulder n ysgwydd, palfais ▸ vt ysgwyddo

shoulder blade n sgapwla, pont yr ysgwydd

shout vb bloeddio, gweiddi ▸ n bloedd, gwaedd

shove vb gwthio

shovel n llwyarn ▸ vt rhofio

show (pt showed, pp shown) vb dangos, arddangos ▸ n arddangosfa, sioe, siew; **show off** vt dangos eich hun ▸ vt (display) arddangos; **show up** vi (inf) ymddangos

shower n cawod, cawad ▸ vb cawodi, bwrw

shower gel n gel cawod

shred n llarp, cerpyn ▸ vb rhwygo, torri'n fân

shrewd adj craff

shriek vb ysgrechian ▸ n ysgrech

shrimp n berdysen ▸ vi berdysa

shrine n creirfa; cysegr, seintwar

shrink (pt shrank, pp shrunk) vb crebachu, cilio

shrivel vb crychu, crebachu

shroud n amdo ▸ vt amdoi, cuddio, celu

Shrove Tuesday n Mawrth Ynyd

shrub n prysgwydden, llwyn

shrug vb codi'r ysgwyddau

shudder n crynfa, arswyd ▸ vi crynu, arswydo

shuffle vb siffrwd; llusgo

shun vt gochelyd, osgoi

shut (pt, pp **shut**) vb cau ▸ adj caeëdig; **shut down** vt cau; **shut up** vt (inf) cau

shutter n caead, clawr

shuttle n gwennol (gwëydd)

shuttlecock n gwennol

shy adj swil ▸ vi osgoi, rhusio

siblings npl brodyr/chwiorydd

sick adj claf; yn chwydu, â chyfog arno; wedi diflasu

sickening adj atgas, diflas, cyfoglyd

sick leave n seibiant salwch

sickly adj afiach, nychlyd

sickness n afiechyd

side n ochr, ystlys; tu, plaid ▸ vi ochri

sideboard n seld

side effect n sgil-effaith

sidetrack vb troi o'r neilltu

sideways adv tua'r ochr, yn wysg ei ochr

siege n gwarchae

sieve n gogr, gwagr, rhidyll

sift vt gogrwn, nithio, hidlo, rhidyllio

sigh vb ochneidio ▸ n ochenaid

sight n golwg, golygfa ▸ vt gweld

sightseeing n taith i weld y wlad

sign n arwydd, argoel ▸ vb arwyddo, llofnodi; **sign on** vi cofrestru

signal adj hynod ▸ n arwydd

signature n llofnod

significance n arwyddocâd, ystyr

significant adj arwyddocaol; o bwys

signify vb arwyddo, arwyddocáu

sign language n iaith arwyddion

signpost *n* mynegbost, arwyddbost

silence *n* taw, distawrwydd ► *vt* rhoi taw ar

silent *adj* distaw, tawedog

silhouette *n* cysgodlun, silŵet

silk *n* sidan

silly *adj* gwirion, ffôl

silver *n* arian ► *vt* ariannu

silver paper *n* papur arian

similar *adj* tebyg, cyffelyb

simmer *vi* lledferwi, goferwi

simple *adj* syml; gwirion, diniwed

simplicity *n* symlrwydd, unplygrwydd

simplify *vt* symleiddio

simply *adv* yn syml; yn ddi-lol; yn wirioneddol

simulate *vt* ffugio, dynwared

simultaneous *adj* cyfamserol, ar y pryd

sin *n* pechod ► *vb* pechu

since *conj* gan, yn gymaint ► *prep* er, er pan

sincere *adj* diffuant, didwyll

sincerely *adv* yn ddiffuant; **Yours sincerely** yr eiddoch yn gywir

sing (*pt* **sang**, *pp* **sung**) *vb* canu

singer *n* canwr, cantwr, cantores

singing *n* canu

single *adj* sengl, dibriod

single bed *n* gwely sengl

single-minded *adj* unplyg, cywir

single parent *n* rhiant sengl

single room *n* ystafell sengl

singular *adj* unigol; hynod

sinister *adj* ysgeler; chwithig

sink (*pt* **sank**, *pp* **sunk**) *vb* soddi, suddo ► *n* sinc

sip *vt* llymeitian ► *n* llymaid, llymeidyn

sir *n* syr

siren *n* corn, seiren

sirloin *n* llwyn eidion

sister *n* chwaer

sister-in-law *n* chwaer yng nghyfraith

sit (*pt*, *pp* **sat**) *vb* eistedd; **sit down** *vi* eistedd

site *n* safle, lle ► *vb* lleoli

sitting *n* eisteddiad

sitting room *n* parlwr, lolfa, ystafell fyw

situated *adj* yn sefyll, wedi ei leoli

situation *n* lle, safle; sefyllfa

six *adj*, *n* chwech

sixteen *adj*, *n* un ar bymtheg, un deg chwech

sixteenth *adj* unfed ar bymtheg

sixth *adj* chweched

sixth form *n* chweched dosbarth

sixth-form college *n* coleg chweched dosbarth

sixty *adj*, *n* trigain, chwe deg

size *n* maint, maintioli

sizzle *vb* ffrio

skate¹ *n* (*fish*) cath fôr

skate² *n* sgêt ► *vb* ysglefrio

skateboard *n* bwrdd sglefrio

skateboarding *n* sgrialfyrddio

skates *n* esgidiau sglefrio

skating *n* sglefrio

skeleton *n* ysgerbwd; amlinelliad

sketch *n* llun, braslun ► *vb* braslunio, tynnu

skewer *n* gwaell, gwachell

ski *n* sgi ► *vb* sgio

skid *vb* llithro (naill ochr)

skier *n* sgiwr

S

skiing n sgïo

skilful adj medrus

skill n medr, medrusrwydd

skilled adj medrus, crefftus

skim vb tynnu, codi (hufen)

skimmed milk n llaeth glas, llaeth sgim

skin n croen ▸ vb blingo

skinhead n pencroen

skinny adj tenau; prin, crintach

skip vi llamu, sgipio

skipper n capten llong

skipping rope n rhaff sgipio

skirt n godre, sgyrt ▸ vt dilyn gyda godre

skive (inf) vi sgelcian; **skive off** vi sgelcian

skull n penglog

skunk n drewgi

sky n wybren, awyr

skyscraper n nendwr

slab n llech

slack adj llac, diofal, esgeulus

slam vb cau yn glats, clepian

slander n enllib ▸ vt enllibio

slang n iaith sathredig, slang ▸ vt difrio

slant vb gwyro, gogwyddo ▸ n gogwydd

slap vt clewtian ▸ n clewt(en), palfod

slash n slaes, hac ▸ vt slasio, chwipio

slate¹ n llech, llechen

slate² vt sennu, difrio

slaughter n lladdedigaeth, lladdfa ▸ vt lladd

slaughterhouse n lladd-dy

slave n slaf, caethwas ▸ vi slafio

slavery n caethiwed, caethwasanaeth

slay (pt **slew**, pp **slain**) vt lladd

sled, sledge, sleigh n car llusg, sled

sledge n sled

sledging n sledio

sleek adj llyfn, graenus

sleep (pt, pp **slept**) vb cysgu, huno ▸ n cwsg, hun; **sleep around** vi neidio o wely i wely; **sleep in** vi cysgu'n hwyr; **sleep together** vi: they're sleeping together maen nhw'n cysgu gyda'i gilydd

sleeper n (person) cysgwr; sliper

sleeping bag n sach gysgu

sleeping pill n pilsen gysgu

sleepy adj cysglyd

sleet n eirlaw

sleeve n llawes

slender adj main

slice n tafell, ysglisen ▸ vt tafellu, ysglisio

slick adj llyfn, tafodrydd, slic

slide (pt, pp **slid**) vb llithro, sglefrio ▸ n llithren, sleid

slight adj ysgafn, eiddil, prin ▸ vt diystyru ▸ n diystyrwch, sarhad

slightly adv ychydig

slim adj main, eiddil

sling (pt, pp **slung**) vt taflu, lluchio ▸ n ffon dafl

slip vb llithro; gollwng ▸ n slip; **slip up** vi llithro

slipper n llopan, sliper

slippery adj llithrig, diafael, di-ddal

slip-up n llithriad

slit (pt, pp **slit**) vb hollti, agennu ▸ n hollt

slog vb gweithio'n galed

slope n llethr, gogwydd ▸ vb gogwyddo

sloppy adj lleidiog; meddal; anniben

slot n agen, twll

Slovakia n Slofacia

Slovenia n Slofenia

slow adj araf ▸ vb arafu; **slow down** vi arafu

slowly adj yn araf (deg)

slug n gwlithen, malwoden

sluggish adj dioglyd

slum n slym

slump n cwymp, gostyngiad; dirwasgiad

slur vb difrïo ▸ n llithriad, cyflusg (cerdd.); anfri

slush n llaid, llaca, eira gwlyb

sly adj cyfrwys, dichellgar

smack n (slap) smac ▸ vb smacio, chwipio

small adj bach, bychan, mân

smart vi gwynio, dolurio ▸ n gwyn, dolur ▸ adj llym, bywiog; ffraeth; crand

smartphone n ffôn clyfar

smash vb torri, malu, chwilfriwio

smear vt iro, dwbio

smell (pt, pp smelt, smelled) n arogl, aroglau ▸ vb arogli

smelly adj drewllyd

smile vb gwenu ▸ n gwên

smirk vi cilwenu, glaswenu ▸ n cilwen

smog n smog, mwgwl

smoke n mwg ▸ vb mygu; ysmygu, smocio

smoke alarm n larwm mwg, larwm fwg

smoked adj wedi ei fygu

smoker n ysmygwr

smoking n ysmygu

smoky adj myglyd

smooth adj llyfn, esmwyth ▸ vt llyfnhau

smother vb mygu, llethu

SMS n SMS

SMS message n neges SMS

smudge n baw, smotyn ▸ vb difwyno, trochi

smug adj hunanol, cysetlyd

smuggle vt smyglo

smuggler n smyglwr

smuggling n smyglo

snack n tamaid, byrbryd

snack bar n lle am damaid

snag n rhwystr, maen tramgwydd

snail n malwoden, malwen

snake n neidr

snap vb clecian; tynnu llun ▸ n clec

snarl vi ysgyrnygu, chwyrnu

snatch vb cipio ▸ n cip; tamaid

sneak (US, pt, pp snuck) vi llechian ▸ n (inf) llechgi

sneer vb gwawdio, glaswenu ▸ n gwawd, glaswen

sneeze vi tisian

sniff vb ffroeni, gwyntio

snigger vb glaschwerthin

snip vb torri, cynhinio ▸ n demyn, toriad

snob n crechyn, snob

snooker n snwcer

snooze vb hepian ▸ n cyntun

snore vi chwyrnu

snort vi ffroeni, ffroenochi

snow n eira, ôd ▸ vb bwrw eira, odi

snowball n pelen eira

snowdrift n lluwch

snowman n dyn eira

s

snow plough n aradr eira
snub[1] vt sennu ▶ n sen
snub[2] adj pwt, smwt
snug adj clyd, diddos

(KEYWORD)

so adv 1 (thus, likewise) felly, fel hyn, yn yr un modd; **if so** os felly; **so do** or **have I** minnau hefyd; **it's 5 o'clock — so it is!** mae'n 5 o'r gloch — ydy wir! or yn hollol!; **I hope so** gobeithio ['n wir, felly, hynny]; **so far** hyd yn hyn

2 (in comparisons etc, to such a degree) mor, cyn; **so big** mor fawr or cymaint; **she's not so clever as her brother** nid yw hi mor ddeallus â'i brawd

3: **so much** (adj, adv) cymaint; **I've got so much work** mae gennyf gymaint o waith; **I love you so much** rwy'n dy garu di gymaint; **so many** cynifer

4 (phrases): **10 or so** rhyw, tua, oddeutu, o gwmpas 10; **so long!** (inf, goodbye) da bo ti! (da boch chi!), hwyl fawr!; **so (what)?** (inf) beth am hynny?, be' wedyn?

▶ conj 1 (expressing purpose): **so as to do** er mwyn gwneud; **so (that)** i or er mwyn i; **she opened the door, so that I might go in** agorodd y drws [er mwyn] i mi gael mynd i mewn

2 (expressing result) fel; **he held me so that I could not move** fe'm daliodd fel na allwn symud; **so that's the reason!** felly dyna'r rheswm!; **so you see, I could have gone** felly rwyt ti'n gweld, fe allwn i fod wedi mynd

soak vb mwydo; slotian
soaking adj gwlyb socian
soap n sebon ▶ vb seboni
soap opera n opera sebon
soap powder n powdr golchi
soar vi ehedeg, esgyn
sob vi igian, beichio ▶ n ig, ebwch
sober adj sobr, sad ▶ vb sobri; **sober up** vi sobri
so-called adj dywededig
soccer n pêl-droed, y bêl gron
sociable adj cymdeithasgar
social adj cymdeithasol
social club n clwb cymdeithasol
socialism n sosialaeth
socialist n sosialydd
socialize vi cymdeithasu
social network n rhwydwaith cymdeithasol
social networking n rhwydweithio cymdeithasol
social security n nawdd cymdeithasol
social work n gwaith cymdeithasol
social worker n gweithiwr cymdeithasol
society n cymdeithas, cyfeillach
sociology n cymdeithaseg
sock n hosan
socket n twll, crau, soced
sofa n soffa
soft adj meddal, tyner; distaw; gwirion
soft drink n diod ysgafn
software n meddalwedd
soggy adj gwlyb, lleidiog
soil[1] n pridd, daear, gweryd

soil² vt difwyno, baeddu

solar adj heulog, solar

solar power n ynni'r haul, ynni haul

soldier n milwr

sole¹ adj unig, unigol, un

sole² n (of foot) gwadn

sole³ n (fish) lleden chwithig

solemn adj difrifol, dwys

solicitor n cyfreithiwr

solid¹ adj solet, cadarn

solid² n solid

solitary adj unig; anghyfannedd

solitude n unigedd

solo n unawd

soloist n unawdydd

soluble adj toddadwy, hydawdd

solution n dehongliad, esboniad; toddiant

solve vt datrys, dehongli

solvent adj yn gallu talu, di-ddyled
  ▸ n toddfa

sombre adj tywyll, prudd

⸻

⟮KEYWORD⟯

some adj 1 (a certain amount or number of) rhyw, peth, rhyw(f)aint o (sometimes not translated); **some tea/water/ice cream** te/dŵr/ hufen iâ; **some children/apples** plant/afalau; **I've got some money but not much** mae gennyf rywfaint o arian ond dim llawer 2 (certain: in contrasts): **some people say that ...** mae rhai/ rhyw(f)rai'n dweud ...; **some films were excellent, but most were mediocre** roedd rhai ffilmiau'n rhagorol, ond gweddol oedd y mwyafrif 3 (unspecified): **some woman was**

⸻

asking for you roedd rhyw fenyw yn gofyn amdanat; **he was asking for some book (or other)** roedd yn gofyn am ryw lyfr (neu ei gilydd); **some day** ryw ddiwrnod; **some day next week** ryw ddiwrnod yr wythnos nesaf
  ▸ pron 1 (a certain number) rhyw, peth, rhyw(f)aint o; **I've got some** (books etc) mae gennyf rywfaint (o lyfrau etc); **some (of them) have been sold** mae rhai (ohonynt) wedi'u gwerthu
2 (a certain amount) rhyw(f)aint, peth; **I've got some** (money, milk) mae gennyf rywfaint (o arian/ laeth); **would you like some?** hoffech chi gael peth?, hoffech chi gael rhywfaint?; **could I have some of that cheese?** ga i rywfaint/ beth o'r caws yna?; **I've read some of the book** rwyf wedi darllen rhyw(f)aint/peth o'r llyfr
  ▸ adv: **some 10 people** rhyw 10 o bobl, tua 10 o bobl

⸻

somebody pron = someone

somehow adv rywfodd, rhywsut

someone pron rhywun

something n rhywbeth

sometime adv rywbryd, gynt

sometimes adv weithiau

somewhat adv go, lled, braidd

somewhere adv (yn) rhywle

son n mab

song n cân

son-in-law n mab yng nghyfraith

soon adv buan

sooner adv (time) ynghynt, yn gynt; **I would sooner do** (preference) soothe

byddai'n well gennyf wneud;
sooner or later yn hwyr neu'n
hwyrach
soothe vt lliniaru, lleddfu, dofi,
tawelu
sophisticated adj soffistigedig
soprano n soprano
sordid adj brwnt
sore adj tost, blin, dolurus ▸ n
dolur
sorrow n tristwch, gofid, galar ▸ vi
tristáu, gofidio
sorry adj drwg gan, edifar; salw
sort n modd; math, bath ▸ vt
trefnu, dosbarthu; **sort out** vt
(problem) datrys; (objects) trefnu
so-so adv gweddol
soul n enaid
sound¹ n sain ▸ vb seinio
sound² n (strait) culfor, swnt
sound³ adj dianaf, cyfan, dilys
soundboard n seinfwrdd
sound effects npl effeithiau sain
soundtrack n trac sain
soup n potes, cawl
sour adj sur ▸ vb suro
source n ffynhonnell, tarddiad
south n deau, de
South Africa n De Affrica
southeast n de-ddwyrain ▸ adj
de-ddwyreiniol
southern adj deheuol
South Pole n: the South Pole
Pegwn y De
southwest n de-orllewin ▸ adj
de-orllewinol
souvenir n cofrodd
sovereign adj pen ▸ n penadur;
sofren
sow¹ n hwch

sow² (pt sowed, pp sown) vt hau
soya n soya
soya beans npl ffa soya
soy sauce n saws soi
space n lle, gwagle, gofod
spacecraft n llong ofod
spaceship n llong ofod
spacious adj eang, helaeth
spade n rhaw, pâl
Spain n Sbaen
spam n sbam ▸ vt sbamio
span n rhychwant ▸ vt
rhychwantu
Spaniard n Sbaenwr
Spanish adj Sbaenaidd ▸ n
(language) Sbaeneg
spank vt slapio, smacio, chwipio
tin
spanner n sbaner
spare adj prin; tenau; sbâr ▸ vt
arbed; hepgor
spare time n oriau hamdden,
amser sbâr
spark n gwreichionen
sparkle vi gwreichioni, pefrio
sparkling adj gloyw, llachar;
byrlymog
sparrow n aderyn y to
sparse adj tenau, prin, gwasgarog
spasm n pwl, gwayw
spate n llifeiriant sydyn
speak (pt spoke, pp spoken) vb
llefaru, siarad; **speak up** vi (raise
voice) siarad yn uwch
speaker n llefarydd, siaradwr
spear n gwaywffon, picell ▸ vt
trywanu
special adj neilltuol, arbennig
special effects npl effeithiau
arbennig

specialist n arbenigwr
speciality n arbenigrwydd
specialize vi arbenigo
specially adv yn arbennig
special needs npl anghenion arbennig
species n rhywogaeth
specific adj penodol
specify vt enwi, penodi
specimen n enghraifft, cynllun
speck n brycheuyn, ysmotyn
specs n (inf) sbectol
spectacle n drych, golygfa
spectacular adj ysblennydd, trawiadol
spectator n edrychwr, gwyliwr
spectrum n spectrwm
speculate vi dyfalu; anturio, mentro
speech n llafar, lleferydd; araith
speechless adj mud
speed (pt, pp **sped**) n cyflymder, buander ▸ vb prysuro, cyflymu;
speed up (pt, pp **speeded up**) vi cyflymu
speedboat n cwch cyflym
speeding n goryrru, gyrru'n rhy gyflym
speed limit n terfyn cyflymder
speedometer n mesurydd cyflymdra
spell[1] n (enchantment) cyfaredd, swyn
spell[2] n sbel, hoe, ysbaid
spell[3] (pt, pp **spelt**, **spelled**) vt sillafu
spellchecker n gwiriwr sillafu
spelling n sillafiad
spend (pt, pp **spent**) vb treulio, gwario

sperm n had
sphere n sffêr; cylch, maes
spice n perlysiau, peraroglau, sbeis
spicy adj blasus; ffraeth, diddorol; coch
spider n corryn, pryf copyn
spike n pig
spill (pt, pp **spilt**, **spilled**) vb colli, tywallt
spin (pt, pp **spun**) vb nyddu; troi, troelli
spinach n pigoglys, sbinais
spin-dryer n trowasgwr
spine n asgwrn cefn; draen, pigyn
spiral adj fel cogwrn tro, troellog
spire n meindwr, pigdwr
spirit n ysbryd; gwirod
spirits n gwirodydd
spiritual adj ysbrydol
spit[1] n bêr
spit[2] (pt, pp **spat**) vb poeri
spite n sbeit, malais ▸ vt sbeitio
spiteful adj maleisus, sbeitlyd
splash vb sblasio, tasgu
splendid adj ysblennydd, gwych, campus
splinter vb ysgyrioni ▸ n ysgyren, fflaw
split (pt, pp **split**) vb hollti, rhannu, gwahanu; **split up** vi hollti
spoil (pt, pp **spoiled**, **spoilt**) n ysbail ▸ vb ysbeilio, difetha
spoiled adj maldodi
spoilsport n surbwch
spoilt adj: **a spoilt child** plentyn sydd wedi cael ei faldodi
spoke n adain olwyn, sbogen, braich
spokesman n llefarwr, llefarydd
spokeswoman n llefaryddes

sponge

sponge *n* sbwng ▸ *vb* ysbyngu

sponsor *n* noddwr

spontaneous *adj* gwirfoddol, digymell

spooky *adj* (*inf*) bwganllyd

spoon *n* llwy ▸ *vb* llwyo; caru

spoonful *n* llwyaid

sport *n* sbort, chwarae, hwyl

sports centre *n* canolfan chwaraeon

sportsman *n* mabolgampwr

sportswear *n* dillad chwarae

sportswoman *n* mabolgampwraig

sporty *adj*: **she's very sporty** mae hi'n hoff iawn o chwaraeon

spot *n* llecyn; brycheuyn, ysmotyn ▸ *vt* mannu, brychu, ysmotio ▸ *adj* ar y pryd

spotless *adj* difrycheulyd, glân

spotlight *n* sbotolau

spotty *adj* smotiog

spouse *n* priod

sprain *vt* ysigo

sprawl *vi* ymdaenu

spray¹ *n* gwlith, tawch, trochion ▸ *vt* taenellu; chwistrellu

spray² *n* (*bouquet*) ysbrigyn, cainc; chwistrellydd

spread (*pt, pp* **spread**) *vb* lledu, taenu, lledaenu, gwasgaru; **spread out** *vt* (*blanket, net*) taenu ▸ *vi* (*get broader*) ymledu

spreadsheet *n* taenlen

spree *n* sbri

spring (*pt* **sprang**, *pp* **sprung**) *vb* tarddu, deillio; llamu, neidio ▸ *n* ffynnon; llam; sbring; gwanwyn

spring-clean *n* glanhau'r gwanwyn

springtime *n* gwanwyn

sprinkle *vb* taenellu, ysgeintio

sprint *vb* gwibio

sprinter *n* gwibiwr

spur *n* ysbardun, swmbwl ▸ *vb* ysbarduno, symbylu

spurt *n* ysbonc

spy *n* ysbïwr ▸ *vb* ysbïo

spying *n* (*espionage*) ysbïaeth

squabble *vi* cweryla, ffraeo ▸ *n* ffrwgwd, ffrae

squad *n* carfan, mintai

squadron *n* sgwadron

squander *vt* gwastraffu, afradu

square *adj*, *n* sgwâr, petryal

squash *vt* gwasgu, llethu ▸ *n* sboncen; **orange squash** sudd oren

squat *vi* swatio, cyrcydu

squeak *n* gwichian ▸ *n* gwich

squeal *vi* gwichian

squeeze *vb* gwasgu; **squeeze in** *vb* gwasgu i mewn

squint *vb* ciledrych, cibedrych ▸ *n* llygaid croes

squirm *vb* gwingo

squirrel *n* gwiwer

squirt *vb* chwistrellu, tasgu ▸ *n* chwistrell, gwn dŵr

stab *vb* gwanu, trywanu

stable¹ *n* ystabl

stable² *adj* sefydlog, safadwy, sad

stack *n* tas, bera; corn simnai, stac

stadium *n* stadiwm

staff *n* ffon; staff

staffroom *n* ystafell staff

stag *n* carw, hydd

stage *n* pwynt; gradd, lefel; llwyfan

stagger *vb* gwegian; syfrdanu

stagnant *adj* llonydd, marw

stag night, stag party *n* noson stag

stain *vb* ystaenio, llychwino ▸ *n* staen

stainless steel *n* dur gloyw

staircase *n* grisiau

stairs *n* grisiau

stake *n* polyn, ystanc

stale *adj* hen; diflas

stalemate *n* sefyllfa ddiddatrys

stalk¹ *vb* torsythu, stelcian, mynd ar drywydd

stalk² *n* gwelltyn, coes

stall *n* côr; stondin; talcen glo ▸ *vb* stolio

stamina *n* saf, ynni

stammer *vb* bloesgi, siarad ag atal arno

stamp *n* stamp, argraff ▸ *vb* stampio; curo traed

stampede *n* chwalfa, rhuthr

stand *(pt, pp stood) vb* sefyll ▸ *n* safiad; eistedddle; stondin; **stand for** *vi (represent)* golygu; *(tolerate)* goddef; **stand out** *vi* sefyll allan; **stand up** *vi* sefyll

standard *n* lluman, baner; post; safon

standard of living *n* safon byw

staple¹ *n (basic item)* prif nwydd; edefyn (gwlân *etc*)

staple² *n* ystwffwl, stapal

star *n* seren ▸ *vb* serennu

starch *n* starts

stare *vb* llygadrythu, synnu

stark *adj* syth, moel, rhonc ▸ *adv* hollol

start *vb* dechrau, cychwyn; **start off** *vi* cychwyn

starter *n (first course)* cwrs cyntaf

startle *vt* brawychu, dychrynu, rhusio

starvation *n* newyn

starve *vb* newynu; fferru, rhynnu

state¹ *n* ystad, cyflwr, ansawdd; gwladwriaeth; talaith

state² *vt* mynegi, datgan

statement *n* mynegiad, datganiad

statesman *n* gwladweinydd

station *n* gorsaf, stesion; safle, sefyllfa

stationary *adj* sefydlog

stationer's *n (shop)* siop bapurau

statistics *npl* ystadegau

statue *n* cerflun

stature *n* uchder, taldra, corffolaeth

status *n* safle, statws

staunch *adj* pybyr, cywir

stay *vb* aros; ategu; atal ▸ *n* arhosiad; ateg; **stay behind** *vi* aros ar ôl; **stay in** *vi (at home)* aros gartref; **stay up** *vi:* **don't stay up tonight** peidiwch ag aros ar eich traed heno

steadily *adv* yn bwyllog, yn gyson

steady *adj* sad, diysgog; cyson, gwastad

steak *n* golwyth, stec

steal *(pt stole, pp stolen) vb* dwyn, lladrata

steam *n* ager, stêm ▸ *vb* ageru

steel *n* dur ▸ *vt* caledu

steep¹ *adj* serth ▸ *n* dibyn, clogwyn, llethr

steep² *vt* mwydo

steeple *n* clochdy

steer *vb* llywio; cyfeirio

steering *n* llywio

steering wheel *n* llyw

stem n corsen, coes, bôn; ach
step vi camu; cerdded ▸ n cam; gris
step- prefix llys-
stepbrother n llysfrawd
stepdaughter n llysferch
stepfather n llystad
stepladder n ysgol risiau
stepmother n llysfam, mam wen
stepsister n llyschwaer
stepson n llysfab
stereo n stereo
stereotype n ystrydeb ▸ vt ystrydebu
sterile adj diffrwyth, sych
sterilize vb diffrwythloni; diheintio
sterling adj ysterling; diledryw, diffuant
stern¹ adj llym, penderfynol
stern² n starn, pen ôl llong
stew vb araf ferwi, stiwio ▸ n stiw
steward n stiward, goruchwyliwr, distain
stewardess n stiwardes
stick¹ n ffon, pric, gwialen
stick² (pt, pp **stuck**) vb glynu; gwanu
▸ **stick out** vi sticio allan
sticker n sticer
sticky adj gludiog, glynol; anodd
stiff adj syth, anhyblyg
stigma n gwarthnod, stigma
still¹ adj llonydd; marw ▸ vb llonyddu
still² adv eto, er hynny; byth
stimulate vt symbylu
stimulus n symbyliad, swmbwl
sting (pt, pp **stung**) vb pigo, brathu, colynnu ▸ n colyn

stink (pt **stank**, pp **stunk**) vi, n drewi
stir vb cyffroi, cynhyrfu, symud ▸ n stŵr, cynnwrf
stitch n pwyth; gwayw, pigyn ▸ vt pwytho, gwnïo
stock n cyff; stoc, ystôr; **stocks** npl cyffion; **stock up on sth** cael stôr o rywbeth
stock cube n ciwb stoc
stock exchange n cyfnewidfa stoc
stocking n hosan
stole n stola
stomach n cylla, stumog
stomach-ache n poen stumog
stone n carreg, maen ▸ vt llabyddio
stool n ystôl
stoop vb plygu, gwargrymu
stop vb atal, rhwystro; stopio, cau; aros, sefyll ▸ n atalfa; atalnod
stoppage n (pay) ataliad; (strike) streic
stopwatch n stopwatsh
storage n stôr, storfa
store n ystôr, ystorfa ▸ vt ystorio
storey, story n llawr
storm n (y)storm, tymestl
stormy adj stormus, tymhestlog
story n hanes, stori; celwydd
stout adj tew, ffyrf; pybyr, gwrol, glew
stove n stof, ffwrn
straight adj union, syth
straighten vb unioni
straightforward adj syml; didwyll, gonest
strain vb straenio, ysigo; tynhau; hidlo ▸ n straen
strainer n hidl(en)

strait adj cyfyng, cul, caeth ▸ n cyfyngder; culfor

strand n cainc (rhaff), edau

strange adj dieithr, estronol, rhyfedd

stranger n dyn dieithr, estron

strangle vt tagu, llindagu

strap n strap, cengl

strategic adj strategol

strategy n strategaeth

straw n gwellt; gwelltyn, blewyn

strawberry n mefysen, syfien

stray vi crwydro, cyfeiliorni

streak n llinell, rhes, rhesen; stremp ▸ vb gwibio

stream n ffrwd ▸ vb ffrydio, llifo

street n heol, stryd

strength n cryfder

strengthen vb cryfhau, nerthu

strenuous adj egniol, ymdrechgar

stress n pwysau, straen

stretch vb estyn, tynhau ▸ n estyniad

stretcher n trestl, stretsier

stretchy adj elastig

strict adj cyfyng, caeth, llym

stride (pt **strode**, pp **stridden**) vb camu, brasgamu ▸ n cam

strike (pt, pp **struck**) vb taro; gostwng ▸ n trawiad, streic

striker n streiciwr

striking adj trawiadol, hynod

string n llinyn, tant, cortyn

strip¹ n llain; **film strip** striplun, stribed ffilm

strip² vb diosg, ymddiosg, ymddihatru

stripe n rhes, rhesen; gwialennod

striped adj rhesog, streipiog

strive (pt **strive**, pp **striven**) vi ymdrechu; ymryson

stroke¹ n dyrnod, ergyd, trawiad; llinell

stroke² vt llochi, dylofi, pratio

stroll vi crwydro, rhodianna

strong adj cryf, cadarn

stronghold n amddiffynfa, cadarnle

strongly adv yn gryf

structure n adeilad, adeiledd, strwythur

struggle vi gwingo; ymdrechu ▸ n ymdrech

stub n bonyn

stubble n sofl

stubborn adj cyndyn, ystyfnig

student n myfyriwr, efrydydd

studio n stiwdio

study n astudiaeth, efrydiaeth ▸ vb myfyrio, efrydu, astudio

stuff n defnydd, stwff ▸ vb stwffio, gwthio

stuffing n stwffin

stuffy adj myglyd, trymllyd, trymaidd

stumble vb baglu, syrthio

stump n bonyn, boncyff

stun vt syfrdanu, hurtio

stunned adj: **to be stunned** (amazed) syfrdan

stunning adj syfrdanol

stunt vt crabio

stuntman n styntiwr

stuntwoman n styntwraig

stupid adj hurt, dwl, twp

sturdy adj cadarn, cryf

stutter vi siarad ag atal arno, bloesgi

S

style n dull, arddull; cyfenw, teitl ▸ vt cyfenwi
stylish adj dillyn, trwsiadus
subconscious n isymwybod ▸ adj isymwybodol
subject¹ n deiliad; pwnc, testun; goddrych
subject² vt darostwng, dwyn dan
subjective adj goddrychol
subjunctive adj dibynnol
submarine adj tanforol ▸ n llong danfor
submission n ymostyngiad; ufudd-dod; cyflwyniad
submit vb ymostwng, ymddarostwng; datgan barn; cyflwyno
subordinate adj israddol ▸ vt darostwng
subscribe vb tanysgrifio, cyfrannu
subscription n tanysgrifiad, cyfraniad
subsequent adj canlynol, dilynol
subsequently adv wedyn, ar ôl hynny
subside vi soddi, ymollwng; darfod
subsidiary adj israddol, ychwanegol, atodol
subsidy n arian cymorth, cymhorthdal
substance n sylwedd, defnydd; da
substantial adj sylweddol
substitute n eilydd ▸ vt rhoi yn lle
subtitled adj gyda isdeitlau
subtitles npl is-deitlau
subtle adj cyfrwys, craff
subtract vt tynnu ymaith
suburb n maestref
subway n isffordd
succeed vb dilyn, canlyn; llwyddo

success n llwyddiant
successful adj llwyddiannus
successfully adv yn llwyddiannus
succession n dilyniad, olyniaeth
successive adj dilynol, olynol
succumb vi ildio, marw
such adj cyfryw, y fath, cyffelyb
such-and-such adj : such-and-such a place y lle a'r lle
suck vb sugno, dyfnu
sudden adj sydyn, disymwth, disyfyd
suddenly adv yn sydyn
sue vb erlyn; erfyn, deisyf
suede n swêd
suffer vb dioddef; goddef, caniatáu
suffering n dioddef
suffice vb bod yn ddigon, digoni
sufficient adj digon, digonol
suffocate vb mygu, tagu
sugar n siwgr ▸ vt siwgro
suggest vt awgrymu
suggestion n awgrym, awgrymiad
suicide n hunanladdiad
suicide bomber n bomiwr hunanleiddiol
suit n cyngaws; siwt ▸ vb siwtio, gweddu
suitable adj addas
suitcase n bag dillad
suite n cyfres; gosgordd, nifer
sulk vi sorri, pwdu
sullen adj sarrug
sulphur n sylffwr
sultanas npl swltanas
sum n swm ▸ vt crynhoi, symio; sum up vt, vi crynhoi
summarize vb crynhoi
summary adj byr, cryno ▸ n crynodeb

summer n haf
summertime n haf
summit n pen, copa
summon vt gwysio, dyfynnu
sun n haul ▸ vt heulo
sunbathe vb torheulo, bolaheulo
sunbed n gwely haul
sunblock n eli atal haul
sunburn n llosg haul
sunburnt adj wedi cael llosg haul
Sunday n dydd Sul
Sunday school n ysgol Sul
sunflower n blodyn yr haul
sunglasses npl sbectol haul
sunlight n golau'r haul
sunny adj heulog
sunrise n codiad haul
sunroof n to haul
sunscreen n eli atal haul
sunset n machlud haul
sunshine n heulwen
sunstroke n ergyd (yr) haul
suntan n lliw haul
superb adj ysblennydd, godidog
superficial adj arwynebol, bas
superintendent n arolygwr, arolygydd
superior adj uwch, gwell; uwchraddol ▸ n uchafiad, uwchradd
superlative adj uchaf; eithaf
supermarket n archfarchnad
supernatural adj goruwchnaturiol
superstition n coelgrefydd, ofergoeliaeth
superstitious adj coelgrefyddol, ofergoelus
supervise vt arolygu
supervision n arolygiaeth

supervisor n goruchwyliwr, arolygydd
supper n swper
supple adj ystwyth, hyblyg
supplement n atodiad ▸ vt atodi
supplier n cyflenwr, cyflenwydd
supplies n cyflenwadau
supply vt cyflenwi, cyflawni ▸ n cyflenwad
supply teacher n athro llanw
support n cynnal ▸ n cynhaliaeth
supporter n cefnogwr, cefnogydd
suppose vt tybio, tybied, bwrw
suppress vt llethu, gostegu; atal; celu
supreme adj goruchaf, prif, pennaf
surcharge n gordal, gordoll ▸ vb codi gormod
sure adj, adv siŵr, sicr; diamau, diau
surely adv yn sicr, yn ddiau
surf n traethfor, beiston; gorewyn ▸ vb brigo, brigdonni
surface n wyneb, arwynebedd
surfboard n astell feiston
surfing n syrffio
surge vi ymchwyddo ▸ n ymchwydd
surgeon n llawfeddyg
surgery n llawfeddygaeth; meddygfa
surname n cyfenw ▸ vt cyfenwi
surpass vt rhagori ar, trechu
surplus n gormod, gwarged
surprise n syndod ▸ vt synnu
surprised adj syn, wedi synnu
surprising adj syn, rhyfedd
surrender vb traddodi, ildio
surrogate mother n mam fenthyg
surround vt amgylchu, amgylchynu

s

405

surroundings *npl* amgylchoedd

surveillance *n* arolygiaeth, gwyliadwriaeth

survey *vt* edrych, arolygu; mesur ▸ *n* arolwg

survival *n* goroesiad

survive *vb* goroesi

survivor *n* goroeswr

suspect *vt* drwgdybio, amau ▸ *n* un a ddrwgdybir

suspend *vt* crogi; gohirio, atal

suspended sentence *n* dedfryd wedi'i gohirio

suspense *n* pryder, petruster, oediad

suspension *n* ataliad

suspension bridge *n* pont grog

suspicion *n* drwgdybiaeth, amheuaeth

suspicious *adj* drwgdybus, amheus

sustain *vt* cynnal; dioddef

swallow¹ *n* gwennol

swallow² *vt* llyncu ▸ *n* llwnc

swamp *n* cors ▸ *vt* gorlifo, boddi

swan *n* alarch

swap *vb* ffeirio

swarm *n* haid ▸ *vi* heidio, heigio

sway *vb* siglo, gwegian; llywio ▸ *n* llywodraeth, swae

swear (*pt* **swore**, *pp* **sworn**) *vb* tyngu, rhegi

swearword *n* rheg

sweat *n* chwys ▸ *vb* chwysu

sweater *n* cot wlan, sweter

sweatshirt *n* crys chwys

sweaty *adj* chwyslyd

Swede *n* Swediad

swede *n* rwden, sweden

Sweden *n* Sweden

Swedish *adj* Swedaidd; *(language)* Swedeg

sweep (*pt*, *pp* **swept**) *vb* ysgubo ▸ *n* ysgubiad; ysgubwr

sweet *adj* melys, pêr, peraidd ▸ *n* pwdin

sweetcorn *n* corn melys

sweetheart *n* cariad

swell (*pt* **swelled**, *pp* **swollen**, **swelled**) *vb* chwyddo ▸ *n* chwydd, ymchwydd; gŵr mawr

swelling *n* chwydd(i)

swerve *vi* gwyro, osgoi

swift *adj* cyflym, clau

swim (*pt* **swam**, *pp* **swum**) *vb* nofio ▸ *n* nawf

swimmer *n* nofiwr

swimming *n* nofio

swimming pool *n* pwll nofio

swimming trunks *npl* trowsus nofio

swimsuit *n* dillad nofio, gwisg nofio

swing (*pt*, *pp* **swung**) *vb* siglo ▸ *n* sigl, siglen, swing

swipe card *n* cerdyn sweip

swirl *vb* troi, chwyldroi, chwyrndroi

Swiss *n* Swisiad ▸ *adj* Swisaidd

switch *n* swits, botwm ▸ *vb* troi, newid; **switch off** *vt* diffodd; **switch on** *vt* dodi, troi ymlaen; cychwyn

switchboard *n* switsfwrdd

Switzerland *n* y Swistir

swivel *n* bwylltid ▸ *vb* troi

swollen *adj* chwyddedig, wedi chwyddo

swoop *vb* dod ar warthaf, disgyn

swop *vt* cyfnewid, ffeirio

sword *n* cleddyf

swot n swot ▸ vi swotio
syllable n sillaf
syllabus n rhaglen, maes llafur
symbol n symbol
symmetrical adj cymesur
symmetry n cymesuredd
sympathetic adj cydymdeimladol
sympathize vi cydymdeimlo
sympathy n cydymdeimlad
symphony n symffoni
symptom n arwydd
synagogue n synagog
syndicate n cwmni
synonym n (gair) cyfystyr
Syria n Syria
syringe n chwistrell ▸ vt
  chwistrellu
syrup n surop; triagl (melyn)
system n system
systematic adj cyfundrefnol

tab n tafod, llabed
table n bwrdd, bord; tabl
table-cloth n lliain bord (bwrdd)
tablespoon n llwy fwrdd
tablet n llechen, llech; tabled
table tennis n tennis bwrdd, ping
  pong
taboo n ysgymunbeth;
  gwaharddiad, tabŵ
tack n tac, pwyth, brasbwyth
  ▸ vb tacio
tackle n taclau, offer; (in rugby)
  tacl, taclad ▸ vb ymosod ar,
  taclo
tact n tact, doethineb
tactful adj doeth, pwyllog
tactics npl cynlluniau, tactegau
tactile adj cyffyrddol
tactless adj di-dact, annoeth
tadpole n penbwl, penbwla
tag n clust, dolen
tail n cynffon, cwt
tailor n teiliwr

take (*pt* **took**, *pp* **taken**) *vb*
cymryd; **take after** *vt*: to take
after sb bod yn debyg i rywun;
take apart *vt* datgymalu; **take
away** *vt* mynd â; **take back** *vt*
mynd yn ôl â; **take down** *vt*
(*dismantle, remove*) tynnu i lawr;
(*make a note of*) nodi; **take in** *vi*
(*grasp*) deall; **take off** *vi* (*plane*)
esgyn, mynd i'r awyr ▸ *vt* (*remove*)
tynnu; **take out** *vt* (*produce,
remove*) tynnu; **take over** *vi*
cymryd drosodd; **to take over
from someone** cymryd lle rhywun
takeaway *n* (*food*) bwyd parod;
(*shop*) siop bwyd parod
tale *n* chwedl, clec, clep
talent *n* talent
talented *adj* talentog
talk *vb*, *n* siarad
talkative *adj* siaradus
tall *adj* tal, uchel
tambourine *n* tambwrîn
tame *adj* dof, gwâr ▸ *vt* dofi
tamper *vi* ymhél(â), ymyrryd(â)
tampon *n* tampwn
tan *vb* trin lledr; llosgi, melynu
tangerine *n* tanjerîn
tangle *vb* drysu, cymysgu ▸ *n*
dryswch, cymhlethdod
tank *n* dyfrgist, tanc
tanker *n* tancer, llong olew
Tanzania *n* Tansania
tap¹ *vb* taro yn ysgafn
tap² *n* tap, feis
tape *n* tâp, incil
tape measure *n* tâp mesur
tape recorder *n* recordydd tâp,
peiriant recordio
tapestry *n* tapestri

tar *n* tar; llongwr, morwr
target *n* nod, targed
tariff *n* toll; rhestr taliadau, rhestr
prisiau
tarmac *n* tarmac
tarpaulin *n* tarpolin
tart¹ *n* tarten, pastai
tart² *adj* sur, surllyd
tartan *n* brithwe, plod
task *n* gorchwyl, tasg ▸ *vt* rhoi
tasg
taste *vb* blasu, profi ▸ *n* blas;
chwaeth
tasty *adj* blasus
tattoo *n* tatŵ ▸ *vb* torri llun (yn
y croen)
taunt *vt* edliw, dannod, gwatwar
▸ *n* gwaradwydd, sen
Taurus *n* y Tarw
taut *adj* tyn
tax *n* treth ▸ *vt* trethu
taxi *n* tacsi
taxi driver *n* gyrrwr tacsi
taxi rank *n* lloc dacsi
tea *n* te
tea bag *n* bag te, cwdyn te
teach (*pt*, *pp* **taught**) *vt* dysgu,
addysgu
teacher *n* athro
teaching *n* dysgeidiaeth; dysgu
teaching assistant *n*
cynorthwyydd dysgu
teacup *n* disgl de, cwpan te
tea leaves *n* dail te
team *n* gwedd, pâr, tîm
teapot *n* tebot
tear¹ *n* deigryn, deigr
tear² (*pt* **tore**, *pp* **torn**) *vb* rhwygo,
llarpio ▸ *n* rhwyg
▸ **tear up** *vt* rhwygo

tearful *adj* dagreuol
tease *vt* pryfocio, plagio, poeni
teaspoon *n* llwy de
teatime *n* amser te
tea towel *n* lliain sychu llestri
technical *adj* technegol
technician *n* technegydd
technique *n* techneg
technology *n* technoleg
teddy, teddy bear *n* tedi, tedi bêr
tedious *adj* blin, poenus
teenage *adj*: **a teenage boy** bachgen yn ei arddegau
teenager *n* un yn yr arddegau
teens *n* arddegau
telegram *n* teligram
telephone *n* teliffon, ffôn
telephone box *n* bocs ffonio
telephone call *n* galwad ffôn
telephone directory *n* cyfeirlyfr ffôn
telescope *n* ysbienddrych, telisgob
televise *vb* teledu
television *n* teledu
tell (*pt, pp* **told**) *vb* dweud, adrodd; cyfrif, rhifo; **tell off** *vt* dweud y drefn wrth, cystwyo
telly *n* (*inf*) teledu
temper *n* tymer, naws ▸ *vt* tymheru
temperament *n* anianawd
temperamental *adj* gwamal, oriog, di-ddal
temperature *n* tymheredd
temple¹ *n* (*building*) teml
temple² *n* (*Anat*) arlais
temporary *adj* dros dro, tymhorol
tempt *vt* temtio, profi
temptation *n* temtiad, temtasiwn
tempting *adj* deniadol

ten *adj, n* deg
tenant *n* deiliad, tenant
tend *vi* tueddu
tendency *n* tuedd, gogwydd
tender *adj* tyner, tirion, mwyn; meddal
tendon *n* gewyn
tennis *n* tennis
tennis ball *n* pêl dennis
tennis court *n* cwrt tennis
tennis player *n* chwaraewr tennis
tennis racket *n* raced tennis
tenor *n* cyfeiriad, tuedd, rhediad; tenor
tenpin bowling *n* bowlio decbinnau
tense¹ *adj* tyn
tense² *n* amser (berf)
tension *n* tyndra, pwysau
tent *n* pabell
tentative *adj* arbrofiadol, dros dro; ansicr
tenth *adj* degfed
tepid *adj* claear
term *n* terfyn; term; teler; tymor ▸ *vt* galw, enwi
terminal *adj* terfynol, termol
terminally *adv*: **terminally ill** gydag afiechyd terfynol
terminate *vb* terfynu
terminology *n* terminoleg
terminus *n* terfynfa
terrace *n* rhes dai, teras
terraced *adj*: **terraced house** tŷ rhes
terrain *n* tir
terrestrial *adj* daearol
terrible *adj* dychrynllyd, ofnadwy, arswydus
terribly *adv* yn ofnadwy

t

terrier

terrier *n* daeargi
terrific *adj* dychrynllyd, arswydus
terrified *adj* mewn arswyd; **to be terrified of sth** arswydo rhag rhywbeth
terrify *vt* brawychu, dychrynu
terrifying *adj* brawychus, dychrynllyd
territorial *adj* tiriogaethol
territory *n* tir, tiriogaeth
terror *n* dychryn, braw, arswyd
terrorism *n* terfysgaeth
terrorist *n* terfysgwr, brawychwr
test *n* prawf ▸ *vt* profi
testicle *n* caill, carreg
testify *vb* tystio
testimony *n* tystiolaeth
test tube *n* tiwb prawf
tetanus *n* gên glo, tetanws
text¹ *n* testun, adnod
text² *vt* tecstio
textbook *n* gwerslyfr
textile *adj* gweol
text message *n* neges destun
texture *n* gwead, cyfansoddiad
Thailand *n* Gwlad Thai
Thames *n* Tafwys
than *conj* na, nag
thank *vt*, *n* diolch
thankful *adj* diolchgar
thanks *npl* diolch, diolchiadau
thanksgiving *n* diolchgarwch

that *adj* (*pl* **those**) (*demonstrative, after masc. n.*) hwnnw (hynny), *pl*, yna, acw; (*after fem. n.*) honno (hynny), yna, acw; **that book** y llyfr hwnnw, y llyfr yna (*within sight*) y llyfr acw; **those books** y llyfrau hynny, y llyfrau yna (*within sight*)

y llyfrau acw; **that one** hwnyna (honyna), hwnna (honna)
▸ *pron* **1** (*pl* **those**) (*demonstrative*) hwnyna (honyna), hwnna (honna); **who's that?** pwy yw hwnna?, pwy yw honna?; **what's that?** beth yw hynny?; **is that you?** [ai] ti sydd yna?; **I prefer this to that** mae'n well gen i hwn/hon na hwnna/honna; **that's what he said** dyna a ddywedodd; **will you eat all that?** a wnei di fwyta hynny i gyd?; **that is (to say)** hynny yw **2** (*relative: subject*) a (*plus inflected form of verb: all tenses,*) or (*in present tense*) yr hwn, yr hon, y rhai sydd yn + *vn*; **the book that I read** y llyfr a ddarllenais; **the books that are in the library** y llyfrau sydd yn y llyfrgell; **all that I have** y cyfan sydd gennyf; **the box that I put it in** y blwch y rhoddais y peth ynddo; **the people that I spoke to** y bobl y siaredais â nhw **3** (*relative: of time*): **the day that he came** y diwrnod y daeth e
▸ *conj* bod; **he thought that I was ill** roedd yn credu fy mod yn sâl
▸ *adv* (*demonstrative*): **I don't like it that much** dwy ddim yn ei hoffi gymaint â hynny; **I didn't know it was that bad** wyddwn i ddim ei bod hi gynddrwg â hynny; **it's about that high** mae tua mor uchel â hynny

thaw *vb* dadlaith, dadmer, meirioli

the *def art* **1** (*gen*) y, yr, 'r; **the boy** y bachgen; **the apple** yr afal; **the**

history of the world hanes y byd;
give it to the postman rhowch e
i'r postmon

2 (+ adj to form n): **the rich and the
poor** y cyfoethogion a'r tlodion; **to
attempt the impossible** mentro'r
amhosibl

3 (in titles): **Elizabeth the First**
Elisabeth y gyntaf; **Peter the Great**
Pedr Fawr

4 (in comparisons): **the more he
works, the more he earns** mwya'n
y byd y mae'n gweithio, mwya'n y
byd y mae'n ei ennill

theatre n theatr; maes, golygfa
theft n lladrad
their pron eu
theirs pron yr eiddynt, eiddynt
hwy
them pron hwy, hwynt, hwythau
theme n thema
theme park n parc thema
themselves pron eu hunain
then adv y pryd hwnnw, yna
▸ conj yna
theology n diwinyddiaeth
theory n damcaniaeth, tyb
therapy n therapi

⸻ KEYWORD ⸻

there adv **1**: **there is**, **there are** mae
yna; **there are 3 of them** (people,
things) mae yna 3 ohonynt; **there
is no-one here/no bread left** nid
oes neb yma/bara ar ôl; **there has
been an accident** mae damwain
wedi digwydd

2 (referring to place) acw, yna, yno;

it's there mae e acw; **in/on/up/
down there** yn/ar/i fyny/i lawr
[yn y] fanna; **he went there on
Friday** aeth yno ddydd Gwener; **I
want that book there** y llyfr yna yr
hoffwn ei gael; **there he is!** dyna fe!

3: **there, there!** (esp to child)
dyna ni!

thereafter adv wedyn
thereby adv trwy hynny
therefore conj gan hynny, am
hynny
thermal adj thermol
thermometer n thermomedr,
mesurydd gwres
these adj pl y rhai hyn, y rhai yma
thesis n gosodiad; traethawd,
thesis
they pron hwy, hwynt, hwynt-hwy
thick adj tew, praff, trwchus
thicken vb tewhau, tewychu
thickness n trwch, tewder
thief n lleidr
thigh n clun, morddwyd
thin adj tenau, cul, main; anaml,
prin ▸ vb teneuo
thing n peth, dim
think (pt, pp **thought**) vb
meddwl
third adj trydydd, trydedd
thirdly adv yn drydydd
Third World n Trydydd Byd
thirst n syched ▸ vi sychedu
thirsty adj sychedig; **I am thirsty**
mae syched arna i
thirteen adj, n tri (tair) ar ddeg, un
deg tri (tair)

thirteenth adj trydydd (trydedd) ar ddeg

thirty adj, n deg ar hugain, tri deg

<KEYWORD>

this adj (pl **these**) (demonstrative) hwn m, hon f, hyn pl or indeter; **this man/woman** y dyn hwn/y fenyw hon; **this one** hwn, hon, hyn
▸ pron (pl **these**) (demonstrative) hwn, hon, hyn (not that one) hwn yma, hon yma, hyn yma; **who's this?** pwy yw hwn?; **what's this?** beth yw hwn?; **I prefer this to that** mae'n well gennyf hwn yma na hwn yna; **this is where I live** dyma ble rwy'n byw; **this is what he said** dyma'r hyn a ddywedodd; **this is Mr Brown** (in introductions) dyma Mr Brown (in photo) dyma Mr Brown (on telephone) Mr Brown yn siarad
▸ adv (demonstrative): **it was about this big** roedd tua'r maint yma; **I didn't know it was this bad** wyddwn i ddim ei bod hi gynddrwg â hyn

thistle n ysgallen
thorn n draen, draenen; pigyn
thorough adj trwyadl, trylwyr
those adj pl y rhai hynny, y rhai yna
though conj er
thought n meddwl
thoughtful adj meddylgar, ystyriol
thoughtless adj difeddwl, anystyriol
thousand adj, n mil
thousandth adj milfed
thrash vt dyrnu, ffusto, curo

thread n edau, edefyn
threat n bygwth, bygythiad
threaten vt bygwth
threatening adj bygythiol
three adj, n tri, tair
threshold n trothwy, rhiniog
thrill vb gwefreiddio ▸ n ias, gwefr
thrilled adj: **I'm thrilled** dw i wrth fy modd; **she was thrilled to hear that** roedd hi wrth ei bodd o glywed hynny
thriller n stori iasoer
thrilling adj cyffrous, gwefreiddiol
throat n gwddf
throb vi dychlamu, curo
throne n gorsedd, gorseddfainc
through prep trwy ▸ adv trwodd
throughout prep trwy, trwy gydol ▸ adv trwodd
throw (pt **threw**, pp **thrown**) n tafliad ▸ vb taflu, lluchio; **throw away** vt taflu, lluchio; **throw out** vt taflu; **throw up** vi taflu i fyny
thrush n bronfraith
thrust (pt, pp **thrust**) vb gwthio ▸ n gwth
thud n twrf, sŵn trwm
thug n llindagwr, dihiryn
thumb n bawd ▸ vt bodio
thump vb dyrnodio, pwnio
thunder n taran(au), tyrfau, trystau ▸ vb taranu
thunderstorm n storm dyrfau
Thursday n dydd Iau
thus adv fel hyn, felly
thwart vb rhwystro
thyme n teim
tick[1] n tipian, tic
tick[2] vt (mark) ticio ▸ n tic
ticket n tocyn, ticed

ticket collector n tocynnwr

ticket inspector n arolygwr tocynnau

ticket office n swyddfa docynnau

tickle vb goglais, gogleisio ▸ n goglais

ticklish n gogleisiol; anodd, dyrys

tide n llanw, teid; **high tide** penllanw; **low tide** trai

tidy adj taclus, twt, destlus; **tidy up** vt tacluso

tie vt clymu, rhwymo ▸ n clwlwm, cadach; **tie up** vt clymu

tier n rhes, rheng

tiger n teigr

tight adj tyn, cryno, twt; cyfyng

tighten vb tynhau

tightly adv yn dyn

tights npl teits

tile n priddlech, teilsen

till prep, conj hyd

tilt vb gogwyddo

timber n coed, pren

time n amser ▸ vt amseru

timely adj amserol, prydlon

timetable n amserlen

timid adj ofnus, llwfr

timing n amseriad

tin n alcam, tun

tinfoil n ffoel alcam

tingle vi ysu

tinker n (inf) tincer ▸ vb tincera

tinned adj mewn tun, tun

tin opener n agorwr tuniau

tint n lliw, arlliw, gwawr ▸ vt lliwio

tinted adj wedi ei liwio

tiny adj bychan, bach, pitw

tip¹ n (point) blaen, pen

tip² vb troi, dymchwelyd; gwobrwyo ▸ n tip, tomen; cyngor; gwobr, cil-dwrn

tiptoe n: **on tiptoe** ar flaenau ei draed

tire¹ vb blino, lluddedu, diffygio

tire², **tyre** n teiar

tired adj blinedig

tiring adj blinedig

tissue n meinwe

tissue paper n papur sidan

title n teitl

(KEYWORD)

to prep (with noun/pronoun) 1 (direction) i; (towards) tua; at; **to go to France/London/school** mynd i Ffrainc/i Lundain/i'r ysgol; **to go to John's** mynd i dŷ John, mynd i weld John; **to go to the doctor's** mynd at y meddyg; **the road to Edinburgh** y ffordd i Gaeredin 2 (as far as) i, hyd at; **to count to 10** cyfrif i 10, cyfrif hyd at 10; **from 40 to 50 people** o 40 i 50 o bobl 3 (with expressions of time): **a quarter to 5** chwarter i 5; **it's twenty to 3** mae'n ugain munud i 3 4 (for, of): **the key to the front door** allwedd y drws blaen; **a letter to his wife** llythyr at ei wraig 5 (expressing indirect object) i; **to give sth to sb** rhoi rhth i rn; **to talk to sb** siarad â rhn; **to be a danger to sb** bod yn berygl i rn 6 (in relation to) i; **3 goals to 2** 3 gôl i 2; **30 miles to the gallon** 30 milltir i'r galwyn 7 (purpose, result): **to come to sb's aid** cynorthwyo/helpu rhn, dod i

413

toad

gynorthwyo/helpu rhn, dod i roi cymorth i rn; **to sentence sb to death** dedfrydu rhn i farwolaeth; **to my surprise** er syndod i mi
▸ *prep* (*with vb*): **1** (*simple infinitive*): **to go/eat** bwyta/mynd
2 (*following another vb*): **to want/try/start to do** dymuno/ceisio/dechrau gwneud
3 (*with vb omitted*): **I don't want to** nid oes arnaf eisiau [gwneud]
4 (*purpose, result*) i; **I did it to help you** fe'i gwneuthum i'ch helpu
5 (*equivalent to relative clause*): **I have things to do** mae gennyf bethau i'w gwneud; **the main thing is to try** y peth pwysig yw rhoi cynnig arni
6 (*after adjective etc*): **ready to go** parod i fynd; **too old/young to ...** rhy hen/ifanc i ...
▸ *adv*: **push/pull the door to** gwthio/tynnu'r drws

toad *n* llyffant du dafadennog
toadstool *n* caws llyffant, bwyd y boda
toast *n* tost; llwncdestun ▸ *vb* tostio
toaster *n* tostiwr
toastie *n* (*inf*) brechdan grasu
tobacco *n* tybaco, baco
toboggan *n* tybogan, car llusg
today *adv* heddiw
toddler *n* plentyn bach
toe *n* bys troed; blaen carn ceffyl
toffee *n* taffi, cyflaith
together *adv* ynghyd, gyda'i gilydd
toilet *n* trwsiad, gwisgiad; ystafell ymolchi, tŷ bach

toilet paper *n* papur tŷ bach
toiletries *n* pethau ymolchi
toilet roll *n* rholyn toiled, rholyn tŷ bach
toilet water *n* dŵr Groeg
token *n* arwydd, argoel; tocyn
tolerant *adj* goddefgar
tolerate *vt* goddef
toll[1] *n* toll, treth
toll[2] *vb* canu (cloch, cnul)
tomato *n* tomato
tomb *n* bedd, beddrod
tomboy *n* hoeden, rhampen
tomorrow *adv* yfory
ton *n* tunnell
tone *n* tôn, oslef ▸ *vb* tyneru, lleddfu
tongs *npl* gefel
tongue *n* tafod; iaith
tonic *n* meddyginiaeth gryfhaol, tonic
tonic water *n* dŵr tonig
tonight *adv* heno
tonsil *n* tonsil
tonsillitis *n* llid y tonsil
tonsils *n* tonsiliau
too *adv* rhy; hefyd; **too much** gormod
tool *n* arf, erfyn
tooth *n* dant
toothache *n* dannoedd
toothbrush *n* brws dannedd
toothpaste *n* sebon dannedd, past dannedd
toothpick *n* pic dannedd
top *n* pen, brig, copa ▸ *vt* tocio; rhagori ar; **top up** ail-lenwi; **to top up one's mobile (phone)** rhoi credyd ar eich ffôn symudol
topic *n* pwnc

topical adj amserol

topple vb syrthio, cwympo, dymchwel

torch n torts, ffagl

torment n poen, poenedigaeth ▸ vt poeni, poenydio

torn adj wedi ei rwygo, rhwygedig

tornado n hyrddwynt, corwynt

torpedo n torpedo

torrent n cenllif, llifeiriant, rhyferthwy

torrential adj llifeiriol, trwm

tortoise n crwban

torture n dirboen, artaith ▸ vt arteithio

Tory n Tori, ceidwadwr ▸ adj toriaidd

toss vb taflu, lluchio

total adj hollol, cyflawn ▸ n cyfan, cyfanswm

totalitarian adj totalitaraidd

totally adv yn llwyr, yn gyfan, yn ei grynswth

touch vb teimlo, cyffwrdd ▸ n teimlad

touched adj dan deimlad

touching adj teimladwy

touch-line n yr ystlys

touchpad n pad cyffwrdd

tough adj gwydn, caled, cyndyn

tour n tro, taith

tourism n twristiaeth

tourist n teithiwr, ymwelydd, twrist

tourist office n swyddfa twristiaid

tournament n twrnamaint

tow[1] n carth

tow[2] vt llusgo, tynnu

toward, towards prep tua, tuag at

towel n lliain sychu, tywel

tower n twˆr ▸ vi esgyn, ymgodi, sefyll yn uchel

town n tref

town centre n canol(y) dref

town clerk n clerc y dref

town council n cyngor y dref

town hall n neuadd y dref

toxic adj gwenwynig

toy n tegan ▸ vi chwarae, maldodi

trace vt olrhain, dilyn

track n ôl, brisg; llwybr ▸ vt olrhain; **track down** vt dod o hyd i

tracksuit n tracwisg

tract n (of land) ardal, rhandir

tractor n tractor

trade n masnach; crefft ▸ vb masnachu

trade-mark n nod masnach

trader n masnachwr

trade-union n undeb llafur

tradition n traddodiad

traditional adj traddodiadol

traffic vb masnachu, trafnidio ▸ n masnach, trafnidiaeth

traffic jam n tagfa

traffic lights npl goleuadau traffig

traffic warden n warden traffig

tragedy n trasiedi, trychineb

tragic adj trychinebus, alaethus

trail n ôl ▸ vb llusgo

trailer n ôl-gerbyd, cart; rhaglun (ffilm)

train vb hyfforddi, ymarfer ▸ n gosgordd, godre; trên, cerbydres

trainee adj, n hyfforddedig

trainer n hyfforddwr

trainers npl esgidiau ymarfer, treners, trenars

training n hyfforddiant, disgyblaeth

training course n cwrs hyfforddiant

training shoes npl esgidiau ymarfer

trait n nodwedd

traitor n bradwr, teyrnfradwr

tram n tram

tramp vb crwydro, trampio ▸ n crwydryn

trample vb sathru, sangu

trampoline n trampolîn

tranquil adj tawel, llonydd, digyffro

tranquillizer n tawelyn, tawelydd

transaction n trafodaeth

transcript n copi, adysgrifiad

transfer vt trosglwyddo ▸ n trosglwyddiad

transform vt trawsffurfio

transformation n trawsffurfiad

transfusion n trosglwyddiad (gwaed), trallwysiad (gwaed)

transit n mynediad dros, trosiad

transition n trosiad, trawsgyweiriad

transitive adj anghyflawn

translate vt cyfieithu

translation n cyfieithiad

translator n cyfieithydd

transmission n trosglwyddiad

transmit vt anfon, trosglwyddo

transmitter n trosglwyddydd

transparent adj tryloyw

transplant vt trawsblannu

transport vt trosglwyddo; alltudio ▸ n trosglwyddiad; cludiant; perlewyg, gorawen

trap n trap, magl; car bach ▸ vt dal, maglu

trash n (inf) sothach, gwehilion, ysbwriel

travel vb teithio, trafaelio ▸ n teithio

travel agency n swyddfa deithio

travel agent n asiant teithio

traveller n teithiwr, trafaeliwr

traveller's cheque n siec deithio

travelling adj teithiol

travel sickness n salwch teithio

tray n hambwrdd

treacherous adj twyllodrus

treacle n triagl

tread (pt **trod**, pp **trodden**) vb sathru, sengi, troedio ▸ n sang

treasure n trysor ▸ vt trysori

treasurer n trysorydd

treasury n trysorfa, trysordy, y Trysorlys

treat vb trin; tretio; traethu ▸ n gwledd, amheuthun

treatment n triniaeth, ymdriniaeth

treaty n cyfamod, cytundeb

treble adj triphlyg ▸ n trebl ▸ vb treblu

tree n pren, coeden

trek vi mudo ▸ n mud, mudo

tremble vi crynu

tremendous adj dychrynllyd, ofnadwy, anferth

trench n ffos, rhych ▸ vb ffosi

trend vi tueddu ▸ n tuedd, gogwydd

trendy adj trendi

trespass vi tresmasu ▸ n tresmasiad

trial n prawf, profedigaeth, treial

trial period n cyfnod prawf

triangle n triongl

triangular adj trionglog

tribe n llwyth, tylwyth, gwehelyth

tribunal *n* tribiwnlys

tribute *n* teyrnged, treth

trick *n* tric, cast, ystryw ▸ *vt* castio

trickle *vi* diferu, diferynnu

tricky *adj* ystrywgar; anodd

tricycle *n* treisigl

trifle *n* gronyn, mymryn; treiffl ▸ *vt* ofera, cellwair

trigger *n* cliced, triger

trim *adj* taclus, twt ▸ *vb* taclu, trwsio ▸ *n* diwyg, trefn

trio *n* triawd

trip *vb* tripio, maglu; disodli ▸ *n* trip, tro

triple *adj* triphlyg

triplets *n* tripledi

tripod *n* trybedd

triumph *n* gorfoledd, buddugoliaeth ▸ *vi* gorfoleddu; buddugoliaethu

triumphant *adj* buddugoliaethus

trivial *adj* dibwys, diwerth

trolley, trolly *n* troli

trombone *n* trombôn

troop *n* torf, mintai ▸ *vb* tyrru; **troops** *npl* lluoedd, minteioedd

trophy *n* gwobr, tlws

tropical *adj* trofannol

trot *vb* tuthio, trotian ▸ *n* tuth, trot

trouble *vt* blino, trafferthu ▸ *n* blinder, helbul, trafferth

troubled *adj* anesmwyth, pryderus

troublemaker *n* codwr twrw

troublesome *adj* blinderus, trafferthus

trough *n* cafn

trousers *npl* trowsus, trwser

trout *n* brithyll

truant *n* triawnt, mitsiwr

truce *n* cadoediad

truck *n* trwc, gwagen

true *adj* gwir, cywir

truly *adv* yn wir, yn ddiau, yn gywir

trumpet *n* trwmped

trunk *n* cyff, cist; corff; duryn, trwnc

trust *n* ymddiriedaeth; ymddiriedolaeth ▸ *vb* hyderu, ymddiried

trustworthy *adj* y gellir dibynnu arno

truth *n* gwir, gwirionedd

truthful *adj* geirwir

try *n* ceisio, treio; **try on** *vt*: **to try sth on** trio rhywbeth amdanoch chi; **try out** *vt*: **to try sth out** rhoi rhywbeth ar brawf

trying *adj* poenus, anodd, blin

T-shirt *n* crys-T

tub *n* twba, twb

tube *n* tiwb

tuberculosis *n* darfodedigaeth, dicáu, diclein

tuck *vt* cwtogi, plygu ▸ *n* plyg, twc

Tuesday *n* dydd Mawrth

tug *vb* llusgo, tynnu

tuition *n* addysg, hyfforddiant

tulip *n* tiwlip

tumble *vb* cwympo ▸ *n* codwm, cwymp

tumble dryer *n* peiriant sychu dillad

tumbler *n* gwydryn

tummy *n (inf)* bola

tumour *n* tiwmor

tuna *n* tiwna

tune *n* tôn, tiwn, cywair ▸ *vb* cyweirio

tunic *n* crysbais, siaced

Tunisia

Tunisia n Tunisia
tunnel n ceuffordd, twnnel
turbulence n terfysg, cynnwrf
turf n tywarchen
Turk n Twrc
Turkey n Twrci
turkey n twrci
Turkish adj Twrcaidd
turmoil n trafferth, ffwdan, berw
turn vb troi ▶ n tro, trofa; **turn
  back** vi troi yn ôl; **turn down**
  vt (lower) troi i lawr; (refuse)
  gwrthod; **turn off** vt difodd; **turn
  on** vt troi ymlaen; **turn round**
  vi troi o gwmpas; **turn up** vb
  troi i fyny
turning n tro; tröedigaeth
turning point n trobwynt
turnip n erfinen, meipen
turnout n cynulliad
turnover n trosiant
turquoise n maen glas
  (gwerthfawr)
turtle n crwban môr
tusk n ysgithrddant, ysgithr
tutor n athro, hyfforddwr ▶ vt
  hyfforddi
tutorial adj tiwtorial
TV n abbr teledu
tweed n brethyn gwlân, twid
tweezers n gefel fach
twelfth adj deuddegfed
twelve adj, n deuddeg, un deg dau
twentieth adj ugeinfed
twenty adj, n ugain
twice adv dwywaith
twig n brigyn, ysbrigyn, impyn
twilight n cyfnos, cyfddydd
twin n gefell
twinkle vi serennu, pefrio

twinned adj gefeilliedig
twin town n gefeilldref
twist vb nyddu, cyfrodeddu; troi
  ▶ n tro; edau gyfrodedd
twit (inf) n dannod, edliw; un ffôl
twitch vb tymhigo, brathgnoi ▶ n
  tymig
two adj, n dau, dwy
type n math, teip
typewriter n teipiadur, peiriant
  teipio
typhoid n twymyn yr ymysgaroedd
typhoon n corwynt
typical adj arwyddol,
  nodweddiadol
typist n teipydd
tyre n teiar

u

UFO n UFO
Uganda n Uganda, Iwganda
ugly adj hagr, hyll
UK n abbr (= United Kingdom) Deyrnas Unedig, DU
ulcer n wlser
ultimate adj diwethaf, olaf, eithaf
ultimately adv o'r diwedd
ultimatum n y gair olaf, y rhybudd olaf
umbrella n ambarél, ymbarél
umpire n dyfarnwr, canolwr
unable adj analluog
unacceptable adj anghymeradwy, annerbyniol
unanimous adj unfrydol
unarmed adj diamddiffyn, heb arfau
unavoidable adj anorfod
unaware adj anymwybodol
unawares adv yn ddiarwybod
unbearable adj annioddefol
unbelievable adj anhygoel

unbutton vb datod, datfotymu
uncalled-for adj di-alw-amdano
uncanny adj rhyfedd
uncertain adj ansicr
uncle n ewythr
uncomfortable adj anghysurus
uncommon adj anghyffredin
unconditional adj diamod
unconscious adj anymwybodol
uncontrollable adj aflywodraethus
unconventional adj anghonfensiynol
uncover vb datguddio
undecided adj petrus, mewn penbleth
undeniable adj anwadadwy
under prep tan ▸ adv tanodd, oddi tanodd
underage adj dan oed
underestimate vb prisio'n rhy isel
undergraduate n myfyriwr israddedig
underground adj tanddaearol
underline vb tanlinellu, pwysleisio
undermine vb tanseilio
underneath adv oddi tanodd ▸ prep tan
underpants n trôns
underpass n ffordd danddaearol, tanffordd
understand vt deall, dirnad
understanding n amgyffred, dealltwriaeth
understatement n tanosodiad
undertake vb ymgymryd
undertaker n ymgymerydd; saer (coffinau)
undertaking adj ymrwymiad
underwater adj tanddwr

underwear n dillad isaf
underworld n annwn
undesirable adj annymunol
undisputed adj diamheuol
undo vt dadwneud; datod; andwyo, difetha
undress vb dadwisgo
uneasy adj anesmwyth
unemployed adj di-waith, segur
unemployment n diweithdra, anghyflogaeth
unequal adj anghyfartal
uneven adj anwastad
uneventful adj diddigwyddiad
unexpected adj annisgwyliadwy
unexpectedly adv yn annisgwyl
unfair adj annheg
unfaithful adj anffyddlon
unfamiliar adj anghyfarwydd
unfashionable adj anffasiynol
unfasten vb datod
unfavourable adj anffafriol
unfinished adj anorffenedig
unfit adj anghymwys; afiach
unfold vb datblygu
unforgettable adj bythgofiadwy
unfortunate adj anffodus
unfortunately adj yn anffodus
unfriendly adj anghyfeillgar
unfurnished adj diddodrefn
ungrateful adj anniolchgar
unhappiness n anhapusrwydd
unhappy adj anhapus
unhealthy adj afiach
uni n abbr (= university) prifysgol
uniform adj unffurf ▸ n gwisg swyddogol
unify vt unoli, uno
unimportant adj dibwys
uninhabited adj anghyfannedd

unintentional adj anfwriadol
union n undeb; uniad
Union Jack n: the Union Jack Jac yr Undeb
unique adj dihafal, digymar
unit n un, rhif un; uned; undod
unite vb uno
united adj, n unol, unedig; the United Kingdom y Deyrnas Unedig; the United States yr Unol Daleithiau
United Kingdom n: the United Kingdom y Deyrnas Unedig
United Nations n: the United Nations y Cenhedloedd Unedig
United States n: the United States yr Unol Daleithiau
unity n undod
universal adj cyffredinol
universe n bydysawd
university n prifysgol
unjust adj anghyfiawn, annheg
unkind adj angharedig
unknown adj anadnabyddus, anenwog
unlawful adj anghyfreithlon
unleaded petrol n petrol di-blwm
unless conj oni, onid
unlike adj annhebyg
unlikely adj annhebygol
unlimited adj diderfyn
unload vb dadlwytho
unlock vb datgloi
unlucky adj anlwcus
unmarried adj dibriod
unmistakable adj digamsyniol
unnatural adj annaturiol
unnecessary adj diangenraid
unpack vb dadbacio
unpaid adj di-dâl, didal

unpleasant adj annymunol

unplug vt: **to unplug sth** tynnu plwg rhywbeth

unpopular adj amhoblogaidd

unprotected adj diamddiffyn

unqualified adj heb gymhwyster

unrealistic adj afrealaidd, afrealistig

unreasonable adj afresymol

unrelated adj amherthnasol; heb berthyn

unreliable adj annibynadwy

unroll vt dadrolio

unruly adj afreolus

unsafe adj anniogel

unsatisfactory adj anfoddhaol

unscrew vt agor; llacio; datroi

unsettled adj ansefydlog

unsightly adj diolwg, blêr

unskilled adj anghelfydd

unstable adj ansefydlog

unsteady adj ansefydlog

unsuccessful adj aflwyddiannus

unsuitable adj anaddas

untidy adj anniben

untie vb datod

until prep, conj hyd, hyd oni, nes, tan

untrue adj celwyddog

unusual adj anarferol

unveil vb dadorchuddio

unwell adj anhwylus

unwilling adj anfodlon, amharod

unwise adj annoeth

unwittingly adv yn ddiarwybod

unwrap vt dadlapio

(KEYWORD)

up prep: he went up the stairs/ the hill aeth i fyny'r grisiau/bryn;

the cat was up a tree roedd y gath ar ben coeden; they live further up the street maent yn byw ymhellach ar hyd y stryd; go up that road and turn left ewch ar hyd y ffordd honno a throwch i'r chwith

▸ adv 1 i fyny; (upwards, higher) up in the sky/the mountains i fyny yn yr awyr/y mynyddoedd put it a bit higher up rhowch y peth ychydig yn uwch; to stand up (get up) sefyll, codi (be standing) sefyll; up there i fyny [yn y] fanna; up above uchod, uwchben, uwchlaw

2: to be up (out of bed) bod wedi codi (prices) bod wedi codi (finished) when the year was up pan oedd y flwyddyn ar ben

3: up to (as far as) hyd at; up to now hyd yn hyn

4: to be up to (depending on) it's up to you mater i chi yw e (equal to) he's not up to it (job, task etc) nid yw'n gallu ei wneud, nid yw'n abl i'w wneud, nid yw'n ddigon o ddyn i'w wneud (inf, be doing) what is he up to? beth mae e'n ei wneud, beth sydd ganddo ar y gweill?

▸ n: the ups and downs of life troeon yr yrfa

upbringing n magwraeth

upheaval n cyffro, terfysg

uphill adj i fyny

upload vt llwytho i fyny

upon prep ar

upper adj uwch, uchaf

upper sixth n: the upper sixth y chweched uchaf

upright *adj* syth, unionsyth

uprising *n* terfysg, gwrthryfel

uproar *n* terfysg, cythrwfl, dadwrdd

upset *vb* troi, dymchwelyd; cyffroi, gofidio

upside-down *adj, adv* (â'i) wyneb i waered

upstairs *n* llofft

up-to-date *adj* cyfoes

upward, upwards *adj, adv* i fyny

uranium *n* wranium

urban *adj* dinasol, dinesig

urge *vt* cymell, annog

urgency *n* brys

urgent *adj* taer, pwysig, yn gofyn brys

urine *n* troeth, iwrin

US *n abbr* (= *United States*) UD, Unol Daleithiau

us *pron* ni, nyni, ninnau; 'n

USA *n abbr* (= *United States of America*) Unol Daleithiau America, UDA

use *n* iws, defnydd ▸ *vb* iwsio, defnyddio; **use up** *vt* defnyddio'r cyfan o, defnyddio'r cwbl o

used *adj* arferedig, mewn arfer; (*car*) ail-law

useful *adj* defnyddiol

useless *adj* diwerth

user *n* defnyddiwr

user-friendly *adj* hawdd ei drin

username *n* enw defnyddiwr

usual *adj* arferol, cynefin

usually *adv* fel arfer, fel rheol

utensil *n* offeryn, llestr

utility *n* defnyddioldeb, budd, lles; cyfleustod

utilize *vt* defnyddio

utmost *adj* eithaf, pellaf

utter[1] *adj* eithaf, pellaf; hollol, llwyr

utter[2] *vt* yngan, dywedyd

U-turn *n* tro pedol

V

vacancy n lle gwag, swydd wag, gwacter
vacant adj gwag
vacate vt ymadael â, gadael yn wag
vacation n seibiant, gwyliau
vaccination n y frech, brechiad
vaccine n brech
vacuum n gwagle, gwacter
vacuum cleaner n sugnydd llwch
vagina n fagina
vague adj amwys, amhenodol
vain adj balch, coegfalch; ofer
Valentine card n cerdyn Ffolant
Valentine's Day n Dydd Sant Ffolant
valid adj dilys
valley n dyffryn, cwm, glyn
valuable adj gwerthfawr
value n gwerth ▸ vt gwerthfawrogi, prisio
valve n falf
vampire n sugnwr gwaed

van n men, fan
vandal n fandal
vandalism n fandaliaeth
vandalize vt fandaleiddio
vanilla n fanila
vanish vi diflannu, darfod
vanity n gwagedd, gwegi, coegfalchder
vapour n tawch, tarth
variable¹ adj cyfnewidiol, anwadal, oriog
variable² n newidyn (rhifyddiaeth)
variant n amrywiad
variation n amrywiad
varied adj amrywiol
variety n amrywiaeth
various adj gwahanol, amrywiol
varnish n barnais, farnais ▸ vt barneisio, farneisio
vary vb amrywio; newid
vase n cwpan, cawg
Vaseline® n faselin, eli
vast adj dirfawr, anferth
vat n cerwyn
vault n daeargell, claddgell; cromen ▸ vb neidio, llamu
veal n cig llo
veer vb troi, cylchdroi; trawshwylio
vegan adj feganaidd, figanaidd ▸ n fegan, figan
vegetable n daeargell llysieuol ▸ n llysieuyn ymborth
vegetarian n llysieuwr
vegetation n tyfiant llysiau, llystyfiant
vehicle n cerbyd; cyfrwng
veil n gorchudd, llen ▸ vt gorchuddio
vein n gwythien
velvet n melfed

vending machine n peiriant gwerthu

vendor n gwerthwr

Venetian blind n llen Fenis

vengeance n dial, dialedd

venison n cig carw, fenswn

venom n gwenwyn

vent n agorfa, twll, arllwysfa ▸ vt arllwys, gollwng

ventilation n awyriad, gwyntylliad

venture n anturiaeth, mentr ▸ vb anturio, mentro

venue n man cyfarfod

Venus n Gwener, duwies serch

verb n berf

verbal adj berfol; geiriol

verdict n dyfarniad, rheithfarn

verge n min, ymyl ▸ vi ymylu

verify vt gwiro, gwireddu

versatile adj amryddawn

verse n adnod, pennill; prydyddiaeth

version n fersiwn; esboniad

versus prep yn erbyn

vertical adj fertigol

very adj, adv iawn, pur, tra

vessel n llestr

vest n gwasgod, crys isaf ▸ vb arwisgo, cynysgaeddu

vet vb arholi, archwilio ▸ n milfeddyg

veteran n un hen a chyfarwydd

veto n gwaharddiad ▸ vt gwahardd

via prep trwy, ar hyd

viable adj abl i fodoli, dichonadwy

vibrate vb crynu, dirgrynu

vibration n dirgryniad

vicar n ficer

vice¹ n drygioni

vice² n (tool) gwasg, feis

vice- prefix rhag-, is-

vice-chairman n is-gadeirydd

vice-versa adv i'r gwrthwyneb

vicinity n cymdogaeth

vicious adj drygionus, gwydus

victim n aberth, ysglyfaeth

victor n gorchfygwr

victorious adj buddugol, buddugoliaethus

victory n buddugoliaeth

video n fideo

video camera n camera fideo

video game n gêm fideo

vie vi cystadlu, cydymgeisio

Vienna n Fienna

Vietnam n Fietnam

Vietnamese n (person) Fietnamiad; (language) Fietnameg ▸ adj Fietnamaidd; (in language) Fietnameg

view n golygfa, barn ▸ vt edrych

viewer n gwyliwr (teledu)

viewpoint n safbwynt

vigilant adj gwyliadwrus

vigorous adj grymus, egniol

vile adj gwael, brwnt

villa n fila

village n pentref

villager n pentrefwr

villain n cnaf, adyn, dihiryn

vine n gwinwydden

vinegar n finegr

vineyard n gwinllan

vintage n cynhaeaf gwin

viola n fiola

violate vt torri, troseddu, treisio

violation n treisiad, trosedd

violence n ffyrnigrwydd, trais

violent adj treisgar

violet n fioled, crinllys

violin n ffidil

virgin n gwyryf, morwyn

Virgo n y Forwyn, y Wyryf

virtual adj rhinweddol

virtually adv i bob pwrpas

virtual reality n rhith-wirionedd, rhithrealiti

virtue n rhinwedd

virus n firws

visa n fisa

visible adj gweladwy, gweledig

vision n gweledigaeth; golwg, gweled

visit vt ymweld, gofwyo ► n ymweliad

visitor n ymwelwr, ymwelydd

visitor centre n canolfan ymwelwyr

visual adj gweledol, golygol; **visual aids** cyfarpar gweld

vital adj bywiol, hanfodol

vitality n bywyd, bywiogrwydd

vitamin n fitamin

vivid adj byw, clir, llachar

viz. adv sef (talfyriad o *videlicet*)

vocabulary n geirfa

vocal adj lleisiol, llafar

vocational adj galwedigaethol, gyrfaol

vodka n fodca

vogue n arfer, ffasiwn, bri

voice n llais, lleferydd; *(grammar)* stad

voicemail n *(message)* neges lais

void adj gwag; ofer, di-rym ► n gwagle ► vt gwagu, gollwng; gwacáu

volatile adj anwadal, gwamal; anweddol

volcano n llosgfynydd, mynydd tân

volleyball n pêl-foli

volt n uned grym trydan, folt

voltage n foltedd

volume n cyfrol; swm, crynswth, cyfaint (mathemateg)

voluntary adj gwirfoddol

volunteer n gwirfoddolwr ► vb gwirfoddoli

vomit vb chwydu, cyfogi

vote n pleidlais ► vb pleidleisio

voter n pleidleisiwr

voucher n tocyn

vow n adduned, diofryd ► vb addunedu

vowel n llafariad; **vowel affection** affeithiad; **vowel mutation** gwyriad

voyage n mordaith ► vb mordeithio, mordwyo

vulgar adj cyffredin; isel, di-foes, aflednais

vulnerable adj archolladwy, hyglwyf, hawdd ei niweidio

vulture n fwltur

W

waddle *vi* siglo, honcian
wade *vb* beisio, rhydio
wafer *n* afrlladen
wag *vb* ysgwyd, siglo
wage *n* cyflog, hur
wagon *n* men, gwagen
wail *vb* cwynfan, wylofain, udo
waist *n* gwasg, canol
waistcoat *n* gwasgod
wait *vb* aros; gweini ► *n* arhosiad;
  wait up *vi*: **don't wait up**
  peidiwch ag aros ar eich traed
waiter *n* gweinydd
waiting list *n* rhestr aros
waiting room *n* ystafell aros
waitress *n* gweinyddes
wake (*pt* **woke**, **waked**, *pp*
  woken, **waked**) *vb* deffro ► *n*
  gwylmabsant; gwylnos; **wake
  up** *vb* deffro
Wales *n* Cymru

walk *vb* cerdded, rhodio ► *n*
  rhodfa; tro
walker *n* cerddwr
walkie-talkie *n* set radio symud
  a siarad
walking *n* cerddediad; cerdded;
  walking stick ffon gerdded
walking stick *n* ffon gerdded
wall *n* mur, wal ► *vt* murio
wallet *n* ysgrepan, gwaled
wallpaper *n* papur wal
walnut *n* cneuen Ffrengig
walrus *n* morfarch
waltz *n* wols
wand *n* hudlath
wander *vb* crwydro, cyfeiliorni
want *n* angen, eisiau, diffyg ► *vb*
  bod mewn angen
war *n* rhyfel ► *vb* rhyfela
ward *n* gward; gwarchodaeth ► *vt*
  gwarchod, amddiffyn
warden *n* gwarden, gwarcheidwad
wardrobe *n* cwpwrdd dillad,
  gwardrob
warehouse *n* warws
warfare *n* milwriaeth, rhyfel
warm *adj* cynnes ► *vb* cynhesu;
  warm up *vb* cynhesu
warmth *n* cynhesrwydd
warn *vt* rhybuddio
warning *n* rhybudd
warrant *n* gwarant, awdurdod
  ► *vt* gwarantu, cyfreithloni
warrior *n* rhyfelwr
warship *n* llong rhyfel
wart *n* dafad, dafaden
wary *adj* gwyliadwrus, gochelgar
was *vi* oedd, bu
wash *vb* golchi ► *n* golchiad,
  golchfa; golchion; **wash up** *vt*

golchi ▸ vi (do dishes) golchi'r llestri
washbasin n basn ymolchi
washcloth n lliain ymolchi
washing n golch
washing machine n peiriant golchi
washing powder n powdr golchi
washing-up n: to do the washing-up golchi'r llestri
washing-up liquid n sebon golchi llestri
wasp n cacynen, gwenynen feirch
waste vb gwastraffu ▸ n gwastraff
wastepaper basket n basged sbwriel
watch vb gwylio, gwylied, gwarchod ▸ n gwyliadwriaeth; oriawr, wats; **watch out** vi bod yn ofalus
water n dwfr, dŵr ▸ vb dyfrhau
watercolour n dyfrlliw
watercress n berwr dŵr
waterfall n rhaeadr, pistyll
watering can n can dŵr
watermelon n melon dŵr
waterproof adj diddos
water skiing n sglefrio ar ddŵr
watt n wat, uned pŵer trydan
wave vb chwifio; tonni ▸ n ton
waver vi anwadalu, gwamalu
wax n cwyr ▸ vt cwyro
way n ffordd, modd
we pron ni, nyni, ninnau
weak adj gwan, egwan
weaken vb gwanhau, gwanychu
weakness n gwendid
wealth n golud, cyfoeth
wealthy adj cyfoethog

weapon n arf
wear (pt **wore**, pp **worn**) vb gwisgo, treulio ▸ n traul; gwisg
weary adj blin, blinedig ▸ vb blino
weasel n gwenci, bronwen
weather n tywydd, hin ▸ vt dal, dioddef
weather forecast n rhagolygon y tywydd
weave (pt **wove**, pp **woven**) vb gwehyddu; plethu
web n gwe; **the (World-Wide) Web** y We (Fyd-Eang)
web address n cyfeiriad gwe
web browser n porwr gwe
webcam n gwe-gamera
web page n tudalen we
website n gwefan, safle gwe
wed (pt, pp **wedded**) vb priodi, ymbriodi
wedding n priodas
wedge n cŷn, gaing, lletem ▸ vt cynio; gwthio i mewn
Wednesday n dydd Mercher
wee adj bach, bychan, pitw
weed n chwynnyn, chwyn ▸ vb chwynnu
week n wythnos
weekday n diwrnod gwaith
weekend n dros y Sul, penwythnos
weekly n (publication) wythnosolyn ▸ adj wythnosol ▸ adv yn wythnosol
weep (pt, pp **wept**) vb wylo, wylofain, llefain
weigh vb pwyso; codi (angor)
weight n pwys, pwysau
weir n cored
weird adj annaearol, iasol

W

427

welcome *excl, n* croeso ▸ *vt* croesawu ▸ *adj* derbyniol, dymunol

weld *vt* asio

welfare *n* llwydd, lles

welfare state *n* gwladwriaeth les

well¹ *adv* yn dda ▸ *adj* da, iach ▸ *excl* wel

well² *n* ffynnon, pydew

well-balanced *adj* cytbwys

well-behaved *adj* ufudd

wellingtons *npl* esgidiau glaw

well-known *adj (person)* adnabyddus; *(fact)* hysbys

well-off *adj* cefnog, da ei fyd

well-paid *adj* â chyflog da

Welsh *adj* Cymreig; Cymraeg ▸ *n* Cymraeg

Welshman *n* Cymro

Welshwoman *n* Cymraes

west *n* gorllewin ▸ *adj* gorllewin

westbound *adj (line, lane)* am y gorllewin; *(vehicle)* yn mynd i'r gorllewin

western *adj* gorllewinol

West Indian *n* Caribïad ▸ *adj* Caribïaidd

West Indies *npl:* the West Indies India'r Gorllewin

wet *adj* gwlyb ▸ *vt* gwlychu ▸ *n* gwlybaniaeth

whack *vb* llachio, ffonodio

whale *n* morfil

wharf *n* porthfa, llwythfa

(KEYWORD)

what *adj* **1** *(in questions)* pa; **what size is he?** pa faint yw e?; **what**

colour is it? pa liw yw e?; **what books do you need?** pa lyfrau sydd arnoch eu hangen?

2 *(in exclamations):* **what a mess!** am lanast!; **what a fool I am!** dyna ffŵl ydw i!, am ffŵl ydw i!

▸ *pron* **1** *(interrogative)* beth; **what are you doing?** beth rydych chi'n ei wneud?; **what is happening?** beth sy'n digwydd?; **what are you talking about?** am beth rydych chi'n siarad?; **what are you thinking about?** am beth rydych chi'n meddwl?; **what is it called?** beth yw ei enw e?, beth mae dyn yn ei alw e; **what about me?** beth amdana i?; **what about doing ...?** beth am wneud ...?

2 *(relative, subject)* yr hyn, y peth; *(direct object)* yr hyn, y peth; *(indirect object)* yr hyn, pa beth; **I saw what you did/was on the table** gwelais yr hyn a wnaethoch/a oedd ar y bwrdd; **tell me what you remember** dywedwch yr hyn yr ydych yn ei gofio; **what I want is a cup of tea** cwpanaid fyddai'n dda

▸ *excl (disbelieving)* sut!, beth!

whatever *pron* beth bynnag

whatsoever *pron* pa beth bynnag

wheat *n* gwenith

wheel *n* olwyn, rhod, troell ▸ *vt* olwyno, powlio

wheelbarrow *n* berfa (drol), whilber

wheelchair *n* cadair olwyn

wheeze *vi* gwichian ▸ *n* gwich

when adv pryd, pa bryd; **when did he go?** pa bryd yr aeth e?

▶ conj 1 (at, during, after the time that) pan; **she was reading when I came in** roedd hi'n darllen pan ddeuthum i mewn

2 (on): (at which) **on the day when I met him** y diwrnod y cyfarfûm ag ef

3 (whereas) tra; **I thought I was wrong when in fact I was right** roeddwn yn meddwl fy mod yn anghywir tra oeddwn yn gywir mewn gwirionedd

whenever adv pa bryd bynnag
where adv ym mha le; yn y lle, lle
whereabouts adv ymhle
whereas conj gan, yn gymaint â
whereby adv trwy yr hyn
whether conj ai, pa un ai

which adj 1 (interrogative; direct, indirect) pa; **which picture do you want?** pa ddarlun hoffech chi ei gael?; **which one?** pa un?

2: **in which case** ac os felly; **we got there at 8pm, by which time the cinema was full** fe gyrhaeddon ni erbyn 8pm, ac erbyn hynny roedd y sinema'n llawn

▶ pron 1 (interrogative) pa un, pa rai pl; **I don't mind which** nid oes gwahaniaeth gennyf ba un; **which (of these) are yours?** pa rai (o'r rhain) sy'n perthyn i chi?; **tell me which you want** dywedwch ba un

yr hoffech ei gael

2 (relative, subject) a plus conjugated verb form; (in present tense) sydd + yn + vn (often contracted to sy'n + vn); (object) a; (indirect object) y; **the apple which you ate/which is on the table** yr afal a fwyteaist/sydd ar y bwrdd; **the chair on which you are sitting** y gadair yr ydych yn eistedd arni; **the book of which you spoke** y llyfr y buoch yn siarad amdano; **he said he knew, which is true** dywedodd ei fod yn gwybod, sy'n wir; **after which** ac ar ôl hynny

whichever pron, adj pa un bynnag
while n ennyd, talm, amser ▶ vt treulio ▶ adv tra
whilst adv cyhyd, tra
whim n mympwy, chwim
whine vb swnian crïo, cwynfan
whip vb chwipio, fflangellu ▶ n chwip, fflangell
whipped cream n hufen chwip
whirl vb chwyrlïo, chwyrnellu, chwyrndroi
whisk n tusw ▶ vb ysgubo; chwyrlïo
whiskers npl blew, barf
whisky n chwisgi
whisper vb, n sibrwd, sisial
whistle vb chwibanu ▶ n chwiban, chwibanogl
white adj gwyn; (ethnicity): **White person** person gwyn
whiteboard n bwrdd gwyn
whitewash n gwyngalch ▶ vb gwyngalchu
whiting n gwyniad

W

429

Whitsun, Whitsunday n
 Sulgwyn
whittle vt naddu, lleihau
who pron a, pwy
whoever pron pwy bynnag
whole adj cyfan, holl; iach, holliach
 ▸ n cyfan
wholemeal adj â'r grawn cyfan,
 cyflawn
wholesale n cyfanwerth ▸ adj yn
 y crynswth
wholly adv yn hollol, yn gyfan
 gwbl, yn llwyr

(KEYWORD)

whom pron 1 (interrogative) pwy;
 whom did you see? pwy welsoch
 chi?; **to whom did you give it?**
 i bwy y'i rhoesoch?
 2 (relative) a..., yr hwn m a..., yr hon
 f; y rhai pl a...; **the man whom I
 saw** y dyn a welais
 3 (indirect obj. and after prep.,
 positive) y ... iddo/iddi/iddynt, y ...
 ohono/ohoni/ohonynt; (negative)
 na/nad ... iddo/iddi/iddynt, na/
 nad ... ohono/ohoni/ohonynt;
 the man to whom I gave the book
 y dyn y rhoddais y llyfr iddo

whore n (infl!) putain, hŵr

(KEYWORD)

whose adj 1 (possessive;
 interrogative): **whose book is this?
 whose is this book?** llyfr pwy
 yw hwn?, pwy biau'r llyfr hwn?;
 whose pencil have you taken?
 pensel pwy gymerest ti?; **whose

daughter are you?** merch pwy
 wyt ti?
 2 (possessive; relative): **the man
 whose son you rescued** y dyn yr
 achubaist ei fab; **the girl whose
 sister you were speaking to** y
 ferch y buoch yn siarad â'i chwaer;
 the woman whose car was stolen
 y fenyw y cafodd ei char ei ddwyn
 ▸ pron: **whose is this?** pwy biau
 hwn?; **I know whose it is** rwy'n
 gwybod pwy a'i piau

(KEYWORD)

why adv pam; **why not?** pam lai?
 ▸ conj: **I wonder why he said that**
 pam dywedodd e hynny, tybed?;
 that's not why I'm here nid dyna
 pam rwyf i yma; **the reason why** y
 rheswm pam
 ▸ excl dew!, duwcs!, jiw jiw!; **why,
 it's you!** dew, chi sy yna!; **why,
 that's impossible!** mae hynny'n
 amhosibl, debyg iawn!

wicked adj drwg, drygionus,
 ysgeler
wicket n wiced, clwyd
wide adj llydan, eang, helaeth
widely adj yn eang
widen vb lledu, llydanu
widespread adj cyffredinol
widow adj gweddw ▸ n gwraig
 weddw, gwidw
widower n gwidman
width n lled, ehangder
wield vt llywio, rheoli; trin
wife n gwraig, gwraig briod,
 priod

Wi-Fi *n* Wi-Fi
wig *n* gwallt gosod, wig
wild *adj* gwyllt ▸ *n* diffeithle
wilderness *n* anialwch
wildlife *n* bywyd gwyllt

(KEYWORD)

will *aux vb* **1** *(forming future tense)*:
I will finish it tomorrow byddaf yn
ei orffen yfory; **I will have finished
it by tomorrow** byddaf wedi'i
orffen erbyn yfory; **will you do it?
— yes I will/no I won't** a wnewch
chi ef? — gwnaf/na wnaf
2 *(in conjectures, predictions)*: he
will *or* **he'll be there by now** fe fydd
yno erbyn hyn; **that will be the
postman** y postmon fydd yno
3 *(in commands, requests, offers)*:
will you be quiet! wnewch chi fod
yn ddistaw!, tewch!, byddwch
ddistaw!; **will you help me?**
wnewch chi fy helpu?; **will you
have a cup of tea?** gymerwch chi
gwpanaid o de?; **I won't put up
with it!** wna i ddim goddef y peth!
▸ *vt (pt, pp* **willed**) to will sb to
do mynnu bod rhn yn gwneud
rhth; **he willed himself to go on**
mynnodd fynd yn ei flaen
▸ *n* **1** ewyllys *f*; **against one's will** yn
erbyn eich ewyllys
2 *(document)* ewyllys *f*

willing *adj* ewyllysgar, bodlon
willingly *adj* o wirfodd
willow *n* helygen, pren helyg
willpower *n* grym ewyllys
win *(pt, pp* **won**) *vb* ennill

wince *vi* gwingo
wind[1] *n* gwynt
wind[2] *(pt, pp* **wound**) *vb* dirwyn,
troi
windfall *n* lwc, ffawd dda
windmill *n* melin wynt
window *n* ffenestr
windowpane *n* cwarel
windscreen *n* ffenestr flaen
windscreen wiper *n* braich law
windsurfing *n* bordhwylio
windy *adj* gwyntog
wine *n* gwin
wineglass *n* gwydr gwin
wing *n* adain, asgell; *(rugby)*
asgellwr
wink *vb* wincio, cau llygad ▸ *n*
winc
winner *n* enillydd
winning *adj* enillgar, deniadol
winter *n* gaeaf ▸ *vb* gaeafu
winter sports *npl* chwaraeon
y gaeaf
wintertime *n* tymor y gaeaf
wipe *vt* sychu; **wipe up** *vt* glanhau
wire *n* gwifr, gwifren
wireless *n* radio ▸ *adj* di-wifr;
wireless network rhwydwaith
di-wifr
wiring *n* weiro
wisdom *n* doethineb
wise *adj* doeth
wish *vb* dymuno, chwennych ▸ *n*
dymuniad
wistful *adj* awyddus, hiraethus
wit *n* synnwyr; arabedd; rhywun
ffraeth
witch *n* dewines, gwrach

W

KEYWORD

with prep 1 (in the company of): gyda, efo; (at the home of) we stayed with friends buom yn aros gyda ffrindiau; **I'll be with you in a minute** byddaf gyda chi mewn munud, dof atoch mewn munud 2 (descriptive): **a room with a view** ystafell â golygfa; **the man with the grey hat/blue eyes** y dyn â'r het lwyd/llygaid glas 3 (indicating manner, means, cause): **with tears in her eyes** â dagrau yn ei llygaid; **to walk with a stick** cerdded â ffon; **red with anger** yn goch gan ddicter; **to shake with fear** crynu gan ofn; **to fill sth with water** llenwi rhth â dŵr 4 (in phrases): **I'm with you** (I understand) rwy'n deall, rwy'n gweld; **to be with it** (inf) (up-to-date) bod yn ffasiynol

withdraw vb tynnu yn ôl, encilio; codi arian
withdrawal n enciliad
wither vb gwywo, crino
withhold vt atal, cadw yn ôl
within adv, n, prep i mewn, o fewn
without prep heb, di- ▸ adv, n tu allan
withstand vt gwrthsefyll
witness n tyst; tystiolaeth ▸ vb tystio
witty adj arab, arabus, ffraeth
wizard n swynwr, dewin
wobble vi siglo, honcian, anwadalu
woe n gwae
wolf n blaidd

woman n gwraig, merch
womb n croth, bru
wonder n rhyfeddod, syndod ▸ vi rhyfeddu, synnu
wonderful adj rhyfeddol
wood n coed, coedwig; pren
wooden adj o goed, o bren; trwsgl, trwstan
woodwind npl chwythoffer pren
woodwork n gwaith coed, gwaith saer
wool n gwlân
woollen adj gwlanog, gwlân
woolly adj gwlanog
word n gair ▸ vt geirio
wording n geiriad
word processing n prosesu geiriau, geirbrosesu
word processor n prosesydd geiriau
work n gwaith ▸ vb gweithio
worker n gweithiwr
work experience n profiad gwaith
working-class adj dosbarth gweithiol
workman n gweithiwr
workout n sesiwn ymarfer
worksheet n taflen waith
workshop n gweithdy
workspace n gweithle
workstation n gweithfan
world n byd
worldwide adj byd-eang
worm n pryf, abwydyn; llyngyren ▸ vb ymnyddu
worn adj treuliedig
worn-out adj wedi blino; wedi treulio
worried adj pryderus, gofidus

worry *vb* poeni ► *n* pryder
worse *adj* gwaeth
worsen *vb* gwaethygu
worship *n* addoliad ► *vb* addoli
worst *vt* gorchfygu, trechu
worth *n* gwerth, teilyngdod
worthless *adj* diwerth
worthy *adj* teilwng ► *n* gŵr o fri
wound *n* archoll, clwyf ► *vt*
    archolli, clwyfo
wrap *vt* plygu, lapio; **wrap up** *vt*
    lapio
wrapping paper *n* papur lapio
wreath *n* torch
wreck *n* llongddrylliad ► *vb*
    llongddryllio
wren *n* dryw, dryw bach
wrench *vt* rhwygo ymaith, tyndroi
    ► *n* tyndro
wrestle *vi* ymgodymu, ymaflyd
    codwm
wrestler *n* ymgodymwr, taflwr
    codwm
wrestling *n* ymgodymu
wretched *adj* truan, truenus
wriggle *vb* gwingo, ymnyddu
wring (*pt, pp* **wrung**) *vt* troi,
    gwasgu
wrinkle *n* crych, crychni ► *vb*
    crychu
wrist *n* arddwrn
write (*pt* **wrote**, *pp* **written**) *vb*
    ysgrifennu; **write down** *vt* nodi
writer *n* ysgrifennwr, awdur
writing *n* ysgrifen; ysgrifennu
writing paper *n* papur ysgrifennu
wrong *adj* anghywir, o'i le ► *n* cam
    ► *vt* gwneud cam â, niweidio

X

Xmas *n* Dolig
X-ray *n* pelydr X ► *vt* tynnu llun
    pelydr X
xylophone *n* seiloffon

yacht n llong bleser, iot
yard¹ n llath, llathen; hwyl-lath
yard² n (enclosure) iard, buarth, clos
yarn n edau, edafedd; stori, chwedl
yawn vi dylyfu gên, agor ceg
year n blwyddyn, blwydd
yearly adv blynyddol
yearn vi hiraethu, dyheu
yeast n burum
yell vb ysgrechian ▸ n ysgrech, nâd
yellow adj, n melyn
yes adv ie, do, oes etc
yesterday n, adv doe
yet conj, adv er hynny, eto
yew n yw, ywen
Yiddish n Almaeneg Iddewaidd
yield vb ildio ▸ n cynnyrch
yoga n ioga
yoghurt n iogwrt
yolk n melyn wy, melynwy

you pron 1 (subject) ti; (polite form) chi; (plural) chi; **you are very kind** rydych yn garedig iawn; **you enjoy your food** rydych yn mwynhau'ch bwyd; **you and I will go** fe ei di a minnau; **there you are!** dyna chi! 2 (object, direct, indirect) di, chi; **I know you** rwy'n d'adnabod di or rwy'n eich adnabod chi; **I gave it to you** fe'i rhoddais i ti 3 (stressed) tydi, chwychwi; **I told you to do it** wrthyt ti or wrthych chi y dywedais am wneud y peth 4 (after prep, in comparisons) ti; chi; **it's for you** i ti or i chi y mae e; **she's younger than you** mae hi'n iau na thi or chi 5 (impersonal; one) chi; **fresh air does you good** mae awyr iach yn gwneud lles i chi; **you never know** dydych chi byth yn gwybod; **you can't do that!** allwch chi ddim gwneud hynny!

young adj ifanc, ieuanc
youngster n bachgennyn, plentyn
your pron eich, 'ch
yours pron eiddoch, yr eiddoch
yourself pron eich hun(an)
yourselves pron eich hunain
youth n ieuenctid; llanc
youth club n clwb ieuenctid
youthful adj ieuanc, ieuengaidd
youth hostel n hostel ieuenctid

Z

zany *adj* gwirion
zeal *n* sêl, brwdfrydedd
zebra *n* sebra
zebra crossing *n* croesfan sebra
zero *n* dim, sero; gwagnod
zest *n* awch, blas, afiaith
zigzag *adj, n* igam-ogam
Zimbabwe *n* Zimbabwe
zinc *n* sinc
zip¹ *n* sip
zip² *vt (file)* sipio
zip file *n* ffeil sip
zipper *n* sip
zodiac *n* sidydd
zone *n* cylch, parth
zoo *n* sw
zoology *n* milofyddiaeth, swoleg